THE AMERICAN WAY

ANNOTATED TEACHER'S EDITION

NANCY W. BAUER

University of Pennsylvania

in consultation with

Nancy J. Allbaugh
Administrative Assistant, Curriculum
Abington School District
Abington, Pennsylvania

Irving E. Sigel
Senior Research Psychologist
Educational Testing Service
Princeton, New Jersey

Holt, Rinehart and Winston, Publishers
New York • Toronto • London • Sydney

NANCY W. BAUER, Ph.D., is adjunct associate professor at the Graduate School of Education, University of Pennsylvania, and is associated with the College of General Studies. She is a historian and author of history and social studies textbooks. Dr. Bauer has been a classroom teacher for 15 years and was coordinator of Social Studies, K-12, in the Birmingham, Michigan, school system. She received her B.A. from Smith College, an M.A. in humanities and education from the University of Michigan, and a Ph.D. in curriculum research from Michigan State University, where she was a fellow of the Learning Systems Institute. Dr. Bauer is well-known as a curriculum designer and consultant for schools. She has published extensively in the curriculum field, including articles for professional journals and *Revolution and Reaction: The Impact of the New Social Studies*. She is actively involved in social studies and citizen education, including the work of the Social Science Education Consortium, the National Council for the Social Studies, the Asia Society, and the Alliance for Citizen Education.

NANCY J. ALLBAUGH is the administrative assistant, curriculum, for the Abington School District in Abington, Pennsylvania. Before receiving her Ph.D. from the University of Iowa, she taught for seven years. Dr. Allbaugh also supervised the School for Inpatients at the University of Iowa, where she trained over 80 teachers in how to teach the emotionally disturbed. Dr. Allbaugh has published papers on reading in the social studies. Her contributions to *The American Way* include the reading, section review, and chapter review questions.

IRVING E. SIGEL is presently senior research psychologist at the Educational Testing Service and director of the Child Care Research Center. He received his Ph.D. from the University of Chicago. Dr. Sigel's publications are concerned with childrens' intellectual development and the factors that influence it. For *The American Way*, Dr. Sigel prepared the special skills features that focus on how people learn.

The feature on page 495 was written by Dr. Shirley Brice Heath of the University of Pennsylvania.

Teacher Reviewers for THE AMERICAN WAY

Maryann Cusack, Junior High School Social Studies teacher, Cambridge, Massachusetts
Miriam Glessner, Junior High School Social Studies teacher, Columbus, Ohio
Alida C. Kratnoff, History Department Coordinator, Palisades Park, New Jersey
William W. Strong, Resource teacher for the academically talented, Charlotte-Meckenburg, North Carolina
David W. Wolfe, Supervisor of Social Studies, K-12, Shawnee Mission, Kansas

Copyright © 1979 by Holt, Rinehart and Winston, Publishers
All Rights Reserved
Printed in the United States of America
ISBN: 0-03-040746-X
 9012 039 98765432

TABLE OF CONTENTS

THE AMERICAN WAY

Everything you've ever had in a social studies text, plus a lot more!

- Reading Questions focus attention on the main ideas

- Special Skills Features teach how to learn

- Photographs and Art create a picture of the times

- Tests for every chapter and unit

- Maps are clear, easy to read, and develop geography skills

- Six Themes weave the narrative into a coherent story

- An Annotated Teacher's Edition with teaching suggestions, objectives, and answered reading questions, section, chapter, and unit reviews

- Chronological Format reveals history the way it happened

- A Workbook to check student progress

THE AMERICAN WAY HELPS TEACHERS TEACH

How the text is organized . . .

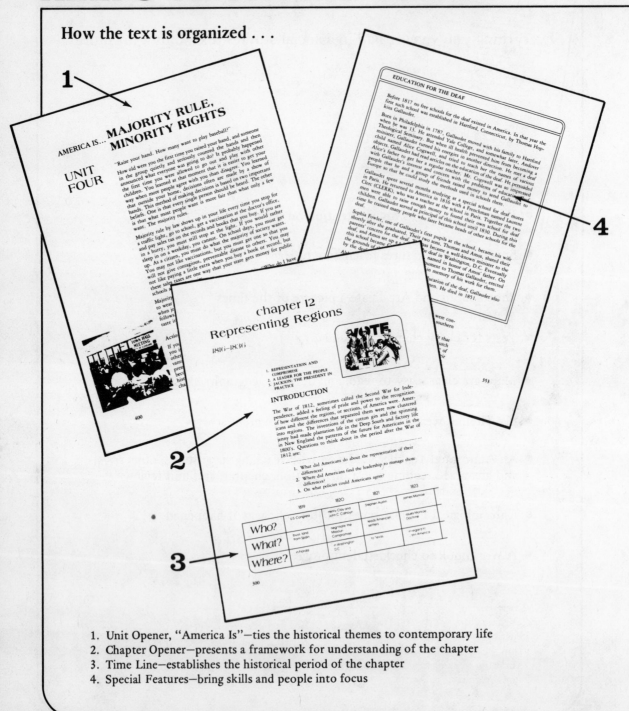

1. Unit Opener, "America Is"—ties the historical themes to contemporary life
2. Chapter Opener—presents a framework for understanding of the chapter
3. Time Line—establishes the historical period of the chapter
4. Special Features—bring skills and people into focus

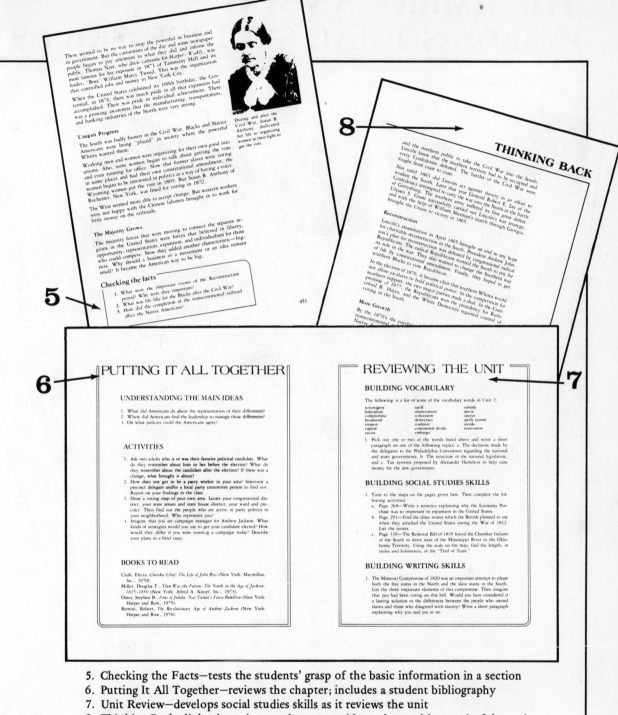

There seemed to be no way to stop the powerful in business and in government. But the cartoonists of the day and some newspaper people began to pay attention to what they did and inform the public. Thomas Nast, who drew cartoons for *Harper's Weekly*, was most famous for his exposure in 1871 of Tammany Hall and its leader, "Boss" William Marcy Tweed. This was the organization that controlled jobs and money in New York City.

When the United States celebrated its 100th birthday, the Centennial, in 1876, there was much pride in all that expansion had accomplished. There was pride in the individual achievement. There was a growing awareness that the manufacturing, transportation, and banking industries of the North were very strong.

Uneven Progress

The South was badly beaten in the Civil War. Blacks and Native Americans were being "placed" in society where the powerful Whites wanted them.

Working men and women were organizing for their own good into unions. Also, some women began to talk about getting the vote and even running for office. Now that former slaves were voting in some places and had their own constitutional amendment, the women began to be interested in politics as a way of having a voice. Wyoming women got the vote in 1869. But Susan B. Anthony of Rochester, New York, was fined for voting in 1872.

The West seemed more able to accept change. But western workers were not happy with the Chinese laborers brought in to work for little money on the railroads.

The Majority Grows

The majority forces that were moving to connect the separate regions in the United States were forces that believed in liberty, opportunity, representation, expansion, and individualism for those who could compete. Now they added another characteristic—bigness. Why should a business or a movement or an idea remain small? It became the American way to be big.

During and after the Civil War, Susan B. Anthony dedicated her life to organizing women in their fight to get the vote.

Checking the facts

1. What were the important events of the Reconstruction period? Why were they important?
2. What was life like for the Blacks after the Civil War?
3. How did the completion of the transcontinental railroad affect the Native Americans?

451

THINKING BACK

and the northern public to take the Civil War into the South. Lincoln knew that the southern territory had to be occupied and every Confederate defeated. The battles of the Civil War were fought from coast to coast.

Not until 1863 did Lincoln act against slavery in an effort to weaken the South. Later that year General Robert E. Lee of the Confederacy attempted to carry the war into the North at the battle of Gettysburg. The southern army suffered its first great defeat. Ulysses S. Grant successfully carried out Lincoln's war strategy, and with the help of William Sherman's march through Georgia, brought the Union to victory in 1865.

Reconstruction

Lincoln's assassination in April 1865 brought an end to any hope for charitable reconstruction in the South. President Andrew Johnson's plan for reconstruction was defeated by congressional radical Republicans. The radical Republicans wanted the South to pay for its role in the war. They also wanted to change the Southern way of life by constitutional amendment. Finally, they hoped to get southern Blacks to vote Republican.

In the election of 1876, it became clear that southern Whites would not allow ex-slaves to hold political power. In the competition for southern support, the two major parties made a deal. In the Compromise of 1877, the Republicans won the presidency for Rutherford B. Hayes, and the White Democrats regained control of voting in the South.

More Growth

By the 1870's the purchase...
transcontinental...
Native American...

PUTTING IT ALL TOGETHER

UNDERSTANDING THE MAIN IDEAS

1. What did Americans do about the representation of their differences?
2. Where did Americans find the leadership to manage those differences?
3. On what policies could the Americans agree?

ACTIVITIES

1. Ask two adults who is or was their favorite political candidate. What do they remember about him or her before the election? What do they remember about the candidate after the election? If there was a change, what brought it about?
2. How does one get to be a party worker in your area? Interview a precinct delegate and/or a local party committee person to find out. Report on your findings to the class.
3. Draw a voting map of your own area. Locate your congressional district, your state senate and state house district, your ward and precinct. Then find out the people who are active in party politics in your neighborhood. Who represents you?
4. Imagine that you are campaign manager for Andrew Jackson. What kinds of strategies would you use to get your candidate elected? How would they differ if you were running a campaign today? Describe your plans in a brief essay.

BOOKS TO READ

Clark, Electa, *Cherokee Chief: The Life of John Ross* (New York: Macmillan, Inc., 1970).
Miller, Douglas T., *Then Was the Future: The North in the Age of Jackson, 1815–1850* (New York: Alfred A. Knopf, Inc., 1973).
Oates, Stephen B., *Fires of Jubilee: Nat Turner's Fierce Rebellion* (New York: Harper and Row, 1975).
Remini, Robert, *The Revolutionary Age of Andrew Jackson* (New York: Harper and Row, 1976).

REVIEWING THE UNIT

BUILDING VOCABULARY

The following is a list of some of the vocabulary words in Unit 2:

sovereignty	tariff	subsidy
federalism	impressment	specie
compromise	concession	caucus
bicameral	democracy	spoils system
treason	coalition	secede
capital	continental divide	reservation
excise	embargo	

1. Pick out one or two of the words listed above and write a short paragraph on one of the following topics: a. The decisions made by the delegates to the Philadelphia Convention regarding the national and state governments, b. The structure of the national legislature, and c. Tax systems proposed by Alexander Hamilton to help raise money for the new government.

BUILDING SOCIAL STUDIES SKILLS

1. Turn to the maps on the pages given here. Then complete the following activities:
   a. Page 268—Write a sentence explaining why the Louisiana Purchase was so important to expansion in the United States.
   b. Page 291—Find the three routes which the British planned to use when they attacked the United States during the War of 1812. List the routes.
   c. Page 319—The Removal Bill of 1835 forced the Cherokee Indians of the South to move west of the Mississippi River to the Oklahoma Territory. Using the scale on the map, find the length, in miles and kilometers, of the "Trail of Tears."

BUILDING WRITING SKILLS

1. The Missouri Compromise of 1820 was an important attempt to please both the free states in the North and the slave states in the South. List the three important elements of this compromise. Then imagine that you had been voting on this bill. Would you have considered it a lasting solution to the differences between the people who owned slaves and those who disagreed with slavery? Write a short paragraph explaining why you said yes or no.

5. Checking the Facts—tests the students' grasp of the basic information in a section
6. Putting It All Together—reviews the chapter; includes a student bibliography
7. Unit Review—develops social studies skills as it reviews the unit
8. Thinking Back—links the units together to provide students with meaningful transitions from unit to unit

THE AMERICAN WAY
BUILDS SOCIAL STUDIES SKILLS

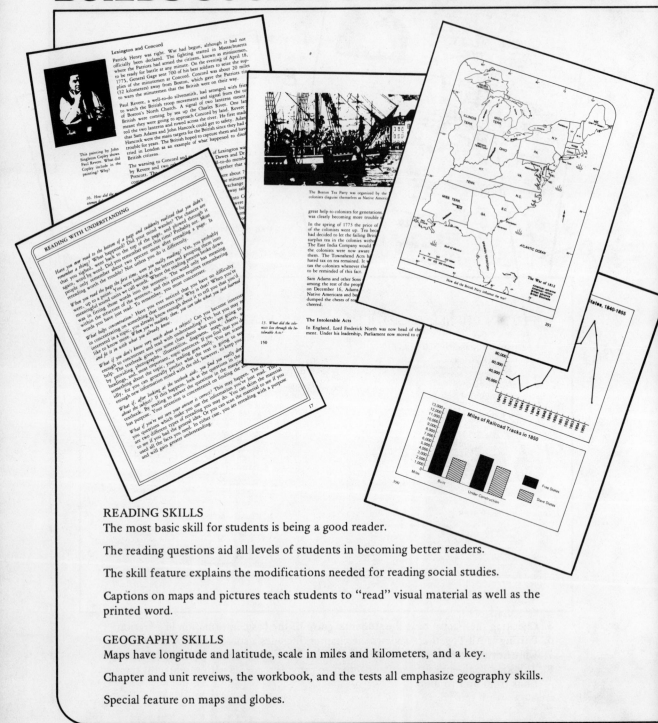

READING SKILLS
The most basic skill for students is being a good reader.

The reading questions aid all levels of students in becoming better readers.

The skill feature explains the modifications needed for reading social studies.

Captions on maps and pictures teach students to "read" visual material as well as the printed word.

GEOGRAPHY SKILLS
Maps have longitude and latitude, scale in miles and kilometers, and a key.

Chapter and unit reveiws, the workbook, and the tests all emphasize geography skills.

Special feature on maps and globes.

supplies cheaper and never run out. There was so much public concern about the influence of big corporations that laws were passed by Congress to protect smaller businesses from unfair competition and consumers from unfair pricing and unfair service policies. Congress also set up a commission on corporations to report on the activities of the large businesses that crossed state lines. In a 1905 report on meatpackers, the Commission commented that Swift and Company kept the highest standards by careful supervision of all its employees nationwide.

Checking the facts

1. What changes did Swift make in supplying meat to customers throughout the nation?
2. How did Swift come up with the idea of a nationwide big business?
3. How did Swift's big business affect other businesses?

3. OTHER BUSINESSES ORGANIZE NATIONWIDE

Other companies, like Swift, followed the new way of organizing their businesses nationwide. They, too, moved to form organizations which could own the raw materials, the processing and packaging factory, and the distributing and selling operations. They, too, cut their costs by cutting the profits made by others at each step along the way. They, too, made sure that there would be supplies for every step of the process.

The United Fruit Company used a nationwide distributing and selling organization to introduce bananas brought all the way from Central America. United Fruit actually persuaded the American public to like bananas and to include them in their diet.

Organizing the Sales

Methods of national marketing were not only applied to foods. Singer Sewing Machines were sold in branch offices all over America and in foreign countries by people employed by the Singer Company. This was a new way of organizing the sales of a manufactured product. Before this time, factories signed up with independent agents who represented many different companies and many different products. These "manufacturers' agents" traveled from customer to customer and town to town selling from their long list of manufactured products.

Do you think this picture would make a good advertisement for sewing machines? Why or why not?

472

BUILT FOR SUCCESS

<u>Section Titles</u> tell the student what is coming up in the section.

<u>Boldface Subtitles</u> focus on specifics.

<u>Open Format</u> makes the text easy to read and encourages the students to read on.

<u>Pictures</u> are an important part of the students' learning process.

THE AMERICAN WAY PROVIDES

NAME _____

CLASS _____ DATE _____

UNIT SIX   America Is . . .
TRYING TO PRESERVE, TRYING TO IMPROVE

Chapter 21
Reform in Modern America

UNDERSTANDING WHAT YOU READ

Below are a list of questions that will be helpful in understanding the main ideas in Chapter 21.
Using your textbook, answer the following questions.

1. What are some of the reforms Progressives accomplished? *Secret ballot; women's suffrage;*
   initiative, referendum, and recall; regulation of railroads, specialists in government, etc.

   (pp. 542–546) _____

2. Give a short biography of Theodore Roosevelt. *He was a member of the New York State*
   Assembly, a commissioner of civil service, police commissioner of New York City, assistant
   Secretary of the Navy, a hero of the Spanish-American war, the governor of New York,
   and Vice-President before becoming President. (p. 547) _____

3. List at least three instances when Theodore Roosevelt acted to strengthen the United States
   role in world affairs. *Panama Canal (p. 557); Venezuela and Dominican Republic (p. 560);*
   Roosevelt Corollary (p. 561); Russo-Japanese peace (p. 562). _____

4. How were the Japanese discriminated against by the United States? *Oriental children were*
   placed in separate schools. (p. 563) _____

A WORKBOOK
- The workbook reinforces the students' understanding of the historical facts and concepts presented in <u>THE AMERICAN WAY</u>.

A Package of Material Ready for Teacher Use
- mapping
- chronology
- graphing
- chart reading
- time lines
- cause and effect
- reading comprehension
- how to use the library effectively
- how to use the textbook

TEACHING RESOURCES

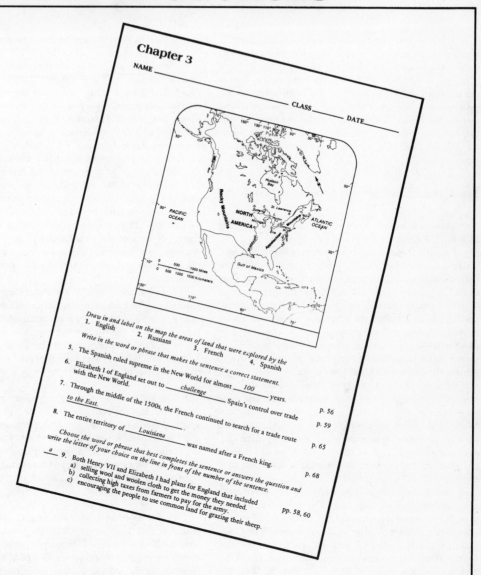

Chapter 3

NAME _____

CLASS _____ DATE _____

Draw in and label on the map the areas of land that were explored by the
1. English
2. Russians
3. French
4. Spanish

Write in the word or phrase that makes the sentence a correct statement.

5. The Spanish ruled supreme in the New World for almost _____100_____ years.

6. Elizabeth I of England set out to _____challenge_____ Spain's control over trade with the New World.   p. 56

7. Through the middle of the 1500s, the French continued to search for a trade route to the East.   p. 59

8. The entire territory of _____Louisiana_____ was named after a French king.   p. 65

Choose the word or phrase that best completes the sentence or answers the question and write the letter of your choice on the line in front of the number of the sentence.   p. 68

_a_ 9. Both Henry VII and Elizabeth I had plans for England that included
   a) selling wool and woolen cloth to get the money they needed.
   b) collecting high taxes from farmers to pay for the army.
   c) encouraging the people to use common land for grazing their sheep.   pp. 58, 60

A COMPLETE EVALUATION PROGRAM

CHAPTER AND UNIT TESTS
- recall
- fill-in
- mapping
- matching
- vocabulary development
- page references are provided for all the answers.

THERE IS AN AMERICAN WAY

The American people have created a unique nation. It is unique in its strengths and its problems, its goals and its vision. What makes it special, however, is not new. Some of its special qualities date back to the beginning of human life in North and South America. Although great changes have occurred, some of those qualities have been the ones that are the dynamics of the people who live here now and shape the American Way. This book maintains that America is special and that its special qualities can be understood.

Six Great Themes in American History

This book selects six of these qualities as six great themes in America's growth and development.

The first theme is *variety and shared values* (Unit One). There has always been variety among the Native Americans, Europeans, and Africans who came to America. They settled in geographically different areas of North America. Together the people and the geography created a varied population long before the idea of a continental nation formed. The values that became dominant were shared by those who—by choice or by conquest—came later. Those shared values were liberty, opportunity, and a desire to control the environment and the future.

How could such a variety of people protect their liberty, increase their opportunities, and make decisions about their own lives? The second great theme is *representation* (Unit Two). Americans are represented in local, state, and national government, and through citizen's organizations. Americans who differ have nevertheless joined in making compromises and decisions for the good of the whole society.

America held the promise of opportunity, particularly the possibility of owning land. The continent was big enough to contain the variety. Opportunity found expression in the nation's third great theme, *expansion and individualism* (Unit Three). Americans, including the new immigrants, were excited by the possibilities of the West. New land became available through the Mexican War. The discovery of gold in California encouraged people to go west and "fill in the nation" with settlements. Some Blacks, women and immigrants could not compete. This did not bother many people. The critical concern was the seemingly limitless opportunities for liberty and land for the majority of the people who were represented and could afford to compete.

It was not long before the warnings of some came true. Unregulated expansion and individualism caused problems in representation. The power of the majority made decisions for the minority—which included southerners, Mexi-

can Americans, Blacks, and Native Americans.

The years before and after the Civil War were years of compromise, agony, and manipulation of power over the issue of *majority rule and minority rights* emerged (Unit Four). The growth of the West and the transcontinental railroad only served to deepen the problems of maintaining liberty, opportunity, control, and representation, for expansion and individualism had brought more to some. Representation in Congress was unable to promote equal protection for permanent minorities under the law.

Still, expansion continued, and not just westward. The networks of buying and selling were linked into nationwide organizations with national owners and managers. It was an era when both private and public institutions became big. Thus *"bigness"* (Unit Five) is the fifth great theme. It became the prime characteristic of modernday America: big business: big labor: big government: big plans overseas: and the idea that bigness, or more, was best for America.

It is a characteristic of the American way, however, not to ignore or gloss over inequalities of liberty and opportunity, control of land, expansion of national territory, and participation in the big institutions. Minority rights cannot be ignored in America. Americans who have benefited most as well as those who have benefited less are aware of the difficulties of using liberty to create justice and equality.

The sixth theme is *trying to preserve; trying to improve* (Unit Six). It is the theme of twentieth-century America in which Americans work through government regulations and by means of a regulatory bureaucracy to preserve the five earlier themes of the American past, broadening their application for everyone. The present century has been one of balancing priorities and trying new methods of improving our present without losing anything gained in our past.

In *The American Way* these six great themes are presented as they grow into each other. History is seen as a continually developing tapestry depicting human life. If we stand far enough back we can see the great themes. From up close we see the individuals who made them happen, and the accompanying benefits and suffering.

Each theme is an idea or a belief. Every society has its beliefs that guide the actions of its people, individually and in groups. This textbook presents America to young Americans as a living example of great ideas that have grown into each other. These great ideas or themes guide the ways Americans at every stage of their history reacted to their geography, to other peoples, to newcomers to their land, and to all those whom they believed were too different to belong. These ideas guide the way Americans try to solve their problems.

Chronology: Time and Timing

The American Way describes the development of people. It illuminates the history of the United States with strict attention to chronology. It shows students why the passage of time and the order in which events, people, and ideas occur may be crucial. It is important for young people to begin to develop an abstract sense of time and a lively appreciation of what it means to be timely.

Students need to know how many generations passed from the invention of the railroad to the building of a national railroad system. They need to know how long it took from the first idea that the Stamp Act meant loss of liberty to the declaration that liberty meant independence. They need to know that ideas and actions require lengthy and creative attention before they can become institutions like our constitutional government.

The Past: Alive and Well

The American Way begins each unit with a look at the detailed evidence that shows how each of the six great ideas or themes is present in American life and is recognizable today. The events of the past do not repeat themselves, but the governing ideas and traditional values that make the American Way unique are continuous and continuing.

Why should students understand the past? Because to understand the past is to understand why we are what we are. There is no great mystery to America. There is no reason for turning it over to someone else to run. It is not too complicated to understand. There is no reason to panic over problems or wail over failures. There are reasons for them too. Some of them have had a long history. There are reasons for great pride.

Analysis: Step-by-Step

To solve problems Americans have to know what these problems consist of. To do this on a concrete, practical, unfrightening level is to look at them one piece at a time.

But to introduce a problem for the first time in its modern form requires familiarity with a special vocabulary and many concepts that most students do not have. Any social studies textbook is confronted with the issue of how to see the parts, not oversimplify the whole and avoid an impossible level of abstraction. *The American Way* shows (not tells) students how the problems Americans faced and the institutions to deal with the problems developed in the first place.

Chronological order alone is not always helpful; it can be mindless. But chronological order that focuses on the building up of strengths, issues, problems, and institutions step-by-step makes it possible for even the students who are the slowest to conceptualize to end up understanding the world in which they live.

A Web—Not a Chain

One of the problems of writing historical narrative is how to include presidents, laws, treaties, and wars, all of which can be pegged to definite dates, while at the same time adequately describing what the rest of society in a variety of regions was doing, thinking, and feeling.

The American Way achieves coverage without destroying the structure, organization, and the readable flow of the narrative. It does this by continually watching how earlier themes weave into and through newer ones. This enables the students to get a picture of the complexity of American history while also recognizing their own present and future in it. The idea that cause and effect consists of one single event following upon another is thus avoided. By the end, students will be able to understand that all these various themes, groups, races, regions, and individuals together form not a chain but a web.

The American Way builds the picture of America around the philosophical core of American life. The book employs a strict chronology and a realistic sense of the significance of time. It is not necessary to double back to pick up concurrent events. The emphasis on personal biographies also makes history come alive by focusing on the actual decisions, judgments, tastes, and mistakes of various individuals.

THE STRUCTURE OF THE NARRATIVE

The Writing Style

The American Way has a narrative writing style designed to capture the reader's imagination and keep student attention. The text is made readable by the use of short sentences and carefully controlled vocabulary.

Good writing for unsophisticated readers requires more words, linked together closely. The best word is often too abstract or assumes too much background for this level reader. Writing for schools does not permit the writers to use metaphors based on adult experience or images that are restricted to some groups or regions. Rhythm of sentences, parallel construction, closely constructed sequences of facts and ideas, and detailed descriptions must carry the reader along.

The American Way makes students aware of the details around them and of the importance of people, time, space, and ideas. It is the goal of this book that its readers will understand America, be proud of its strengths, be pleased in its determination to improve, and welcome the opportunity to join as active citizens in *The American Way*.

How a Unit Works: Its Structure and Function

The Opening: America Is . . .

Each of the six units of *The American Way* begins with a modern look at the detailed evidence of a theme in American life that is characteristic of the American way. Each of these essays is entitled America Is . . . It is followed by the theme that is the focus of the chronological period in history that is about to be studied. This opening feature of the unit ends with "how and when did this theme become a major characteristic of the American way?"

Why does each unit open with the modern observation? The book encourages *awareness* that there is an American way and that despite distances and diversity each American is a part of it. The unit opener presents the *least vicarious and most concrete presentation of the abstract theme*. Students in this age range can handle abstractions. The developmental learning theory behind this textbook is that students get a realistic, grownup look at America if they can relate the abstractions of a theme to the practical examples of it in the world they live in. This book teaches through description, not definitions. The historical account of how a theme came to be also is descriptive. The student watches that theme being built into the American way piece by piece. Historical figures are vividly pictured as alive in their world of real options, perceptions, conditions, and values.

America Is . . . can easily and effectively be read aloud in class to enhance awareness of modern times as living history and history as the dynamics of a continuing human experience.

Chapter Organization

Each chapter is tied to the theme of the unit in a short introduction. The chapter introduction reinforces the theme and reminds the students of the setting of time and place they are about to study. It serves as a kind of overview of when and where they are in the narrative of America's history.

The chapter introduction asks several specific questions about the content of the chapter. Those same questions often appear at the end of each chapter for review.

Section and Subsection

Each chapter is divided into sections and each section is divided into boldface subheads. In this way students can stay alert to what is coming next and can use the survey and reinforcement techniques that enhance reading comprehension.

Pronunciations

Unfamiliar words and names are pronounced for the student when they first occur. The pronunciation is not repeated with each succeeding occurrence of the word. The following pronunciation key has been used throughout:

	Pronunciation Key
map	Alaska (uh LASS kuh)
date	Maine (MANE)
father	Nevada (neh VAH duh)
wet	Texas (TECK suss)
tip	Britain (BRIT'n)
toe	Ohio (oe HIE oe)
boy	Detroit (di TROIT)
humid	Utah (YOO taw)
sun	Kentucky (ken TUCK ih)

Reading for Study and Understanding

Questions in the Margin

Even good readers need to learn to adjust their reading speed and style to the nature of the reading. This text is a narrative. It is a story focused on six themes; each theme grows into the next and is continuously recalled. But all textbooks have the responsibility for comprehensive chronological coverage. The book must be read slowly and thoughtfully for the information to sink in. The student can then go beyond remembering to understand and finally to independent thought.

Every classroom, no matter how homogeneous, contains students who have vastly different reading abilities. In order to help all kinds of readers get the most out of their reading, *The American Way* has reading questions that help the student read for understanding and meaning. These questions are numbered sequentially and are designed to help students attach each new subsection to the last one and earlier ones. Good readers assimilate new information by making room for it and checking it against what they already know. They then make accommodation for the information, and it becomes part of their storehouse of information and ideas.

The margin questions are a continuing reminder of the need to process the new facts and ideas as the student proceeds through the textbook. They require low-level inferences and can be useful to different levels of readers in different ways.

Different Levels of Readers

The competent reader. Some students can take the book home and read a section or two. They will read it as a narrative, enjoying a good story. For these students the margin questions can be read afterward, as they go back to review the content.

The word reader. Most students will be able to read the words in this book without difficulty. The vocabulary and sentence length have been carefully controlled. Many, however, do not process the words or put them together into a meaningful picture without help. These are students who do not think about meaning or apply their reading to their own lives.

These students should read the margin questions for each subhead first and then proceed to read, stopping to think about the answers to each question as they go.

The student who has difficulty identifying words. These are the students who need to read with a partner or have their books read aloud in class. A margin question can be asked aloud by the teacher. Then the part of the book relating to that question can be read by the students as the answer to the question. Bit by bit the bigger story and the bigger picture can be created in a joint effort by the whole class. Together they can build a much more comprehensive and thoughtful picture than any of them could have done alone.

The Importance of Continuing Review

The American Way uses advance organizers to keep the students aware of what's coming. The book also uses a number of features to recap where the student has been and how that fits the expected outcomes. Each section has an opportunity for reviewing with checking the facts.

Each chapter has a feature called Putting It All Together. There the student is asked to understand the main ideas of the chapter and do some activities. The activities reinforce the use of maps and globes as representations of information. Each set of chapter activities also makes it possible for students to get much needed practice in expository writing. The end of the chapter also features additional reading for students to pursue their special interests. Fiction and nonfiction books are included.

The unit ends with a review. This is called Reviewing the Unit. It consists of an exercise in defining and using important words, called Building Vocabulary. A second exercise is Building Social Studies Skills, particularly those representational ones—maps, globes, charts, and graphs. The third part is Building Writing Skills, which has questions requiring the use of thinking skills, for example, comparisons, and the recognition of cause and effect.

A feature essay called Thinking Back follows each unit. This essay reviews the content coverage of the previous unit from the point of view of the unit's theme and the previous themes.

The American Way provides students with tools to help them learn. The narrative itself is written at an appropriate reading level. The sentences are descriptive. The use of readable materials encourages reading. The margin questions and Checking the Facts questions are two specific ways students can check to see whether they are getting the important data in the narrative. The development of the themes provides a method of introducing new material and reinforcing previously learned materials. *The American Way* is structured for the student and the teacher to provide the basic equipment for successful learning.

SKILLS: LEARNING WHY AND HOW YOU LEARN

In *The American Way* students will gain three kinds of learning skills. They are given the unusual opportunity to find out what it really takes to be able to "read" a map, a globe, a chart, a graph, and a time line. Students will learn these skills and how to use them easily. These are skills requiring abstract symbolic thought. Students will learn that there are skills for gathering information, such as interviewing and observing. And, finally, that there are efficient ways of learning to remember. Adolescents are old enough to be allowed "in" on what is happening to them as they learn. These skills features help them to understand the learning process.

Reporting Information: An Abstract Task

Current research on the intellectual development of children and teaching has shown that children learn more easily with some advance organizers. Further, it has been shown that even by grade eight many children have not yet mastered the basic cognitive skills to handle abstract materials such as maps, globes, and time lines. It may come as a surprise to read that statement, and so it should be explained. Many students can recite what a time line is or what a map is or even what the difference is between a map and a globe. They can conceptualize the difference, but they do not understand the difference, nor do they know how to use these tools. Ask students to explain the difference between a map and a globe or the pros and cons in using each, or which is the appropriate one and for what purpose. It may come as a surprise that they have never given much thought to such issues. Asking about the differences between maps and globes is important primarily as a way for the teacher to identify whether students understand their meaning and how they think about them. Can they make the necessary abstractions? If they can, that means they truly understand the difference. They have the intellectual ability to handle ideas on a somewhat abstract level.

Maps and globes involve abstractions. Charts and graphs are abstractions as well as pictures used to show an idea. While a map or globe represents the earth, a chart or a graph is the outcome of a set of complex transformations. For example, to understand a graph depicting economic growth, the student must understand that the symbols on the graph represent some other set of numbers, e.g., amount of income, which is in itself an abstraction denoting an amount of money. So the graph reflects first the transformation of real amounts of money into averages and then again into symbols on the graph.

Charts and graphs demand that students understand relationships. The set of relationships depicted on a chart represents the interaction of two things. For example, a chart intended to show the increase in average income in the United States from 1900 to 1970 will contain one dimension of time (years) and the other of average income (dollars). The principle is that as time changes, income increases; this is a relationship between time and income.

What the student has to understand in reading the graph is not only the meaning of the symbols but also the meaning of the abstract relationships represented in the graph. Again the student must understand the logic of the graph or the chart. The teacher may describe the elements so the student will come to grasp at the simplest level what it is all about. However, as with maps and globes, until students verbalize the conceptual base, they will not understand and be able to use that understanding in analyzing and creating other graphs and charts.

Exercises in chart building for whatever dimensions are of interest, e.g., the relationship between the number of horses in the United States and the number of cars from 1900 to 1978, or the number of cars and the growth of the city, or the increase in the production of cotton over the years, etc. Each of these examples represents a real change in the society. Depicting them on a graph or chart is an economical way to communicate the information. For the students to understand the message they must have the experience of constructing graphs and explaining the construction to someone else. Maps, globes, charts, and graphs depict abstract or representational events. They do not necessarily present the chronological relationship between events.

Chronology can be depicted on a time line. This is usually done by the teacher. The student is expected to come to understand the how of chronology through a time line. A time line may appear as a very concrete presentation. A time line should be understood by the student as a way of depicting temporal relationships. A time line, and a scale on a map, try to achieve the same goal. Each represents distance either in time or in space.

Relationships between concurrent events or events at different time points might provide the opportunity to examine such critical issues as why some things happen and what might be some of the background features that influence a certain event. For example, charting time of people's birth and charting some social events might demonstrate the relationship between particular people and social events. This would set the stage for a discussion of the "great person" theory of history, and the question: Did the time create the person or did the person create the time?

Gathering Information

The previous sections have referred to how data can be reported in charts or graphs and how the physical world can be represented. Another area of consideration is how some data or information about the physical and social world can be generated.

Two of the key tools that students can employ in social science and history are observation and interviewing. Observation is a basic data-gathering tool used by all of us. We are all observers of ourselves, of the society, and the physical environment. Research has demonstrated that though observation is common, if we observe the same event or phenomenon we do not usually see it the same way nor do we report it the same way. The phenomenon of observer disagreement is common knowledge to lawyers, teachers, and in fact everyone who has been somewhat thoughtful about the question. Seeing is not necessarily the way to truth. Yet much of what is reported is based on observations. In the accompanying textbook there are examples of historical events that have been reported by more than one individual.

Students can observe the same event and report on it in order to come to the conclusion that seeing is not necessarily the way to truth. Ask students to report on a common experience; it will yield important information showing them how many differences emerge even when all individuals see the same thing.

Observations, of course, do not tell what people are thinking or how they reason. It becomes necessary to interview: our second method. Interviewing, like observation, is a data-gathering procedure. It is often used in journalism or in political analysis. Virtually every student has seen some interview on television. Students doing their own interview can quickly come to learn about individual differences in thinking, reasoning, belief systems, etc. They may have discovered that while in their observation, people are seen acting in a similar way, with interview information they would discover it is done for different reasons. For example, just observing a hijacker would not tell you whether that person is an ideologue or an adventurer. Interviews can provide a rich data base students can analyze. They can see the value of the material, the trustworthiness of it, the degree to which the interviewee is biased, and a host of other issues.

Interviewing is a very useful way for the students to get into the act of generating their own knowledge base where appropriate. There is much to be gained in this process.

Learning to Comprehend: Learning to Remember

All is for naught with these data-gathering strategies if the student does not know how to use and organize materials, and how to proceed in an orderly fashion in mastering knowledge and integrating it with experience.

All the previously described skills come to their ultimate value to the degree that they facilitate the pupils' learning and retention of that material. Exercises in asking students to make these relationships—not in a mechanical manner, but by letting them discover the way events are related or by asking them to explain the rationale for their answers—bring them into direct contact with a need to explain, to justify, and to meet challenges. These engagements or dialogues can benefit the student by helping to organize the material, and in so doing facilitate retention.

Specifically asking students, for example, to relate to daily life the different kinds of information they studied in the text about the growth of their particular city, town, or village may facilitate retention and articulation of what is learned. By rooting their learning in their experience, namely living in the community and trying to identify its historical roots, the students should get a sharper picture of their town in its historical setting.

Unless students can learn how to use the information they have acquired by themselves and through teacher-generated activities, their learning will be less effective. By appropriate discussion emphasizing relationships such as causal connection, statements indicating relationships and, in essence, testing hypotheses, students will expand their own horizons as learners and as thinkers.

Teachers have their own teaching styles and ways of working with students. We all know there are many ways of doing the teaching job well. Many of the suggestions present here are intended to offer alternatives to help the student grow from a learner to a problem solver.

FOR CHILDREN WITH SPECIAL NEEDS

Public Law 94 142, the Education for All Handicapped Children Act, enacted November 29, 1975, changed the manner in which basic education was delivered to students with special needs. This change has three essential ingredients.

1. A handicapped student must be educated in the least restrictive environment. This is interpreted as an environment where educational needs are met with as little segregation or separation from the mainstream as possible.
2. An individual educational plan must be prepared for the handicapped student. The parent or guardian reviews the plan with the school and must agree to its contents.
3. The handicapped student is protected by due process. The parent or guardian is able to initiate a set of procedures if there is disagreement with the school placement and/or program.

The law also required the United States Office of Education to write a set of regulations to implement it. These are the regulations that hold the school accountable for the education of all handicapped students in the least restrictive environment. De facto segregation is no longer admissible.

This is accomplished through documented team meetings. The team comprises the teacher(s), the school psychologist, a central administrator. It may also include other appropriate specialists, such as the guidance counselor, the reading specialist, the speech or language specialist, the vision or hearing specialist, and so on. The team's purpose is to reach consensus on what is best for each student.

Through this process, then, the team defines the least restrictive environment for each student. A student's mainstream initially could be the self-contained classroom. As the team monitors the student's progress, the student could be assigned to a regular classroom in some areas. Another student may be assigned to a special education or resource room for part of the time and to regular classrooms at other times. A different student may remain in the regular classroom with some modifications in his or her program. All students, however, receive whatever supportive services they require.

The supportive services may be provided directly or indirectly to the student. He or she may need counseling (with the guidance counselor or school psychologist), reading or speech therapy, or perhaps adaptive physical education. There must be a variety of special services available to the handicapped student.

The Function of the Team

The regulations are very specific about how handicapped students are identified, about how their programs are developed, and about how their progress is monitored.

Delivery of Supportive Services

By calling for mainstreaming in the least restrictive environment, the regulations have changed the delivery system of the supportive services. In addition to providing direct assistance to the student, they provide for indirect services. The classroom teacher may need some assistance from the specialist in modifying curriculum and/or instruction for the handicapped student.

The handicapped student, as stated, has been assigned to the classroom by the team. He or she has been segregated from the mainstream in social studies and is now ready for re-entry. This, of course, does not mean that a handicap no longer exists. It does mean, however, that the student has been taught some techniques to compensate for it. The classroom teacher can assist the handicapped student by creating a climate where these coping mechanisms can be used. The student has the ability to learn.

The physically handicapped student can now attend school as it has been modified for accessibility and safety. This generally does not require further modifications in the classroom unless the student is also handicapped in other ways. If the student is unable to write, for instance, his or her responses can be dictated to a volunteer recorder or the responses can be recorded on a cassette or tape.

The Visually Impaired

The visually impaired student must rely primarily on listening skills to learn in and out of the classroom. The time and cost of transcribing a text into Braille, if that is the student's form of reading, is prohibitive. In many cases, however, a high intensity lamp and/or a magnifying glass may be of assistance.

Recording the text on cassette or tape, however, is within the realm of possibility. Parent or student volunteers could be solicited for this purpose. Some schools have marshaled senior citizen volunteers for such activities. If a Braille typewriter is unavailable for the student's written assignments, these would either need to be recorded or read to the student. In either case, the student's responses should be recorded, so that they may be replayed and adjusted as needed.

This would also provide the teacher with an opportunity to analyze the longer responses more carefully. If the student has some vision, the assignment should be typed on a primer typewriter or printed in large letters with a black felt-tip pen.

The Hearing Impaired

The hearing impaired student is in the regular classroom because of her or his lip-reading ability. Furthermore, that student knows how to read the alphabet system. This is especially important because, if the student is deaf, the alphabet becomes a second language.

The system we read is based on spelling words with the letters of the alphabet. The spelling pattern tracks sound, which represents meaning. The hearing impaired student then must often go from the visual to its association without the benefit of the sound symbol (phonics). In other words, the sound of a letter or letters to assist the student in recognizing unknown words cannot always be relied on. Each word must therefore be memorized visually. As a result, reading may be a slow process.

The hearing impaired student in the regular classroom can, however, put together speech sounds with a combination of a hearing aid and lip movements. Depending upon the nature of the loss, some sounds may be more difficult to distinguish than others. The hearing therapist will provide the teacher with that information and some suggestions for compensation. The teacher will need to inform the other students as to how they may assist during large-group and small-group sessions. In general, extraneous noises would mask speech sounds for the student. She or he would also benefit from slow, distinct speech with natural pauses between phrases to enhance meaning.

The Socially and Emotionally Disturbed

The socially and emotionally disturbed student has experienced difficulties in learning that cannot be explained by intellectual, sensory, or health factors. That student has probably been assigned to the self-contained special education classroom where the teacher is trained to handle his or her interpersonal problems, anxiety, depression, or inappropriate types of behavior. By keeping the student on task through a behavior—modification program, the teacher has helped the student acquire the necessary basic academic and personal skills to be mainstreamed.

The social studies teacher needs to study the records carefully and consult with all members of the team to deal with these fragile personality structures. The primary difficulty for these students is in how they view their individual worlds. They have no doubt been dealt with inconsistently by the meaningful adults in their lives. Consequently they do not know where their limits are, and this has led to insecurity. For young people to feel secure, their world must be predictable to them. The socially and emotionally disturbed students test adults in attempts to find those limits.

The teacher, then, must be very specific and consistent with the socially and emotionally disturbed student. It is especially important that praise be both specific and deserved. A global compliment, such as "That's good," is noninstructive. The student needs to know why. Saying that a task was done well when it was not makes the teacher appear less than congruous. This fails to promote the trust this student lacks with adults.

The socially and emotionally disturbed student may need an opportunity and a place for "time out." This is a mechanism whereby the student may retreat when feelings and/or behavior cannot be kept under control. Security is then provided because the student knows that he or she can retreat from circumstances until returning is comfortable. Sometimes the teacher must ask if the student wants to stay with the group or take "time out." The tacit understanding is that, if the student remains, she or he stays on task. The "time out" area could be the resource room or the guidance office, where counseling could be given if necessary.

The Learning Disabled

The student with a learning disability has a deficiency in acquiring basic skills. This may be in the ability to reason, think, read, write, spell, or do mathematical calculations. The student may also exhibit such conditions as brain damage or minimal brain dysfunction. Any adjustment problems in this case are considered to be results of that individual's problems with learning. The learning disabled student is distinguished from the educable mentally retarded student, who exhibits some of the same learning problems, in that intellectual functioning is average or above.

The learning disabled student generally has difficulty with associative learning. This can manifest itself, in reading, by an inability to identify the visual cluster of letters that track a sound or an inability to blend sounds together to track a meaning-bearing unit. As with the deaf, learning disabled students must often be taught to respond to the whole word. Sometimes this can be accomplished only through a total sensory imprint method known as visual-auditory-kinesthetic-tactile. The student first traces the word while saying it and then writes the word while saying it.

The reading required in a social studies classroom may be difficult for the learning disabled student. The taping of material required for the visually impaired may also be beneficial for the learning disabled student. However, this student should be encouraged to read along in the text to foster the sensory imprint method of learning. The student may have difficulty with expressive language as well. Responses from this student may be better if she or he dictates to a volunteer or into a tape recorder. Such a student has difficulty in copying material from the chalkboard, in formulating written sentences, and in spelling. Anxiety over trying to accomplish these tasks may interfere with the communication of what this student already knows.

Team Decision

It is the responsibility of the team, of which the social studies teacher is a part, to determine how much modification is possible for any one student in any one classroom. Other members will observe the student and make suggestions. The team also decides how the student is to be evaluated, i.e., relative to classmates or to some other criterion. The team may in fact decide that the mainstreaming effort is too ambitious for the student at this time.

Use of Problem Solving

The law has required mainstreaming and with good reason. The student needs remediation in the basic skills, but this can be determined as well, because the handicapped student is deprived of the social benefits from learning in a group. If the teacher is using the problem-solving approach to learning, group performance may be superior to that of the individual for the following reasons:
1. A broader background of experience is represented, and more and varied suggestions are made.
2. The diversity of viewpoints is more likely to be representative of the problem.
3. More criticisms of proposals are made, and the bases for rejecting them are offered.
4. More interstimulation is offered.
5. More interpersonal dynamics are experienced.

Thus the teacher has provided a group experience for individual responses.

For Students with Special Needs

How *The American Way* Can Help

The philosophy behind mainstreaming is similar to the philosophy of *The American Way*. Americans have to accept differences and build on strengths in what is a common national experience. We are a variety of people with shared values.

Every strong program in history and social studies must be held responsible for opportunities to increase the skills and understanding of all the students, including the academically gifted and the handicapped. While giving opportunities for growth to the strongest, what can *The American Way* do to help teachers reach everyone? What features of *The American Way* make it easier for teachers to handle differences within the single classroom?
1. The message of *The American Way* is that we are a nation of variety and shared values. A classroom of differences is the American way.
2. The text anchors the learning in concrete experiences recognizable to every child. From their own experience, all will be aware of the themes in modern America that open each unit. That feature is called *America Is*.
3. The text tells the readers in advance what the big idea or theme is—and then builds it step by step. Advance organizers in every unit, chapter, and section recap and compare earlier facts and recurring themes. All of these

aspects of the text work together to keep the learner's attention and enhance motivation through expectation.

4. The margin questions provide needed structure by guaranteeing the close attention of the reader paragraph by paragraph and subsection by subsection. Through activities such as gaming, simulations, and role playing, or by observing someone else engaged in such activities, the handicapped student may gain a better understanding of a complex situation. Furthermore, she or he would benefit from the opportunity to demonstrate strengths that may not be obvious in a large group discussion or in a reading-writing format.

In general, handicapped students will experience some difficulty in reading and in writing the assignments. Students, of course, require reteaching in how to use the learning aids in the book to help in reading comprehension.

The introduction and the paragraph, section, and chapter headings give the student the reasons for reading. However, students often fail to use pictures, charts, graphs, and tables effectively. These would be another tool to aid the handicapped student in reading.

Written assignments, as stated, can be extremely difficult for the handicapped student. Expository writing is the presentation of information in a logical order. It requires that the student know the facts, see their relationships, and know how to present them to an audience. Overlaying this thinking process is sentence construction and mechanics. If the team decides that the student should have some writing, some specific suggestions should be made. The philosophy of special education is to compensate by first building on strengths. Once these strengths are identified, then the student has the confidence to work in new areas.

UNIT FOCUS, CHAPTER CONTENT, OBJECTIVES, AND ANSWERS TO: CHECKING THE FACTS, PUTTING IT ALL TOGETHER, AND REVIEWING THE UNIT

Unit One—Variety and Shared Values

Focus

In this unit students are asked to focus on the variety that became America. They are asked to look at as a large group of people from far off in time and space. The unit explores: the different relationships of people to their environment: the meaning of spiritual life and belief to people's daily lives: the interaction of organization of society and its values: the outside conditions that restricted people or became opportunities for them.

Chapter 1. Variety Among Native Americans

Content
● Earliest Native Americans, their social organization, their relation to land use, and their need to live with nature
● What Native Americans valued, as seen through their rituals
● The migration of peoples from Asia, and the tools scientists use to support theories of migration

Objectives
Students will be able to:
—make a chart that compares groups of Native Americans by means of their location, language groups and land use
—identify the kinds of artifacts that can be used for evidence
—trace on a map the movement of early people in North and South America
—recognize the idea of spiritual belief, as the core of outward ritual and mythology
—recognize and identify the fixed geographical conditions that some people have to live with rather than control

Checking the facts, page 16

1. Why did the earliest people come across the Bering land bridge?
They followed the animals that they relied upon for food.
2. How did the increasing knowledge of plants change the lives of the early Americans?
Once they came upon fertile areas, these first Americans stayed in one place for longer periods of time to grow and harvest the new plants they found. They organized themselves within settlements for the common good. The concept of land ownership developed in America.
3. "The civilizations of the early American people were less advanced than those of Europe or Asia." What facts would you use to agree with this statement? What facts would you use to disagree?
The student could defend the positive view by citing the development of metal tools and vehicles for transportation in Europe and Asia. On the other hand, a student could defend the negative view by citing how the early Americans adapted to and used their environment in a highly organized way.

Checking the facts, page 30

1. Choose two language families from different geographic areas. Describe how each adapted to its environment.
The student should mention how the tribe used the available food or produced food, and also how the tribe used whatever materials for housing and clothing were available.
2. Compare the roles of men and women in hunting and farming tribes.
The roles were fairly consistent in the hunting tribes; men hunted game while women prepared the meat for food and the hides for clothing, etc. But in agricultural tribes these roles were not always consistent. In some, women planted and harvested the crops while in others men performed these tasks.
3. What was special about the Native Americans' beliefs about nature?
Because they were dependent on nature, the Native Americans believed that spirits were responsible for producing the plant life that was necessary to keep people and animals alive. Thus, the spirits were in all things that produced life and had to be treated with respect. Also, people were never alone, since they shared their lives with these many spirits in nature.

Putting It All Together, page 31

Understanding the Main Ideas

1. Where did Native Americans come from?
Archaeological evidence suggests that they came from various places in Asia across the land bridge that existed thousands of years ago between what is now Siberia in Russia and Alaska.
2. Where did they settle?
They spread into the flat areas of what is now the United States, Canada, and South America.
3. What kind of society did Native Americans build in Mexico and Peru? How was this society different from the society of northern Native Americans?
The Native Americans of Mexico and Peru had a more organized society than those of North America. They planted food, developed agriculture, and settled in communities. Community life demanded that they organize to build roads, bridges, and irrigation ditches. They built temples for worship. They produced works of art in stone and gold. Those Native Americans of North America who lived in areas where it was easy to grow crops also set aside land for farming, built villages, and organized their lives around special duties and ceremonies that they believed would yield a good harvest.
Some Native Americans of North America lived by hunting. Because they did not stay in one place for very long, they did not develop the community structures of the people who settled in villages.
4. How did the climate and land affect the people of North America?
The fertility of the land and the amount of rainfall determined whether they lived by farming or hunting. Agricultural communities developed more complex societies than did nomadic tribes.

Activities
Student answers will vary.

Chapter 2. Europeans Reach Out

Content
● During the Middle Ages connections developed among political, economic, and social structures. This was supported by knowledge and values that formed the web of European society in the Middle Ages and early modern period
● The relationship of trade, war, and governmental organization in Europe and the connections between Europe and Africa
● The development of Spanish and Portuguese explorations in the Americas
● The Spanish in the New World, their relationship to Native Americans, and the political and social organizations they developed

Objectives
Students will be able to:
—name the major exploring nations in Europe
—identify geographic and demographic conditions that influenced the discoverers to explore new lands and settle them in a particular style
—compare in at least two ways the different manners in which Europeans and Native Americans thought about universal values or the meaning of life
—identify at least three of the results of the conquest of one culture by another
—locate on a map the European exploring nations and the areas the European discoverers found

Checking the facts, page 38

1. What were the forces that made Europe become a society of traders?
The land produced more food than could be consumed locally. European producers wanted to trade their surplus food. Both Moslems and Christians conquered new lands that became markets for goods and sources of raw material.
2. How did trade among nations affect the lives of Europeans?
Europeans became dependent on eastern goods, such as spices. Europeans produced wool, fur, and lumber that they traded with the East. People left their farms to manufacture products. Manufacturers bought food from farmers, and farmers bought products from manufacturers. Money became the medium of exchange in trade. Europe soon became a society of towns and traders.
3. Why do historians believe the Norse, or Vikings, explored North America?
There are remains of Viking villages in North America. Norse writing describes land that resembles America.
4. What benefits came from trade among the different parts of the East?
A trading chain was established. A desire for a sea route to the East became the preoccupation of European traders. Through

Marco Polo's travels, Europe learned about business and social activity in the East.

Checking the facts, page 54

1. How did geography determine which nations would explore the New World?
The nations that explored the New World were located on the Atlantic coast. They had developed good sailors, seaworthy vessels, navigation skills, and knowledge of other lands and people in the course of their trading operations.
2. What were the circumstances that led to Columbus's voyage in 1492?
Some Europeans wanted to find a sea route to India. Others wanted to convert the rest of the world to Christianity. Queen Isabella and King Ferdinand of Spain wanted to find gold and silver to secure the unification of their country. Columbus wanted to make the first voyage to the "Indies." Those motivating forces provided the impetus for Columbus' voyage in 1492.
3. How did the Spanish explorations change the lives of people in the New World?
The Spanish introduced the horse to the New World. It gave the Native Americans mobility and enhanced their hunting capability. The Spanish introduced their form of government and the encomienda system of land ownership. Missionaries introduced Christianity and schooling in their attempts to convert the Native Americans and to condition them to living under Spanish rule.

Putting It All Together, page 55

Understanding the Main Ideas
1. Why did Europeans want to reach out to new lands?
They wanted more land for production. They wanted wealth represented by precious metals found outside the Continent. They wanted to establish trading networks with colonies. And they wanted to introduce their religions and their forms of government to people living in other lands.
2. How did life in Europe expand beyond its borders?
The Vikings founded settlements in Newfoundland and in North America. European Christians went on Crusades to gain control of the Holy Land from the Moslems in a war that lasted over 200 years. Trade developed between the East and the West.
3. How did Spain organize its explorations?
It sent explorers to find a passage to the East. The explorers were to exercise complete control over any land and people that they claimed in the name of Spain. They were to explore for gold and silver. When they found new lands, Spain sent more explorers to continue exploring new territory.
4. How did the Spanish behave towards the Native Americans?

The Spanish conquered the Native Americans. They tried to convert them to Christianity. The Native American civilizations were destroyed and replaced with Spanish organizations, structures of government, and education.

Activities
Student answers will vary.

Chapter 3. France and England Compete

Content
● The development of England and France in the 1500's
● How the English became so distinctive in their trade, agriculture, shipping, religion, and representative government
● How the French brought their ways to North America

Objectives
Students will be able to:
—identify the differences among the French, English, and Spanish organization of colonies in America
—identify the common elements of the newly organized nation-states in Europe as part of the history of the settlement and culture in the Americas
—locate the areas the French explored and colonized

Checking the facts, page 64

1. Why were England and Spain such bitter enemies?
England needed to explore and conquer new lands in order to develop trade. Spain was engaged in the same activity. England had broken away from the Roman Catholic church and formed its own Protestant religion. Spain remained Roman Catholic and wanted England to rejoin the Catholic church.
2. How was England's approach to the New World different from Spain's?
Spain ruled the Native Americans with a few conquistadors. England sent colonists to form permanent settlements. The area that Spain found was rich in natural resources and contained an organized civilization living in permanent settlements. The area England formed was forest land without apparent wealth or settlers.
3. How did England become a world power?
During the reign of Elizabeth, explorers were sent to claim land for England in the New World. Settlements were started, pirates such

as Drake were encouraged to raid Spanish treasure ships, and the rival Spanish fleet, the Armada, was defeated.

Checking the facts, page 70

1. Why did the French arrive late in the New World?
They were busy fighting religious wars in France. When Henry IV, a Catholic convert, decreed that the harsh treatment of Protestants be stopped, the French turned their attention to exploring the New World.
2. How did the French attempt to settle the New World?
They granted individuals the right to explore certain territories. The individual was responsible for outfitting ships, supplying the expedition, setting up farms, and trading with France. The French converted the Native Americans to Christianity. They tried to get French nobles to come to the New World by giving them land and inducing peasants to settle and work on the land.
3. What was the continent of North America like after 300 years of exploration and settlement?
It contained the civilizations of several European nations. Spain and France tried to rule their colonies from home, whereas England governed its colonies indirectly. The Native Americans' lives had changed because of the tools, animals, clothing, and cultures that the Europeans had introduced. The Native Americans had their land, their culture, and often their freedom, taken from them.

Putting It All Together, page 71

Understanding the Main Ideas
1. How did England become strong enough to explore new land?
It improved trade by raising sheep and exporting wool. It reduced its dependency on other nations by building a fishing fleet, and developing its capacity, and encouraging people to eat more fish. It grew rich from piracy on the high seas.
2. Why did England organize settlements in the New World?
England wanted to establish colonies with which it could trade. Trade was considered the most effective means of increasing the resources and the power of the island.
3. How did the French organize their efforts in the New World?
They sent explorers who were to claim land for France and to set up fur trading posts with the Native Americans. The explorers were given grants to explore certain territories.
4. How did the French and English behave toward the Native Americans?
The French learned the languages of the Native Americans, married them, and trapped their animals. The English brought families to settle Native American land.

Activities
Student answers will vary.

Chapter 4. Settlements and Choices

Content
● An up-close look at the variety within the English colonial policy of North America
● The settlement of Jamestown: including its trade, labor, the introduction of Blacks, English survival, and conflict with Native American survival
● The settlement of New England: including the role of the Protestant churches, the separation of new churches through emigration, the organization by hierarchy, and the place of women

Objectives
Students will be able to:
—list how the English worked through the conditions of their first settlements, describe the choices available to them and the cause-and-effect relationship of their decisions to conditions, and describe in a paragraph the relationship of fixed conditions to change of leadership
—describe how unplanned-change affected the colonists
—contrast the differences in motivation between common loyalties of the Mayflower Compact and individual reasons for emigration
—chart and compare different leadership roles, use of power, and reason for settlement in the Jamestown and the Puritan settlements in America
—locate Jamestown and Plymouth colonies on a map

Checking the facts, page 84

1. How did the English change their plans after sending people to settle Jamestown?
They developed a quasi-military plan. Settlers were told that they had to work together and support one another in order to survive. They were recruited on the strength of their commitments to leave England forever and settle in the New World.
2. What changes came about because of growing tobacco?
Tobacco was a good cash crop that grew in poor land. Little knowledge of farming was required to raise this crop, and so settlers were attracted to land where tobacco could be grown. A new system of government became necessary as the number of settlers increased. The Native Americans began attacking the settlers as they took over more and more land.
3. Describe the first representative government in the New World.
The House of Burgesses was made up of two people from each of the small settlements in the Jamestown area. It was based on English law. It dealt with decisions regarding the growing, pricing, and selling of tobacco and arguments that settlement owners could not resolve.

Checking the facts, page 89

1. Why did the Puritans disagree with the leaders of the Church of England?

The Puritans did not want to worship in the orthodox way prescribed by the king, the head of the Church of England. Puritan ministers refused to acknowledge the religious authority of the king.

2. What held the Puritans together as a group during the first years at Plymouth?

They had made an agreement, or a compact, about how they would govern themselves. They realized that they needed to work together in order to survive. They were convinced that settling in the New World was the right thing to do.

3. What were the main ideas behind the Mayflower Compact?

Leadership was not to be exercised by one individual but was to be the preserve of the congregation. Decisions were to be made by majority vote. The Mayflower Compact provided for a civil, political body that was to make "just and equal laws."

Checking the facts, page 96

1. What did the Puritans think about equality, work, and government?

Only White male householders who were God's chosen people were authorized to make decisions for the community. Hard work was evidence that a man was chosen by God. Work was valued by the congregation. Decisions made by the government should be for the good of the whole congregation.

2. What was the role of the selectmen in Puritan colonies of New England?

They watched over the activities of the congregation and gave advice at town meetings.

3. What did women do in Puritan New England?

They made the cloth and clothing for the household. They cooked, preserved, and stored food. They provided health service to the community. They helped their husbands in their trades. They often served as the town undertakers. They set up schools to teach other women how to spin and weave.

4. What were the reasons for the success of the New England colonies?

The Pilgrims were committed to establishing a new way of life. The Native Americans helped them to plant for the second winter. They invited people with necessary skills to help the congregation. They had a strong belief that they were doing what God wanted them to do.

Putting It All Together, page 97

Understanding the Main Ideas

1. Why did the English come to America?

They came for various reasons. Some hoped to become traders. Some
hoped to find riches. Some hoped to convert the Native Americans to Christianity. Some wanted the freedom to worship as they pleased.

2. What did the English find when they arrived?

At Jamestown they found a mosquito-ridden and malarial swamp surrounded by poor farming land and many Native Americans. At Plymouth they found a cold, rocky coast. There were few Native Americans in New England, but they showed the settlers how to farm.

3. What did they save from their life in England?

They retained the laws, their religion, and the notion of freedom of opportunity.

4. What changes in their lives did they have to make in America?

They had to devise organizations that would produce cooperative living and working arrangements, and they had to learn to understand the Native Americans and be understood by them.

5. What did the settlers think was most important?

The settlers thought that self-government was most important. In Jamestown the settlers believed that their decision to grow tobacco was more important than the king's belief that the settlers should supply raw materials to England. In Massachusetts the settlers thought that the special people of God had the right to run their colony.

Activities

Student answers will vary.

Chapter 5. New Settlements, Other Choices

Content

- The development of greater variety in America through policy decisions by the Dutch in New York and the English in Maryland, Pennsylvania, the Carolinas, and Georgia
- The importance of the existence of many religions in the colonies
- The English Civil War's effect on colonization
- The English conflict with the Dutch in New York
- The comparison and contrast of the early and later colonies
- The immigrants to America from nations other than England and France

Objectives

Students will be able to:

—compare the differences between the early and late colonies

—make a chart that shows the geographical conditions, organization, and timing of the colonial settlements for Maryland, Connecticut, Rhode Island, the Carolinas, New York, New Jersey, Pennsylvania, and Georgia

—describe the different religious groups in America including Protestants, Catholics and Jews

—guess at the implications of this for the development of the continent, the lives of individuals, and of groups
—locate the colonies on a map and identify who settled them

Checking the facts, page 104

1. For what reason was the Dutch colony of New Netherland set up?
It was established for the purpose of trading and acquiring riches.
2. Why did other colonies in New England develop?
Some colonists disagreed about the right way to worship and to run a religious community. They left to form new colonies, taking their followers with them.
3. What did the Fundamental Orders of Connecticut provide for?
The Fundamental Orders of Connecticut was a constitution that embodied a detailed plan of government that everyone agreed to support.

Checking the facts, page 112

1. What was the triangular trade?
The colonists took their ships, horses, grain, pork, and beef to such places as the Caribbean islands and Africa, where they sold them for sugar or slaves. They sold the products that they had purchased to other nations. The rationale behind the triangular trade was to sell products and transportation to other traders.
2. How did William Penn plan for a successful colony?
He sent a surveyor to America to map the colony and lay out cities, streets, and public parks. He sent word to the Native Americans, informing them of his respect for them and of his wish to buy some of their land. He wrote rules for settlers that required the fair treatment of Native Americans. He advertised in Europe for settlers, describing the beauty of the country and the operations of a representative government that would guarantee freedom of worship.
3. What was special about the Georgia colony?
James Oglethorpe wanted to establish a colony for poor people imprisoned in England for not paying their debts. He planned to pay for their voyages and give them 50 acres of land when they arrived in the colony. Few debtors arrived. Instead people searching for land and wealth went to Georgia and shaped the development of the colony.

Checking the facts, page 116

1. What made the French Huguenots different from other settlers?
They spread out and adopted the way of life around them rather than clustering together and preserving their own distinct culture.

2. Why did the Germans settle in the colonies?
Farmland in Germany had been ruined by a generation of warfare, and so the poor came to establish farming communities. The Mennonites, who had broken away from the Lutheran church in Germany, came for religious freedom.
3. Why was Rhode Island Colony a center for Jews?
The Jews tended to live in Rhode Island where there existed the separation of church and state. The Jews had religious freedom in Rhode Island.
4. What were some of the contributions of the Scotch-Irish?
They used their skills as weavers of wool and linen and as furniture makers. They fought for their right to have equal representation in the legislatures of the colonies. They believed in a classical education and founded the College of New Jersey, later known as Princeton.

Putting It All Together, page 117

Understanding the Main Ideas
1. What did these colonists learn from the experiences of earlier settlers?
They learned that they would have to recruit people who had the desire and the skills to work the land. They settled where they could learn from and trade with older colonies.
2. How were the later colonies influenced by changes in England and Europe?
Charles I of England asked Roman Catholics who were resisting the Church of England to leave the country. They founded Maryland. The Civil War in England prevented emigration, and the New England colonies began trading with other lands to compensate for the loss of markets represented by the decline in immigration. The farmlands of Germany were ruined by a generation of warfare, and so many German farmers immigrated to the colonies. The Scots-Irish emigrated when England tried to keep them from competing with English weavers.
3. What choices were open to non-English settlers?
They could go almost anywhere they wanted to in the colonies. Their skills and their customs were welcomed. If they immigrated for religious reasons, there were especially well received in Rhode Island and in Pennsylvania.

Activities
Student answers will vary.

Chapter 6. Colonies in a Strong Empire

Content
● The development of class differences from 1700 to 1763 and how they depended on geographic location and the timing of the arrival of the colonists
● The development of slavery as a system in the agricultural South

- The development and growth of Southern cities
- The development of church organizations and educational institutions
- The importance of the triangular trade for the Northern colonies' economic development
- How the French and Indian War created a sense of being "American"

Objectives
Students will be able to:
—identify the interconnections of land, social class, time, and individual people in determining dominant lifestyle in any one region
—describe the cause-and-effect relationships of British policy toward trade, and the economic life-style developing in the colonies
—use the maps in the text for evidence to describe the conflicts developing among the French, English and Americans on the North American continent

Checking the facts, page 127

1. How did the mercantile system affect the growth of cities in the South?
Southern colonies produced certain crops such as tobacco, rice, and indigo. In a predominantly agricultural economy, a city only grew up if it was a port for storing or shipping crops.
2. Why were slaves needed in the South?
Slaves were used on plantations. Prices for agricultural products were low because so much was available for sale. Farmers needed to grow substantial quantities to make profits. Cheap labor was needed, and to southerners this meant slaves.
3. What was the South's specialization?
Tobacco, planted and harvested by slaves, grew easily.

Checking the facts, page 132

1. Why did so many settlers come to live in the New England colonies?
The Europeans did not need New England's crops, and the colonists traded with the West Indies. This trade created a need for shipbuilding and for ports. Cities developed around the port facilities. The development of cities created jobs for newcomers who could buy land that made them recognized members of the community.
2. What views did the North hold regarding slavery?
Some people, such as the Quakers, were opposed to slavery on religious grounds. White city workers were worried that the slaves would take their jobs. Some thought that there were too many slaves. Others objected to the profit made from slavery.
3. How did some Blacks succeed in the North?
They could buy their freedom, and many worked as farmers, in crafts, and at trades. Some towns provided schooling for Blacks.

4. What had Americans accomplished by mid-century?
They had prospered and had more individual freedom than Europeans could exercise. They produced far-reaching thinkers such as Benjamin Franklin who founded what was to become the University of Pennsylvania. Franklin formulated a plan for "one general government" for all the British colonies in America.
5. What was the purpose of the Albany Plan of Union?
Franklin proposed a general government for all the British colonies. The colonies as a whole would be able to pass laws and raise money for settlement and defense.

Checking the facts, page 138

1. Why did the English colonists want the land west of the Appalachians?
Furs were abundant in the area west of the Appalachians. The English colonists wanted to trade those furs but the land was held by the French.
2. How did the French react to the actions of the colonists?
The French told Washington that they planned to take over the entire Ohio Valley. They used Native Americans to help them fight the British.
3. What were the results of the Treaty of Paris?
The French and Indian War ended. The land east of the Mississippi, except New Orleans, was given to England.
4. How did the British gain control of the North American continent?
They defeated France in North America, in the West Indies, and in India. The Treaty of Paris gave them all of North America east of the Mississippi River except New Orleans.

Putting It All Together, page 139

Understanding the Main Ideas
1. How did the colonies develop economically within the British Empire?
The colonies in the South grew tobacco, indigo, and rice, which England wanted. The farm products were sent directly to England in exchange for manufactured goods. The colonies in the North produced fish, lumber, and cereals, which England did not want. They traded their products with the West Indies for sugar. The sugar was then sent to England and traded for manufactured goods.
2. Which of the various differences among the English colonies grew stronger in the 1700's?
The South maintained a system of slavery that provided cheap labor on the plantations. The North had few slaves. Several northern towns educated Blacks and encouraged them in trades. The South had a few cities that were considered good ports for shipping. The North had many small towns and a few cities. The needs of White people in the South were met on the plantations, and the needs of people in the North were met in the small towns and cities. In the South laws were made by a few. In the North, espe-

cially in New England, White male householders gathered at town meetings and voted on laws.

3. Which values did the colonists share?
They were proud to be residents of their colonies and members of the British Empire. They believed in hard work and equality of opportunity.

Activities
Student answers will vary.

Chapter 7. The Idea of Liberty

Content
● The Stamp Act and the actions taken during the crisis
● Parliament's decision to tax the colonies
● The American boycott of English tea
● The strengthening of local Committees of Correspondence
● The roles of Henry, Adams, Paine, Jefferson as leaders in the colonies
● Action and reaction between Britain and the colonies over trade, taxes, and local government
● The fighting at Lexington and Concord
● The decision to declare independence
● An analysis of the Declaration of Independence

Objectives
Students will be able to:
—discuss the power of the idea of liberty and back up their arguments with examples from the text
—explain the idea of consent and the reasons for the idea of constitution
—recognize the relationship between the origin of ideas, the importance of ideas, and the quality of writing
—list in chronological order the steps that moved the colonies toward independence
—identify the different groups within the colonies that supported independence and their reasons for doing so
—locate the battlefields of Lexington and Concord

Checking the facts, page 152

1. Why were the colonists having difficulty settling the West?
Native American uprisings were killing thousands of settlers. Parliament passed a law forbidding colonists to settle west of the Appalachians.
2. How was the English Parliament responsible for the development of American independence?
Before 1763, when Parliament passed legislation to raise money from the colonies and to exercise greater control over them, each colony thought only of its own interests. After 1763, the colonies joined together to act against their common enemy, England.

3. What decisions were made by the delegates at the First Continental Congress?
The delegates decided not to obey the Intolerable Acts. They pledged to take up arms if necessary. They appointed a committee to supervise a boycott of all goods imported from England as well as a ban on goods exported to England. The committee operated in every colony and maintained contact with all of the colonies.

Checking the facts, page 164

1. Why did the Second Continental Congress meet?
The colonies met to help Massachusetts and to plan the fight against England.
2. What actions did the Second Continental Congress take?
The delegates selected John Hancock president of the Congress. They made Congress an official organization by giving it the right to make decisions. They created a continental army with George Washington as its commander. The Second Continental Congress issued bills of credit that could be used as money throughout the colonies. It initiated trade with nations. It permitted privateers to attack English ships on the high seas. It asked each colony to adopt a constitution and to form a state government. It declared the colonies' independence from England.
3. How did the Declaration of Independence reflect the colonists' feelings about "taxation without representation"?
It declared that "governments are instituted among men, deriving their just powers from the consent of the governed." The colonists rejected Parliament's contention that it had the right to make laws for them without their consent.

Putting It All Together, page 165

Understanding the Main Ideas
1. What made the colonists think of themselves as separate from other English people?
For six generations they had made their own laws and governed themselves. The only regulation that had been imposed by Britain had been that of trade through the Navigation Acts.
2. How did the idea of liberty become so important?
In 1763 Parliament began to pass a series of measures to raise money from the colonies and to exercise greater control over them. The colonists believed that those decisions, made without their consent, took away their liberty.
3. What did liberty mean?
Liberty meant all of the values that had become associated with self-government.
4. How did Americans organize to get liberty?
They convened the First Continental Congress to send Great Britain a list of their rights and grievances, to organize a boycott of English goods, and to take up arms if necessary. They convened the Second Continental Congress to organize an army and to issue

bills of credit to be used throughout the colonies in order to supply the army. They declared their independence from Great Britain.

Activities
Student answers will vary.

Chapter 8. Liberty in Action

Content
● The organization of troops, leadership, and materials to fight the Revolutionary War
● The organization of men and women to participate in the war effort
● The major battles and the development of a strategy in winning the war
● The Articles of Confederation as a way of governing for liberty, not to unify the nation

Objectives
Students will be able to:
—discuss the ideas of liberty, rights, constitution, organization, and trust—describing how they are connected in creating an environment that supports a war
—explain how variety among Americans strengthened the idea and values of liberty for and trust in individuals
—use the map to locate the movement of troops throughout the war
—define diplomatic, general, revolution
—identify the people who worked as diplomats during the war and describe their contributions
—identify the major problems of the Articles of Confederation

Checking the facts, page 179

1. Why did some colonists remain loyal to Britain?
Back-country Scots did not want to be left to the mercy of east coast power groups. Wealthy merchants knew that their businesses depended on trade with England. The officers of the empire wanted to remain loyal to England.
2. What was the attitude of the states toward the Articles of Confederation?
The states distrusted giving power to a central government. Some states loaned money to the Congress, but others did not.
3. What did other nations do to help the colonists win the war?
Frederick von Steuben of Germany trained the Americans to deploy the most modern techniques of warfare and strategy. Pulaski and Kosciusko from Poland aided the army. The French declared war against England and sent troops. Spain declared war against England and attacked its fort at Gibralter in the Mediterranean. The Dutch sold supplies to the Americans, provoking England to declare war against them.

Checking the facts, page 187

1. How did the Articles of Confederation operate?
The Confederation was made up of one body, the legislature. The legislature was limited to making decisions about war and peace, raising an army, making treaties and alliances with other countries, and settling disputes between the states. Each state made all other decisions; states had more power than the Confederation.
2. What economic problems was the Confederation having?
It did not have the right to tax to raise money to pay its debts. Because it could not tax, it could not borrow money. It was buying more than it was selling to other nations.
3. How was the question of public lands settled?
The states agreed upon a plan whereby Congress made and enforced laws until 5,000 people lived in a territory. The adult males could elect a legislature and send a nonvoting delegate to Congress. With a population of 60,000 the territory could become a state. It could write its own constitution as long as it provided for a democratic government that rejected slavery.
4. Why was another convention called in Philadelphia?
Another convention was called to revise the Articles of Confederation, to promote trade, to levy and collect taxes, and to enforce the laws that were passed.

Putting It All Together, page 188

Understanding the Main Ideas
1. How did Americans organize to fight?
The 13 colonies had to learn to plan and work together. Congress could not tax, and so states and individuals had to supply the Continental Army, which was made up of untrained volunteers. There was no navy. They learned to organize most effectively when circumstances forced them to do so.
2. What caused the American military victory?
The British troops had to be supplied from across the ocean. It took four months for orders to reach the British generals in America. France declared war on England and sent troops to aid the colonists. Spain declared war on England and attacked Gibralter. France, Spain, and Holland gave financial aid to the colonies.
3. What could the Confederation do? Why could it not do more?
The Confederation provided for a weak central government. It could make war and peace, raise an army, make treaties and alliances, and settle disputes between states. It could not tax or regulate interstate commerce because the states had not given the central government that power. The states refused to create an executive and a court system.
4. Why could the Articles not guarantee liberty for all?
The basic weakness of the Articles was voluntary compliance with the laws passed by Congress. The Articles made no provision for enforcing compliance with those laws.

Activities
Student answers will vary.

Reviewing the unit, page 189

Building Vocabulary

Student answers will vary.

Building Social Studies Skills

a) 41° latitude, approximately
   74° longitude
b) approximately 40 miles
   64 kilometers
c) France lost all the territory on the continent. The northeastern part of the land became British territory. The
   western section became Spanish territory.

Building Writing Skills

1. Student answers will vary.
2. Student answers will vary.

Unit Two—Variety, Liberty and Representation

Focus

In this unit students are asked to focus on representation as the way the government handled the variety of
American people and their demands for liberty. Students
will see that this developed in America from the English
tradition.

Chapter 9. Out of Many—A New Nation

Content

● The Constitutional Convention and the discussions
  which led to the Constitution
● How the Constitution was created, the people who
  were present, their arguments, and the compromises
  reached
● The images of the American way as they appear in the
  Constitution
● The Constitution itself, considered article by article

Objectives

Students will be able to:
—list the grounds for agreement among the people who
  wanted to shape the new nation
—identify the people and the contributions of key members of the Constitutional Convention
—explain the need for compromise in building new organizations and institutions
—describe the Great Compromise and the Three-Fifths
  Compromise
—read the Constitution
—be able to define Constitution, covenant, convention

Checking the facts, page 200

1. What did the delegates from the Philadelphia Convention agree on from the start?
*They wanted the government to have the right to take action. They
wanted to make sure that no one person or group had too much
power. They wanted to preserve the differences among the 13 separate states. They wanted to preserve liberty for everyone.*
2. What ingredients were needed for this new recipe called
   federalism?
*A system of checks and balances was needed so that no level of
government could get too much power. The sovereignty of the 13
states had to be guaranteed. Procedures for determining representation and majority rule had to be established.*
3. What is the system of checks and balances?
*The Congress, the President, and the Court can check one another,
thus keeping the power of the central government in balance.*

Checking the facts, page 206

1. Who were "We, the people" in the late 1700's?
They were all White males who could vote.
2. How did the makers of the Constitution provide for
   expansion of "We, the people"?
They built into the Constitution mechanisms for amending it.
3. What was the importance of the Great Compromise?
*It satisfied the five smallest states that they would be represented
fairly. This assurance was necessary in order to ensure that their
votes would be included in the 9 votes that were required to ratify
the Constitution.*

Checking the facts, page 210

1. Why was Patrick Henry against the Constitution?
*He believed that the Constitution created too strong a govern-
ment.*
2. Why did Hamilton, Jay, and Madison write The Federalist Papers?
*Opinion in New York State was divided between the upstate farm-
ers who were opposed to ratification and the merchants of Manhattan who supported the creation of a strong central government. New
York's ratification of the Constitution was considered essential to
the success of the new government. Hamilton, Jay, and Madison
wrote a series of newspaper articles to convince New Yorkers to
support the Constitution.*
3. Why was it important for the future country to have
   Virginia ratify the Constitution?
*It was the home state of George Washington and other prominent
Americans. Without Virginia the new government would be
deprived of the services of many of the country's most influential
leaders.*

Putting It All Together, page 241

Understanding the Main Ideas

1. How did the delegates to the convention find a way to organize the 13 states into one whole nation?
They developed the idea of a federation—a union demanding as much loyalty as that required by local and state governments. The federation would give the states the power to achieve new strength together. The federation would prevent one state, one lawmaker, one assembly, and one popular leader from exercising unlimited power. The federation would permit each citizen to continue to be a member of her or his state.

2. How did the delegates find a way that would not force any part of the area to give up its way of living?
The small states demanded equal power. The South wanted to maintain its economic system, which depended on slave labor. Through the Great Compromise, a bicameral legislature was established. The House of Representatives was based on population; the Senate was based on the equal representation of each state. A formula was devised that permitted the slave states to count the slaves for the purpose of determining taxation and the number of representatives in the House. At the expiration of 20 years, the slave states were to stop importing slaves and thus be prevented from gaining new representation through the operation of that system.

3. How did the delegates find a way that could guarantee that everyone would be heard and that everyone would be represented in the decisions of a nation?
The membership of the House of Representatives was based on the population of the states. Members were to be elected directly by the people. The President was to be the "guardian of the people," and the people were given the right to elect the President.

4. How did the delegates try to find a way that would last through the years to come?
The delegates made provisions for amending the Constitution, they did not want their compromise plan for governing to be frozen.

5. How did they try to make their plan of governing strong enough to make decisions for all the states, yet representative enough to take care of all the variety, and flexible enough to change when necessary?
The new government claimed certain powers for the national government, including the printing and the coining of money and the control of interstate commerce. Representation in the House was based on population so that when population shifted, so would representation. They built in a system of checks and balances.

Activities

Student answers will vary.

Chapter 10. One Purpose for All?

Content
- Washington's administrations and the debate over what representation really meant to Hamilton and Jefferson
- Policy making and methods of governing under the Constitution
- Washington's options for the presidency
- The Adams administration, and the issues raised by the Alien and Sedition Acts
- How Jefferson's coalition brought about a shift in the control of politics
- The Supreme Court and its role in *Marbury* v. *Madison*

Objectives
Students will be able to:
—identify what Washington, Adams, Hamilton and Jefferson contributed toward making policy
—list the functions of the President
—describe the role of public opinion and political leadership, as Adams had to deal with each of these in his foreign policy with regard to France
—diagram the cause-and-effect connections in the making of policy toward one of the following: the United States Bank, the French Revolution, the Alien and Sedition Acts
—define foreign policy, minister, administration, presidency, Cabinet

Checking the facts, page 251

1. What was Washington's view of the presidency?
Washington named a Cabinet of advisers to perform the special tasks of the government. He wanted to strike a balance between being formal and informal. He believed that only members of Congress as the representatives of the people should formulate laws. He believed that he should not veto a bill unless it contradicted his conception of the Constitution.

2. Why were Hamilton and Jefferson in conflict?
Hamilton wanted the union to amass capital, make investments, tax revenues, and help private business. Jefferson wanted the union to bind people together and to prevent them from being dominated by people like the English king.

3. How did the conflict between the Hamilton and Jefferson followers affect politics in the United States?
National and state leaders developed factions. Eastern merchants sided with Hamilton, whereas western farmers sided with Jefferson. Washington won reelection in 1792, and Jefferson's supporters won a majority of the seats in the House. Representation was no longer used only to guarantee freedom. It had become a way of helping one group over another.

Checking the facts, page 256

1. Why did France expect help from America?
France had helped America fight for independence.

2. What problems did the central government have in the western frontier?
Native Americans fought the continuing spread of settlements.

Checking the facts, page 262

1. What circumstances brought Jefferson to the presidency?

France began attacking American ships, but the United States was not strong enough to fight back. Adams' followers in Congress passed the Alien and Sedition Acts to define disloyalty against the government. Adams made peace with France. The Jeffersonians contended that the Alien and Sedition Acts were not repealed because Adams intended to use the acts to silence their opposition.

2. What major changes took place during the Jefferson presidency?

He convinced people from different economic and social backgrounds to work together for common causes. In his second term he chose a running mate for the vice-presidency. The Supreme Court ruled that it had the right to declare laws unconstitutional.

3. Why did Adams believe that the Alien and Sedition Acts were needed?

Adams believed that the national government was being unduly influenced by foreigners. The newspapers were attacking Adams and his way of handling the French. Adams believed the Alien and Sedition Acts were a way of eliminating criticism and thus of letting him deal with France.

4. How were the results of the treaties signed by Jay and Pinckney different?

Jay won some concessions from the British but not all of the concessions that the American people wanted. Jay's treaty resulted in a treaty with Spain. Pinckney was able to get greater concessions from Spain than Jay had extracted from England. The United States was given the right to navigate the Mississippi River and to use New Orleans as a port for depositing its goods. The Pinckney Treaty was more popular than the Jay Treaty.

Putting It All Together, page 263

Understanding the Main Ideas

1. What actions did the national or federal government take?

The federal government established a court system, proposed a Bill of Rights, made treaties with England and Spain, used troops to stop the whiskey rebellion, and presided over the passage of power from one administration to another.

2. Did a powerful, active federal government help or hurt the states?

This question asks for an interpretation of facts. All answers should be supported by facts from the text.

3. How did the nation organize itself to make decisions?

Congress made laws for the country as a whole, the Supreme Court, in Marbury v. Madison, *established the right of judicial review. A party system developed around different points of view about how to govern the nation. These parties competed with each other to control national and local politics.*

Activities

Student answers will vary.

Chapter 11. Problems for Representation

Content

- Jefferson's decision to buy Louisiana, the Burr conspiracy, the Barbary pirates
- The reasons for the purchase of the Louisiana territory and its exploration by Lewis and Clark
- The different economic development within the nation
- The regional development of cotton, factories, roads, canals
- The effects of Madison's leadership during the War of 1812

Objectives

Students will be able to:

—define orally the President's decision to buy Louisiana

—locate the area of the Louisiana Purchase on the map

—describe the lands Lewis and Clark explored

—identify the causes within the nation for the Embargo and the effect of it on foreign and domestic affairs

—list the new inventions and their impact on the economy

—describe the role of cotton in the Southern economy, how it was tied to slavery, its relation to trading centers

—name two major internal improvements and explain how each affected the economic growth of America

—argue for and against the American participation in the War of 1812

—define the Monroe Doctrine, describe its elements and its effect on Latin America

Checking the facts, page 271

1. Why was Napoleon willing to sell the Louisiana Territory?

He could not reimpose French power in Santo Domingo, which was the key to his plan to create a powerful French empire, because a yellow fever epidemic had wiped out his army there. He needed all the money that he could get from the sale of Louisiana to carry out his plan to go to war against England.

2. What was the importance of the Louisiana Purchase?

The United States gained one third of a continent and 50,000 future citizens through peaceful means. The United States paid in government bonds, which meant that its credit was recognized and its economic future seemed to be secure.

3. What did the Lewis and Clark expedition accomplish?

The expedition established the boundaries of the new territory. The members of the expedition made detailed maps of the area. They cataloged the plant and animal life and analyzed environmental conditions that could conduce to growth. They surveyed the Native Americans and the conditions under which they lived.

Checking the facts, page 274

1. What actions did Jefferson take during his second term in office that divided the people?
He meddled in Burr's trial by offering aid to anyone who would testify against Burr. He persuaded Congress to pass the Embargo Act that put people out of work and raised the prices of goods.
2. What was Burr's conspiracy?
Burr plotted with members of the Federalist party to establish a confederacy in New England. Three years later, in 1807, he plotted with Governor Wilkinson of Louisiana to establish a separate nation out of the western territory of the United States.
3. Why did Jefferson decide to put an embargo on British trade?
Both Britain and France had imposed blockades against one another. The United States was selling to both sides. Britain began seizing American ships that were trading with France and the West Indies. Jefferson thought that the best way to stay neutral was to impose an embargo on all trade.

Checking the facts, page 288

1. Why was the invention of the cotton gin so important?
The South was able to compete with Egypt in selling cotton to England. The cotton gin increased the need for slaves. The profits derived from cotton created jobs and increased the amount of goods and services that people could buy throughout the United States.
2. What conditions were necessary for a network of factories to grow?
People had to learn how to make machines. A labor market was needed. A water supply was necessary to power the machines. A transportation network was also needed.
3. How did transportation change in the early 1800's?
Turnpikes were built enabling merchants to transport goods from town to town. The invention of the steamboat meant that goods could be carried upstream. The development of canal systems made it possible to take produce directly to cities on rivers.

Checking the facts, page 298

1. Why did some Americans want war with Great Britain?
Westerners and other Americans who wanted to settle the West thought that the Native Americans, who refused to surrender their land to the settlers, were receiving help from the British in Canada. The War Hawks thought that the British seizure of American ships and the impressment of American seamen had put America's honor at stake.
2. Why were the Americans able to fight the British to a standstill?
The Americans were fighting on their own territory. They won some important naval battles early in the war, despite having only a small navy. In 1813 Perry destroyed British ships on Lake Erie; then he ferried Harrison's troops to attack the British in Canada. Tecumseh was killed, and the Native Americans gave up the fight. The British were engaged in a two-front war, fighting in America and fighting against Napoleon in Europe.
3. What was the importance of the treaty with Great Britain and the battle of New Orleans?
Americans believed that their honor had been saved by fighting the British to a standstill. Much needed trade with Great Britain could begin again. The battle of New Orleans boosted American morale and made Andrew Jackson a national hero. In the next few years, the Americans were able to settle by negotiation the boundaries of the United States. The British agreed to an unarmed border with Canada.

Putting It All Together, page 299

Understanding the Main Ideas

1. How did the West fit into the total picture of the nation?
The West attracted people from the South and the East to settle its farm land. A transportation network established links between the West and the Northeast. The West became an area where the interests of the South and the East competed.
2. How might the different regions be tied together?
The transportation system of canals, railroads, and turnpikes established networks that tied the regions together. Settlers from one region often had families in other regions. The national government tried to hold all three regions together.
3. What foreign policy did American leaders think was best for the regions of the nation?
The West wanted war with Great Britain because western leaders believed that Great Britain was encouraging Native Americans to attack American settlers. The East, on the other hand, had developed a strong trading relationship with Great Britain. Eastern leaders did not want a war to disrupt this relationship. The War Hawks, including Henry Clay of Kentucky and John C. Calhoun of South Carolina, wanted to defend the nation's honor by declaring war against Great Britain.

Activities
Student answers will vary.

Chapter 12. Representing Regions

Content
● The regional differences as shown in the tariff, the bank, western lands
● The reason for and results of the Missouri Compromise
● The meaning of the Era of Good Feelings in America
● The election of 1824 and how it illuminates the developing sectionalism
● A description of Clay's American System

- The election of John Quincy Adams
- Jackson as a new type of candidate with his image of the winner

Objectives
Students will be able to:
—locate on a map the regions within the United States
—explain the connections between regional economics and political sectional rivalry
—describe the problems of representation when the sections compete for national resources
—characterize the role of the charismatic President and large political parties organized for winning
—write a short biography of President Jackson

Checking the facts, page 306

1. Why was the American System for developing a national interest needed?
The American System proposed by Henry Clay was needed to make the nation less dependent on trade with foreign nations. Through the development of the system, the nation would become strong, rich, and independent because every need would be met within its borders.

2. Why did slavery become an issue in Congress?
Slavery became an issue in Congress when the territories applied for statehood and Congress had to decide whether to admit them as free states or as slave states. The South supported Missouri's request to enter the Union as a slave state. Northern leaders did not want slaves competing with paid laborers. Nor did they want the new states to be admitted as slave states and thus change the balance of power in Congress by giving the South a majority.

Checking the facts, page 313

1. How did John Quincy Adams get elected?
Because none of the five candidates had received a majority of votes in the electoral college, the election had to be decided by the House of Representatives. Clay, the candidate who had received the fewest electoral votes, persuaded his supporters in the House to vote for Adams. Congress elected Adams even though Jackson had received more electoral votes than had Adams.

2. How did Andrew Jackson avoid being defeated a second time?
He organized a national party whose members soon became known as Democrats. During his campaign he said nothing about such controversial issues as the tariff and thus avoided offending each section of the country. The Democrats not only elected Jackson to the presidency, they also elected so many of their candidates to Congress that the new party constituted a majority in each house.

3. How did Calhoun's Doctrine of Nullification point out differences among the regions of the United States?
The North wanted the tariff and the South did not. The North,

represented by Webster, believed that the law of the country transcended regional concerns. Calhoun asserted that whenever a state believed that a law was unconstitutional, it could declare it null and void. The issue of the tariff, which led to the Doctrine of Nullification, epitomized the conflicting economic interests of the regions.

Checking the facts, page 321

1. What changes did Jackson make in the presidency?
He used a "Kitchen Cabinet," or a group of friends, as advisors. He used the spoils system to appoint his friends and supporters to government jobs. He vetoed bills that he thought the people did not want, and he used the pocket veto frequently.

2. How did Jackson and Calhoun differ on states' rights?
Jackson believed that the union was more important than any single state. Calhoun believed that a state could nullify any action of the federal government that it didn't agree with.

3. How was the Native American question resolved?
The reaction to this problem in the 1820's was to uproot the Native Americans from their land. They were driven westward to the Oklahoma territory. Many Native Americans died in the process of forcible resettlement.

Putting It All Together, page 322

Understanding the Main Ideas

1. What did Americans do about the representation of their differences?
The Tariff Bill of 1816 pitted the merchants of New England who traded with Europe against northerners and westerners who wanted to promote more manufacturing in the United States. The Missouri statehood bill pitted northerners who did not want another slave state against Southerners who did. The Tariff Bill of 1828 pitted northerners and westerners who wanted a tariff on wool, hemp, flax, fur, and liquor against New Englanders and southerners who did not. Easterners thought that government land in the West should not be sold too rapidly, while the southerners and westerners wanted cheaper prices for the land. In each of these cases the proponents of sectional interests elected representatives who articulated their points of view.

2. Where did Americans find the leadership to manage those differences?
The fundamental issue was whether the states or the union was more important. Calhoun believed that South Carolina had the right to pass a law that would declare a law of Congress null and void. Adams from Massachusetts and Jackson from Tennessee believed that the union was more important than any state.

3. On what policies could the Americans agree?
They agreed that compromise was necessary in order to preserve the union. They believed that each section should get its share of federal tax dollars. They believed in national political parties as a way of reconciling their differences.

Activities

Student answers will vary.

Reviewing the Unit, page 323

Building Vocabulary

1. Student answers will vary.

Building Social Studies Skills

1. a. Student answers will vary.
   b. The British planned to attack
      1) through the Great Lakes,
      2) through Washington, D. C.,
      3) and through New Orleans.
   c. The Cherokees traveled approximately 825 miles, or 1,320 kilometers.

Building Writing Skills

1. Student answers will vary.

Unit Three—Expansion and Individualism

Focus

This unit focuses on what happened to people when the mood of the nation encouraged its geographic expansion and its individualism. Different groups and individuals responded in unique ways to the expansion of the nation. The social history of the period requires a look at the systems that developed and the personalities who emerged within this period.

Chapter 13. Greater Growth–Stronger Ties

Content

● The development of the system of manufacturing
● The division between people born in America and the new immigrants
● How trade affected life in the cities
● The rise of reformers, including women's rights at Seneca Falls and the abolitionists
● The growth of regionalism in the South
● The growth of the factory system in the North and slavery in the South

Objectives

Students will be able to:
—describe how the American manufacturing system was built on agricultural products

—write a historical fiction about an Irish immigrant family in Boston
—define strike, blacklist, suffrage, slums, abolition, temperance, monopoly, factors

Checking the facts, page 344

1. How did the development of transportation affect the New England and Atlantic states?

They had the streams, the labor force, and the capital to become major manufacturers. The development of roads, canals, steamboats, and railroads to bring raw materials to the factories and to transport finished goods to markets throughout the country transformed those states into important manufacturing centers.

2. What effect did the wave of Irish immigration have upon labor and industry?

Many businesses began in New England because of the availability of the cheap Irish labor force. Wages remained low and the hours of work remained long because there was a surplus of immigrant laborers who needed jobs. More machines were invented to make use of the cheap, unskilled labor. Many Irish workers replaced protesting women workers in many New England mills.

3. What social and labor reforms were attempted during this period?

Women workers struck to get higher wages in the New England mills. Men and women workers tried to get shorter working hours in factories. The Quakers and other nonslaveowners worked to abolish slavery. Some reformers were concerned with the plight of the urban poor. Horace Mann set up the first school to train teachers and improve the quality of public education. Thomas Gallaudet established special schools for the deaf, Samuel Gridley Howe did the same for the blind, and Dorothea Dix got special hospitals built for the insane. Some reformers wanted a law passed making the drinking of liquor illegal. They claimed that drinking was the cause of social problems.

Checking the facts, page 350

1. How did the settlers of Cincinnati regard opportunity, religion, education, and race?

The settlers of Cincinnati became the owners of the best land and of the key businesses. Their descendants became the upper classes and controlled the wealth. They seemed to believe in opportunity prescribed by the boundaries of religion, national origin, race, and social class. For example, all religions were respected. The churches and synagogues were built in neighborhoods to represent the national origin, race, and social class of their members. The city offered many opportunities for the people to better themselves through education. There was free public education for children and for adults, a system of higher education, and parochial, private, and segregated schools. Blacks were not slaves, but they lived in segregated housing and went to segregated schools. They worked at low-paying, unskilled jobs.

2. What did the cities of Buffalo, Cleveland, Chicago, Detroit, and Milwaukee have in common?
They were chartered in the 1830's and became the trading centers of the Great Lakes. They passed laws to control safety, order, and sanitation. They competed for settlers by advertising in the East. The economic system of each city was based on competition, and businesses engaged in trade were licensed to prevent the emergence of monopolies. Because of their sparse populations and the absence of wealth that could be taxed to provide municipal services, the settlers of those cities became volunteer fire fighters, police officers, street repairers, and so forth.

Checking the facts, page 354

1. How was the South different from the other regions at mid-century?
The cotton industry and slavery constituted the major aspects of economic and social life that distinguished the South from the other regions at mid-century. During that period, there was a steady rise in the demand for cotton. As cotton production rose so did the price of slaves. Paralleling the growth of the cotton industry, slave trading became a big business. Small farmers were priced out of the slave market, and by 1850, only 250 people owned 200 or more slaves.
2. What was life like for the Blacks in the South at mid-century?
Slaves were considered valuable property, not human beings. Free Blacks in the cities were forced to live under a series of regulations that kept them segregated from Whites. They lived in segregated houses, attended segregated schools, were treated in segregated hospitals, and were imprisoned in segregated jails. They had special sections in theaters and were not allowed in public parks. Blacks chose to form separate churches. There they developed independent thought, community activities, and religious, cultural, and political leadership.
3. Why was cotton so important for the growth of the economy of the South?
Cotton was America's most profitable export. Using the unpaid labor of slaves and the greatly increased yields that resulted from the use of the cotton gin, southern plantation owners were able to meet the demand for cotton that arose during the mid-1850's and transform the marginal enterprise of slave trading into a lucrative big business.

Putting It All Together, page 355

Understanding the Main Ideas
1. In what ways did the American system expand to take in so much new land and so many new people?
America had all of the resources necessary to become a major manufacturer—power to run the machines, raw materials, cheap immigrant labor, customers, and capital to create a transportation system. Manufacturing created profits that provided the capital for

new investments. As settlers moved west and bought cheap government land, investors followed to supply their needs.
2. How did people learn to live in the new cities?
They found that regulations had to be devised so that they could live comfortably. They learned that they had to volunteer their services so that the cities would become clean and safe.
3. What happened to the Blacks and women during this period?
Some people, such as the Quakers, were trying to convince people that slavery was wrong. In the South, the value of the slaves increased as the value of cotton increased. Plantation owners considered the slaves valuable property. Women were hired at very low wages to work in the factories and mills of New England. They were recruited from the farms and brought to the mill towns where they were placed in crowded boarding houses that impinged on their social lives. If they left before the expiration of their one-year employment agreements, the factory owners blacklisted them and no one else hired them. When they protested their low wages and long hours of work, they were ridiculed by the entire community, including newspapers editors and church leaders. When the Irish immigrated to New England, they replaced the women working in the mills. The women either became sales clerks or else returned to the farms.

Activities
Student answers will vary.

Chapter 14. Many Cultures—One Destiny

Content
● The migration to the West, especially into Mexico
● The Spanish culture and its differences from Anglo culture
● The development of different presidential policies toward Mexico
● The United States strategy in regard to the Mexican War and the generals who fought the war
● The emergence of peace groups that protest the war

Objectives
Students will be able to:
—make a two-column list of the pros and cons of issues, for example: Should the United States annex Mexico, or should the United States go from ocean to ocean
—identify the differences between Anglo- and Spanish-American cultures and describe the difficulties in combining cultures with conflicting customs
—give examples of government policies that must involve political pressures
—identify Thoreau and how he was a protestor within the American system
—locate the geographic area that became part of the United States between 1836 and 1850

Checking the facts, page 364

1. What changes did the independent Mexican government bring about?

Mexico encouraged Americans from the southern United States to settle in its northern provinces. The Mexicans wanted settlers to protect them from hostile Native Americans. They also wanted American manufactured goods.

2. What circumstances led up to the battle of the Alamo?

The Anglos had no intention of changing their culture, language, religion, or their use of slaves. General Santa Anna declared himself President of Mexico and put the country under military rule. After fighting broke out between the Anglos and the Mexicans one year later, Santa Anna brought an army of 6,000 into Texas.

3. Why was there a delay in annexing Texas?

President Jackson was afraid that such an action would bring war with Mexico. Instead, he recognized Texas as a new foreign nation. Almost a decade elapsed between the granting of recognition to Texas as a foreign state and its annexation by the United States because it was feared that the controversy over whether to admit Texas as a slave state or as a free state.

Checking the facts, page 380

1. Why did the Webster-Ashburton Treaty become necessary? What were the provisions?

Americans and Canadians were in conflict over the boundary between Maine and Canada. Under the Webster-Ashburton Treaty a peaceful border was established from the Great Lakes to the Lake of the Woods, Minnesota. The United States received 6,500 square miles (16,900 square kilometers) of territory rich in iron ore.

2. Why was the treaty with Britain over the Oregon Territory necessary? What were the provisions?

In his campaign for the presidency Polk had implied that he would be willing to go to war against Britain over the territory. The British knew they could not hold on to the area. Under the treaty, the United States got all of the land south of the 49th parallel. The British retained Vancouver Island and the right to use the Columbia River. Each nation acknowledged the right of the other to use the Strait of Juan de Fuca.

3. How did Texas finally become a state?

Calhoun's statements about Texas forced the Democratic party to take a stand in favor of annexing Texas; Polk ran for the presidency on the issue. The Whigs lost the election. Three days before he left office, Tyler asked Congress to approve the admission of Texas to the Union.

4. How did the Americans react to the Mexican War?

The Mexican War was popular in the West. But as the distance from the frontier increased, so did the intensity of the opposition expressed. A peace movement was formed in the Northeast where the abolitionists believed that taking more southern territory was an invitation to extend slavery. Thoreau was arrested for refusing to pay his taxes to support the army. In "Civil Disobedience" he wrote about his opposition to the war, reasoning that the moral right of an individual to act in accordance with his or her conscience may well transcend the political right of the majority to rule. The debate in Congress reflected the range of opinion expressed throughout the country.

5. How did the gold rush affect the West?

St. Louis and St. Joseph, Missouri, became important cities, for travelers bought equipment and supplies there before heading West. Some towns in California lost their entire populations as people moved to localities that were accessible to the gold mines. Within two years of the discovery of gold, the population in California had grown from 15,000 to 93,000. By 1852 California contained 250,000 people, most of whom lived in the north. Many people found gold, but many more found hardship.

Putting It All Together, page 381

Understanding the Main Ideas

1. In what form did the American cultures arrive in the West?

The American cultures in the West consisted of three forms or patterns of development: the Native American form, the Spanish-Mexican form, and the English-American form.

2. What was the form of the Spanish-Mexican culture?

The Spanish form of culture came to the New World with Columbus and Cortés. During 300 years of colonial rule, Spanish values did not change. Spanish-Mexican development followed that pattern of tight government control and government support of the Roman Catholic church.

3. What were the results of the meeting of the two cultures for the Americans, the Mexicans, and for the Native Americans of the Southwest?

Serious problems developed between the Anglos and the Mexicans in Texas. The English-American culture supported diversity, whereas the Spanish-Mexican culture valued uniformity. The clash between the two cultures became manifest in the Anglos' rejection of the Mexican law that required immigrants to be Catholic. The Anglos did not speak Spanish and showed no interest in giving up their culture. The Mexican government did not like slavery and passed a law against it. The Anglos freed their slaves but then signed Blacks to lifetime contracts as indentured servants. After ten years of conflict between the two cultures, the Mexican government announced that no immigrant could enter Texas. The Mexicans also tried to enforce restrictions on the Anglos who lived in Texas. But it was too late. The Anglos from the American South considered themselves Texans. They had no intention of obeying the laws of the Mexican government. Armed fights broke out between the Mexican authorities and the Anglos. The struggle between the two cultures ultimately led to war between Mexico and the United States. The treaty that ended the war showed no mercy to the Native Americans by either side.

Activities
Student answers will vary.

Chapter 15. The Nation at Mid-Century

Content

- The extension of the regional questions to the West, specifically slavery
- The election of 1848; Taylor's victory against a party split over slavery
- The admission of California and Clay's Compromise of 1850
- The roles of Calhoun, Webster, and Stephen Douglas at mid-century
- The cultures of the Far West, missions, Easterners, Mexicans, Utah, New Mexico, Texas, Anglo-Eastern majority, their separate identity and the conflicts of interaction

Objectives

Students will be able to:

—list the problems of political leadership in the compromise

—describe the role of Clay, Calhoun, and Webster in the compromise and their personal sacrifices to bring about compromise

—identify on an outline map of the United States in 1850 cultural differences in geographic locations

Checking the facts, page 389

1. What were the provisions under the Compromise of 1850?
California entered the union as a free state. Slave trading was ended in the District of Columbia. The rest of the Mexican territory was divided into two areas that could become states in the future: Utah and New Mexico. Texas entered the union as a slave state. The fugitive slave law required northern states that harbored fugitive slaves to return them to their owners.

2. What was Calhoun's response to the Compromise?
Because it looked as if the western territory would enter the union as free states, Calhoun suggested a constitutional amendment to preserve the balance between the North and the South. He believed that the system of majority rule had to be abandoned. He contended that if that system were maintained, the South would have no choice but to secede from the union.

3. What was Webster's response to the Compromise?
He agreed with Calhoun that one section would have to give in. But to him the separation of the North and the South was unthinkable. He supported the Compromise even though many northerners believed that to do so was to support slavery.

Checking the facts, page 395

1. How did the movement of the Anglo population westward affect the lives of the Mexicans?
The culture of the Anglos and that of the Mexicans did not blend in California and Texas. They lived side by side. But the Anglos controlled the jobs and elections. In New Mexico life continued in the Spanish style. Anglos did not immigrate because there was no gold there. Those who went to New Mexico assumed the comfortable, quiet life of the Spanish-Americans.

2. How did the Anglos regard education?
In the East Horace Mann encouraged education supported by taxes so that all could benefit. Some easterners who went west supported public education. They believed that schools should be for the miners, farmers, and ranchers. Some people in San Francisco preferred a cultural approach to education—universities, libraries, and theaters.

Putting It All Together, page 396

Understanding the Main Ideas

1. How did the national government try to represent the unexpected results of expansion? Could the differences of a whole continent be represented by the same federal government?
California applied for statehood within two years of the discovery of gold. It voted to enter the union as a free state, but the granting of that status would upset the balance between the North and the South in the Senate. Once again Clay was called to resolve the differences between the North and the South. In the Compromise of 1850 California entered as a free state and slave trading in Washington, D.C. was ended. The South had succeeded in having Texas admitted as a slave state and succeeded in getting a federal law passed that made it unlawful for states to harbor fugitive slaves. The slavery issue was dividing the nation. Calhoun continued to call for the South to secede from the union if it were not given equal representation in Congress regardless of its population. Webster continued to assert the validity of the union and supported Clay's compromise. Many northerners did not agree with Webster. They contended that supporting the compromise was tantamount to supporting slavery.

2. How could the desire of individuals to live as they please exist at the same time as their desire to benefit from the wealth of each section?
In the southwest and California the conflict was most apparent. The influx of Anglo-Americans into the territory previously owned by Mexico epitomized the conflict. Individuals from each group wanted to live differently. Nevertheless, the majority determined the prevailing life style.

3. In the midst of the congressional debate about political unity, what happened to the mixture of the cultures of the Anglos and the Spanish-Americans?
In California and Texas the Spanish culture was destroyed. The Anglos immigrated in such numbers that they soon controlled the land, the wealth, and the government. The Mexicans retained only their religion, language, and life style and were considered foreigners. Relatively few Anglos settled in New Mexico. They adapted their life styles to that of the Spanish, and the two cultures blended harmoniously.

Activities

Student answers will vary.

Reviewing the Unit, page 397

Building Vocabulary
1. Student answers will vary.

Building Social Studies Skills
a. The United States got about one and a half times more land than Great Britain.
b. Students should locate the place.
c. *Amphibious* means an operation in which troops attack from both land and water.

Unit Four—Majority Rule Minority Rights

Focus
This unit focuses on the development of the railroads and the telegraph. It shows how they linked cities in a trading network. The differences between the North and South are explored. The Civil War is fought for different reasons in different ways by the two cultures, neither of which can find equal representation in the national government.

Chapter 16. Technology Brings Change

Content
● The development of the railroads through unpopulated areas of the country; the relationship between the telegraph and railroad lines
● How cities grow up in the transportation and industrial network
● How investment capital is made available for railroad construction
● Activity in Central America and the Far East
● The growth of southern cities
● The distinctions between the economic development of the North and the South
● How the South was unable to catch up to northern growth

Objectives
Students will be able to:
—list in chronological order the ingredients of the national technological network
—diagram interlocking developments of the following: cities, the West, the desire for land, new farm machinery, railroads, and capital
—make a chart that shows the increasing gap between the South and the North

Checking the facts, page 410

1. What effect did the Mexican War have upon the development of the West?
The United States won vast new public lands in the West. Americans began to move westward in search of opportunity. The railroad was constructed and settlers followed in its path. More people moved west because the railroad could carry their farm produce to eastern markets. Cities grew up along the railroad lines.
2. What made the development of the north and west railroad network possible?
The states assigned their public lands to the railroads to build lines. The development of iron rails attached to wooden ties gave the rails a longer life and the trains a smoother ride. The development of the pilot wheel placed in front of the drive wheel enabled trains to go around bends and travel long distances. Coal was found, mined, and used to heat the water for steam locomotion. The telegraph made it possible for dispatchers to send out trains on schedule and to warn their engineers of dangerous conditions on the track. The railroads permitted investors to buy stock on the installment plan, providing capital for further construction. The invention of the steel plow and the reaper made more farm production possible, increasing the need for railroads to transport produce to markets.
3. Why didn't the South develop an extensive system of railroads in the 1850's?
In 1850 the dominant enterprise in the South was the production and sale of cotton and tobacco. Southern plantation owners shipped those products to the North and to Europe by waterways that flowed through the South.

Checking the facts, page 417

1. How did the Compromise of 1850 come to be repealed?
Stephen Douglas, a senator from Illinois and also a director of the Illinois Central Railroad, wanted the railroad to build a transcontinental line from Chicago through Nebraska. The South wanted a railroad from Mobile and New Orleans to Texas and Santa Fe, New Mexico. Douglas knew that Congress would not spend money for more than one railroad at a time. To win southern support for his railroad plan, Douglas changed the bill dealing with the Nebraska territory. The territory was divided into two parts—Kansas and Nebraska—and the people in each part were permitted to decide whether their territory should become a slave or a free state. This provision of the bill replaced that section of the Compromise of 1850 that proscribed slavery in the northern part of the territory.
2. Why was the Republican party formed?
The bloodshed in Kansas over its status as a free or a slave state angered many antislavery northerners. Some formed a political party that opposed the extension of slavery.
3. What actions were the abolitionists taking during this time in American history?
The abolitionists wrote books, the most popular of which was Uncle Tom's Cabin, to make people realize that slaves were individual human beings. They helped slaves escape from the South

on the Underground Railway, a chain of houses and hideouts whose occupants were willing to hide escaping slaves by night and send them on to the next hideout before morning. They also lectured to persuade people that slavery was wrong.

Checking the facts, page 424

1. What made it possible for Lincoln to be elected President?
Lincoln had gained national exposure through his debates with Douglas. The northern and southern Democrats split. By running separate presidential candidates, they divided their vote, facilitating the election of Lincoln.
2. Why did the election of 1860 bring about the break up of the Union?
Several southern states seceded from the Union when Lincoln won because the Republican platform included the provision that slavery would not be allowed in the territories. Lincoln believed that it was unconstitutional for a state to secede from the Union. He believed that in order for the Union to survive, all must be loyal to it. When the Confederates fired on Fort Sumpter on April 12, 1861, Lincoln called for 75,000 volunteers and thus presided over the war to save the Union.
3. What was Lincoln's attitude about secession?
Lincoln was opposed to secession, an action that he believed was illegal. He wanted to work within the framework of the Union to resolve sectional conflicts.

Putting It All Together, page 425

Understanding the Main Ideas
1. How did the railroad affect the development of natural resources in the United States?
The states assigned their public lands to the railroads in order to build lines. The railroads sold land to finance construction projects. More and more people settled in the West to farm the lands. Iron ore mining increased when iron and steel rails were developed. Coal mining increased when the coal-burning steam engine was developed.
2. What effect did the railroad have on where and how people lived in the North, South, and West?
In the North the railroads were built where cities already existed. With the network of transportation systems that the roadways and canals provided, the cities became the major manufacturing and trading centers. The railroad did not exert much effect on the South. Because their rivers and streams were able to provide cheap transportation for products going to the port of New Orleans, southern leaders did not feel impelled to change their mode of transportation. The railroad made the western lands accessible to increasing numbers of people. As Americans moved westward, the railroads followed. The development of the railroads attracted farmers to settle in the West because they provided a system of transporting farm produce to eastern markets. As trade increased, cities grew up along the railroad lines.

3. What effect did the added power and wealth of the United States have on its relations with foreign nations?
When the United States became a Pacific nation, Great Britain and the United States signed a treaty to build a two-nation canal across the narrowest part of Central America. Commodore Perry sailed to Japan and was instrumental in opening six ports to American trade in 1858.
4. What leadership was able to help a divided nation?
Lincoln had the insight to know that secession was a constitutional issue, not an issue of slavery. He believed that minority rights were protected by majority rule and that the American people had to accept the consequences of free elections. He took the country into the Civil War in order to preserve the Union.

Activities
Student answers will vary.

Chapter 17. War and Peace: For What?

Content
- The outbreak and fighting of the Civil War
- The advantages and disadvantages of the Union and Confederate armies
- The various important battles of the war
- The military theory of the war from the point of view of the North and South
- The Reconstruction of the South by the North, including the emancipation of and new roles for Blacks
- The completion of the transcontinental railroad; the disruption and reaction of Native Americans
- Urban political bosses like Tweed

Objectives
Students will be able to:
— trace the military strategy of the war on a map
— write a biography of one of the leaders of the war
— make a time line of the importance of individual events and how they change history
— list the changes in the South after it lost the war and organize the list into the changes brought about by outsiders and the ones originating in the South

Checking the facts, page 440

1. How did the South and the North differ in the way they conducted the war?
The South had no desire to conquer the North; southerners fought primarily to defend their borders. The North sought to bring every individual and every acre back into the Union, which meant conquering the South.

2. What advantages did the North have over the South in the war?

There were 20 million northerners, as compared to 9 million southerners. One third of the population of the South was composed of slaves, who were not allowed to carry guns. Manufacturing was concentrated in the North, so the Union had the resources to supply its army. The North controlled the navy, with which it blockaded the southern ports to prevent the Confederacy from getting supplies. The war was concentrated in the South, where the fields were burned to destroy food crops.

3. What were the results of the Civil War?

Some 600,000 people perished. Two thirds of the South's railroads were destroyed. Crops, fields, and cotton stored for shipment were burned. Slavery was abolished. Lincoln was assassinated by John Wilkes Booth, who belonged to a group of proslavery fanatics.

Checking the facts, page 451

1. What were the important events of the Reconstruction period? Why were they important?

President Johnson thought that reconstruction was complete when he pardoned the states in which 10 percent of the citizens had taken loyalty oaths to the United States, when southerners were readmitted to Congress, and when the Thirteenth Amendment was passed freeing all slaves. The slaves were freed, but the southern states passed a series of Black Codes that restricted their freedom. Congress passed the Fourteenth Amendment guaranteeing Blacks due process and equal protection of the law. Congress passed the Fifteenth Amendment guaranteeing suffrage irrespective of race. The Republican party abandoned reconstruction in the Compromise of 1877 that resulted in the awarding of the disputed election to its presidential candidate, Rutherford B. Hayes.

2. What was life like for the Blacks after the Civil War?

Their movements were restricted by the Black Codes. They tended to remain on the plantations working for slave wages that were equivalent to food and clothing allowances. They had the right to vote but in many cases were prevented from using it.

3. How did the completion of the transcontinental railroad affect the Native Americans?

When the Homestead Act was passed, settlers moved out West rapidly, taking the buffalo grazing land. The buffalo herd migration patterns were destroyed by the railroad. Native Americans lost their livelihood and banded together to fight the settlers. Eventually they had to surrender. They were cast onto reservations and subjected to a life of confinement that destroyed their hunting culture.

Putting It All Together, page 452

Understanding the Main Ideas

1. What did the war between the states achieve?

The North conquered the South, forcing it back into the Union. The economic base of the South—its cotton and tobacco fields and its railroad system and manufacturing facilities—was destroyed.

The slaves were freed and were given citizenship rights. The twelve-year reconstruction period delayed the economic recovery of the South and humiliated southerners whose sense of dignity was offended by the northern occupation of their land and the administration of their affairs.

2. How did the North, South, and West develop during and after the war?

The completion of the transcontinental railroad connected the North and the West, enabling many people to move west and take advantage of the Homestead Act. The development of the West gave the manufacturing North more markets and enabled the farmers in the West to send their farm products to the East. Both sections of the country prospered. The development of the West destroyed the way of life of the Native Americans. The homesteaders took over the grazing land of the buffalo herds, and the transcontinental railroad destroyed their migration patterns. Native Americans banded together to fight the White settlers, but they eventually surrendered and were forced to endure reservation life for which they were not suited.

3. How much did political leadership achieve for Blacks and Native Americans when the war was over?

Blacks were supposed to benefit from three constitutional amendments. The Thirteenth freed them, the Fourteenth gave them citizenship rights, and the Fifteenth guaranteed male suffrage. But many Blacks were prevented from exercising their rights. Native Americans were confined to government reservations.

Activities
Student answers will vary.

Reviewing the Unit, page 453

Building Vocabulary
1. Student answers will vary.

Building Social Studies Skills
1. Most railroads were in the North. This mode of transportation was important in the war because trains moved troops and material quickly. They also provided the North with access to the major cities of the South.
2. *Southern Victories*
   Bull Run
   Fredericksburg
   Chancellorsville

   Northern Victories
   Shilo
   Antietam
   Gettysburg
   Appomattox
   Atlanta was the final, decisive battle.

Building Writing Skills
Student answers will vary.

Unit Five—Big

Focus

This unit focuses on the change in organization and management of American society. This particular view is of the building of a national marketing network to match the transportation and communication network. The idea of bigness, from national development to infrastructure, pervades America's thinking.

Chapter 18. Organizing Nationwide

Content

- Organizations and big business, including news, farms, cattle, go west
- The development of Swift, a nationwide beef industry
- Carnegie and the growth of U.S. Steel
- United Fruit and Nabisco as two examples of advertising nationwide
- The growth of nationwide professional managers
- Innovative business structures, like the vertical organization
- Cities and the growth of mass media, entertainment, and housing
- Immigration into urban neighborhoods and its impact on schooling and language

Objectives

Students will be able to:

—list ten important changes in America that were a result of organizing nationwide. Using one of the ten, students will identify the reasons for change

—use a map to describe the changes in Indian land ownership

—use a map to hypothesize about the relationship of natural resources to industrial centers

—identify several major events in the history of the Swift Company

Checking the facts, page 466

1. Why was the railroad a lifeline to those who settled in the West?
After the Civil War, gold and silver were discovered in the areas of the Great Plains and the Rocky Mountains. Prospectors flocked to the areas, and settlers followed them. Some mining towns grew up. They needed supplies, and so railroads developed to accommodate their needs. Farms and ranches grew up around the towns to supply food, and before long, railroads formed a network similar to the system that evolved in the East.

2. How did farming grow big?
The prairie did not receive enough rainfall, nor did the soil retain water. Only large estate owners could afford the machinery necessary to cultivate the soil and to bring in wood to build fences and houses. Estate owners grew so much grain that they could demand good rates from the railroads for transporting it.

3. What was the policy regarding the Native Americans in the western lands?
In 1887 Congress passed the General Allotment Act that authorized the breaking up of tribal reservations. It gave each head of household 160 acres of land and each adult 80 acres. It was hoped that Native Americans would become assimilated in American society. Government agents were afraid of Indian religious ceremonies and supervised them closely. In effect, Native Americans were not free on their own land.

Checking the facts, page 472

1. What changes did Swift make in supplying meat to customers?
Swift bought the cattle at its source, slaughtered it, and sent the meat east in refrigerated cars to packing houses. The refrigerated cars guaranteed its freshness. Swift's method of operation enabled him to sell his meat cheaply.

2. How did Swift develop the idea of a nationwide big business?
When local butchers refused to buy his meat, he put his own employees in branch houses. The branch houses stored and marketed the meat. He began a system of communication among the branch houses for the purpose of standardizing the time and number of people required to do a particular job. In time he developed a vertical organization that enabled him to control the purchasing, processing, and marketing of his products.

3. How did Swift's big business affect other businesses?
Swift sold his products much more cheaply than did small businesses because he controlled all of the steps in the process and ran his business more efficiently. Small businesses went out of business or else merged with Swift.

Checking the facts, page 478

1. How did the advertising business change during this expansion period?
Advertising was originally concerned with "keeping the name before the people." The National Biscuit Company spent $1 million to tell the public about its new product. This campaign signaled the emergence of big advertising to match big business. C. W. Post was one of the first to use advertising to introduce a substitute coffee and breakfast cereal.

2. Why did business have difficulty in remaining small?
Small businesses experienced difficulty in maintaining supplies for their customers. If they were unable to fill orders, their customers would go to larger suppliers who could. To prevent loss of customers due to unavailability of goods, many small businesses often kept too many supplies that they would eventually have to sell at a loss. Large businesses could afford to sell at a loss until they secured for

themselves the customers of small businesses. Small businesses were thus forced to close or to consolidate their operations through mergers.

3. What are the advantages and disadvantages of big business to the consumer?

Through the expenditure of large sums of money for advertising, big business can inform consumers about new products. The consumer can be sure that the product is made according to certain standards. Because of its volume, big business can sell its product cheaply. The disadvantages are that the consumer has fewer choices because small businesses have merged with larger businesses. Once large businesses control products, they can raise their prices.

Putting It All Together, page 479

Understanding the Main Ideas

1. How did mining, cattle raising, and farming in the West develop during the last 20 years of the nineteenth century?

Gold and silver were discovered in the regions of the Great Plains and Rocky Mountains. After the Civil War, miners went west and many mining towns grew up. By the 1880's the mines in Colorado and in the Dakotas were controlled by large corporations whose stockholders lived in large cities. Only through those organizations could expensive equipment be bought to extract gold and silver from the deep veins in the rock. The small cattle rancher was forced out of business by large cattle corporations. During the open range ranching period, corporations bought large tracts of land to secure access to water. Then they enclosed tracts of land with barbed wire so that they could raise beef cattle under controlled conditions. The farms developed by the first settlers on the Great Plains were sold to the estate builders who could afford the machinery necessary to break up the tough sod, put up fencing to keep out the cattle, build houses for the farm families and workers, and get good prices for transporting grain by rail to markets.

2. What connections did ranchers and farmers in the West have to the rest of the nation?

As mining towns grew up, ranches and farms grew up around them to supply them with food. Railroads connected them with trading centers. From railroad centers, excess food was shipped to customers in the East.

3. How did business organizations tie the entire nation together?

Business organizations tied the nation together through the means that they used to create national markets for their products: advertising that used standardized terms to communicate sales messages, railroads that formed a transcontinental system of transportation, and corporations that created standardized methods of producing, selling, and distributing their products across the nation.

4. How did bigness in business cause the rise of new kinds of organizations and new kinds of jobs?

Because of the scope of their activities, big business evolved a unique form of organization. They were organized vertically to conform with the step-by-step process associated with the manufacture, sale, and distribution of products. As businesses enlarged, they created

jobs for accountants, advertisers, national sales forces, transportation networks, and so forth.

Activities
Student answers will vary.

Chapter 19. Cities and Big Business

Content
● The role of the cities
● The changing role of the wealthy in philanthropy
● The growth of social workers in an urban setting
● Labor conditions in the sweatshop
● The response of the cities to new immigrants, in housing, education, citizenship, and ward politics
● Schooling for the new immigrants
● The rise of middle-class specialists

Objectives
Students will be able to:
—write a historical fiction about life in a city in 1900
—define immigrant, sweatshop, quota, muckraker, tenement
—use the pie graph on page 489 to discuss who came to the United States and guess why the people came from where they did
—role-play a conversation between Jacob Riis and Andrew Carnegie about what should be done for immigrants
—discuss the role of the school in 1900 and compare it with that of schools today

Checking the facts, page 485

1. What kinds of entertainment did big cities offer? What made them possible?

The trolley and elevated trains made it possible for more people to see the sights of the city and its environs. The railroad made it possible for people from one city to see their sports teams play against teams from other cities. The electric light bulb made it possible for people to attend the theater and to sightsee at night.

2. What made new ways of communicating possible?

The invention of the automatic typesetter provided an eager market in cities for more newspapers and magazines.

3. What was one author's impression of the new elevated trains in New York City? What was special about them?

William Dean Howells believed that the view of life through people's windows was better drama than what could be seen at the theater.

Checking the facts, page 487

1. What was meant by "the survival of the fittest"?

According to Carnegie, the fittest were those people who had won the competition for mergers, customers, and profits.

2. Why did the wealthy practice philanthropy?

The wealthy practiced philanthropy for psychological, sociological, humanitarian, and economic reasons. The donation of money could show how successful certain people had been at their work or how generous they were in contributing a part of their legacies. Some rich people felt impelled to give the money that they had made back to society in the form of gifts that other people could not afford. Philanthropy was a way of satisfying humanitarian impulses. There was no income tax, and so the very wealthy had money to spend on philanthropic causes.

Checking the facts, page 500

1. List the features of life for new immigrants to America.

They lived in crowded slum neighborhoods in large cities with people who spoke the same language and shared the same culture. They lived in crowded tenements and worked at low-paying jobs. They valued education and the opportunities afforded by work. They formed groups to help each other.

2. What evidence is there that large cities cared about the new immigrants?

The public schools made special efforts to teach immigrant children the language, customs, and system of government. The public schools offered evening classes in practical subjects for adults. The settlement houses provided classes and recreation for the family.

3. What were some of the ways in which immigrant children were exposed to new ways of living in the cities?

They encountered other cultures in school, in cities, and at settlement houses and camps.

Checking the facts, page 501

1. Compare John Dewey's view of education with that of Jane Addams. How did they differ? How did they agree?

They agreed that schools should educate students to become ethical or moral citizens. Jane Addams believed that students should also be taught to use and to value both their heads and their hands.

2. How would both Dewey and Addams disagree with Charles Thurber's view on education?

Thurber believed that students should be educated to value a "spirit of commercial ambition." Dewey and Addams did not agree that a business society required business courses in school.

3. Who was able to go to college during this time period?

Usually the children of well-to-do, established families.

4. What was the general attitude about education for women at this time?

Most females were not expected to go to college. They were expected to help their families.

Checking the facts, page 506

1. What goals and requirements did the organizations of specialists all have in common?

They contained members from all over America. They established standards for their professions, and they convinced colleges and state legislatures to enforce those standards.

2. What would belonging to a national professional organization do for the individual specialist?

It would enable a specialist to contact other specialists throughout the United States. Membership would give a specialist more knowledge about his or her profession.

3. How did organizations of specialists help improve American life?

Organizations of specialists served to transmit knowledge through their members to the general public. Through the application of specialized knowledge, both the pure and the applied sciences developed in the United States.

Putting It All Together, page 507

Understanding the Main Ideas

1. Why were cities so important at the turn of the century?

Cities had the factories, businesses, and transportation systems that created job opportunities for immigrants. An influx of immigrants meant that more building was required. More building created more jobs and attracted more people to the cities. The labor of the immigrants built the cities. That experience created a new national consciousness that transformed immigrants from diverse nations into American citizens.

2. What caused the differences among city people in America?

Poor workers lived in the central business, factory, and dock sections of the cities. They lived in tenement housing close to their work places. Because the poor were separated from those who were more affluent than they, they did not understand or trust other economic groups.

3. Which Americans were grouped together within cities because of the new ways of life? Which were separated from each other? How did these groupings happen? Why did they happen?

The immigrants were grouped together in ethnic neighborhoods because they came to the United States to stay with relatives and friends from the old country. Those who spoke the same language could help each other find jobs and learn how to get along in the new country. The immigrants were also grouped together near the factories because they could not pay for transportation to get to work. The immigrants were grouped together in crowded tenements because they could not afford better housing. The immigrants were separated from Americans who enjoyed higher standards of living.

Activities

Student answers will vary.

Chapter 20. Action on a Bigger Scale

Content

- The development of various labor unions, how they organized, the use they made of strikes, volunteers, and the immigrants' involvement with labor
- The organization of women in the labor market
- The changing role of the farmers
- Government response to the growth of big business and labor in the Sherman Antitrust Act
- The growth of the People's Party
- The United States involvement in Hawaii, the Spanish-American War, and the Open Door policy
- The protests against American foreign policy

Objectives

Students will be able to:

—make a chart that compares the actions of muckrakers, labor unions, the Grange, women workers, and the government between 1886 and 1899

—use the map on page 530 to identify American possessions after 1899 and also to locate Japan and Panama

—define a reformer, and then write a description of the qualities of a reformer

—identify the sources of some of today's conflicts that have their roots in the early 1900's

Checking the facts, page 512

1. How was the Knights of Labor different from craft unions?

It cut across crafts in recruiting members from all over the nation. The Knights of Labor welcomed skilled and unskilled workers and women as well as Blacks.

2. What contributions did Samuel Gompers make to the labor movement?

Gompers was the first president of the American Federation of Labor. During the 34 years of his presidency, the A.F. of L. grew from 150,000 to more than 1 million members. He believed that only with a large, loyal union membership could there be amassed enough dues to pay for a strike. He considered the strike the workers' most important weapon in their common struggle to attain their demands. His conception that labor was a group within the American system that deserved recognition, rights, and justice provided the rationale for American labor unions.

3. How did businesses react to the major strikes of workers during the late 1800's?

Businesses brought in scab labor to replace striking workers. They hired private guards or asked that federal troops be sent to protect the scabs. They asked the courts to issue injunctions against the strikes. They did not rehire the strikers.

Checking the facts, page 520

1. How did the National Women's Trade Union League get organized?

Women workers were paid less than were men. Samuel Gompers of the A.F. of L. approved the formation of a separate organization for women. A meeting of men and women workers from several trade unions was called in Boston in 1903. The League was formed and elected its first officers.

2. What were the goals of the League?

The League wanted self-government in shops, better working conditions, and a living wage. Its members wanted equal opportunity with males in trades and technical training with equal pay. They wanted representation on important committees. They wanted to inform the public about the purposes of their movement.

3. What were the results of the women workers' first major strike?

They got shorter working hours and four paid holidays a year. Their work was distributed so that they could work during the off season. They got free needles and the free use of electricity.

Checking the facts, page 528

1. How did the political machines operate in the large cities?

Ward leaders operated political machines through neighborhood precincts. They provided services to the immigrants, who in turn were expected to vote for city officials. The officials gave the ward leaders favors for these votes, making some of them rich and powerful. Ward leaders and other political bosses put their friends in office by using their connections. Many of them used their power to ensure that city contracts were awarded to those who were willing to give them kickbacks.

2. How did the federal government take on the role of regulator of industry?

In 1887, the Interstate Commerce Commission was established as an agency of the executive branch to set and enforce equal treatment for all railroad customers. The Sherman Antitrust Act in 1890 made trusts illegal.

3. Why did government civil service examinations become necessary?

Jobs in all levels of government went to people who worked for and contributed money to the campaigns of the winning candidates. The Pendleton Act of 1883 set up a civil service commission that administered competitive exams to people seeking certain government positions. The act made it illegal for the party in power to ask for campaign contributions from government workers.

4. For what issues were the national political parties failing to propose solutions?

Although they challenged the railroads and the trusts, the political parties failed to deal with child labor or with regulating businesses that crossed state lines.

Checking the facts, page 533

1. How did the United States acquire Hawaii?

American sugar producers objected to allowing Hawaiian sugar to be imported without subjecting it to a tariff. American residents wanted Hawaii to become a territory of the United States. With the help of American marines, they seized the Hawaiian government and deposed its ruler. For four years, Cleveland, who objected to the use of force, and American sugar producers kept Hawaii from becoming a territory. The Senate finally voted to accept Hawaii as a territory to protect America's Pacific interests when the United States went to war with Spain.

2. What were the results of the war with Spain?

The United States became the last Western nation to acquire an empire. It controlled Cuba, Puerto Rico, the Philippine Islands, and Guam.

Putting It All Together, page 534

Understanding the Main Ideas

1. What made working men and women and farmers organize?

Men and women workers worked long hours for low wages in bad working conditions. Often they had to pay for their own tools, for the use of electricity, and for damaged goods. Farmers had problems with the railroads, which charged them more for short hauls. They could not get lower prices on other lines, for the railroads fixed prices.

2. How successful were they? What problems did they have?

The American Federation of Labor was formed to cut across all craft unions. Its first president Samuel Gompers convinced union members that they should fight for their common goals. He believed that the strike was the workers' most important weapon and that a large, loyal membership was necessary to pay for a strike. During his leadership, the A.F. of L. grew from 150,000 members in 1886 to more than 1 million in 1901. The government aided big business to suppress strikes. The National Women's Trade Union League was formed in Boston in 1903. It supported the first major strike in the garment industry against the Triangle Shirtwaist Company. The workers settled for shorter hours, four paid holidays a year, some work during the off season, and free needles and electricity. The farmers convinced Congress to act against the unfair practices of the railroads. Congress passed the Interstate Commerce Act that established an agency in the executive branch to set and enforce equal treatment for all railroad customers.

3. What did government do? What reasons did leaders have for the action they took and for the action they refused to take?

State governments were reluctant to pass laws, for they feared that factories would move to other states in retaliation against regulatory legislation. Congress did have the power to regulate interstate commerce, a power that it finally invoked when it passed legislation regulating the railroads and making trusts illegal. But the judicial and the executive branches supported big business through Supreme Court decisions and through the use of federal troops in labor disputes. The leaders of both political parties seemed incapable of dealing with the problems created by the expansion of busi-ness. The parties were weak after taking sides on the slavery issue, and the rapidity of events strained their capacities to formulate effective responses.

Activities

Student answers will vary.

Reviewing the Unit, page 535

Building Vocabulary

Student answers will vary.

Building Social Studies Skills

1. Student answers will vary.
2. Like the European nations, the United States became concerned with protecting its colonies and maintaining the balance of power.

Building Writing Skills

1. Immigrants 1) went to school, 2) joined churches, 3) joined labor unions, 4) became involved in politics, 5) read newspapers, 6) became citizens, 7) learned English, 8) joined associations, 9) went to settlement houses.

Unit Six—Trying To Preserve, Trying To Improve

Focus

This unit shows that all the early themes are a part of the 20th century. The desire to improve is based on the past. The unit shows how Americans have balanced, rebalanced, and rearranged priorities. Both the development of today's bureaucracy and regulations and changing attitudes toward them are examined.

Chapter 21. Reform in Modern America

Content

● The Progressive movement and its impact on election reform, urban management, state reform, and experts in business and industry
● The Progressives' push for scientific government and regulation
● Theodore Roosevelt's plan for reform in the national interest
● Government action against trusts, the food and drug industry, and protection of people's interests
● The actions of the United States in Panama, Venezuela and the Dominican Republic

- The Roosevelt Corollary to the Monroe Doctrine
- The policy of the United States toward East Asia

Objectives

Students will be able to:
—list and define the reforms introduced by the Progressives
—write a biography of President Theodore Roosevelt that includes an explanation of the importance of presidential leadership and appeal
—make a chart of the actions Roosevelt took within the United States
—define a muckraker
—explain the reasons Roosevelt built the Panama Canal
—discuss United States policy toward Latin America
—explain how race influenced policy for Asian immigrants

Checking the facts, page 547

1. What job do lobbyists do?
Lobbyists work with government agencies and with lawmakers to have legislation passed that will be good for the businesses for which they work.
2. What are the initiative, the referendum, and the recall?
The initiative is the process by which the voters get a law on the ballot by signing petitions. The referendum is the process by which the voters record their approval or disapproval of a law passed by the legislature. The recall is the process by which the voters can remove an official from office by presenting a petition to the legislature calling on it to remove the official and to hold a special election.
3. What areas of American life did state government change?
They changed how elections were conducted, how some businesses operated, and the conditions under which women and children worked.

Checking the facts, page 551

1. Theodore Roosevelt was known as "the trust buster." Is that an accurate label? Explain your answer.
The answer calls for a value judgment that should be supported by the facts. Roosevelt was not against all trusts, only those that used their power unfairly. More trusts were formed during his term of office than had been established before.
2. What was Roosevelt's view of big corporations?
He was not against all big businesses. He was against those that broke the law, that treated their workers badly, and that cheated their customers.
3. How did Roosevelt use newspapers to make contact with the American people?

He created news on Sunday when very little happened. He made the Monday morning headlines and was the subject of many cartoons.

Checking the facts, page 555

1. Why was it necessary for government to interfere with business?
More government regulation was necessary to protect the public from the misuse of power by some corporations. Privately owned businesses were not able to control their own activities.
2. What practices of the meat-packing industry were attacked by Upton Sinclair?
He exposed the unsanitary and unsafe working conditions in that industry.
3. What was Roosevelt's stand on conservation?
He used his power to set aside 150 million acres of government forest land as part of the national treasure. He spoke out against those who used up the resources of the nation because they owned the land on which those resources were found.

Checking the facts, page 564

1. Why was building the Panama Canal important to Roosevelt?
Roosevelt believed that building a canal through Central America would make it possible for the United States to move its navy quickly from the Atlantic Ocean to the Pacific Ocean. The canal would also show the world how powerful the United States was. Building a canal would demonstrate power without involving the country in a costly war that could not be won.
2. What concerns made American business leaders want to see the United States take a more active role in world affairs?
They looked at the rest of the world as a market for their products and as a vehicle for increasing their profits. They knew that their investments in other countries needed the backing of a nation that others considered powerful.
3. What was the Roosevelt Corollary?
This statement reinforced the Monroe Doctrine of 1823. In the corollary, Roosevelt declared that the United States would use its "international police powers" whenever it thought that Latin American countries were guilty of wrongdoing.

Putting It All Together, page 565

Understanding the Main Ideas
1. What worked well in the American system in the early 1900's?
Big business had organized the country nationwide. Big business had prospered wherever it created jobs that could be filled by all newcomers.

2. What needed to be reformed in the American system in the early 1900's?

Reforms were needed to make sure that all Americans could vote to elect good people to the government. Methods of persuasion had to be developed to convince representatives to pass laws to ensure that employers would be fair to their workers. Regulations were needed to make sure that big businesses did not break the law.

3. What did government do to make the American system work better?

Some states improved city and state government, improved working conditions, and regulated businesses. But those reforms needed to be done on a national level to be effective. The national government created the Department of Commerce and Industry to collect information about unfair practices by industries that operated within states or across state boundaries. Roosevelt directed the Justice Department to file suit against the Northern Securities Company, a huge railroad trust, for charging unfair rates and for violating the Sherman Antitrust Act. The Hepburn Act gave the Interstate Commerce Commission the power to decide what railroads should charge.

4. What did government do to help other countries solve their problems and still help America?

The government recognized Panama and assisted the rebels in gaining their independence from Colombia. The United States then made an agreement with Panama to finish building the canal. The government helped to settle the dispute between Venezuela and its English and German creditors. It also took over the customs of the Dominican Republic to help that country pay its debts. These actions helped to establish the United States as the policeman of the Western Hemisphere, a role that many European nations respected. Roosevelt was asked to be the peacemaker in the Russo-Japanese War over Manchuria.

Activities

Student answers will vary.

Chapter 22. Should Government Do More?

Content

- The organizations of groups that were unhappy with modern developments, including the I.W.W., muckrakers, socialists, and minorities
- The leadership that emerged among Blacks concerned with segregation and lack of opportunities for Blacks, including Washington, Du Bois, and the NAACP
- The election of Taft, his administration and policy, including the political activity of the Progressives in the election of 1912, and the amendments to the Constitution that provided for direct taxing by the federal government and the election of Senators
- Wilson's policy of the New Freedom
- Wilson's policy at home toward federal banks, trusts, and workers
- The United States' actions in Mexico

- The United States' entry into World War I and the idea of freedom in the world

Objectives

Students will be able to:

—compare the way Roosevelt, Taft, and Wilson assumed the role of President, how each was a political theorist, leader, and philosopher

—write a paragraph that compares Booker T. Washington's and W.E.B Du Bois' plans for integration

—trace the United States' relationship with Mexico from 1914 to the Zimmermann note

—discuss national goals and the issue of fighting for them

—list in chronological order the sequence of events that brought the United States into World War I

—define socialist, dollar diplomacy, alliance

—explain the differences between a liberal and a conservative

—use the maps on pages 589 and 590, to compare Europe before and after World War I

Checking the facts, page 570

1. What had Roosevelt failed to do for all workers?
He failed to push Congress to pass laws that would protect women and children who worked in interstate businesses.

2. How did Lincoln Steffens find the big city political machines to be alike?
Steffens found that people with money controlled local governments. Big city political machines were financed by corrupt people whose money made it possible for machine politicians to steal elections and thereby keep themselves in office.

3. How did Booker T. Washington and W.E.B. Du Bois differ in their opinions on how to help Blacks?
Washington believed that because Whites had all the power, they were the people who had to change. Until they did so, Blacks would have to play secondary roles. Therefore, they should be trained for industrial, agricultural, and manual work, for Whites had no objection to Blacks' holding those kinds of jobs. Du Bois believed that Blacks should achieve political rights through government influence. He believed that the most talented 10 percent of the Black population should receive the same college education as that obtained by the best White students.

Checking the facts, page 576

1. What qualities did Taft lack as President?
Taft did not have the charm, the public image, or the sense of how far the government could push for action. He did not understand the importance of public relations. He spent little time on his speeches and failed to get his ideas across to the people.

2. What was accomplished during Taft's administration?
The Department of Commerce and Labor was divided into two

executive departments. The Bureau of Mines was established. The Children's Bureau was formed. The Post Office began operating a savings bank and was allowed to handle packages. Alaska got its own territorial government; New Mexico and Arizona became the forty-seventh and the forty-eighth states. The Sixteenth Amendment, providing for direct federal taxing of yearly incomes, and the Seventeenth Amendment, providing for the direct election of United States senators, were passed.

3. Why were the Republicans divided at their convention?

The reformers wanted to nominate a leader who would continue Roosevelt's progressive policies. Those who did not want to change things too much wanted to renominate Taft.

Checking the facts, page 582

1. How did Wilson regard the government and the economic system?

Wilson believed strong leadership from the president was needed to unify the complex American economic system. He thought that industrial success could continue to characterize the economy but that the government would have to pass laws to provide safe, healthful working conditions for American workers.

2. How did Wilson put his beliefs into practice?

He persuaded Congress to lower tariffs on foreign goods so that American business would have to compete. He got Congress to pass a graduated income tax, providing the government with additional revenue that could be spent to help people with low incomes. He got Congress to establish the Federal Reserve system to control the flow of money and to promote new businesses. The Clayton Antitrust Act was passed to prevent price fixing, unfair competition, and business leaders from directing the activities of more than one corporation. A Federal Trade Commission was set up to investigate the behavior of corporations. Wilson convinced Congress that labor unions should not be regulated as large corporations. He had a law passed that forbade the sale of goods made by child labor. The Adamson Act gave interstate railway workers an eight-hour work day. Federal money was spent to train workers for careers in industry and farming. Federal aid to build highways was begun.

3. What was the status of Blacks in America in 1913?

In general, Blacks were poorly treated in both the North and the South, although some owned homes and businesses. In the 50 years since emancipation, 70 percent of all Blacks had become literate. Their strongest organizations were the churches. Many did not vote; workers in the government were segregated and the NAACP protested these conditions.

4. How did the Federal Reserve system work?

Federal Reserve banks charged interest for providing loans to local banks. By raising the rate of interest, the Federal Reserve banks kept local banks from loaning too much money. Federal Reserve banks are run by 12 officers appointed by the President.

Checking the facts, page 590

1. How did Wilson's foreign policy with small nations break down with Mexico?

Wilson took the side of revolutionary leaders if they established democratic governments. When one of the revolutionaries, Pancho Villa, killed several Americans, Wilson sent troops to capture him.

2. Why did the Great War come about?

The nations of Europe had fought each other for land, ports, and trade for hundreds of years. The new competition created by modern industry and the need for natural resources created more feelings of nation against nation. Many alliances were formed to protect national interests and to maintain the balance of power. In 1914 Archduke Ferdinand was assassinated, and the Europeans lined up into two groups that fought to impose a new balance of power.

3. Why did the United States get involved in World War I?

The United States traded heavily with European nations. It increased its trade with the Allies after England blockaded German ports. The German navy began attacking Allied passenger and cargo ships. When the Germans sank the English ship, the Lusitania, 128 Americans were killed. The British got hold of a note from the German minister of foreign affairs to the president of Mexico in which he promised that New Mexico, Arizona, and Texas would be returned to Mexico if that country fought against the United States. Wilson became convinced that the United States had to enter the war to save Western civilization.

Putting It All Together, page 591

Understanding the Main Ideas

1. What had the Progressives accomplished under Roosevelt's leadership?

The Progressives convinced the nation that there was a public interest greater than that of the interests of individual groups. They used legislation and the courts to bring about reform. They convinced the nation that the American system was basically sound but that the government should regulate and control private industry to prevent big businesses from abusing their power.

2. How did Taft differ from Roosevelt in his view of the presidency? What were the results of his presidency?

Taft was afraid of putting too much power into the hands of the President. He avoided exercising the power of the presidency. Thus Congress acted on its own authority and passed laws that supported Roosevelt's progressive ideas.

3. How did Woodrow Wilson's beliefs influence the actions he took as President?

Wilson proposed many laws that supported his belief that strong leadership was needed from the President to unify a complex system. He convinced Congress to pass many laws that protected the public interest, such as reducing tariffs, the graduated income tax, the Federal Reserve system, the Clayton Antitrust Act, and the formation of the Federal Trade Commission.

4. What were Wilson's contributions to the nation?

He got Congress to pass many laws to protect the public interest. He proposed a League of Nations that would work for cooperation rather than conflict among nations. He insisted that the American government should help Americans and people throughout the world to help themselves.

Activities

Student answers will vary.

Chapter 23. America Tires of Improving

Content

● The postwar reforms of Prohibition and suffrage
● Marcus Garvey and opportunity for Blacks
● The emergence of intolerance, the Red Scare, and the Ku Klux Klan
● The limitation of immigration
● The presidencies of Harding and Coolidge
● The integration of the radio, automobile, movies, and airplane into American life
● The great crash, the Depression, and Hoover's response

Objectives

Students will be able to:
—look at the photographs on pages 594–599 and use them to discuss the areas of reform
—identify changes in the national mood
—write a history of women's suffrage
—use the event of the crash and make a diagram of how it affected various parts of the country

Checking the facts, page 601

1. How did the formation of laws and organizations reflect the mood of the people after World War I?
Many people believed that the cause of evil and war was liquor. They convinced Congress to pass the Eighteenth Amendment that made the sale of alcoholic beverages illegal. In recognition of women's work during the war, Congress passed the Nineteenth Amendment that gave women the right to vote. Blacks formed organizations to help one another. Because of the Red Scare, Congress passed a new immigration law that established quotas to maintain the ethnic balance of 1920. From its base in the South, the Ku Klux Klan established a national organization to combat what it considered alien or un-American influences represented by Jews, Catholics, foreigners, and Blacks.

2. What were the cities like in this postwar period?
They contained many poor people. Many Blacks who had migrated to the cities during the war lost their jobs when the war ended. The immigrant population decreased after the quota system was established.

Checking the facts, page 606

1. How did the Harding and Coolidge administrations reflect the nation's feelings about government and business?
Those administrations believed that the federal government should not regulate or control business. They wanted to reduce taxes on income and on corporations so that business could expand and hire more workers. They developed no plan to help the poor. A new tariff helped new businesses in the United States but it did nothing to improve the economic position of farmers who had lost their European markets. They paid back much of the money that had been borrowed during the war years, but they did not spend much to improve the conditions of individual Americans.

2. What changes did new inventions make in the American way of life?
Nearly everyone went to the movies. The automobile allowed people to live outside of the city, away from their work places. The radio made it possible for people all over the United States to hear the same music, the same sermons, and the same political speeches. The airplane brought distant places such as Europe into closer communication with the United States.

3. How had the role of women changed during the years following World War I?
Women worked for personal satisfaction as well as to feed their families. They changed their styles of dress and social activities and considered themselves more liberated than they had been before the war.

4. How did this change affect the work force?
The number of married women who were willing to work outside their homes increased the work force and added to the source of cheap labor that single working women provided. Women were paid lower wages than men were paid to do the same jobs.

Checking the facts, page 612

1. What factors helped the cities of the South grow?
The cities of the South grew when they were tied to the national transportation system of railroads. They grew when Federal Reserve banks were located near them. The major ports for shipping cotton and oil grew until they became the principal cities of the South.

2. What caused the business depression?
The boom in inventions and investing encouraged people to buy stocks on credit. Businesses used the money to expand, but no new market was developed. On October 24, 1929, so many people began to sell their stocks that there were no buyers for them. The stock market crashed. The owners of factories produced less. They laid off workers from their jobs. Workers then spent less. This caused lower production, more layoffs. This cycle of business failures and unemployment resulted in the depression.

3. Why did people become discontented with Hoover?
Hoover believed that the federal government should only get things started, loaning money, but not giving food and money. People without jobs on the breadlines thought that Hoover was not doing enough to help them.

Putting It All Together, page 613

Understanding the Main Ideas

1. What seemed to be the main goals of the American people after World War I?

Enjoying their prosperity, extending the suffrage to women, and limiting immigration seemed to be their major goals.

2. How did they go about achieving those goals?

Their style of living marked the postwar period as "the roaring twenties". By campaigning for women's suffrage and working hard during the war, women finally convinced Congress to pass the Nineteenth Amendment. An immigration law was passed that set nationality quotas.

3. What changes took place in American life after World War I?

Movies, automobiles, radios, and airplanes excited Americans, improved their means of communicating with one another, made it possible for some Americans to move to the suburbs and to travel, and produced a uniform culture.

4. How did these changes influence the way that Americans live today?

Most Americans still enjoy movies, automobiles, radios, and the use of airplanes. But as their accessibility increased, they became commonplace rather than exciting. Movies, automobiles, radio, airplanes, and television have made it possible for Americans to know how people live in other parts of the world.

5. What role did the government play after World War I?

Congress and the President believed that most people thought there was enough representation to preserve individual liberty. They believed that the federal government should not regulate business.

Activities

Student answers will vary.

Chapter 24. The Government Leads

Content

● The election of Franklin Roosevelt and his plan for a New Deal
● Government action to change structure of society: the reforms and programs introduced
● The shifts in the farm programs
● The role of the President in determining policy
● Economics: understanding productivity and employment

Objectives

Students will be able to:

—recognize and explain in a discussion the connections between employment or unemployment, profits, taxes, and welfare
—conduct an interview with someone who lived through the Depression
—use the chart on page 617 to discuss the changes the New Deal brought to the United States
—recognize the individual style of presidential leadership

Checking the Facts, page 624

1. How was Roosevelt different from Hoover in his approach to helping people?

Hoover believed in making loans to help people get started again. Roosevelt believed that the government should take more direct action to provide relief for those who were suffering.

2. What actions did Roosevelt take to provide relief for those who were suffering?

The Works Progress Administration was created to pay people to work. The Public Works Administration was created to employ people on big construction projects called public works. The Civilian Conservation Corps was created to employ young people to plant forests and to develop national parks.

3. What actions did Roosevelt take to insure a better future for the people?

He closed the banks and only reopened those that had enough reserves to pay depositors and good management to insure continued operation. The Federal Deposit Insurance Corporation was created to insure bank accounts in properly run banks. The Home Owners Loan Corporation was created to make sure that homes would not be taken away if people had trouble paying their mortgages. The National Recovery Administration was created to persuade businesses to compete less with each other, to keep wages up, and to produce as much as possible. The National Labor Relations Board was set up to prevent unfair labor practices. The Wagner Act enabled unions to organize, to bargain for higher wages and better working conditions, and to strike. The Agricultural Adjustment Act cut farm production, raised prices, and paid farmers not to plant.

Checking the Facts, page 628

1. What were Roosevelt's plans for developing the Tennessee Valley? Why did some people oppose those plans?

Roosevelt wanted to establish the Tennessee Valley Authority so that it could work across state lines and use its surplus money to start new ventures. Such ventures included building more dams and developing more industries. Some people thought that the government should not own a business. Private electric companies were afraid that the government would be able to sell electricity cheaper than they could.

2. What methods did Roosevelt use to make his plans known to the public? Why were his methods successful?

He held press conferences twice a week to explain his approach toward solving the nation's problems. He got along well with reporters and was a masterful speaker. He used the radio to conduct what he called fireside chats during which he treated his audience as members of a family.

3. What issues brought Roosevelt into conflict with the Supreme Court?

The Court declared some New Deal programs unconstitutional. Roosevelt tried to get a law passed that would have allowed him to appoint a justice for every member of the Court who was over 70 years of age. Roosevelt claimed that they were so old that they did not understand that the American people's thinking had changed. Congress rejected the President's proposal.

Putting It All Together, page 629

Understanding the Main Ideas

1. How did Americans try to solve their problems during the depression?

They elected Roosevelt President. Although he did not solve the problems of America, he seemed to care about the victims of the depression. He encouraged people and gave them hope. Many Americans supported Roosevelt's ideas. Under his leadership, Congress passed many laws that were designed to help people.

2. How did government spending of tax dollars help private citizens?

To pay for the programs of the New Deal, Congress taxed the wealthy more heavily. Programs were designed to give immediate relief to the hungry and the homeless, to provide jobs for the unemployed, and to train the unemployable. Congress also passed laws to provide for a more secure future.

3. Whom should government help today?
Student answers will vary.

Activities
Student answers will vary.

Chapter 25. A World War for Survival

Content
● The United States' response to Hitler
● Roosevelt's election in 1940 and the issue of a third term
● The entry of the United States into World War II
● Economic and social change in the United States as a result
● The wartime strategy for winning World War II
● The role of black and Japanese Americans during the war
● Migration to urban centers to work in wartime industries, and the new problems it raised for Blacks
● The decision of Truman to drop the atom bomb and end of war

Objectives
Students will be able to:
—identify and explain the changes in American attitudes toward foreign affairs as Germany, Italy, and Japan expanded beyond their national boundaries

—recognize the importance of World War II to the economic recovery in America
—list the changes in urban life as rural southern Blacks and Whites go to cities
—write a historical fiction of someone on December 7, 1941
—explain how women participated in World War II
—debate the issue of relocating the Japanese Americans during World War II
—identify the strategy and moral issues involved in dropping the atom bomb
—use the map on page 633 to trace the overall military strategy of the Allies

Checking the facts, page, 635

1. How did the United States support the Allies in the early years of World War II?

At first the United States agreed to sell them arms if they sent their own ships to carry the supplies and paid cash for them. After Denmark, Norway, Holland, Belgium, and France had fallen, only Great Britain remained free. Congress passed the Lend-Lease Act in 1941 under which the United States provided supplies to Britain in return for the leasing of British bases.

2. How did Americans react to the war in Europe?

Some were against war, some were against Jews, and some were in favor of the Nazis. Some thought that Hitler was going to win. Some were only interested in their own country. Most supported the Allies.

3. What event brought Americans into the fighting?

The Japanese attacked the American naval base at Pearl Harbor, Hawaii, on December 7, 1941. Two thousand, three hundred thirty-five American soldiers and sailors were killed; 1,178 were wounded; over 200 planes were destroyed or damaged, and 8 battleships, 3 cruisers, and 3 destroyers were damaged or sunk. At the moment of the attack, two Japanese ambassadors were sitting in the office of the American secretary of state to talk about peaceful agreements.

Checking the facts, page 638

1. How did Americans organize themselves in the effort to win the war?

They rationed meat, sugar, coffee, butter, tires, and gasoline so that the troops would be supplied. They drafted men into the armed forces; many men and women volunteered their services. The WACS and the WAVES were formed as women's branches of the armed services and did important work throughout the war. Labor unions called off strikes. People bought war bonds to lend the government money. They paid higher income taxes to pay for the war.

2. Which side won the first battles of World War II in the Pacific?

The United States lost Pearl Harbor as a supply base, and so Japan seized the initiative and won the first battles of the war.
3. What was the Allied plan for the invasion of Europe? The Allied plan called for invading North Africa, securing its ports, and crossing the Mediterranean to invade southern Italy. The Allies planned to launch another attack by sending forces across the English Channel onto the beaches of Normandy, France.

Checking the facts, page 644

1. While the United States was fighting for freedom in Europe and Asia, what was happening to freedom at home?
So many Black and White Americans from the rural South went to the North looking for factory jobs that the cities became overcrowded. Blacks did not get equal opportunities in jobs, in the armed forces, or in government programs that trained the unemployed. Roosevelt issued an executive order making discriminatory practices in government programs illegal after Randolph planned a march on Washington.
2. What were the major factors in the Allied victory?
The Allied line held against the Germans' offensive in the Belgium-Luxembourg area. Berlin fell. The Allies crossed the Rhine River from the west and from the east.

Putting It All Together, page 645

Understanding the Main Ideas
1. How did Americans respond to the threat of dictatorship abroad?
Their attitudes were very different from what they had been in World War I. It was clear to most Americans that Hitler and Mussolini intended to destroy the free nations of the world. They debated their role in the war and decided to help the Allies.
2. How did Roosevelt unite the American people behind the war effort?
He got them to agree to the draft, to rationing, to suspend strikes, to lend money to the government, and to pay higher income taxes.
3. In the war years, what happened to minorities in America?
Blacks did not receive equal opportunity in jobs, in the armed forces, or in government programs that trained the unemployed until Roosevelt issued an executive order making discrimination illegal. Rural Americans got better jobs, but Mexican Americans were treated badly. Japanese Americans were interned in camps surrounded by barbed wire because the government feared that they would support Japan in the event that the enemy tried to invade the West Coast.

Activities
Student answers will vary.

Chapter 26. Preserving: A New Challenge

Content
● Truman's postwar policy of the Fair Deal
● The challenge of Communism in the Soviet Union and China
● The American response in the Marshall Plan
● The Truman Doctrine and containment as a national foreign policy
● Communist challenges to the democratic life in Yugoslavia, Germany, Korea, and Taiwan
● The fighting in Korea and the role and issues of MacArthur
● Joseph McCarthy and the accusations about communism within the United States government
● The election of 1952 and the Eisenhower presidency
● The new policy of peaceful coexistence with Communist countries
● The Cold War development in the areas of space exploration and Third World aid in the Middle East
● The internal issues of civil rights, the Warren Court, and the integration of southern schools in Little Rock, Arkansas
● Life in the fifties, the growth of the suburbs, and the increase in the number of people who got a formal education
● Hispanic minorities, the Puerto Rican migration into the United States, its advantages and disadvantages, and Mexican-American issues
● The election of John F. Kennedy in 1960

Objectives
Students will be able to:
—identify the following people and list their contributions to the postwar environment: Harry Truman, George C. Marshall, General MacArthur, Senator Joseph McCarthy, Margaret Chase Smith, Dwight D. Eisenhower, Earl Warren, Martin Luther King
—discuss the issues of the Soviet Union's nationalism and the appeal of Communism to Third World countries
—explain the Marshall Plan and what it hoped to accomplish
—make a chart that compares the areas where the United States and the Communist nations were in conflict, locate the geographic area of conflict, and explain how the conflict was resolved
—explain the ideas of McCarthy and explain how he lost power
—debate the issues surrounding integration in Little Rock, Arkansas
—describe the changes in the American life-style in the 1950's for Whites, Blacks, and Hispanic Americans

Checking the facts, page 653

1. How did the Taft-Hartley Act come to be enacted?
Truman used the army to take over the coal mines in order to provide enough fuel for industry and to prevent an economic recession. The President also threatened to order the army to run the railroads if a nationwide strike were called. In 1946 the voters elected more Republicans than Democrats to both the House and Senate. In reaction against the industrial strife of the postwar period, the Republican-dominated Congress passed the Taft-Hartley Act.

2. How did Truman meet the Communist challenge abroad?
The President announced the "Truman Doctrine," which committed the United States to providing aid to nations that were threatened by Communist aggression. To prevent the Communists from fomenting revolution among the poverty-stricken victims of the war, the Marshall Plan was formulated. The United States offered economic aid to all European nations to help them rebuild their factories, houses, and means of transportation. Acting on the orders of the Soviet Union, the Communist nations rejected Marshall Plan aid. When the Soviet Union blockaded Berlin, the President ordered the air force to fly supplies into Berlin. The success of the airlift convinced the Soviets to lift the blockade a year after it was imposed.

Checking the facts, page 659

1. What circumstances led to American involvement in Korea in the 1950's?
The Soviets had exploded their first atomic bomb, and the Communists had defeated the Nationalists in China. When the Communist army of North Korea crossed the border into non-Communist South Korea, the United States decided that it was time to contain communism in Asia.

2. What is meant by the "McCarthy era"?
Americans were afraid of communism and did not know what to do about it. They were afraid to criticize the government because they feared that they would be considered disloyal. In such a climate, Senator McCarthy presided over Senate hearings in which many people were accused and virtually convicted of being members of or sympathizing with the Communist party. The realization that an individual's reputation could be ruined in an extralegal proceeding fueled the climate of suspicion and fear that characterized the McCarthy era. Many people refused to speak out against McCarthy for fear that he would attack them next.

Checking the facts, page 665

1. What ended the McCarthy era?
McCarthy accused the army of harboring subversives, and held committee hearings that were televised. Many people began to question his credibility when he implied that no one in the government
was hard enough on communism. When the army's counsel, Joseph N. Welch, succeeded in persuading many Americans that McCarthy sought publicity rather than the adjudication of his charges in the federal courts, the Senate voted to censure McCarthy. His fall from power ended the McCarthy era.

2. How did Eisenhower conduct his foreign policy regarding communism?
Believing that the Communists would never give up, Eisenhower negotiated a cease-fire that ended the fighting in Korea. He proposed a policy of peaceful coexistence with the Soviet Union. He advocated competition rather than conflict with the Soviet Union and its Communist allies. He proposed an "open skies" accord with the Soviets, whereby each nation would take aerial photographs of the other to monitor troop movements or other preparations for war. The United States launched a space program to keep pace with the Soviets, who had succeeded in launching a satellite into space. Eisenhower subscribed to the domino theory, which provided the rationale for the United States policy of containment.

3. What actions did Eisenhower take in support of equal rights?
He appointed Earl Warren Chief Justice of the Supreme Court. The Warren Court ruled that most of the provisions of the Bill of Rights limited the powers of the states as well as those of the federal government. The Court declared that separate schools for Blacks were unconstitutional, and ruled that reapportionment had to be based on "one man, one vote." Eisenhower sent the army to protect nine Black students who were refused admission to the all-White Central High School, in Little Rock, Arkansas.

Checking the facts, page 670

1. How were the Puerto Ricans different from other immigrants in the United States?
They were American citizens when they arrived on the mainland. The Puerto Rican government worked with local governments and businesses in many mainland towns and cities to make sure that Puerto Ricans would have jobs and housing accommodations when they arrived. But like other newcomers, they were the first to be laid off in periods of economic retrenchment. Many Puerto Ricans could not find low-skilled jobs, for their lack of money made it impossible for them to commute to or live in the suburbs, where many factories had relocated. Many Puerto Ricans lived in housing projects that were scattered across the city and they could not offer each other neighborhood support. They did not want to be identified with Black Americans who were discriminated against, and so they kept their Spanish language to set themselves apart. They banded together to get political power.

2. Why were the Mexican American workers having trouble getting help?
Some workers came as contract farm laborers to fulfill agreements between the Mexican government and American employers. Some workers came illegally and had to accept lower wages than those paid to the contract laborers. Some Mexicans took factory jobs in northern cities, making it difficult for them to organize themselves into an occupational pressure group.

Putting It All Together, page 671

Understanding the Main Ideas

1. How did Truman meet the challenge of communism?
He developed the Truman Doctrine, which served as the rationale for his policy of containing communism. He and Secretary of State George Marshall developed a plan to promote the recovery of Europe. He ordered the air force to fly supplies to the French, English, and American zones of Berlin to break the Soviet blockade of that divided city. Under his direction, the United States formed NATO, a collective security agreement that created an alliance among the nations of the North Atlantic region.

2. What was the reaction of Americans to the Korean War?
Many Americans were unhappy about fighting another war, but war seemed to be necessary to prevent a Communist victory in Asia. Some Americans did not want the war to be extended to China because they thought that it was impossible to conquer such a large country. Some Americans were opposed to the war because they thought that communism was a good idea. They believed that communism produced social justice, even if the price that people had to pay was loss of freedom.

3. How did Senator Joseph McCarthy first attract public attention?
He accused State Department officials serving in China of being Communists, and he blamed them for "losing" China to communism. He based his accusations on the fact that those officials had written reports praising the economic policies of the Communists. He spoke from the floor of the Senate, where he did not have to prove his charges. The newspapers printed his speeches, and thus his public crusade was launched.

4. What improvements were made in American life during the 1950's? For whom?
Blacks gained recognition of their civil rights in several rulings of the Warren Court that required the states to apply many provisions of the Bill of Rights to all their citizens. The Supreme Court also ruled that separate schools for Blacks were unconstitutional. Americans living in urban areas were given equal representation when the Court ruled that reapportionment had to be based on "one man, one vote." Increasing numbers of Americans were finishing high school, going to college, and enrolling in continuing education.

Activities
Student answers will vary.

Chapter 27. Improving By Finding New Ways

Content
- The Kennedy Administration, its trouble with Congress on government aid, civil rights, and freedom marches
- The foreign activities of the government in Cuba: the Bay of Pigs and the missile crisis
- The United States involvement in Vietnam
- The continued Cold War
- The rise of new Black leadership in Martin Luther King, Jr. and Malcolm X
- Minority demands for greater participation
- The Kennedy assassination and the assumption of the presidency by Lyndon Johnson, and his plans for the Great Society
- The demands for equality by women in the 1960's and the development of the National Organization for Women

Objectives
Students will be able to:
—discuss the relationship between congressional power and government policy
—identify the important minority organizations and explain the reasons for which they organized and their plans of action
—make a time line of the United States involvement in Vietnam and Cuba
—interview three people about what they were doing when Kennedy was assassinated
—use the chart on page 683 to discuss the role women are playing in the labor force

Checking the facts, page 681

1. How did Kennedy meet the challenge of communism?
Kennedy endorsed the CIA plan to use Cuban exiles to invade their homeland. He committed the United States to increasing its aid to the government of South Vietnam and sent the Green Berets to advise and train the army of South Vietnam. He got Congress to appropriate money for the development of sophisticated weaponry and for the training of astronauts to explore the moon. He blockaded Cuba to force the Soviet Union to remove its missiles.

2. How did Kennedy use Eisenhower's idea of peaceful coexistence with Communist nations?
He signed a treaty with the Soviet Union that banned the testing of nuclear weapons. A direct telephone line was set up between the White House and the Kremlin to facilitate communications and to defuse hostility. Kennedy agreed to sell surplus wheat to the Soviet Union.

3. What progress were minority groups making during Kennedy's administration?
Through the protection accorded by the federal government, a Black, James Meredith, entered the University of Mississippi. A peaceful march of 200,000 Blacks and their White supporters converged on Washington to demand jobs and freedom. César Chávez of the National Farm Workers Association led a six-year strike against the owners of the California vineyards before the strike and a national boycott of grapes grown in their vineyards convinced them to accept the workers' demands. The Spanish Americans of New Mexico formed Alianza Federal de Mercedes to get

back land that had been taken from their families. Second-generation Puerto Ricans who held professional jobs formed ASPIRA to promote the education and training of young Puerto Ricans.

Checking the facts, page 684

1. What goals of Kennedy's did Johnson meet?
Medicare, which gave hospital insurance to people over 65, was passed. One billion dollars in aid to public and parochial schools was approved. The Voting Rights Act authorized the federal government to send registrars to the South to register Blacks who had been prevented from voting.
2. What were the accomplishments of the "war on poverty"?
Special training was provided for people who could not get jobs. Over one million children from poor families were given special lessons in the Headstart preschool educational program. The Neighborhood Youth Corps paid for 500,000 part-time jobs for teenagers. A Peace Corps for Americans, VISTA, was established. Nine billion dollars was spent to help Appalachia, a poverty-stricken rural area in the Southeast.
3. How had the thinking changed in the women's movement in the mid-1960's?
The women's movement was for all women, those who wanted to stay home, those who wanted to work, and those who had to work. It was for men as well, because feminists believed that the liberation of women would be conducive to the freedom of men.

Putting It All Together, page 685

Understanding the Main Ideas
1. What did Kennedy accomplish in dealing with communism?
The Soviets began a massive build-up of missiles in Cuba. Kennedy imposed a blockade to prevent shipments of supplies to Cuba. The Soviets removed their missiles. After the Cuban missile crisis, the Americans and the Soviets decided to take steps to prevent the cold war from degenerating into a hot war. They signed the Nuclear Test Ban Treaty and set up a direct telephone line between the White House and the Kremlin. The United States agreed to sell its surplus wheat to the Soviet Union.
2. What did minorities accomplish in their fight for equal opportunity?
César Chávez of the National Farm Workers Association led a six-year strike against the owners of the California vineyards. The successful prosecution of the strike gave migrant workers the right to bargain collectively. Senior citizens got federal medical insurance when the Medicare bill was passed. The Voting Rights Act of 1965 reinforced the voting rights of Blacks. The "war on poverty" provided education, housing, and health services to the poor.
3. What government programs were developed to help the disadvantaged?
Special training was provided for people who could not get jobs. Children from poor families were given special lessons in the Head-

start preschool educational program. The Neighborhood Youth Corps and a Peace Corps for Americans, VISTA, were established. Medicare provided health insurance for retired people on fixed incomes.

Activities
Student answers will vary.

Chapter 28. More Challenges for Americans

Content
● President Johnson and the escalation of the war in Vietnam, the use of guerrilla warfare, and the North and South Vietnamese leadership
● The development of the American protest movements
● The riots of 1967
● The assassination of Robert Kennedy and Martin Luther King, Jr.
● The election of Richard Nixon, his policies in Vietnam
● Nixon and illegal action against critics, the Watergate scandal, the Senate hearings, and his resignation
● The foreign policy innovations with China and the Soviet Union
● President Ford's use of the veto
● The election of President Carter and the issues of holding the tension between paying the bills and solving problems
● The Panama Canal Treaty

Objectives
Students will be able to:
—continue the time line on Vietnam
—recognize and discuss the policy dilemma of supporting freedom and anti-Communists
—debate the moral and legal issues of Nixon's use of power
—describe the importance of rivalry between China and Russia to U.S. foreign policy
—discuss the advantages of government action and local organized citizen action for improving and preserving the American way
—make a collage of the themes of *The American Way*

Checking the facts, page 693

1. How did Americans react to the United States' lengthy involvement in Vietnam?
Students rioted on college campuses. Many young men burned their draft cards and left the country rather than be sent to Vietnam.

2. Why was the involvement in Vietnam the longest in United States history?

The enemy was hard to identify. No difference in appearance distinguished the North Vietnamese and the Viet Cong from the people of South Vietnam. The enemy excelled at guerilla warfare, which bombing could not combat. The South Vietnam government was corrupt and did not have the support among the Vietnamese people. The United States and its Vietnamese ally could not agree with the North Vietnamese on the terms of a peace settlement.

Checking the facts, page 698

1. What resulted from Nixon's trip to China and Russia?

The United States withdrew its objection to the entry of the People's Republic of China into the United Nations. Trade between the two nations resumed after 20 years of hostility. The United States and the Soviet Union agreed to work together in space and to develop joint programs in public health, cancer and heart research, and pollution control. They also agreed to limit their production of missiles for a period of five years.

2. What circumstances led up to Nixon's resignation from the presidency?

Nixon became suspicious of people who opposed his policies. He established an illegal special investigation unit that reported directly to him. He ordered his staff to draw up a list of enemies whose names were given to the FBI and the Internal Revenue Service, so that their activities could be investigated. A unit headed by the security officer of the Committee to Reelect the President burglarized Democratic party headquarters in the Watergate building. Nixon tried to cover up these activities by denying any knowledge of them, by refusing to turn over tapes of his conversations with his staff, and by firing the special prosecutor who had subpoenaed the tapes. The House Judiciary Committee voted three articles of impeachment against him. The Committee recommended that the House concur in its judgment that Nixon should be charged with obstructing justice, abusing the powers of his office, and treating Congress with contempt.

Checking the facts, page 703

1. What issues did Ford have to face when he took office?

Ford had to decide how to put Watergate behind the nation. He had to decide how to pay the debts of the Great Society and those arising from the Vietnamese War. He had to deal with the recession, as well as with unemployment, inflation, and the energy crisis.

2. Why was Carter elected?

He was an outsider. Many Americans supported his candidacy because they believed that their leaders in Washington had let them down. Carter promised that he would form a more efficient government, so that taxes could be lowered. He favored federal aid for the

unemployed, but thought that business should be entrusted with the major responsibility of creating jobs.

3. Why was Carter having difficulty mobilizing the nation behind his programs?

Big programs run from Washington had turned out to be wasteful, so minorities and other groups wanted money paid directly to community organizations. There was disagreement about whether the goals of improving and increasing productivity could be achieved at the same time. There was disagreement about whether farmers should be guaranteed prices that would raise the cost of food. There was disagreement about how much responsibility women should assume in supporting themselves and in taking care of their families. There was disagreement about energy policy. There was disagreement about how much power Congress and the President should have.

Putting It All Together, page 704

Understanding the Main Ideas

1. What questions faced Americans as they became more deeply involved in the war in Vietnam?

They found it difficult to support an anti-Communist government led by dictators who used American aid to make themselves rich. They wondered if the United States could save a government that its own people did not support. They wondered if the cost of trying to contain communism was worth the expenditure of limited resources that could be used at home.

2. How did programs aimed at helping the poor suffer because of government spending on the war?

As the government put more and more money into the war effort, less money was available to help the poor in the United States.

3. What kinds of illegal actions did the Nixon administration take part in?

The first article of impeachment was obstruction of justice. Nixon "made it his policy" to cover up the Watergate burglary. The second article accused the President of "massive and persistent abuse of power for political purposes." The third article charged him with contempt of Congress for defying its subpoenas.

4. How did Presidents Ford and Carter plan to deal with the nation's problems?

They realized that to pay the debts of the Great Society and the Vietnam War and to fund new programs for the needy, new tax money would have to be obtained from private business. This source of revenue could not be realized until business earned higher profits and workers increased their rates of productivity. Carter believed that taxes could be lowered if the government eliminated waste.

5. What kinds of citizen action have appeared since the 1960's?

New self help programs have emerged. Government aid is still sought but not relied on. Most citizens seem to accept the notion that programs that train people for jobs are the most successful.

Activities

Student answers will vary.

Reviewing the unit, page 705

Building Vocabulary
Student answers will vary.

Building Social Studies Skills
1. They are Communist.
2. With its missiles on Cuban soil, ninety miles from Florida, the Soviets could launch a surprise attack on the United States.

Building Writing Skills
Student answers will vary.

TEACHER BIBLIOGRAPHY

Unit 1

Becker, Carl. *The Declaration of Independence: A Study in the History of Political Ideas.* New York: Knopf, 1958.

Caffrey, Kate. *The Mayflower.* New York: Stein & Day, 1974.

Catton, Bruce. *American Heritage Book of the Revolution.* New York: Simon & Schuster, 1966.

Churchill, Winston S. *A History of the English-Speaking Peoples.* Vol. 3, *The Age of Revolution.* New York: Dodd.

Forbes, Esther. *Paul Revere and the World He Lived In.* Boston: Houghton Mifflin, 1962.

Hamilton, Alexander. *The Federalist: A Commentary on the Constitution of the United States.* New York: Modern Library, 1964.

Jameson, J. F. *The American Revolution Considered As a Social Movement.* Princeton: Princeton University Press, 1940.

Jensen, Merrill. *The Articles of Confederation.* Madison: University of Wisconsin Press, 1940.

Judd, Barbara, and Daniel Josephs. *Women in the United States.* Glenview, Ill.: Scott, Foresman, 1975.

Lancaster, Bruce, and John H. Plumb. *American Heritage Book of the Revolution.* New York: Dell.

Lengyel, Cornel. *Four Days in July.* New York: Bantam, 1976.

Malone, Dumas. *The Story of the Declaration of Independence.* New York: Oxford University Press, 1976.

Morrison, Samuel Eliot. *The European Discovery of America: The Northern and Southern Voyages.* New York: Oxford University Press, 1975.

Pearson, Michael. *Those Damned Rebels: The American Revolution As Seen Through British Eyes.* New York: G. P. Putnam's Sons, 1972.

Preston, John Hyde. *Revolution 1776, A Short History of the American Revolution,* New York: Washington Square Press, 1976.

Quarles, Benjamin. *The Negro in the American Revolution.* New York: Norton, 1973.

Scheer, George, and Hugh F. Rankin. *Rebels and Redcoats.* New York: T. Y. Crowell, 1972.

Unit 2

Adams, Abigail. *New Letters of Abigail Adams.* Westport, CT: Greenwood, 1973.

Baker, Leonard. *John Marshall: A Life in Law.* New York: Macmillan, 1974.

Bestor, Arthur E., Jr. *Backwoods Utopias.* Philadelphia: University of Pennsylvania Press, 1971.

Billington, Ray Allen. *The Far West Frontier, 1830–1860.* New York: Harper & Row, 1956.

Bowen, Catherine Dunker. *Miracle at Philadelphia.* Boston: Little, Brown, 1966.

Debo, Angie. *A History of the Indians of the United States.*

Tulsa: University of Oklahoma Press, 1970.

DeVoto, Bernard. *The Journals of Lewis and Clark*. Boston: Houghton Mifflin, 1953.

Kelly, Alfred J., and Winfield A. Harbison. *American Constitution*. 3d ed. New York: Norton, 1970.

Madison, James. *Notes of Debates in the Federal Convention of 1787*. New York: Norton, 1969.

Schlesinger, Arthur M., Jr. *The Age of Jackson*. Boston: Little, Brown, 1945.

Van Doren, Carl. *The Great Rehearsal: The Story of the Making and Ratifying of the Constitution of the United States*. New York: Viking, 1971.

Unit 3

Alcaraz, Ramon. *The Other Side: Or Notes for the History of the War Between Mexico and the United States*. St. Clair Shores, MI: Scholarly Press, 1976.

Coit, Margaret L. *John C. Calhoun: An American Portrait*. New York: Sentry, 1961.

Daughterty, James. *Trappers and Traders of the Far West*. New York: Random House, 1952.

Katcher, Philip. *The Mexican American War, 1846–48*. New York: Hippocrene, 1976.

Riegel, Robert, and Robert Athearn. *America Moves West*. New York: Holt, Rinehart and Winston, 1971.

Sterling, Dorothy. *Freedom Train: The Story of Harriet Tubman*. Garden City, NY: Doubleday, 1954.

Schroeder, John H. *Mr. Polk's War: American Opposition and Dissent*. Madison: University of Wisconsin Press, 1973.

Turner, Frederick. *1830 to 1850,* New York: Norton, 1965.

Underhill, Ruth M. *Red Man's America: A History of Indians in the United States*. Chicago: University of Chicago Press, 1971.

Ware, Norman. *The Industrial Worker, 1840–1860*. New York: Quadrangle, 1964.

Unit 4

Backmaster, Henrietta. *Let My People Go: The Story of the Underground Railroad and the Abolition Movement*. New York: T. Y. Crowell, 1959.

Bennett, Lerone, Jr. *Before the Mayflower: A History of the Negro in America*. New York: Penguin, 1962.

Catton, Bruce. *This Hallowed Ground*. New York: Pocket, 1961.

Commager, Henry S., ed. *The Blue and the Gray*. Glouster, MASS: Peter Smith, 1960.

Coutler, E. Merton. *The South During the Reconstruction, 1865–1877*. Baton Rouge: Louisiana State University Press, 1947.

Franklin, John Hope. *From Slavery to Freedom*. New York: Knopf, 1974.

Genovese, Eugene D. *The Political Economy of Slavery: Studies in the Economy and Society of the Slave South*. New York: Vintage, 1965.

McPherson, James M. *The Struggle for Equality: Abolitionists and the Negro in the Civil War and Reconstruction*. Princeton: Princeton University Press, 1964.

Oates, Stephen. *To Purge This Land with Blood: A Biography of John Brown*. New York: Harper & Row, 1970.

Quarles, Benjamin. *The Negro in the Civil War*. Boston: Little, Brown, 1969.

Stampp, Kenneth M. *The Era of Reconstruction, 1865–1877*. New York: Knopf, 1965.

———, Englewood Cliffs, N. J.: *The Peculiar Institution*. New York: Knopf, 1965.

Wiley, Bell I. *Common Soldier of the Civil War*. New York: Charles Scribner's Sons, 1975.

Unit 5

Addams, Jane. *Twenty Years at Hull House*. New York: Macmillan, 1966.

Baxandell, Rosalyn, et al., eds. *America's Working Women*. New York: Random House, 1976.

Bontemps, Arna. *The Harlem Renaissance Remembered*. New York: Dodd, 1972.

Chu, Daniel and Samuel. *Passage to the Golden Gate: A History of the Chinese in America to 1910*. Garden City, NY: Doubleday, 1967.

Glaab, Charles, and Theodore A. Brown. *A History of Urban America*. New York: Macmillan, 1967.

Hanlin, Oscar. *Boston's Immigrants*. New York: Atheneum, 1974.

———. *The Uprooted*. Boston: Little, Brown, 1973.

Josephson, Matthew. *The Robber Barons*. New York: Harcourt Brace Jovanovich, 1962.

Lewis, Marvin, ed. *The Mining Frontier*. Tulsa: University of Oklahoma Press, 1967.

National Geographic Society. *Those Inventive Americans*. Washington, DC: National Geographic Society, 1971.

Schlesinger, Arthur M. Jr., and Dixon Ryan Fox. *Rise of the City, 1878–1898*. New York: Franklin Watts, 1971.

Smedley, Agnes. *Daughter of Earth*. Westbury, NY: The Feminist Press, 1963.

Woodward, C. Vann. *Reunion and Reaction*. Boston: Little, Brown, 1966.

———. *The Strange Career of Jim Crow*. New York: Oxford University Press, 1974.

Unit 6

Alford, Harold J. *The Proud Peoples, The Heritage and Culture of Spanish-Speaking Peoples in the United States.* New York: McKay, 1972.

Allen, Frederick Lewis. *Only Yesterday: An Informed History of the 1920's.* New York: Harper & Row, 1957.

Bernstein, Irving. *The Lean Years: A History of the American Worker, 1920–1933.* Boston: Houghton Mifflin, 1960.

Chafe, William Henry. *The American Woman: Her Changing Social, Economic and Political Roles, 1920–1970.* New York: Oxford University Press, 1974.

Clark, Kenneth B. *Dark Ghetto: The Dilemmas of Social Power.* New York: Harper & Row, 1965.

Friedan, Betty. *The Feminist Mystique.* New York: Norton, 1963.

Goldman, Eric. *Rendezvous with Destiny: A History of Modern American Reform.* New York: Knopf, 1952.

Harrington, Michael. *The Other America.* New York: Macmillan, 1970.

Hofstadter, Richard. *The Age of Reform: From Bryan to FDR.* New York: Vintage, 1960.

Martin, George W. *Madame Secretary: Frances Perkins.* Boston: Houghton Mifflin, 1976.

Meier, M. S., and Feliciano Rivera. *The Chicano: A History of Mexican Americans.* New York: Hill & Wang, 1972.

Mowry, George E., ed. *The Twenties: Fords, Flappers and Fanatics.* Englewood Cliffs, NJ: Prentice-Hall, 1962.

Uchida, Yoshiko. *Journey to Topaz: A Story of the Japanese-American Evacuation.* New York: Charles Scribner's Sons, 1971.

White, Theodore. *Breach of Faith: The Fall of Richard Nixon.* New York: Atheneum, 1975.

FILMS

The following is a list of 16 mm films available for purchase or rental.

Unit 1

America: A Personal History of the United States, from Time-Life Films, color, 13 films each 52 min., discussion guide available.

The Beginnings of Exploration, from EBE, color, 15 min.

Benjamin Banneker: Man of Science, from EBE, color, 9 min.

Colonial Life in the South, from Cornet Films, color, 12 ½ min.

Deborah Sampson: A Woman in the Revolution, from BFA, color, 15 min.

Early Settlers in New England, from EBE, b/w, 11 min.

The English and Dutch Explorers, from EBE, color, 11 min.

The First Americans—Indians of the Southland, from International Film Foundation, color, 15 min.

The French Explorers, from EBE, color, 11 min.

Jamestown Colony, from Cornet Films, color, 16 min.

Man and the State: Burke and Paine on Revolution, from BFA, color, 28 min.

Missions of California: New Ways in the New World, from BFA, color, 15 min.

The Mystery of the Maya, from WNET Media Services, color, 60 min.

Paul Revere's Ride, from BFA, color, 22 min.

Plymouth Colony, from Cornet Films, color, 15 ½ min.

The Treason of Benedict Arnold, from BFA, color, 22 min.

Why the New World Was Explored, from BFA, color, 11 min.

Unit 2

Administration of Thomas Jefferson, from Cornet Films, color, 13½ min.

Alexander Hamilton, from EBE, b/w, 18 min.

Catlin and the Indians, from Contemporary McGraw-Hill Films, color, 24 min.

The Constitution, from Contemporary McGraw-Hill Films, color, 21 min.

Gibbons v. Ogden, from McGraw-Hill, color, 36 min.

Lewis and Clark at the Great Divide, from BFA, color, 22 min.

McCulloch v. Maryland, from McGraw-Hill, color, 36 min.

Man and the State: Hamilton and Jefferson on Democracy, from BFA, color, 26 min.

Marbury v. Madison, from McGraw-Hill, color, 36 min.

People of the Buffalo, from EBE, color, 15 min.

War of 1812, from Cornet Films, color, 13½ min.

Unit 3

The American Parade: The 34th Star (a family in Kansas, 1820–1865), from BFA, color, 34 min.

The Big Push West—America Expands, from Graphic Curriculum, color, 24 min.

Black People in the Slave South, 1850, from EBE, color, 11 min.

The Chinese Americans—The Early Immigrants, from Handel, color, 20 min.

The Gold Rush, from EBE, color, 24 min.

The Oregon Trail, from BFA, color, 31 min.

Saga of the Erie Canal, from Cornet Films, color, 10 min.

Santa Fe and the Trail, from EBE, color, 20 min.

Trail of the Forty-Niners, from Cornet Films, color, 10½ min.

Unit 4

The Background of the Civil War, from BFA, color, 21 min.

Frederick Douglass, from EBE, color, 9 min.

Harriet Tubman and the Underground Railroad, from BFA, color, 21 min.

The Nomination of Abraham Lincoln, from BFA, color, 22 min.

The Plantation South, from EBE, color, 17 min.

The Reconstruction—A Changing Nation, from Graphic Curriculum, color, 25 min.

The Record Ride for the Pony Express, from BFA, color, 21 min.

Shiloh, from BFA, color, 15 min.

Slavery and Slave Resistance, from Cornet Films, color, 23½ min.

Unit 5

Booker T. Washington, from BFA, color, 23 min.

Growth of Farming in America, 1865–1900, from Cornet Films, b/w, 14 min.

Inventions in America's Growth II—1850–1910, from Cornet Films, color, 10½ min.

The Rise of the American City, from EBE, color, 34 min.

The Rise of Big Business, from EBE, color, 27 min.

The Rise of Industrial Giants, from McGraw-Hill, color, 25 min.

"Separate But Equal," from EBE, color, 8 min.

The Trial of Susan B. Anthony, from BFA, color, 22 min.

Unit 6

The American Experience: Becoming an American, from BFA, color, 30 min.

The American Parade: FDR—The Man Who Changed America, from BFA, color, 30 min.

The American Parade: We the Women, from BFA, color, 30 min.

The Bill of Rights in Action (Series), from BFA, color 18–21 min.

Boom or Bust—Between the Wars, from Graphic Curriculum, color, 25 min.

Chicano, from BFA, color, 23 min.

The Farmer in a Changing America, from EBE, color, 30 min.

Five Presidents on the Presidency, from BFA, color, 25 min.

George Washington Carver, from BFA, b/w, 11 min.

"I Have a Dream . . .": The Life of Martin Luther King, from BFA, b/w, 35 min.

Indian Boy of the Southwest, from BFA, color, 15 min.

Man and the State: Roosevelt and Hoover on the Economy, from BFA, color, 25 min.

The Mystery of Amelia Earhart, from BFA, color, 22 min.

The New South (part 1 and part 2), from WNET 13 Media Services, color, 30 min. each.

Ordeal of a President (Wilson), from BFA, color, 22 min.

The Rise of Labor, from EBE, color, 30 min.

The United States in the Twentieth Century, from Cornet Films:

1) *1900–1912,* b/w, 11½ min.
2) *1912–1920,* b/w, 12 min.
3) *1920–1932,* b/w, 18 min.
4) *1932–1940,* b/w, 21 min.

World War I, A Documentary on the Role of the U.S.A., from EBE, b/w, 28 min.

World War II, Prologue U.S.A., from EBE, b/w, 29 min.

Maps

Latitude, Longitude and Time Zones, from Cornet Films, color, 13 min.

Maps Add Meaning to History, from Cornet Films, color, 10 min.

Maps and Their Uses, from Cornet Films, color, 10½ min.

A NOTE ON THE ANNOTATIONS IN THE TEACHER'S EDITION OF *THE AMERICAN WAY*

The annotations at the top and bottom of each page are suggested places in which the author as teacher might "stop by," "open up the text for discussion," let the meaning of the words "sink in." The annotations would probably be used after the text has been read.

The teacher should use the annotations in a manner which best suits his or her teaching style.

The margin questions (blue) are designed to keep the slowest students' attention focused on the meaning of the reading. The annotations (red) are comments and questions from the teacher to the students to help make the continuing transition from concrete to abstract understanding of *The American Way*.

THE AMERICAN WAY

NANCY W. BAUER
University of Pennsylvania

in consultation with

Nancy J. Allbaugh
Administrative Assistant, Curriculum
Abington School District
Abington, Pennsylvania

Irving E. Sigel
Senior Research Psychologist
Educational Testing Service
Princeton, New Jersey

Historical Consultant

Educational Consultant

Sheldon Hackney
President
Tulane University
New Orleans, Louisiana

Joseph D. Baca
Social Studies Education Specialist
State Department of Education
Santa Fe, New Mexico

Holt, Rinehart and Winston, Publishers
New York ● Toronto ● London ● Sydney

NANCY W. BAUER, Ph.D., is adjunct associate professor at the Graduate School of Education, University of Pennsylvania, and is associated with the College of General Studies. She is a historian and author of history and social studies textbooks. Dr. Bauer has been a classroom teacher for 15 years and was coordinator of Social Studies, K-12, in the Birmingham, Michigan, school system. She received her B.A. from Smith College, an M.A. in humanities and education from the University of Michigan, and a Ph.D. in curriculum research from Michigan State University, where she was a fellow of the Learning Systems Institute. Dr. Bauer is well-known as a curriculum designer and consultant for schools. She has published extensively in the curriculum field, including articles for professional journals and *Revolution and Reaction: The Impact of the New Social Studies*. She is actively involved in social studies and citizen education, including the work of the Social Science Education Consortium, the National Council for the Social Studies, the Asia Society, and the Alliance for Citizen Education.

NANCY J. ALLBAUGH is the administrative assistant, curriculum, for the Abington School District in Abington, Pennsylvania. Before receiving her Ph.D. from the University of Iowa, she taught at the elementary and university levels as well as special education classes. In addition, Dr. Allbaugh has trained elementary classroom teachers, special education teachers, and reading specialists. Dr. Allbaugh has published papers on reading in the social studies. Her contributions to *The American Way* include the reading, section review, and chapter review questions.

IRVING E. SIGEL is presently senior research psychologist at the Educational Testing Service and director of the Child Care Research Center. He received his Ph.D. from the University of Chicago. Dr. Sigel's publications are concerned with childrens' intellectual development and the factors that influence it. For *The American Way*, Dr. Sigel prepared the special skills features that focus on how people learn.

SHELDON HACKNEY is president and professor of history at Tulane University, New Orleans, Louisiana. Dr. Hackney received his Ph.D. from Yale University in 1966. His specialty is southern history. Dr. Hackney was the historical consultant for *The American Way*.

JOSEPH D. BACA is the social studies specialist for the Department of Education in Santa Fe, New Mexico. He has been involved in education for 15 years as a classroom teacher and an administrator. Mr. Baca reviewed *The American Way*.

Grateful acknowledgment is made for the following:
An excerpt from "I Have a Dream,"
copyright © 1963 by Martin Luther King, Jr.

Photo Credits are on page 726.

CONTENTS

MAPS

CHARTS AND GRAPHS

FEATURES

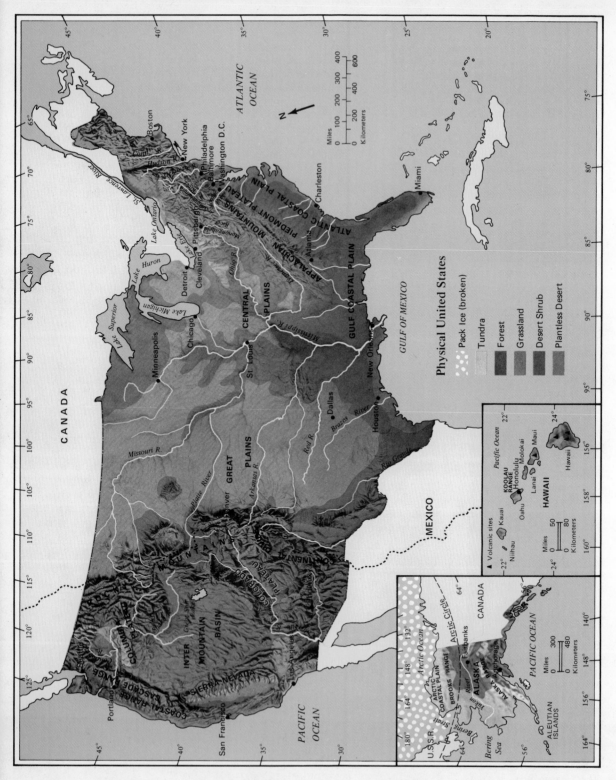

Physical United States

- Pack Ice (broken)
- Tundra
- Forest
- Grassland
- Desert Shrub
- Plantless Desert

CANADA

ATLANTIC OCEAN

Boston
New York
Philadelphia
Baltimore
Washington D.C.
Charleston
Miami

Lake Ontario
Lake Erie
Lake Huron
Lake Michigan
Lake Superior

St. Lawrence River
Hudson River

Detroit
Cleveland
Pittsburgh
Atlanta

APPALACHIAN MOUNTAINS
PIEDMONT PLATEAU
ATLANTIC COASTAL PLAIN

Minneapolis
Chicago

CENTRAL PLAINS

St. Louis
Ohio R.
Mississippi R.

GULF COASTAL PLAIN

GULF OF MEXICO

New Orleans
Dallas
Houston
Red R.
Brazos River
Rio Grande
Missouri R.

GREAT PLAINS

Platte River
Arkansas R.
Denver

ROCKY MOUNTAINS
CONTINENTAL DIVIDE

COLORADO PLATEAU
INTER MOUNTAIN BASIN

SIERRA NEVADA
CASCADE RANGE
COASTAL RANGE
COLUMBIA PLATEAU

Portland
San Francisco
Los Angeles

PACIFIC OCEAN

MEXICO

HAWAII

Pacific Ocean
Kauai
Niihau
Oahu
KOOLAU RANGE
Honolulu
Molokai
Lanai
Maui
Hawaii

▲ Volcanic sites

Miles 0 50
Kilometers 0 80

ALASKA

U.S.S.R.
Arctic Ocean
Arctic Circle
CANADA
ARCTIC COASTAL PLAIN
BROOKS RANGE
Fairbanks
Yukon River
ALASKA RANGE
Anchorage
PACIFIC OCEAN
Bering Strait
Bering Sea
ALEUTIAN ISLANDS

Miles 0 300
Kilometers 0 480

Miles 0 100 200 300 400
Kilometers 0 200 400 600

N

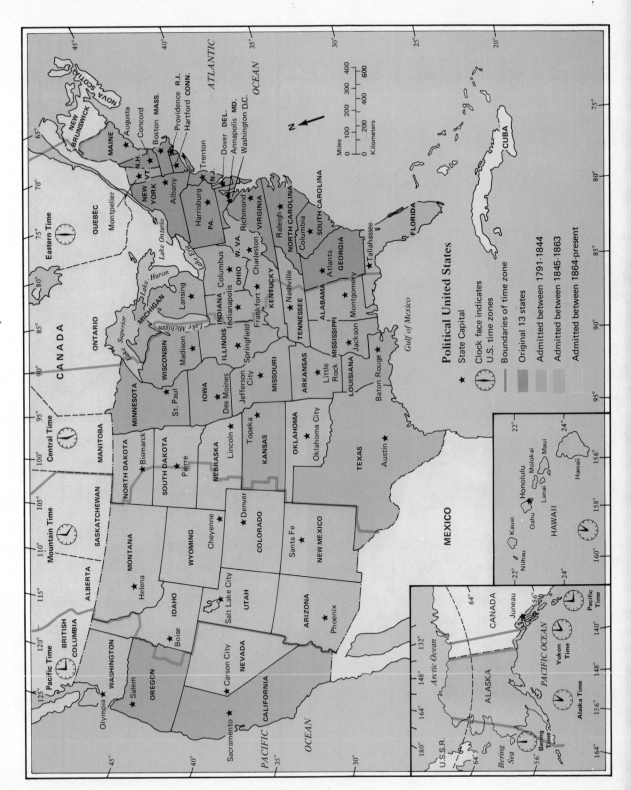

Political United States

★ State Capital

🕐 Clock face indicates
U.S. time zones

⎯ Boundaries of time zone

Original 13 states

Admitted between 1791-1844

Admitted between 1845-1863

Admitted between 1864-present

ATLANTIC OCEAN

Augusta
Concord
Boston MASS.
Providence R.I.
Hartford CONN.
Dover DEL.
Annapolis MD.
Washington D.C.
Trenton
N.J.
NEW YORK Albany
Montpelier
MAINE
N.H.
VT.
Harrisburg PA.
W. VA.
Richmond VIRGINIA
Charleston
Raleigh
NORTH CAROLINA
Columbia
SOUTH CAROLINA
Atlanta GEORGIA
Tallahassee FLORIDA
Montgomery ALABAMA
Nashville TENNESSEE
Frankfort KENTUCKY
Columbus OHIO
Indianapolis INDIANA
Springfield ILLINOIS
Jefferson City MISSOURI
Little Rock ARKANSAS
Baton Rouge LOUISIANA
Jackson MISSISSIPPI

Eastern Time

QUEBEC

Lake Ontario
Lake Erie
Lake Huron
Lake Superior
Lake Michigan

NEW BRUNSWICK
NOVA SCOTIA

CANADA

ONTARIO

Lansing MICHIGAN
Madison WISCONSIN
St. Paul MINNESOTA
Des Moines IOWA

Central Time

MANITOBA

Bismarck NORTH DAKOTA
Pierre SOUTH DAKOTA
Lincoln NEBRASKA
Topeka KANSAS
Oklahoma City OKLAHOMA
Austin TEXAS

SASKATCHEWAN

Mountain Time

ALBERTA

Helena MONTANA
Cheyenne WYOMING
Denver COLORADO
Santa Fe NEW MEXICO

Boise IDAHO
Salt Lake City UTAH
Phoenix ARIZONA

Pacific Time

BRITISH COLUMBIA

Olympia WASHINGTON
Salem OREGON
Carson City NEVADA
Sacramento CALIFORNIA

PACIFIC OCEAN

Gulf of Mexico

MEXICO

CUBA

Pacific Time — HAWAII
Honolulu
Kauai
Niihau
Oahu
Molokai
Lanai Maui
Hawaii

Pacific Time
Yukon Time
Alaska Time
Bering Time

ALASKA
CANADA
Juneau
PACIFIC OCEAN
Arctic Ocean
Bering Sea
U.S.S.R.

ix

THE AMERICAN WAY

AMERICA IS...

VARIETY AND SHARED VALUES

UNIT ONE

How many people can you describe in any way, although you have never met them? Five thousand? A million? A billion? How many people have you seen with your own eyes? Three thousand? Twenty thousand? How many people have you actually met? One hundred? Four hundred? How many people do you know well? Twenty? Fifty? How many people do you understand? Ten? Two?

History is a way of describing people so that they can be understood. If you were asked to describe one person you know well, it would probably take you a long time to do it. Because you know so many details about the person, you have to decide where to begin and how to put all the details together to form an accurate picture. To describe people you know well, you need to describe how they talk, what they talk about, what they like to do, and what they hope to do in the future.

It is harder to describe people you see only once in a while. These are people you may see regularly but always in the same place—such as at a church or synagogue, a gym, or a skating rink. All that you know about them is how they behave in certain activities. They do not stand out so clearly in your minds.

It is even more difficult to describe clearly whole groups of people. How would you describe all the people in your school or neighborhood? You might begin by describing the behavior, beliefs, and physical characteristics that are shared by almost everyone in the group. Those are the details that are repeated often enough to apply to almost everyone, most of the time.

When people describe groups, they have to leave out the details that make one person stand out from another. A group description is useful, but it is not an accurate description of any one individual who belongs to that group.

Describing people is partly a matter of choosing a place from which to view them. When seen up close, the details about a single person are clear to the viewer. The farther away from a person the viewer gets, the harder it is to see details. But from far away it is easier to tell what groups people move in, where they live, who else lives nearby, and when and where their lives meet. From far away you can see the landscape of a place. You have to move in closer to be able to see hills, water, and traffic patterns of the same place.

Looking at people in time also involves deciding whether to look at them from far away or up close. If you back away from people

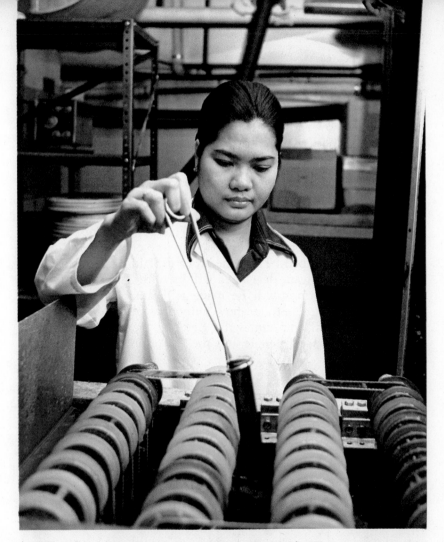

Americans have their roots in every nation in the world. Where can you see this variety in your community?

in time, you can see how long they have lived in a certain place, why they came to live there, and whom they have met along the way. In fact, the farther back in time you step, the more easily you can notice changes in other people's lives. Stepping back has some advantages. But when you do it, you have to be careful not to miss important details.

Studying people is like looking at a large painting or at a tapestry, a woven picture. The closer you get, the more detail you can see and recognize. The farther away you get, the more parts of the big picture you can take in at one time. But the tiny details, the brush strokes, the threads or stitches do not show. Large patches of color show from farther away. But up close you can tell what those colors are made of. Up close, you can even notice different shades of gray.

Describe another person. Describe a group of people. What is one difference in what you can see? Can a reader picture the person and group you have described?

Ask each student to describe a picture or hand-held object from close up and then, again, after stepping back.

Studying Americans

There are over 200 million people living in the United States of America. People's lives are tied to each other in many ways. People need to know how and why they are connected. They need to know what other Americans are like. They need to know what being connected means.

But what would you do if someone asked you to describe Americans? Not just one American or a town full of Americans. You would have to describe all the people who have been and are called Americans within the United States. That is what this textbook will try to do. In each unit, a particular way of looking at Americans will be described. Then the story explaining how that way of looking at Americans developed will be told. The distances from which the descriptions will be made will differ. Sometimes the view will be up close—to see how individual people have thought and felt and acted. Sometimes the view will be from far away, in order to see groups of people and the important changes in their lives.

America Is a Variety of People

The first way in which this book will describe Americans is by stepping back and looking at the variety among them. Americans are a variety of languages, skin colors, habits, and customs.

Freedom of religion is an American value. How has this American value influenced your life?

Americans live and work in small towns and large cities. What can you see in this picture that shows what is important to Americans?

Even the first Americans—Native Americans—were not one people. They were and are a variety of people. The groups of Europeans who later came from across the Atlantic Ocean to explore America were also different from each other. And the Europeans who came still later and settled the land were a variety, too. In looking at the earliest years, when only Native Americans lived here, and in looking at the years when Native Americans and Europeans met, it is possible to see that America is—and always has been—a variety of people. Yet even with such variety, there were some beliefs and goals that became the shared or common ones for Americans.

In the study of people, you—as the viewer, or observer—have to choose the best distance for what you want to see. As you do this in this first unit, think about the following questions:

1. How did the land and climate in different areas affect the way people lived?
2. What were some of the beliefs and values that guided people's daily lives?
3. How were individuals in one area connected to one another?
4. Which beliefs and ways of living have lasted and are part of people's lives today?

These questions might be written on the board for ready reference or put on newsprint for students to add answers as they read.

5

chapter 1
Variety Among Native Americans

30,000 B.C.—A.D. 1300

1. THE EARLIEST PEOPLE IN THE AMERICAS
2. THE TRIBES OF NORTH AMERICA

INTRODUCTION

To describe the history of the earliest people in North and South America, you have to choose a distance from which to view them. You would have to make the same decision if you wanted to describe people in the United States today. For both descriptions you need to see the land the people lived on, the climate, the kind of food they ate, and the way they changed. You need to find out what difference time and place made in their lives.

You need to try to figure out why people moved and why their lives changed. Did change come about because people set out to find something new? Or did change come about because someone came from outside and caused it? Or did change come about as a reaction to something that happened by mistake? These are examples of questions to be asked from far away. When you try to describe a group of people, you also try to get as close as you can

Give an example of each of these kinds of change.

	c. 30,000-10,000 B.C.	c. 9000-1500 B.C.	c. 1000 B.C.	c. 200 B.C.-400 A.D.	
Who?	the first Americans	Folsom culture	Southern and Central Native Americans	Hopewell culture	
What?	arrive in North America	hunt, make tools	plant food, irrigate crops	build mounds	
Where?	across the land bridge from Asia	from Alaska to the Great Plains	in Peru, Honduras, Mexico	in southern Ohio, Illinois	

What are the three basic categories of the time line?

Which dates are the earliest? How do you read this time line?

and still see all the people in the group. In describing early Native Americans, you want to know how they are the same and how they are different from each other. You want to know what they thought was important and what their goals were. You also want to know what they believed people could and should do. These are examples of close-up questions.

The answers to these questions will make it possible for you to know how Native Americans were and are, on the whole, alike or different from other people. As you read this chapter about Native Americans before they met Europeans, think about the following questions:

1. Where did Native Americans come from?
2. Where did they settle?
3. What kind of society did Native Americans build in Mexico and Peru? How was this society different from the society of the northern Native Americans?
4. How did the climate and land affect the people of North America?

1. THE EARLIEST PEOPLE IN THE AMERICAS

The earliest people who lived in North and South America did not belong to one group. These people came at different times across a land bridge from Asia and settled in very different places. They left no written record. The record is in bones, tools, and art work that remain today. People lived near sources of food. Their settlements and the paths that they traveled can be traced by the bones of the animals they killed. Scientists called archeologists use these bones to tell us about life long ago.

c. 200 A.D.	c. 1000 A.D.	c. 1300 A.D.	c. 1300-1492	c. 1500
the Pueblos	Woodland Tribes	Iroquois tribes	Aztecs, Incas	Apacheans
a basket-making culture emerged	farm, make pottery	form a league of five nations	establish empires	learn farming from the Pueblos
in Arizona, New Mexico, Colorado, and Utah	in Nebraska, central Kansas	in central and western New York	in Mexico, Peru	in southwest of North America

How can you tell what someone thinks is important? How can you tell about a group's goals?

7

People Arrive

At the bottom of a cliff at Cape Prince of Wales, Alaska, is a big pile of bones. They are the bones of the woolly mammoth, a kind of elephant that lived in *prehistoric* times. From the size of the pile of bones, it is easy to see that they did not get there by accident. These animals were stampeded over the cliff. From these remains scientists and historians have learned about the earliest people in the Americas. They say that people who were used to hunting and eating meat probably caused the stampede of the woolly mammoths over the cliffs. But which people? Scientists and historians believe that the earliest people in the Americas, the ones who hunted the woolly mammoths, must have come from somewhere else.

1. How did the people probably get to the Americas?

They probably came over the land bridge between what is now Siberia in Russia and Alaska in North America.

Because the Americas are almost totally surrounded by water, the people would have to have come from some nearby land. What land is nearest to the American continents? *Geologists*—scientists who study land formations—think that thousands of years ago there was a land bridge between what is now Siberia in Russia and Alaska in North America. Today there is a narrow body of water separating Russia and Alaska, called the Bering Strait. In the Bering Strait there are two islands that were probably once part of that land bridge.

When could people have crossed that land bridge? Geologists believe that at one time much of North America was covered by large sheets of moving ice, or *glaciers*. This Ice Age lasted for about a million years. But it was only at the time of the last of these glaciers, known as the Wisconsin Glacier, that there was an ice-free corridor east of the Rocky Mountains that humans could easily travel through.

2. Why do scientists use a 10,000- to 30,000-year estimate of when the earliest people crossed the Bering strip?

That expanse of time coincides with the melting of the Wisconsin glacier. Scientists have based their calculations on comparisons between the age of some of the mammoths killed by humans and the dates of the glaciers.

3. How do we know that the earliest people in the Americas came from elsewhere?

Scientists and historians believe that the earliest people in the Americas, those who hunted the woolly

By looking at the age of the bones of the mammoths killed by humans and the dates of the glaciers, it is possible to figure out about what time the first humans arrived in North America. If they came after the last glacier melted, it would be about 10,000 to 12,000 years ago. Or they might have come during one of the periods of melting that took place within the time of the glacier. These periods happened every 5,000 years or so. This would mean that the date of the first entry of humans into the Americas could be 20,000 or even 30,000 years ago.

The Culture of the Native Americans

The arrival of people in the Americas was thousands of years before any highly organized way of life, or civilization, had developed anywhere. The first such civilization discovered so far was in the Middle East, in the land known today as Iraq. This civilization developed at least 13,000 years after the first people arrived in the Americas.

mammoths, must have come from somewhere else. They base their assumptions on their examinations of the bones of those prehistoric animals that, they conclude, were stampeded over the cliff at Cape Prince of Wales, Alaska.

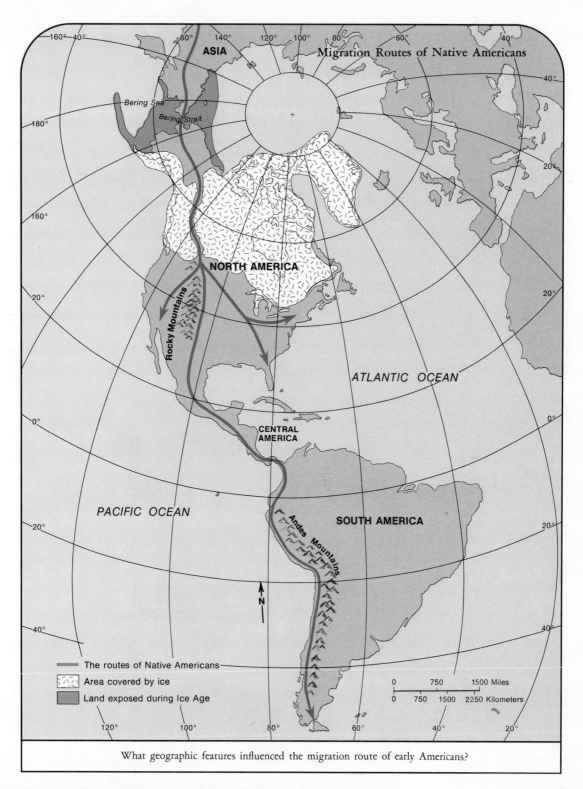

Migration Routes of Native Americans

ASIA

Bering Sea

Bering Strait

NORTH AMERICA

Rocky Mountains

ATLANTIC OCEAN

CENTRAL AMERICA

PACIFIC OCEAN

SOUTH AMERICA

Andes Mountains

N

The routes of Native Americans

Area covered by ice

Land exposed during Ice Age

0		750		1500 Miles
0	750	1500	2250	Kilometers

What geographic features influenced the migration route of early Americans?

The Native Americans traveled across areas covered by ice, through mountain valleys, and along the course of rivers.

Try to imagine the great distances people traveled. A person on foot can travel 15–50 miles (24–80 kilometers) per day depending on the terrain, and the weather, etc.. Does it make a difference if a person has a destination?

The first Americans therefore developed cultures without outside influence. They were isolated from the other continents before the races and cultures you know about today were even formed.

Spreading Out

These first people in the Americas followed the wildlife—and there was a great deal of it. Not only woolly mammoths, but other kinds of elephants, musk oxen, caribou, mountain sheep, and the bison, or buffalo. The people left behind a trail of chipped stone points, which they used to spear the animals. One of their routes followed the foothills of the Brooks Range in Alaska, then down the Mackenzie River, and into the open land, or plains, east of the Rocky Mountains. There was also a trail through the Yukon Valley, which followed the Peace and Laird rivers. With the Rockies before them, it is no wonder that groups turned in other directions, and headed south and east. Before the last glacier ended, there were people as far south as New Mexico. The Southwest, which is dry desert today, was big-game country 6,000 years ago. Remains of animals like the ground sloth, which had come from South America, have been found there. So have bones of native animals, such as the horse, which disappeared in the Americas after the Ice Age.

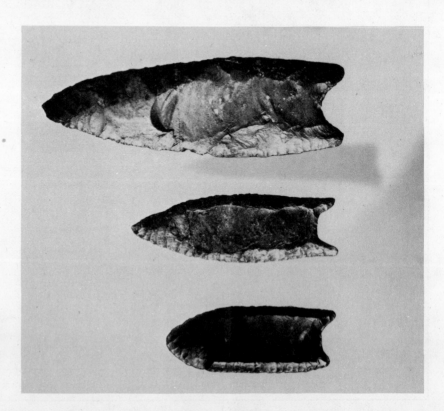

4. How do we know that the first Americans developed cultures on their own?

The first civilization discovered was in the Middle East. This civilization developed at least 13,000 years after the first people arrived in the Americas. The first Americans therefore developed cultures on their own.

Arrowheads have been found in every region of North America. What skills did the tribes use to make arrowheads?

10

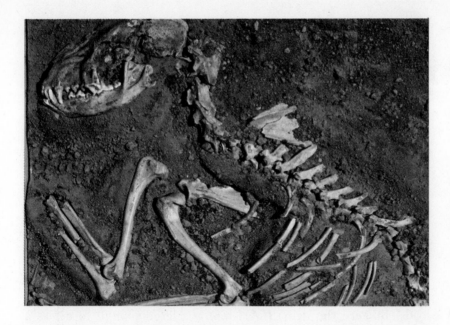

This is a mummy of an ancient dog. What can archæologists learn from this kind of evidence?

Some groups of early Americans traveled along the flat plateau of Mexico, across the *Isthmus* of Panama, and down along the Andes Mountains. There was enough plant and animal life to provide food all the way to the tip of South America.

5. *Why did the people migrate in a southeastern direction?*

1) They followed the wildlife. 2) The wildlife followed the river beds away from the Rocky Mountains. 3) There was enough plant and animal life for food.

The Land and the Lives of the People

Once the ice had melted, these people were able to spread out all over the two continents. They spread into the flat areas of what is now the United States and down to South America. There was a difference in the ways the lives of these early people developed. Much of the difference was due to the variety of native plants the people found.

The most *fertile* part of the Americas was the central part—the areas known today as Mexico, Central America, and the northern part of eastern South America. These areas were nearest the *equator*. There the climate is warm and the rainfall steady. In these areas *botanists*, or plant scientists, have found remains of many root plants: sweet potatoes, potatoes, manioc, Jerusalem artichokes, and arrowroot. There were beans, chili peppers, corn (maize) of several kinds, pineapples, pumpkins, squash, tomatoes, and cashew nuts. Plants used for medicine, such as quinine and ipecac, grew there.

How did early ways of life develop by chance? How much chance is left in your life?

Chicle for chewing gum, tobacco for smoking, and cotton for making clothing also grew there.

6. How did these early people develop agriculture?

People carried the knowledge of growing and using native plants from one settlement to another.

Once people discovered the value of a particular plant, the use of it spread. Knowledge of plants was carried by people who lived at the edge of one group's settlement to the people at the edge of a different settlement. The growing of corn, for example, spread to wherever it could be grown. *Agriculture*, or the planned growing of food, therefore grew up with the cultures of the people of the Americas.

What Was Different?

The people of the Americas were skilled at agriculture. But they did not develop the tools and transportation that gave Europeans and Asians more control over the land, the climate, and one another. There were two main reasons for this. First, there was no hard metal easily found in the Americas. Second, there were no animals big enough and able to be tamed that could carry heavy loads. In Peru the llama (LAH-ma) was large enough to use as a pack animal. But it was not large or strong enough to pull anything very heavy. Perhaps the absence of large animals and the fact that the land in Peru was mountainous were reasons the wheel never came into use there. Like plants, animals were used in very special ways. For example, in Peru the llama was sheared for its wool, but it was never milked.

Farther north, in Central Mexico and the Yucatan peninsula, there were no beasts of burden at all. *Anthropologists*—scientists who study how and why behavior develops among groups of people—believe that this fact helps explain why the wheel never developed in the Americas. These scientists reason that since people in ancient Mexico made toys with wheels on them for children, they knew about the idea of a wheel. But to develop the idea further for transportation of heavy materials required animals strong enough to pull a load.

The Most Organized Early Americans

The Incas of the Andes Mountains, the Mayas of Central America, and the Aztecs of Mexico had the most highly organized civilizations in the Americas. They built irrigation ditches to water the land. They also built roads and bridges. To accomplish these projects, they had to organize themselves.

These people chose chiefs and priests to rule over them. The priests were trained in *astronomy*, so they could tell people when to plant crops. The priests were also in charge of religious life. Like other early peoples, the Incas, Mayas, and Aztecs believed that the world

When do people learn new ways of doing things? How do they learn them? Give an example of something you have learned.

Some ideas take organization. Name a few.

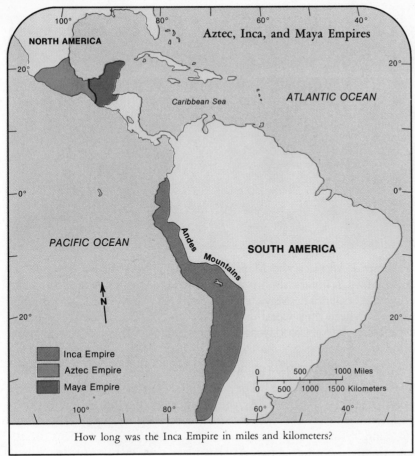

Aztec, Inca, and Maya Empires

NORTH AMERICA

ATLANTIC OCEAN

Caribbean Sea

PACIFIC OCEAN

Andes Mountains

SOUTH AMERICA

N

Inca Empire
Aztec Empire
Maya Empire

0   500   1000 Miles
0 500 1000 1500 Kilometers

How long was the Inca Empire in miles and kilometers?

The Inca Empire was approximately 2,750 miles, or 4,400 kilometers, long.

was filled with spirits. The more powerful spirits were worshipped as gods. To keep on the good side of the gods, people made sacrifices to them. These sacrifices were both human and animal. The priests were responsible for the sacrifices. In addition, they helped the leaders rule over everyone else. Those who were not priests or rulers were farmers and craftspeople. Accounts were carefully kept of who did what work and how much each worker had to give to the leaders.

In the land of the Incas, people had the same jobs as their parents. This ensured that certain skills would be carried down over the years. For example, groups of Incan artists built temples, made beautiful ornaments of gold, and, for reasons unknown today, dug out the outline of large animals in the soil for miles across. The ability of the Incas to organize helped them spread their control over other areas. Soon they had an empire, which, at its largest, ran from present-day Colombia to Chile. The empire was controlled from the city of Cuzco, in what is now Peru.

What do you think makes some people spend more time and effort doing something than others do?

What customs helped people survive? What customs help us today?

What skills did the Inca gold makers need to make the cups?

In Central America the Mayas developed a very advanced civilization. Maya scholars set up a way to tell time using the sun and created a calendar. Maya artists built big stone faces and huge temples where they worshipped their gods. The remains of a Maya center can be seen today at Chichen Itza, in the Yucatan area of Mexico.

The Aztecs arrived in the Americas later than the Mayas. They were a wandering tribe. They entered Central America from the north around A.D. 1200. As they migrated they fought with other people for control of land. According to their *mythology*, they were to wander until they came upon an eagle with a serpent in its mouth, sitting on a cactus. At that place they were to settle. When the Aztecs found this sacred land in the central valley of Mexico, they fought and won a battle over it. The land was surrounded by a lake. The Aztecs built their capital city (now Mexico City) on this naturally protected island. Their rulers and priests lived there. Farms were located on nearby land.

7. What were the features of these highly organized civilizations?

1) They developed irrigation. 2) They built roads and bridges. 3) They assigned jobs to individuals and kept records of what they did.

Like the Mayas and Incas, the Aztecs developed a very high level of civilization. They constructed a calendar more accurate than that developed by the Europeans. They were also skilled builders and gold workers. They built huge "step" *pyramids* that were used as religious temples. The Aztecs worshipped the sun. They also considered their own leaders to be gods.

Ideas Are Traded

The ideas developed by advanced civilizations of the Aztecs, Mayas, and Incas were passed on to people living in the north. These people used the ideas that were suited to where they lived. One of the ideas they used was a way of clearing the land of trees. They made a deep cut in the base of a tree, causing it to die and fall to the ground. Then they burned the tree stump and left the wood ash on the soil. Because the minerals in the wood ash improved the soil, people were able to grow crops on the cleared area for three or four years in a row. When the minerals in the ground were used up, the people cleared new fields.

What does this Maya temple complex tell you about the skills and beliefs of the Maya people?

8. *Why was the "milpa" system used all over the world?*

The "milpa" system was practiced all over the world because this method of clearing the land used resources that were found everywhere.

This method of clearing the land was called the *milpa system*. Under one name or another, the milpa system was used by people all over the world. When a practice appears in several locations, does that mean there was contact between the people in these locations? Not necessarily. Not every practice is developed in only one place. When people use the resources around them, those with similar resources may discover similar ways of living.

Checking the facts

1. Why did the early people come across the Bering land bridge?
2. How did the increasing knowledge of plants change the lives of the early Americans?
3. "The civilizations of the early American people were less advanced than those of Europe or Asia." What facts would you use to agree with this statement? What facts would you use to disagree?

2. THE TRIBES OF NORTH AMERICA

The Native Americans that lived on the land now known as the mainland of North America were as great a variety as any other people anywhere. You have seen that, from the time of the last Ice Age, people came to this continent and spread out along the routes where food was available. To look at all the Native Americans of what is now the United States requires that you look from a distance.

There are two major ways in which you can get a view of all the Native Americans and, at the same time, note their differences. One way is to look at how they lived on the land. The other way is to look at their language. From what is known of geography and language, it is possible to take a close-up view of Native Americans. The close view shows that people were grouped according to their language. These language families were called tribes. Within the tribes there were sections. The daily life in each of these sections was different from the daily life in other sections.

The Native Americans of North America were divided into six major language families. Each family lived in a different geographical region. Some happened to settle where it was fairly easy to grow crops. They built villages, set aside land for farming, and organized their lives around special duties and ceremonies they believed would guarantee a good harvest. Others, however, arrived

9. *What determined whether Native Americans lived in agricultural communities or in wandering communities?*

The amount of rainfall in the area determined whether crops would grow. When

there was adequate rainfall, agricultural communities emerged.

16

READING WITH UNDERSTANDING

Have you ever read to the bottom of a page and suddenly realized that you didn't remember a thing? What happened? Did your mind wander? The chances are that you sighed, went back to the top of the page, and plowed through it again, word by word. Did you remember more this time? Probably not. Most people only remember about two percent more after rereading a page. Is rereading worth the trouble? Not unless you do it differently.

When you read the page the first time, were you really reading? Yes, you probably were, up to a point. You were looking at the letters and grouping them into meaningful sound units we call words. Where the reading process broke down was in fitting those words into the sentence. The word only has meaning within the structure of the sentence, and this process requires remembering words you have just read. To remember, you must concentrate.

What helps concentration? Have you ever noticed that you have no difficulty in concentrating on something that interests you? Why is that? When you're interested in a topic, you already know enough about it to tell you that you'd like to know more. *When you're reading, then, you can take what you just learned and fit it in with what you already know.*

What if you don't know very much about a subject? Can you become interested enough to concentrate and read with understanding? Yes, but you may need help. The textbook gives you some clues about what you are going to read by providing photographs, illustrations, diagrams, maps, charts, section headings, and, most important, topic sentences. If you find that you do know something about the topic, your reading goes easily. You are scanning rapidly, for you can generally predict what the text is going to say. There's enough new information mixed with the old, however, to keep you interested.

What if, after looking at the textbook aids, you find you really don't know much about the subject? If this happens, look at the questions in the margin of the textbook. By reading to answer the questions in the margins, your reading has purpose. Your attention is concentrated on finding the answers.

What if you're not sure your answer is correct? This may happen. The text asks you questions which make you use the information you've just read. There are two different types of rereading you may do. You can skim the material to see if you had the general idea. Or you can scan the material to see if you used all the facts you need. In either case, you are rereading with a purpose and will gain greater understanding.

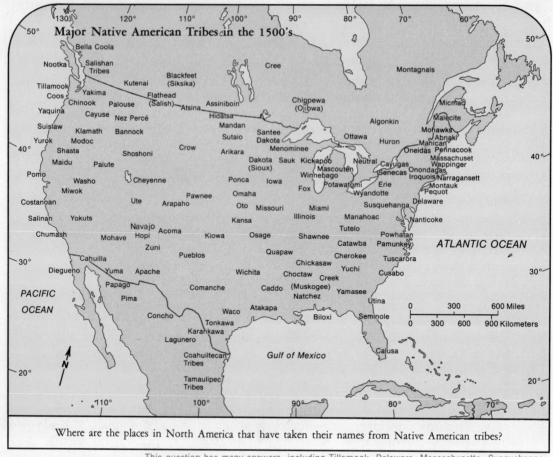

Major Native American Tribes in the 1500's

Where are the places in North America that have taken their names from Native American tribes?

This question has many answers, including Tillamook, Delaware, Massachusetts, Susquehanna, Ottawa, Dakota, Iowa, Erie, Yakima, Missouri, and Waco.

in areas without enough rainfall for agriculture. These people had to keep moving to find enough food. They hunted for food. Because they did not stay in one place for very long, they could not organize their lives as much as the people who settled in villages could.

10. How do we know how the Native Americans lived?
The best clues are the artifacts that remain, arrowheads, bones, tools, and art work. The ceremonies and stories handed down from generation to generation also give us clues.

Some of the Native American tribes were near enough to the advanced cultures of Central America to get ideas from them. Some tribes were isolated. In both cases, knowledge about Native Americans comes from their tools, art work, ceremonies, and stories that have been handed down from generation to generation. Their languages were not written down. But a great deal of detail was preserved and passed on from speaker to speaker. Historians use this information and compare it with descriptions written by the Europeans who first met the Native Americans.

The Southeastern Tribes

The tribes of the area known today as Mississippi, Georgia, Ala-

18

bama, Tennessee, and northern Florida spoke the same or similar languages. These were the Creek, Chickasaw, Choctaw, and Cherokee tribes.

How did they live on the land? They settled in an area of dense forests from the Mississippi River east to the Atlantic Ocean. Rivers ran through the area. The Native Americans' main goal was survival, as it is for everyone. To survive, these people fished, hunted, and gathered berries, nuts, and roots. What little farming they did was around a central place that was almost like a town. In the settled farming area, each family had its own plot of land. In addition, there was a common, or town, plot that went to the tribal leader.

11. How did the Southeastern tribes use their environment?

1) They fished in the rivers and hunted in the forests. They gathered berries, nuts, and roots from the forests for food. 2) They grew food on their land. 3) They lived along the creeks in bark-covered houses built from the trees in the forests.

This wooden deer head was carved by a member of the Caluse tribe. The ears could be moved by pulling strings. The head was probably used in ceremonies and as a lure for game. Can you think of other ways it might have been used?

12. *How were the families organized?*

1) Ownership of the family plot came from the woman's side of the family. 2) The man was the head of the family. 3) The mother's brother had the right to discipline the children.

Families lived along the creeks in bark-covered houses. It was the English who called the people the Creeks. The family groups, or *clans*, were organized around the women. Ownership of the family plot came from the woman's side of the family. But the men held the final responsibility for the family. The man was the head of the family. The mother's brother could hand out punishment to the children of the family.

Besides food gathering and growing, the business of these southeastern tribes was war. Boys grew up to be warriors. Men took pride in being able to endure pain. Games were supposed to be as rough as possible. Facing danger and possible bodily harm was part of the excitement of life for the men.

These Native Americans believed that nature was filled with spirits. Each form of life, such as plants and animals, had a spirit. Earth and air held spirits, too. People were never alone. They shared their lives with the spirits of nature.

The Algonkians

The Algonkian (al-GAHN-kee-un) language family was so widespread that it included hunters in the far north of present-day Canada and corn growers as far south along the Atlantic Coast as the region that is now the Carolinas. The Algonkians lived in a huge area that stretched from Hudson Bay all the way across North America to Labrador, Canada. From that northern source, two streams of Algonkians moved south.

The Canadian tribes were hunters of deer, elk, and caribou. They traveled in small groups when they hunted. For water journeys they used birch-bark canoes.

The Canadian tribes were not highly organized. The leader of the groups would decide when and where to move. The leader also watched to make sure that no one disturbed the spirits. Like other Native Americans, these hunters believed that plants and animals had spirits. They thought that when animals were killed, their spirits lived on. These spirits might return at any time to make sure that the bones of the animals were respected. Native Americans also communicated with the spirit world through dreams, or *trances*. The medicine man or drum person, the *shaman*, was believed to have supernatural powers.

Farther south the Algonkians were more than just hunters. They gathered nuts and berries and fished along the coast. In summer they planted corn. They put chopped-up fish heads, which were rich in minerals, into the ground with the corn seeds to make the soil more fertile.

These Native Americans from Virginia are cooking fish. Notice that it is the men who do the cooking. What other jobs did the men have to do in order to prepare the fish?

Money is anything people agree has value and are willing to use as something to trade for. Why do you think wampum was used as money? What other items might be used for money?

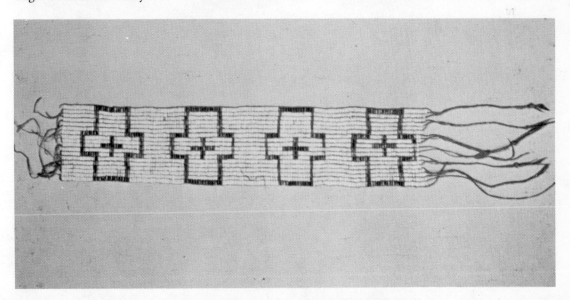

Notice that anything people agree on can be used for money. It is the agreement that gives the object value.

21

Power is the ability to have one's plans carried out. Power does not have to come through war.

13. What did Algonkian women do?

They were responsible for planting in the spring, for catching and drying fish in summer, and harvesting in the fall.

14. How did the Algonkian tribes of the north use their environment?

1) They hunted deer, elk, and caribou for food. 2) They traveled in small groups when they hunted. 3) They used the bark of birch to build canoes.

These Algonkian tribes lived a much more settled life. They set up villages with many huts made of elm bark. Two or three families often lived in one hut. These people used the same tools as the northern tribes. They also made pottery and woven baskets. And valuable shells were used to make *wampum*. Wampum was then used for money, decoration, and pledges of friendship.

In these tribes men and women had different roles. The men were the hunters. They supplied their own families with food, but they also had to give the first animal killed on each hunt to someone else in the village. Women were responsible for planting in the spring, for catching and drying fish in summer, and harvesting in the fall. Wives were chosen because they were hard workers. Work and family life were tied together.

Compared to the northern tribes, the many tribes of the Atlantic seaboard were much more organized. They had leaders who inherited their positions through the male line. Each leader tried to get more power, usually by taking over nearby villages and making them pay a tax, or tribute, in animal skins, corn, or pottery beads. Some leaders held power over only two or three villages. Others had as many as 30. This rivalry for power meant that the tribes were constantly at war with one another.

Look closely at the picture. How many different activities are the Native Americans doing?

22

In all, there were 11 major tribes in the Algonkian language family. Each of these was a loose grouping, or *confederacy*, of other clans and tribes. The 11 Algonkian groups were the Abenaki (a-buh-NA-kee), Massachusett, Narragansett (nar-ruh-GAN-set), Wampanoag (wahm-puh-NOE-ag), Pennacook, Pequot (PEE-kwat), Mahican, Wappinger, Montauk, Delaware or Lenape, and Powhatan (POW-uh-tan) tribes.

The Iroquois

The Iroquois were another language group that settled in the forests of the northeast. They arrived later than the Algonkians, and they pushed these older tribes apart. Iroquois territory included western New York, Pennsylvania, the land around Lakes Ontario and Erie, the Ohio Valley, and lands in the south.

The Iroquois built stockades to protect themselves from outsiders. Inside the stockades they built sturdy houses, 50 to 100 feet (1,500 to 3,000 centimeters) long. Eight to ten families lived in each house, with every two families sharing a fireplace. These long houses were covered with elm bark, which was also used for many utensils and for canoes.

Some tribes lived by hunting. Others lived by farming. When the Iroquois went out to kill game, they organized into hunting parties. During the winter they would send out a large hunting party, under the direction of a leader. The leader made all the plans and was in charge of dividing up the spoils of the hunt. The Iroquois also organized in teams to build dams to catch fish.

The farmers among the Iroquois used the milpa method to clear huge areas of land. They grew many varieties of corn, beans, squash, strawberries, and herbs. Their cornfields often stretched for long distances along a stream. In the fields older women supervised the harvesting of the crops.

Besides working in the fields, women also cooked and made pottery. The Iroquois valued women. Women owned the houses and the fields, and women also arranged marriages and selected the chief of the tribal council.

Some of the spirits the Iroquois believed in were female. These were the spirits who guided the planting and growing of the three main crops—corn, beans, and squash. Other spirits controlled hunting and warfare. All these spirits were part of an invisible force that flowed through nature. The Iroquois called this force *orenda*.

The Iroquois had detailed and carefully organized ceremonies. These ceremonies matched the seasons. At harvest time there was a ceremony of thanksgiving, and in the winter one for warfare.

Notice that these people did not worship plants and animals. They recognized that there was a force or spirit that all living things shared.

15. How were the tribes organized?

1) The Iroquois organized teams to hunt and fish. 2) Each team had a leader who made its plans.

16. How did the Iroquois get their food?

1) They hunted game and built dams to catch fish. 2) They used the slash-and-burn method to clear huge areas for growing many varieties of corn, beans, squash, strawberries, and herbs.

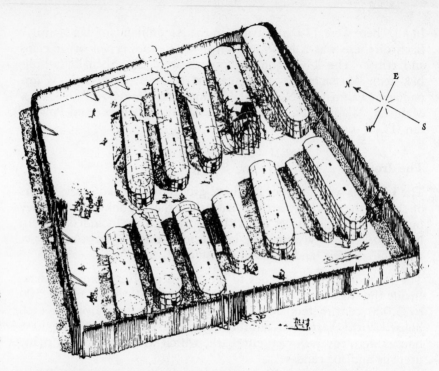

This picture shows Iroquois longhouses. What are the advantages of living in houses like these?

17. How did the Iroquois become powerful?

1) They formed a League of Five Nations that kept them from warring against each other. 2) They developed trade with the Algonkians.

At first the different Iroquois fought among themselves. Later on, however, they organized into a union. By A.D. 1300, the Iroquois had formed the League of Five Nations. The League was made up of the Onondagas (ah-nahn-DAH-gahs), the Cayugas (kee-YOO-gahs), the Mohawks, the Oneidas (oe-NEI-dahs), and the Senecas. The Tuscaroras (tus-cuh-ROAR-rahs) joined the League in 1711. The League dealt only with making war and peace. Tribes could act independently within their own tribal organizations, but the League kept them from warring against each other.

The Iroquois became the most powerful of the eastern woodland Indians. They developed trade with the Algonkians. They traded their dried corn for Algonkian tobacco, birchbark canoes, arrowheads, and wampum. The Iroquois also had much variety among their tribes. There were the hunters with their shamans, who interpreted signs of nature. And the farmers had their trained leaders and group ceremonies.

The Tribes of the Western Great Lakes

The Native Americans who lived along the upper Mississippi River and the western Great Lakes—Huron, Michigan, and Superior— were Algonkian speakers who had migrated south and west. They moved to a different land with different neighbors, and they learned much from both the land and the other people.

Why do people unite?

Why do people trade? What does trading do to people's ways of living?

The shores of the Great Lakes were flat and windy. The weather was too cold for much agriculture, except in protected places. So the tribes that pushed into this area had to hunt and fish. They also collected sap from the trees to make sugar when the season allowed. And in late summer they gathered wild rice along the banks of ponds and streams. Families had their own gathering territories, hunting lands, and sugar maples.

From their new neighbors—the tribes of the open land, or *prairies*, across the Mississippi, and the tribes to the south—the Algonkians of the western Great Lakes learned to grow corn in the summer and to hunt buffalo in the fall. Some tribes were able to kill 200 buffalo a day in the fall. During that time all the men hunted. The women packed the meat, dried it, and tanned the hides while the hunt continued. When winter came, the tribes could take a rest.

18. How did the Algonkians use the buffalo?

1) They ate the meat. 2) They dried and tanned the hides for clothing and housing material.

These Algonkians carved beautiful pipe bowls. Each bowl was fitted to a long reed stem, and the stem was decorated with feathers— red for war and white for peace. These pipes were called *calumets* by the Native Americans. Later, European settlers called them peace pipes. They were a sign of protection and agreement. No one would harm the possessor of one of the tribe's calumets.

The tribes of the western Great Lakes were the Ojibwa (o-JIB-way), who were also called the Chippewa, the Ottawa, Potawatomi (pot-uh-wah-TAH-mee), Menomini (men-NAH-min-nee), Mascouten, Winnebago, Sauk, Fox, Kickapoo, Illinois, Miami, Shawnee, and Sautee Dakota tribes.

As they settled down, these tribes organized into clans. Each clan had a peace chief and a war chief. The tribes believed that it was better to die in battle than to be taken prisoner and tortured.

The Native Americans of the Plains

Across the Mississippi River, from South Dakota to Oklahoma and Texas, was the area of the Plains. This was open country. Because it was suited for hunting and agriculture, the area could support both wandering, or *nomadic,* tribes, and settled village tribes. There were two major language groups that lived on the Plains. The Sioux (SOO) -speaking nomads were the Dakota, Crow, and Black-foot tribes. The Algonkian-speaking nomads were the Cheyenne (shy-YAAN), Arapaho (uh-RAP-uh-hoe), and Plains Cree tribes.

1) Whole villages hunted buffalo. When a village moved, the people used dogs to carry packs or drag supplies on a frame attached to two poles. 2) The village tribes built houses of logs and sod and grew corn, beans, and squash along the river banks. 3) The clans of both the hunters and the villagers were well organized.

19. How did the Plains tribes organize?

The men of these tribes hunted deer and elk. Whole villages hunted buffalo when the season came. The buffalo, or bison, were large beasts that stood about six feet (1.8 meters) high. They were never tamed to be used as beasts of burden. When a village moved from one place to another, the people used dogs rather than buffalo to carry packs or drag supplies on a frame attached to two poles. The village tribes of the Plains were the Mandan, Sioux, Arikara, and Pawnee groups. Their houses consisted of ditches in the flat soil, with logs built up above the ditches and covered with sod. The people grew corn, beans, and squash along the river banks. The clans of both the hunters and the villagers were well organized.

Southwest Native Americans

In the hundreds of years after the Ice Age, the land of the Southwest changed from lakes and forests, alive with bison, to bare hills and sandy plains. Today this land includes Arizona, New Mexico, part of Nevada, Utah, Colorado, and part of northern Mexico.

20. In what ways were the Pueblos influenced by their environment?

1) Their settlements were built on hilltops with steep sides and flat tops called mesas. 2) Their buildings were made of stone or sun-dried clay, or adobe. 3) They believed that there were cloud-beings and rain-beings. Because there was little rainfall in the Southwest, many of their religious ceremonies were designed to please these beings.

Three major groups of Native Americans moved into the Southwest. They were the Pueblos, the Apaches, and the Navajos. The Pueblos were the first to arrive. They were given their name by the Spanish, who came into the area much later. In Spanish the word *pueblo* means "village." The Pueblos lived in large settlements, consisting of stone or sun-dried clay, or adobe (uh-DOE-bee), buildings. Often the settlements were built on top of hills with steep sides and flat tops, called *mesas*. In the Pueblo villages, all the people lived as equals. Every person had the same responsibility for the survival of the group. The men were in charge of the spirits that might bring rain. The Pueblos believed that there were cloud-beings and rain-beings called the *kachina*. Because there was little rainfall in the area, many of the religious ceremonies of the Pueblos were designed to please these beings.

The women had an important position. They owned the fields and the houses, and they headed the family groups or clans.

The Pueblo lived by farming. They grew squash, kidney beans, and corn. They also grew cotton, which they wove into cloth on their looms. In addition, they made pottery.

The Hopi (HOE-pee), Zuñi (ZOO-nyee), and Acoma tribes of Arizona and western New Mexico were all Pueblo peoples. They were not warlike. War was considered a form of madness. The Pueblos went to war only if they were attacked by other Native Americans, such as the Apaches.

The Apaches and the Navajos came into the Southwest after the Pueblos. When they entered the area, they introduced a new language group, Uto-Aztecan. The peoples in this language group stretched from Utah and Colorado to Mexico. The Apaches were nomads who fought other Indians. They only organized into a large group under a single leader for purposes of warfare. Otherwise,

In what way did the Pueblos make sure that every person could be relied on? In what way did they recognize events beyond their power?

These Pueblo houses were made from available resources. Compare this photograph with the illustration of the North Carolina tribal village on page 22. What different resources did each tribe use?

they lived in small bands of related families. Some Apaches farmed, others gathered wild foods, and others hunted buffalo. They lived in *wickiups*, or circular-shaped buildings with thatched roofs.

Unlike the Apaches, the Navajos borrowed many of their customs and ceremonies from their neighbors, the Pueblos. From them they learned to farm and weave. Besides farming, the Navajos also raised sheep, goats, horses, and cattle, after these animals had been brought over by the Europeans. They did not live together in large settlements like the Pueblos. Instead, their *hogans*, or dome-shaped houses built of logs and mud, were spread over a wide area.

Northwest Native American Tribes

The Northwest tribes settled in what is now Oregon, Washington, British Columbia, and Alaska. Some lived near the coast. Others lived inland. The Nootka, Tillamook, Bella Coola, and Coo were

What are the advantages of meeting people who live differently from oneself?

some of the Northwest tribes. They depended on the many streams in the area for salmon and other fish. The thick forests supplied them with nuts and berries.

These Northwest tribes were famous for their cedar *totems*. A totem was a tall, carved wooden statue used to identify and protect a family. The totems were carved from hardwood trees and inlaid with sea shells.

21. How did the North-west tribes celebrate?

At winter celebrations, or potlatches, with neighboring tribes, rival chiefs entertained one another by giving gifts.

Families among the Northwest tribes belonged to different social classes, depending on how wealthy they were. Having wealth required catching many fish. Many families had fishing stations, away from the tribe, which they used during the summer months. During the winter social activities and warfare took place. At winter celebrations, or *potlatches*, with neighboring tribes, rival chiefs entertained one another by giving gifts. Tribes went to war to increase their wealth, by capturing people to be used as slaves or by taking property from other tribes.

Why did the Northwest tribes use wood for their carvings?

How many different reasons for war have you noticed? E.g., as a game, as training, for power, for prestige, or status.

THE MOUND BUILDERS

A number of mounds dot the country from the Mississippi River to the East. *Archeologists*—scientists who study the life and culture of ancient people—think some of these mounds were built between 200 B.C. and A.D. 400 as graves for burials. Archeologists have given a name to the builders of these mounds—the Hopewell culture.

The Hopewell culture extended from present-day Kansas to New York and from the Gulf of Mexico to Wisconsin. The mounds were built by these people. Their purpose is still a mystery. Some mounds were used as graves, but not all of them. The building of the mounds probably took much time and human labor. People had to carry basket after basket of dirt until the great mound was formed. The Serpent Mound, in Ohio, extends 1,300 feet (39,000 centimeters) in length. Other mounds vary in size from 8 to 40 feet (240 to 1,200 centimeters) high. Some of the more famous burial mounds are the Great Serpent Mound, near Hillsboro, Ohio; the Temple Mound, near Madison, Wisconsin; the Etowah Mounds, near Cartersville, Georgia; and the Hopewell Site, in south central Ohio. One of the burial mounds showed the remains of more than 1,000 burials. Along with the bones, archeologists have found offerings. These include arrowheads, copper, shell jewelry, bear teeth, pottery, pipes, hoes and spades, weapons, needles made of animal bone, and wood and stone carvings of humans and animals.

From these remains, or artifacts, archeologists have tried to put together a picture of the lives of the early Native Americans. The arrowheads and bone needles suggest that they hunted for meat and used animal skins as clothing. Hoes, spades, and pipes seem to indicate that these Native Americans might have farmed corn and tobacco. Since copper and grizzly bear teeth come from the Rocky Mountain area, it would seem that the people buried with them in Ohio must have traded with people in the West.

Other Mound Builders invented temple mounds. These mounds had flattened tops and served as platforms for temples and sacred buildings. Archeologists think that the Native Americans who lived along the Mississippi River built these mounds between A.D. 700 and 900. Archeologists have named the Temple Mound Builders the Mississippian culture. By about A.D. 1200 this culture seems to have spread east. By 1500 it reached Georgia, South Carolina, and the Gulf Coast of Florida. Hernando de Soto saw and described these temple mounds in the 1500's. Examples of temple mounds can be seen at Monk's Mound, Illinois; Macon, Georgia; Moundsville, Alabama; and Greenville, Mississippi. Temple mounds were built by the Natchez, Chickasaw, Cherokee, and Creek tribes until the eighteenth century. Did the arrival of the White settlers cause the end of the mound-building era?

What is it important to study these mounds?

Why is it important to keep records? Do you keep records?

The mounds shown here are 1,300 feet (390 meters) long. How do you suppose they were built? How long do you think it took to build them?

22. What was of value to the Native Americans?

1) They valued nature. They believed that the land and its plant life had to be shared with the animals and the spirits. 2) Although some valued warfare, others were not interested in war.

The Americas—a Variety over a Long Period of Time

Life among the Native Americans of North America was varied, but it was still strongly influenced by the need to live within the limits of nature. Each of the tribes within each of the six great language groups made its own adjustment to the land and climate where that tribe lived. The land and its plant life had to be shared with the other inhabitants of the earth—the animals and the spirits. The Native Americans developed many ways of keeping themselves alive and in good relationship with the spirits. In every tribe there were separate jobs for men and women, although the jobs were different in different tribes. There was growth and movement and change from tribe to tribe. But as a group, Native Americans developed differently from people who lived on other continents at the same time.

Checking the facts

1. Choose two language families from different geographic areas. Describe how each adapted to its environment.
2. Compare the roles of men and women in hunting and farming tribes.
3. What was special about the Native Americans' beliefs about nature?

What are the differences between living with nature as the early Americans did and "going back to nature" as some modern people have tried to do?

PUTTING IT ALL TOGETHER

UNDERSTANDING THE MAIN IDEAS

1. Where did the Native Americans come from?
2. Where did they settle?
3. What kind of society did Native Americans build in Mexico and Peru? How was this society different from the society of northern Native Americans?
4. How did the climate and land affect the people of North America?

ACTIVITIES

1. What Native Americans have lived in your area? Use your local library or historical association to find out. If there was more than one group, put their arrival on a time line. If new groups arrived, find out what caused them to move. What language group or groups do the Native Americans belong to?
2. Find out where Native Americans settled in your area before the Europeans arrived. Place the original Native American areas on a map of your state. Then locate the areas where the first Europeans settled on the same map.
3. Plan a visit to your local museum or historical society. Look at the art work of the different Native Americans. What can you tell about the materials they had to work with? What do you think they valued?
4. It has been said that the most organized settlers, the English, came upon the least settled Native Americans, the eastern hunting and gathering tribes. What difference might it have made in the history of the Americas if the Spanish had come to Plymouth and the English had met the Aztecs and the Mayas?

BOOKS TO READ

Karen, Ruth, *Kingdom of the Sun; the Inca: Empire Builders of the Americas* (New York: Four Winds Press, 1975).

White, Anne Terry, *The American Indian* (New York: Random House, 1975).

Whitlock, Ralph, *Everyday Life of the Maya* (New York: G. P. Putnam and Sons, 1976).

chapter 2
Europeans Reach Out

800–1696

1. EUROPEANS DEVELOP TRADE
2. PORTUGUESE AND SPANISH EXPLORATIONS

INTRODUCTION

During the hundreds of years when the Native Americans of North America were developing their many ways of life, the people of Europe were part of a totally different kind of development. Human beings can and do live in almost any environment. They live as they must, when there are no choices. But when new possibilities appear, men and women begin to reach out for them. In Europe from the year A.D. 1000 on, changes happened very fast, especially in comparison with the slowness of change of the hunters and corn growers of North America.

The changes that took place in Europe caused Europeans to reach out beyond the Atlantic Ocean for something new. For almost 600 years, what happened in Europe had little effect on developments in North America. At the end of that time, events on the two continents became closely related.

	1492	1500	1513	1519-1522
Who?	Christopher Columbus	Pedro Alvarez Cabral	Ponce de Leon	Fernando Magellan and the Spanish fleet
What?	set sail to find the Indies	claims land for Portugal	explores for Spain	sail around the world
Where?	finds Hispañola	in Brazil	in Florida	to Spain, South America, Philippines

Compare the time lines in Chapters 1 and 2 for the enormous differences in the time span covered. This comparison may help explain why Native American and European cultures developed so differently.

As you read this chapter, think about the following questions:

1. Why did Europeans want to reach out to new lands?
2. How did life in Europe expand beyond its borders?
3. How did Spain organize its explorations?
4. How did the Spanish behave toward the Native Americans?

1. EUROPEANS DEVELOP TRADE

Life in Europe during the Middle Ages (A.D. 800–1100) had been closely tied to the land. The land was owned by powerful individuals who gave protection to others who farmed for them. The owner was the lord of the manor. The others were serfs who promised the lord their loyalty, obedience, and their work.

War was also the business of many of these people. The strong lords used their armies to take over more land and more serfs. Their tools of war were made of steel. Horses made it possible for them to go to war far from home.

1. Why were both war and trade the business of people in the Middle Ages?

1) Lords who owned the land wanted more. 2) They used their armies to take over more land and more serfs. 3) They had to protect their own land and serfs. 4) They produced more food than the people could eat.

Perhaps the greatest difference between life in the old world of Europe and Asia and life in the Americas was extra food. Farms on the fertile soil and in the mild climate could produce more than people could eat. There was a surplus. And surpluses meant having something to trade. By the year 1000, there were people all over Europe and Asia who were organized for both trade and conquest.

The Vikings

The Vikings, or Norse, were the first to reach out across the Atlantic Ocean. They lived in northern Europe, on the peninsula now known as Scandinavia (skan-duh-NAY-vee-uh). The Vikings were farmers and seagoing warriors. From A.D. 800 to 1000 they sailed the seas and sent settlers to faraway lands. There were Norse villages

1519-1522	1530-1532	1539-1543	1542	1598
Hernando Cortés	Francisco Pizarro	Hernando de Soto	Juan Rodriquez Cabrillo	Juan de Oñate
conquers the Aztecs	conquers the Inca	explores for Spain	sails from Mexico	explores North America's interior
in Mexico	in Peru	interior of North America	to the California coast	establishes Santa Fe

The Native Americans also had organized ways of guaranteeing loyalty, obedience, and work. But they did not have metals, horses, and surplus food. Both war and peace were vastly different.

This picture shows a Viking ship. The crew sometimes had to row the ship if there was no wind.

2. Why are there remains of Viking villages only in Vinland?

1) Fighting broke out and the Vikings were forced back to Greenland. 2) They never returned.

in France, England, Scotland, and Ireland. There were Norse villages to the east, in Russia. The Norse also crossed the North Atlantic and left settlers in Iceland and in Greenland.

The most famous Norse explorer was Leif Ericson. He set out from Greenland in search of other lands. What was he looking for? Perhaps for places for farming that would be less covered with ice than Greenland was. Leif and his men landed on an island that is now called Newfoundland. They stayed there awhile, and then continued on. Norse writings about land on which wild grapes grew and cattle fed have led historians to believe that Leif and his fellow Vikings may have traveled as far south as present-day Massachusetts. In their writings the Norse called this land Vinland.

After Leif Ericson, other Vikings sailed to Vinland. They found people already living there, and for a time the Vikings and these people lived peacefully together. Finally, however, fighting broke out. The Vikings were forced to go back to Greenland. They never returned to Vinland.

Trade with the East

About 100 years after the Vikings' voyage to America, other Europeans began to be interested in another part of the world—the

Far East. Their interest started with the competition for land and trade. It was fired by a competition of beliefs. Religious beliefs were represented by people who wanted to conquer the world in the name of their religion. It was the fight between the Moslems and the Christians that sent people out into new territory. Each group believed it was right. Each group believed that it should teach its beliefs to others—even at the point of a sword. These religious wars between the Moslems and the Christians were called the Crusades. They were blessed by the Roman Catholic Church, which was headed by the bishop of Rome, the pope.

3. Why were the Crusades fought?

1) Moslems and Christians were competing for land and trade. 2) Each group thought it should teach its beliefs to others.

The Moslems had great success in spreading their power and religion in the area around the Mediterranean Sea. By A.D. 900 they had conquered North Africa and the Iberian Peninsula (the peninsula of Spain). They also controlled the Holy Land of Palestine, or modern-day Israel.

Meanwhile, the strongest Christian lords, or nobles, of Europe built up armies to go to the Holy Land and take it away from the Moslems. The Crusades began in A.D. 1095 and continued on and off for over 200 years. The Europeans were never able to capture the Holy Land, but they did begin to develop trade with the Middle East and eventually the Far East. The people who came back from the Crusades told stories of wonderful lands with great riches. Merchants went to these lands to exchange their goods for things like salt, spices, figs, oranges, steel swords, rare stones, rice, rugs, and fine silks. They journeyed as far as India in search of trade.

4. What resulted from this 200-year war?

1) The Moslems controlled the area around the Mediterranean Sea. 2) The Christian Europeans developed trade with the Middle East and the Far East. 3) Spices became a necessity to Europeans, who used them to cover up the taste of spoiled meat.

Such spices as pepper, cinnamon, ginger, cloves, and nutmeg became necessities in Europe. Europe did not then produce food for cattle in winter. The cattle had to be killed every year, and the meat had to be saved. The spices were used to cover up the taste of spoiled meat.

Europe Changes Because of Trade

The Europeans wanted more and more of the goods from the East. They had to have more products to sell to the East in order to be able to trade. Otherwise, they had to pay gold and silver for the goods they wanted.

5. What did the use of money do for trade?

Sellers could deal with buyers whose trade goods they did not want.

One European product that sold well was fine woolen cloth. Another was furs. Lumber from the forests of Europe was also prized in places in the Near and Far East that were hotter and drier and did not have such forests. Once they were sure of customers, or a steady market, Europeans were encouraged to leave their farms and move to town. There they could help to manufacture the goods that would sell. Town life grew. When more people lived in towns, the people on farms had customers for their food. Buying and

Notice that the Crusades and travel were a way of life for over six generations. Contrast with Native Americans.

35

selling, with money as the means of exchange, became popular. Money made it possible to sell goods to someone who had nothing that the seller wanted in trade. Europe soon became a society of towns and traders. During this time, the population of Europe increased, creating more buyers and sellers.

Eventually a chain of buyers and sellers spread from east to west. No one trader took the goods all the way from one area to the next. Each sold to the next trader in the trading chain. In that way the civilizations of the East and West traded with one another. In the 1100's there were great civilizations elsewhere that were much older than the one in Christian Europe. There were ancient cultures in the Middle East, in India, and in China. Each of these groups believed that its way of living and thinking was the best. Each of these cultures looked to trade to bring extra wealth.

The ships from the Italian cities of Venice and Genoa carried goods to overland traders at the eastern end of the Mediterranean. These traders were usually Moslems. The Moslems took the goods on pack animals across the deserts and the mountains of Asia.

6. How was trade carried on between the East and the West?

1) Each trader sold goods to the next trader in the trading chain. 2) Ships from Venice and Genoa carried goods to overland traders at the eastern end of the Mediterranean. 3) These Moslems took the goods on pack animals across the deserts and the mountains of Asia.

While in China, Marco Polo was made an official of the Chinese government. This picture shows him at the court of Kublai Khan.

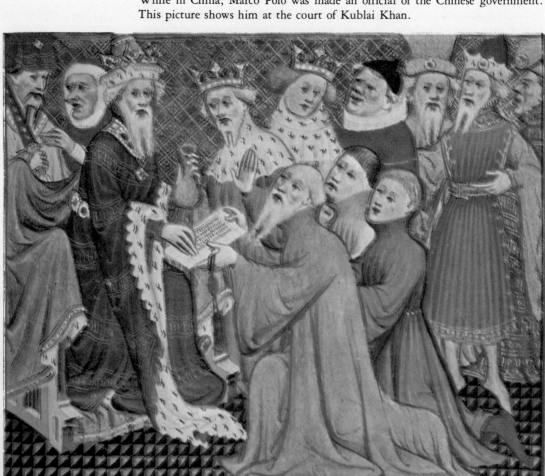

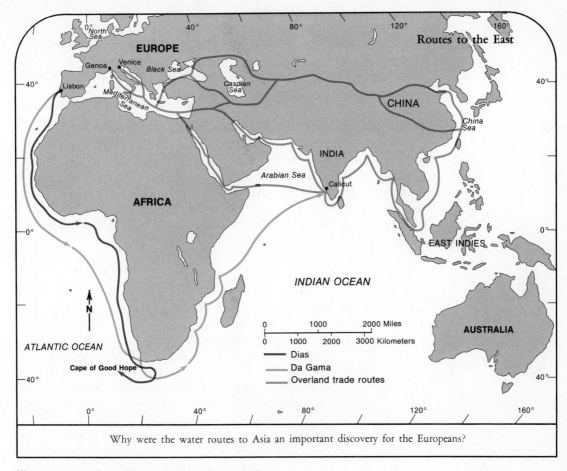

Routes to the East

Why were the water routes to Asia an important discovery for the Europeans?

Water routes were faster, less dangerous, and more profitable.

Marco Polo

Two brothers, Maffei (mah-FEY) and Niccolo Polo, and Niccolo's 17-year-old son, Marco, actually made the trip from Europe to China and Japan. They left in 1271, with the blessing of the pope. The Polos were merchants on the lookout for products to buy and sell. The travelers were away for 20 years. In that time they traveled through land taken over by the Mongols. The Mongols were a group of warriors who, in the thirteenth century, swept out of what is today southern Russia and conquered Russia, eastern Europe, much of the land held by German-speaking tribes, western India, and all the Moslem lands as far as Egypt. The Mongols, through their conquest, had connected Europe and China.

When Marco Polo returned to Europe, he wrote a book about the trip. His book excited Europeans. They were thrilled by his descriptions of great wealth—of jewels, gold, silks, and spices, and of dinners for 10,000 people which lasted ten days. Marco Polo's book further encouraged trade between the Europeans and the East.

7. What was the importance of Marco Polo's trip?

1) He wrote a book which described the East. 2) This book encouraged trade between the Europeans and the Asians.

37

Trade Cutoff

In the middle of the fifteenth century, the trading chain between the East and West was broken. A group of Moslems, the Ottoman Turks, began a new wave of conquest in the East. They took over the land between Europe and Asia—some 10,000 miles (16,000 kilometers) of it. Through their conquests, the Ottoman Turks controlled the Indian Ocean and stopped ships that tried to sail across it to the East.

European nations were not going to give up the chance to have the riches they wanted. New ways to the East had to be found. New ways of organizing and paying for ships and sailors had to be developed. Europeans were anxious to spread their religion and their power as far as trade and warfare could take them. As a result, they made great changes that changed the world.

Checking the facts

1. What were the forces that made Europe become a society of traders?
2. How did trade among nations affect the lives of Europeans?
3. Why do historians believe the Norse, or Vikings, explored North America?
4. What benefits came to Europeans from trading with the different parts of the East?

2. PORTUGUESE AND SPANISH EXPLORATIONS

Getting to the East

How could traders bring their goods all the way from Europe to the East? How could Europeans keep the goods from changing hands too often and thus get a big profit? How could they avoid crossing the area ruled by the Ottoman Turks? Now that Europeans knew about the East and wanted to trade there, the problem was how to do this.

The answer might have been to sail around Africa and bypass the Mediterranean Sea. But no one had yet taken this route. Whoever tried it would need knowledge as well as the money and support of a government. There was one person who had all three of these things. He was Prince Henry of Portugal. In 1415 and 1418 he explored the western coast of Africa. Prince Henry found out how difficult it was to take long sea trips.

Notice one great opportunity to trade blocked by two problems that needed three factors to solve them.

PRINCE HENRY OF PORTUGALL

CEUTA

Prince Henry of Portugal set up a special school to study the sea and navigation. How did the school influence Portuguese exploration?

Because they didn't know how to find *longitude*, sailors often could not tell how far east or west they had sailed. People didn't know how to build seagoing ships, either. And the coast of Africa was not yet explored or mapped. In 1419 Prince Henry left the court and created a new settlement at Sagres, on the coast of Portugal. There he gathered astronomers, mapmakers, Moslem and Jewish mathematicians, shipbuilders, captains, and sailors. They collected all the latest knowledge and tried out new instruments. They built an observatory and recorded the changing position of the sun and the stars.

8. Why did Prince Henry create a new settlement at Sagres?

1) He brought together astronomers, mapmakers, mathematicians, ship builders, captains, and sailors to study ocean travel.
2) He wanted to teach sailors how to plot longitude, build seagoing ships, and map the coast of Africa.

African Trade

Prince Henry's captains sailed west to the Madeira and Canary Islands and then south along the African coast. They were on the lookout for ways to trade directly with the African kingdoms of Ghana, Mali, and Songhai (SONG-hie). (See map, page 41.)

9. What did Prince Henry hope to accomplish by exploring the African coast?

Notice the importance of one person with knowledge, money, and the authority to carry out a plan. How can we solve such problems in our democracy today?

By selling African gold, ivory, and slaves, the Portuguese would raise enough money for their travels to the East.

The African empires were highly developed. Their rulers had conquered much of the interior of Africa, from the Gulf of Guinea to the edge of the Sahara Desert. In the course of the conquest, they took prisoners and made them slaves. They had cities, agriculture, metal tools, and armies. They had developed the arts as well as trade. Those who traded with the Moslems to the north used the Arabic written language.

Prince Henry and his followers hoped that by selling African gold, ivory, and slaves, the Portuguese could raise enough money to pay for their travels to the East. By the time Henry died in 1460, the Portuguese had explored the West African coast as far as present-day Sierra Leone.

Portugal Succeeds

10. How did Portugal get an empire of islands in the Indian Ocean?

Dias sailed around the tip of Africa into the Indian Ocean.

In 1481 John II became king of Portugal. He sent explorers even farther south along the West African coast. By 1488 Bartholomeu Dias (bar-TOL-o-mew DEE-az) had sailed around the Cape of Good Hope at the tip of Africa and had continued all the way to the Indian Ocean. Vasco da Gama took four ships to India in 1497. (See map, page 37.) When he returned two years later, he had a full cargo of pepper and cinnamon. By 1520 Portugal had an empire of islands in the Indian Ocean.

These bronze works of art were made by the Benin culture. The heads hold ivory elephant tusks with carved designs. Why did Europeans want to establish trade with Africans?

Notice that Portugal's development depended on itself and on African development.

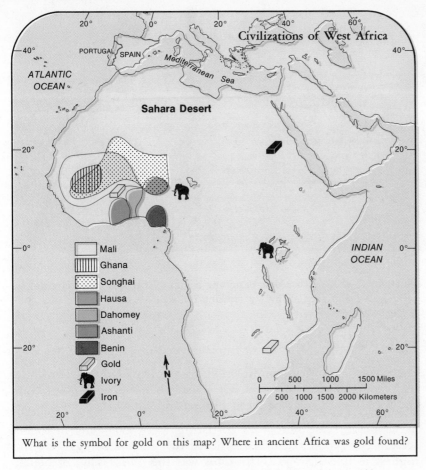

Civilizations of West Africa

PORTUGAL SPAIN
ATLANTIC
OCEAN
Mediterranean Sea
Sahara Desert

Mali
Ghana
Songhai
Hausa
Dahomey
Ashanti
Benin
Gold
Ivory
Iron

INDIAN
OCEAN

N

0   500   1000   1500 Miles
0 500 1000 1500 2000 Kilometers

What is the symbol for gold on this map? Where in ancient Africa was gold found?

The symbol for gold is a yellow-colored bar. It is found in Mali and southeastern Africa.

Competition from Spain

Other Europeans were interested in the wealth that was coming to Portugal. Especially interested were the rulers of the newly organized nations of Europe. Actually, these rulers were no more than the strongest of the lords and nobles. And they were constantly fighting with the other nobles, who also wanted to be the most powerful. The best way to get power was to get hold of gold and silver. The money paid for armies. Armies could keep the other nobles in their places. The rulers of Spain, England, and France were all interested in and in need of more money for more power at home.

Like Portugal, Spain, England, and France all bordered on the Atlantic Ocean. If they could find an even shorter way to the East, they would find a shorter way to wealth and power. If it were true, as some believed, that the world was round, then ships could also

11. Why did the other European nations compete with Portugal?

1) The rulers wanted more territory. 2) They needed gold and silver to pay for their armies. 3) They wanted to find a shorter way to the East and its riches. 4) They wanted to try out their power over others.

Notice what it took to begin to build up the resources to explore and trade: gold, armies, ships, and tight organization.

This picture shows two people designing a ship. What special features did an ocean-going ship need? Why was crossing the ocean in one of these ships dangerous?

sail around it in the other direction. They calculated that the world was about half the size it is. Of course they did not know about the Americas that lay between Europe and China.

What made these Europeans so daring was their belief in themselves. The people of Europe believed that human beings were the highest form of life on earth. This was the philosophy, or belief, of *humanism*. It was combined with a growing interest in technology, or tools and their uses. The Europeans believed that by using their intelligence, they could develop new ways to do things. They thought that they could control plants, animals, and each other.

Columbus—At the Right Moment

12. Why did Columbus think he could find a sea route to the East?

1) He believed that people could do anything if they knew enough and tried enough. 2) He was an excellent navigator. 3) He had sailed the Mediterranean Sea and the Atlantic Ocean.

At the end of the 1400's, a sailor appeared who wanted power and control. He had the humanist's belief that people could do anything if they knew enough and tried hard enough. He wanted to make that first voyage west to the East or, as it was called then, the "Indies." He was Christopher Columbus, an Italian from Genoa who had sailed the Mediterranean Sea and the Atlantic Ocean. Columbus had sailed on a number of Portuguese ships and was known as an excellent navigator. But when Columbus asked the king of Portugal to pay for a voyage to the East in 1486, the king refused. Columbus spent eight years trying to get someone to support his idea with money.

Why do some people try new activities? What makes them think it worth the risk?

What made 1492 the right moment? Has timing ever been important in your life?

Notice that Columbus could rule new lands in the same way the rulers commanded Spain.

Finally, Columbus found the right people to sell his idea to, at the right moment. In 1492 Queen Isabella and King Ferdinand of Spain wanted to get control over all of Spain. By marrying, they had just united their two kingdoms. A 700-year war between the Spanish and the Moslem invaders, called Moors, had just ended. Spain had won. But the rulers wanted to gain absolute control over all life in Spain. To do this they forced out all the Moors and Jews. To unite Spain they needed an army. To pay the army they needed gold and silver. Columbus offered a possible way to get it.

In August 1492 Columbus left the port of Palos, Spain, with his three small ships—the *Niña*, the *Pinta*, and the *Santa Maria*. Ninety sailors took the trip with him. Their goal was to find a new way to the East.

Columbus was promised absolute control over the lands and the people he would claim for Spain. He was to convert the natives to Christianity and to get 10 percent of whatever gold and silver he found. This was the European way to do business, to govern, and to spread beliefs.

What Columbus Found

The trip took two months. The sailors were often at the point of mutiny. Finally they sighted land, an island that they called San

13. How did Columbus get money to pay for his trip?

1) Columbus found the right people to sell his idea to. 2) Queen Isabella and King Ferdinand wanted to get control of all Spain. 3) They needed gold and silver to pay for their army.

14. What were the terms of agreement between Spain and Columbus?

1) He was to find a new way to the East. 2) He was to have absolute control over the people and the lands he could claim for Spain. 3) He was to convert the natives to Christianity. 4) He was to get 10 percent of whatever gold and silver he found.

This picture shows Columbus leaving for America. What kinds of activities are taking place here?

43

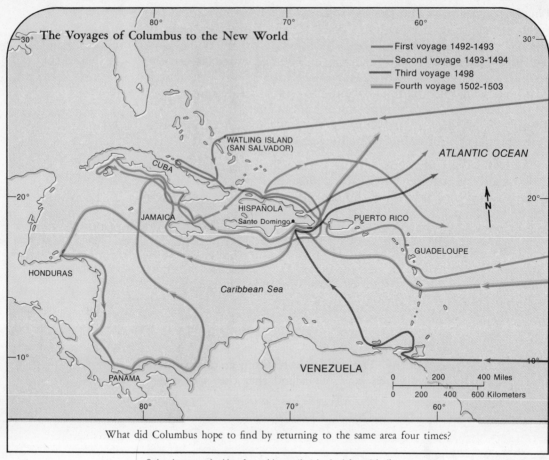

The Voyages of Columbus to the New World

— First voyage 1492-1493
— Second voyage 1493-1494
— Third voyage 1498
— Fourth voyage 1502-1503

WATLING ISLAND
(SAN SALVADOR)

ATLANTIC OCEAN

CUBA

JAMAICA

HISPAÑOLA
Santo Domingo

PUERTO RICO

GUADELOUPE

N

HONDURAS

Caribbean Sea

PANAMA

VENEZUELA

0   200   400 Miles
0   200   400   600 Kilometers

What did Columbus hope to find by returning to the same area four times?

Columbus was looking for evidence that he had found India.

Salvador. The natives of the island came out to meet them in their canoes. After years of hoping and trying, Columbus believed that he had arrived in the Indies. He called the natives Indians.

15. What did Columbus accomplish?

He touched the coasts of Cuba, Hispañola, Puerto Rico, Jamaica, Venezuela, Panama, and Honduras.

Columbus searched for gold and silver on nearby islands. He explored Cuba, thinking it was the land Marco Polo had described in his book. At the end of three months, he returned to Spain. Columbus made three more trips across the Atlantic Ocean. (See map, above.) He explored Hispañola, Puerto Rico, and Jamaica. He went as far south as Venezuela, on the coast of South America. He even sailed west as far as Panama and Honduras, in Central America. All the time he believed these were the outer edge of Asia.

No Challenge to Spain

Two nations that might have challenged Spain in the New World were Portugal and England. The Portuguese, however, did not

What was the Spanish attitude toward the natives? Why?

believe that Columbus had found the Indies. They were more interested in keeping Spain out of their rich trade with Africa. So the Portuguese asked the pope in Rome to divide the world between the two nations. To the pope this was a reasonable idea. Both nations wanted to convert other people of the world to the Christian faith. Either way the Church would benefit. So the pope took a map of the world and drew a line from north to south separating Spanish land from Portuguese land. This line was called the Papal Line of Demarcation. Everything west of the line—including all the people who already lived there—was declared the possession of Spain. Everything east of the line belonged to Portugal. The only land in Portugal's half of the world that was in the Americas was the land we now call Brazil.

The Spanish were too powerful for both Portugal and England, however. They had strong rulers and a strong, well-organized Catholic Church. The Spanish also happened to explore the only parts of the Americas where there was gold and silver.

The Search Continues

After Columbus' last trip to what Europeans were now calling the New World, the Spanish tried for 20 years to find a way through these new lands to the East. The first explorer to realize that this was going to be more difficult than it seemed was Amerigo Vespucci (ves-POO-chee). (See chart, page 49.) An Italian in the service of Spain, Vespucci made several trips to the New world. He visited South America and realized that it was a new continent lying between Europe and Asia. He made maps of the new continent. Later, in 1507, another mapmaker honored Vespucci by attaching his name to the land. Now it was called America.

Another explorer found out what was on the other side of the new lands. Vasco Núñez de Balboa left the colony of Hispañola with a search party to look for gold in Central America. In 1513 he crossed Central America and saw the Pacific Ocean. The Spanish then began a search for a way through to the new ocean by ship. Because the land between the two oceans was so narrow, they thought it would be easy to find.

The eastern coast of Latin America was fairly well known, so the Spanish decided to send an expedition around the southern end of the continent. They hired a Portuguese navigator, Ferdinand Magellan. His task was to sail around the world! Magellan was killed in the Philippines, but his crew finished the trip in 1522. Magellan's trip proved to the world that the earth was round.

As a result of this latest knowledge, Spain stopped trying to compete with the Portuguese for the trade in the East. The Pacific

16. Why was the Papal Line of Demarcation drawn?

Portugal asked the pope to divide the world between the two nations.

17. Why did the Papal Line of Demarcation favor the Spanish?

Their area was west, and they found gold in the Americas.

18. From whom did America get its name?

Amerigo Vespucci made maps of the new continent and put his name on them.

Magellan set out to prove that it was possible to sail around the world. Why was this important?

Which do you think was the most important: luck, bravery, or power?

45

Discuss: When the Spanish and the Aztec cultures met, there was war. Why?

Do you think two cultures with different weapons could ever live together peacefully right from the first meeting? How?

19. Why did King Charles V of Spain send Black African slaves to the New World?

1) The Spanish had little success with forced Indian labor. 2) The Indians preferred to fight than to do forced labor. 3) Many Indians died from European diseases.

Ocean was too wide. What Spain did instead was to concentrate on trying to get wealth out of the New World. The Spanish had little success in raising cattle and sugar on the islands with forced Indian labor. The Indians fought back. Many also became ill and died from European diseases. In 1517 King Charles V of Spain allowed the purchase of 15,000 Black Africans, to be shipped to Santo Domingo. These were the first Black slaves in the New World.

Cortés and the Aztecs

By 1518, the Spanish had decided to send a force of soldiers into the mainland of the Americas. The plan was to conquer the Aztecs and bring them under Spanish control. Whatever riches the soldiers found would be theirs.

20. How did Cortés conquer the Aztecs of Mexico?

1) Their leader, Montezuma, thinking Cortés was a god, invited him to court. 2) The Spanish attacked, and the Aztecs, blaming their leader, put him to death. 3) After two years the Spanish defeated the Aztecs with the aid of horses, muskets, and cannons. 4) Many Aztecs died from diseases brought by the Spanish.

In 1519 the Spanish sent a force of about 550 men to Mexico under the leadership of Hernando Cortés. Cortés and his men discovered the highly organized civilizations of Central America. The Aztecs ruled part of Mexico. (See map, page 13.) They had conquered many tribes and had brought them under the rule of their leader, Montezuma. Some of the tribes that had been conquered by Montezuma welcomed Cortés. Many, including Montezuma, thought he was a god. The Spanish horses were thought to be mysterious spirits.

Montezuma made the mistake of allowing Cortés to come to his court. The Spanish took Montezuma prisoner. Then, when the Aztecs rebelled against the foreigners, the Spanish made Montezuma speak to his people. The Aztecs were so disappointed with their ruler that they stoned him to death. Afterward, they drove the Spanish out.

But the gold-hungry Spanish would not give up. For two years they fought the Aztecs. They had horses, muskets, and cannon. Nothing the Aztecs had could compete with them in battle. Also, many of the Aztecs died from diseases brought by the Spanish on their first visit. Finally they had to surrender. Cortés made the defeated Aztecs work in the gold and silver mines. They were also forced to accept Christianity.

Spanish Values

21. How did the Aztecs regard gold?

To them it was just a beautiful metal that had been given to the earth.

The Spanish were surprised to realize that the Aztecs did not value gold in the same way they did. The Aztecs had no buying and selling system, dependent on money. To them, gold was just a beautiful metal that had been given to the earth. And the Aztecs were the users of it. With such totally different ways of seeing the

46

Notice that the Spanish and the Central Americans were all empire builders. They had all conquered others.

yeqtla ti tetzavitl
yn mal ques.

This is a copy of an Aztec manuscript. It shows the defeat of the Aztecs by the Spanish. Why do you think the Spanish were successful?

world and each other, it was no wonder that Montezuma misunderstood the Spanish. Too late he found out that the Spanish would kill for gold.

Other Spanish Conquests

After bringing the Aztecs under their control, the Spanish armies tried to conquer the oldest and most highly developed of all the American civilizations, the Mayas. This expedition was not successful at first. It took almost 20 years for the Spanish to conquer the Mayas.

The Spanish had quicker success against the Incas. In 1532 Francisco Pizarro (pih-ZAHR-oh) took a small group of Spanish soldiers south into the land controlled by the Incas in the Andes. (See map, page 13.) There they found the gold and silver mines of Peru. They killed the Incan emperor and many of his people. Others died from diseases like smallpox, which the Spanish brought with them. Within a relatively short time, Pizarro was able to declare himself head of an empire of almost 8 million Incas.

22. What other conquests did the Spanish make?

1) They conquered the Mayas, who had the oldest and most highly developed of all the American civilizations.
2) They conquered the Incas of Peru and found gold and silver mines.

The Spanish got rich from the silver in the New World. This picture shows a silver mine in Bolivia. The Native Americans are doing the work.

The Spanish in North America

Once word had spread about the gold and silver mines and the great cities of Central America, many Spaniards were ready to go to other parts of the Americas. One of the earliest to explore North America was the Spanish governor of Puerto Rico, Juan Ponce de León. He had made a personal fortune in gold and slaves. But he wasn't satisfied. The Native Americans told him about a magical fountain. They said that a drink from the waters of this fountain could keep a person young forever.

Ponce de León believed this story and traveled to the mainland of North America to look for the fountain of youth. He landed on the coast of North America in 1513. He named the place where he landed Florida, and claimed it for the King of Spain. But he didn't find the fountain of youth. Nor was he able to colonize Florida. When Ponce de León returned several years later, he was

1) He landed on the coast of North America and claimed Florida for Spain. 2) The Spanish later established St. Augustine, the first permanent settlement in what is now the United States.

23. What was the importance of Ponce de Leon's search?

Note that each of the Spanish explorers had to have permission from the ruler of Spain for every trip. They all kept in close touch with the ruler, although they traveled far.
Who found the most land? Which country did the most exploring? What 10-year period was the busiest? Who were the luckiest explorers?

EUROPEAN EXPLORERS

Explorer	Date of Voyage	Discoveries
Explorers for Spain		
Christopher Columbus	1492	Discovers America, returns and tells the story of his discovery
Amerigo Vespucci	1499–1501	Finds that the New World is not part of Asia
Vasco Núñez de Balboa	1513	Crosses the Isthmus of Panama and sees the Pacific Ocean
Hernando Cortés	1519–1521	Conquers the Aztecs in Mexico
Ferdinand Magellan	1519–1522	Sails around the world
Álvar Núñez Cabeza de Vaca	1527–1536	Explores the west coast of South America, conquers Inca Empire
Hernando de Soto	1530–1542	Explores the southern part of North America, including, Florida, Oklahoma, and Georgia
Francisco Vásques de Coronado	1540	Searches for gold and silver in southwestern North America
Explorers for Portugal		
Vasco da Gama	1497	Sails around Africa to India
Pedro Álvares Cabral	1500	Explores the coast of Brazil
Explorers for France		
Giovanni da Verrazano	1524	Explores the northeast coast of North America. First European to see New York harbor
Jacques Cartier	1534	Locates the St. Lawrence River
Samuel de Champlain	1608–1615	Travels through the St. Lawrence River to the Great Lakes
Explorers for England		
John Cabot	1497	Reaches Newfoundland
Francis Drake	1577–1580	Sails around the world
Martin Frobisher	1576–1579	Looks for a Northwest Passage through Labrador and Baffin Island
George Weymouth	1602–1606	Explores New England coast
Henry Hudson (also sailed for The Netherlands)	1610	Searches for a Northwest Passage

killed in battle with the Indians. Not until 1565 were the Spanish able to establish the first permanent settlement in what is now the United States. They named the settlement St. Augustine. It was in Florida, located near the spot where Ponce de León had first landed.

24. Why was De Vaca disappointed?

He wanted to set up a colony in Florida, but he was shipwrecked off the coast of Texas. He made his way to Mexico City and returned to Spain by ship.

Another tough but disappointed Spaniard was Álvar Núñez Cabeza de Vaca (day VAH-kuh). He came directly to Florida from Spain, hoping to set up a colony. From Florida he and other explorers sailed across the Gulf of Mexico. Several of the ships were lost at sea. Cabeza de Vaca, a Black explorer named Estévanico (es-TAY-vah-nee-koe), and two others were shipwrecked near the coast of Texas. They then traveled on foot through what is now New Mexico, Arizona, and Texas. They finally found their way to Mexico City and returned to Spain by ship. By this time there was enough travel back and forth between Spain and the New World to excite the imagination of other would-be explorers.

25. What was to be De Soto's fate?

1) He didn't find the Seven Cities of Cibola. 2) He died after exploring the southeastern part of North America.

Hernando de Soto was one of these explorers. In 1539 he set out to find the Seven Cities of Cibola (SEE-bo-lah). These were places of great wealth that the Spanish had heard about from the Native Americans. De Soto was given permission to search the southeastern part of North America for the cities. De Soto and his men walked

This is a mural of the viceroy's palace in Mexico City. What differences can you see between the Native Americans and the Spanish?

FOOD SUPPLIES ON A SHIP

What food did a ship need when it set out for the New World? The journey would take three months. The captain had to figure out how much food and drink would be needed. The sailors knew the trip to the New World involved the risks of starvation and disease. The following is a list of the supplies for 190 sailors as they set out for the New World.

8,000 pounds of salt beef
2,800 pounds of salt pork
A few beef tongues
600 pounds of haberdine (salted codfish)
15,000 brown biscuits
5,000 white biscuits
30 bushels of oatmeal
40 bushels of dried peas
1½ bushels of mustard seed
1 barrel of salt
100 pounds of suet (fat)
1 barrel of flour
11 firkins (small wooden casks) of butter
1 hogshead (large cask) of vinegar
10,500 gallons of beer
3,500 gallons of water
2 hogsheads of cider

The supplies for the captain were different from the supplies for the rest of the crew. They included the following items: cheese, pepper, currants, cloves, sugar, ginger, prunes, bacon, marmalade, almonds, cinnamon, wine, and rice.

through present-day Georgia, North and South Carolina, Tennessee, and Alabama. They crossed the wide Mississippi River, walked along the shore of the Arkansas River, and traveled into what is now Oklahoma. There they decided to turn back. De Soto died on the return trip and was buried in the Mississippi River.

Francisco Vásquez de Coronado (kor-oe-NAH-doe) also tried to find the cities of gold. In 1540 he started out from Mexico. With

26. What did Coronado discover?

The Grand Canyon.

Coronado was Estévanico, who had been with Cabeza de Vaca years before. He led a small group of men ahead of the rest of the party. When he got close to what he believed were the seven cities, he sent word to Coronado. But before Coronado could reach him, Estévanico was killed in battle with the Indians. The cities he had found did not have any precious jewels. Coronado and his men traveled as far as the Kansas River looking for riches. They discovered the Grand Canyon and came upon great herds of buffalo. But they did not find any gold. Disappointed, Coronado returned to Mexico.

The Spanish Establish and Organize Their Colonies

To govern the vast areas of land taken over by the conquerers, or *conquistadores* (con-KEYS-tah-dor-es), the Spanish brought their form of government to the New World. The local leaders were vice-kings, or viceroys. They ruled over everything and everyone in the name of the king of Spain. A royal council made all the laws. And the laws were the same for everyone.

27. How was the encomienda system different from slavery?

The Native Americans who lived on the land belonged to it and could be sold along with the land.

To divide up the land, the Spanish had a system of giving an area to one man. He not only became the owner of the land, he also became the lord of the people who lived on that land. This was called the *encomienda* system. The Native Americans who lived on the land were not owned as slaves. They came along with the land and could be sold with the land if the owner decided to sell it. They had no power.

In the Spanish colonial organization, which was run from Spain, there were absolute levels of power. At the top were the Spanish-born officials. Then came the Creoles, American-born Spaniards. Following them were the mestizos, children of marriages between the Spanish and the Native Americans. The Native Americans were at the bottom of the structure. And in the islands of the Caribbean Sea, there were the Black slaves.

28. How was the government organized?

1) Levels of power ran downward from Spanish to Creoles, to Mestizos, to Native Americans. 2) Territories were divided into two vice-royalties, one governed from Peru and the other from Mexico City. 3) The Spanish built forts, towns, and missions, and schools where priests converted the Indians to Christianity.

The Spanish territories were divided into two viceroyalties. One, which included parts of South America, was governed from Lima, the capital of Peru. The other, extending up from Mexico into New Mexico and California, was ruled from Mexico City.

Within each of these viceroyalties, the Spanish established settlements. They built *presidios* (pray-SID-ee-oes), or forts, and *villas*, or towns. They also built missions. The missions were run by Catholic priests from Spain. Through persuasion or force the Indians came to live at the missions. The priests converted them to Christianity and set up schools for them. They also tried to improve conditions for the Native Americans living under Spanish rule.

Native Americans and the Church

When the Spanish had first arrived, they had killed and tortured many Native Americans. They had made slaves out of those who survived and had forced them to work in the gold and silver mines. But soon the Spanish priests began to argue with the soldier governors over the harsh treatment of the Native Americans. They took their case to the pope in Rome. In matters of concern to the Church, the pope could tell even the king what to do. By 1537 one friar, Brother Bernadino, had persuaded the pope to outlaw Native American slavery.

In 1542 the best known of the priests in the New World, Bartolomé de Las Casas, convinced the pope to pass laws to get rid of the encomienda system. To Las Casas the system was a way of enslaving the Native Americans by making them work for one master. These new laws said that the Indians had to be freed after the original owners had died. And in 1551 about 160,000 Native Americans were freed from forced labor in the Mexican mines. This was not the freedom they had known before the Spaniards came. But it was an improvement over the first 30 years of Spanish rule. The church actually set up courts for the protection of Native American rights.

Another priest, Father Kino, also tried to help the Native Americans. He set up a string of missions in lower California and present-day Arizona. Before each settlement was established, he would send cattle and wheat on ahead. This was partly a gift to the Native Americans and partly to support the mission once it was started. Father Kino was also careful not to interfere with the family life and customs of the people he had come to help.

Although most Spanish rulers did little to preserve the Native American culture, priests like Father Kino and Bartolomé de Las Casas at least tried to make life less painful for the Native Americans once they had been conquered.

Spanish Settlement and the Revolt of the Pueblos

The most serious attempt to colonize North America and not just search for gold was in 1598. Four hundred Spaniards with 7,000 head of animal stock moved into the Rio Grande Valley. The Spanish took prisoners and held trials for any Native Americans who refused to give in. One common form of punishment was to cut off one foot—and thereby force the Native American into permanent slavery. Women and children were given 20-year terms as slaves. The worst of the leaders of this Spanish settlement came about 15 years after its founding. He was Don Juan de Onate, the son of a rich mine owner. He had married the great-granddaughter

29. What did Spanish priests do for the Native Americans?

1) In 1537 Brother Bernadino persuaded the pope to outlaw slavery. 2) In 1542 the priest Bartolomé de Las Casas convinced the pope to pass laws to get rid of the encomienda system. 3) Father Kino set up a string of missions in lower California and present-day Arizona.

30. Why did the Pueblos revolt?

1) The Spanish forced them into slavery. 2) Don Juan de Oñate was especially cruel to them.

of Montezuma. His treatment of the Native Americans was so cruel that the Spanish priests who were part of the settlement made formal complaints to Spain.

In 1680 the Pueblos, under the leadership of a man named Popé, organized resistance to the Spanish in their *kivas*, or underground ceremonial rooms. For 12 years the Pueblos were able to drive the Spanish out from their settlement at Santa Fe, New Mexico, to what is now El Paso, Texas. But in the four-year period from 1692 to 1696, the Spaniards reconquered the Pueblo territory. Only the Hopi tribe was left alone. The other tribes, including the warlike Apache, were badly beaten and never rose again.

What Were the Results of the Spanish Conquest?

31. How did the horse change life for the Native American?

1) The Native American could now hunt on horseback. 2) Tribes could now migrate to buffalo-hunting territory.

The Spanish spread their way of life up through Mexico into New Mexico and California. With each army fort, or presidio, they built a mission with a church. The priests built schools for the Native Americans. The invaders brought horses, which the Native Americans did not have. And when the Spanish horses escaped and ran wild, they were caught and tamed by the Native Americans who lived on the Plains. The village Native Americans left their village culture to become hunters on horseback. When other tribes heard about the horses, they migrated to the buffalo-hunting territory. The Blackfoot, Arapaho, and Cheyenne tribes came from the east. The Comanches came from the west. From the Mississippi River culture came the Crows. The Teton Dakotas, also called the Sioux, came to the Plains from Minnesota.

32. What role did the church play in village life?

It was the religious, medical, and recreation center.

Life for the Spanish Americans in the land west of the Rocky Mountains was much like life in Spain. Buildings were Spanish in style but were built with American materials. Family life was similar to family life in Spain. The daily life of the village revolved around the church. The church served as a medical center and was also the center of recreation for the community.

Checking the facts

1. How did geography determine which nations would explore the New World?
2. What were the circumstances that led to Columbus' voyage in 1492?
3. How did the Spanish explorations change the lives of people in the New World?

Notice how long the Spanish conquest of Native American culture took. What would not have happened if the Spanish conquest had failed?

PUTTING IT ALL TOGETHER

UNDERSTANDING THE MAIN IDEAS

1. Why did Europeans want to reach out to new lands?
2. How did life in Europe expand beyond its borders?
3. How did Spain organize its explorations?
4. How did the Spanish behave towards the Native Americans?

ACTIVITIES

1. This activity requires that you do some research on a European nation. Go to the library and look at a book of the paintings and architecture of the 1500's in Spain and Portugal. What kind of lives did the people live? What did they think was worth painting or writing about?
2. Write an essay on the following topic: "From the time of the European settlement, America has been part of modern European history." Support your findings by giving examples. What did European settlers in the New World own. What did they know? What did they care about? How did they behave toward each other?
3. Read a book about Prince Henry the Navigator. What kinds of discoveries did the people in his employ make? What information do navigators and ship builders need today?
4. Who were the first European explorers to come to your area? When and why did they come? What route did they travel? Find this information in your local library or historical society and put it into a chart.

BOOKS TO READ

Gerson, Noel B., *Passage to the West: The Great Voyages of Henry Hudson* (New York: Julian Messner, Inc., 1968).

Hirsch, Carl S., *Mapmakers of America; From the Age of Discovery to the Space Era* (New York: Viking Press, 1970).

Keating, Bern, *Famous American Explorers* (Chicago: Rand McNally, 1972).

Morison, Samuel Eliot, *Christopher Columbus, Mariner* (Boston: Little, Brown and Co., 1955).

chapter 3
England and France Compete

1265–1720

1. ENGLAND JOINS IN THE
   EXPLORATIONS
2. THE FRENCH IN AMERICA

INTRODUCTION

For almost 100 years the Spanish ruled supreme in the New World. Other countries, such as France and England, were jealous of the amounts of gold and silver Spain was getting from the Americas. They wanted to share in the wealth. But how could they do so? Spain was the most powerful country in Europe. It was organized for colonizing because it had a stronger army. The army was paid for with gold and silver from the New World. Spain had a stronger army and more money than any other country. England and France were afraid to challenge Spain. Yet even as Spain's power reached its height changes were taking place. Spain was spending gold and silver on wars in Europe. Isabella and Ferdinands' grandson, Charles V, fought the Protestants in Germany and the Netherlands. In 1588 Spain armed a huge fleet to engage the English. The Spanish fleet was destroyed. England began to come to the fore.

	1497	1524	1534-1543	1540	
Who?	John Cabot	Giovanni da Verrazano	Jacques Cartier	Native Americans	
What?	claims land for England	sails for France	explores for France	begin to use the horse	
Where?	in Maine	sees New York Harbor	in Quebec and Montreal	in the southwest of North America	

Notice that American history rises out of the story of modern Europe.

As you read this chapter keep these questions in mind.

1. How did England become strong enough to explore new land?
2. Why did England organize settlements in the New World?
3. How did the French organize their efforts in the New World?
4. How did the English and French behave towards the Native Americans?

1. ENGLAND JOINS IN THE EXPLORATIONS

What was happening in England would later have a great deal to do with the future of North America. For this reason, students of American history have to know how the English got to be so different from the Spaniards and the French. American students need to look at how the differences that came about within the European nations affected the settlers who came to North America.

In order to look at those changes within England, we need to drop back in time to the end of a long period of warfare. A new ruling family had come to power in England in 1485, just seven years before Ferdinand and Isabella of Spain sent Columbus on his first voyage. The first of the Tudor family to rule England was called Henry VII. He was king of England for almost 25 years, and he had the same problems all the nations of Europe faced in the fifteenth and sixteenth centuries. How could he join the people within England together, so that they could win battles and find riches outside their own borders?

In order to build strength, Henry built special friendships with commoners, people who were not nobles. They became part of the

1. What problem did Henry VII have?

To unite the English people, he needed to win battles and find riches outside of England.

1558	1576-1606	1588	1608-1611	1603-1633
Queen Elizabeth	Martin Frobisher, John Davis	English navy	Henry Hudson	Samuel de Champlain
takes over the throne	search for a Northwest Passage	defeats the Spanish Armada	finds the Hudson River and Delaware Bay	secures French claims to North America
in England	through North America	in the English Channel	in North America	during trips to Canada

57

This is a portrait of King Henry VIII. What did he do to change England?

2. How did Henry VII go about solving his problem?

1) He built special friendships with commoners. 2) He increased trade by having people raise more sheep and sell more wool. 3) He encouraged fishing. The English began to eat fish and have less need for spices from the East. 4) He sent John Cabot to explore the coast of North America.

group of lawmakers in the Commons. The Commons was one of the houses of the English parliament. The English had had a parliament since 1265. The existence of a group of lawmakers made up of common people was unusual for any nation. It remained an important part of English government ever after.

Getting enough money was as much a problem for Henry as making friends in Parliament. To win battles a king had to have a strong army. To build a strong army a king had to have money. Money for armies usually came from taxes paid by the people. How were the English people to earn enough money to pay taxes for the king's army? Since England was an island, there was a limit to what the people could do besides farming. Perhaps they could trade with other places. But what could they sell? The answer was wool.

In order to get money from trade, King Henry urged landowners to fence in the land that villagers used in common. In this way sheep would graze on the land without wandering away. With more sheep, there would be more wool. Of course, enclosing the common land meant that peasants who did not own a lot of land could not graze their animals anymore. It also caused herders to lose work, since the sheep were enclosed. But more wool brought more trade and more wealth to England.

Henry's other plan was to encourage the people to turn to fishing to make a living. Then the English would not have to depend on the ships from Venice, on the Mediterranean, or the ships from the cities in the north of Europe, on the Baltic Sea. England would have its own fishing fleet. In this way, the culture of England changed a great deal. Not only did the English diet change to include fish and mutton, but the English also became less interested in the spices of the East.

With his new-found wealth Henry VII was able to send an Italian sea captain, John Cabot, to the New World. In 1497 Cabot explored the coast of North America. His explorations gave England a claim to part of the continent. But the English were not yet ready to take up this claim. First they had to become stronger.

A New English Church

Henry VII's son, Henry VIII, who became king in 1509, also gained more power for England. He broke away from the Roman Catholic Church. Henry and his wife, Catherine, a Spanish princess, had only a daughter. But Henry wanted a son to succeed him on the throne. Henry asked the pope to annul, or cancel, their marriage. When the pope refused, Henry asked Parliament to break

Why do people trade? What is needed in order to trade?

the connection between the Catholic Church in Rome and England. The Church of England was set up. The ruler of England became the head of the new church as well.

The split was more than a religious one. Henry took all English land away from the Roman Catholic Church. Since that church owned a great deal of land, its officials had collected a great deal of rent on it. When Henry took that land and sold it, more and more people became landholders. Then more land was used to raise sheep for the wool trade. The money from the sale of land made Henry VIII's power secure and also helped to make England stronger. And it made England a seagoing, trading nation.

England Against Spain

Henry's break with the Church of Rome made an enemy out of Spain. It was at this point that Spain's power in the New World and England's growing strength began to be part of the same story. The gold that Spain collected in America was being spent in fighting Protestants in Europe, especially after Philip II of Spain became king in 1556. Philip was a very religious Catholic. He had been married to Henry VIII's daughter, Mary Tudor. Mary was a Roman Catholic. As queen, she tried to make England Catholic again. She had members of the Church of England captured, jailed, and executed to reach this goal. She became known as Bloody Mary. Her half-sister, Elizabeth, however, was loyal to the Church of England. When Elizabeth became queen of England in 1558, she set out to challenge Spain's 50-year control over trade with the New World.

3. How did the split with the Catholic Church in Rome affect England?

1) Henry VIII became the head of the Church of England. 2) He sold the lands the church had owned. 3) More land was available for raising sheep for the wool trade. 4) England became a seagoing, trading nation.

4. Why did Philip II especially dislike England?

1) He was a religious Catholic. 2) He had been married to Mary Tudor who had tried, but failed, to make England Catholic again.

Elizabeth I was queen during the beginning of England's expansion overseas. What did she do to encourage and support this action?

5. How did Queen Elizabeth solve her problem?

1) She became the secret partner of sea pirates. 2) They attacked Spanish ships on the high seas and took their gold and silver cargo.

Elizabeth's plan was to sell woolen cloth and slaves to Spain's colonies in America. The Spanish would pay the English traders in gold. Gold was accepted as payment for goods everywhere in the world. But there were some problems with this plan. Elizabeth had no fleet of ships of her own with which to reach the colonies. And the Spanish navy controlled the seas.

Hawkins and Drake

Elizabeth solved these problems by becoming the secret partner of private citizens who sailed the seas in their own ships. The first of these was John Hawkins. He carried 300 Black slaves from West Africa and traded them in Hispañola for cattle hides. These he took to Europe, where he sold them at a higher price. He made a large profit.

England had a chance to benefit from trade with the Spanish colonies. But then Spain closed this trade to outsiders in 1569. It wanted to keep all the money for itself. Not to be stopped, the English set out to trade illegally and smuggled goods in and out of the Spanish colonies. When smuggling took too much time, the English simply attacked Spanish ships on the high seas and took their gold and silver cargo. They acted with the unspoken consent of Queen Elizabeth.

Francis Drake was the most successful of these English pirates. In 1577, with secret orders and money from Queen Elizabeth, Drake crossed the Atlantic Ocean in his ship, the *Golden Hind*. He then sailed south around South America through the Straits of Magellan and north up the coast of South and North America. Along the way, Drake captured an entire shipful of Spanish silver from Peru and claimed the whole of North America for England!

John Hawkins, Sir Francis Drake, and Thomas Cavendish are shown here. These men raided the Spanish fleet and took the money for England.

Drake then crossed the Pacific Ocean and sailed for England by way of the East Indies. After buying several tons of cloves there, he sailed around Africa. When he returned in 1580, the excitement in England was incredible. The queen herself came down to his ship and made him a knight. The whole world, including the Spanish, knew then that England was a power to be noticed.

Elizabeth Supports Raleigh's Colony

Elizabeth gave licenses, or charters, to private businesses to trade in Europe, in the Mediterranean with the Greeks and the Turks, in Africa, and in the East Indies. These charters promised that if anyone interfered with these companies or put them in danger, they would get help from the English government.

Elizabeth helped Humphrey Gilbert and Walter Raleigh, who were trying to send English people to the New World to start a colony.

Elizabeth helped the pirates and traders. Their services helped strengthen her government in England.

SIR FRANCIS DRAKE—PIRATE OR HERO?

Sir Francis Drake was an English sea captain who was admired for his spirit of adventure and daring. With no fear of the unknown, he sailed around the world attacking and robbing Spanish ships along the way.

Drake grew up in a farming community. His father was a preacher who disagreed with the established religion. So he preached his own beliefs. As a result, the Drake family lived in poverty and was not accepted by the community. Francis learned reading and writing from his father and then worked for a ship owner. He learned how to handle a ship properly and became a captain.

In 1566 Drake sailed on slave trade voyages to the Spanish West Indies. On one trip his partner's ship was attacked by the Spanish ships and destroyed. From then on Drake hated the Spanish and robbed Spanish ships wherever he went. Since relations between England and Spain were not good at this time, Drake's adventures made him very popular in England. The queen even gave permission for the raids. She may have secretly given him money to carry them out. For the sake of diplomacy, however, Drake's raids appeared to be his own private ventures.

Drake received many honors for his adventures. He was the first English captain to sail around the world. Queen Elizabeth honored him by making him a knight. In 1584 he was elected a member of Parliament.

As tensions grew between Spain and England, Drake and his ships acted as the English navy. Queen Elizabeth sent him, with a fleet of 20 ships, to capture and loot Spanish-owned Santo Domingo and Cartegena. On the way home Drake managed to destroy a Spanish fort in Florida. He also stopped at Roanoke Island to pick up discouraged settlers who wanted to return to England.

Drake's missions against Spain continued. In 1587 he destroyed more than 20 ships in Cadiz harbor, in Spain. This attack played an important role in history because it delayed Spain's war preparations against England for one year. In 1588, when the Spanish Armada sailed against England, Drake, serving as vice-admiral, defeated it in the English Channel. This was the highlight of Drake's career. In the years following, Drake continued to raid Spanish ships but met with disaster several times. On January 28, 1596, during one of these expeditions, he lost his life and was buried at sea.

Although Drake's adventures on the sea were pirate-like, he never thought of himself as a pirate. He was admired by the English nobles, merchants, and sailors.

Europeans valued the achievements of individuals.

Why was the time just right for Drake's success?

The idea of exporting people to become the other end of two-way trade was an English idea.

The English way of colonizing, like the Spanish, was formed at home and then made to work abroad.

For his colony Raleigh wanted people who could survive in the New World by using whatever they found there. He hoped the colony would become successful enough to trade with England. There might not be any gold in North America, but at least the colonists could supply England with raw materials like lumber for ships.

Raleigh sent several groups of colonists to the New World. The first group only stayed one winter and then returned to England. In 1587 Raleigh chose John White to lead a group of about 100 people willing to risk a new life in America. He bought three ships and loaded them with supplies. These were supposed to last until the people could fish and grow food in order to keep themselves alive. The settlers landed on Roanoke Island, off the coast of what is today North Carolina, in July, 1587.

6. What happened to Raleigh's colony?

1) John White returned to England for supplies. 2) When he returned, the settlers had disappeared.

In a matter of months, before they could grow enough food to support themselves, the settlers ran out of supplies. John White took one of the ships and returned to England for the necessary food, clothing, and tools. He left behind his own family, including his granddaughter, Virginia Dare. She was the first baby born to English parents in America.

War between England and Spain prevented White from returning to the Roanoke colony for three years. When he finally returned, there was not a single person left on the island. Not a clue existed as to what happened to them. The only thing White found were the initials "CRO" carved on one tree, and the word "Croatan" carved on another. Was this a message left for him? What did it mean? No one has ever found out.

7. What was the English plan for settlement?

They let people migrate who were interested in coming to America to form permanent settlements.

The English plan for settlement, colonies, and trade was very different from the Spanish plan. The Spanish had never set up colonies of families who would live on their own. The Spanish way had been to run colonies from Spain with as few Spaniards as possible. Spanish women and children were not encouraged to migrate to the New World. And the people who did go were sent to take over the Native American mines for the benefit of Spain. They went to the New World to spread the Roman Catholic religion, but also for the power it would bring to the Roman Catholic organization in Spain and in Rome. The English were the only people who were interested in coming to America to live. And no country but England had a system of trading, a religion of its own, and a history of paying attention to the common people.

The Spanish Fleet Destroyed

The war that kept John White from returning to Roanoke grew out of Spanish anger. King Philip II of Spain was determined to

The Spanish believed their armada would defeat the English. What happened to prove them wrong?

stop English piracy of Spanish treasure ships. His plan was to enter the narrow channel of water between England and France with so many ships that the English fleet would be easily defeated.

But Philip's plan didn't work. The Spanish ships were too big and bulky. Spanish captains had to send home for orders. Without them they didn't know how to respond to the surprise English attack. In an eight-day battle in July of 1588, the smaller, lighter, more easily maneuvered English ships defeated Spain's so-called invincible (unbeatable) armada. The Spanish ships that were not sunk sailed north. They hoped to circle the British Isles (England, Scotland, and Ireland) to get home to Spain. But a storm off the coast of Ireland shipwrecked the rest of the fleet.

8. How was the Spanish fleet destroyed?
1) They entered the English channel, and the English surprised them with an attack. 2) Without orders, the Spanish didn't know how to respond. 3) The lighter, more easily maneuvered English ships had the advantage in the narrow channel. 4) A storm off the coast of Ireland shipwrecked the rest of the fleet.

The English in 1603

With the armada destroyed, the English were free to roam the Atlantic and capture great numbers of Spanish and Portuguese cargoes. By the time Elizabeth died in 1603, England had a tightly organized government under a ruler who also headed the tightly organized Church of England.

The English people were used to living off trade and used to sailing to strange lands. They had more to say in their government than any other people on earth. Their parliament was run by the people who owned the land and the merchant ships and who supported their ruler in government policies.

How important was the one big naval battle? How much was planning? How much was luck?

Why is the "English Renaissance"—the "Elizabethan Age"—so exciting and so admired?

9. Why did the English have the right to be proud?
1) They had a tightly organized government under a ruler who also headed the tightly organized Church of England. 2) They had more to say in their government than any other people on earth. 3) They had produced great works of literature.

The English were a proud and productive people. The years of Elizabeth's rule were the years of great works of literature and great pride in the English language. These were the years of Shakespeare. When Elizabeth died James Stuart of Scotland became King James I. There were only 3 million English subjects. But they were ready for a new place in the world.

Checking the facts

1. Why were England and Spain such bitter enemies?
2. How was England's approach to the New World different from Spain's?
3. How did England become a world power?

2. THE FRENCH IN AMERICA

The year after the English defeated the Spanish Armada, the religious wars in France began to come to an end. The Catholic rulers of France had no sons to succeed them. So the French crown went to another branch of the family. The man who became Henry IV of France had been a Protestant, a Huguenot. But to become king of France, he converted to the Catholic faith. However, the harsh treatment of Protestants was stopped by special royal decree in 1598.

These changes in France changed France's attitude toward the rest of the world. The French now had time to think of other policies and of becoming richer and more powerful. Would they, too, turn to the New World for wealth? What they did was to allow those French Catholics who wished to explore North America to do so. But they gave them very little support. It was still not a major concern of the rulers of France.

The French, like the English, believed in trade as a way to wealth. They wanted the rest of the world to buy French goods in exchange for gold and silver. They did not share the English idea that a nation could set up colonies with its own people in other parts of the world as trading partners with the home country.

The French were like the English in wanting to trade. But they were more like the Spanish in the way they organized their lives. The French kings of the 1600's were out to build their power by controlling the nobles and telling the people exactly what they must or could do. The Roman Catholic Church in France was a strong ally of the kings.

Notice how the events in one part of the world cause changes in faraway places.

The French would not let many Protestants leave France to form colonies. The Catholics did not wish to leave, since all the power was at the king's court. To leave the court was a mistake. To stay at court was expensive. The kings of France had thought of a system that could bring France wealth and an army. But they were not going to send French families abroad, where they would have to be protected and supported at great cost. They might even want to rebel once they were out of the king's sight.

French Explorers

The French system of exploration in America was to grant certain individuals the right, or patent, to explore. This plan would keep too many people from competing in one territory. The owner of the patent would outfit the ships, supply the expedition, set up farming, and decide what there was of value to be sent back to France to be sold.

The French had been fishing off the shores of Newfoundland for years. From them came the news that there were fur-bearing animals and timber that could also bring a good price in the markets of France. This was shortly after John Cabot's voyage in 1497.

But at the time the French were still hoping to find a trade route to the East. In 1524 the French ruler, Francis I, sent out an Italian explorer, Giovanni da Verrazano, to find such a route (see chart on page 49). Verrazano sailed across the Atlantic to what is now the coast of North Carolina. Continuing north, he came to a harbor at the mouth of the Hudson River, where later the city of New York would be built. From there Verrazano sailed along the coast of New England to Newfoundland. When he returned to Europe, Verrazano claimed to have found a sea route that would lead to China.

Although Verrazano had found nothing of the sort, the French continued to search for a water route to the East. In 1534 a French seaman, Jacques Cartier (kar-TYAY), sailed for America. He came to the coast of Newfoundland and journeyed up the gulf of the St. Lawrence River. (See map, page 67.) Back in France, Cartier told Francis I about the gulf of the St. Lawrence. Convinced that this was the long-sought seaway to the East, Francis made Cartier go back. Cartier explored the St. Lawrence valley, which the Indians called Canada. The Native Americans told him about a city up the river, so he went there, hoping to find riches. But the city, located near present-day Montreal, was only a poor Indian village.

Champlain

Cartier had paved the way. But another adventurer and explorer was the most important moving force for the French. Samuel de

10. Why didn't the French send families to the New World?

1) The French king didn't want to pay the cost of protecting and supporting colonies. 2) The king wasn't sure he could control them.

11. Why did France want to explore the New World?

1) They wanted to look for riches. 2) They wanted to find a trade route to the East.

12. What did Verrazano and Cartier think they had found?

A sea route to the East.

This drawing shows the fortress of Quebec built by Champlain.

Try to imagine how it feels to find the mouth of a great river and to begin to follow it to its source.

65

LES VOYAGES DE LA NOVVELLE FRANCE OCCIDENTALE, DICTE CANADA,

This is the cover of a book written by Champlain about his voyages to Canada. Why was it important not only to visit a country, but to write about it after the voyage?

1) The nobles liked life better in France. 2) The settlers did not like being tied to the nobles. 3) The Protestant Huguenots were not allowed settlements of their own.

13. Why did Champlain fail to get more settlers to America?

Champlain had traveled to the West Indies, Mexico, and Canada. When he returned to France, he wrote about what he had seen. In 1604 Champlain set out to chart the territory and begin a colony. The colonists were to trade with the Native Americans for furs or to trap the animals themselves. Beaver hats were becoming fashionable in Europe. The more animals they caught, the wealthier the colonists could become.

After three tries, Champlain and the explorers who went with him founded a colony in Quebec (kay-BEC) in 1608. Few settlers came in the first years. Most of those who did were men who hunted and traded in the forests, *coureurs de bois* (koo-RUR duh BWAH), and *voyageurs* (voi-ya-JUHR), who lived in the more open areas of the woods and fields. These men often married Native American women and learned their languages.

French traders, trappers, and hunters traveled north to Hudson Bay in Canada and then followed the Susquehanna River south to Chesapeake Bay. They claimed the land they crossed for the king of France and named it New France. But since no French settled on it, those claims were good only until someone challenged them.

The challenge came first in 1620 with the arrival of English settlers in Cape Cod and then in 1625 with the arrival of Dutch settlers in New Amsterdam, or, as it later came to be known, New York. At that point the settlers were not fighting one another. They were competing to take over the fur trade with the Native Americans. In return for furs the Native Americans received tools, blankets, guns, and beads from the Europeans. The idea of price for numbers of items was introduced to Indians for the first time.

The French Make Another Try at Settlement

Champlain thought that the way to get more settlers to go to French territory in America was to make it worthwhile for nobles to go. To lure them away from the French court, they were offered free land along the riverfronts and lakes. The lords could then bring over settlers who could farm the land for them. The plan of organization was much like life in France. The settlers had to pay dues to the landlord. They had to pay to grind their grain into flour at the lord's mill. They also had to work six days a year to keep the lord's road in good repair.

Some nobles and some settlers did come to the New World under this arrangement. But most nobles liked life better in France. All the power was at court. And settlers did not like being tied to the nobles. The land remained thinly populated. Not enough people became farmers. Most preferred the life of a trader or trapper. The people who might have liked to get out of France, the Protestant Huguenots, were not allowed independent settlements.

Notice that the Native Americans learned about the idea of price for value when they discovered more than one group of European settlers.

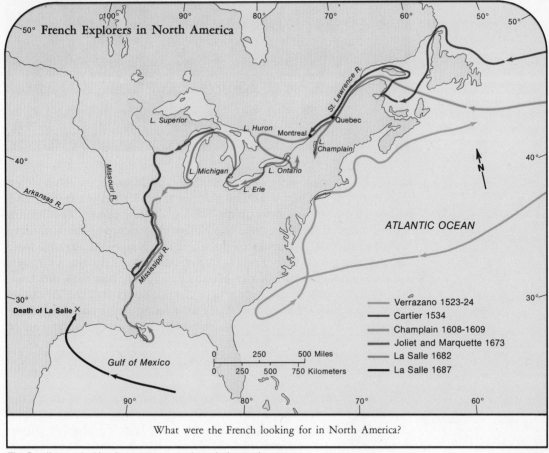

French Explorers in North America

L. Superior

L. Huron

Montreal

Quebec

St. Lawrence R.

L. Champlain

L. Michigan

L. Ontario

L. Erie

Missouri R.

Arkansas R.

Mississippi R.

Death of La Salle ✕

Gulf of Mexico

ATLANTIC OCEAN

N

——	Verrazano 1523-24
——	Cartier 1534
——	Champlain 1608-1609
——	Joliet and Marquette 1673
——	La Salle 1682
——	La Salle 1687

0 250 500 Miles

0 250 500 750 Kilometers

What were the French looking for in North America?

The French were looking for a water route through the continent.

The French Travel the Mississippi River

Quebec was the chief French settlement in North America. But trade from Quebec on the St. Lawrence River was a problem because the river was frozen over for half of every year. What could the French do to build their power? The French king, Louis XIII, who had come to the throne in 1643, thought he knew the answer. The French had discovered the waterways of the eastern half of North America. They had also learned how to be friends with the Native Americans. Together these two factors could give France a firm hold on the land and also halt the advance of the English and the Spanish.

The French plan was to send a representative of the king to New France to encourage priests and traders to explore the rivers. They were to claim the shores and all the land between the rivers for France. Along the way they were to set up trapping stations and trading posts for fur trade with the Native Americans.

1) They were to claim the shores and all lands between rivers for France. 2) They were to set up trapping stations and trading posts for fur trade with the Native Americans. 3) They were to convert the Indians.

14. Why were priests and traders encouraged to explore the rivers?

Following the rivers on a large physical map can give you a sense of where the geography led the explorers.

Notice another variety of culture and another way in which cultures met.

This painting by George Catlin shows La Salle meeting with the Taensa Indians.

15. *What did Joliet and Marquette discover?*

1) They found the place where the Missouri and Arkansas rivers joined the Mississippi. 2) They learned from the Native Americans that there were Spanish settlements at the other end of the river.

In 1672 two men went out to explore the Mississippi River. (See map, page 67.) They were Louis Joliet (zjoh-LYEH), a trader, and Father Jacques Marquette (mahr-KET), a Jesuit priest. The Jesuits were interested in converting the Native Americans to Christianity. They found that job easier to do when the Native Americans were trading their furs with French traders. On this trip the two men did not get to the end of the Mississippi River, but they did float far enough south to discover where the Missouri and the Arkansas rivers joined the Mississippi. They also found out from the Native Americans that there were Spanish settlements at the other end of the river.

La Salle

Ten years went by before the next major trip was taken down the Mississippi River. The leader was Robert Cavelier, Sieur de La Salle (roe-BARE kah-vuh-LYAY, SYUHR duh la SAL). In his group were 23 French citizens and 31 Native Americans. They wisely used the Native Americans' method of travel, lightweight canoes.

16. *What did La Salle's trip accomplish?*

1) He found the mouth of the Mississippi River. 2) He claimed the Louisiana Territory for France. 3) The French were able to settle New Orleans near the mouth.

When the difficult trip was over, La Salle planted both a cross and the flag of France at the mouth of the river. Then he made an enormous claim. He said that all the land watered by any river or stream that emptied into the Mississippi River belonged to France. He named the entire territory Louisiana, after Louis XIV.

After La Salle's death, the French finally did build their settlement near the southern end of the Mississippi River. In 1718 they selected a site far enough up the river to be protected from attack and from storms. But it was still the place where river trade and seagoing trade could meet. The French called the settlement New Orleans.

Between New Orleans and Quebec were many scattered forts and trading posts—all set up under French colonial rule and helped by the work of the French priests. But a French way of life never developed. Nor did the French ever find a way of organizing themselves to use the land.

What ways did the priests use to introduce Christianity? Why do some beliefs spread? Why do other beliefs not take hold?

Notice how much land is watered and drained by the Mississippi River.

North America—Variety from the Start

If you step back far enough to see the whole of North America at the beginnings of exploration and settlement, what do you see? You have learned that the continent of North America held within its boundaries the civilizations of several European nations and many Native American tribes. (See maps, pages 70 and 18.) When the Europeans came, they were separated by so much land for such a long time that they had very little effect on one another's development in the New World.

If we look over the long span of time between the voyages of Cortés and the founding of French New Orleans, what do we see? We see that the Spanish tried to rule the New World from home. The policy worked well for them as long as all Spain wanted was gold and silver. The policy also worked for France, as long as all it wanted was trade goods that could bring a high price quickly.

But the Europeans did have an effect on the Native Americans they met. The Native Americans made use of the tools, weapons, and clothing that the Europeans brought. They often used these items in their own ways. Copper kettles were cut up for spear points. Swords were made into knives, and mirrors were used for signalling. Beads became symbols of peace and were used in treaty making by the Native Americans.

The Native Americans made changes when the changes suited their way of life. They welcomed the horse because they could hunt better with it. They used guns to give themselves more power in their own practices of hunting and making war. In the exchange with the Europeans, the Native Americans lost as well as gained. They had to give up their land to the settlers. And sometimes they had to give up their freedom as well. Guns and disease took many Native American lives. Highly organized, settled tribes like the Pueblos held out against the Europeans as long as they could.

This picture shows a French convent in Quebec. What changes had the French brought to North America?

How many kinds of people from various places are represented on this map?

How important are ideas and beliefs in the way people behave?

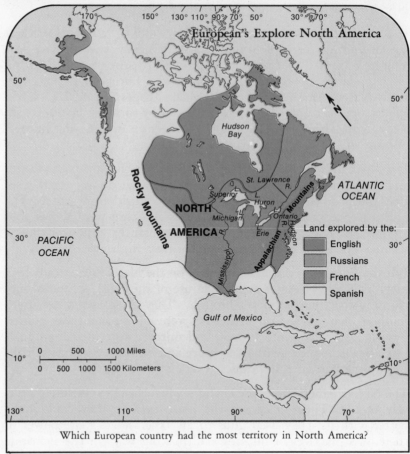

European's Explore North America

Land explored by the:
- English
- Russians
- French
- Spanish

Which European country had the most territory in North America?

The French had the most land in North America.

In the end North America was conquered by beliefs as much as by people. The Europeans believed in the power of individuals. They brought with them the ideas of humanism. They also brought with them the idea of *nationalism*. The Europeans believed in the strength of their new nations, and they believed in their churches. They were convinced that they must win new people to their religions. They also believed, as most Native Americans did, that it was all right to fight anyone who got in their way. As they pushed into the new lands the Europeans were ready to fight anyone who got in their way. And the Native Americans were often in their way.

Checking the facts

1. Why did the French arrive late in the New World?
2. How did the French attempt to settle the New World?
3. What was the continent of North America like after 300 years of exploration and settlement?

PUTTING IT ALL TOGETHER

UNDERSTANDING THE MAIN IDEAS

1. How did England become strong enough to explore new land?
2. Why did England organize settlements in the New World?
3. How did the French organize their efforts in the New World?
4. How did the French and English behave toward the Native Americans?

ACTIVITIES

1. Use your school or local library to find out the meaning of the term "sea dog." Then name the "Sea Dogs" of the late 1500's. Who were they? What did they do to help England? How were they regarded by the English ruler?
2. Write a biographical essay on Sir Walter Raleigh. What made him so special? How did he fit into the picture of English settlement in America?
3. Read about the French *coureurs de bois* and *voyageurs*. Who were these early settlers? Did any settle or explore in your area? What was their life like? Present your findings in a brief oral report.
4. Look at a map of areas explored by the French in North America. How many of these places have French names? Can you find out what they mean? Are they the names of people or geographic features? Locate the places on a current map of the United States.

BOOKS TO READ

Guillet, E., and M., *The Pathfinders of North America* (New York: St. Martin's Press, 1970).

Kjelgaard, Jim, *Explorations of Père Marquette* (New York: Random House, Inc., 1968).

Viereck, Phillip, *The New Land: Discovery, Exploration, and Early Settlement of the Northeastern United States, from the Earliest Voyages to 1621* (New York: Day Publishing Co., 1967).

chapter 4
Settlements and Choices

1606–1640

1. THE FIRST ENGLISH
   SETTLEMENT: JAMESTOWN
2. THE FIRST SETTLEMENTS:
   NEW ENGLAND
3. MORE PURITANS: BETTER
   RESULTS

Here we begin a much closer look at the tapestry of history. More differences will now show up.

INTRODUCTION

The settlers who came to North America from Europe came from different cultures. They were used to different ways of being governed. They belonged to a variety of churches. They came from fairly new nations that were competing with each other for riches and power. They were alike in that all were sure their religion was the best. They all wanted to spread it to others. When necessary, force was used to reach this goal.

As you take a closer look at the settlers from Europe, think about how their cultures made them different from each other. Think about when they came to the New World and how this made a difference. Also, think about where they made their settlements and why their choices were important.

	1607	1608	1619	1619	
Who?	The London Company	Samuel de Champlain	The House of Burgesses	The first Blacks	
What?	sends settlers	establishes a colony	meets for the first time	arrive on a Dutch ship	
Where?	to Jamestown, Virginia	in Quebec	at Jamestown	from the West Indies	

Why do you think the timing of an event is important?

Why do you think the geographical place is important?

The English sent the most settlers to North America. They took the idea of permanent settlement much more seriously than other Europeans. Since these English settlements finally became the United States, you will take an even closer look at them. Americans from every background have inherited some of the English story. It is the story of different groups of English settlers who came at different times, built their new lives in different places in North America and in different ways. All Americans have some of the values these early English brought with them. As you look at the history of the English settlements in North America, answer the following questions:

1. Why did the English come to America?
2. What did they find when they arrived?
3. What did they save from their life in England?
4. What changes in their lives did they have to make in America?
5. What did the settlers think was most important?
6. What did all English settlers have in common?

1. THE FIRST ENGLISH SETTLEMENT: JAMESTOWN

Why Go to America?

In the 1600's, the English king, James I, government leaders, church leaders, merchants, and the people agreed on setting up colonies in America. They believed that it was good for England to have colonies. They wanted colonies for different reasons. Some

1. Why did the English want to set up colonies in America?

1620	1630	1634	1636	1636-37
The Pilgrims	The Puritans	Anne Hutchinson	The Puritans	John Endecott and the Pequots
leave England to settle	establish a colony	is banished from the Massachusetts colony	establish Harvard College	fight the Pequot War
in the New World	called Massachusetts Bay	and settles in Rhode Island	in Cambridge, Massachusetts	in Connecticut

Compare this time line with the ones in previous chapters. How many generations have passed since Columbus sailed to the New World?

1) To set up trade, 2) to find riches, 3) to convert Native Americans to Christianity, and 4) to spread English culture, in which they had pride.

hoped to set up trade while others wanted to find riches. Even others hoped to find converts to Christianity among the Native Americans.

Pride in their nation was another reason why the English wanted colonies. They were sure that their way of living and believing was the best way.

The First Plan for Settlement

2. What was the worth of a share in a joint stock company?

Each shareowner would get a share of the profits the same size as the share of capital he or she had invested.

The English were already used to the kind of business organization that could pay for a settlement overseas. Companies, such as the East India Company, were already organizing and paying for fleets of ships to trade with the Far East. The owners were individuals. Each bought a part or a share of what it would take to get the business started. This was called putting in risk capital. After the bills were paid each shareowner would take out of the leftovers, or *profits,* the same size share he or she had originally put in, or invested. These businesses were called joint stock companies— joint, meaning together, stock, meaning shares, companies meaning businesses. The more successful a company or business was, the larger the profits of the shareholders.

3. How did James I work with business?

1) He granted charters to merchants to colonize North America. 2) He appointed a Royal Council, on which those merchants had seats, to supervise the companies.

Two different groups of merchants formed joint stock companies and asked James I for licenses or charters to colonize a part of North America called Virginia. James agreed and gave out two charters, one to the London Company and one to the Plymouth Company. The two groups of merchants had to find their own settlers. In addition to granting the charters, James set up a Royal Council to supervise both the London and the Plymouth companies. The merchants of both joint stock companies had seats on the council, and could make decisions and choices for their settlements in North America.

The First English Settlers

4. Why did the James-town settlers have many difficulties?

1) The settlement was a mosquito-ridden, malarial swamp. 2) The surrounding land was poor for farming. 3) Many settlers were not interested in or capable of farming and fishing. 4) Many grew ill and died.

The merchants of the London Company sent 105 men and no women on the first ship to North America in 1606. It was around Christmas when they left England. Twenty-nine of the future settlers were listed as gentlemen and 12 were listed as laborers. The others were skilled in the kinds of services people who live in a town or city would need. One was a surgeon, while others were a blacksmith, a barber, a stonemason, a bricklayer, a tailor, and a drummer! There were no farmers, hunters, or soldiers aboard.

The colonizers arrived in Virginia five months later. When they arrived in North America, they looked carefully for a place to build their settlement. Above all, they wanted a spot that could be easily protected from the Native Americans since they didn't know how

Capitalism rewards the people who take the risk as well as paying those who do the work.

they would be met. To avoid the Native Americans, they chose a place that was near the water. Unfortunately, the place they chose was a mosquito-ridden, malarial swamp. The land around it was poor for planting seeds and growing food. The settlers for the London Company called their new home Jamestown to honor the king.

In their first year in Virginia almost two thirds of the Jamestown settlers died. They sent back word to London for more settlers and more supplies, and they got them. Again, the wrong kind of settlers for the location came over. For example, the second group of ships brought two goldsmiths to Jamestown instead of workers who would be willing to farm and fish. Jamestown needed people who planned to spend the rest of their lives there. For this purpose, women were needed to start family life.

The first women to arrive in the Virginia colony were Anne Forrest, the wife of one of the first settlers, and her maid, 13-year-old Anne Buras. They came in 1608. The next year 20 women came. The year after that, 100 women came. Sickness, attacks by Native Americans, and starvation were common during the first years in Virginia.

A Second Plan for a Colony

If a colony were to survive in Virginia, it would have to be made up of people who were willing to leave England forever. The new settlers would have to live according to a strict plan.

This picture shows Jamestown in 1619. What were the advantages of building a town like this?

5. What qualities did settlers need to survive in Virginia?
1) They had to be willing to leave England forever, to live according to a strict plan, and learn to feed themselves.

In 1609, one man was able to make this message clear to his fellow settlers and to the company owners back in London. He was 27 year old John Smith. Smith had been a soldier and an adventurer. Past experience had taught him how to organize people. John Smith knew that the settlers were going to have to learn to feed themselves if they were to survive. Riches were only a dream; survival was the real problem. "A plain soldier that can use a pickaxe and a spade is better than five nobles," he said.

6. What was the basis for the new set of rules for Virginia?
The London Company hoped that the strict rules and schedule would help the Jamestown settlers succeed.

On the advice of John Smith, the English made a new set of rules for Virginia. Every person was given specific duties. Rules spelled these duties out in detail. Supervisors could use gunpoint to make sure the jobs were done. In the new plan, the settlers were to be divided into groups of 10 or 20. Every day, records would be kept of how much work was done and by whom. At the end of the week each group would report. At the end of the month, all the reports were checked before new supplies were given out. The rules said that each person was to be given enough food to prevent arguments among the settlers. The London Company hoped that this army-style schedule would help the Jamestown settlers succeed.

John Smith and the Native Americans

Organization was one problem for the Jamestown settlers. Understanding the Native Americans and being understood by them was another. John Smith made the closest contacts with the Powhatans. They showed the settlers how to grow the plants that were native to the area. They also showed the English how to slash and burn the trees to clear the land.

7. How did the English misunderstand the structure of the Powhatan confederacy?
1) The English expected the chief to control his subjects.
2) The English didn't understand that the members had a sense of loyalty to each other, but did not have to obey the chief.

The Powhatans were the leaders of a confederacy of over 200 villages. The chief, whom the settlers called Powhatan, built the entire confederacy in his own lifetime. The English were never sure how much control Powhatan had. They assumed that he was a king and they expected him to control his subjects. The English thought they had done the right thing when, in 1608, they had the King of England declare Powhatan an independent king within the English territory. James I sent him a copper crown to wear, a red woolen robe, and an English bed! Powhatan wanted to make sure that he was known as a king, equal to James in power. He made the English bring the gifts to him. He refused to bow his head to receive the crown. Powhatan saw the whole ceremony as an exchange of gifts from one leader to another. He said, "If your king has sent me presents, I also am a king, and this is my land."

The Powhatan confederacy was held together by a sense of loyalty to each other. Members of the confederacy did not have to obey the chief. When members of the confederacy raided English set-

Both Powhatan and James I show how hard it is to understand the way another culture looks at the world.

tlements, the settlers blamed Powhatan. Records show that Powhatan probably did not even know about the raids.

Relations between the English and the Native Americans changed from time to time. John Smith was sometimes on friendly terms with them. Sometimes he was captured by them or they by him. The famous story which Smith told was that he was about to be put to death when Powhatan's daughter, Pocahontas, saved him. The English and the Native Americans now lived in the same place. But the differences in their experiences and their values made it impossible to see each other's actions clearly and to understand.

Pocahontas and the English

Pocahontas was a regular visitor to Jamestown. She was kidnapped by the English when she was 17 years old. Although she was married to a Powhatan she became the wife of a Jamestown settler. John Rolfe and Pocahontas married a year after her capture perhaps to provide the English with protection against Indian attack. John Smith wrote of Pocahontas that "she, under God, was the person

This engraving shows Pocahontas saving the life of John Smith. She is kneeling alongside Smith.

Ætatis suæ 21. Aᵒ. 1616.

This is a portrait of Pocahontas, made when she was in England. What do you think life was like for a Native American at Queen Elizabeth's court?

8. *What role did Pocahontas play in Jamestown?*

With her there, the settlers hoped that the Powhatans would not attack them.

able to preserve this colony from death, famine, and utter confusion." There was obviously a great deal of all three at Jamestown. Rolfe took Pocahontas to London where she was the subject of much curiosity and fame. She met the Queen and an English artist painted her portrait. Pocahontas died at the age of 21.

Tobacco Makes a Difference

In Jamestown, John Rolfe found a new plant that could be grown easily and sold at a good price in England. This was a mild tobacco that had been grown in the West Indies. It caused enormous changes in peoples' lives in Jamestown.

9. *How did tobacco make a difference?*

1) It was easy to grow, and the Jamestown colonists were poor farmers. 2) Tobacco was becoming popular, and it could be sold for cash in Europe.

The Jamestown colonists were poor farmers, as John Smith had pointed out. But the new tobacco was easy to grow. It satisfied the needs of the Virginia settlers who wanted to get rich, because it could be sold for cash. The cash would buy the manufactured goods the settlers were used to. King James and the London Company owners were not as pleased with tobacco as the settlers. They thought of tobacco as a useless product, not one that could be used as raw material for making other goods. The king thought smoking was a "vile habit."

But the colonists ignored the complaints from England. Those who had been in Jamestown for seven years had a strong claim on the land. They grew the tobacco and liked the profit it brought. Luckily for the Virginia growers, smoking tobacco was becoming a habit in Europe. The demand was on the rise and for ten years, the number of customers grew and grew.

Tobacco growing needed a great deal of land. That was easy to provide in America. In fact, the colonists were so excited about the money-making possibilities of growing tobacco that they grew it in the streets of Jamestown.

More People Needed

Raising tobacco required a worker for every two or three acres (.8 to 1.2 hectares) of land. To continue growing tobacco, Virginia needed more people. So in 1619, a plan was set up to lure more English people to Virginia. Settlers were offered something they could not get in the growing villages and towns of their native England—free land.

10. *What was the "headright" system?*

Each person who came to Virginia or who paid for the voyage of someone else got free land. One hundred acres (40 hectares) went to anyone who had come over before 1616. Fifty acres (20 hectares) went to anyone who paid for the voyage of someone else. As stated

Tobacco turned out to be more important to the Jamestown way of life than all of John Smith's rules or the king's statements.

in the plan, land was given out "per head." The plan of land grants was called the "headright system."

Tobacco ruled family life in Virginia. As the colony began to have success, there were more Virginians who wished to marry and settle down.

To encourage women to come to America, they, too, were given shares of land. But that did not last long. For some reason women with land did not marry fast enough. Women were then brought in as servants to work for those who had paid 120 pounds (54 kilograms) of tobacco for their voyage. The women who came to Virginia in this way were required to do the laundry and other household duties. After a time, a woman could decide whether or not to marry. In the settlers' view, marriage was the only purpose for having women in the colony.

Servants

The headright plan was very successful in bringing more settlers to Virginia. But most free workers who came to Virginia by the headright system would not stay as workers for long if free land could be had. What the Virginia planters needed were people who would be bound to the job of raising and gathering tobacco. The

One hundred acres of free land were given to anyone who came to Virginia and 50 acres were given to anyone who paid for the voyage of someone else.

11. Why were women brought to Virginia?

1) More Virginians wanted to marry and settle down. 2) More Virginians needed servants.

12. How did the indenture system work?

1) The servant signed a seven-year labor contract with a planter to pay for the trip to America. 2) After seven years the servant was free, and entitled to clothing, livestock, tools, and a small piece of land.

Women were first brought to Virginia in 1608. Why was family life important to the settlers?

The idea of such a contract for an indentured servant is an English idea. Individual freedom and the right to land and property were also English ideas.

The arrival of the first Blacks was not part of a major plan or scheme.

London Company thought of a solution to this problem in Virginia. It shipped out of England poor men and women to be sold as servants to Virginia planters. The servants signed a contract of *indenture* by which they had to work for the planter for about seven years as payment for their trip. After the time of the contract was up, the servant was free to start a life of his or her own.

The former servant was entitled to freedom dues. These were clothing, livestock, tools, and a small piece of land, something to begin a free life on. By the indenture method, the labor shortage was solved and the increased profits of the Virginia planters was assured.

Tobacco had made farmers out of the Jamestown settlers. Tobacco, however, had not made Jamestown settlers into a close-knit farming community. How to get more land, more servants, and more money were goals on every mind.

The First Blacks

13. How were the first Blacks treated in Virginia?

They were treated just like the White indentured servants.

1619 was the date of the arrival of the first Black servants in Virginia. It was the governor of the colony and a merchant who bought the first Blacks from a private Dutch ship that had been unsuccessful in the pirate business against the Spanish. The Dutch ship had slaves aboard and needed supplies. So a trade was arranged. About 20 Black servants were exchanged for those supplies.

The engraving shows the arrival of the first Blacks in America. Why were Blacks brought to Virginia?

There is no evidence that these Black servants were thought of any differently from the White servants who had come by contract, bond, or indenture. The term "bought" was used for the White servants as well as the Blacks. There is evidence that some of those first Blacks became free of their bonds in a few years.

Organizing for Business

So many people were going into business for themselves in Jamestown that they forgot about the system of military-type government set up by John Smith. Virginians were now making so much money that they wanted new laws about who could sell to whom. They especially wanted rules about prices. There was so much competition that people wanted to make sure that everyone competed by the same rules. And, of course, everyone wanted a voice in making those rules.

The Jamestown landowners turned to the English way of making decisions about laws. They added an assembly of the people to the colony's organization for governing. Obviously, there were too many people for everyone to come to every meeting to make the rules. But all people needed to feel that what they wanted for their families or their tobacco sales would be heard at the meeting. The assembly, therefore, was to be made up of two people from each of the small settlements that had grown up in the Jamestown area. This assembly, called the House of Burgesses, or villagers, was, a *representative assembly*. It was begun in 1619 and was the first representative government in America. Most of its decisions had to do with the growing, pricing, and selling of tobacco. It also took up arguments over servants, land, and animals when it seemed that owners could not settle their disagreements themselves.

14. What kinds of decisions did the House of Burgesses make?

1) Most concerned the growing, pricing, and selling of tobacco. 2) Others had to do with servants, land, and animals.

Native Americans Attack

The new chief of the Powhatans hated the English from the start. As the growth of tobacco and the headright system of giving land began to send English settlers farther and farther into Powhatan land, the chief planned and carried out an attack in 1622.

The official report from the colonies described what happened.

15. What was the importance of the massacre of 1622?

It was a signal to the White settlers that the Native Americans were a danger to their new way of life.

> "As they had on other days before, they came unarmed
> into our houses, without bows or arrows or other
> weapons, with deer, turkey, fish, fur, and other
> provisions to sell and trade with us for glass, beads,
> and other items. Yet in some places, they sat down at
> breakfast with our people at their tables, whom they
> murdered, not sparing men, women, or children. . . ."

The Indians killed 347 people in the attack. The Massacre of 1622 was the signal to the White settlers that the Native Americans were a danger to their new way of life. From then on, it was open warfare between the English settlers and the Native Americans of the Southeast.

English Values in the New Land

16. Where did power lie in the Virginia colony?

In the hands of the early settlers, who had the best land for tobacco and seats in the House of Burgesses.

In 1624, King James I put Virginia directly under his rule as a crown colony. In the years from 1607 to 1624, the English settlers had succeeded in setting up a money-making colony of people who competed with one another. They settled their arguments by English law in their English-style representative assembly. And they worked hard to control the land, gain wealth, and get the newcomers to work for them. The newcomers used their votes to elect settlers who had come earlier to the House of Burgesses. By 1640 a look around Jamestown and the other towns in that Virginia colony showed that early settlers had the best land. This land was near the ocean and the mouths of the great rivers. From there the tobacco growers could ship their plants directly to England.

Latecomers to Virginia got land in the back woods, farther and farther from the rivers and the oceans. They had to sell their tobacco through the growers who lived near and owned the docks.

The early settlers worked hard to keep their power in Virginia. When a newcomer, Nathaniel Bacon, tried to lead a rebellion of newcomer White farmers in 1676, the old-timers fought hard against him. The older leaders were on the lookout for anyone who might try to take away some of their land, their money from tobacco, or their voting power in the House of Burgesses.

New Power—In Owning Slaves

Another change came with the new wealth in Virginia. People were beginning to make distinctions between White and Black servants. In 1630, the records of the House of Burgesses show that the laws about servants referred separately to "Negroes." Other laws from that time established an even greater difference between White servants and Black servants.

17. Why was a series of laws passed to keep the Blacks separated from the Whites?

The reason for this change is a long and complex story. Irish newcomers to Virginia were growing scarce. Life in England, Scotland, and Ireland was improving, and fewer people were coming to the colonies as bond servants. By 1661, the Negroes, and only the Negroes, were referred to as "slaves."

In 1667, a law was passed to make it clear that although slaves became Christians, they were still not free. By 1680, it was not

82

It was in Virginia where relations between Whites and Blacks first changed. Black slaves became the servants.

"lawful for any Negro or other slave to carry or arm himself with any club, staff, or gun, sword, . . . nor to go or depart from his master's ground without a certificate from his master." By 1691, runaway "Negroes, mulattos, or slaves" were all put into one classification group. Runaways were to be returned, and if they put up a fight it was lawful to kill them.

By making the Blacks slaves, the tobacco planters got the cheap labor they needed.

Finally, to keep the races separate in the future, marriages between Blacks and Whites was cause for removal from the colony forever.

These laws were not the cause of Black slavery. These laws are descriptions of a way of life that grew up over two generations. And then the laws were passed to keep the Whites separate from Blacks and Native Americans. Getting cheap labor had always been a desire of the Virginia colonists. By making slaves out of Blacks, the tobacco growers could have the cheap labor they wanted.

New Arrivals; New Wealth

About 1680, after Black slavery had been recognized by law, Virginia got a new kind of settler. Rich people from England came to live in the colonies. They did not need the headright system. They came with money, and they immediately bought land and slaves. Their letters show the life they were used to. They sent home for feather beds, furniture, and fine linen cloth. They bought more Black slaves, including children who would grow up in their service.

18. What did the rich settlers bring with them to the colonies?

1) They brought money and bought land and slaves. 2) They sent to England for featherbeds, furniture, fine linen, and the workers needed to build fine houses.

Some of these new settlers sent to England for bricklayers and carpenters to build their new houses in Virginia. The houses of these families were richly decorated, especially for a territory that had been wilderness to the Europeans and home to the Indians just 80 years before.

English Settlements in the South

By the 1700's the English in the southern part of Virginia had built their success on opportunity for individuals, control of the land, and the desire for money. They ran their own businesses and competed with each other. They settled their differences through their representative assembly.

America was for them a land of opportunity. But there was more opportunity for those who either got an early start or came later with the wealth to buy land and Black slaves. By 1700 Virginians were used to running their own businesses and their own government. The freedom they had to manage their lives had grown out

19. How did the English in the southern part of Virginia differ from those in England?

They owned slaves.

Note the timing of the arrival of new wealthy families and the laws about Black slaves—almost three generations after the first settlement.

This painting shows a whole plantation. The yellow building is a mill. What other buildings can you identify?

of their English traditions of trade and government. Their freedom was also tied to their use of slavery. It was a strange new combination in the world.

Checking the facts

1. How did the English change their plans after sending people to settle Jamestown?
2. What changes came about because of growing tobacco?
3. Describe the first representative government in the New World.

Notice the development of a definite English way of life in Virginia. The Native Americans of the southeast had lost out.

2. THE FIRST SETTLEMENTS: NEW ENGLAND

Disagreeing with the King

20. How did the English disagree with King James over the law?

1) They considered the law more important than the king or Parliament. 2) James believed kings were chosen by God and that whatever a king said was the law.

Understanding the English who came to North America must begin with understanding government and religion in England itself in the early 1600's. When James came from Scotland to become King of England in 1603, he tried to tell the Parliament what to do. He insisted on his ideas about the right kind of Protestant church for England. James believed that kings ruled because they were selected by God. Therefore whatever the king said was the law. When James became king, England had a long history of the law being more important than either the king or the Parliament. Many important English people spoke out against the king's opinion, or simply ignored it.

84

1600 again—English history, the king, and the church are an important background for New England.

What was harder for the English people to ignore was James' opinion about the church. The Church of England had taken the stand that there was one true faith in Jesus Christ, but that the form of the church service and the organization of the church government could be different in different places. However, James said that since he was the head of the Church of England, he could decide what the proper form of church service ought to be and how the individual churches should be governed. Among those opposed to James' point of view were Roman Catholics who hoped to be left alone by the Protestants, and groups of Protestants who wanted to make their church services as simple as possible. These Protestants wanted to keep it pure from any traces of the Roman Catholic Church. These Protestants were called Puritans.

The king, the Parliament, and the churches were arguing much of the time. Some people who could not stand the king's policies any longer left England.

One great difference between being English and French or Spanish was clear. In Spain and France people who disagreed with their rulers would never have been trusted to leave. English people who disagreed with their ruler were allowed to go, with the king's blessing. From the king's point of view, it was a good way to keep them loyal to England and, at the same time, keep them from making trouble at home.

What Is a Pure Church?

In England there was a great debate over what form the church service should take. Everyone wanted the Church of England to be the perfect church with the true beliefs. But who was to say what was perfect or true? King James was sure that whatever he said was correct. But there were those Puritans who thought that James' ideas were too much like the Roman Catholic Church. There were other Puritans who went so far as to say that the members of a church group, or *congregation* should decide for themselves what was the perfect or true belief. The government should stay out of it entirely. To these Puritans, government should be totally separate from the church. Puritans who held these beliefs were called Separatists.

The Pilgrims Leave England

One group of Puritans was so certain of being right about how to worship and so sure the king was wrong that they left England in 1608 to live in Holland. They had been there 12 years when they decided that they did not like their children to speak Dutch.

21. How did the English disagree with King James on religion?

1) They thought that they should be able to conduct church services as they liked. 2) King James claimed the right to decide what the proper form was to be.

22. Why did the king permit those who disagreed with him to leave England?

The king believed that 1) it would keep them loyal to England, and 2) it would keep them from making trouble at home.

23. What separated the Puritans from other English people?

1) Some thought that the king's ideas were too much like the Roman Catholic Church. 2) Some, called Separatists, believed that government should be totally separate from the church.

24. Why did the Puritans leave Holland?

Puritans were free to leave. They left in order to practice their religion without interference from the king.

85

The Pilgrims left Plymouth, England, for the New World. What did the Pilgrims hope to find in America?

1) They wanted their children to speak English. 2) They wanted to preserve their English customs. 3) They couldn't find jobs.

They found they did not like having to give up their English customs. They also had trouble finding jobs. These Puritans applied to the Virginia Company for the right to go to Virginia to live. They formed the Plymouth Company with some English people who had money to invest. In 1620, some 35 of these Puritans from Leyden in Holland, and 67 others left Plymouth, England on the ship *Mayflower*. They called themselves Pilgrims because of their many travels.

25. Why did the Pilgrims remain where they first landed?

1) It was too late in the winter to start down the coast looking for Virginia. 2) They were ill.

The *Mayflower* sailed in the fall of the year and was blown off course on its way to Virginia. It was December when land was sighted. A few men under the leadership of Miles Standish set out in a small boat to find out where they were. There were no English settlements in sight. The place they found was certainly not Virginia. It was later to be called Massachusetts after the Massachusett Indians. The Pilgrims had little choice about what to do. It was too late in the winter and they were too ill to start looking down the coast for their original destination. So they decided to stay where they were.

The first winter for the Pilgrims was a horror. They dug pits for houses and covered them with sod, or layers of earth. Some lived in caves. Half the group died that winter. On any one day there might be as few as six or seven adults well enough to take care of

How were the Jamestown colonists and the Pilgrims different?

the rest of the group. In addition to starvation and pneumonia, they had scurvy—a disease that comes from poor diet.

But in spite of the Pilgrim's terrible conditions, there was something different about the Plymouth group. The settlers had come over with their families. They had come to stay. Finally, they had come to live as a group. Eighteen women and 37 children had been on the *Mayflower*. The records show that only four of the women lived through the first winter. However all 11 girls and 20 of the 26 boys lived. That was a surprisingly good survival rate. It shows that the adults took care of the children first. By doing this they expected the settlement to have a future.

26. How do we know that the Pilgrims had come to stay?

1) They had come to live as a group. 2) They had brought their families with them. 3) They took special care of the children, who represented the future of their colony.

The Mayflower Compact

The Plymouth Colony was a group within a group. These Separatists felt that they were special. Their religious belief gave them a feeling of strength. Those beliefs also separated them from the rest of the English colonists. While still aboard the *Mayflower*, the men in the group met together to decide how they were going to organize themselves. Since they were not going to join the Virginia colony as planned, they would have to come to some sort of agreement about governing. So they took an idea out of their church

27. What was the Mayflower Compact?

It was an agreement signed by the Plymouth settlers to govern their colony by majority rule.

This painting shows the signing of the Mayflower Compact. Why did the Pilgrims decide to sign the Compact?

Can you give a modern example of people freely getting together to help the whole group?

organization. They made an agreement that they would act as equals and decide together for the good of the group. This was a *compact* or *covenant*. This meant that free people would use their freedom to decide. The Plymouth settlers decided to rule together, by majority rule. On board their ship, they signed the Mayflower Compact.

The Mayflower Compact was a very English kind of agreement. It was also a very Separatist Puritan kind of agreement. It did not look to a single leader or council for leadership but to the whole group of members. It was like a church congregation. The 41 signers of the compact pledged:

> To "combine ourselves together into a civil (that is, not a religious) body politic, for our better ordering and preservation . . . And we do frame such just and equal laws. . . . from time to time . . . as shall be thought most (right) and convenient for the general good of the colony; unto which we promise all due submission and obedience."

The land they decided to rule would be ruled very differently than New Spain or New France. It was called New England by the Pilgrims.

The Land and the Native Americans

28. How did the Native Americans help the Pilgrims survive?

1) The Wampanoags gave them seed and taught them to grow corn, pumpkins, and beans. 2) They knew how to farm. 3) They knew how to build thatch-roofed log cabins. 4) There were few Indians to compete with for land.

The Pilgrims had come to a land where there were few Native Americans left. The ones who were left had met European and English fishing ships from season to season for years. John Smith from the Virginia colony had explored the area in 1614. One of the Wampanoag Indians, named Tisquantum, had been captured by a slave ship, escaped to England and made the trip back to New England. He was at Plymouth when the Pilgrims landed. Squanto, as the English called him, spoke English. He introduced them to his local chief, Samoset. Samoset, in turn, made the Pilgrims known to the great chief, Massosoit.

The Wampanoag Indians gave the English settlers seed and showed them how to grow corn, pumpkins, and beans. Unlike the first people to go to Jamestown, these settlers knew how to farm and how to build thatch-roofed log cabins. With help from the Native Americans and with skilled settlers who had come to stay, the Plymouth Colony was able to survive.

For a long while, the colonists had no major trouble from the local Indians. This was partly because there were so few Indians to compete for the land. In 1616 there had been a terrible epidemic, probably of smallpox. After three years it had run its course and

Native Americans of the northeast had been meeting European sailors for many years.

How important was organization and religious belief to the Pilgrims?

List the various peoples who lived in North America as of 1650. Why did these people come to America?

killed an estimated 9,000 Indians. Only about 1,000 were left in the northeast area of Massachusetts.

The Pilgrims Survive

The Pilgrims were skilled at survival in their new situation. The future was not an easy one. There were no rivers to follow upstream. There were no beavers to provide furs to wear, or to sell. But in spite of the Pilgrims' difficulty in making a living, they had a strong sense of why they were there.

They had strength in their leader, William Bradford. With all of their troubles, Bradford and the members of the Plymouth colony tried to be fair. They divided the land according to the number of people in each household. Women worked in the fields with the men. But the Pilgrims could find nothing else to do for a living but just work to survive. The Plymouth colony never was able to support itself very well. After ten years, they had just 300 people. In 1640, the whole colony only owned one plow.

But the settlers felt that they had done the right thing by migrating. The Pilgrims had a religious purpose in coming to New England. They were serious about their duty and they hoped to be a success.

29. What was the colony like after ten years?

1) It could only farm for a living. 2) It didn't support itself very well. 3) It had only 300 people. 4) The settlers felt they had done the right thing by coming.

Checking the facts

1. Why did the Puritans disagree with the leaders of the Church of England?
2. What held the Puritans together as a group during the first years at Plymouth?
3. What were the main ideas behind the Mayflower Compact?

3. MORE PURITANS: BETTER RESULTS

Puritans Leave England

Charles I became king of England in 1625. Five years later King Charles and his newly appointed archbishop decided that all people must worship exactly as the king and the Church of England wished. This was a challenge to churches and Parliament, which did not want the king to have that much power. It was a complicated struggle, with religion and politics mixed.

The Puritan ministers were watched closely by agents of the king. They were given strict orders about when prayers would be said,

1) King Charles and his archbishop demanded that all people worship as the king and church decreed. 2) Agents of the king watched the Puritan ministers closely to see if they were following orders.

30. How were the Puritans pressured into leaving England?

List the advantages of the Puritans who arrived with John Winthrop. What advantages did they have over earlier settlers?

whether the Sabbath started on Saturday evening or Sunday morning, and whether Thursday was a market day or a day of prayer. The pressure on Puritans as a group and on individual Puritans was great—so great that they felt they had no choice but to leave England. This is what the king and the archbishop seemed to have in mind.

31. How did the Puritans organize to leave?

1) A group got a grant from King Charles to start a colony. 2) They took the charter with them. The settlers had the necessary skills for building a new community.

32. What marked the success of the movement?

1) A dozen settlements were built by 1632. 2) Some 10,000 Puritans went to Massachusetts during the first ten years of the colony.

A group of Puritans had a grant from King Charles to start a colony between the Charles and the Merrimack Rivers in present-day Massachusetts. These were people who had money and wanted to make more. But in 1630, they realized that they would have to leave England for America if they wanted to practice their religion. They took their charter from the king with them. By doing this, all the control for the colony would be in America.

The leader of this group of Puritans was John Winthrop. He gathered 1,000 Puritans to make the trip. They came in family groups, because they knew they could not go back to England. The company saw to it that the settlers had the necessary skills for building

This is a portrait of John Winthrop. He was the first governor of the Massachusetts Bay colony. What can you tell about Winthrop's qualities as a leader, using this portrait as evidence?

a whole new community. There were weavers, tailors, barrelmakers (coopers), animal breeders (husbandmen), and carpenters.

By 1632, there were a dozen Puritan settlements built in the Massachusetts Bay area. Unlike Jamestown, which had to depend on giving away land to get people to grow tobacco, the Massachusetts Bay Colony was able to get thousands of Puritans who wanted to come. Ten thousand Puritans went to Massachusetts within the first ten years of the colony. Like the earlier Pilgrims, they had a great sense of belonging.

Beliefs in Common

The Puritans were practical business people and hard workers. They were also religious. The beliefs they held before they left England were part of what made New England very different from Virginia. Massachusetts Bay was established with a mission for the whole world. To carry it out, the Puritans were to obey the rules of their church in every detail. The Puritans organized themselves around the church. Their officers of the church believed they were chosen, or ordained, by God to lead others. There were Ruling Elders, Elders, Pastors, and Teachers. The Elders made the rules. The Pastors gave advice. The Teachers explained the beliefs or truths to the rest of the people.

All citizens of the colonies had to go to church, although over half of them were not allowed to become church members. Only the settlers who were examined and found fit for church membership were permitted to be voting members of the church. Only men were chosen. The Puritans did not think of their way of choosing members as unequal or unfair. It was, they said, just recognizing that some people were better than others. The Puritans believed that God made people unequal.

The Value of Work

The Puritans believed that one of the ways a person could know whether she or he was among God's chosen, or elect, was to be a hard worker. The Puritans were certain that hard workers would be successful. Workers were needed so badly in the colonies that it often happened that anyone who learned his or her trade well and worked hard at it would do well.

Puritan life was one of hard work for adults and hard study for young people. It was important for young people to study hard, because God's chosen could not be lazy. For the Puritans there was a close connection between education, work, church membership, and being chosen by God. In 1636, the Puritans established Harvard College so that young men could become educated—especially if they were to be ministers.

33. How did the Puritans organize themselves?

1) They organized around the church. 2) Elders, Pastors, and Teachers were believed to be chosen by God to lead others. 3) Only worthy men were chosen to be church members. 4) The church members elected all church officers and voted on important questions.

34. Why did the Puritans consider work to be important?
1) Hard work could show that a person was one of God's chosen. 2) It would make an individual a success.
35. How did the Puritans regard poor people?
1) Jobs were plentiful and well paid; to be poor was a disgrace. 2) They passed laws to prevent poor people from having time to waste. 3) They only welcomed hard workers.

Anthropologists and historians say that every part of our lives is connected to all the other parts. Do you agree?

MAPS AND GLOBES: PICTURES OF THE WORLD

What Is a Map? What Is a Globe?

A map is flat and has length and width. We say it has two dimensions. A globe is a sphere like a ball. We use both maps and globes to stand for, or represent, the world.

A globe gives us a picture of the whole earth. It is more accurate than a map because it shows the earth as a sphere, which is what it is.

When the astronauts took pictures of the earth, they saw it as a ball floating in space. When you see a map you have to imagine that it is a flattened globe.

Accurate Maps

People who make maps, the *cartographers*, must keep everything they show on a map in proportion. This is called making maps to scale. Scale means that islands are smaller than continents, etc. For example, when you draw a person you draw the person to scale. You make the head smaller than the body, and the ears smaller than the head. Everything is reduced in size, but the size of each portion of the body is in proportion to all of the others. Maps are made to scale as is a globe. Scale is shown on the maps in this textbook in miles and kilometers.

Because they can't make a map 800 miles (1,280 kilometers) long to show the distance between New York and Chicago, cartographers draw eight half-inch lines, or four inches on the map. Every half-inch stands for 100 miles (160 kilometers). If you put a ruler on a map in this textbook and measure the distance between one point and the other, you will get a measurement on your ruler. Now look for the scale on the map. Find out how many inches equal a mile or kilometer. This will tell you the actual distance.

Maps and globes also tell us which places are near each other, and where they are located in relation to other places and spaces. Maps also are made with directions. There are four major directions, north, south, east, and west. The cartographer tells you where north is by drawing a directional indicator on the map. This is an arrow pointing north. See the map on page 124 for an example. If the north is the top, then south is at the bottom. The arrow usually points to the top of the map to show us where north is. Then to the right (where your right hand is) is the east; to the left (where your left hand is) is the west.

You need to know how to find both direction and distance to be able to locate a place on a map or a globe. It also helps if you know whether a place is near water or mountains or a river or some large feature that is easy to spot quickly.

Since Puritans believed that success and wealth were signs of being one of God's chosen, it followed that they also believed that the poor brought their poverty on themselves. The shortage of workers in America simply made this belief stronger. In a land where jobs were plentiful, to be poor was a disgrace. After all, workers in New England were paid 30 to 100 percent higher wages than the same jobs brought in England. The only way to help the poor was to keep them from having any spare time to waste. Laws were passed against bowling, shuffleboard, and drinking. Strangers to the New England communities were carefully watched. Only hard workers were welcome.

Puritan Government: Being Represented

Puritan church organization also controlled the government. Since the Puritans of Massachusetts Bay believed that the adult White males who were chosen to be church members were chosen by God, it is not surprising that the same people were the ones trusted to make the non-church, or *civil,* law. The church members chose their own representatives to what was called the General Court. They also elected the governor. What power they now had compared to their lives in Charles I's England! In Puritan America, even the local church congregations could elect their own ministers.

36. How did the Puritans govern themselves?

The church members chose their own representatives to the General Court and elected the governor.

The English idea of representation had been established in Virginia in the House of Burgesses over questions of tobacco and trade. This same idea appeared in Puritan Massachusetts as the right of the special people of God to run their colony in the best way they knew how. In both Virginia and Massachusetts, it was the English idea of the peoples' vote that had been extended to more groups of people than in England itself. More and more people had the opportunity to manage their lives and behave as they chose. Representative government was based on trust. When people were trusted with their own lives, they could choose whomever they wished to represent them.

37. What makes a representative government work?

It works when people trust those they choose to represent them.

Towns and Town Meetings

Towns spread fairly rapidly in Massachuetts Bay. And the idea of self-government spread with them. By 1640 it was a regular happening that all male householders in a town would come together to make decisions for the whole town. They acted as if they were a church congregation making decisions for the whole church group.

There was so much discussion at town meetings that special committees were set up to deal with special tasks, such as building

38. What was the purpose of the town meeting?

Not everyone was equal in the Puritan scheme. The chosen were trusted and free to decide on behalf of the others.

93

This is a restoration of a New England kitchen. Notice the pot and kettle over the fire and the metal plates and cups on the table. Why was the kitchen the center of home life?

1) The town meeting dealt with special tasks, such as building fences and roads and taking care of the poor. 2) The community acted together to take care of its problems.

39. How was the community governed?

A board of officers was chosen to watch over the activities of the community and give expert advice.

fences and roads and taking care of the poor. These were common worries that no one family could take care of by itself. It seemed natural to the people of Massachusetts that the community should act together to take care of community jobs and make community plans.

Usually a board of officers was chosen or selected to watch over the activities of the community. They were called selectmen and were highly thought of by people in the community. They were expected to become experts and give advice when the members of the town meeting disagreed.

One of the rules the selectmen required was that every male householder attend the town meetings. No one was allowed to walk out of a meeting without saying out loud that he was leaving. The selectmen had to give permission for him to leave or he had to pay a fine. Government by the people was not only valued in Massachusetts. It was required.

What Did Women Do?

Women were important in colonial New England. They were, however, not included in the church and government organization.

40. What was the importance of women to colonial life?

Should people be required to take part in our government?

Their place was within their families. Family life was perhaps the most important organization of all. In all of the colonies, most of what a family ate and wore was made at home. For example, all colonial women made their family's clothing from spinning yarn to dying, weaving, cutting, and final sewing. The coarse fabric cloth worn by the colonists was called *homespun.*

Getting through the winter was a family activity and a major problem. It was the women's responsibility to plan for all the needs of the family. The family was usually made up of three generations. Indentured servants and apprentices to the husband's work were also part of the household. Food and supplies had to be stored for all those people. This included butter, cheese, bread, candles, and soap. Wild herbs were collected and dried. The kitchen was the center of the home. That meant that women had to keep the fire going in the open fireplace as well as carry water from the town well.

Colonial women also gave health service to the community. They were the doctors and midwives who delivered the babies. They were also expected to help their husbands in their trades. Shoe-makers, tinsmiths, and operators of sawmills and flour mills often had their wives run the machines while they were out selling or delivering to customers. Women are known to have worked in slaughterhouses, print shops, cloth or dry goods stores, tobacco shops, drug shops, and general stores. They painted houses, made eyeglasses, made rope and remade old clothing. They were often the town undertakers.

Among the differences between men and women in daily economic life of a colonial community was the way they were trained. Boys were sent outside the home to become apprentices to become skilled in a trade. Women learned their skills in much less formal manner. They learned by helping at home. However, they were still expected to learn well and work hard.

In the 1640's the New England colonies decided to produce their own cloth. So much money was going to England for finished cloth or textiles, that the colonists decided to set up businesses of their own. Women were asked to set up spinning schools to teach other women and girls how to spin and weave. Then the government would tell each family how much cloth they were to produce at home. People who were better at it had to produce more. In addition to everything else she had to do, a woman might take a whole year to make a suit for her husband—from yarn to finished product.

1) They made cloth and sewed clothing for family and servants. 2) They made and stored supplies and food for the household. 3) They provided health services to the community. 4) They helped their husbands in their trades.

41. What jobs did women hold?

1) Women were the doctors and midwives. 2) They were tradespeople. 3) They were often undertakers.

This picture shows a Puritan woman and her daughter. The painting was done in the 1600's. Why would a family have its portrait painted?

Why do boys and girls have the same education in our society?

95

New England Settlements and Choices

The Plymouth and Massachusetts Bay colonies had built strong communities on strong beliefs. They had organized themselves into congregations. They held town meetings in the belief that God's chosen should make decisions together.

42. What did strong belief mean for the Puritan way of life?

It meant 1) doing good deeds and working hard, 2) teaching the world how to live better and more prosperous lives, 3) governing for the good of the whole community.

Their strong beliefs in doing good deeds and working hard made their early years much less difficult than those of the Virginia colony. In spite of New England's rocky soil, cold weather, and lack of rivers for navigation, the Puritans did well. Part of their success was due to the strength of the families that took care of the young, old, sick, and newcomers. Part of their success was also caused by the fact that there were many newcomers. One of the steady kinds of businesses in New England was selling land and supplies and livestock to new settlers. As long as the population grew, there was a constant supply of new customers.

By the time the English king thought that New Englanders had too much independence, it was too late to do anything about it. The colonies were too strong to be stopped. At least the king was pleased that he had been able to get the discontented out of the country and still keep them happy as trading partners with England. More trade would help keep England strong.

The New England colonies shared the wish for opportunity and wealth. They shared the wish to control the land and their lives. But they added something else to America. This was the church congregation's belief that decisions made by government should be made for the good of the whole community. They also added the belief that their community was supposed to teach the world how to live better and more prosperous lives.

Checking the facts

1. What did the Puritans think about equality, work, and government?
2. What was the role of the selectmen in the Puritan colonies of New England?
3. What did women do in Puritan New England?
4. What were the reasons for the success of the people of the New England colonies?

Notice the values that are beginning to show up in more than one settlement. Why do they show up in several places?

PUTTING IT ALL TOGETHER

UNDERSTANDING THE MAIN IDEAS

1. Why did the English come to America?
2. What did they find when they arrived?
3. What did they save from their life in England?
4. What changes in their lives did they have to make in America?
5. What did the settlers think was most important?

ACTIVITIES

1. John Smith organized the Jamestown settlers for work in the Virginia Colony. Imagine that you are trying to get a group of friends together to accomplish some goal. How can you organize their work so everyone achieves the goal? Write down your ideas in a short outline. Try them out on a group of friends or classmates. What happened? Why do you think having objectives is important?
2. Write a brief essay in which you imagine yourself to be Powhatan or Pocahontas. Describe your way of living, the values of your tribe, your first meeting with the English settlers and their beliefs and attitudes. How are they different from yours?
3. Do some research in your school or local library on the history and growing of tobacco. Where in the United States is it grown? How is it grown? What sort of conditions are important for tobacco to grow? Include your findings in a brief written report.
4. Do some research on the beginning of slavery in the United States. Using history books in your library, find out the names and locations of the African kingdoms where Black slaves came from. What kind of life did Blacks have in Africa before the rise of the slave trade? Describe some of the achievements of the civilizations of West Africa.

BOOKS TO READ

Daugherty, James, *Landing of the Pilgrims* (New York: Random House, Inc., 1968).

Jacobs, W. J., *William Bradford of Plymouth Colony* (New York: Watts Publishing Co., 1974).

Latham, Jean, *This Dear-Bought Land* (New York: Harper and Row, 1957).

Malloy, Anne, *The Years Before the Mayflower: The Pilgrims in Holland* (New York: Hastings House Publishing Co., 1972).

chapter 5
New Settlements, Other Choices

1624–1746

1. OTHER SETTLEMENTS
2. CIVIL WAR IN ENGLAND: A
   NEW STRENGTH IN THE
   COLONIES
3. OTHER EUROPEANS MAKE A
   DIFFERENCE

INTRODUCTION

Each English and European colony had its own style. For the most part other colonies did not have the pain of simply trying to survive that was so much a part of the choices made in Jamestown and Plymouth. And no other colony had both the sense of religious mission and close community of Massachusetts Bay.

In this chapter you will focus on the same questions asked in Chapter 4. In addition, think of the following questions:

1. What did the new colonists learn from the experience of others?
2. How were the later colonies affected by changes in England and Europe?
3. What choices were open to non-English settlers?

	1624	1634	1644	1649	
Who?	Dutch colonists	English Catholics	Roger Williams	Puritans	
What?	set up a colony	settle in North America	gets a charter from the king	gain control of the government	
Where?	in New York	in Maryland	for Rhode Island and Providence Plantation	in England	

1. OTHER SETTLEMENTS

The Dutch in America

The English were not the only ones to colonize North America. In 1624 the Dutch sent 30 families from the Netherlands or Holland to set up a colony in North America. They followed the river that Henry Hudson had explored in 1609 and named after himself. At the south end of the river they built New Amsterdam. Then they bought the island of Manhattan from the Indians in a treaty ceremony in 1625. And much farther up the river they built Fort Orange (Albany), named for the family of the ruling king of the Netherlands.

The Dutch colony of New Netherland was set up only for trade and making money. Some people from every nation came to live there. By 1644 some 18 different languages were spoken in New Netherland.

The main business for the men was fur trading. The women ran the farms, the businesses, and a hospital. The Dutch had wanted to set up large farms along the Hudson River. In 1629 they started a *patroon* system. This system was to guarantee settlement in New Netherland by giving huge grants of land to anyone who would bring over at least 50 other people. Five patroonships were created but most failed. The only really successful estate was Rensselaerswyck (ren-sah-LEER-wick), owned by a rich merchant. Despite their failure to settle the land, the Dutch control of the Hudson River did manage to keep the French from surrounding the English settlements. This turned out to be a great help to the English.

This is a Dutch woman from New Amsterdam. What does her clothing tell you about everyday life in the city of New Amsterdam?

Catholics in Maryland

The Puritans were not the only English people who caused trouble for King Charles I. The stiff rules for church organization and

	1649	1664	1675	1676	1732
	The Annapolis colonists	Soldiers sent by James, Duke of York	Metacon	Nathaniel Bacon	George Oglethorpe
	pass a Toleration Act	take over the Dutch colony	leads Indian troops against the colonists	leads a frontier rebellion	starts a debtor colony
	in Maryland	in New York	in New England	in Virginia	in Georgia

Notice how the English colonial policy created more variety in North America.

Calvert's colony in Maryland learned from Virginia.

behavior which the king and the leaders of the Church of England had tried against the Puritans also made life worse for the Roman Catholics. So the king invited the Catholics to colonize in the same way that he had invited the Puritans of Massachusetts Bay.

1. How was the new colony different from that of the Puritans of Massachusetts Bay?

1) The charter went to one person rather than to a church group. 2) It was near Virginia, enabling the settlers to learn from and trade with the Virginians.

The new colony was different, however, in several ways. In the first place, the charter for the Roman Catholic colony did not go to a church group like the Puritans, but to one man, George Calvert, Lord Baltimore. Calvert was well known and the king trusted him. He had been interested in colonies ever since he had been a shareholder of the London Company. He actually had owned a colony in Newfoundland.

Since Calvert was a Catholic, he wanted his new colony to be a safe place for members of his faith. When George Calvert died suddenly in 1632, the charter was given to his son Cecilius. It was a charter for one owner, or proprietor. The first group of Catholic settlers came to North America in 1634.

The new Catholic colony was north of Virginia and close enough for the new colonists to learn from the Virginians nearby. In fact they bought supplies from them and got advice on how to grow tobacco. Becoming a successful tobacco growing colony was not hard. The colony was named Maryland after the Queen of England, Henrietta Maria, who was a Catholic.

The Maryland Act of Toleration

2. What did freedom of religion mean in the colonies of the English?

1) In Maryland, any Christian who believed in the Father, the Son, and the Holy Ghost was free to worship as she or he pleased. 2) No one was tolerated who was not a Christian or had no religion at all.

Calvert knew from the beginning that there were not going to be enough Catholics to fill his colony. Protestant settlers came to live there and they soon outnumbered Catholics. They became the majority. Calvert wanted to protect the Catholic minority. In 1649 a law was passed promising protection, or toleration, to all Christians who believed in the Father, the Son, and the Holy Ghost.

Lord Calvert sent surveyors to find out where to put Baltimore. Why was surveying the land important?

This was called the Toleration Act. However, there was no toleration for anyone who was not a Christian.

Freedom of religion in the colonies did not mean that people were free to have no religion at all. People in the 1600's took religion very seriously. The problem was that there were more and more religions in America every year. Each one believed in its own idea of truth and its own ways of worshipping. Each religion also had its own organization. If people who were so different from each other wanted to be part of the same New World of farming and trade, they would have to leave each others' religions alone.

Differences Among the Puritans

The Puritans thought they had the only answer to the right and proper way to worship God and the right and proper way to run a church community. But some Puritans were in disagreement with each other about the methods to be used. Since Puritans took each rule so seriously, they found it hard to disagree and stay in the same community. Some of them moved out and took their followers with them. Several colonies in New England were founded that way.

Some Puritans Move Elsewhere: Connecticut

Those Puritans who thought it was wrong to keep non-members of the church from voting moved out of Massachusetts Bay. They formed three separate towns of Hartford, Windsor, and Wethersfield along the Connecticut River. These towns were combined into one colony under the leadership of Thomas Hooker. In 1639 the followers of Hooker drew up an agreement called the *Fundamental Orders.* It was a written plan of government, a *constitution.* It was the first written constitution in America.

The idea was new that people could get together and write down a detailed plan of governing that everyone agreed to support. It was an important step in bringing together people who needed to work together. Since the people in Connecticut could not know each other well or see each other daily, they needed some way to show that they could count on each other for protection. The Fundamental Orders of Connecticut which each town signed was a promise and a sign that each could be trusted to protect the others. It was also a reminder to each town to be trustworthy.

In England there had been no written constitutions. They had not been needed in a society which had fewer differences within it. Nor was the land an unfamiliar wilderness like America. Therefore, the written constitution of the Fundamental Orders was a sign that a connection existed between people that were different from each other in many ways.

3. Why were some New England colonies founded?

1) Some Puritans disagreed with each other on the proper way to worship God and to run a church community. 2) Some moved out and took their followers with them.

4. Why was there no written constitution in England?

It was not needed in English society, which had fewer differences within it than America had.

Recall the Mayflower Compact. Notice how the idea of agreement and trust among free citizens has grown.

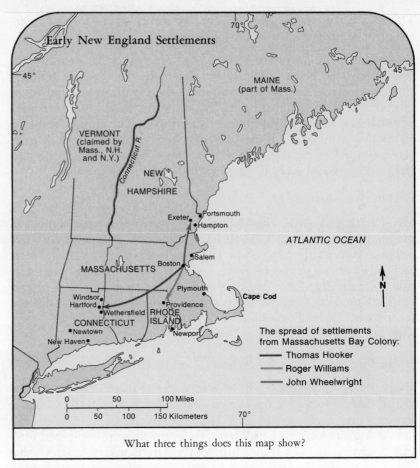

Early New England Settlements

MAINE
(part of Mass.)

VERMONT
(claimed by
Mass., N.H.
and N.Y.)

NEW
HAMPSHIRE

Exeter • Portsmouth
• Hampton

ATLANTIC OCEAN

Boston • Salem

MASSACHUSETTS

Windsor
Hartford
• Wethersfield

CONNECTICUT
Newtown
New Haven

Plymouth

Cape Cod

Providence

RHODE
ISLAND

Newport

N

The spread of settlements
from Massachusetts Bay Colony:
—— Thomas Hooker
—— Roger Williams
—— John Wheelwright

0   50   100 Miles
0   50   100   150 Kilometers

What three things does this map show?

The map shows 1) who settled Connecticut and New Hampshire, 2) the names of the settlements, and 3) the location of the three colonies.

Roger Williams and Rhode Island

5. What made Rhode Island different from other New England colonies?

1) Everyone in the colony had religious freedom. 2) There was a legal separation of church and state.

Roger Williams had a religious disagreement with Massachusetts Bay. Williams was a minister who argued that the Puritan Church in Massachusetts was not a part of the Church of England. He wanted to make the church separate from the government. He also wanted every congregation to speak for itself and govern itself. Williams said in public that the Indians should not have their land used or taken without agreement or payment. For these beliefs Williams was ordered to leave Massachusetts Bay in 1635. He had to run away to safety among the Narragansett Indians. Soon friends and supporters followed him and together they built a village called Providence. This became the center of present-day Rhode Island. In 1644 Roger Williams was able to get a charter from the king for Rhode Island and Providence Plantation. Everyone in the colony had religious freedom. There was absolute separation of church and state. It was the law.

What are some major arguments in the debate over separation of church and state?

ANNE HUTCHINSON

Born in Lincolnshire, England, Anne Hutchinson became one of the most controversial religious thinkers in colonial America. The daughter of a Puritan minister, she carefully studied the Bible. In fact, she learned every chapter by heart. She even got some formal education. In 1612 she married a merchant named William Hutchinson. They had 14 children. Although she and her family enjoyed a comfortable life in England, they settled in the Massachusetts Bay colony in 1634. They moved to follow their minister, John Cotton, whose ideas were very important to Hutchinson.

John Cotton became one of the most popular ministers in the Massachusetts Bay colony. Cotton disagreed with the popular opinion that those who attended church and prayed regularly would become saints. He wanted his congregation to lead decent lives and go to church and pray on a regular basis. Anne Hutchinson carried this belief one step further. She believed that saintly people could have direct, personal contact with God. They did not always need to communicate with God through a minister. A saintly person would only need to follow her or his own conscience.

Anne Hutchinson was very outspoken about these beliefs. She had many followers. They came to weekly religious talks. The meetings held at her home became very popular. At times as many as 60 people came. Soon the colony was divided over this controversial issue. Among Hutchinson's supporters were Henry Vane, a colonial leader, John Cotton, and the majority of Boston. She was opposed by many townspeople and the clergy. In 1638 Governor John Winthrop took her to the General Court.

Court records suggest the verdict was decided long before the trial ended. Anne Hutchinson defended herself. John Cotton and William Hutchinson refused to defend her. When she tried to explain her beliefs by describing divine revelations, she lost the case. In 1637 she was banished from the colony. In 1638 she was expelled from the church.

She and her family moved to Rhode Island. When her husband died, she moved to the Long Island wilderness where she would be able to work with the Native Americans. But in 1634, in what is now called Pelham Bay, New York, she and all but one of her children were killed by Indians.

Although Anne Hutchinson was persecuted for expressing her religious beliefs, she always will be remembered for her courage and her contribution to freedom of religious thought.

In this picture, Anne Hutchinson is preaching in her own home. What did she do that angered the leaders of Boston?

The king of England allowed the Rhode Island colonists to follow their beliefs. After all, the colonists stayed loyal to England. A new idea of how to keep so many differences alive in one place had its first try.

Checking the facts

1. For what reason was the Dutch colony of New Netherland set up?
2. Why did other colonies in New England develop?
3. What did the Fundamental Orders of Connecticut provide for?

2. CIVIL WAR IN ENGLAND: A NEW STRENGTH IN THE COLONIES

The great wave of Puritan immigrants that had come to America slowed down in 1642. No new colonies were started while a civil war was fought in England between the Puritans and King Charles I. The Puritans came to power in 1649. They set up a government with Oliver Cromwell as Lord Protector of the Commonwealth. The Puritans stayed in power in England until 1660.

The king expected loyalty. After that, people were free to disagree with each other and to run their own lives.

A Change in New England's Business

Without the newcomers from England to sell to, the New England colonists had to find other ways to make a living. The New England farmers found something else to do. They looked around to see what they had which could be used as resources to make money. All they saw were forests and the ocean. So they built ships out of lumber from the trees, went to sea in their ships, and fished. Ships carried lumber to far-off places, carried goods back to New England, and fished the waters of the North Atlantic.

New England ships carried and sold codfish, strips of wood, or staves for barrelmaking, wooden plates, horses, grain, pork, and salt beef. Tar, pitch, and rope for ship repairs (called naval stores) was also cargo. Often the traders sold the oak ship itself. The ships brought back sugar from the Caribbean Islands and iron, salt, wine, oranges, and grapes from Spain. The main idea behind this three-cornered or triangular trade was to sell both products and transportation to other traders.

Soon the New Englanders had a transatlantic trade. By the end of the 1600's the New Englanders were making sugar into rum. Boston, Massachusetts was the town which produced the most rum. Then the traders took the rum to Africa, where they traded it for slaves. Newport, Rhode Island, was the biggest port for slave ships. More than one triangle of trade developed.

New England Changes

The New England merchants who owned the ships became the wealthy and powerful people of New England by the end of the 1600's. Now they were ready to show the world both what to believe and how to make a world-wide success.

In New England, values in the 1700's did not change. People were still very religious. But they were attached to new ways of living. Being a tradesperson or a shop owner was thought to be not only important, but good. By the middle of the 1700's the children and grandchildren of the New England merchants became leaders in the army and in the legislature. The next step up was the college education of a child. They believed this to be progress. The best future of all was to have a child or grandchild married to the children or grandchildren of the ministers who founded Harvard College. Business, money, religion, and education combined in New England to become American Yankee values.

After the Civil War—More Colonies

Charles II became king of England in 1660, after the Puritans lost power. With the king restored to his proper place, trade began to

6. How did the New England colonists find other ways to make a living using the resources around them?

1) They built ships and traded codfish, wood, horses, grain and other products. 2) They participated in the triangular trade.

7. What became American Yankee values?

Business, money, religion, and education combined to become Yankee values.

What effect did the civil war have on the American colonies?

Harvard College was named after John Harvard, a Puritan teacher. Why was schooling important to the Puritans?

pick up. People in England began new business ventures in the American colonies that would be part of the transatlantic trading system.

Most of those who wanted to start colonies were rich people who wanted business investments. There were not great numbers of English people waiting to escape to North America. The time of religious warfare was over.

Carolina

The first big effort to colonize for money was made by eight nobles to whom the king gave large grants of land south of the Virginia colony. The nobles' plan was to make money by growing products that would sell in the triangular trade. They would not do the work themselves. They would give out to others the right to make unusual products, such as wine, silk, olives, and olive oil. Then the holders of the land grants, the proprietors, would take a percentage of the profits. Their plan was to attract people from the other colonies who wanted to make money. The colony they founded was called Carolina after Charles II.

Carolina was founded to make money. It was not a religious community. It was not to be a representative democracy. It was an almost *medieval system* in which lords were to get titles to land that could be handed down to their children. The people to be lords

8. How were the new settlers different from the original ones in New England?

They came for profit rather than religious freedom.

9. What was different about the colony known as Carolina?

1) It was founded to make money. 2) It was not meant to be a representative democracy. 3) It was a large area and attracted many kinds of people.

Why do some groups value education more than others?

The Carolinas had to be later colonies. They depended for settlers and trade on the earlier ones.

were not hard to find. But peasants were not available in England's new American colonies.

Carolina was a large area and it attracted different kinds of people. In 1670 English settlers came from Barbados in the Caribbean. In 1680 the port city of Charles Town was founded. Then a group of settlers from Virginia moved south. People who settled around Charles Town traded in furs and sold food to the West Indies. One of the major food stuffs sold was rice. In the north there were mostly poor farmers. By 1712, the two groups separated into North and South Carolina.

The English Against the Dutch

Trade across the Atlantic was becoming very profitable for the English. Their competitors were the Dutch who also had a cloth industry and a shipping fleet. One move made by the English during Oliver Cromwell's time was a law requiring English goods to be carried on English ships. This Navigation Act of 1651 meant a great deal to the builders and owners of English ships. Now they could keep out the Dutch competition.

When Charles II came to the throne of England, one of his aims was to pull the colonies and England into one huge trading system. New navigation acts were passed which required certain products to be sold only to English customers such as, tobacco, sugar, ginger, indigo, and tree bark from which dyes could be made. This was a great help to most of the colonies because it guaranteed more buyers and sellers. In addition, all goods brought into, or imported into, the English colonies had to be shipped from an English port. New Englanders built more ships to take advantage of this new situation. And the English navy promised to keep pirates away from the English shipping lanes. It was a help to the growing colonies to be part of England's empire, especially when the empire was growing stronger all the time.

The idea behind the Navigation Acts was called *mercantilism*. This idea held that building a profitable trade was important to a nation. If a nation could sell more goods to other nations than it bought from them, then that nation could build power. England could avoid buying goods from Spain, for example, if it could buy the same goods from its colonies in America. Trade, then, between America and England became carefully regulated. England used the Navigation Acts to achieve this goal.

Capturing New Amsterdam

In 1664 Charles II made a bold move to show the Dutch who had the most strength in the colonies. Charles gave the land between

10. How did the colonies benefit from the Navigation Acts?

1) They became part of one huge trading system. 2) Certain products were to be sold only to English customers, which guaranteed the colonists more buyers and sellers. 3) All goods brought into the English colonies had to be shipped from an English port, requiring colonists to build more ships. 4) The English promised to protect colonial ships from pirates.

11. What was meant by mercantilism?

1) It meant the building of power through a profitable trade, in which a nation sold more goods to other nations than it bought from them. 2) The colonial trade was regulated in order to ensure that the colonies traded only with England.

A reminder that the differences developing in North America were very much a part of the plan for a growing English empire.

107

Peter Stuyvesant was the last Dutch director-general of New Amsterdam. In 1664 he surrendered the city to the British.

Connecticut and Maryland to his brother James, Duke of York. This included the Dutch landholdings along the Hudson River and on Manhattan Island.

The English captured the settlement at New Amsterdam with only four ships. The Dutch governor, Peter Stuyvesant, gave up quickly. The English renamed the colony New York, after James who was Duke of York. In one easy step, the English had acquired a fine port city. And a group of people lived there who were already interested in the busy life of trading. As for the Dutch landholders along the Hudson River, James let them keep their property.

New Jersey

In 1664, the same year in which New York was established, the Duke of York gave part of his land grant to two of his friends, John, Lord Berkeley and Sir George Carteret. Berkeley and Carteret wanted more settlers to come to their colony, so they made the land cheap and the rules easy. People could worship as they pleased and would have a representative assembly. Settlers were glad to come and a good many of them were Puritans from other areas.

After ten years Berkeley sold his share of New Jersey to two Quakers. Quakers were a group of Separatists who believed that any individual could experience a divine Inner Light from God. This meant that Quakers did not believe that any person stood higher than anyone else in the eyes of God. For this belief, they had been persecuted in England. They were also a threat to the clergy in New England. In fact, the Puritans in Massachusetts Bay had killed six Quakers who refused either to obey Puritan rules of worship or to leave their colony. New Jersey welcomed the Quakers. For their part, the Quakers were glad to have a colony of their own in which they could guarantee everyone freedom of belief and trial by other citizens.

12. Why did Quakers settle in New Jersey?

People could worship as they pleased and have a representative assembly.

13. What ended Native American power in New England?

A chief, Metacom, was killed, and hundreds of his followers were sold as slaves to the West Indies.

The End of Indian Power in New England

In the late 1600's English power was growing everywhere in the colonies. The Native Americans had a hard time trying to hold onto any land at all, as the colonists moved westward, farm by farm. In New England the Indian chief was Metacom, called King Philip by the English. He was the son of Massasoit. In 1675 Metacom led a group of Wampanoags and Narragansetts in a battle against the English and their Indian allies. The war between Metacom and the English was called King Philip's War. It was a terrible war and lasted a year. There were now guns on both sides. And both were determined to win. Fifty-two of the 90 towns in New England were attacked by Indians. Over a dozen were de-

The more solid the English colonies became, the worse it was for the Native Americans.

stroyed and 600 people killed. The Puritans in Massachusetts under their leader, Reverend Increase Mather, now felt that part of their holy mission was to wipe out the Native Americans.

Metacom, or King Philip, was killed in the last battle of the war. His head was placed on a pole as a sign of victory and his wife and son were sold as slaves to the West Indies, as were hundreds of his followers. Native American power was over in New England.

Pennsylvania—A Different Picture

Differences were great among the English colonies. The British Empire had grown stronger since 1607 when Jamestown was established. Later colonies had strong trading partners in England and in Europe to begin with. But this did not mean that each colonial picture was alike. Each had its own style and its own history.

In 1674 New Jersey became a home for Quakers. In 1681 another Quaker colony was founded. The land was given as a grant to one man, William Penn. Penn's father had been an admiral in the English navy and loaned money to the king. The land in North

14. What did the king accomplish by giving a land grant to William Penn?

1) The land grant repaid the money Penn's father had loaned the king. 2) It helped to remove the troublesome Quakers from England.

Edward Hicks painted this picture in 1840. It shows Penn buying the land that became Pennsylvania. What kinds of items are Penn and his followers offering the Native Americans in trade?

The Native Americans of the northeast had lost out in a little more than 50 years. Notice the force of modern government, financing, and weapons.

America was the king's way of repaying the loan. It was to be called Pennsylvania (meaning Penn's woods) in honor of Penn's father.

Founding Pennsylvania was also England's way of dealing with troublesome Quakers. William Penn had become a Quaker. It was surprising that he had been able to stay on good terms with the king, because Quakers refused to pay taxes to the government or the church. They held different views from the rest of the society and the government. For example, they would not own slaves and they believed that men and women were equal. These were strange and upsetting beliefs to most English people. And the fact that the Quakers preached their beliefs on the street did not make life easier for them.

15. What did Penn do to guarantee a successful colony?

1) He sent a surveyor to map the area where the Schuylkill and the Delaware rivers meet. 2) He worked out the colonial plan, including the cities, streets, and public parks.

William Penn planned carefully to make his colony a safe place for Quakers. He sent a surveyor to America to map the area where the Schuylkill (SKY-kill) and the Delaware Rivers meet. Penn worked out every part of the colonial plan, including the cities, streets and the public parks. The city, called Philadelphia (meaning brotherly love), was laid out in a checkerboard or grid pattern. Streets that ran from north to south were given numbers. The ones that ran east and west were named for trees. Every quarter of the city had land reserved for everyone's use as a public park.

16. What else did Penn do to guarantee a successful colony?

1) He sent messages of friendship to the Indians, bought land from them, and wrote rules for their fair treatment. 2) He advertised in Europe for settlers, guaranteeing beautiful land, a free government, and freedom of worship.

Penn knew how important it was to have peaceful relations with the neighboring people. He sent word ahead of time to the Indians expressing his respect for them. Penn bought the land from the Indians and wrote out rules for settlers requiring the Indians to be treated fairly. Anyone who cheated an Indian was to be severely punished. Penn was also interested in making a profit. He advertised in Europe, telling people how beautiful and fertile the land was. He told them that people in Pennsylvania would have a free government and the freedom to worship. Freedom of religion for Penn, as for Roger Williams, meant separation of church and state.

17. Why did Pennsylvania become the wealthiest colony on the North American continent?

1) Many settlers came because Penn had planned his colony carefully. 2) The colony produced grain and shipped it abroad. 3) It had the best location, the most freedom, and the greatest variety of settlers.

Penn was interested in fair treatment for all. The laws were to be thought up by the governor and his council. The people's representative assembly could vote yes or no on these laws. This was called veto power. Because of these attractions people from many countries came to Pennsylvania. English and Germans came as well as Swedes and Finns who had been living near the Delaware River. Penn got an additional grant west of the Delaware River for a port. It later became the state of Delaware. Pennsylvania became the wealthiest colony in North America. By 1691 the city of Philadelphia had almost 4,000 settlers. In the entire English empire, Philadelphia was second in size only to London. Pennsylvania made its early wealth by producing grain—wheat, corn, and rye—and shipping it abroad, especially to the West Indies.

Neighbors often helped each other in colonial times. The people in this picture have gathered for a "scutching bee." They are paddling flax into linen thread. Why do you think people gathered to share the work?

Pennsylvania had the best planning, the best location, the greatest freedom of worship, separation of the church from the government, and the greatest variety of English and European settlers. It benefited from being the last of the colonies to be founded in the 1600's. It was the center or keystone of the English settlement on the east coast of North America.

Georgia

About 50 years after the founding of Pennsylvania, another colony was created. This one was started by James Oglethorpe and some friends in 1732. They wanted to set up a colony for poor people trapped in English prisons for not paying their debts. Because they could not get out of prison, these debtors could not work and pay back what they owed. Oglethorpe planned to pay for their voyage and give them 50 acres (20 hectares) of land when they arrived in America. Liquor and slaves were forbidden to encourage good habits and hard work.

Georgia also served another purpose. From the king's point of view, the colony would keep the Spanish and the Florida Indians away from the Carolinas. Oglethorpe hoped to get many poor people from England to settle in Georgia but few came. Instead people searching for land and wealth became colonists. The settlers found out quickly that the way colonists lived in South Carolina was not only to be envied, but copied. And soon they had large landholdings, rum, slaves, and a new government reporting to the king.

18. What happened to Oglethorpe's dream?

1) Few poor people came to settle in Georgia. 2) The settlers copied the South Carolina plan of large land holdings, rum, slaves, and a new government reporting to the king.

What was the importance of planning? What was the importance of luck?
In what ways was it better to be an early colony? In what ways was it better to be a later one?

111

What qualities did people need to live successfully in the colonies?

Which was more important to success within a colony—the values of the individual, opportunity, and control, or knowing the language and customs? Why?

Differences and Similarities in 1700

The English colonies had grown and prospered although the original founders of the earliest colonies had suffered greatly. The Indians lost out. But those people who joined the English colonies in eastern North America found a variety of ways of being successful. While the Spanish moved their civilization up the western coast, the English way was being set up in the east. English colonies had a variety of ways of being represented. Yet the values of the individual, opportunity, and control had become central parts of life in every colony.

Checking the facts

1. What was the triangular trade?
2. How did William Penn plan for a successful colony?
3. What was special about the Georgia colony?

Georgia was the last colony to be set up. The key at the bottom of the engraving tells the plan for the town. How is this town different from the plan for Jamestown on page 75?

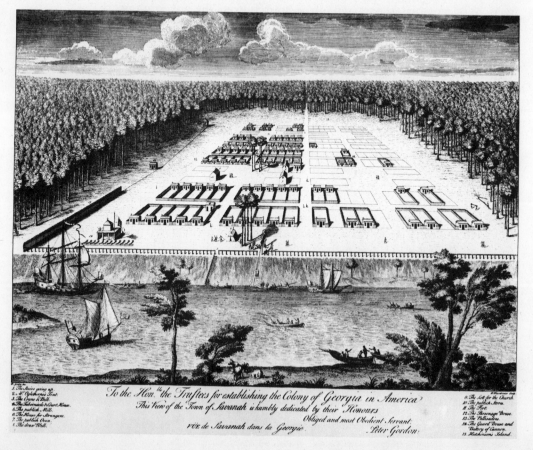

To the Hon.ble the Truftees for establishing the Colony of Georgia in America

This View of the Town of Savanah is humbly dedicated by their Honours

Obliged and most Obedient Servant

vüe de Savanah dans la Georgie.   Peter Gordon.

3. OTHER EUROPEANS MAKE A DIFFERENCE

By 1700 the North American continent held people from very different backgrounds and cultures. The English organized governments and ran the major trading businesses. Other people from Europe were filling up the land away from the coast. They brought their own way of life to these areas.

The Swedes and Huguenots

Swedes who settled in the Delaware River Valley developed the notched log cabin. Settlers moving west used this type of housing because it was cheap and easy to put together. The Huguenots were Protestant settlers from France. They were welcomed in South Carolina, Pennsylvania, New York, and Boston, because they worked in crafts and were highly skilled. Their work was valued by other settlers. The French tended to spread out and take on the characteristics of the English around them. In the south, the Huguenots even joined their church with the Anglican or Church of England. They did this because the Church of England was the most important church in the southern colonies.

19. What made the French Huguenots lose their identity as a group?

They tended to spread out and take on the characteristics of the English around them.

The Germans

There were many more Germans than French in the English colonies. By the middle of the 1700's, there were said to be 100,000 German-speaking people in Pennsylvania alone. They came in response to Penn's advertising which had been translated into German and distributed along the valley of the Rhine River. There had been a whole generation of warfare in central Europe during which time the farmland had been ruined. German farmers were glad to leave for America. In America the Germans did not spread out and try to melt into the English city life. They lived together and tried to create German communities.

20. What reasons brought the Germans to the English colonies?

1) Central European farmland had been ruined by a generation of warfare. 2) The Mennonites had broken away from the Lutheran Church in Germany. 3) The poor came as indentured servants.

Some Germans were members of a peace-loving group, the Mennonites, that broke away from the Lutheran Church. Mennonites came to join the Quakers who seemed to be much like themselves. The first group of Germans to come to America were led by Francis Daniel Pastorius. Their land grant, given by Penn in 1685, was just two miles (3.2 kilometers) northwest of Philadelphia. They called it Germantown. Pastorius brought hard-working people with him. There were doctors, bakers, seamstresses to name a few. They were followed by the Rittenhouse family who built the first paper mill in the colonies. The Germans planted fruit trees, cleared the land for farming, and showed everyone how small communities could produce almost everything they needed.

The Germans did not lose native characteristics. Many of them lived outside the cities. What is the connection between these two facts?

113

A later group of Germans came in the early 1700's and they were poor. They came as indentured servants and helped to provide the great profits in farming made by the large landowners. Within the ten years from 1737 to 1746, some 67 ships brought 15,000 Germans to Philadelphia alone. When their period of service was over, they moved even further west. This was the pattern in most colonies. Other Germans who came went to South Carolina and to Virginia. Wherever there was vacant land, the owner wanted Germans or German-speaking Swiss to settle on it because they worked so hard and so well.

The Moravians, a small group of settlers from Austria came first to Georgia. But because they were so afraid of attacks by the Spanish, they moved to Pennsylvania and set up the towns of Bethlehem, Nazareth, and Lititz. They set up missions to convert the Indians and church schools. Every British colony had Germans in it. But in Pennsylvania there were even counties where German was the chief language.

Jews

21. What privileges did the Jews enjoy in the English colonies?

They enjoyed the same privileges as the other inhabitants.

The Jews who came to the English colonies were mostly the descendants of the Spanish Jews that had been thrown out of Spain in 1492. They were called Sephardim. They had settled in Holland. The first group to come to America settled in New Amsterdam as early as 1654. There were Jews in every colony, but they were most welcome in Rhode Island which allowed freedom of worship. Newport, Rhode Island was the center for Jews in the northern colonies. They built a synagogue in 1763, which was paid for by contributions from Jews throughout the British colonies in America. Other important Jewish congregations were in Charleston, Philadelphia, and New York. Peter Kalm, a Swedish scientist who traveled in the colonies in the mid-1700's was surprised at the success of the Jews in America and of the freedom they had, compared to Jews in Europe. What surprised Kalm, because it was so unusual in Europe, was that in Kalm's words "Jews enjoy all the privileges common to the other inhabitants of this town and province."

The Scotch-Irish

22. What did the Scotch-Irish value?

1) They wanted to be able to worship as Presbyterians.
2) They wanted equal representation in the legislature.
3) They wanted formal education.

After 1700 a great number of people came to the English colonies from Scotland. The English had moved many Scots into northern Ireland in the 1600's in order to keep the Irish under control. But in the 1700's, English policy toward the Scots changed. The English wanted to keep the Scottish weavers from competing with the English ones. So the Scots began to leave for America. They also had a religious reason for leaving. The Scots living in northern Ireland were Protestant Presbyterians.

What qualities did the Scotch-Irish have in common with the English colonists?

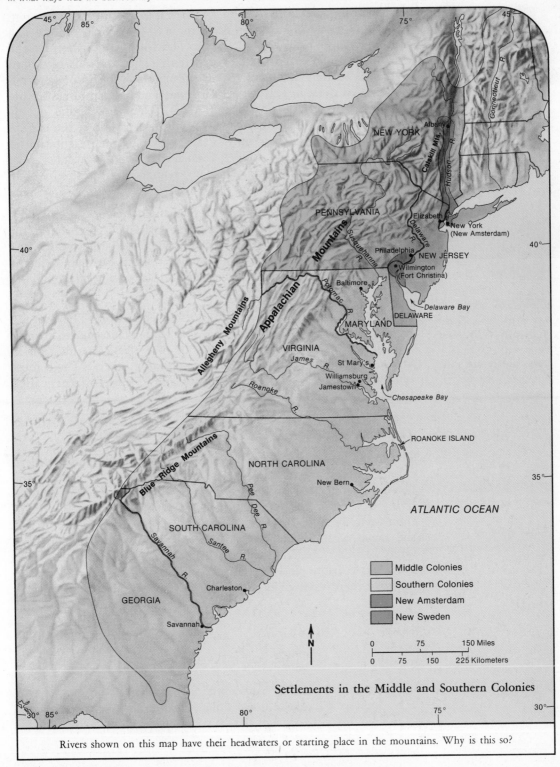

NEW YORK

Albany

Catskill Mts.

Hudson R.

Connecticut R.

PENNSYLVANIA

Mountains

Susquehanna R.

Elizabeth

Delaware R.

New York
(New Amsterdam)

Philadelphia

NEW JERSEY

Wilmington
(Fort Christina)

Appalachian

Allegheny Mountains

Potomac R.

Baltimore

Delaware Bay

DELAWARE

MARYLAND

VIRGINIA

James

St. Mary's

Roanoke R.

Williamsburg
Jamestown

Chesapeake Bay

ROANOKE ISLAND

NORTH CAROLINA

New Bern

ATLANTIC OCEAN

Blue Ridge Mountains

Pee Dee R.

SOUTH CAROLINA

Santee R.

Savannah R.

Charleston

GEORGIA

Savannah

	Middle Colonies
	Southern Colonies
	New Amsterdam
	New Sweden

N

| 0 | 75 | 150 Miles |
| 0 | 75 | 150 | 225 Kilometers |

Settlements in the Middle and Southern Colonies

Rivers shown on this map have their headwaters or starting place in the mountains. Why is this so?

Rainfall and snow in the mountain areas collect into water that becomes rivers and streams
that flow toward the sea.

This photograph shows a Jewish cemetery. It was established in the mid-1600's in New York City. Why did Jews settle in the American colonies?

And the English had tried to make them join the Anglican Church. Almost a quarter of a million Scots came to the colonies in the first 30 years of the 1700's. Because they had lived in northern Ireland they are often referred to as Scotch-Irish. They did not like New England. So they settled in the western back country of Pennsylvania, New Jersey, Maryland, Virginia, and the Carolinas. From there they fought against the Indians. They also spoke openly against the people who ran the colonial government in the eastern cities. They wanted their rights, especially equal representation in the legislature. The first Scotch-Irish settlers were weavers of wool and linen and furniture makers. They had their greatest success in trading with the Indians.

In 1707, the Scottish and English parliaments were united. From then on England was known as Great Britain. All through the 1700's business people from Scotland who had some wealth and learning came to America. They set up trading companies in the eastern cities. They became very successful, especially in the buying and selling of tobacco.

These Scots were a big force for formal education. They set up schools and sent out teachers who rode from plantation to plantation. They believed in the importance of a classical education in Greek and Latin for their ministers and for others. Their most famous college was the College of New Jersey, later called Princeton.

The Non-English Made a Difference

The other European newcomers helped the middle and southern colonies spread westward and become wealthy in the 1700's. The non-English settlers made the biggest difference in the ways of living of the middle colonies. In the South they developed a life of their own, because they were isolated by both the mountains and the slave-owning society of the coastal area. So, the colonies of Great Britain were not just English. The colonists made use of each other's inventions and customs. All colonists shared a desire to improve their lives.

Checking the facts

1. What made the French Huguenots different from other settlers?
2. Why did the Germans settle in the colonies?
3. Why was Rhode Island Colony a center for Jews?
4. What were some of the contributions of the Scotch-Irish?

PUTTING IT ALL TOGETHER

UNDERSTANDING THE MAIN IDEAS

1. What did these colonists learn from the experiences of earlier settlers?
2. How were the later colonies influenced by changes in England and Europe?
3. What choices were open to non-English settlers?

ACTIVITIES

1. Look at the maps in this chapter. Locate the places where settlements were started, for example, Providence, Rhode Island; Hartford, Connecticut; the Hudson River Valley; and Charlestown, South Carolina. What geographic features attracted settlers to each place? How did geography influence the way of life there? Include your comments in an oral presentation to the class. Try to use a wall map in your presentation.
2. Do a research report on the Moravians who settled in Pennsylvania. Focus your research on the city of Bethlehem, Pennsylvania. Why is it a center of Moravian culture? What kinds of traditions are still carried on from the early Moravians? Use your local or school library for information.
3. Work with three classmates for this activity. Find out about trading ships in colonial New England. Some items to research would be: the skills needed to build a ship, what was carried on board a ship (in terms of cargo and people), how long a voyage across the Atlantic Ocean might take, some of the dangers of being aboard a ship, how a person trained to be a sailor, etc. Divide the task of researching among your classmates. Give each one a specific time in which to complete his or her research. Findings could be incorporated into a series of short papers, or drawings or pictures of famous old ships. Package all of this material into a portfolio for presentation to your library or social studies resource center.

BOOKS TO READ

Baker, Betty, *A Stranger and Afraid* (New York: Macmillan, 1972).
Crouse, A., and B., *Peter Stuyvesant of Old New York* (New York: Random House, Inc., 1958).
O'Dell, Scott, *The King's Fifth* (Boston: Houghton Mifflin, 1966).
Vining, Elizabeth Gray, *Penn* (New York: Viking Press, 1938).

chapter 6
Colonies in a Strong Empire

1700–1763

1. THE REGIONS DEVELOP
   DIFFERENTLY: THE SOUTH
2. THE NORTH GROWS
   STRONGER
3. WAR FOR EMPIRE

INTRODUCTION

By the end of the 1600's, the future looked bright to the English. In the Glorious Revolution of 1688, they had replaced the Catholic king, James II, with two Protestants—James's daughter, Mary, and her husband, William of Orange, the ruler of Holland.

Parliament had asked William and Mary to come to the throne. Parliament had made them promise in a Bill of Rights that they would not tax the people without its consent. The English now had a very powerful legislature. The English in the colonies were as proud of Parliament's power as were the English at home.

Parliament used its new power to help the trading system. In the late 1600's, more navigation acts were passed to make sure that shippers had to pay taxes or customs duties when they set sail. To prevent cheating, colonial shipowners had to pay the tax before they left the port in the colonies.

	1705	1728	1735	1744	
Who?	British colonists	the British Army	John Peter Zenger	Eliza Lucas Pinckney	
What?	set up a slave code to keep the Blacks under control	builds Ft. Oswego to attract Indian fur traders away from Montreal	goes on trial and wins a battle for freedom of the press	sends indigo to England	
Where?	in the colony of Virginia	on Lake Ontario	in New York City	from her plantation in South Carolina	

By the time most of the English colonies had been founded, English people had more self-government than any other country in Europe.

A law was passed to make sure that the colonies only produced raw materials. All of the manufacturing would be done in England. In 1699, the Woolen Act was passed to make sure that finished woolen goods were not made in the colonies.

The English were also becoming more successful in fighting the Spanish and the French. This meant less trouble for the English colonists, because the other nations could do little to strengthen their colonies.

This chapter describes how the various people in the colonies in North America developed in the 1700's. As you read about these years, think about the following questions:

1. How did the colonies develop within the British Empire?
2. Which of the various differences among the English colonies grew stronger in the 1700's?
3. Which values did the colonists share? How did those values show up in the lives of the people?

1. THE REGIONS DEVELOP DIFFERENTLY: THE SOUTH

The colonial system that England practiced was successful in the colonies for 150 years. Except for the clothing manufacturers of New England and the owners of the iron works in Pennsylvania, most colonists liked sending to England for the goods they could afford. Ninety percent of the colonists in the middle of the 1700's were in farming. And agriculture was good business in an empire, when crop surpluses resulted in greater numbers of customers in the home country.

1. What was the South's relationship to the home country?

1) Crop surpluses were sent to England for sale. 2) Colonists bought goods they could afford from England.

1754	1756	1759	1762	1763
6 Nations of the Iroquois Confederacy and 6 British colonies	The French and English	General James Wolfe	France	England, Spain, and France
send delegates to the Albany Congress	declare war	defeats the French	gives land to Spain as payment for its friendship during the war with England	end the French and Indian War
Albany, New York	in North America	on the Plains of Abraham in Quebec	all land west of the Mississippi R. and New Orleans	by signing the Treaty of Paris

England's colonists were farmers and traders. Farming was slower and surer than looking for gold or trapping furs.

Notice the tie-in of family life to geography, social class, and the economy.

Fewer slaves or more slaves was not a moral question to slave owners. Owning slaves was guaranteed labor—even for those who felt it was wrong.

Growing Tobacco in the South

2. How was most of the tobacco grown?

It was grown on small family farms using four or five servants or slaves, who helped harvest the tobacco.

Tobacco continued to bring profits even when great amounts of tobacco caused the price to drop. Lower prices simply meant that the larger growers planted more. People used their profits to buy more land.

The wealthiest of the growers lived near the *tidewater* rivers. Ocean-going ships could sail right to their docks. These large farms were called plantations. They provided for the owner's family and the workers all the services that northerners found in towns. Plantations often had smokehouses for meat, a blacksmith shop, a laundry, and stables. But the small farmers actually grew over half of the tobacco crop. Most of Virginia and Maryland was farmed by people who did not have large farms. These farmers had no more than four or five servants or slaves. And they often worked along with the servants. Their services were sometimes provided by neighbors who went from farm to farm.

In the South, tobacco was almost all that was grown. There were some iron mines, some flour mills. Trees were cut for lumber and for barrel-making. Barrels were one of the few items made in the South. Almost every other manufactured item came from England.

The slave ships that made the middle passage packed in as many slaves as possible. Many of the slaves died during the trip. This drawing shows how many slaves could be held on the ship.

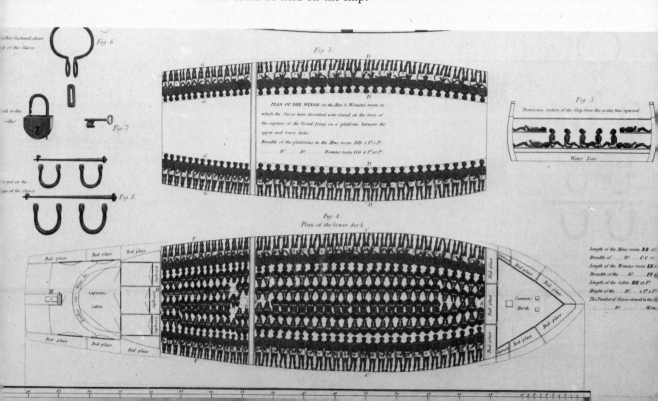

The System of Slavery

For the richer people who owned bigger farms, another way to keep profits coming in while prices dropped was to use cheaper labor. Slave labor was the cheapest labor available. Buying bigger farms and owning slaves became part of the way of life in the South. People thought they had to own slaves. How else could they continue to do well and prosper? Some people who owned slaves disapproved of it. But most accepted it because it meant the success of their farms. It was a system southerners and some northerners had come to depend on even though many hated it.

3. Why was the system of slavery used?

Cheap labor was needed to maintain profits when the price of tobacco dropped.

How did Black slaves respond to this way of life? In diaries and letters, people have described some of the ways Blacks behaved. To object to their situation and still survive, slaves often slowed down the job, pretended to be humble, or pretended to be happy. Some ran away or attacked their owners. But the slaves were locked into the system with the owners.

4. How did slaves protest against their owners?

1) They slowed down on their job. 2) They ran away. 3) They attacked their owners.

Slavery and the Law

Benjamin West, a New Englander, traveled to South Carolina in the 1700's. He described the hard labor of slaves in the fields and wrote how Black slaves were punished under the law. West wrote:

> "They have a way of trying Negroes for major crimes. The court consists of one justice and two freeholders, who order the Negro before them at any place, try him, and hang him up immediately. Few Negroes would be sentenced in this way were it not for some other reasons. When a Negro is hanged by the local justice, the government pays his master full value. If the master shoots his slave he loses the money he invested in him."

Life Under Slavery

All slaves were bound by the same laws. But not all of them lived the same way. They had different owners and they were assigned different tasks. For the slaves who lived in the cities and worked in the houses, life was often easier. Some slaves were treated fairly. Others were often whipped and beaten.

5. What brought so many slaves to the Carolinas?

The boom in rice production encouraged the importation of slaves there.

Life was probably hardest for the Blacks who had recently arrived from Africa. They were new to the cruelty of the system. They did not have the skills developed by those who had grown up in the southern colonies. But with the growth of farms in the South, more slaves were needed and more were brought from Africa. For example, with the boom in rice production came a rise in the number

ELIZA LUCAS PINCKNEY

In the 1670's, English colonists tried to grow indigo near Charleston. The dark blue dye produced by this plant was used by British cloth manufacturers. The colonists hoped to be able to supply England with it. But they were unable to grow the plant successfully. Seventy years later, a young woman succeeded where they had failed.

Eliza Lucas Pinckney was the oldest of four children. Her father, George Lucas, was a lieutenant colonel in the British army. He was stationed in the West Indies. In 1738 he moved his family to a plantation in South Carolina. A year later, he had to return to his military post in the West Indies. Seventeen-year-old Eliza was left in charge of the plantation where the family lived and two other plantations as well.

Occasionally, Eliza left the plantation for a taste of Charleston society. But her main interest was in the land. Encouraged by her father, she began to experiment with different kinds of crops. Indigo was one of them.

When Eliza began her experiments with indigo, she had no idea how to grow it. She didn't know what the proper season for sowing the plant was, nor did she know what the best soil was. But she kept trying. Finally, her efforts paid off. In 1744 six pounds of indigo from the Lucas plantation were sent to England. The English were quite enthusiastic. They said this indigo was better than that which they had been buying from the French. Eliza gave seeds from her indigo plants to other planters. Two years later, South Carolina planters were shipping almost 40,000 pounds (18,000 kilograms) of indigo to England. By 1747 the shipments had risen to almost 100,000 pounds (45,000 kilograms). Parliament voted to pay a special bounty on all indigo that came from the colonies. For the next three decades, right up until the Revolutionary War, indigo sales helped to keep the Carolina economy going.

As for Eliza, in the same year of her great success with the indigo plant, she married Charles Pinckney. After her marriage, she continued her experiments in agriculture. She brought silk worms to her husband's plantation, and she set up her own private silk factory. When her hustand died 14 years later, she took charge of the land he owned.

Eliza's last years were spent at her daughter's plantation. There, in 1791, she greeted President Washington as he journeyed through the South. When she died two years later, President Washington served as one of the pallbearers at her funeral.

of slaves in South Carolina. In 1700 there were 2,400 slaves. The number doubled by 1710, and tripled again by 1720. By 1740 there were 30,000 slaves in that one colony. The slaves outnumbered the Whites two to one.

Success in South Carolina

In addition to the boom in rice production, the other crop from which South Carolina planters made so much money was *indigo*—the plant which produced blue dye. It was introduced in the 1740's by Eliza Lucas Pinckney. Indigo was a successful second cash crop. It could be grown on high ground, and gathered in the seasons when rice did not require work. Between raising rice and indigo, slaves were kept busy all year round.

6. Why was indigo considered to be a second cash crop?

It could be grown on high ground and gathered in the seasons when rice did not require work.

The Colonies Become Specialized

Southern growers seldom met their customers. They sold their produce to agents, or *factors*. They were content with being paid at once by the factors. The factors decided when to sell for a higher price and when to hire New England ships to carry the produce to England.

7. What advantage was there to selling crops to factors?

1) Growers were paid immediately. 2) They did not have to get their produce to the markets, which left them time for tending their crops.

This engraving shows slaves working on an indigo plantation. The slaves are cutting, soaking, and drying indigo. Why was the sale of indigo important to the southern colonies?

Notice the importance of understanding the details of how a business works; for example, year-round use of land and labor.

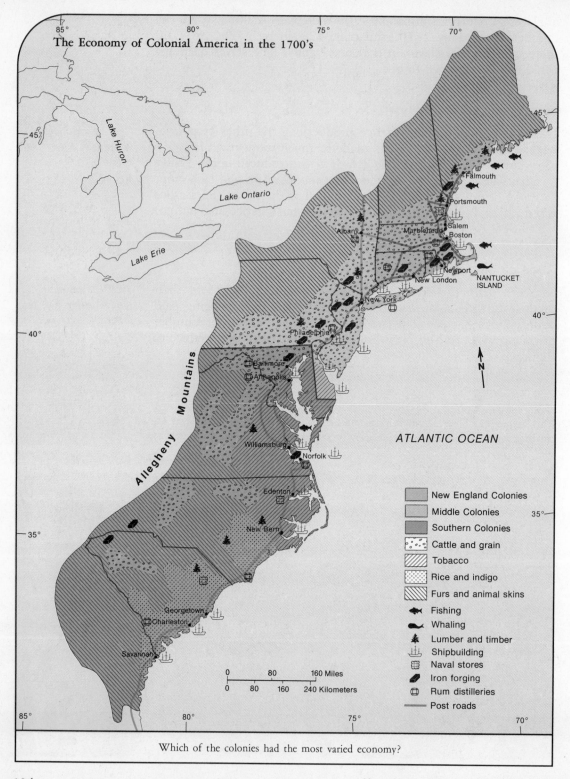

The Economy of Colonial America in the 1700's

Lake Huron

Lake Ontario

Lake Erie

Allegheny Mountains

Albany

Falmouth
Portsmouth
Marblehead
Salem
Boston
Newport
New London
New York
NANTUCKET ISLAND

Philadelphia

Baltimore
Annapolis

Williamsburg
Norfolk

Edenton

New Bern

ATLANTIC OCEAN

N

Georgetown
Charleston

Savannah

	New England Colonies
	Middle Colonies
	Southern Colonies
	Cattle and grain
	Tobacco
	Rice and indigo
	Furs and animal skins
Fishing	
Whaling	
Lumber and timber	
Shipbuilding	
Naval stores	
Iron forging	
Rum distilleries	
Post roads	

0 80 160 Miles
0 80 160 240 Kilometers

Which of the colonies had the most varied economy?

Massachusetts had the most varied economy.

The English colonies in North America became specialized very rapidly. The southerners were growers. As long as they made money and could buy what they wanted, the southern English colonists did not worry about being dependent on someone else for manufacturing or shipping.

Cities in the South

The South was mostly rural. Because of southern farming and trade with England, there was no reason for cities to grow other than the few along the coast. Most of the crops from the back country were sent by river to the Atlantic coast city of Charleston. Cities like Charleston served as storage places for crops before they were loaded on ships and sent to England, the Caribbean, or other colonies. They were also buying and selling points for rice, tobacco, indigo, and slaves. There was no reason for people living away from the coast to move to the cities. The services they needed were either supplied by the plantation or by local people who would serve as a *blacksmith* or *miller* to the families in their neighborhoods.

8. Why did most people live in the rural areas?

1) There was no reason for inland cities to develop in the South. 2) Most people produced farm products to be sold in England.
3) Services they needed were supplied, either by the plantation or by local people.

Farther up the coast geography controlled most of the growth of cities. In Maryland and Virginia there were so many rivers that it was hard to have either one system of transport or one port where ships could gather. Land travel between cities was even a problem. To travel the 120 miles (192 kilometers) from Williamsburg, Virginia, to Annapolis, Maryland, meant one dozen ferry rides over many rivers. Cities grew where services were needed to supply transportation.

9. Why was land travel often difficult?

There were many rivers, which had to be crossed by ferry.

Baltimore, Maryland became the storage place and shipping port for grain and flour. It competed with Philadelphia for the grain business. Those farmers who lived west of the Susquehanna River found travel to Baltimore easier than the long ride to Philadelphia. Maryland had built roads into its back country area. Pennsylvania's legislature was not interested in links west.

Although Philadelphia was not a southern city, it was part of the trading system of the upper South. Philadelphia had even greater storage places for grain than Baltimore. In addition, it had people who could lend money. There were also wealthy buyers who would pay a high price for grain. Philadelphia had merchants, manufacturing, and banking. Philadelphia was one of the reasons the southern colonies never developed very large cities.

10. Why was Philadelphia part of a trading system of the South?

1) Philadelphia had storage places for grain. 2) It had wealthy buyers for the grain, merchants, manufacturing, and banking.

Charleston, South Carolina, had the largest population of the southern cities. Located on two rivers and having a good harbor, it became a center for trade. But even so, its population of 10,000 in 1770 was small when compared with other colonial cities. The population changed from season to season. People would move to

Why was it important for cities to be close to farmland and waterways?

An Exact Prospect of CHARLESTOWN, the Metropolis of the Province of SOUTH CAROLINA

Charles Town, later called Charleston, was an important city in South Carolina. Why do you think so many ships are in the harbor?

Charleston in the summer to avoid the heat and the malaria of their swampy lands. The ocean breezes kept Charleston cool. The salt water prevented the mosquitoes from breeding. But when autumn came, people went back to their plantations.

The Southern Way

11. What did the rural way of life mean for the people?

1) Rural life meant that there were few town centers, schools, libraries, or hospitals. 2) The rich hired tutors or sent their children to England for education. Most others didn't learn to read and write. 3) Organized religion was not strong, as people had to travel great distances to churches. 4) The rich and powerful people on the coast developed close business and cultural ties to England, while those in the piedmont area did not.

The rural way in which most people in the South lived meant that there were few town centers, few schools, libraries, or hospitals. The College of William and Mary was founded in 1693. But there were almost no primary and secondary schools. The rich hired private tutors for their children or sent them to England to be educated. Most of the small farmers and the slaves never learned to read and write.

The Church of England was the main church. But it did not have much power because the people were so scattered over the countryside. The Presbyterians and Baptists who arrived in the 1700's built churches and traveled long distances to get to them. But these people were not the older and richer families of the east coast.

The rich and powerful people in the South developed close business and cultural ties to England. Great differences grew up between the back country, or *piedmont* area, and the east coast, or *tidewater* area. The South grew wealthy in its own special way. Slavery and cash crops made it possible. The South grew up within the empire's trading laws. These laws were best for its business. But the southern colonists, like northerners, also wanted the right to make their own local decisions.

Notice the tie-in between church, school, family life, trade, and geographical location.

Checking the facts

1. How did the mercantile system affect the growth of cities in the South?
2. Why were slaves needed in the South?
3. What was the South's specialization?

2. THE NORTH GROWS STRONGER

The New England and Middle colonies grew and became wealthier through several triangles of trade that had developed. (See map, page 128). At the beginning, the West Indies were the most important corner of the triangles. The West Indies were a natural market for the New England and Middle colonies. They had only one crop—sugar. They needed the dried fish, lumber, and cereals produced in the colonies. Since Europeans had all the barley, rye, and fish they could eat, the colonists could not sell their products to England. But Europe wanted sugar. So the ships from Boston, Salem, Newport, Portsmouth, and Philadelphia carried their fish, lumber, or cereals to the West Indies. There they exchanged their products for sugar and molasses, a by-product of the sugar refining process. The sugar went to England where it was traded for English goods. As for the molasses, it was made into rum by the distilleries of New England.

The ships also bought sugar from the French and Spanish islands and sold it to England. The British sugar islands objected. They convinced Parliament to pass the Molasses Act of 1733. The law placed a high tax on any sugar or molasses bought from anyone who was not British. The result of the tax was that the colonial shippers smuggled the French and Spanish sugar and molasses to England and to the distilleries in North America. From the colonist's point of view the law seemed too strict. Colonial officials did little to enforce it.

New England ships also were involved in the slave trade. Another triangle of trade took them to Africa with goods to be exchanged for slaves. From there they made the terrible middle passage to the West Indies or to the colonies on the mainland of North America. As many as two-thirds of the slaves might die on one of these trips. In the West Indies, the slaves were exchanged for more sugar and molasses.

The fishing industry grew in New England in the 1700's. Over 150 new fishing ships were built each year during this period.

12. How were the West Indies important in a triangle of trade?

1) The West Indies was a market for the goods of the New England and middle colonies. 2) The colonies traded dried fish, lumber, and cereals for sugar. 3) The sugar was then taken to England and traded for goods. 4) Molasses was brought to New England, where it was made into rum.

13. What resulted from the Molasses Act of 1733?

The colonial shippers smuggled the French and Spanish sugar and molasses to England and to the distilleries in North America.

14. How did Africa figure in the triangle of trade?

1) Africans bought colonial goods with slaves. 2) The slaves were exchanged in the West Indies for sugar and molasses.

To do business there have to be buyers and sellers and transportation. Distance was no barrier to traders. How did slavery fit into the southern way of life?

The length of the routes were approximately: the British colonies to Africa, 4,000 miles, 6,400 kilometers; Africa to the West Indies, 4,000 miles, 6,400 kilometers; the colonies to England, 3,000 miles, 4,800 kilometers; England to the West Indies, 4,250 miles, 6,800 kilometers; the colonies to the West Indies, 1,800 miles, 2,880 kilometers.

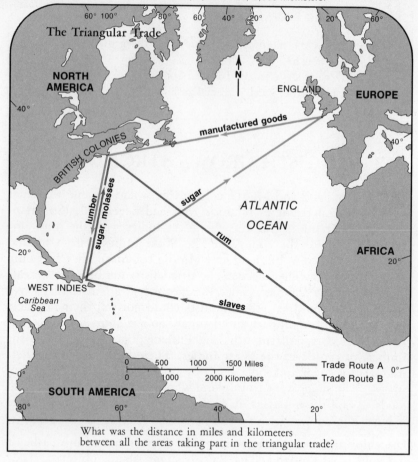

What was the distance in miles and kilometers between all the areas taking part in the triangular trade?

Whaling was a profitable business, especially for the people of Nantucket Island and Marblehead, Massachusetts.

15. How did the colonists get the news?

1) They read the newspapers. 2) They gathered in the taverns to talk.

The North had cities, and city life was different in each one. Newspapers were printed in cities and made it possible for people to share public events daily. In 1725 there were only five newspapers in the British colonies. By 1765 there were 25. Cities also had taverns where people could gather to talk. Cities were places of ideas and jobs for newcomers.

16. How did the towns make their laws?

1) Everyone who owned property could attend the town meetings. 2) At the meetings rules were passed by a majority vote.

Although the North had many cities, 95 percent of the colonists still lived on farms. Most towns held no more than 2,500 people. In northern colonies the newcomers became instant members of the community if they owned property. Because there were town meetings, the newcomers had a place to go and be heard. Since the meetings passed rules by majority vote, the support of new people was needed and looked for by others. The system of small towns in New England meant that there was a more democratic chance for people to speak up than there was in other American colonies.

The cities were the centers of change. Towns and cities made it possible to organize people for change.

Blacks in the North

Although northern society received many newcomers as landowners and voters, Blacks, both slave and free, were not a major part of life in the North. In New England they never numbered more than 3 percent of the population. Free Black colonists held a wide variety of jobs in the north. They were farmers, crafts workers, and tradespeople.

Black colonial women worked outside their homes as spinners, weavers, dressmakers, hat makers, hairdressers, and printers. Many worked in households as servants. Black women could, and did, hold any jobs that were open to women in colonial New England. Some Blacks who lived in the North went to school, although some towns refused to let Native Americans and Blacks be educated. Many Blacks became well known in the northern colonies. Benjamin Banneker was a Black astronomer, mathematician, and mechanical genius. He was born in Maryland in 1731. In 1791 he published an almanac of observations made from astronomy. Another Black, Lucy Terry became well known in the North. She was born in Africa in 1730 and grew up as a slave in Deerfield, Massachusetts. She wrote a poem that described the famous Deerfield Massacre. When she was 26, Lucy Terry married a Black freeman, who bought her freedom. When her son was refused admission to

17. What determined the life of northern Blacks?

1) Some towns permitted Blacks to go to school.
2) Some Black slaves were educated by their owners.
3) The life of a northern Black depended a great deal on personal connections to Whites in the community.

The people and the land have always had a close connection in America.

This painting shows a farming community in Pennsylvania. Can you tell anything about the farmers from the look of the land?

Phillis Wheatley was brought to the United States from Africa as a child. She learned to read and write and was finally freed. She was the first Black American to have a book of poems published.

Williams College, in Massachusetts, only because he was Black, Lucy Terry made a speech in his defense to the school officials. But even so, the college refused to take a Black student. Another famous Black colonial woman was Phillis Wheatley. She was sold in the slave market in Boston in 1759 to a merchant and his wife. Mrs. Wheatley, the master's wife, taught Phillis reading, writing, mathematics, astronomy, history, and Latin. Phillis Wheatley's first book of poems was published in England. But the rest of her life was a sad one. When her friend and mistress died, Phillis married a grocer. Her life was spent after that in poverty.

The life of a Black in the northern colonies tended to depend a great deal on personal connections to Whites in the community who cared about them.

Opinions About Slavery

By 1770, there were 700,000 Blacks in all the colonies out of a total population of 2½ million. This large number of Blacks caused some Whites to think that the slave trade should be stopped.

People opposed slavery for several reasons. The Quakers were opposed to slavery on religious grounds, although there were Quakers who owned slaves. White workers in the cities opposed slavery because of jobs. If people could own slaves, they argued, then free workers would have to work for very low wages in order to get any job. A third group opposed slavery because of the profits the slave trade brought to England.

Land and Social Class in New England

18. What social classes existed in New England?

According to one observer, there were gentlemen, freeholders, and "the lower classes," but no beggars.

By the middle of the 1700's there were strong differences in wealth and power among New Englanders. These differences were described in a book called *Animal Husbandry,* published in London

The Quakers came to the colonies from England. They were looking for religious freedom. They had many customs that were different from most colonists'. What makes this Quaker woman different from other colonial women?

in 1775. Each of the American social classes described in the book was shown to be living in a land of opportunity. American farmers were especially lucky:

> "The gentlemen . . . have more liberty . . . and pay what may be almost called no taxes . . . They also have the advantage of living in a country where their property is constantly on the increase value . . . "

A second class, the freeholders, were described as: "a very happy people; they enjoy many of the necessaries of life upon their own farms . . . but few of the luxuries of it."

The book also compared the American "lower classes" to lower classes elsewhere:

> "There is scarcely any part of the world in which they are better off. The price of labor is very high and the farm worker can buy his own land with money he saves."

The book was startled to find no beggars in New England, just poor newcomers working hard to move up to the next higher class.

An American View at Mid-Century

In the 50 years since the founding of Jamestown and Plymouth, the ideals of the American colonists had come true in different ways. Trade in the British Empire had grown stronger and the colonists had prospered.

The practical colonists now had time to look to the future. One of the people most able to do this was a man from Philadelphia. Benjamin Franklin was a printer, an inventor, an experimenter in science, and a publisher. In 1749, Franklin looked to a bright future in British America. He recommended that a school, or academy, be founded for the education of youth. His plan for the academy included a library, equipment for scientific experiments, and equipment for teaching about mechanics and building construction. Students were to be taught good handwriting, as well as reading, writing, and speaking proper English. Both classical history and the history of commerce would be taught. Franklin's plan left room for other details. Every student was to have good food and planned time for exercise. This academy was set up in 1751, and became the University of Pennsylvania forty years later.

Franklin had more plans for the 13 colonies. He founded the American Philosophical Society in 1744. It was to meet in Philadelphia, and bring together the best minds to share the latest ideas. The society exists today with this same purpose in mind.

Benjamin Franklin has been called an American genius. He was a scientist, diplomat, scholar, and inventor. He founded the Union Fire Company, as well.

What can you learn from studying about great individuals? What can you learn from studying about the not-so-great?

131

Many people shared Franklin's hopes for the future, although none were as full of plans as he. These were years of progress and excitement for the British colonies in America.

A Plan for Cooperation

19. Why did the British want the friendship of the Iroquois?

The Iroquois helped protect the British from the Hurons and other tribes who were helping the French.

20. Why was the Albany Plan of Union rejected?

The colonial assemblies did not see themselves as a group, apart from being part of the British Empire.

Growing wealth and hope for the future were part of colonial life in the mid-1700's. But fighting between the British and French along the St. Lawrence River, in the years from 1744 to 1748, was a concern to all the colonies. For their part the British worked to keep the friendship of the Iroquois Confederacy. The members of the confederacy protected the British from the Hurons and other tribes who were helping the French.

In 1754 a meeting was called in Albany, New York, to consider a treaty with the Iroquois. At that meeting, Benjamin Franklin proposed a plan for one general government for all the British colonies. In his plan, each colony would keep its own government. A president-general would be appointed and paid for by the king, and a grand council would be elected by the representative assemblies of each of the colonies. Colonies with bigger populations would be allowed more representatives. The grand council would pass laws and raise money for wars against Native Americans, settlement of new lands in the west, and defense of the colonies. Treaties with the Native Americans would be made by the new government on behalf of all the colonies. Franklin's plan was called the Albany Plan of Union.

The colonial assemblies did not see themselves as one group in 1754. In their view, each colony was a part of the British Empire. So they rejected Franklin's plan. Although it wasn't used, the Albany Plan of Union did show that someone was thinking about the colonies as one group.

Checking the facts

1. Why did so many settlers come to live in the New England colonies?
2. What views did the North hold regarding slavery?
3. How did some Blacks succeed in the North?
4. What had Americans accomplished by mid-century?
5. What was the purpose of the Albany Plan of Union?

3. WAR FOR EMPIRE

The only nation in the path of England's power in the world was France. For years Britain and France were rivals in Europe. Each tried to get other nations to join in alliances. They also competed for trade, colonies, and raw materials in India, the Caribbean, and North America.

War broke out again between Britain and France at the time that Franklin proposed his Albany Plan of Union.

The first battles occurred when English fur trappers moved west into territory which the French claimed. The French attacked these traders in western Pennsylvania. French forces built a string of forts south from Lake Erie. They were Fort Presque Isle (PRESK-eel), Fort Le Boeuf (leh-BUF), and Fort Venango (vuh-NANG-go). (See map, page 135.) The French were trying to build a wall of forts between the West and the growing English population.

Young Washington

France and Britain had legal claims to the western territory, home of many Native Americans. Champlain, Marquette, and La Salle had explored the rivers that drained the area and claimed it for France. Pennsylvania, Connecticut, and Virginia all had charters from English kings for the same land. Each charter stated that the land extended "west and northwest to the Pacific." The Lieutenant Governor of Virginia was particularly interested in the territory because he had stock in the Ohio trading company. In 1753 he sent out a young surveyor, George Washington, to warn the French that the property belonged to Virginia.

Washington had no experience in public life, and certainly none in dealing with foreigners. The French commander of Fort Le Boeuf told Washington that they planned to take over control of the entire Ohio River Valley. George Washington took this message back to Virginia.

Six months later, Washington was appointed lieutenant colonel, with 150 colonial soldiers. He was supposed to occupy that point at which the Allegheny and Monongahela Rivers met to form the Ohio River. This was just south of the French forts. Washington's orders were to stop the French from reaching the Ohio River. However, the French also knew the importance of that spot and had already built Fort Duquesne (due-KANE) there. The French also outnumbered Washington's troops four to one. Washington

21. Why did war break out between Britain and France in the continent of North America?

They were rivals for trade, colonies, and raw materials in India, the Caribbean, and North America.

22. Why did the French build a string of forts south of Lake Erie?

They were trying to build a wall of forts between the West and the growing English population.

23. How was Washington defeated?

1) The French outnumbered Washington's troops four to one. 2) Washington had to set up a post at a spot that was hard to defend. 3) He was surrounded and captured.

What can you tell about George Washington as a person from his early career?

The death of General Braddock in the French and Indian War was a setback for the British and the colonists.

This war captured the feelings of all the colonists. Why?

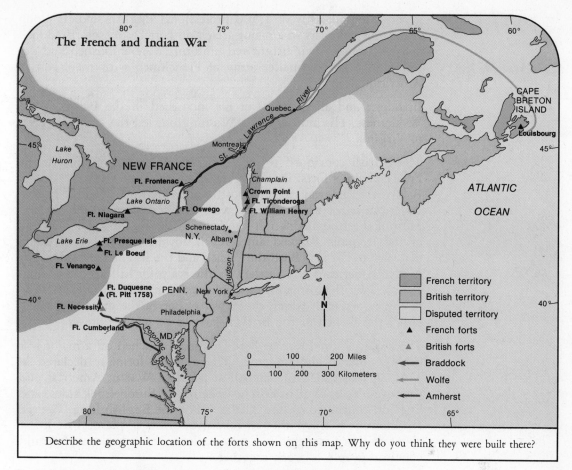

The French and Indian War

Lake Huron · NEW FRANCE · Ft. Frontenac · Lake Ontario · Ft. Oswego · Ft. Niagara · Lake Erie · Ft. Presque Isle · Ft. Le Boeuf · Ft. Venango · Ft. Duquesne (Ft. Pitt 1758) · PENN. · Ft. Necessity · Ft. Cumberland · MD. · Potomac · Quebec · St. Lawrence River · Montreal · L. Champlain · Crown Point · Ft. Ticonderoga · Ft. William Henry · Schenectady · N.Y. · Albany · Hudson R. · New York · Philadelphia · ATLANTIC OCEAN · CAPE BRETON ISLAND · Louisbourg

N

French territory
British territory
Disputed territory
▲ French forts
▲ British forts
← Braddock
← Wolfe
← Amherst

0   100   200 Miles
0   100   200   300 Kilometers

Describe the geographic location of the forts shown on this map. Why do you think they were built there?

The English forts were built to protect English colonists from Native American attack. They also protected the western territory of England and France.

was forced to set up his post at a spot which was hard to defend. It was such a poor location that he called it Fort Necessity. The French easily surrounded the fort and captured Washington and his men. Washington was forced to sign a confession that he had killed one of the French officers. He and his troops were then freed and sent back to Virginia.

This event was a defeat for the English, but a victory for the young Washington. He had fired the first shots at the French. And his name became known throughout the colonies.

Braddock and the British Army

The British had a hard time organizing in the early years of the war. It was difficult to coordinate both the colonists and the regular British army as one team in 1755. Edward Braddock, a British

24. How was Braddock defeated?

Why did the French and English fight each other in these locations?

He was ambushed by a smaller band of Frenchmen and Native Americans.

general, led an army of 1,500 professional English soldiers along with some colonists in a major attack on Fort Duquesne. Braddock and his men in their bright red uniforms were ambushed and defeated by a much smaller army of Frenchmen with their Native American allies.

Braddock and all but 500 of his men died in the Battle of the Wilderness. His aide, George Washington, led the survivors back to Virginia.

25. What was the importance of this war?

1) Each empire fought to wipe out the power of the other. 2) This war touched off a major war between France and England.

The British continued to lose battles at many key points in the French chain of forts: Fort Niagara, the gateway to the west, Crown Point, the gateway to the north, and Montreal. Those Native American tribes who had sided with the French fought ferociously. Most of the Iroquois nation fought with the English. The location of the Iroquois blocked any French advance from Fort Niagara eastward to the sea. Both the French and the English offered to pay Native Americans and settlers by the scalp for killing the enemy. It was easier than organizing a volunteer army. Both sides thought of this as a war in which the power of one of the great empires—either the French or the British—would be wiped out.

The defeat of Braddock at Fort Duquesne touched off a major war between France and England. The war was formally declared in 1756. It was called the French and Indian War in America, and the Seven Years War in Europe. The rest of Europe took sides, and England continued to lose battles. Then the English king, George II, allowed William Pitt to take over the war plans. Pitt knew about military strategy and was a great public speaker. He could convince people to work together.

Attacking The French in Canada

26. What was Pitt's strategy?

1) Pitt poured men and money into the fight against the French. 2) He chose brilliant young generals to lead the troops.

Pitt believed that North America was important to the future of England and Europe. So he poured men and money into the fight against the French. Pitt was a good judge of leaders and chose brilliant young generals to head the British troops. This strategy worked well and the English began to win battles. In 1758, Fort Duquesne was captured and renamed Fort Pitt. In 1759, Major General Jeffrey Amherst took Crown Point. And then the most brilliant of them all, James Wolfe, age 31, sailed up the St. Lawrence to attack Quebec.

27. What resulted from the battle of Quebec?

1) Both Wolfe and Montcalm died. 2) Quebec fell to the British. 3) After Montreal fell, the French gave control of Canada to the British.

Quebec was a difficult place to capture for two reasons. First it was protected on the riverfront by steep cliffs and hills. Second, it was defended by one of the finest French generals, Louis Montcalm. In September 1759, Wolfe and his army landed opposite the city, crossed the river, and managed to climb the steep cliffs during the night when the French could not see them. The next morning, the two armies faced each other on a grassy meadow known as the Plains of Abraham. They fired their muskets at each other and finally the French retreated. Quebec fell to the English in this important battle. Both Wolfe and Montcalm died in that fight. The next year, 1760, Montreal fell, and the French gave control of Canada to the British.

The Treaty of Paris

The war ended officially in 1763 after the French had lost battles in the West Indies and in India. The Treaty of Paris granted the British all of North America east of the Mississippi River except for New Orleans. That city went to Spain along with the territory west of the Mississippi River. This was to make up for the fact that Spain, as France's ally in the war, had been forced to give Florida to the English. (See map, page 138.)

The Treaty of Paris was a turning point in the history of North America. As a famous American historian, Francis Parkman, said, "Half the continent had changed hands at the scratch of a pen."

28. What were the conditions of the Treaty of Paris?

1) The British got North America east of the Mississippi River. 2) Spain got New Orleans and the territory west of the Mississippi River.

29. Why was the Treaty of Paris a turning point in the history of North America?

This picture shows the British victory at the battle of the Plains of Abraham. The British troops arrived by barge, climbed the cliffs, and fought the battle. What kind of leadership was needed to accomplish this victory?

What relationships do you see between this military success and the political power?

1) Huge amounts of territory changed hands. 2) The British were now free of their enemy, the French. 3) The colonists could look toward the new western lands.

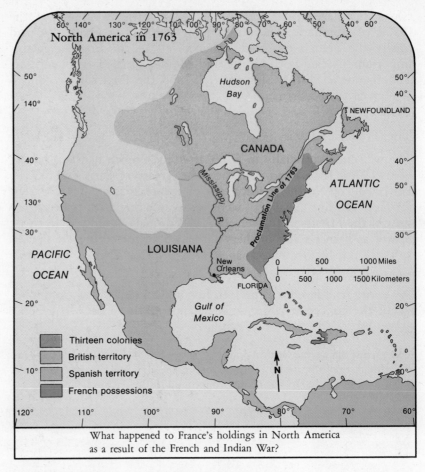

North America in 1763

Hudson Bay

NEWFOUNDLAND

CANADA

ATLANTIC OCEAN

Mississippi R.

Proclamation Line of 1763

PACIFIC OCEAN

LOUISIANA

New Orleans

FLORIDA

Gulf of Mexico

500   1000 Miles
0   500   1000   1500 Kilometers

Thirteen colonies
British territory
Spanish territory
French possessions

N

What happened to France's holdings in North America as a result of the French and Indian War?

The French lost almost all of their holdings in North America.

The British colonists in America went wild with joy. The continent as far as they knew it was free of their worst enemies. This meant they had more freedom to run their lives within the empire. Now there would be more opportunity and more prosperity. Control of the new western lands was the next goal colonists desired.

Checking the facts

1. Why did the English colonists want the land west of the Appalachians?
2. How did the French react to the actions of the colonists?
3. What were the results of the Treaty of Paris?
4. How did the British gain control of the North American continent?

What variety of people were in North America in 1763? Which were new since 1650? Which have disappeared since then?

PUTTING IT ALL TOGETHER

UNDERSTANDING THE MAIN IDEAS

1. How did the colonies develop economically within the British Empire?
2. Which of the various differences among the English colonies grew stronger in the 1700's?
3. Which values did the colonists share? How did those values show up in the lives of the people?

ACTIVITIES

1. Have your librarian at school or in your community help you with this activity. Read a detailed diary or first hand account of life on a southern plantation. What were the people concerned about each day? What seemed to make them happy? List your findings in a book report.
2. Read a detailed account of the conditions aboard a slave ship and on plantations. What did Blacks in the South do to survive? Ask your school or local librarian to help you find this information.
3. Write a short essay on the subject: Diaries as Historical Evidence. Why do diaries help historians? Why should historians be cautious of diaries? Answer these questions in your essay.
4. The poetry of Phillis Wheatley describes how it felt to be a slave in colonial times. Read her *Memoirs and Poems* for this information. Ask your school or local librarian to help you find Phillis Wheatley's poetry.
5. Read some accounts of the strategy of the Americans in the French and Indian War. What was special about their plans? How did they succeed? How did they fail? Present your findings in a brief oral report to your class.

BOOKS TO READ

Alter, Robert E., *Listen, The Drum* (New York: G. P. Putnam and Sons, 1970).

Gallman, Robert E., *Developing the American Colonies, 1607-1783* (Chicago: Scott, Foresman and Co., 1964).

Lawson, Don, *The Colonial Wars* (New York: Abelard-Schuman Ltd., 1972).

chapter 7
The Idea of Liberty

1763–1775

1. THE IDEA OF LIBERTY
   GROWS
2. SPEAKING OUT FOR LIBERTY

INTRODUCTION

While the colonists fought together against the French and the Native Americans, they slowly began to realize that they shared a common future. After the French and Indian War, the colonists became more aware of themselves as English people with rights. They began to speak of ways to keep all they had gained from England. The period from 1763 to 1787 brings to light the way in which something American rose out of the colonists' English background. Important questions to focus on in this period are:

1. What made the colonists think of themselves as separate from other English people?
2. How did the idea of liberty become so important?
3. What did liberty mean?
4. How did Americans organize to get liberty?

	1763	1765	1767	1769	
Who?	The British Government	Grenville and Parliament	John Dickinson	George Washington	
What?	issues the Proclamation stopping settlement	pass Stamp Act	writes to oppose the Townshend Act	introduces a resolution calling for only Virginia governor and legislature to be able to tax	
Where?	west of the colonies	to collect money from the colonies	in pamphlet distributed in the colonies	in House of Burgesses	

1. THE IDEA OF LIBERTY GROWS

The English victory over the French gave England more power. The British government now had to rule over a much larger area of the world. It had learned during the Seven Years' War that managing a world-wide empire took planning, money, and coordination. To govern North America properly, the British had to solve major problems. For one thing, the colonists had to be able to live in peace with the Native Americans.

Pontiac's War

The English knew that the Native Americans had been treated well by the French. They also knew that the British colonists in their rush to establish settlements and farms had not treated the Native Americans fairly. Fearing trouble, the British government decided that the Native Americans and the colonists should be separated. In the spring of 1763, the very time that this decision was being made, there was a highly organized, very successful uprising on the part of the Native Americans. The Ottawa chief, Pontiac, led an attack against the British fort at Detroit. At the same time other tribes attacked every British fort west of Niagara. All the British forts except Pitt and Detroit were destroyed within a few weeks. Then word of the uprising spread to Indian tribes in the east. Settlements were destroyed all along the frontier. By the end of the summer, over 2,000 settlers had been killed.

The Native Americans fought a kind of *guerrilla* warfare. They attacked in small groups and always by surprise. If the British counterattacked, the Native Americans would immediately pull back. As soon as the British relaxed, the Native Americans would attack again. Finally, however, the English managed to crush the uprising. They signed a peace treaty with Pontiac. But they were concerned about the future. How could they keep peace along a 1,500-mile-long (2,400 kilometers) frontier?

This engraving shows Pontiac in council with members of his tribe. Why did the Ottawa and other tribes attack the settlers?

1. How did the Native Americans organize their uprising?

1) They attacked every British fort west of Niagara at the same time. 2) They attacked in small groups and always by surprise. 3) If the British counterattacked, they pulled back. 4) When the British relaxed, they attacked again.

1770	1772	1773	1774	1775
Crispus Attucks	Sam Adams	Sons of Liberty	Representatives of the colonies	American minutemen and British regulars
first American killed fighting the British	issues a call for a Committee of Correspondence	dump British tea	meet at first Continental Congress	engage in battle
in Boston, Massachusetts	in Boston, Massachusetts	in Boston harbor	in Philadelphia, Pennsylvania	in Lexington and Concord

Pontiac did not know about the new English policy. How did his not knowing trigger new events and prevent peace?

The Proclamation of 1763

2. Why did the British government pass the Proclamation of 1763?

The British wanted to freeze English settlement at the frontier. 2) This order limited contact between colonists and Indians by requiring trading licenses.

In the fall of 1763, the British government issued an order or proclamation. No colonists were to settle west of the Appalachian Mountains. With this proclamation the government in England thought it could freeze the edge of English settlement at the frontier. Anyone who wanted to trade with Native Americans must have a license, and only a limited number of licenses would be given out. The frontier settlers, the colonial legislatures, and the fur traders were angry. They felt that the proclamation was unfair, and many of the colonists refused to accept it.

The Sugar Act

3. How did England and the colonists differ on the Sugar Act?

1) England wanted a greater share of the wealth of the colonies. 2) The colonists wanted Britain's protection but wanted to keep their local power.

The colonists had looked forward to going west. They had also believed the victory over France would be good for trade. But here they were disappointed. In 1764 Parliament passed the Sugar Act. This law made trading with the French West Indies more difficult. The tax or customs duty on French molasses was lowered, but the tax on sugar was raised. The Sugar Act was the first law ever passed by Parliament for the specific purpose of raising money from the colonies. As the colonies became wealthier, England wanted a greater share of their wealth. Was that not the whole purpose of the empire in the first place?

As for the colonists, they saw themselves as a part of the empire. They were glad to have Britain's protection and the boost to business that came under the Navigation Acts. But the colonists viewed the empire from their shore, plantation, or town. They did not think of the empire as a whole.

A Belief and a Reason

4. What did being free mean to the colonists?

It meant having a say in what power the government had over a person's life.

The educated colonists had read the writings of John Locke, a British philosopher. Locke said people were born with certain rights. He argued that government should never use its power to take away those rights. Locke used taking away a person's property as an example of the wrong use of power. Being free meant having a say in what power the government had over a person's life.

"Freedom," "liberty," and "consent of the governed" were new words added to the colonists' vocabulary. But some of the colonists wondered how a person could be free and be governed at the same time.

The Stamp Act

In 1765, while some of the colonists had begun to discuss rights, freedom, and government, the British Parliament passed a law that spotlighted the issues. The Chancellor of the Exchequer (the treasurer) Mr. Grenville, suggested a new kind of tax. The colonists could pay this tax by buying a stamp for every letter, will, contract, newspaper, pamphlet, pack of cards, and set of dice. Unlike customs duties the Stamp Act placed a tax on goods and services actually produced in the colonies. Grenville felt that such a tax would be less expensive to collect. He had found that it cost more to hire customs tax collectors in the colonies than the collectors actually took in. With the Stamp Act the British treasury hoped to make the colonies pay their share of the cost of running the empire.

To the colonists the Stamp Act was an annoyance. It seemed to them that the act was another attempt to control their lives from across the ocean. The colonists and their leaders did not see the Stamp Act merely as a way to collect taxes. They saw it as a loss of their freedom. They said it was illegal. According to the English system of government, free people elected their own representatives. Only these representatives had the right to tax the property of a free people. The Stamp Act, argued the colonists, was not passed by their representatives. It was not passed with their consent. Therefore, they did not have to obey it.

Each idea was linked to the next one in the colonists' argument. The phrase "taxation without representation" became their charge against Parliament. Parliament, they said, was too far away to represent them. Parliament represented the voters in Great Britain. Only their colonial legislatures could represent the colonists. The

5. How did the colonists react to the Stamp Act?

1) They declared that it was "taxation without representation." 2) They refused to buy the stamps.

THE REPEAL.___ or the Funeral Procession, of MISS AMERIC-STAMP.

This cartoon shows the repeal of the Stamp Act. It is a funeral procession for Miss Americ-Stamp.

Someone might make a flowchart on the board of how the feeling of freedom in 1764 led to the idea of liberty, of consent, and of "taxation without representation."

143

English argued that the colonists were represented by Parliament since Parliament was the symbol of representation for everyone. The colonists said this idea was nonsense. For them representation meant being able to vote for someone from their home area who knew what they wanted.

The colonists thought that there was a British plot against them. Therefore, they took whatever action they could to stop the Stamp Act. Crowds gathered to prevent the stamp distributors from taking office. The merchants and people who owned property had no intention of giving in to the stamp tax. They refused to buy the stamps.

This picture is entitled "Burning the Stamps." Why were the colonists especially angry about the Stamp Act?

The Stamp Act Congress

Now the colonies were ready to act together. Nine colonies sent representatives to a Stamp Act Congress in October, 1765. The Congress stated in a petition to the king and to Parliament that the colonies were not opposed to regulation of trade. What they were opposed to was taxation without representation.

They asked that the law be repealed, and warned that they were prepared to *boycott,* or refuse to buy, British goods until the act's repeal. One man in particular saw this moment in history as something special. John Adams of Massachusetts, then 34 years old, wrote: "The year 1765 has been the most remarkable year of my life . . . the Stamp Act, has raised and spread through the whole continent a spirit that will be recorded to our honor with all future generations. . . . The people even to the lowest ranks have become more concerned with their liberties, more interested in them and more determined to defend them than they were ever before known or had occasion to be. . . . So triumphant is the spirit of liberty everywhere. Such a union was never before known in America."

The boycott worked so well that British merchants were losing business. Now they wanted the Stamp Act cancelled, or repealed. In the spring of 1766 the act was repealed, but the colonists had not won their main point. Parliament also passed a law called the Declaratory Act that said Parliament had the right to make laws for the colonies "in all cases whatsoever." A new idea had grown in the colonists' minds. This was the idea that an unconstitutional law, or one that was not right according to custom, did not have to be obeyed. Over the years the colonists had become used to thinking of law based on written charters like theirs. They began to use the word "constitution" the way they had used the word "charter." And the word "constitution" came to have a new meaning. It became a symbol for rights and a symbol for correct, fair methods of governing.

More Taxes—More Problems

Other actions by the British government made the colonists think harder about the future of their freedom to act within the empire. The Quartering Act, passed in 1765, required colonists to help pay for the British soldiers who were stationed, or quartered, in the colonies. New York had more British soldiers quartered there than any other colony. When the New York legislative assembly refused to pay for them, the Governor, appointed by the King, ruled that the legislature could not meet!

In June of 1767 Parliament also put a tax on glass, lead, paints, paper, and tea imported to the colonies. The new taxes were part

6. What did the Stamp Act Congress accomplish?

The colonists boycotted British goods until the Stamp Act was repealed.

7. What other taxes did the British place on the colonists?

Explain in your own words the connection between liberty, union, and the constitution. Notice that "constitutional" means correct and fair as well as legal.

1) The Quartering Act of 1765 required the colonists to help pay for the British soldiers who were quartered in the colonies. 2) In 1767 Parliament passed the Townshend Acts (import duties on various British goods) to pay for British officials in the colonies. 3) The Townshend Acts also established new courts without juries to try merchants caught smuggling and to permit a search in the home of anyone suspected of not having paid duties.

of the Townshend Acts, named after the Chancellor of the Exchequer, Charles Townshend. These laws were a way of raising money in a hurry for the British treasury. But they had another purpose as well. The money was to be used to pay the salaries of British officials in the colonies. These salaries had previously been paid by the colonial assemblies. But the English wanted to change this practice because they felt it gave the assemblies too much power over their officials.

Another of the Townshend Acts set up boards of customs officials in the colonies, especially in Boston where the smuggling business was so successful. New courts without juries were established to try merchants caught smuggling. Colonial courts were given the power to issue *writs of assistance.* With these documents British officials could search the home of anyone they suspected of not having paid the customs duties.

Organized Opposition Grows

Many colonial merchants reacted to the Townshend Acts with *non-importation agreements.* They refused to buy British goods, and began to plan manufacturing in the colonies, so that in the future they would be less dependent on trade with England.

The Massachusetts legislature realized that the colonies must learn to work together in order to stop the English Parliament from clamping down on their freedom. A letter was drawn up by Sam Adams. It was known as a Circular Letter because it was sent to the other legislatures. This letter outlined plans for taking action against the new taxes.

In November of 1767, a Pennsylvanian named John Dickinson published a series of articles which he called *Letters from a Farmer in Pennsylvania to the Inhabitants of the British Colonies.* In these "letters," he said that a loyal colonist should oppose taxes which were levied for raising money and not for regulating trade. To stand up to Parliament's new laws was to stand for liberty. The articles were published in newspapers all over the colonies. Ten printings of them in pamphlet form appeared in the colonies and in Europe. The question of freedom of the colonies was now a public question.

8. Why was the Sons of Liberty formed?

They kept up the arguments against the English and tried to cause as much annoyance as possible.

Throughout the colonies men organized into groups called Sons of Liberty. They kept up the argument against the English and tried to cause as much annoyance as possible. Such men were Samuel Adams, cousin to John Adams, and John Hancock, a merchant who was also a well-known smuggler. These men tried to keep the argument in front of the public. Months and even years went by in this way with no improvement. Britain refused to change its policies.

Pamphlets, letters, and newspaper articles connected the educated people to each other from colony to colony. Is that important today?

The Boston Massacre

On March 5, 1770, the anger between the Sons of Liberty in Boston and the British soldiers stationed there broke out into open fighting. It began with a fist fight between a soldier and a worker. Then groups of people began to move around the town looking for trouble. One of these groups was headed by Crispus Attucks, a Black sailor known for his ability to fight. The crowd moved toward the customs house which was guarded by British soldiers. Someone threw a brick at one of the soldiers and knocked him to the ground. The soldier fired into the crowd, and so did the other soldiers. Five Boston citizens were killed. Crispus Attucks was one of them.

Sam Adams called the incident the "Boston Massacre." He hoped that the massacre would rouse the colonists to take action that would lead to a complete break with England. But there were people throughout the colonies who, although they were angry at

Crispus Attucks was the first American to die in a fight against the British.

The Boston Massacre was one of the first fights between the British army and the colonists. Why didn't the Boston Massacre cause the colonists to take further action?

the British, were more afraid than Sam Adams. They did not like mobs and riots. They hoped for a better solution.

New Trouble—Two Years Later

9. How did the colonists begin to work together?

These difficulties between Britain and its colonies wore away the close relationship which had grown up over 163 years. Since the end of the French and Indian War ten years before, the colonists had tried to patch up the ill feelings after each incident. Yet they

---

CRISPUS ATTUCKS

Compared to most men, Crispus Attucks was a giant. At a time when the average height was 5′5″ he stood tall at 6′2″. Crispus Attucks was a runaway slave. He had been born in nearby Framington, Massachusetts, the son of a Natick Indian and a Black woman. (The name Attucks or Ah-tuck comes from a Massachusetts Indian word for deer.) For 27 years Crispus Attucks had lived as a slave. Then in 1750 he had run away from his master, a man named Browne. Thereafter he lived the rough life of a sailor. In March of 1770, he had just come off a whaling ship, and was in Boston awaiting passage to South Carolina.

On the Boston docks Attucks fell in with other angry and discontented men. Some were slaves, some were manual workers, some were apprentices, and some were sailors like himself. They had little money, often went hungry, and were poorly clothed and sheltered. They blamed their troubles on the British. The British were taking work away from them by cracking down on Boston's profitable smuggling trade. The British had stationed soldiers in their city. These soldiers were offering to do work for pennies less a day. The time had come to strike out against the redcoats.

Before the evening of March 5 there had been clashes between the British soldiers and the citizens of Boston. But on that night the resentment on both sides boiled over into violence. A crowd of citizens and British soldiers exchanged angry words and threats in front of the customs house. They were joined by Attucks and his followers from the docks. Each of these men carried a heavy club. As Attucks pushed his way to the front of the crowd, he let out a blood-chilling yell. He threw himself into the line of soldiers, pushing a bayonet aside and swinging his club. In the confusion that followed, a gun went off, and then another gun. Attucks was hit in the chest by two lead balls. He fell bleeding onto the snow. When the "massacre" was over, Attucks was taken to a nearby tavern. There he died—among the first victims of the fight for independence.

What are the biographical facts of Crispus Attucks's life? What did he do for America?

were still determined to keep their freedom of action under the empire. They wanted to belong to the empire, but without being told what to do by the government in England.

Troubles began again in 1772 when a British ship, the *Gaspee,* was sent into Narragansett Bay to stop the smuggling. One night when the *Gaspee* ran aground, a mob boarded the ship, wounded the captain, and set fire to the ship. When the British government demanded information about those responsible—and offered huge rewards for the information—not one person in the colony admitted to knowing anything about the incident. The colonists were beginning to act together.

Committees of Correspondence

One way in which the colonists began to act together was through Committees of Correspondence. The idea was for people in each town to choose a committee to correspond, or exchange letters, with people in other towns and, eventually, with other colonies. This would give the colonists a chance to discuss important questions with each other. Committees of Correspondence were set up in six colonies. For the first time, the leaders in both the North and the South were actively in touch with each other. This network of communication would prove very important in the event of future trouble. That trouble was not long in coming.

In Massachusetts the governor announced that from then on he and the judges in the courts would be paid by the Crown instead of the colonial legislature. This would have caused the legislature to lose its greatest power—paying the salaries of the king's officers.

This announcement, combined with a banking failure in England, caused the colonists to change their thinking. They would have to take action against the British soon. Many merchants and all the planters were in debt. The failure of so many English banks meant that they could not borrow money when they needed it. These merchants and planters were also most powerful members of their colonial legislatures. Now they began to talk of "being free." That is, they wanted to be free from having to go to England to borrow money or get credit. Each person's idea of freedom of action was different. It depended a great deal on what people did for a living and what part of North America they lived in.

The Boston Tea Party

The colonists were slowly learning about their rights and the difficulty of doing business under the British Parliament. The protection of trade within a worldwide British Empire had been a

1) A mob burned the British ship *Gaspee*, sent to stop smuggling. 2) Not one person admitted to knowing anything about the incident.

10. Why were the Committees of Correspondence needed?

The colonists needed a chance to discuss important questions with each other through letters.

11. What further action of the British disturbed the colonists?

1) The governor of Massachusetts announced that he and the court judges would be paid by the Crown, causing the legislature to lose much of its power.
2) Bank failures in England prevented colonial merchants from borrowing money when they needed it.

12. Why did the Boston Tea Party occur?

Being free in the empire was beginning to shift to being free from the British government. Notice how slowly this happened.

149

The Boston Tea Party was organized by the Sons of Liberty. Why did the colonists disguise themselves as Native Americans?

1) Tea became cheaper because Parliament let the failing British East India Company sell its surplus tea to the colonies without having to pay British duties. 2) The Townshend Acts had been repealed, but the tax on tea remained. 3) This reminded the colonists that the British could tax them whenever they wished.

great help to colonists for generations. But by 1773, this protection was clearly becoming more trouble than it was worth.

In the spring of 1773 the price of tea went down, and the anger of the colonists went up. Tea became cheaper because Parliament had decided to let the failing British East India Company sell their surplus tea in the colonies without having to pay British duties. The East India Company would have all the trade, a *monopoly*. But the colonists were now aware of England's attempts to control them. The Townshend Acts had been repealed in 1770, but the hated tax on tea remained. It was a reminder that the British could tax the colonists whenever they wished. The colonists did not wish to be reminded of this fact.

Sam Adams and other Sons of Liberty found support for their ideas among the rest of the people of Boston. In the middle of the night on December 16, Adams and his group disguised themselves as Native Americans and boarded the tea ship *Dartmouth*. While they dumped the chests of tea into Boston Harbor, the crowds on shore cheered.

The Intolerable Acts

13. What did the colonists lose through the Intolerable Acts?

In England, Lord Frederick North was now head of the government. Under his leadership, Parliament now moved to control the

Why is it important for us to take a close look at each event and to notice the passage of time?

colonies. In 1774, it passed a series of laws known in the colonies as the Coercive or Intolerable Acts. One act closed the port of Boston to all trade until the tea was paid for. Another act said that court cases could be tried outside Massachusetts whenever the governor chose. A further act stated that town meetings could not be held without the previous written consent of the governor. Also, issues had to be approved by the governor in order to be discussed at the town meetings.

In addition to the Boston laws Parliament passed the Quebec Act. This act extended Canada's border south to the Ohio River. It was a plan that gave the people very little representation. It also granted religious toleration to Roman Catholics in Quebec. The colonists disliked the Quebec Act because several colonies had claims to the land now being given to Canada. Also, Protestant New Englanders were not happy with the idea of religious toleration for Roman Catholics.

If Parliament were trying to lose an empire, it could have done no better. The English did not understand the colonists' desire for more freedom to act within the empire. Instead they simply made more rules requiring absolute obedience. England had forgotten how over six generations the colonies had been allowed the freedom to become different from England and from each other.

They lost the right to 1) keep the port of Boston open to trade, 2) hold town meetings when they chose, 3) discuss what they pleased at town meetings, 4) claim the land now being given to Canada. 5) The governor of Massachusetts could order court cases tried elsewhere. 6) Colonists lost in their demands for freedom to act within the empire.

The First Continental Congress

The Intolerable Acts were mostly aimed at Massachusetts. But now the colonies were ready to act together. They had come to be united against England. Their view had changed a great deal since they turned down Franklin's plan in 1754. Now, twenty years later, representatives from all the colonies except Georgia decided to meet together and discuss what should be done. The First Continental Congress, as it was called, met in Philadelphia in September, 1774. The delegates included Patrick Henry and George Washington from Virginia, and Sam Adams and John Adams from the colony of Massachusetts.

An important shift in position came at this meeting. The colonists no longer would settle just for taxation with representation. Now they did not want England's Parliament to pass laws of any kind about life in the colonies. John Adams, the Boston lawyer, said that all people have the right to be represented in their own law-making body. Parliament was that body for people living in England and Scotland. But in the colonies the colonial legislatures were equal to Parliament. England could continue to set the rules of trade for the empire, only because trade was bigger than all of the parts of the empire and applied to everyone.

14. How did the colonists decide to take action together?

1) Delegates from all colonies except Georgia met at the First Continental Congress in Philadelphia in 1774. 2) They decided that England could only set rules of trade for the empire. 3) They decided not to obey the Intolerable Acts. 4) They signed a promise to take up arms if necessary. 5) They appointed a committee to supervise a boycott of all goods imported from England and a ban on goods exported to England. 6) The committee would operate in every colony and keep all the colonies in touch with each other.

John Adams, Gouverneur Morris, Alexander Hamilton, and Thomas Jefferson were the leaders of the Continental Congress. Why was this congress important?

The Continental Congress denounced the Intolerable Acts and said that the colonists would not obey them. It also criticized other British actions taken since 1763, and presented Parliament with a list of the rights of the colonists and of their colonial legislatures. Then the members of the Congress organized themselves to take the consequences. They signed a promise to take up arms if necessary. They also appointed a committee to supervise a boycott of all goods imported from England, and a ban on goods exported to England. The committee would operate in every colony and would keep all colonies in touch with one another.

John Adams said later that at that moment the "revolution was complete in the minds of the people." Something had happened to the thinking of the colonists. In the past, they had associated the idea of liberty with the representative system of England. Now that idea of liberty had become attached to a new feeling. They were Americans now.

Checking the facts

1. Why were the colonists having difficulty settling the West?
2. How was the English Parliament responsible for the development of American independence?
3. What decisions were made by the delegates at the First Continental Congress?

Notice the development of the idea of liberty and of the events.

The leadership helped people to organize around the idea of liberty.

Can you think of an idea today that has recently caused an organization to form?

2. SPEAKING OUT FOR LIBERTY

The First Continental Congress had set the terms for a continuing relationship with England. Now it was up to Parliament to decide whether or not to agree to the terms. There was a debate in Parliament over how much freedom the colonies should be allowed to have. The British statesman Edmund Burke warned that tightening control on the colonies would mean losing them. He said that the time had come to give them more freedom and thus keep their loyalty. But in January, 1775 Parliament voted 270 to 78 to punish the colonies instead. The people of Massachusetts were declared to be in open rebellion, and a law was passed restricting that colony's trade. At the same time a letter was sent to the general in charge of the British forces in the colonies. It said to use force if necessary to put down the rebellion.

It took four months for the letter authorizing the use of troops against the colonists to reach the British general in charge. General Gage had been part of Braddock's army in the terrible defeat in the French and Indian War. Now he was head of all the British armies in the North American colonies and governor of Massachusetts besides.

The Colonists Take Action

The timetable was speeding up for the colonists. During those four months they began to organize themselves for armed resistance to the British. In New England the Patriots, as the leaders of the opposition called themselves, formed volunteer armies, or *militias*. They took supplies of guns and ammunition from storage in the armory. With these guns they drilled right out in the open on the village greens. In the South, the governor of Virginia fled and asked all people who were loyal to Britain to follow him. He asked Blacks to fight for the British side. After the war they would have their freedom, he promised.

In Virginia, the leaders of the fight against Britain called a convention. There they heard one of the most fiery speakers of all time, Patrick Henry. He told them:

> "The war is actually begun! . . . Our brethren are already in the field! Why stand we here idle? Is life so dear, or peace so sweet, as to be purchased at the price of chains and slavery? Forbid it, Almighty God! I know not what course others may take; but as for me, give me liberty or give me death."

Patrick Henry knew that revolution, even for the right of liberty, had to be successful or the patriots would be jailed as rebels.

15. How did Parliament react to the decision of the First Continental Congress?

Parliament voted to punish the colonies. It restricted Massachusett's trade and authorized the use of force, if needed.

Patrick Henry is shown here with the words "Liberty or Death" around his head. Why were these famous words startling to many colonists?

Lexington and Concord

This painting by John Singleton Copley shows Paul Revere. What did Copley include in the painting? Why?

16. How did the minutemen fight the British?

1) The minutemen fought the British from a bridge near Concord. 2) They also attacked the British from behind trees as the British marched to Boston.

17. How did the colonists react to their early success?

Patrick Henry was right. War had begun, although it had not officially been declared. The fighting started in Massachusetts where the Patriots had armed the citizens, known as minutemen, to be ready for battle at any minute. On the evening of April 18, 1775, General Gage sent 700 of his best soldiers to seize the supplies of the minutemen at Concord. Concord was about 20 miles (32 kilometers) away from Boston, which gave the Patriots time to warn the minutemen that the British were on their way.

Paul Revere, a well-to-do silversmith, had arranged with friends to watch the British troop movements and signal from the tower of Boston's North Church. A signal of two lanterns meant the British were coming by sea up the Charles River. One lantern meant they were going to approach Concord by land. Revere spotted the two lanterns and rowed across the river. He first made sure that Sam Adams and John Hancock could get to safety. Adams and Hancock were the main targets for the British since they had caused trouble for years. The British hoped to capture them and have them tried in London as an example of what happened to disobedient British citizens.

The warning to Concord and to the town of Lexington was carried by Revere and two other riders, William Dawes and Dr. Samuel Prescott. The others, like Revere, were well-to-do members of the community. People of every class worked together that night.

The fighting started on Lexington Green where about 70 minutemen were faced with the large British force. The minutemen started to retreat when someone fired a shot. In the exchange of gunfire, eight of the minutemen died. The others got away safely.

The next encounter was at the North Bridge into Concord. The minutemen, from their position on the bridge, were able to hold back the redcoats. The British captured some guns but never found the main supply. Fourteen soldiers of the king's army were killed at Concord. As the British marched back to Boston, they found themselves attacked by militia all the way. April 19, 1775 was the first day of the American Revolution. One hundred Americans and 273 British soldiers were killed or wounded that day.

The Excitement and the War Spread

Men and women alike took to the streets in excitement over their success. There were members of the Daughters of Liberty marching along with the men. They were an active part of the petitions, the boycotts, and the letter writing. When one British sympathizer tried to stop a mass meeting of the Daughters, they grabbed him, took off his coat and shirt, covered him with molasses, and poured

Notice that the fight for liberty cut across classes and included men and women.

flour on him! It was everyone's fight. Working men and women took part with the wealthy merchants in Boston. In the South, the meetings were quieter, but women and men also participated together in making plans against the British.

The news of Lexington and Concord was heard in Vermont where a hot-tempered commander of a group of patriots took up the fight. Ethan Allen and his Green Mountain Boys attacked Fort Ticonderoga on Lake Champlain just weeks after the news about Massachusetts had arrived.

The Second Continental Congress

On May 10, 1775, the day Fort Ticonderoga fell, the colonial delegates to the Continental Congress met again. Like the delegates to the First Continental Congress these were a distinguished group of well-to-do leaders who were now ready to take the final steps against England. There were merchants, businessmen, and planters. Among them were John and Sam Adams from Massachusetts, Patrick Henry, Richard Henry Lee, Thomas Jefferson, and George Washington from Virginia. Washington came to the meetings in his army uniform.

Benjamin Franklin was also there, ready to assume leadership. He had been an agent for the colonies in London, and he knew the British well. The Boston merchant John Hancock was honored by being made President of the Congress. The members of Congress were people of power from every colony. They now knew each other and were ready to plan the fight against England together.

The immediate task was to save Massachusetts. The Congress made itself into an official organization with the right to make decisions. It created a Continental Army and sent George Washington to command it. Six companies of soldiers were started in Pennsylvania, Maryland, and Virginia.

The Congress also issued bills of credit that could be used for money throughout the colonies. Agreement was needed on this issue so that the colonies could buy and sell from each other. Also, the Continental Congress needed to purchase supplies for Washington and his army.

Breed's Hill

In June, 1775, before Washington took his command, the Americans in Boston moved to fortify Breed's Hill. They were trying to stop the British forces from occupying land outside the city. But before the Americans had a chance to finish building their fort, the British attacked. After three assaults the British were able to drive

1) They took to the streets, excited. 2) They held meetings and made plans. 3) Ethan Allen and his Green Mountain Boys attacked Fort Ticonderoga on Lake Champlain.

18. What happened at the Second Continental Congress?

This is a portrait of John Adams.

155

1) John Hancock was made president of the Congress. 2) It made itself an official organization with the right to make decisions. 3) It created a Continental army with George Washington as its commander. 4) It issued bills of credit, which could be used as money throughout the colonies.

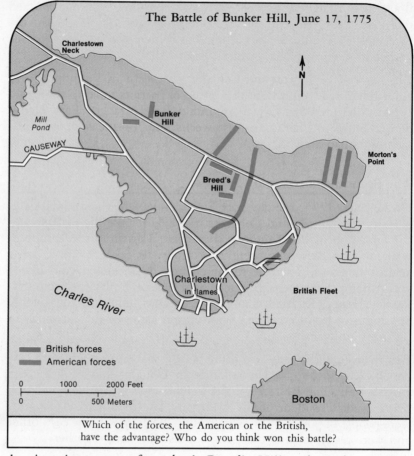

The Battle of Bunker Hill, June 17, 1775

Charlestown Neck

N

Mill Pond

Bunker Hill

CAUSEWAY

Morton's Point

Breed's Hill

Charlestown in flames

British Fleet

Charles River

British forces
American forces

0   1000   2000 Feet
0   500 Meters

Boston

Which of the forces, the American or the British, have the advantage? Who do you think won this battle?

the Americans away from both Breed's Hill and nearby Bunker Hill. The Americans had run out of ammunition. But the British lost almost 2,500 men in a few hours of fighting. The Americans lost 400 at the end of the battle.

No Peaceful Way Out

19. Why was the battle of Bunker Hill important to the American colonists?

1) It marked the end of any chance of coming to peaceful terms with the British. 2) The British navy was ordered to capture colonial ships at sea. 3) The king declared the colonies to be in open rebellion.

The battle of Bunker Hill, as it came to be called, marked the end of any chance of coming to peaceful terms with the British. George III removed General Gage and made Sir William Howe commander of the British troops. The navy was ordered to capture colonial ships at sea. The king declared the colonies to be in open rebellion.

The Continental Congress tried to put off a final declaration of separation from England. As wrong as England had been, there were a good many colonists who were not at all sure that they could win a war against the most powerful empire in the world. They were also not sure that they could govern themselves without a king.

While they debated how far to push their formal relationship with the British Empire, the Continental Congress carried on the war. They sent an army to Canada to attack the British there. Montreal was taken in November, 1775. But when a small army under Benedict Arnold tried to take Quebec on New Year's Eve, they failed. Arnold was wounded, and about half of the American troops were captured. With the arrival of fresh British troops, the Americans had to give up the idea of taking Canada.

Meanwhile, the army under Washington's command was enjoying better success. With cannons and guns brought all the way from Fort Ticonderoga, Washington was able to fortify the hills south of Boston. In March of 1776 the British left Boston for Nova Scotia in Canada in order to gather a larger army and better supplies.

The winter was also the time when the British hired German-speaking troops, known as Hessians, to fight against the colonies. Britain was afraid to send too many of its own soldiers to America. The island nation might not have enough protection from Europe. The news of the hired soldiers, or *mercenaries*, angered the colonists. After all, it was a war among English citizens over English rights.

20. What was the Continental army doing?

1) After the army's loss at Quebec, Americans had to give up the idea of taking Canada. 2) Washington was able to fortify the hills south of Boston, forcing the British to go to Nova Scotia for a larger army and better supplies. The British hired Hessians to fight the Americans.

"The Battle of Bunker Hill" by Jonathan Trumbull shows one of the first battles of the Revolution. At the top right is the smoke from the burning of Charlestown. Peter Salem is shown at the lower right with a rifle.

Recall that the colonists were fighting for rights and values, not for independence as a separate country.

Thomas Paine wrote *Common Sense*. Why did Americans read this book?

Common Sense

Event after event sharpened feelings among the colonists. One of the most important events of the winter of 1776 was the publication of a pamphlet which brilliantly attacked King George III himself. The pamphlet, entitled *Common Sense,* was written by a newcomer to the colonies. Thomas Paine, the author, was totally caught up in the revolutionary spirit. He was not only against the laws passed by Parliament. He took the argument a final step. No one ought to live under a king, he said. Monarchy, or rule by one person, was wrong because it took away the natural rights of every individual to be part of his or her own government. Tom Paine called the king a tyrant, and a number of colonists agreed with him. Some 150,000 copies of *Common Sense* were sold. This meant that almost every person in the colonies had either read the pamphlet or heard about it.

Month by month the Second Continental Congress increased the action against England and took greater charge of colonial business. Trade was begun with other nations. Privately-owned American ships, or *privateers*, were allowed to attack English ships on the high seas. And each colony was asked to make a constitution of its own and form a state government.

Declaring Independence

21. Why was it necessary to draft a written statement of American aims?

1) The rest of the world needed to know there was a new nation with which to trade and make new alliances. 2) The colonies needed to know in advance what they were agreeing to. 3) The statement could be sent throughout the colonies to help persuade people to support the long war that was ahead.

All of these actions showed that the colonists believed that there could be no liberty for them as part of the British Empire. They must make the break, and stand alone in the world. Their English values of liberty and representation finally led them to the decision to declare publicly the separation from Britain. Not everyone in the colonies agreed, however. In fact, about 10 to 15 percent of the colonists did not want separation. They were the Loyalists, or Tories. But the leaders of the Continental Congress represented a sizeable and powerful majority. They took the step, realizing that there would be disagreement among the colonists.

On June 7, 1776, Richard Henry Lee of Virginia put a resolution before the Congress. The resolution said that the colonies should become free and independent states. The Congress then chose a committee to draft a statement of American aims. The statement had to be written down because the rest of the world needed to know that there was a new nation with which to trade and make alliances. It had to be written down because there were so many differences among and within the colonies that they needed to know what they were agreeing to. In addition, the Declaration of

158

The Declaration was the last step in recognizing that a colony could not have the kind of freedom the Americans wanted.

Independence was needed in writing so that it could be sent everywhere throughout the colonies to help persuade people to support the long war that was most certainly ahead.

The youngest member of the Continental Congress was the man chosen to write the Declaration. Thomas Jefferson was 33 years old, but he was already known for his ability to write. The Declaration was his work, with some changes made by Benjamin Franklin and the Congress.

Jefferson explained that the Declaration was not an invention of new ideas. His goal was to "place before mankind the common sense of the subject, in terms so plain and firm as to command their assent (agreement)." And he did just that.

Reading the Declaration of Independence

When Jefferson said he wanted people to believe that declaring independence from Britain was "common sense," he showed that he was aiming the document at the mass of the people. It was not written in difficult language. But it was written to catch the readers at the very beginning and carry them through in a carefully planned step-by-step order. Even the sounds of the words and the rhythm of the sentences were written to carry the reader from point to point.

The Declaration has been called one of the greatest prose poems in the English language. It has even been set to music and sung without having to change one word. Be sure to read it aloud without stopping, both before and after you discuss it. Notice how many words are used to explain the Declaration. Then look for the kinds of words Jefferson used in creating it.

What was Jefferson's goal for the Declaration of Independence?

The Declaration of Independence

PREAMBLE

When, in the course of human events, it becomes necessary for one people to dissolve the political bonds which have connected them with another, and to assume, among the powers of the earth, the separate and equal station to which the laws of nature and of nature's God entitle them, a decent respect to the opinions of mankind requires that they should declare the causes which impel them to the separation.

22. The Americans and the English already are two peoples. They are separate and equal under the laws of nature and the laws of God. The separation is necessary. The public deserves to know the causes of separation.

23. *Some truths do not need to be proved: all people are created equal and have certain God-given rights.*

24. *The purpose of government is to protect the God-given rights of the individual.*

25. *When government harms the rights of people, the people may act to change or do away with that government.*

26. *People should not change their government for unimportant reasons. But when a government tries to be a dictatorship over a long period of time, people have the right to change it.*

27. *This is what has happened in these colonies. This is why they have no choice but to change their government.*

28. *These are the 27 actions that the king has taken against the colonists. [Not all were the king's fault, but each action damaged the rights of the colonists. The Americans no longer recognized Parliament as having any power outside Great Britain. Only the crown had legal power, and George III used that power to take away the rights of the colonists.]*

New Principles of Government

We hold these truths to be self-evident: that all men are created equal, that they are endowed by their Creator with certain unalienable rights, that among these are life, liberty, and the pursuit of happiness.

That, to secure these rights, governments are instituted among men, deriving their just powers from the consent of the governed;

That whenever any form of government becomes destructive of these ends, it is the right of the people to alter or to abolish it, and to institute new government, laying its foundation on such principles, and organizing its powers in such form, as to them shall seem most likely to effect their safety and happiness. Prudence, indeed, will dictate that governments long established should not be changed for light and transient causes; and accordingly all experience hath shown that mankind are more disposed to suffer while evils are sufferable, than to right themselves by abolishing the forms to which they are accustomed. But when a long train of abuses and usurpations, pursuing invariably the same object, evinces a design to reduce them under absolute despotism, it is their right, it is their duty, to throw off such government, and to provide new guards for their future security.

Reasons for Separation

Such has been the patient sufferance of these colonies; and such is now the necessity which constrains them to alter their former systems of government. The history of the present king of Great Britain is a history of repeated injuries and usurpations, all having in direct object the establishment of an absolute tyranny over these states. To prove this, let facts be submitted to a candid world.

He has refused his assent to laws the most wholesome and necessary for the public good.

He has forbidden his governors to pass laws of immediate and pressing importance unless suspended in their operation till his assent should be obtained; and when so suspended, he has utterly neglected to attend to them.

He has refused to pass other laws for the accommodation of large districts of people, unless those people would relinquish the right of representation in the legislature, a right inestimable to them, and formidable to tyrants only.

He has called together legislative bodies at places unusual, uncomfortable, and distant from the depository of their public records, for the sole purpose of fatiguing them into compliance with his measures.

He has dissolved representative houses repeatedly, for opposing, with manly firmness, his invasions on the rights of the people.

He has refused, for a long time after such dissolutions, to cause others to be elected; whereby the legislative powers incapable of annihilation, have returned to the people at large for their exercise; the state remaining, in the mean time, exposed to all the dangers of invasion from without and convulsions within.

He has endeavored to prevent the population of these states; for that purpose obstructing the laws of naturalization of foreigners, refusing to pass others to encourage their migration hither, and raising the conditions of new appropriations of lands.

He has obstructed the administration of justice, by refusing his assent to laws for establishing judiciary powers.

He has made judges dependent on his will alone for the tenure of their offices, and the amount and payment of their salaries.

He was erected a multitude of new offices, and sent hither swarms of officers to harass our people and eat out their substance.

He has kept among us, in times of peace, standing armies, without the consent of our legislature.

He has affected to render the military independent of, and superior to, the civil power.

He has combined with others to subject us to a jurisdiction foreign to our constitution and unacknowledged by our laws, giving his assent to their acts of pretended legislation:

For quartering large bodies of armed troops among us;

For protecting them, by a mock trial, from punishment for any murders which they should commit on the inhabitants of these states;

For cutting off our trade with all parts of the world;

For imposing taxes on us without our consent;

For depriving us, in many cases, of the benefits of trial by jury;

For transporting us beyond seas, to be tried for pretended offenses;

For abolishing the free system of English laws in a neighboring province, establishing therein an arbitrary government, and enlarging its boundaries, so as to render it at once an example and fit instrument for introducing the same absolute rule into these colonies;

For taking away our charters, abolishing our most valuable laws, and altering, fundamentally, the forms of our governments;

For suspending our own legislatures, and declaring themselves invested with power to legislate for us in all cases whatsoever.

He has abdicated government here, by declaring us out of his protection and waging war against us.

He has plundered our seas, ravaged our coasts, burned our towns, and destroyed the lives of our people.

He is at this time transporting large armies of foreign mercenaries to complete the works of death, desolation, and tyranny already begun with circumstances of cruelty and perfidy scarcely paralleled in the most barbarous ages, and totally unworthy of the head of a civilized nation.

He has constrained our fellow-citizens, taken captive on the high seas, to bear arms against their country, to become the executioners of their friends and brethren, or to fall themselves by their hands.

He has excited domestic insurrections among us, and has endeavored to bring on the inhabitants of our frontiers the merciless Indian savages, whose known rule of warfare is an undistinguished destruction of all ages, sexes, and conditions.

In every stage of these oppressions we have petitioned for redress in the most humble terms; our repeated petitions have been answered only by repeated injury. A prince whose character is thus marked by every act which may define a tyrant is unfit to be the ruler of a free people.

Nor have we been wanting in attention to our British brethren. We have warned them, from time to time, of attempts by their legislature to extend an unwarrantable jurisdiction over us. We have reminded them of the circumstances of our emigration and settlement here. We have appealed to their native justice and magnanimity; and we have conjured them, by the ties of our common kindred, to disavow these usurpations, which would inevitably interrupt our connections and correspondence. They, too, have been deaf to the voice of justice and of consanguinity. We must, therefore, acquiesce in the necessity which denounces our separation, and hold them, as we hold the rest of mankind, enemies in war, in peace, friends.

A Formal Declaration of War

We, therefore, the representatives of the United States of America, in General Congress assembled, appealing to the Supreme Judge of the world for the rectitude of our intentions, do, in the name and by authority of the good people of these colonies, solemnly publish and declare, that these united colonies are, and of right ought to be, free and independent states; that they are absolved from all allegiance to the British crown, and that all political connection between them and the state of Great Britain is, and ought to be, totally dissolved; and that, as free and independent states, they have full power to levy war, conclude peace, contract alliances, establish commerce, and to do all other acts and things which independent states may of a right do. And, for the support of this declaration, with a firm reliance on the protection of Divine Providence, we mutually pledge to each other our lives, our fortunes, and our sacred honor.

Is there any wonder that people throughout the world who wanted freedom have turned to the Declaration of Independence? Americans still use the beginning paragraphs as a standard by which to measure the actions of their governments and themselves. Notice how many of the ideas had arrived with the European settlers. Notice how many were part of the British past.

Independence was declared on July 2, and the Declaration of Independence in its final form was adopted on July 4, 1776. It was then read throughout the colonies. Jefferson had created a work of art and a work of spirit, as well as a work of persuasion. Abigail

This painting done in 1785 by Robert Edge Pine shows the signing of the Declaration of Independence. Benjamin Franklin is seated in the center. He joked at the meeting, "We must indeed all hang together, or most assuredly we shall hang separately."

In July 1776, Americans in New York pulled down this statue of George III. They melted the statue and used the metal for bullets.

Adams, wife of John Adams, wrote to her husband in Philadelphia about the celebration in Boston:

" . . . I went with the multitude into King Street to hear the Proclamation for Independence read and proclaimed. . . . The troops appeared under arms, and all the inhabitants assembled there . . . when Colonel Crafts read from the balcony of the State House the proclamation. Great attention was given to every word. As soon as he ended, the cry from the balcony was, 'God save our American States,' and then three cheers rent the air. The bells rang, the privateers fired, the forts and batteries, the cannon were discharged, the platoons followed, and every face appeared joyful. . . . After dinner, the King's Arms were taken down from the State House, and every vestige of him from every place in which it appeared, and burnt in King Street. Thus ends royal authority in this State. And all the people shall say Amen."

Checking the facts

1. Why did the Second Continental Congress meet?
2. What actions did the Second Continental Congress take?
3. How did the Declaration of Independence reflect the colonists' feelings about "taxation without representation"?

Reread the beginning of the Declaration. Which is your favorite part?

PUTTING IT ALL TOGETHER

UNDERSTANDING THE MAIN IDEAS

1. What made the colonists think of themselves as separate from other English people?
2. How did the idea of liberty become so important?
3. What did liberty mean?
4. How did Americans organize to get liberty?

ACTIVITIES

1. Ask three people of different ages to define liberty and to give you an example of what they mean. Then put everyone's lists together by age. Now group the lists by definition and finally by kinds of examples. How are the definitions alike? In what ways do they differ? What can you say about the meaning of liberty to different people?
2. Find the letters of Abigail and John Adams in a book in your library. Read and enjoy them.
3. Write one paragraph in which you name your favorite part of the Declaration of Independence. Why is it your favorite? What idea is important for you? Then take one sentence out of the Declaration and figure out what makes the words, the sounds, and the rhythm so powerful.

BOOKS TO READ

Dobler, Lavina, and Toppin, Edgar, *Pioneers and Patriots* (New York: Doubleday and Co., 1974).

Eaton, Jeannette, *Leader by Destiny* (New York: Harcourt, Brace, Jovanovich, 1938).

Hoehling, Mary, and Randall, Betty, *For Life and Liberty: The Story of the Declaration of Independence* (New York: Messner and Co., 1969).

Morris, Richard B., ed., *Voices from America's Past* (New York: E. P. Dutton and Co., 1963).

Yates, Elizabeth, *Amos Fortune, Free Man* (New York: E. P. Dutton and Co., 1950).

chapter 8
Liberty in Action

1776–1787

1. FIGHTING FOR LIBERTY
2. GOVERNING FOR LIBERTY

INTRODUCTION

The Declaration of Independence marked the early stages of the Revolutionary War. Now Americans had to fight to remain independent. Running the war effort was their first major opportunity to work together. Now they would have no chance to turn back. The war had to be a success although the Americans did not have the government to organize it carefully. In addition, they did not have the aid of experts to train and supply an army. Most importantly, the Americans did not have a government that could use its power to raise taxes and make sure the laws were obeyed. When the Revolutionary War was over, these same problems remained. Americans all agreed that liberty for each person was the most important value. In the years following the war, Americans had a difficult time agreeing on anything else.

As you read about the American Revolution and the first government of the United States, think about the following questions:

	1776	1777	1779	1780	
Who?	Thomas Jefferson	British General Burgoyne	John Paul Jones	Benedict Arnold	
What?	writes the Declaration of Independence	surrenders his army	raids	becomes a traitor	
Where?	in Philadelphia	at Saratoga N.Y.	English ships	and flees to England	

Breaking away was one act, and it took years. Independence took organization and money.

1. How did Americans organize to fight?
2. What caused the American military victory?
3. What could the Confederation do? Why could it not do more?
4. Why could the Articles not guarantee liberty for all?

1. FIGHTING FOR LIBERTY

In July of 1776 a large British force under General Howe arrived in New York. Washington was waiting for them, but he was unable to hold his position. His soldiers still did not act like disciplined troops. Washington was impatient with them when, in September of 1776, he ordered the army to leave New York so as not to be trapped on Manhattan Island. One of the soldiers reported, "The General was so exasperated that he struck several officers in their flight, three times dashed his hat on the ground, and at last exclaimed, 'Have I got such troops as those!' "

The war might have been over in New York if General Howe had pursued Washington's untrained army. Luckily, Howe delayed and after several narrow escapes, the Americans made it across the Hudson River to New Jersey, and from there across the Delaware River to Pennsylvania.

The British spent the winter of 1776 in New York with some outlying troops stationed in New Jersey. The hated Hessian soldiers were camped for the winter at Trenton, New Jersey. Here Washington staged an exciting victory. It was Christmas Eve and the Hessians were celebrating. No one expected the war to start up until spring. During the night Washington led his men by boat across the Delaware River and surprised the Hessians. The Americans took over 900 prisoners on that stormy night. Then they marched to Princeton and scored another victory there.

1. What happened to boost the American spirit?

1) Washington's troops escaped the large British force, under General Howe, which arrived in New York. 2) On Christmas Eve, 1776, Washington surprised Hessians camped at Trenton, N. J., and took more than 900 prisoners. 3) Washington's troops marched on to Princeton, scoring another victory there.

1781	1783	1784	1785	1786
Washington accepts Cornwallis'	Ben Franklin, John Adams and John Jay	John Greene	Congress	Alexander Hamilton and James Madison
surrender	sign a Peace Treaty ending the war	sails Empress of China to open trade	passes Land Ordinance	persuade people to reform the Articles
in Yorktown, Va.	in Paris, France	with China	for Northwest Territories	at the Annapolis Convention

These battles were important for the boost they gave to the American spirit. The army began to think like an army and follow orders like an army. The winter of 1776 was also the time when Tom Paine produced pamphlets to urge everyone to fight. In *The Crisis* he spoke out against those who did not care enough—"the sunshine soldiers and the summer patriots," he called them. The Americans were able to get through that first winter by thinking they had a chance to win.

The Loyalists

2. Who were the Loyalists in the colonies?

1) Loyalists were Americans who did not wish to fight the British. 2) Among the Loyalists, or Tories, were Backcountry Scots who didn't want to be left at the mercy of east coast power groups; wealthy merchants whose businesses depended on trade with England; the officers of the empire who were British.

These were difficult times for the Americans who did not wish to fight the British. How many remained Loyalist, or Tory, is not known for certain. The figures range from just under 8 percent to as high as 33 percent. There were Loyalists in each one of the 13 states. But not everyone became a Loyalist for the same reason. The back-country Scots in the middle and southern colonies joined the Loyalists because they did not want to be left at the mercy of the east coast power groups they had opposed for so long. On the other hand, wealthy merchants in the bigger cities became Loyalists because their businesses depended on trade with England. These two groups along with the officers of the empire sent about 50,000

This picture shows a British camp. The camp was laid out in a grid pattern. Notice the laundry drying on the tents, and the visitors to the camp. What does this picture tell you about life in the British army?

It was difficult to supply the British because they were fighting 3,000 miles (4,800 kilometers) away from home.

men into the war to help the British. Some of the Indians also fought for the British. They feared the colonists and wanted the protection of the British army.

But other Loyalists took no part in the fighting. Some fled while others remained in the country. Throughout the war feelings between Patriots and Loyalists were very strong. Both sides recognized that this was a last chance. When the British finally lost, many of the Loyalists left the country for Canada and the British West Indies.

Managing the War

The split between the Loyalists and the Patriots was not the only problem Americans had to face. The Patriots themselves had to learn to plan and work together. This was a difficult task for thirteen separate brand new governments, with few strong local leaders. Two of the states, New York and Massachusetts, had elected governors with some responsibility. But in most of the states the people were so afraid of powerful governors that they only allowed them a one-year term and very few powers. Pennsylvania had no governor at all. The state was run by a 13-member council.

The states did not trust the legislature totally either. All but two states had a two-house, or *bicameral*, legislature like the English Parliament. But only Maryland and New York let the upper house have a separate vote from the lower one. In those two states the senate or upper house was made of wealthy men who owned a great deal of property. Most of the power was given to the lower house, which was elected by the people. Americans were frightened that they would lose their freedom to the new governments. The voters trusted themselves. That is, they trusted free White men who owned some property. The new state constitutions did reduce the amount of property a person had to own in order to vote. But only two states—Pennsylvania and North Carolina—gave the vote to all male taxpayers, whether they owned property or not. These changes meant that more people could vote. But women and Blacks were still excluded.

Separating Church and State

During the war a number of states also moved to cut ties between church and state. Almost every state had an established church. This meant that the church was supported by tax money. Every person had to pay taxes to the church whether they belonged to it or not. In New York and in the South the established church was the Church of England. People did not want to pay taxes to the king's church anymore so they disestablished it. However, in New

3. Why did the Patriots have difficulty learning to plan and work together?

1) Each of the 13 colonies had a new government. 2) Most states allowed governors only a one-year term and granted them few powers. 3) The states did not totally trust their legislatures. 4) Most voters trusted only themselves—White men who owned property.

4. Why did each state government form a separate government?

The colonists did not want to pay taxes to support an established church, so it was disestablished in many states.

The variety among the churches led to separation of church and government.

England, where most people belonged to the Congregational Church, this church remained the established one for some time.

Written Constitutions

5. *Why did the states form a new government for all the states?*

1) Each state wanted its own written constitution, to prevent the government from acting without the people's consent, and to guarantee that individual rights could not be taken away by the government. 2) The states did not trust each other enough to form a union under one constitution. 3) The states did not want to give away some of their new power to a central government. 4) Each state was concerned with its own future.

It was not surprising that the states decided to have written constitutions. After all that had happened with England, they never again would let a government act without the consent of the people. The states also made sure that their constitutions contained a list of individual rights which no government could take away. These lists or *bills of rights* were something new, just as the written constitutions were new.

For the first time in the history of the western nations, new governments were formed without any difficulty. This was because the states had their constitutions approved by public vote. Americans went back to the wording of the Declaration of Independence which stated that government comes from free people binding themselves together. This was an idea made popular in England by the philosopher John Locke. The people made a contract that they would obey the new government which they had helped to form. Thus the states were formed on a belief of people in each other. Only the vote of a free people could be trusted. Each person would have to agree to follow the laws made by the representatives of the people.

But the people in different states did not trust each other enough to form a union. Throughout the war the Continental Congress, in session at Philadelphia, tried to get the states to form a new government for all of the states. The idea was to join together under a constitution called the Articles of Confederation. But the states kept turning the Articles down, because they did not wish to give away any of their new power. Each state was looking past the war to its own separate future.

Paying for the War

6. *How were the costs of the war met?*

1) Either Congress or the state legislatures paid for the supplies. 2) People loaned money by buying bonds from the Continental Congress. 3) France and Spain gave secret aid to the Americans. 4) The Congress and the states issued paper money.

Food and supplies come from every state. Sometimes these were paid for by the Congress and sometimes by the state legislatures. People with money loaned it by buying *bonds*, or promises to pay, from the Continental Congress. They were to be paid back with interest when the war was won. Money was also borrowed from foreign governments. France and Spain gave secret aid to the Americans, hoping, of course, to weaken the British Empire. Benjamin Franklin spent a good deal of the time in France trying to get help and an alliance, if possible. Without this foreign aid the states would never have been able to pay for running the war.

The order of the battles was: 1) Lexington and Concord, 2) Bunker Hill, 3) Montreal,
4) Oriskany, 5) Bennington, and 6) Saratoga.

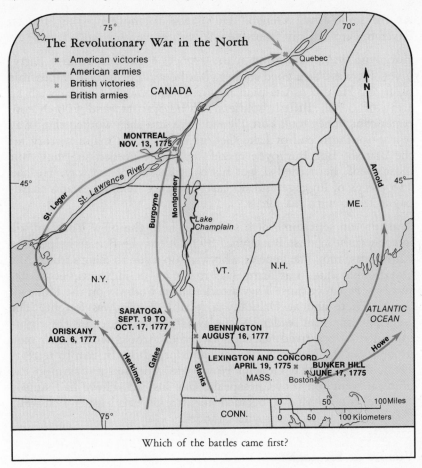

The Revolutionary War in the North

× American victories
— American armies
× British victories
— British armies

Which of the battles came first?

The Continental Congress and each of the states also issued paper money. Because people did not have much faith in the value of paper, sellers raised their prices. More and more money was needed to buy goods. This was *inflation*.

One way of raising money was not used. The Americans never passed tax laws. After all, the first reason for fighting the British was over the right to tax.

The Fight for New England

While the Americans were trying to organize and pay for the war, the British were on the march again. In the spring of 1777 they had a grand plan to cut off New England from the rest of the states by moving an army under "Gentleman Johnny" Burgoyne (bur-GOYN) south from Canada down Lake Champlain to Albany. Another British army was to move east from Lake Ontario to Albany.

1) The army that was supposed to move east from Lake Ontario to Albany left late and was forced to retreat from Fort Stanwix on the Mohawk River. 2) Howe went south to Philadelphia rather than up to Albany from New York, leaving Burgoyne stranded.

7. What happened to the British plan to cut off New England from the rest of the states?

The British general, John Burgoyne.

Joseph Brant, the Mohawk leader, sided with the British. He raided colonial settlements in upper New York. Why do you think he formed an alliance with the British?

At the same time, General Howe was to move up the Hudson River toward Albany from New York.

Burgoyne was a charming man, a poet, a gambler, and a party-lover. He was also a good soldier. But he was put into an impossible position. He did as the plan required. He marched south with an army of 6,000 British soldiers, 650 Loyalists, and 500 Native Americans. They took Fort Ticonderoga and then worked their way to the southern end of Lake George. This was a major victory for the British. But Burgoyne needed help. He needed supplies. But most of all, he needed to get his baggage out of the way. He had 138 pieces of luggage and 30 carts carrying his clothes and champagne to go with his meals.

Washington sent some of his army to help the New York militia in their fight against Burgoyne. By accident the British helped the Americans, too. The general who was supposed to march from Lake Ontario left late. His army was made up of Hessians, Loyalists, and Native Americans. They attacked Fort Stanwix on the Mohawk River. There and at Oriskany a terrible battle was fought. The German-American leader, Nicholas Herkimer, directed the fighting until help arrived. General Benedict Arnold with 1,000 men drove away the Native Americans and forced the British to retreat. Then, the army that General Howe was supposed to bring up the Hudson went south to Chesapeake Bay instead. Howe had simply changed his mind and decided to attack Philadelphia first! His change of plan left Burgoyne stranded.

Victory at Saratoga

Burgoyne knew he was in trouble. But he still hoped to reach Albany. He fought several battles against the American forces under General Horatio Gates, and was forced to retreat to Saratoga. On October 17, 1777 the battle of Saratoga was fought. It was a great victory for the Americans. Burgoyne surrendered his entire army. As he surrendered, the Americans played "Yankee Doodle," the song the British had sung originally to make fun of them.

The British in Philadelphia

In the meantime, Howe won several important battles in the fight for Philadelphia. These victories including the battle of Brandywine, south and west of the city, and the battle of Germantown. Washington had hoped for victory at the latter spot, but his troops lost their way in the fog. The Americans retreated to Valley Forge, Pennsylvania, 20 miles (32 kilometers) northwest of Philadelphia to wait out the winter. The British meanwhile enjoyed the comfort of Philadelphia.

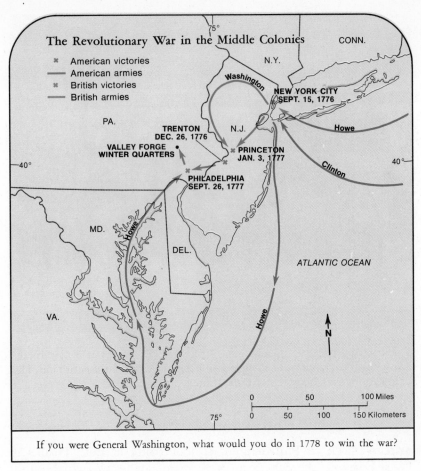

The Revolutionary War in the Middle Colonies

× American victories
— American armies
× British victories
— British armies

CONN.

N.Y.

Washington

NEW YORK CITY
SEPT. 15, 1776

Howe

PA.

N.J.

TRENTON
DEC. 26, 1776

VALLEY FORGE
WINTER QUARTERS

PRINCETON
JAN. 3, 1777

Clinton

40°   40°

PHILADELPHIA
SEPT. 26, 1777

MD.

Howe

DEL.

ATLANTIC OCEAN

VA.

Howe

N

0   50   100 Miles

75°

0   50   100   150 Kilometers

If you were General Washington, what would you do in 1778 to win the war?

Answers will vary.

Lydia Darragh Takes a Message

During the winter they spent in Philadelphia, the British enjoyed an active social life. But at one point they decided to launch a surprise attack on an American camp at Whitemarsh to the north of the city. A Quaker woman named Lydia Darragh happened to overhear them discussing these plans. Using the excuse that her family was out of flour, Lydia left home to go to the mill. She was able to get a pass from General Howe to get through British lines. She did, in fact, go to the mill. But instead of stopping there, Lydia continued on through the snow until she reached the American camp. Her warning delivered, she went back to the mill, picked up her flour sack, and returned home. No one guessed where she had really gone. But when the British arrived at Whitemarsh, they found the Americans ready and waiting. Since the British had counted on a surprise attack, they simply turned around and

8. *How did Lydia Darragh help the American troops?*

1) She discovered plans to launch a surprise attack on the American camp at Whitemarsh, north of Philadelphia. She got a pass through the British lines and warned the Americans.
2) When the British arrived, they found the Americans ready and waiting.

Notice the difference between a detailed incident and the story of an army. What is the value of each to a student?

173

This painting is called "Washington Reviewing His Troops at Valley Forge." The winter the troops spent there was probably the worst of the entire war. How did Washington's troops survive the winter?

Thaddeus Kosciusko was a Polish military leader who helped the Americans. How did other nations help the Americans?

marched back to Philadelphia without firing a shot. Thanks to Lydia Darragh, the Americans were spared an attack, which might have ended disastrously for them.

Washington at Valley Forge

The winter at Valley Forge was harsh. Washington's army had few supplies, because Washington was unable to get Congress or private citizens to provide food and clothing for his soldiers. Some of the men left for home while others joined the British in Philadelphia. Still others remained to die of the cold. If General Howe had attacked the Americans at Valley Forge, the war might have been over. But the British did not fight in the wintertime. While Howe waited for spring, important help came to the Americans. A European military officer, Baron Frederick Von Steuben (STU-ben), arrived to help Washington. He drilled the Americans at Valley Forge in the latest methods of warfare and strategy. Besides Von Steuben, other Europeans like the Polish cavalry officer, Casimir Pulaski (pu-LAS-kee), and Thaddeus Kosciusko (kos-i-US-ko) aided the American cause.

The American fight was seen by many Europeans as a fight for everyone's liberty.

American women also did their part. From their homes women prepared meals and made clothes for the army. They also raised money, and nursed the sick and wounded. Most did not go so far as Deborah Sampson Gannett who, disguised as a man, joined the 11th Massachusetts Regiment. But many did assist their husbands in camp and on the battlefield. Martha Washington joined her husband at Valley Forge, and during other winters of the war as well.

France Joins the War

The French heard of the victory at Saratoga and decided that the Americans could probably win the war. Therefore, it was safe for the French to come out in the open and join the Americans. France declared war on England in the spring of 1778. The Spanish joined the war in 1779 and attacked the British fort at Gibraltar in the Mediterranean. The Dutch sold supplies to the Americans from the West Indies until the British declared war on them. But the Dutch continued to loan the Americans money. Thus Americans received help from the nations which had been England's former rivals in the struggle for empire.

Fighting at Sea

The Revolution was fought at sea as well as on land. The French let Americans use their ports to attack British ships. The most famous American captain was John Paul Jones. His ship, *Ranger*, was the first new gun ship built by Americans. Jones attacked the coast of Britain in 1777. And in 1779, aboard the *Bonhomme Richard*, Jones attacked a much larger British ship, the *Serapis*. Jones' strategy was to tie his ship with grappling hooks to the *Serapis* so that it could not use its big guns. A hand-to-hand battle was fought for hours. When asked if he was about to surrender, Jones was said to reply, "I have not yet begun to fight." At another point he announced, "Yankees do not haul down their colors until they are fairly beaten." The Americans won. Excitement spread through the states and through France.

The American navy was tiny, but the owners of private ships were many. These privateers were sent out, some by the separate states and some by the Continental Congress. They captured over 600 British ships during the war.

Fighting in the West

A thousand miles (1,600 kilometers) west of the main fighting, George Rogers Clark was given a commission by Patrick Henry, Governor of Virginia, to attack the British army north and west

Deborah Sampson enlisted in the colonial army. She fought at the battle of Yorktown and received an honorable discharge.

Martha Washington visited George Washington's headquarters many times during the war.

175

This painting shows the encounter of the *Serapis* and the *Bonhomme Richard* in 1779. How did ships fight at sea?

9. *What important areas did Clark take in 1778 and 1779?*

The British were not expecting an attack 1,000 miles west of the main fighting.

of Kentucky. This was an important area because it controlled the Ohio and Mississippi rivers. With an incredibly small army of 175, Clark took Kaskaskia in Illinois in the summer of 1778, and Vincennes in Indiana in the terrible winter of 1779.

The Fighting Moves South

During the winter at Valley Forge, the Americans had been drilled in the latest methods by von Steuben. This training served them well when they fought the British again in the spring of 1778. By this time Howe had been replaced by General Henry Clinton. Fearing that the French were going to attack Philadelphia from the sea, Clinton left the city and started out across New Jersey for New York. Washington went after him. The two armies met in battle at Monmouth Courthouse in New Jersey. The battle ended in a draw. After it, the center of the fighting moved to the South. In the next year-and-a-half, the British took Savannah and most of Georgia. Charleston fell in May of 1780, and the British captured 5,000 American soldiers. They were quite successful in their effort in the South. But bands of fighters kept up the attack against the British. Their leaders were Francis Marion, known as the Swamp Fox, and Thomas Sumter.

What was the importance of each region to the war effort?

The British generals were Cornwallis, Campbell, and Hamilton. (Note this is not Alexander Hamilton, the American, but another person with the same name.)

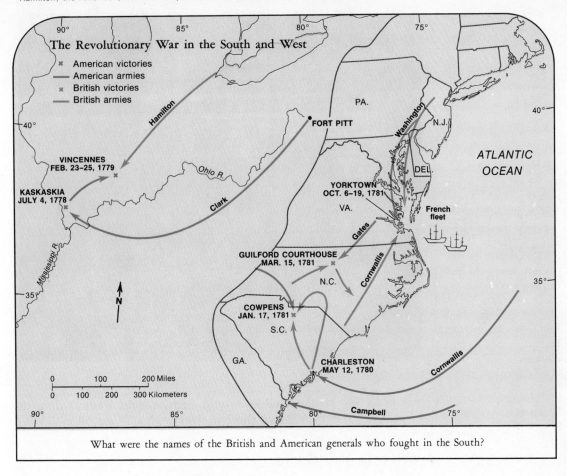

The Revolutionary War in the South and West

- ✶ American victories
- ━ American armies
- × British victories
- ━ British armies

ATLANTIC OCEAN

FORT PITT

PA.

Hamilton

VINCENNES
FEB. 23–25, 1779

KASKASKIA
JULY 4, 1778

Clark

Ohio R.

Mississippi R.

N.J.

Washington

DEL.

YORKTOWN
OCT. 6–19, 1781

VA.

French fleet

Gates

GUILFORD COURTHOUSE
MAR. 15, 1781

Cornwallis

N.C.

COWPENS
JAN. 17, 1781

S.C.

GA.

CHARLESTON
MAY 12, 1780

Cornwallis

Campbell

N

| 0 | 100 | 200 Miles |
| 0 | 100 | 200 | 300 Kilometers |

What were the names of the British and American generals who fought in the South?

Certain that the South was conquered, the British left for New York. The army in the South was left in the command of General William Cornwallis. Washington sent Nathaniel Greene to lead the army there against the 8,000 British soldiers. Greene did not try to attack the main part of the British force, but rather planned and carried out several smaller battles. The Patriots won at King's Mountain, at Cowpens, and at Guilford Court House. Cornwallis retreated to the seaport at Wilmington, North Carolina, and then moved north to Virginia.

In Virginia Cornwallis joined with Benedict Arnold who had joined the British side. Arnold's story was one of the saddest of the war. After a brilliant career leading the Americans, he became disappointed in the recognition he received. He conspired with Major John Andre, a British spy, to turn the American fort at West Point in New York over to the British. But the plot was discovered when Andre was caught by the Americans with plans of the fort. Andre

10. How did Nathaniel Greene force Cornwallis' troops to retreat?

Greene planned and carried out several smaller battles instead of attacking the main force of 8,000 troops.

177

The battle of Monmouth, New Jersey, was fought on a scorching hot day in June 1778. Mary Hays brought water to the soldiers during the battle. She was nicknamed Molly Pitcher. When her husband was wounded, Mary Hays took his place at the cannon.

was tried and hanged while Arnold fled. Arnold went to live in England in 1781 and died there in 1801.

Victory at Yorktown

Cornwallis and Arnold were no match for the Americans under Von Steuben and the Frenchman, the Marquis de Lafayette, who had

Francis Marion was known as the Swamp Fox. He and his men fought in the South. In this picture, Francis Marion is entertaining a British soldier.

178

After their defeat in the North, the British turned to the South. This picture shows the final attack on Yorktown, led by Colonel Alexander Hamilton.

come to help Washington because he believed in the cause of freedom. Cornwallis again retreated to the sea, this time to the peninsula of Yorktown. Washington planned and carried out a brilliant move. He and the French navy commander tricked the British into thinking they were going to attack Clinton in New York. Instead, a combined force of 17,000 French and Americans marched south to Yorktown. At the same time the French fleet sailed into Chesapeake Bay. Cornwallis was trapped. He put up a fight, but was greatly outnumbered. On the 19th of October, 1781, 7,000 British soldiers under Cornwallis' command surrendered. The fighting was over. Americans were free of control of the British army. Now they had to pull themselves together to make a treaty, pay the bills, and manage the peace.

11. How was Cornwallis defeated at Yorktown?

1) Washington and the French naval commander tricked Cornwallis into thinking they were going to attack General Henry Clinton, in New York. 2) A combined American and French force marched south to Yorktown while the French navy sailed into Chesapeake Bay, trapping the British.

Checking the facts

1. Why did some colonists remain loyal to Britain?
2. What was the attitude of the states toward the Articles of Confederation?
3. What did other nations do to help the colonists win the war?

2. GOVERNING FOR LIBERTY

12. Why were the Articles of Confederation finally ratified?

Maryland and Virginia settled their rival claims to territory "west and northwest to the Pacific."

By the time the fighting was over in 1781 the official governing organization for the thirteen states was seven months old. The Continental Congress had tried for four years to get the states to ratify the Articles of Confederation. One reason for the delay was the rival claims to the territory "west and northwest to the Pacific." Maryland had rights from the Native Americans to land in the Ohio River Valley. Virginia had 170-year-old claims to the same land and more from its original English charter. But Virginia agreed to give up claims to land west and north of the Ohio River, if Maryland would give up the claims based on the treaties with the Native Americans. Finally, all states agreed and the new Confederation was proclaimed on March 1, 1781.

Union—But Not Too Close

13. Why did Americans agree to a confederation?

1) Each state was to be on an equal basis with every other state. 2) There was no idea of a nation that was greater than the sum of all the parts. 3) The confederation was a very loose union, allowing states to remain different from each other.

Confederation was a key word. The key part of the word was the prefix "con-." "Con" means with. The idea was that the states would come together on an equal basis with other states. But there was no idea of a nation that was greater than the sum of all the parts. The Confederation was a very loose union of states and the word itself gave comfort to Americans who wanted the right to live as they pleased. Americans were not only different from each other, but they intended to remain so. The small states did not want to be swallowed up by the big ones. While the large ones, like Virginia, New York, Massachusetts, and Pennsylvania, traded with each other, they still saw each other as possible competitors.

The Articles and Liberty

14. What rights did Congress have under the Confederation?

1) It could make war and peace, and raise an army. 2) It could make treaties and alliances with other countries. 3) It could settle disputes between the states.

The Americans wanted guarantees of liberty. They had fought for the right to make their own decisions and they had no intention of giving up that right. They trusted themselves, and they did not trust "government." The less government they had to live with, the better.

The Articles of Confederation were as close to the least amount of government as possible. The union was a "league of friendship," nothing more. Under the Articles, each state kept its *sovereignty* or its right to be the supreme authority on most matters. The states also kept their freedom and independence. Any power or right which was not specifically written down in the Articles was left to the states. Congress could make war and peace, and raise an army. It could make treaties and alliances with other countries, and settle disputes between the states. But Congress had no power over trade between the states, and it had no authority to tax. These two very important powers, as well as every power not specifically given to

When the war was over, what did the colonists know about governing themselves? What was new?
Why did the new 13 states want a joint government?

the Congress, belonged to the states. Also, the Congress was the only recognized branch of government. There was no *executive*, or single person, to carry out the laws of the land. There was no *judiciary*, or group of court officials, to interpret the laws and settle disputes about them. The Congress of the Confederation could not force any individual to obey its laws. Since the Confederation was only a league of states, each state had to ask its citizens to obey laws passed by the Congress.

Paying the Bills

A government with little power had a hard time paying its bills. The states and the Continental Congress owed a great deal of money to wealthy Americans, to state governments, and to foreign governments. But a new government that could not tax had little chance of repaying its debts.

A wealthy Philadelphia merchant, Robert Morris, was put in charge of the finances of the Continental Congress. Morris knew how important the moment was. If he could establish enough faith and confidence in the new government's ability to pay its debts, he would do much toward making the future bright for the American states.

But Morris could not get the states to agree that the Confederation should pay all the state debts. He could not even get them to agree to a tax on imports which would help pay Washington's army. Some of the soldiers were never paid what was owed them. When Morris was able to get loans for Congress, it was usually on his own signature. That is, he personally promised to pay the loan back in case the confederacy did not. One man's credit was better than all the states of this not-very-strong union!

The Peace Treaty

Although the American states had won an important victory at Yorktown, making a treaty was difficult. The government of Great Britain was slow to agree to the idea of independence. The Continental Congress had to consult the other nations that had helped, especially France and Spain. Spain did not want the British to give much land to the new nation, because Spain intended to expand and link up its lands west of the Mississippi River to those in Florida. France had been delighted to help weaken Britain. But after the war, France did not care if the British gave the American states everything they wanted.

John Adams, Benjamin Franklin, and John Jay were sent by the Continental Congress to conduct the peace talks in Paris. Jay had been minister to Spain and was well aware that France and Spain

15. Why was Morris' credit better than that of the Confederation?

The government could not tax the people to pay its debts. Morris had better credit because he was a wealthy and respected merchant.

16. Why did the Americans have to negotiate a separate treaty with Great Britain?

1) The Americans knew that their allies, Spain and France, were not going to push the British to recognize American independence.
2) The Americans knew the British would rather have a weak new country in North America than a rebuilt Spanish Empire.

were not going to push the British to recognize American independence. So the Americans decided to try for a separate treaty with the British without telling the French. They knew that the British would rather have a weak new country in North America than a strong rebuilt Spanish Empire. Besides, the Americans wanted to start buying goods from England again. The Americans began secret negotiations with the British and finally signed a treaty with them right in Paris in November, 1782. In the treaty, the British agreed that the United States were "free, sovereign, and independent." The boundaries of the new nation were set at the Great Lakes, the Mississippi River, and the northern border of Florida.

Once an agreement with England had been reached, the Americans had to tell the French. The French had known about the talks between the Americans and the English all along. They had an elaborate network of spies, one of whom was Franklin's own private secretary. Still, when they heard the news, they pretended to be surprised and angry. But both the French and the Spanish were ready for peace. On January 20, 1783, they signed a separate treaty with England.

17. Why didn't the British leave their fur trading posts?

1) The British did not want to leave the profitable fur trade. 2) The Americans had not kept their agreement to pay their debts or return land taken from the Loyalists.

John Adams stayed on in England as minister from the United States, and Jefferson did the same in France. Franklin remained in France for two more years to work on trade treaties. There was much to be done. Americans were unhappy when the British did not leave the forts and fur trading posts on the other side of the

Benjamin West painted John Jay, John Adams, Benjamin Franklin, Henry Laurens, and William Temple Franklin at the Paris peace talks. Why do you think the British commissioners refused to sit for the painting?

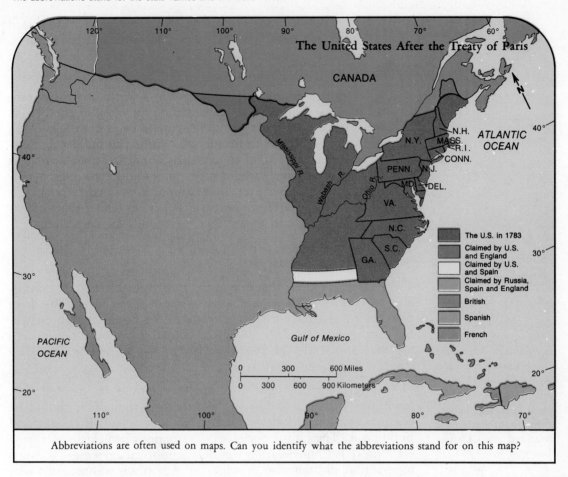

The United States After the Treaty of Paris

CANADA

N.H.
N.Y.
MASS.
R.I.
CONN.
PENN.
N.J.
MD.
DEL.
VA.
N.C.
S.C.
GA.

ATLANTIC OCEAN

Mississippi R.
Wabash R.
Ohio R.

The U.S. in 1783
Claimed by U.S. and England
Claimed by U.S. and Spain
Claimed by Russia, Spain and England
British
Spanish
French

PACIFIC OCEAN

Gulf of Mexico

0   300   600 Miles
0   300   600   900 Kilometers

Abbreviations are often used on maps. Can you identify what the abbreviations stand for on this map?

St. Lawrence River and also on the western frontier around the Great Lakes, in western New York, and along the Ohio Valley. This meant that Americans had to stay out of the Great Lakes region. It also meant that they could not take over the profitable fur trade there. But when the Americans protested the British reminded them that they had not lived up to their part of the bargain either. They had not paid their debts, nor had they returned the lands to the Loyalists as they had said they would in the treaty.

John Adams was also very concerned with trade. The Americans were buying so much more than they could sell that the *economy* of their new country was in trouble. And the British were making life difficult. Britain put a high tariff on American whale oil, and refused to let Americans sell fish to the British West Indies.

In France Jefferson was no more successful in getting the contracts for Virginia tobacco improved. In Spain Jay found that the Spanish had cut down on the amount of American traffic on the lower

18. What problems were the Americans having with trade?

183

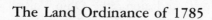

1) They were buying more than they were selling. 2) Britain put a high tariff on whale oil. 3) Britain refused to let Americans sell fish to the British West Indies. 4) The French had not approved the contracts for Virginia tobacco. 5) The Spanish cut down on American traffic on the lower Mississippi. 6) The Spanish taxed all American goods that passed through the port of New Orleans.

Mississippi. They also began to tax all American goods that passed through New Orleans. This was a serious blow to western farmers. They depended on the Mississippi River to get their goods to market inexpensively.

The Americans were now trying to live in a world of strong competitive nations. They no longer had the protection of the British Empire. They did not have the home manufactures nor the banking system to provide credit to people who wanted to build new businesses. Several leaders tried to get the Congress to pass *tariffs*, or taxes on imports, which would raise money and encourage manufacture in America. But even if the Congress wanted to take such action, the states would not agree, or *ratify* it. Under the Confederation, nine states had to agree or there could be no action.

Settling Public Lands

19. How did Americans compromise on what to do with western public lands?
Congress passed the Land Ordinance of 1785.
During and after the war, many Americans traveled west of the Appalachian Mountains. This shows the early fort at Boonesborough, a settlement founded by Daniel Boone.

The Americans knew that one of the most valuable resources available to them was their land west of the Appalachians. This land now belonged jointly to all the states of the Confederation. It was not surprising that they all agreed something should be done to organize and settle the territory. It was not surprising that they could not agree on what to do.

New Englanders thought this territory should be divided into townships with planned towns. Southerners thought it should be open to any settler who wanted to go west, claim the land, and build on it. These differences between regions had existed for generations. The Confederation was only a political agreement to work together. It did not change what the Americans wanted, or make them any more alike.

The Land Ordinance of 1785

The Congress made one decision about the western lands that was acceptable to both sides and was not exactly what either had wanted. It was a compromise. The Land Ordinance (law) of 1785 divided the western lands into six-mile (9.6 kilometers) square townships. These townships in turn were split up into 36 sections, each to be 640 acres (about 256 hectares) or one square mile. In New England fashion, every 16th section of every township was to be set aside to pay for the schools and provide space for the schoolhouse. The rest of the land would then be sold at auction for a dollar an acre (.4 hectare.) But since most frontier families did not have cash, much of the land was to be sold to *speculators*. The speculators were able to buy large amounts of land for as little as a few pennies an acre. Then they cleared it, divided it up, put in roads, and sold it to others a little at a time.

America had spectacular resources in land. American families of all backgrounds wanted land of their own, not cooperation with others.

The Northwest Ordinance of 1787

Land came first in the American list of values, because it meant opportunity. But democratic government to protect the rights of Americans came next. Citizens of the new territories should not lose any of their rights just because they left one of the thirteen original states. Their rights were God-given. Therefore, the rights should go west with the people.

Thomas Jefferson headed the committee that worked out the plan of governing, known as the Northwest Ordinance of 1787. The lands north of the Ohio, east of the Mississippi, and south of the Great Lakes were to be the Northwest Territory. Out of that land were to come not less than three, nor more than five, political or governmental divisions. A governor and three judges appointed by the Congress were to make and enforce the laws until 5,000 people lived there. Then the adult males could elect their own legislature and send a representative as a nonvoting delegate to Congress. When one of the divisions grew to have a population of 60,000, it could become a state and write its own constitution. Each state could organize as it wished, except for two important rules. It must have democratic government and there were to be no slaves.

These land laws were probably the greatest achievement of the Confederation. Never before had new lands been added to a nation without being completely controlled by the old government. Never before had new states been guaranteed equal rights and power with the founding states.

The Question of Slavery

Both the British and the Patriots offered freedom, or *emancipation*, to Black slaves who fought in the Revolution. Blacks had fought on both sides and in every major battle. When the Revolution was over, the slaves who had fought in the war were freed.

Other Blacks won their freedom in a different way. In Massachusetts a slave named Quock Walker took his case to court. He claimed that under the state constitution all persons were free and equal. The court upheld his claims. The result was that all slaves in Massachusetts were freed. Other New England states also did away with slavery, and the states of New York, New Jersey, and Pennsylvania passed laws providing for a gradual freeing of the slaves.

The states reacted differently to Black free people living in their communities. There were a large number of free Blacks living in the upper South, in the old tobacco states of Virginia and Maryland. In Virginia alone, there were about 2,000 free Blacks in 1782. By 1790 there were 10,000.

20. How were the citizens of the western territory guaranteed their rights?

1) A governor and three judges appointed by Congress were to make and enforce laws until 5,000 people lived in a division. 2) Then the adult males could elect their own legislature and send a nonvoting delegate to Congress. 3) When the division's population grew to 60,000, it could become a state and write its own constitution. 4) Each state could organize as it wished as long as it was a democratic government, without slaves.

21. What problems occurred with the emancipation of Black slaves?

1) Wages stayed low where freed Blacks lived. 2) Slave owners were afraid that the free Blacks would help their slaves to run away. 3) Some Whites couldn't bring themselves to see Blacks as equal.

As soon as there were a great many free Blacks in one area, trouble began. More and more people were against the slave trade and the idea of one person owning another. On the other hand, it was difficult having free Blacks and Black slaves living in the same community. Wages stayed low. Slave owners feared that the free Blacks would help their slaves run away. Also, the presence of free Blacks was upsetting to those Whites who could not bring themselves to see Blacks as equal. People tried hard to deal with their revolutionary beliefs in natural rights and liberty. But at the same time, many could not see themselves living in a community of mixed races with no sharp divisions between Whites and Blacks.

In his *Notes on the State of Virginia*, published in 1787, Thomas Jefferson spoke out against owning slaves. Slavery, he said, made tyrants out of the masters and destroyed the spirit of the slaves. But Jefferson also said that he did not think a freed slave could live in the country in which he had been a slave. All Jefferson could offer as a solution was the idea that slaves should be freed and colonized in Africa. Although Jefferson and others who owned slaves spoke against slavery, many people did not believe that a mixed society of equals could work. There the argument remained for generations.

Differences Remain

Americans were pleased with the victory and the peace treaty. But the absence of British rule did not cause Americans to make sacrifices for the good of the new nation. Those to whom the government owed money would have liked to have been paid back. But the other people were not willing to pay taxes to the Congress of the Confederation to help the government pay its debts.

What circumstances led to Shays' Rebellion?

Shays' Rebellion

Individuals within the various states also had trouble paying their debts. There was a shortage of money because gold and silver were going out of the country to pay foreign debts. Some of the states issued paper money to ease the situation. But other states like Massachusetts, refused because they knew the paper money would have little value without gold and silver to back it up. The farmers of Massachusetts objected. Without paper money, they could not pay their debts, and if they did not pay, their farms would be taken away from them. They banded together to keep the courts from taking action against them. Under the leadership of a war veteran, Daniel Shays, a group of farmers marched on Springfield and stopped the state supreme court from meeting. Shays' Rebellion did not get far. But it came at the same moment that others in the colonies were working in order to get the Articles of Confederation strengthened.

How did variety among Americans show itself at the time of the Articles?

Variety and Liberty—How?

In March, 1785, Virginia and Maryland held a meeting at Washington's home in Mount Vernon to decide how to share the shipping on the Potomac River. The problems of trade between states, or *interstate commerce*, were so difficult and so important to the future of business within the states, that Virginia sent out invitations to all the states to meet and discuss trade. The conference was held in September, 1786 at Annapolis, Maryland. Only five states sent representatives. However, the meeting was held in exactly the same month as Shays' Rebellion.

One of the delegates to the trade convention was Alexander Hamilton, a brilliant lawyer from New York who had served in Washington's army as an officer when he was only 21. Hamilton took advantage of the news about Shays. He proposed that another convention be called in Philadelphia to discuss ways to improve the Articles of Confederation. Hamilton and others realized that some way had to be found to establish the credit of the states so that money could be borrowed. Something had to be done to build trade with Europe and to protect Americans who wanted to start manufacturing businesses. Something had to be done to keep peace within and among the states. Otherwise the British would see so much chaos that they might be tempted to reinvade.

Guaranteeing Liberty

Americans were very different from one another. Their differences could no longer be allowed to get in each other's way. One postal system was not enough cooperation. One set of ambassadors was not equal to a strong foreign policy. In order to use the liberty they had won, something had to be done to settle their differences. Americans of all national backgrounds turned to their English and colonial way of making decisions. What was needed was a new, strong system of representative government—one where everyone could be heard. It had to be a government in which differences could be worked out for the good of all.

Americans needed each other. They wanted their liberty. Now they wanted to grow in ways that would require cooperation. Representation was the way they knew they would be able to do both.

22. What was needed to settle the differences among Americans?

A new, strong, representative government was needed, under which everyone could be heard but differences could be worked out for the good of all.

Checking the facts

1. How did the Articles of Confederation operate?
2. What economic problems was the Confederation having?
3. How was the question of public lands settled?
4. Why was another convention called in Philadelphia?

PUTTING IT ALL TOGETHER

UNDERSTANDING THE MAIN IDEAS

1. How did Americans organize to fight?
2. What caused the American military victory?
3. What could the Confederation do? Why could it not do more?
4. Why could the Articles not guarantee liberty to all?

ACTIVITIES

1. Draw a time line for the years 1763-1781. Show the major events leading to the American Revolution and the major battles.
2. Choose one of the battles discussed in this chapter. Make a chart showing the progress of the battle. Who was the victor? Who was defeated? What determined the outcome of the battle? Include this information in your chart.
3. Write a brief essay on Thomas Paine's writings. What influence did he have on the Americans during the war? What happened to him after the Revolution? You may want to do some research on Paine before you begin writing your essay. Ask your school or local librarian for help in finding information on Paine.

BOOKS TO READ

Blackburn, Joyce, *John Adams* (Mountain View, California: World Publications, 1970).

Forbes, Esther, *Johnny Tremain* (Boston: Houghton Mifflin, 1943).

Phelan, Mary Kay, *The Story of the Boston Tea Party* (New York: T.Y. Crowell, 1973).

Raskin, Joseph, *Spies and Traitors; Tales of the Revolutionary War* (New York: Lothrop and Co., 1976).

Tunis, Edwin, *Colonial Living* (Mountain View, California: World Publications, 1972).

REVIEWING THE UNIT

BUILDING VOCABULARY

The following is a list of some of the vocabulary words in Unit 1:

longitude	pyramid	constitution
isthmus	ratify	shaman
wampum	kachina	homespun
blacksmith	milpa system	potlatch
cartographer	congregation	indigo
tidewater	*presidio*	*coureurs de bois*
profits	*conquistadore*	tariff
patroon	indenture	nomadic

1. Pick out four of the vocabulary words listed above and write a short paragraph on one of the following topics: a. the lives of the Native Americans before the arrival of the Europeans, b. the Age of Exploration, or c. life in the first colonies.

BUILDING SOCIAL STUDIES SKILLS

1. Turn to the maps on the pages given here. Then answer the following questions:
   a. Page 67—In 1524 Giovanni da Verrazano became the first European to see what is now New York harbor, at the mouth of the Hudson River. What is the latitude and longitude of the harbor?
   b. Page 102—Roger Williams left Massachusetts Bay Colony in 1635 to found a new colony called Providence. Use the scale to determine how far Williams and his followers traveled.
   c. Page 138—After the French and Indian War, "half the continent changed hands at the scratch of a pen," said an American historian. Using this map, find out what happened to the land controlled by France after the war ended.

BUILDING WRITING SKILLS

1. Use Chapters 1–8 to locate five factors that could explain why the American colonies rebelled. After you have done this, use each factor in a full sentence. Some examples are: the independent spirit of the colonists, the Sugar Act, the Quartering Act, Writs of Assistance, and the Boston Massacre.
2. In this unit you have looked at the problems of women, Native Americans, and Blacks. Choose one group and compare the rights it had at the end of the eighteenth century with those it has now.

The North American continent has had a long history of immigration, struggle for survival, and cultural change. Native Americans and Europeans developed very different ways of living. The English shaped the United States, in particular. People came to live in North America because they wanted to be free.

Native Americans

The first people to arrive in the Americas came over the land bridge from Asia between 30,000 and 10,000 years ago. They came before the organized civilizations of Europe and Asia developed. The life they had depended a great deal on the soil and climate they found. The most organized and highly developed of the Native American cultures in North America were the Aztec and Maya. The hunters and gatherers of the north had a less settled, less organized way of living. The Native American cultures developed over a period of 15,000 to 25,000 years. They developed in their own special way.

Europeans

European development moved beyond survival to control of the environment. Europeans had the advantage of fertile soil and a mild climate. The land could produce a surplus. This meant that surpluses could be traded.

Trade changed Europe. People developed wool and lumber to exchange for spices in the Far East. Trade required towns, money, and a system of prices.

By the mid-fifteenth century, the Ottoman Turks cut off the land trade routes that had been established to the East. The Europeans then turned to finding water routes. The Portuguese developed new methods of navigation. They were the first to go around the continent of Africa. In 1492, the Spanish, under the rule of Ferdinand and Isabella, discovered new lands in the Americas. Soon they came to control the land and the native people of the Americas.

Europeans explored and colonized the New World. The French tried to control large amounts of land without organization and settlement. The English, however, encouraged their citizens to settle in North America and govern themselves.

THINKING BACK

The British Empire and the Idea of Liberty

For 150 years the 13 English colonies developed differently. The British Empire guaranteed them markets for their raw materials and protection from outsiders. The New England colonists became traders and town builders as well as independent farmers. The people in the middle colonies became farmers and traders through their major port cities. The southern colonists developed large plantations which needed large supplies of labor. Labor was supplied first by indentured servants and then by Black slaves from Africa. Non-English people were welcomed. In America, they found that the English beliefs of liberty, property rights, and consent of the governed offered them greater opportunity.

At the end of the French and Indian War in 1763, the colonists found themselves up against a series of British government actions designed to keep control over the empire. From the time of the Stamp Act of 1765, the colonists argued about representation. Leaders with vision saw the development of a union of people around the idea of liberty. The British became more and more intolerant of Americans acting on their own. American leaders began to talk of open resistance against British rule.

The colonists organized two Continental Congresses. They responded to British actions by raising volunteer militias. Pamphlets about liberty were read throughout the colonies. Independence from Britain was finally declared in 1776. The Declaration of Independence tied together the philosophy of liberty and consent of the governed to the specific history of unhappy events between England and the colonies since 1763.

The Revolution was managed by the Continental Congress and its outstanding general, George Washington. Americans, with the help of European officers, the government of France, and some British errors, won the war. The treaty with England was signed by the new United States in 1783.

By 1787 the people in America knew they had to find a way to cooperate. Their goal was to build a stronger nation together. The people turned to their tradition of representative government in creating a new government. They wanted to organize themselves into a nation that could represent variety and opportunity, guarantee liberty, and take action for the good of all.

AMERICA IS... VARIETY, LIBERTY AND REPRESENTATION

UNIT TWO

If you were to make a list of all your activities for a year, you would find that some of them happen over and over again. They are very important. They are the organizers of your life. For instance, large chunks of your time and energy and thinking are spent at home, in your neighborhood, and at school. And yet you cannot be in all of these places at one time. Nor are you expert enough to manage them by yourself.

Standing In For You

Somehow you can count on your home, school, library, zoo, museum, and bus stop to be there when you need them. You know you can count on people to care about you, work to keep you safe, and help you do some of the things with your life that you would like to try.

How is this possible? When you are at school, who stands in for you at home? Who makes sure that the house is safe whether you are there or not? Who is planning tomorrow's day in school? Or next year's? How can they know about your concerns and goals? How can they keep your interests in mind?

Who is helping your neighborhood by making sure the trash is picked up in front of your house or apartment? Who makes sure dams are built so that overflowing rivers don't flood your farm or your house? Who is planning the storage of water so that your needs are met even when there is no rain? Who is doing all this for you?

You have people standing in for you all over the United States. There are people, thousands of miles away, who are trying to improve your school so that you can get a better education. There are people who are planning ways for you to travel to other places in safety and comfort—and to have exciting scenery to look at both along the way and when you get there. There are people who are working to find out how to make sure the things you want to buy are safe, convenient, and workable. There are people who are hoping to help you live longer, stay safe, and be healthy enough to enjoy your life.

Why Should They Care?

All these things are done for you because you are not the only one who wants them done. Because you belong to groups that are made up of many people who want what you want. Together you select people to be responsible for running the school, repairing the road, and fixing up the park and the playgrounds. These people are supposed to know what you and the others in your group want. They are supposed to know how to get things done. And they are supposed to have the skills to do them well. These people act for you. They represent you.

How Representation Works

How can such a variety of Americans ever agree? In the United States, citizens belong to groups. Senior citizens are an example. In recent years, men and women who have retired from business or have reached retirement age have formed organizations. Why? Because they want to pay less taxes than they did when they were working. They want better health insurance for older people who may have more expensive illnesses and yet live on fixed retirement incomes. They want a flexible retirement age. Congress can help in all these matters by passing laws. So these older people have formed organizations such as the Gray Panthers and the American Association of Retired Teachers. The Congress listens to them because they speak up and because they vote.

This is the way in which individual Americans are best represented. No nation on earth ever held so much variety within its borders as ours. No nation on earth ever gave so many individuals of such different backgrounds so much right to speak up. And no nation that promised individual opportunity and control over property had so many groups or so much land in so many regions to unite into one workable organization.

Americans found out that the only way to have both variety and liberty is to make sure that the variety is protected and the liberty is guaranteed. And the way to take action is to do so through local, state, and national representative governments. Americans belong to and are represented by all of these governments at the same time.

The plan that makes it possible for a varied people and their governments to work properly together was created in Philadelphia in 1787. This unit is the story of how America's own combination of variety, liberty, and representation first came to be. It is also the story of how that combination developed through the leaders and events of the next 45 years.

chapter 9
Out of Many—A New Nation

1787–1789

1. THE CONSTITUTION: ITS SETTING AND ITS VALUES
2. READING THE CONSTITUTION
3. RATIFYING THE CONSTITUTION
4. THE CONSTITUTION OF THE UNITED STATES AND WHAT IT MEANS TODAY

INTRODUCTION

In 1787 the American states sent delegates to Philadelphia to repair the Articles of Confederation. Many of the signers of the Declaration, and the older revolutionaries who had successfully managed the war, were not there. John Hancock and Sam Adams were not selected. John Adams was in London, Thomas Jefferson was in Paris. Patrick Henry and Richard Henry Lee were chosen but would not come.

The 55 men who did come to Philadelphia were successful lawyers, merchants, planters, and businessmen. These men were used to leadership in their local communities, but they had a new role to play on a much bigger stage. Among the new names were James Wilson, a lawyer from Pennsylvania, James Madison of Virginia, and Charles Pinckney of South Carolina. These men were ready for a stronger government led by the most talented citizens.

	1783	1784	1785	1786	
Who?	Congress of the Confederation	Captain John Green	Jefferson, Franklin, and Adams	Alexander Hamilton	
What?	ratifies the Articles of Peace ending the War	of the clipper ship <u>Empress of China</u>	negotiate Commercial Treaty	calls for a Convention to look at the government revisions	
Where?	in Philadelphia	sails to Canton, China	in France	at Annapolis Convention in Maryland	

There were others who were equally ready to support a strong government *if*—and it was a big *if*—there were absolute agreement on what the new national government could and could not do. Among these men were Edmund Randolph and George Mason of Virginia and Elbridge Gerry of Massachusetts.

As you read about this important time in American history, think about these questions:

1. How did the delegates to the Convention find a way to organize the 13 states into one whole nation?
2. How did they find a way that would not force any part of the area to give up its way of living?
3. How did they find a way that could guarantee that everyone would be heard and that everyone would be represented in the decisions of a national government?
4. How did they try to find a way that would last through the years to come?
5. How did they try to make their plan of governing strong enough to make decisions for all the states, yet representative enough to take care of all the variety, and flexible enough to change when necessary?

1. THE CONSTITUTION: ITS SETTING AND ITS VALUES

Have you ever been to Independence Hall in Philadelphia? It seems to have set the mood for the achievements that happened there. The room in which the convention met is the east chamber of what was the Pennsylvania State House. You enter it from a dark hallway so that the room itself seems very bright. There are very large

	1786	1787	1787	1787	1788
	Daniel Shays	delegates to Constitutional Convention	The Congress of the Confederation	Madison, Jay, and Hamilton	New Hampshire Convention
	leads Shays' Rebellion	meet to revise the Articles of Confederation	passes the Northwest Ordinance	write the Federalist	becomes the 9th state to ratify the Constitution
	in Massachusetts	in Philadelphia, Pennsylvania	for the territory north of the Ohio River	to distribute to the states	in Manchester, N.H.

arched windows on both the north and south walls. On the east wall are two large fireplaces framed simply, but handsomely, in marble. Between the fireplaces is a desk. On it is a silver inkstand with quill pen. The chair is very straight with a high back which has a carved cockle shell, or sunburst, pattern at the top. It is a fitting chair for George Washington, the hero of the Revolution, and president of the convention.

The building is small by today's standards. But the nation was small in 1787. The big meeting room is 40 feet long and 40 feet high. The leaders of every state could easily see and talk to each other. There was a large round table covered with green cloth for each state delegation. The tables were arranged geographically, from northern to southern states. Thus people were grouped in the room according to the differences they had come to resolve. The delegates sat in armchairs within easy view and hearing range of each other. They were, after all, assembled to talk seriously and to listen carefully. They were there to work together.

The room is a reminder of all that happened there. It recalls the Continental Congress which ran the war, the Declaration of Independence, and the Constitution which marked the beginning of a new nation. Created out of old values and a long tradition in self-government, the constitution offered a sparkling hope for the future of the United States of America.

This photograph shows the restored interior of the Pennsylvania State House. What is the value of preserving historic places?

This shows the building where the Constitution was written. Why do you think the convention met in Philadelphia?

Shared Values

It took the convention four months to make a new plan for governing the American states—a new written Constitution. It was clear from the discussions at the meeting in Philadelphia that the ideas of liberty and representation had been thoroughly tested in the emotional years of the Revolution and in the muddled years of the Confederation. The delegates to the Philadelphia convention were agreed on some things from the start.

On Power

The new plan had to give the government of all the states the right to take action and a workable method to do so. The delegates wanted action that would be good for all the states. They had a new sense of the whole being bigger than the sum of the 13 parts. They wanted a nation, and they wanted their nation to be respected by other nations.

They wanted a strong nation. But they also were afraid of power. From long experience as English citizens, they had learned that if you give too much power to any one person, that person can use it unjustly. So the Constitutional Convention had to think of a way to keep one state, one lawmaker, one assembly, or one popular leader from having all the power. They decided that the power to

1. What were the goals of the delegates to the Philadelphia convention?

1) They wanted a strong nation. 2) They wanted to keep one state, one lawmaker, one assembly, or one popular leader from ever having all the power.

How did this convention's goals differ from the one that wrote the Articles?

197

get things done must be given to more than one part of the government. Then every possible action could be looked at, thought about, and worried over several times before it was taken. If part of Congress, or the President, became carried away by a speech or a mood, the other part of Congress, or the President, or the courts would hear different speeches and be subject to different moods. Each could stop or *check* the other. Each would serve to keep the other in *balance*. This way of dealing with power has been called a system of checks and balances.

On Differences

2. How did the delegates preserve the separateness of states within the national government?

Each citizen would continue to be a member of a state, and states would keep the right to govern themselves.

3. Why was a national government needed?

To give the states power to achieve new strength together.

The delegates agreed that the new national government should not harm the idea of 13 separate states. Americans had developed differently from the beginning of the colonial period. They did not intend to destroy those differences in the Constitution. They made a wise decision because those differences were real. Therefore, they felt, each citizen must remain a member of a state, and the states must continue to have the right to govern, or *sovereignty*.

How was it possible to have both state and national governments that were directly connected to the people? The governments had to be connected to the people because only the people could transfer their natural rights to a government. That was an old English and American belief. It was the heart of the Declaration of Independence. Governments come from the consent of the governed. Americans consented to two levels of government—state government to preserve their differences, and national government to give the states the power to achieve new strength together.

The idea that each person belonged to two governments at the same time was a remarkable idea indeed. It was called *federalism*. Federation was a stronger word than *con*federation. A federal system was not a loose union of states. It was a strong, permanent union to which the people gave as much of their loyalty as they did to their local and state governments.

On Liberty

The hardest question of all had to do with liberty. That was the one value on which every American, rich or poor, and from every background, agreed. But during the years of the Confederation, people often had used their freedom selfishly. Could they be trusted now? Trusting people in one church or one town was hard enough. How could people be trusted to work together if they would not pay for food and uniforms for soldiers from another state?

The delegates, under the leadership of James Madison of Virginia, said that everyone should be free to speak up and try to get laws

How do you know that you are a citizen of a sovereign state and a sovereign nation?

passed. But everyone would have to think beyond selfish, special interests to get others to vote on his or her side. Checks, balances, and majority rule would stop selfish uses of freedom.

A Representative Democracy

Liberty, therefore, was to be guaranteed through representation. This was a new idea in a new nation. And this nation was the size of an empire! Any one group, or faction, would have to give in to some of the other groups in order to win enough votes for its ideas. This method of giving in, called *compromise,* was not only built into the written Constitution, but it also was the method that worked in the hot summer of 1787.

Practical Decisions

In the first days of the convention in Philadelphia, the delegates made a few very wise decisions. They knew well what their differences were. They knew that only frank, open discussion would ever resolve those differences. These were practical men who knew how to bargain. But bargaining is not a public event. Words are said in haste and anger. Things are said to cause other people to compromise. So at the beginning they agreed that the sessions would be closed to the public. To keep them secret there were to be no official minutes published before their work was entirely done. Several members took notes. But James Madison of Virginia decided to write down as precisely as he could every word said by everyone. Those notes were not published for 30 years. But they serve as a source of information for people today.

The delegates made one other practical decision about disagreement. Any decision made by any part of the government could be reopened and voted on again. They realized that each part of the system would be related to all the other parts. People would not be satisfied about the protection of rights or the strength of the government or any other of their goals until they saw the whole Constitution as a package.

As a result of this very open method, the Constitution was not decided on in the same order in which it was finally published. To follow its day by day, four-month-long meetings in which each part was reconsidered from time to time is fascinating, but too time consuming in this study. Therefore, as you look at the Constitution you will be considering each article from three angles: 1) What was the Americans' past experience that influenced this decision? 2) Which of the values so alive among Americans even today were involved in that decision? 3) How did the convention make compromises to reach that decision?

James Madison kept a journal of the meetings of the Constitutional Convention. The journal tells *present-day* historians what went on at the convention.

4. How did the delegates ensure privacy for resolving their differences?

Their meetings were closed to the public.

5. Why weren't the articles of the Constitution approved in the same order in which they appear in the final document?

Since each part of the system was related to the others, decisions about various portions of the document were reconsidered and voted on again.

In the absence of perfect trust or a population of people who are the same the checks-and-balances system was developed.

199

1. What did the delegates from the Philadelphia Convention agree on from the start?
2. What ingredients were needed for this new recipe called federalism?
3. What is the system of checks and balances?

2. READING THE CONSTITUTION

The Constitution is not a long document. As you read through it, you will see a written statement that has remained both solid and lively and yet has grown with the years. The Constitution contains much of the past, present, and future of the United States of America.

The Preamble

6. What role did Morris play in writing the federal Constitution?

1) He organized 23 separate articles into 7. 2) He wrote the preamble to the Constitution, expressing its purpose.

The choice of words for the opening of the Constitution was left to the last. When all the decisions were made, the document was given to the Committee of Style and Arrangement to be put into the clearest and smoothest language. Most of the work was done by the Pennsylvanian Gouverneur Morris. He was given 23 separate articles, and he organized them into seven. It was Morris who made the choice of words to express the purpose of the whole Constitution in the introduction, or preamble.

7. What is the significance of the words "We, the people"?

The federal government has grown out of the consent of the people.

Notice that the preamble says "We, the people," not we the states. This clearly puts forth the idea that the national, or federal, government has grown directly out of the consent of the people. The seven verbs are wonderful examples of what this new and stronger government was supposed to be able to do: form, establish, insure, provide, promote, secure, and ordain. These are symbols of what the United States was going to do for its citizens. The delegates had come a long way from the Articles of Confederation and its expression of their fear of each other.

Article I

Article I is almost half the length of the entire Constitution. It took half the summer of 1787 to put this article together. Most of the major arguments were settled in Article I: How strong would the new government be, and how would the small states be protected from the larger ones? The nine parts of the article must be looked at together.

The Great Compromise

The Convention spent most of its time making changes in a plan presented during the first week by Edmund Randolph of Virginia. It called for a two-house, or *bicameral*, legislature. In the Virginia Plan, both houses would have representation by population. This would give the larger states an advantage in both houses. Two weeks later, the small states, under the leadership of William Paterson of New Jersey, proposed a plan for a one-house legislature. In this plan, each state received one vote no matter how many people lived there or how much wealth the state produced.

8. Why did New Jersey propose a one-house legislature in which each state received one vote?

New Jersey, a small state, wanted the smaller states to have the same representation as the larger states.

Gouverneur Morris lost his leg in an accident. He was in charge of writing the final draft of the Constitution. He pulled together the ideas of the other members of the convention, so the Constitution would be easier to read.

James Madison of Virginia made a speech in which he tore the New Jersey plan apart, item by item. He showed that all the problems of unpaid bills, unpaid soldiers, and Shays' rebellion would rise again under such a weak organization. James Wilson of Pennsylvania was in agreement with Madison. Wilson said, "Why should a national government be unpopular? Has it less dignity? Will each citizen enjoy under it less liberty or protection? Will a citizen of Delaware be degraded by becoming a citizen of the United States?"

The Convention voted immediately to turn down the New Jersey Plan. But it did not agree immediately on how to fill out the details of the Virginia Plan so that the small states would not be pushed around by the larger ones. Also, both large and small states wanted to be sure that the state governments would not be wiped out by the new national government.

James Wilson of Pennsylvania wanted a strong central government. What were the advantages of a strong government?

9. How was a compromise reached?

The House of Representatives would be based on population, and the Senate on equal representation.

10. What other decisions were made possible because of the Great Compromise?

The delegates decided to list what Congress could and could not do, and to list what the states could not do.

It was not until July 16 that the Convention finally voted to approve the Great Compromise. Roger Sherman of Connecticut had offered the idea before. Benjamin Franklin, who did not speak up often, had said, "When a broad table is to be made, and the edges of the planks do not fit, the artist takes a little from both, and makes a good joint. In like manner here both sides must part with some of their demands, in order that they may join in some accommodating proposition." The delegates agreed that the lower house, or House of Representatives, was to be based on population. The upper house, the Senate, was to be based on equal representation of all states no matter what their size.

The Great Compromise made all the others possible. Then the idea was adopted that there would be a list of what Congress could do (Section 8), a list of what Congress could not do (Section 9), and then a list of what the states could not do (Section 10). Through all of these measures in Article I, the major problems of fair representation of differences and fair use of power were decided.

The debate had been long. The arguments were real. But the fear of weakness in the future, and the memory of weakness in the past, finally caused these thoughtful men to find a meeting ground.

North Against South—The Three-Fifths Compromise

11. How was a compromise reached on slavery and representation?

Unfortunately, the Great Compromise did not solve all of the problems. The differences of opinion between the small states and the large states were not the only ones that had to be settled. The southern states and the northern ones also differed on the question of slavery and representation. The North argued that slaves should be counted as part of the population when it came to determining

To make the Great Compromise required trust. The Constitution requires some trust but also lists the don'ts.

each state's share of taxes paid to the national government, but not counted when it came to determining the number of representatives each state could send to the House of Representatives. The South took the opposite position. It wanted slaves counted for representation but not for taxation. Finally, the two sides agreed to a compromise. Each slave would be considered as three-fifths of a person for purposes of both taxation and representation. Also, to calm the fears of the South that the North would try to force it to give up the system of slavery, it was written into the Constitution that Congress could not interfere with or end the slave trade until 1808.

1) Two thirds of the slaves were counted for determining taxation and the number of representatives a state could have in the House. 2) The South was given 20 more years to import slaves.

Checks and Balances

The system of checks and balances was spelled out in Section 7. Every proposed law, or bill, has to be considered by each house and by the President. In addition, the court system allows citizens to challenge laws once they are made.

12. Who considers every law before it is passed?

The three branches are the legislative, executive, and judiciary.

From Experience—Fear

Some of the items in Article I seem very detailed. They are reminders of hated action taken by the English government after the French and Indian War. The convention was afraid of officials with power. The writers of the Constitution wanted to make sure that no one in their new government interfered with the place and time of meeting of Congress or the elections to it.

Therefore the Congress was to be the judge of its own elections and its own behavior. It was also to judge the behavior of all officers of the government. The House could accuse, or impeach. The Senate could try those who had been impeached. The people's representatives had the power to regulate themselves. Also, the House, which was closest to the people, had the only power to begin a tax bill.

13. How did the Constitution ensure that officials would not gain too much power?

1) Congress was to be judge of its own elections, its own behavior, and the behavior of all officers of the government. 2) The House could accuse or impeach. 3) The Senate could try impeachments. 4) Only the House could begin a tax bill.

Congress Under Law

Much of Section 9 also promised that Congress would never take away the rights of an individual. It could not accuse someone of a crime without proper protection of the accused. The government was not as important as the Constitution and the law.

Article I makes sure that the federal government has enough power to carry out three of the goals of the Preamble—domestic tranquillity, the common defense, and the general welfare.

14. In what ways were the rights and privileges of the people protected?

The Right to Vote

Each state was supposed to be able to decide who could vote. This part of Section 2 removed from the convention the problem of resolving the differences between the New England town meetings, the property qualifications in some states, and slavery in others. At the time of the writing of the Constitution, the United States was considered very democratic in allowing all White males with some property to vote. The Convention put its emphasis on people of talent and skill rather than on people who had inherited titles of nobility. The exclusion of women, poor men, Blacks, and Native Americans was an accepted standard of the late 1700's, even in America. In the course of the development of the nation, "We, the people" has come to mean everyone.

Article II

The idea of a single person as the national executive had been proposed to the Convention during its first week. It was part of Randolph's Virginia Plan. Most people agreed that there had to be someone responsible for carrying out the laws. There was disagreement during the four months of the convention, however, on many smaller questions. Should there be one executive or a committee? How long should the term last? Should the executive be reelected? Should the executive have the right to stop legislation, or veto? What happens if the executive dies? Should the executive be impeached for wrongdoing? Should the executive be paid?

But the big question had to do with the nature of the Presidency. Should the executive be someone who carried out the will of the Congress, or would the executive be the guardian of the people against a Congress that acted like a tyrant? In the end, the President was allowed to be both. Through the separation of powers of the President and the Congress, and their need to agree to get anything done, the compromise was brought about. In the years to come, individual Presidents would tend to be more one or the other. Which kind of President is best for the people is still debated.

Why did Edmond Randolph want to add a bill of rights to the Constitution?

There was very little argument about Article II in the convention as a whole. Many of the details actually were written in committee and then presented to the convention with the final draft of the Constitution. The great presidential powers to make treaties and appoint people to government jobs were softened by the fact that those decisions were subject to the "advice and consent of the Senate." Since the Congress had the power, it seemed right to find a way to let the people, rather than the Congress, choose the President. It was the Committee on Style that came up with the idea of the electoral college. In that way, the people, through their state legislatures, could be part of the election process. However, in this new system, only the best people could make the final choice for President.

Once the final draft was presented to the whole convention, there was no further debate on Article II. Some said it passed easily because it was September 12 and everyone wanted to go home. Others felt comfortable letting it pass because they knew George Washington was going to be the first President, and they trusted him completely.

Article III

The delegates agreed from the start on Article III. The new nation had to have a court system. Federal courts were necessary to enforce the federal, or national laws, to which individual citizens would now be subject. They also were necessary to act as umpires when two states, or the citizens of two states, disagreed. The only problem was whether to have lower, or *inferior,* courts in the federal judicial system. Were not state courts perfectly able to serve as lower courts to the Supreme Court of the United States? The compromise on this led to the creation of the Supreme Court. Congress also was given the power to establish lower courts if and when it wished. At its very first session in 1789, Congress set up federal districts, each with its court.

The last three paragraphs of Article III are the strong statement of civil liberties stemming from English law and the American experience. All citizens have a right to trial by jury in the place where the crime was supposed to have been committed. *Treason* is defined as overthrow or attempted overthrow of the government. Criticism of the government or taking legal action to remove people from office could not be called treason against the nation.

Article IV

Article IV pulls the states together within the national union. Only the second sentence of the article caused any debate at all. It gave Congress the right to decide *how* to give "full faith and credit" to state laws. Some delegates were afraid that this statement was too vague and might give Congress too much say. But giving Congress this power was a practical way to make sure that laws in one state were honored by citizens of every state. The rest of the article comes from the Articles of Confederation and the Northwest Ordinance.

Article V

This is one of the great achievements of the convention. It was startling enough that the delegates could compromise on a plan of

Benjamin Franklin was 81 years old when he addressed the convention. James Madison and George Washington are also shown here.

15. What decisions were made regarding the court system and citizens' rights within it?

1) The Supreme Court would enforce national laws and act as umpire between states, or the citizens of two states, 2) Trial by jury was guaranteed.

16. Why was there little controversy over the contents of Article IV?

Article IV pulled the states together within the national union, which was the reason for the convention.

17. Why did the delegates make provisions for amendments to the Constitution?

1) They didn't want their compromises on a plan for governing to be frozen forever. 2) They wanted to add a bill of rights.

governing. But that they would not want their compromise frozen forever is equally surprising. The question before the delegates was whether or not Congress had the power to make changes, or *amendments,* in the Constitution. Two groups were particularly concerned with this question. The southern states were afraid that the federal government would add an amendment prohibiting slavery. The small states were afraid that Congress might decide to change the make-up of the Senate so they would not be on an equal footing with the larger states. In the end, James Madison was the careful author of a compromise on this question. A procedure was set up whereby both the states and the Congress could make amendments to the Constitution.

The first ten amendments were a Bill of Rights, a list of actions Congress could never take against individuals. This list came out of both their English experience and the English and American belief in natural rights. A Bill of Rights was promised to the states if they would agree or ratify the Constitution. And the first Congress proposed them right away.

Article VI

18. What was the relationship of the states to the national government?

1) The states were part of a federal system and were guaranteed their powers. 2) The Union was more important than any of the states.

This is the article that states once and for all that there is a national union and it outranks the states. Federal or national laws made by Congress outrank state laws. State laws also are outranked by treaties. And the Constitution is the last word. This is the famous supremacy clause. It declared absolutely that the Articles of Confederation had been discarded for a new national agreement.

The first step the new national government took was to assume the debts of the Confederation. It also required a loyalty oath of every officer of both state and federal governments. The oath was a better way to guarantee loyalty than to give Congress the power to punish or force loyalty.

In forming Article VI, the convention simply agreed that there was a ladder, or *hierarchy,* of power. The states were part of a federal system and they were guaranteed their powers (see Amendment X), but the Union was more important than any of the states.

Checking the facts

1. Who were "We, the people" in the late 1700's?
2. How did the makers of the Constitution provide for the expansion of "We, the people"?
3. What was the importance of the Great Compromise?

How does the Bill of Rights balance the idea that the Constitution and federal government are supreme?

This painting shows the Constitutional Convention. The artist painted a scene of the rising sun behind George Washington. How did the rising sun represent the new nation?

3. RATIFYING THE CONSTITUTION

Article VII made sure that the new Constitution was not going back to the Congress of the Confederation for agreement. The convention had been meeting in New York. It only took ten days to send the Constitution to the states so that the states could call their special conventions. Special conventions were a clever idea. The regular state legislatures might not have ratified the Constitution. Only Rhode Island, which had not sent delegates to Philadelphia, refused to set up a convention to discuss the Constitution.

The small states were the first ones to ratify. This was a change from the year before. They had been reluctant to join a union then. But the Great Compromise had given them guarantees of enough power to make a difference. The first states to ratify the Constitution were Delaware, New Jersey, Georgia, Connecticut, and Maryland.

In Pennsylvania the opponents from the back country did not want to go to the assembly to vote on a call for a convention. Some of them locked themselves in a boarding house. But a mob of people stoned the house and carried them to the hall. Once the convention was held, it was clear that the opposition was fearful that the

19. How did the delegates guarantee ratification of the Constitution?

They sent the Constitution to each state, calling for special ratifying conventions that by-passed the Confederation Congress and the state legislatures.

20. Why were the small states the first to ratify?

The bicameral legislature guaranteed their power.

21. What was the conflict in Pennsylvania over ratification?

People from the back country thought that the wealthy eastern city dwellers would control the new government.

Hancock felt that government endangered liberty.

Writing is an important skill in a democracy. Why?

wealthy, eastern-city dwellers would control the new government, and they would have even less voice. But the strong leaders—Franklin, Wilson, and Morris—carried the vote.

Much depended on Massachusetts, and the Massachusetts vote depended on John Hancock. Hancock was angry because he thought the Constitution gave too much power over trade to the Congress. He also thought that George Washington had been given too much power at the Constitutional Convention. Somehow Hancock had to be lured into taking a leadership role. First, Sam Adams was won over. Then Adams proposed some amendments and talked Hancock into coming to the assembly to present them. The backers of the Constitution also promised Hancock a nomination to the presidency in case Virginia did not ratify. All this worked. When a vote was taken, Massachusetts ratified the Constitution by a vote

22. Why was Sam Adams the key to ratification in Massachusetts?

He won the support of John Hancock, whose influence was crucial.

This picture shows the cover of *The Federalist Papers.* What did Alexander Hamilton, John Jay, and James Madison hope to accomplish by writing these essays? What did they accomplish?

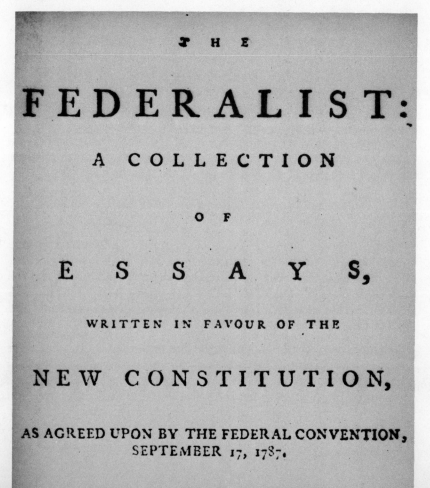

THE

FEDERALIST:

A COLLECTION

OF

ESSAYS,

WRITTEN IN FAVOUR OF THE

NEW CONSTITUTION,

AS AGREED UPON BY THE FEDERAL CONVENTION, SEPTEMBER 17, 1787.

How do you feel about politicians' working in these ways to get a law passed?

What issues in the Constitution caused people to disagree?

of 187 to 168. It passed by only 19 votes. The Massachusetts decision to ratify was important in getting other states to join the new government. On the streets of Boston, the supporters of the Constitution celebrated. They sang a song to the tune of Yankee Doodle. Its last verse showed where the state's interests were:

> So here I end my Fed'ral song,
> Composed of thirteen verses;
> May agriculture flourish long
> And commerce fill our purses!

In Virginia the opposition was led by the Revolutionary War hero Patrick Henry. Henry believed the Constitution created too strong a government. He did not want it to pass. Edmund Randolph also had refused to sign the Constitution because he thought it needed a Bill of Rights. But when Randolph learned that other states had ratified and were prepared to have the first Congress start the amendment procedure for a Bill of Rights, he changed his mind. Randolph was the only one who could sway Virginians against Patrick Henry. Washington stayed at home. He tried not to get involved in the state debate. Virginia also knew that New Hampshire was about to ratify and that South Carolina had done so easily. Virginia wanted to be the ninth state, the one that made the nation come into being. But Virginia narrowly missed. New Hampshire's vote came in before, but not very much before, Virginia's.

23. What historic role did New Hampshire play?

It was the ninth state to ratify the Constitution, the one that brought the nation into being.

The only major state left was New York. In New York the campaign for ratification had been the most carefully planned. A brilliant series of articles had appeared in the press signed by Publius—in reality John Jay, James Madison, and Alexander Hamilton. Hamilton supported strong national government at the convention because he felt that the people were not wise enough to live under weak government. In these newspaper articles, *The Federalist Papers,* Hamilton and the others had written with care, logic, and facts. People throughout the states who supported the Constitution called themselves Federalists. Their opponents became Anti-Federalists. The Federalists used every possible argument to sway the public to support the Constitution. But New York was still caught between the upstate farmers and the merchants of Manhattan Island. Manhattan finally threatened to leave the state and join the union by itself. The threat worked. The vote switched to favor the Constitution, but not by much. It was 30 to 27 or a majority of three!

24. How did the state of New York come to ratify the Constitution?

1) Jay, Madison, and Hamilton published *The Federalist Papers* to convince the public to support ratification. 2) Manhattan threatened to leave the state and join the Union by itself, which brought the upstate farmers into line.

The United States of America was now ready to begin its work. The states of North Carolina and Rhode Island would join later. The Bill of Rights would be added. Ratification had taken ten months and now the Americans had reason to celebrate. There were

People in the states celebrated the new government in many different ways. In New York City they celebrated with floats and parades. Hamilton is honored by having his name on the float.

parades in every city—in Philadelphia there were ships made into floats, the *Union* and the *Constitution*. In Philadelphia, too, the chairman of the arrangements committee for the celebration, Francis Hopkinson, had written a poem. It ended on the note that had sent the states to the Constitutional Convention in the first place:

> "And let the people's motto ever be,
> 'United thus, and thus united, free!' "

Checking the facts

1. Why was Patrick Henry against the Constitution?
2. Why did Hamilton, Jay, and Madison write *The Federalist Papers?*
3. Why was it important for the country to have Virginia ratify the Constitution?

In what ways are you free when you are united with other people?

4. The Constitution of the United States and What It Means Today

(Portions of the text printed in brackets have been changed by amendment or have gone out of date. The text of the Constitution appears in black; annotations appear in blue.)

Preamble

We, the people of the United States, in order to form a more perfect Union, establish justice, insure domestic tranquillity, provide for the common defense, promote the general welfare, and secure the blessings of liberty to ourselves and our posterity, do ordain and establish this Constitution for the United States of America.

The Preamble. The opening is called the *Preamble*, and it states the purpose of the Constitution. Note that it begins, "We, the people," not "We, the states. . . ."

Article 1. The Legislative Branch

Section 1. Congress

All legislative powers herein granted shall be vested in a Congress of the United States, which shall consist of a Senate and House of Representatives.

Section 1. This section states how Congress shall be organized, and that it will have the power to make all federal laws. This clause has been modified in practice to allow certain federal agencies to make regulations that function as federal laws.

Section 2. House of Representatives

1. Election and Term of Members. The House of Representatives shall be composed of members chosen every second year by the people of the several states, and the electors in each state shall have the qualifications requisite for electors of the most numerous branch of the state legislature.

Clause 1. Members of the House serve two-year terms. The term *electors* is used here to refer to voters.

2. Qualifications. No person shall be a Representative who shall not have attained to the age of twenty-five years, and been seven years a citizen of the United States, and who shall not, when elected, be an inhabitant of that state in which he shall be chosen.

Clause 2. A representative must be over the age of 25, a United States citizen for at least 7 years, and a resident of the state from which he or she is elected. The states are divided into congressional districts, each of which elects a representative.

3. Apportionment of Representatives. Representatives [and direct taxes] shall be apportioned among the several states which may be included within this Union, according to their

Clause 3. The number of members in the House of Representatives was to be determined according to the number of "free persons" in each state plus "three fifths of all other persons." This meant that states could count only three fifths

211

respective numbers [which shall be determined by adding to the whole number of free persons, including those bound to service for a term of years, and excluding Indians not taxed, three-fifths of all other persons]. The actual enumeration shall be made within three years after the first meeting of the Congress of the United States, and within every subsequent term of ten years, in such manner as they shall by law direct. The number of Representatives shall not exceed 1 for every 30,000, but each state shall have at least 1 Representative; [and until such enumeration shall be made, the state of New Hampshire shall be entitled to choose 3; Massachusetts, 8; Rhode Island and Providence Plantations, 1; Connecticut, 5; New York, 6; New Jersey, 4; Pennsylvania, 8; Delaware, 1; Maryland, 6; Virginia, 10; North Carolina, 5; South Carolina, 5; and Georgia, 3].

of their Black slaves (see page 202). In the case of Black slaves, this provision was overruled by the 13th Amendment (1865) and Section 2 of the 14th Amendment (1868). Native Americans, however, were excluded from the census until 1940 because they were considered a separate nation.

Since representation was based on population, the Constitution provided for a national head count, or census, every ten years. The United States was the first nation to have a regular census. Every representative must represent at least 30,000 people, but each state is entitled to at least one representative. In 1929, in order to prevent the House of Representatives from growing too large, Congress limited the membership of the House to 435.

4. Vacancies. When vacancies happen in the representation from any state, the executive authority thereof shall issue writs of election to fill such vacancies.

Clause 4. If a member of the House of Representatives dies or resigns, the governor of the state orders a special election to fill the vacant seat.

5. Impeachment. The House of Representatives shall choose their Speaker and other officers; and shall have the sole power of impeachment.

Clause 5. By majority vote, the House can impeach, or accuse, officers of the executive branch or federal judges. The Senate tries all impeachment cases.

Section 3. Senate

1. Number of Members and Terms of Office. The Senate of the United States shall be composed of two Senators from each state [chosen by the legislatures thereof], for six years, and each Senator shall have one vote.

Clause 1. Each state legislature was to elect two members to the Senate. Senators represented states, not people. This system was changed by the 17th Amendment in 1913. Senators are now elected directly by the voters of the state.

2. Classification; Vacancies. [Immediately after they shall be assembled in consequence of the first election, they shall be divided as equally as may be into three classes. The seats of the Senators of the first class shall be vacated at the expiration of the second year, of the second class at the expiration of the fourth year, and of the third class at the expiration of the sixth year, so that one-third may be chosen every second year; and if vacancies happen by resignation, or otherwise, during the recess of the legislature of any state, the executive thereof may make temporary appointments until the next meeting of the legislature, which shall then fill such vacancies.]

Clause 2. Senators serve six-year terms. The paragraph defining "classes" of senators sets up a staggered system whereby one third of the Senate comes up for reelection every two years. If a Senator resigns or dies, the 17th Amendment provides that the state governor call a special election to fill the vacancy or appoint a temporary successor.

212

3. Qualifications. No person shall be a Senator who shall not have attained the age of thirty years, and been nine years a citizen of the United States, and who shall not, when elected, be an inhabitant of that state for which he shall be chosen.

4. The President of the Senate. The Vice-President of the United States shall be president of the Senate, but shall have no vote, unless they be equally divided.

5. Other Officers. The Senate shall choose their other officers, and also a president pro tempore, in the absence of the Vice-President, or when he shall exercise the office of the President of the United States.

6. Impeachments. The Senate shall have the sole power to try all impeachments. When sitting for that purpose, they shall be on oath or affirmation. When the President of the United States is tried, the Chief Justice shall preside; and no person shall be convicted without the concurrence of two-thirds of the members present.

7. Penalty for Conviction. Judgment in cases of impeachment shall not extend further than to removal from office, and disqualification to hold and enjoy any office of honor, trust, or profit under the United States; but the party convicted shall nevertheless be liable and subject to indictment, trial, judgment, and punishment, according to law.

Clauses 4 and 5. The Vice-President serves as the president of the Senate and votes only to break a tie. This is the only vice-presidential duty specified in the Constitution. If the Vice-President is absent or becomes President, the Senate elects a temporary president (pro tempore).

Clauses 6 and 7. The trial of members of the executive or judiciary accused by the House of Representatives takes place before the Senate. A vote of two thirds of the Senate is necessary for conviction. If convicted, the accused is removed from office and is then subject to indictment and criminal proceedings according to the law. Andrew Johnson is the only President who was ever impeached (1868). He was not convicted, since the vote for conviction failed by one vote. Richard M. Nixon was the first President to resign from office. He did so in 1974, when the Judiciary Committee of the House of Representatives recommended that he be impeached. Following his resignation he was granted a presidential pardon, which spared him from possible proceedings.

Section 4. Elections and Meetings

1. Holding elections. The times, places, and manner of holding elections for Senators and Representatives shall be prescribed in each state by the legislature thereof; but the Congress may at any time by law make or alter such regulations, except as to the places of choosing Senators.

2. Meetings. The Congress shall assemble at least once in every year, [and such meeting shall be on the first Monday in December,] unless they shall by law appoint a different day.

Clause 1. The states set the conditions of congressional elections, determining even who can vote. This was modified by the 15th Amendment (1870), which prevents the states from interfering with the right of Blacks to vote; the 19th Amendment (1920), which extends voting rights to women; the 24th Amendment (1964), which forbids collection of poll taxes as a condition for voting; and the 26th Amendment (1971), which lowers the voting age to 18.

Clause 2. The date for Congress to assemble was changed by the 20th Amendment (1933). Congress now meets on January 3.

213

Section 5.   Procedure

1. Organization. Each house shall be the judge of the elections, returns, and qualifications of its own members, and a majority of each shall constitute a quorum to do business; but a smaller number may adjourn from day to day, and may be authorized to compel the attendance of absent members, in such manner, and under such penalties, as each house may provide.

2. Proceedings. Each house may determine the rules of its proceedings, punish its members for disorderly behavior, and with the concurrence of two-thirds, expel a member.

3. The Journal. Each house shall keep a journal of its proceedings, and from time to time publish the same, excepting such parts as may in their judgment require secrecy; and the yeas and nays of the members of either house on any question shall, at the desire of one-fifth of those present, be entered on the journal.

4. Adjournment. Neither house, during the session of Congress, shall, without the consent of the other, adjourn for more than three days, nor to any other place than that in which the two houses shall be sitting.

Section 6.   Privileges and Restrictions

1. Pay and Privileges. The Senators and Representatives shall receive a compensation for their services, to be ascertained by law and paid out of the Treasury of the United States. They shall in all cases, except treason, felony, and breach of the peace, be privileged from arrest during their attendance at the session of their respective houses, and in going to and returning from the same; and for any speech or debate in either house, they shall not be questioned in any other place.

2. Restrictions. No Senator or Representative shall, during the time for which he was elected, be appointed to any civil office under the authority of the United States, which shall have been created, or the emoluments whereof shall have been increased, during such

Clause 1. Both houses have the right to refuse to seat new members. A *quorum* is a majority of members of either house of Congress and is the minimum number required to be present to carry on business. In practice, however, business can be and often is transacted without a quorum, so long as no one objects. Each house can compel the attendance of its members when their presence is needed.

Clause 3. The framers of the Constitution wanted the voters to be kept informed of the activities of Congress. Such a record would also enable the people to find out how their representatives voted on particular issues. Such openness in government was unknown in Europe at the time the Constitution was written. The *House Journal* and the *Senate Journal* are published at the end of each session of Congress. The *Congressional Record* is published for every day Congress is in session and records the action of both houses.

Clause 4. Once Congress has met, the House and Senate must remain at work until both agree on a time to adjourn. Since they work closely together, they must both work in the same place.

Clause 1. This clause aims to enable members to speak freely by providing *congressional immunity* from prosecution or arrest for things they say in speeches and debates in Congress.

Clause 2. This clause underscores the principle of separation of powers. No member of Congress can hold any other government office. If Congress creates a new office or raises the salary of an old one, no member of Congress may fill that office until his or her term expires. This provision was made because in Britain in the 18th century, the king and

time; and no person holding any office under the United States shall be a member of either house during his continuance in office.

his ministers controlled Parliament by promising offices as bribes.

Section 7. Passing Laws

1. Revenue Bills. All bills for raising revenue shall originate in the House of Representatives; but the Senate may propose or concur with amendments as on other bills.

Clause 1. Bills for raising money by taxes must be introduced in the House of Representatives. This was part of the compromise between the large states and the small states. The large states received proportional representation in one house, and that house was also given first authority over money and tax measures. This provision has little practical importance, however, since the Senate can amend such bills.

2. How a Bill Becomes a Law. Every bill which shall have passed the House of Representatives and the Senate shall, before it becomes a law, be presented to the President of the United States; if he approve, he shall sign it, but if not, he shall return it, with his objections, to that house in which it shall have originated, who shall enter the objections at large on their journal, and proceed to reconsider it. If after such reconsideration two-thirds of that house shall agree to pass the bill, it shall be sent, together with the objections, to the other house, by which it shall likewise be reconsidered, and, if approved by two-thirds of that house, it shall become a law. But in all such cases the votes of both houses shall be determined by yeas and nays, and the names of the persons voting for and against the bill shall be entered on the journal of each house respectively. If any bill shall not be returned by the President within ten days (Sundays excepted) after it shall have been presented to him, the same bill shall be a law, in like manner as if he had signed it, unless the Congress by their adjournment prevent its return, in which case it shall not be a law.

Clause 2. Every bill that passes both houses of Congress is sent to the President. If he approves the bill, he signs it into law. His refusal to sign is called a *veto*. A vetoed bill is sent back to Congress with a written statement of the President's objections. If the bill can pass both houses by two-thirds majority (usually very difficult to obtain) Congress can *override* the President's veto and the bill becomes law. If not, the veto is *sustained* and the bill dies. If the President receives a bill and keeps it ten days without acting on it, it automatically becomes law. If, however, Congress adjourns within those ten days, it must be introduced all over again in the next congressional session. This is called a *pocket veto*.

The presidential veto is an important check of the executive branch of the government on the legislative branch. Congress checks the President when it overrides a veto.

3. Presidential Approval or Veto. Every order, resolution, or vote to which the concurrence of the Senate and House of Representatives may be necessary (except on a question of adjournment) shall be presented to the President of the United States; and before the same shall take effect, shall be approved by him, or being disapproved by him, shall be repassed by two-thirds of the Senate and House of Representatives, according to the rules and limitations prescribed in the case of a bill.

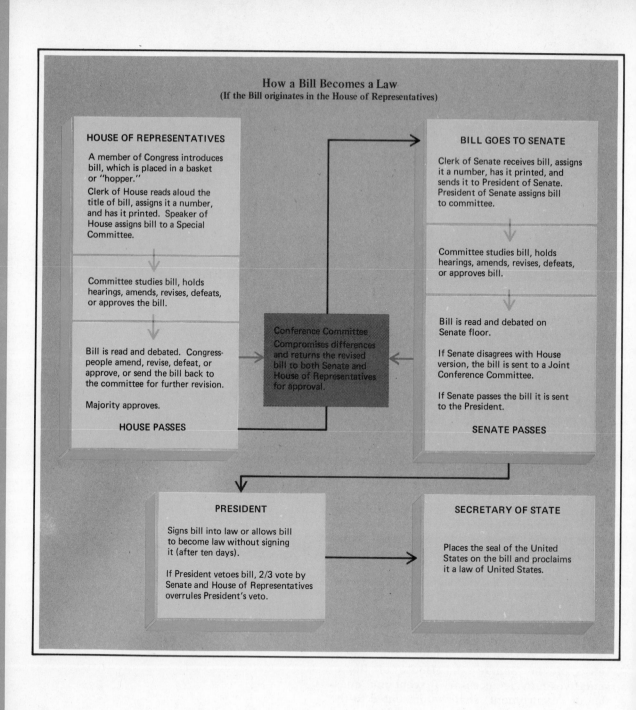

How a Bill Becomes a Law
(If the Bill originates in the House of Representatives)

HOUSE OF REPRESENTATIVES

A member of Congress introduces bill, which is placed in a basket or "hopper."

Clerk of House reads aloud the title of bill, assigns it a number, and has it printed. Speaker of House assigns bill to a Special Committee.

Committee studies bill, holds hearings, amends, revises, defeats, or approves the bill.

Bill is read and debated. Congresspeople amend, revise, defeat, or approve, or send the bill back to the committee for further revision.

Majority approves.

HOUSE PASSES

Conference Committee
Compromises differences and returns the revised bill to both Senate and House of Representatives for approval.

BILL GOES TO SENATE

Clerk of Senate receives bill, assigns it a number, has it printed, and sends it to President of Senate. President of Senate assigns bill to committee.

Committee studies bill, holds hearings, amends, revises, defeats, or approves bill.

Bill is read and debated on Senate floor.

If Senate disagrees with House version, the bill is sent to a Joint Conference Committee.

If Senate passes the bill it is sent to the President.

SENATE PASSES

PRESIDENT

Signs bill into law or allows bill to become law without signing it (after ten days).

If President vetoes bill, 2/3 vote by Senate and House of Representatives overrules President's veto.

SECRETARY OF STATE

Places the seal of the United States on the bill and proclaims it a law of United States.

Section 8. Powers Delegated to Congress
The Congress shall have power

Section 8. This section lists the 18 *delegated* or *enumerated* powers granted to Congress. The first 17 specify clearly areas in which Congress has authority and are called *expressed* powers. The 18th power is the elastic clause. The doctrine of *implied* powers developed from this clause.

1. To lay and collect taxes, duties, imposts, and excises, to pay the debts and provide for the common defense and general welfare of the United States; but all duties, imposts, and excises shall be uniform throughout the United States;

Clause 1. Congress has the power to levy taxes to pay the nation's debts, to provide for national defense, and to provide for the general welfare of the people. All federal taxes must be equal in various parts of the country.

2. To borrow money on the credit of the United States;

Clause 2. The Constitution sets no limit on the amount Congress can borrow—Congress itself sets the national debt.

3. To regulate commerce with foreign nations, and among the several states, [and with the Indian tribes];

Clause 3. Congress has the power to regulate trade with foreign nations. It also has direct control over interstate commerce. This phrase is broad enough to include the power to regulate transportation, the stock market, and even the more modern radio and television broadcasting industries.

4. To establish a uniform rule of naturalization, and uniform laws on the subject of bankruptcies throughout the United States;

Clause 4. Congress can decide how immigrants become citizens. It can also make laws about procedures involved in business failures.

5. To coin money, regulate the value thereof, and of foreign coin, and fix the standard of weights and measures;

Clause 5. Congress can mint coins, print paper money, and set the value of both American money and foreign currency within this country. It can also set standard measurements for the nation.

6. To provide for the punishment of counterfeiting the securities and current coin of the United States;

Clause 6. Congress can make laws fixing the punishment for counterfeiting currency, bonds, or stamps.

7. To establish post offices and post roads;

Clause 7. Congress can designate which highways should be used by the federal mails.

8. To promote the progress of science and useful arts by securing for limited times to authors and inventors the exclusive right to their respective writings and discoveries;

Clause 8. Congress can pass patent and copyright laws to give the sole rights to inventors and artists for their works for a number of years. Anyone who uses patented inventions or copyrighted material without permission may be punished.

9. To constitute tribunals inferior to the Supreme Court;

Clause 9. All federal courts except the Supreme Court are established by acts of Congress.

10. To define and punish piracies and felonies committed on the high seas and offenses against the law of nations;

Clause 10. Congress can decide what acts committed on American ships are crimes and how such acts should be punished. It can also decide the punishment for American citizens who break international laws.

11. To declare war, [grant letters of marque and reprisal,] and make rules concerning captures on land and water;

Clause 11. Only Congress may declare war. However, American forces have engaged in combat in some instances without a congressional declaration of war—for example, in the Vietnamese War. *Letters of marque and reprisal* refers to permission granted to American merchant ships to attack enemy ships, a practice common in early wars. This practice is outlawed by international agreement today.

12. To raise and support armies, but no appropriation of money to that use shall be for a longer term than two years;

Clause 12. All money for the army comes from Congress. However, Congress may not grant money to the army for longer than a two-year period. This is to make sure that civilians will have financial control over the army.

13. To provide and maintain a navy;

Clause 13. There is no two-year limit on naval appropriations because the navy was not considered a threat to liberty.

14. To make rules for the government and regulation of the land and naval forces;

Clause 14. Such rules now include the air force. Since Congress can create the armed forces, it is necessary to give it the power to make rules for the services.

15. To provide for calling forth the militia to execute the laws of the Union, suppress insurrections, and repel invasions;

Clause 15. Congress can call into federal service the state militia forces (citizen-soldiers now referred to as the National Guard) to enforce federal laws and defend life and property. Congress can empower the President to call out the militia, but only for the reasons named here.

16. To provide for organizing, arming, and disciplining the militia, and for governing such part of them as may be employed in the service of the United States, reserving to the states, respectively, the appointment of the officers, and the authority of training the militia according to the discipline prescribed by Congress;

Clause 16. The states may appoint the officers for the militia, but Congress establishes rules for training the militia.

17. To exercise exclusive legislation in all cases whatsoever, over such district (not exceeding ten miles square) as may, by cession of particular states, and the acceptance of Congress, become the seat of government of the United States, and to exercise like authority over all places purchased by the consent of the legislature of the state in which the same shall be, for the erection of forts, magazines, arsenals, dock-yards, and other needful buildings;—and

Clause 17. Congress has control over the District of Columbia as well as all forts, arsenals, dockyards, federal courthouses, and other places owned and operated by the federal government.

18. To make all laws which shall be necessary and proper for carrying into execution the foregoing powers, and all other powers vested by this Constitution in the government of the

Clause 18. The framers were very careful to ensure that Congress would be able to meet the needs of a changing society. Sometimes called the elastic clause of the Constitution, this clause enables Congress to frame new laws that

United States, or in any department or officer thereof.

are related to specific powers already listed in the Constitution. For instance, as part of its power "to raise and support armies," Congress might undertake the construction of roads to transport its armies. Such roads are "necessary and proper" for maintaining an army.

This elastic clause has enabled Congress to meet the changing needs of society over two centuries. The power that has proved most expandable in this regard is the power to regulate interstate trade and commerce. In the 20th century, Congress has used this power to pass Civil Rights Acts (protecting the free movement of people and trade) and labor legislation that guards the right of unions to organize (strikes interfere with interstate commerce).

Section 9. Powers Denied to the Federal Government

1. [The migration or importation of such persons as any of the states now existing shall think proper to admit shall not be prohibited by the Congress prior to the year 1808; but a tax or duty may be imposed on such importation, not exceeding $10 for each person.]

Clause 1. "Such persons" refers to slaves. This clause was the result of a compromise between northern merchants and southern planters. The Constitutional Convention gave Congress powers to regulate commerce and to tax imports, while also providing that the importation of slaves would not be prohibited prior to 1808 and that there would not be an import tax of more than $10 per person. The importation of slaves was prohibited in 1808.

2. The privilege of the writ of *habeas corpus* shall not be suspended, unless when in cases of rebellion or invasion the public safety may require it.

Clause 2. A *writ of habeas corpus* protects citizens from arbitrary arrest. It is an order demanding that a person who is arrested be brought before a court so a judge can decide if he or she is being held lawfully.

3. No bill of attainder or *ex post facto* law shall be passed.

Clause 3. A *bill of attainder* is a law that declares an individual guilty of a crime without a court trial. An *ex post facto* law makes an act a crime after the act has been committed.

4. [No capitation or other direct tax shall be laid, unless in proportion to the census herein before directed to be taken.]

Clause 4. Congress must divide direct taxes among the states according to their populations. This provision was included to keep Congress from abolishing slavery by taxing slaves. The 16th Amendment (1913) makes it possible for Congress to levy a tax on individual incomes without regard to state population.

5. No tax or duty shall be laid on articles exported from any state.

Clause 5. Southern delegates to the Constitutional Convention opposed a tax on exports because they exported goods, such as tobacco and cotton, to Europe. The Constitution permitted Congress to tax imports for revenue, but not exports.

6. No preference shall be given any regulation of commerce or revenue to the ports of one state over those of another; nor shall vessels bound to, or from, one state, be obliged to enter, clear, or pay duties in another.

Clause 6. No port in any state is to have preference over any other. Ships going from state to state may not be taxed by Congress.

7. No money shall be drawn from the Treasury, but in consequence of appropriations made by law; and a regular statement and account of the receipts and expenditures of all public money shall be published from time to time.

8. No title of nobility shall be granted by the United States; and no person holding any office of profit or trust under them, shall, without the consent of the Congress, accept of any present, emolument, office, or title, of any kind whatever, from any king, prince, or foreign state.

Section 10.   Powers Denied to the States

1. No state shall enter into any treaty, alliance, or confederation; grant letters of marque and reprisal; coin money; emit bills of credit; make anything but gold and silver coin a tender in payment of debts; pass any bill of attainder, *ex post facto* law, or law impairing the obligation of contracts, or grant any title of nobility.

2. No state shall, without the consent of the Congress, lay any imposts or duties on imports or exports, except what may be absolutely necessary for executing its inspection laws; and the net produce of all duties and imposts, laid by any state on imports or exports, shall be for the use of the Treasury of the United States; and all such laws shall be subject to the revision and control of the Congress.

3. No state shall, without the consent of Congress, lay any duty of tonnage, keep troops, or ships of war in time of peace, enter into any agreement or compact with another state, or with a foreign power, or engage in war, unless actually invaded, or in such imminent danger as will not admit of delay.

Article 2. The Executive Branch

Section 1.   President and Vice-President

1.   Term of Office. The executive power shall be vested in a President of the United States of America. He shall hold his office during the term of four years, and together with

Clause 7. Only Congress can grant permission for money to be spent from the treasury. This provision permits Congress to limit the power of the President by controlling the amount of money to be spent to run the government.

Clause 8. This clause prohibits the establishment of a noble class and discourages bribery of American officials by foreign governments.

Clause 1. The clauses in this section limit the powers of the states. Most of these limitations stemmed from complaints the Nationalists had had against the states during the Confederation period. The prohibition of laws "impairing the obligations of contracts" was intended to prevent the sort of relief laws the states had passed during the hard times of the 1780's (the time of Shays' Rebellion). These laws protected debtors against law suits. A debt or other obligation was a contract, and a state could not interfere with it.

Clause 2. States cannot interefere with commerce by taxing goods, although they may charge fees for inspecting such goods. Any such inspection fees must be paid into the treasury of the United States. Also, all tariff revenue goes to the national government and not to the states.

the Vice-President, chosen for the same term, be elected as follows:

2. Electoral System. Each state shall appoint, in such manner as the legislature thereof may direct, a number of electors, equal to the whole number of Senators and Representatives to which the state may be entitled in the Congress; but no Senator or Representative, or person holding an office of trust or profit under the United States, shall be appointed an elector.

3. Former Method of the Electoral System. [The electors shall meet in their respective states, and vote by ballot for two persons, of whom one at least shall not be an inhabitant of the same state with themselves. And they shall make a list of all the persons voted for, and of the number of votes for each; which list they shall sign and certify, and transmit sealed to the seat of the government of the United States, directed to the president of the Senate. The president of the Senate shall, in the presence of the Senate and House of Representatives, open all the certificates, and the votes shall then be counted. The person having the greatest number of votes shall be the President, if such number be a majority of the whole number of electors appointed; and if there be more than one who have such majority, and have an equal number of votes, then the House of Representatives shall immediately choose by ballot one of them for President; and if no person have a majority, then from the five highest on the list the said House shall in like manner choose the President. But in choosing the President the votes shall be taken by states, the representation from each state having one vote. A quorum for this purpose shall consist of a member or members from two-thirds of the states, and a majority of all the states shall be necessary to a choice. In every case, after the choice of the President, the person having the greatest number of votes of the electors shall be the Vice-President. But if there should remain two or more who have equal votes, the Senate shall choose from them by ballot the Vice-President.]

4. Time of Elections. The Congress may determine the time of choosing the electors, and

Clauses 2 and 3. The framers of the Constitution did not want a President chosen directly by the people. They felt the voters could not be familiar with the qualifications of people living in distant states. So they suggested an electoral college. The electors, it was hoped, would be prominent individuals acquainted with leaders in other states. They would thus be able to make a wise choice for President. Originally, the state legislatures chose the electors, but since 1828 they have generally been nominated by the political parties and elected by the people. The electors from all the states make up the electoral college. Each state has as many electors as it has senators and representatives.

This system provided that each elector vote for two candidates, with the person receiving the largest number of votes (providing it was a majority) becoming President and the one who was runner-up becoming Vice-President. In 1800 the two top candidates tied, making it necessary for the House to choose the President. The 12th Amendment (1804) was passed to prevent this situation from happening again.

Clause 4. Elections for President are held on the first Tuesday after the first Monday in November. The electors cast

the day on which they shall give their votes; which day shall be the same throughout the United States.

their votes on the first Monday after the second Wednesday in December.

5. Qualifications for President. No person except a natural-born citizen [or a citizen of the United States, at the time of the adoption of this Constitution], shall be eligible to the office of the President; neither shall any person be eligible to that office who shall not have attained to the age of thirty-five years, and been fourteen years a resident within the United States.

6. Filling Vacancies. In the case of the removal of the President from office, or of his death, resignation, or inability to discharge the powers and duties of the said office, the same shall devolve on the Vice-President, and the Congress may by law provide for the case of removal, death, resignation, or inability, both of the President and Vice-President, declaring what officer shall then act as President, and

Clause 6. If the presidency becomes vacant, then the Vice-President takes the office. Congress may decide by law who will become President when neither the President nor the Vice-President is able to serve. In the present succession law, the speaker of the House is next in line and then the president pro tempore of the Senate. The 25th Amendment (1967) has been passed to deal further with the inability of Presidents to discharge their duties.

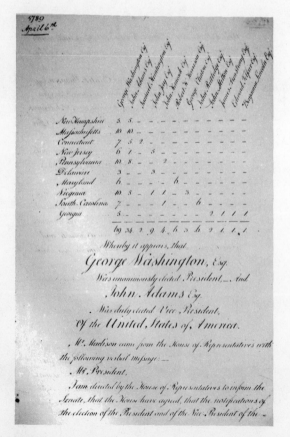

Only ten states voted in the first presidential election. Rhode Island and North Carolina had not yet ratified the Constitution, and New York had not yet set up a system for choosing electors. Do you think the results would have been different if all states had voted?

such officer shall act accordingly, until the disability be removed, or a President shall be elected.

7. Salary. The President shall, at stated times, receive for his services, a compensation, which shall neither be increased nor diminished during the period for which he shall have been elected, and he shall not receive within that period any other emolument from the United States, or any of them.

8. Oath of Office. Before he enter on the execution of his office, he shall take the following oath or affirmation:—"I do solemnly swear (or affirm) that I will faithfully execute the office of President of the United States, and will to the best of my ability, preserve, protect, and defend the Constitution of the United States."

Section 2. Powers of the President

1. Military Powers. The President shall be Commander in Chief of the Army and Navy of the United States, and of the militia of the several states, when called into the actual service of the United States; he may require the option, in writing, of the principal officer in each of the executive departments, upon any subject relating to the duties of their respective offices, and he shall have power to grant reprieves and pardons for offenses against the United States, except in cases of impeachment.

Clause 1. The President, who cannot be a member of the military, heads the armed forces. This places the armed forces under civilian control. The President can ask the heads of executive departments for written opinions about matters related to their departments. This clause provides a constitutional basis for the cabinet.

2. Treaties and Appointments. He shall have power, by and with the advice and consent of the Senate, to make treaties, provided two-thirds of the Senators present concur; and he shall nominate, and by and with the advice and consent of the Senate, shall appoint ambassadors, other public ministers and consuls, judges of the Supreme Court, and all other officers of the United States, whose appointments are not herein otherwise provided for, and which shall be established by law; but the Congress may by law vest the appointment of such inferior officers, as they think proper, in the President alone, in the courts of law, or in the heads of departments.

Clause 2. The President can make treaties with foreign countries, but they must be approved by two thirds of those present at a session of the Senate. Note that this is a power given to the Senate, but not to the House, and is also a part of the checks and balances system.

The Senate must also approve the appointment of American foreign representatives abroad, judges of the Supreme Court, and any other government officials not already provided for in the Constitution. However, Congress may make laws allowing either the President, the courts, or heads of departments to appoint minor government officials.

3. Filling Vacancies. The President shall have power to fill up all vacancies that may happen during the recess of the Senate, by granting commissions which shall expire at the end of their next session.

Clause 3. If vacancies occur in appointive federal offices when the Senate is not in session, the President may make temporary appointments.

Section 3. Duties of the President

He shall from time to time give to the Congress information of the state of the Union, and recommend to their consideration such measures as he shall judge necessary and expedient; he may, on extraordinary occasions, convene both houses, or either of them, and in case of disagreement between them, with respect to the time of adjournment, he may adjourn them to such time as he shall think proper; he shall receive ambassadors and other public ministers; he shall take care that the laws be faithfully executed, and shall commission all the officers of the United States.

Section 3. The President must give Congress information about the condition of the country. It has become customary for the President to deliver a "State of the Union" message to Congress every January. If the need arises the President may call either or both houses of Congress into special session. The President has the power to end a session of Congress if the two houses cannot agree on an adjournment date. The President is to receive foreign representatives, see that the laws of the federal government are carried out, and commission all officers of the armed forces.

Section 4. Impeachment

The President, Vice-President, and all civil officers of the United States, shall be removed from office on impeachment for, and conviction of, treason, bribery, or other high crimes and misdemeanors.

Section 4. (See annotation for Article 1, Section 2, Clause 5, and Section 3, Clauses 6 and 7.)

Article 3. The Judicial Branch

Section 1. Federal Courts

The judicial power of the United States shall be vested in one Supreme Court, and in such inferior courts as the Congress may from time to time ordain and establish. The judges, both of the Supreme and inferior courts, shall hold their offices during good behavior, and shall, at stated times, receive for their services a compensation, which shall not be diminished during their continuance in office.

Section 1. Instead of precisely limiting the President, the Constitution seeks to control the President's power with a system of "checks and balances." Each branch of government—legislative, executive, and judicial—has certain checks against the other two. The President can veto acts of Congress, but Congress (in particular, the Senate) must approve the President's appointments and consent to the President's treaties. The judiciary is an extremely important part of this system of balanced government.

Section 1 authorizes a Supreme Court and such lower courts as Congress shall establish. Both President and Congress have checks on the courts. Congress determines the number of judges on the Supreme Court and creates by law all other courts. The President appoints all federal judges, with the consent of the Senate. Federal judges hold office for life.

Section 2. Jurisdiction of Federal Courts

1. General Jurisdiction. The judicial power shall extend to all cases, in law and equity, arising under this Constitution, the laws of the United States, and treaties made or which shall be made, under their authority; to all cases affecting ambassadors, other public ministers and consuls; to all cases of admiralty and maritime jurisdiction; to controversies to which the United States shall be a party; to controversies between two or more states; [between a state and citizens of another state;] between citizens of the same state claiming lands under grants of different states, and between a state or the citizens thereof, and foreign states, citizens, or subjects.

Clause 1. Over the years the courts have defined their jurisdiction and established some checks of their own. In 1803 Supreme Court Justice John Marshall asserted the power of the Court to determine the constitutionality of acts of Congress. If the Court finds a law unconstitutional, it can declare it to be of no effect. By that ruling the Court made itself the primary interpreter of the Constitution. The Supreme Court has several times declared that the President too is "under the law" as interpreted by the Court. Only once has there been an open confrontation. In 1950 President Truman, acting in the emergency of the Korean War, seized the nation's steel mills. The Supreme Court, declaring that he had exceeded his constitutional powers, ordered him to return them to their owners. He did.

2. Supreme Court. In all cases affecting ambassadors, other public ministers and consuls, and those in which a state shall be a party, the Supreme Court shall have original jurisdiction. In all the other cases before mentioned, the Supreme Court shall have appellate jurisdiction, both as to law and fact, with such exceptions, and under such regulations as the Congress shall make.

Clause 2. "Original jurisdiction" refers to the right to try a case before any other court hears it. Actually, very few cases come directly to the Supreme Court. Most federal court cases begin in the district courts. They can be appealed to the circuit courts and finally carried up to the Supreme Court. "Appellate jurisdiction" refers to the right to try cases carried by appeal from lower courts. Most cases reaching the Supreme Court are taken to it on appeal. The Supreme Court has original jurisdiction in cases involving foreign representatives or in cases involving disputes between states.

3. Conduct of Trials. The trial of all crimes, except in cases of impeachent, shall be by jury; and such trial shall be held in the state where the said crimes shall have been committed; but when not committed within any state, the trial shall be at such place or places as the Congress may by law have directed.

Clause 3. Except for impeachment cases, anyone accused of a federal crime has the right to a trial by jury. The trial must be held in the state where the crime was committed.

Section 3. Treason

1. Definition. Treason against the United States shall consist only in levying war against them, or in adhering to their enemies, giving them aid and comfort. No person shall be convicted of treason unless on the testimony of two witnesses to the same overt act, or on confession in open court.

Clause 1. Treason is the only crime defined by the Constitution. Notice how strict the requirements are—there must be two witnesses to the same overt (open) act. The framers did not want anyone tried for treason merely for criticizing the government.

2. Punishment. The Congress shall have power to declare the punishment of treason, but no attainder of treason shall work corruption of blood or forfeiture except during the life of the person attained.

Clause 2. Congress has the power to fix the punishment for treason. But the families and descendants of a person found guilty of treason cannot be punished for his or her crime.

225

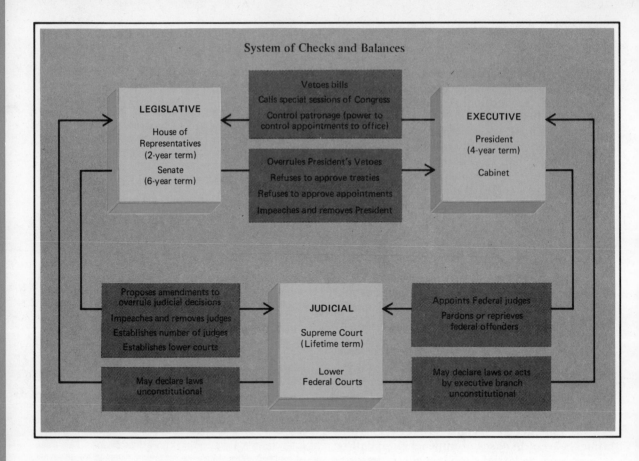

System of Checks and Balances

LEGISLATIVE

House of
Representatives
(2-year term)

Senate
(6-year term)

Vetoes bills
Calls special sessions of Congress
Control patronage (power to
control appointments to office)

Overrules President's Vetoes
Refuses to approve treaties
Refuses to approve appointments
Impeaches and removes President

EXECUTIVE

President
(4-year term)

Cabinet

Proposes amendments to
overrule judicial decisions
Impeaches and removes judges
Establishes number of judges
Establishes lower courts

JUDICIAL

Supreme Court
(Lifetime term)

Lower
Federal Courts

Appoints Federal judges
Pardons or reprieves
federal offenders

May declare laws
unconstitutional

May declare laws or acts
by executive branch
unconstitutional

Article 4. Relations Among States

Section 1. Official Acts

Full faith and credit shall be given in each state to the public acts, records, and judicial proceedings of every other state. And the Congress may by general laws prescribe the manner in which such acts, records, and proceedings shall be proved, and the effect thereof.

Section 1. Each state must respect the laws, records, and court decisions of other states. If this were not the case, a person might move to another state to avoid legal punishment in the first state. The "full faith and credit" clause avoids much of the confusion arising from different state regulations.

Section 2. Privileges of Citizens

1. Privileges. The citizens of each state shall be entitled to all privileges and immunities of citizens in the several states.

Clause 1. This clause gives a person moving into a state the same rights the state gives to its own citizens. The state may still require a person to meet its own residence requirements for voting and holding office.

2. Extradition. A person charged in any state with treason, felony, or other crime, who

Clause 2. If a suspect flees to another state, the governor of the state where the crime was committed may request

shall flee from justice, and be found in another state, shall on demand of the executive authority of the state from which he fled, be delivered up, to be removed to the state having jurisdiction of the crime.

3. Fugitive Slaves. [No person held in service or labor in one state, under the laws thereof, escaping into another, shall in consequence of any law or regulation therein, be discharged from such service or labor, but shall be delivered up on claim of the party to whom such service or labor may be due.]

that he or she be returned. Sending escaped suspects back for trial or punishment is called *extradition*. In the vast majority of cases, the suspected criminal's return is automatic, but in a very few cases state governors have refused to return the fugitives.

Clause 3. This clause provided the constitutional basis for slave owners to have their escaped slaves returned to them. The 13th Amendment (1865) ended slavery, making this clause obsolete.

Section 3.   New States and Territories

1. Admission of New States. New states may be admitted by the Congress into this Union; but no new state shall be formed or erected within the jurisdiction of any other state; nor any state be formed by the junction of two or more states, or parts of states, without the consent of the legislatures of the states concerned as well as of the Congress.

Clause 1. The Constitution specifically gives Congress power to govern the western territories. It can admit new states to the Union, but old states cannot be subdivided without their consent. Subdivision has happened only three times. Kentucky was separated from Virginia in 1792. Maine was split off from Massachusetts in 1820. And during the Civil War (1863), West Virginia separated from Virginia and joined the northern Union.

2. Powers of Congress Over Territories and Other Property. The Congress shall have power to dispose of and make all needful rules and regulations respecting the territory or other property belonging to the United States; and nothing in this Constitution shall be so construed as to prejudice any claims of the United States, or of any particular state.

Clause 2. Congress may govern and make regulations for the territories and properties of the United States. "Territories" here refers to lands not under the control of any state.

Section 4.   Guarantees to the States

The United States shall guarantee to every state in this Union a republican form of government, and shall protect each of them against invasion; and on application of the legislature or of the executive (when the legislature cannot be convened) against domestic violence.

Section 4. In practice, Congress determines whether a state has a republican form of government. The Constitution also requires the federal government to protect a state against invasion and, upon request of the proper state authorities, to protect it against rioting and violence. Sometimes Presidents have ordered federal intervention without the state's request when federal laws were being violated.

Article 5. Methods of Amendment

The Congress, whenever two-thirds of both houses shall deem it necessary, shall propose amendments to this Constitution, or, on the application of the legislatures of two-thirds of the

Article 5. The framers of the Constitution recognized that later generations would need to make some changes in the Constitution. They wanted to make the process of change difficult, however, so that the Constitution would not be battered by every popular trend. According to Article 5, Congress can propose an amendment by a two-thirds vote of both houses. Or, if two thirds of the state legislatures request it,

several states, shall call a convention for proposing amendments, which, in either case, shall be valid to all intents and purposes, as part of this Constitution, when ratified by the legislatures of three-fourths of the several states, or by conventions in three-fourths thereof, as the one or the other mode of ratification may be proposed by the Congress; provided that [no amendments which may be made prior to the year 1808 shall in any manner affect the first and fourth clauses in the Ninth Section of the First Article; and that] no state, without its consent, shall be deprived of its equal suffrage in the Senate.

Congress is to call a convention to propose an amendment. So far, all amendments have been proposed by Congress. An amendment must be approved by three fourths of the state legislatures or by conventions in three fourths of the states.

Considering the enormous changes in American society, there have been remarkably few amendments to the Constitution. The first ten (known as the Bill of Rights) were approved within two years, but there were only two more amendments before the Civil War. There have been 26 amendments in all.

Article 6. General Provisions

1. Public Debts. All debts contracted and engagements entered into, before the adoption of this Constitution, shall be as valid against the United States under this Constitution, as under the Confederation.

Clause 1. All debts and treaties made under the Articles of Confederation are recognized by the United States. This action was favored by Alexander Hamilton and was one of several steps taken by Congress to establish the credit of the new government.

2. The Supreme Law. This Constitution, and the laws of the United States which shall be made in pursuance thereof, and all treaties made, or which shall be made, under the authority of the United States, shall be the supreme law of the land; and the judges in every state shall be bound thereby, anything in the constitution or laws of any state to the contrary notwithstanding.

Clause 2. This clause is the basic statement of national authority in the Constitution. It makes the national government, rather than the states, the supreme power. It required many years, however—even a Civil War—before the precise relationship between the federal government and the states was worked out.

3. Oaths of Office. The Senators and Representatives before mentioned, and the members of the several state legislatures, and all executive and judicial officers, both of the United States and of the several states, shall be bound by oath or affirmation, to support this Constitution; but no religious test shall ever be required as a qualification to any office or public trust under the United States.

Clause 3. All the officials listed must pledge themselves to support the Constitution. But such a pledge, or oath, cannot include any religious test or requirement that a person belong to a particular religious faith. This provision results from the principle of separation of church and state in the United States.

Article 7. Ratification

The ratification of the convention of nine states shall be sufficient for the establishment of the Constitution between the states so ratifying the same.

Article 7. The final article sets up the process of ratification. The framers knew they had to submit their document for popular approval. But they wished to avoid the state legislatures, which might resent the powers of the federal government.

DONE in Convention by the unanimous consent of the States present the seventeenth day of September in the year of our Lord one thousand seven hundred and eight-seven and of the independence of the United States of America the twelfth. In witness whereof we have hereunto subscribed our names,

G. Washington—President and deputy from Virginia

As a result, they provided for specially elected ratifying conventions, one in each state. And when nine states approved, the Constitution would be considered in effect. Of the 55 people who attended the Constitutional Convention in the summer of 1787, 39 signed the Constitution.

NEW HAMPSHIRE
John Langdon
Nicholas Gilman

NEW YORK
Alexander Hamilton

DELAWARE
George Read
Gunning Bedford
John Dickinson
Richard Bassett
Jacob Broom

NORTH CAROLINA
William Blount
Richard Dobbs Spaight
Hugh Williamson

MASSACHUSETTS
Nathaniel Gorman
Rufus King

NEW JERSEY
William Livingston
David Brearley
William Paterson
Jonathan Dayton

MARYLAND
James McHenry
Daniel of St. Thomas Jenifer
Daniel Carroll

SOUTH CAROLINA
John Rutledge
Charles Cotesworth Pinckney
Charles Pinckney
Pierce Butler

CONNECTICUT
William Samuel Johnson
Roger Sherman

PENNSYLVANIA
Benjamin Franklin
Thomas Mifflin
Robert Morris
George Clymer
Thomas FitzSimons
Jared Ingersoll
James Wilson
Gouverneur Morris

VIRGINIA
John Blair
James Madison

GEORGIA
William Few
Abraham Baldwin

Amendments to the Constitution

(The first ten amendments constitute the Bill of Rights. They became an official part of the Constitution in 1791. They limit the powers of the federal government but not the powers of the states.)

Amendment 1. Freedom of Religion, Speech, Press, Assembly, and Petition (1791)

Congress shall make no law respecting an establishment of religion, or prohibiting the free exercise thereof; or abridging the freedom of speech, or of the press; or the right of the people peaceably to assemble, and to petition the government for a redress of grievances.

Amendment 1. This amendment guarantees to Americans the most essential freedoms. Freedom of religion guarantees the right to worship as one chooses without interference from Congress. The Supreme Court has interpreted this amendment as a guarantee of separation of church and state. Freedoms of speech and press are limited only when they extend to slander and libel (false and malicious statements) or statements that might be injurious to the general welfare of the nation. The First Amendment also entitles the people to hold meetings and to request the government to respond to their grievances.

Amendment 2. Right to Bear Arms (1791)

A well-regulated militia, being necessary to the security of a free state, the right of the people to keep and bear arms shall not be infringed.

Amendment 2. The states have the right to maintain armed militias for their protection. However, the rights of private citizens to own guns can be, and are, regulated by federal and state legislation.

Amendment 3. Housing of Troops (1791)

No soldier shall, in time of peace, be quartered in any house, without the consent of the owner; nor in time of war, but in a manner to be prescribed by law.

Amendment 3. One source of bitter complaint in the colonies had been the British practice of housing their troops in American homes. The Third Amendment guarantees that no soldier will be quartered in a private residence during peacetime, or even in wartime unless under specific congressional legislation.

Amendment 4. Searches and Seizures (1791)

The right of the people to be secure in their persons, houses, papers, and effects, against unreasonable searches and seizures, shall not be violated; and no warrants shall issue but upon probable cause, supported by oath or affirmation, and particularly describing the place to be searched, and the persons or things to be seized.

Amendment 4. This amendment came in response to the British writs of assistance—blanket search warrants permitting officers to search any house at any time. For an American home to be searched, a warrant must be issued by a judge and it must state precisely what the official expects to find.

Amendment 5. Rights of Accused Persons (1791)

No person shall be held to answer for a capital, or otherwise infamous, crime, unless on

Amendment 5. In a federal court no person can be held for a serious crime unless indicted, or charged, by a grand jury. A grand jury is a group of 23 persons who hear in secret the charges against the accused and then decide whether or not the person should be tried in court. "Twice put in

a presentment or indictment of a grand jury, except in cases arising in the land or naval forces, or in the militia, when in actual service in time of war or public danger; nor shall any person be subject for the same offense to be twice put in jeopardy of life and limb; nor shall be compelled, in any criminal case, to be a witness against himself; nor be deprived of life, liberty, or property, without due process of law; nor shall private property be taken for public use, without just compensation.

jeopardy," or double jeopardy, means that no person can be tried twice in federal courts for the same crime.

People cannot be forced to give evidence against themselves that will help prove their guilt. This provision goes back to earlier history when persons were tortured in order to make them confess. This clause allows people on trial to refuse to answer questions when they fear that their answers might convict them of the crime.

"Due process of law" has become quite complicated, but the framers wished to guarantee proper judicial procedures for a person accused of a crime (see Amendment 6). The taking of private property for public use is called the right of "eminent domain." The government cannot take such property without giving owners a fair price for their property. The price is determined by a court.

Amendment 6. Right to a Speedy, Fair Trial (1791)

In all criminal prosecutions, the accused shall enjoy the right to a speedy and public trial, by an impartial jury of the state and district wherein the crime shall have been committed, which district shall have been previously ascertained by law, and to be informed of the nature and cause of the accusation; to be confronted with the witnesses against him; to have compulsory process for obtaining witnesses in his favor, and to have the assistance of counsel for his defense.

Amendment 6. This amendment defines the rights of the accused under due process of law. A person has the right to be informed of the charges against him or her and to a speedy and public trial by jury. Witnesses for and against the accused may be compelled to appear in court to give evidence. The accused is entitled to confront these witnesses and to be represented by an attorney.

Amendment 7. Civil Suits (1791)

In suits at common law, where the value in controversy shall exceed $20, the right of trial by jury shall be preserved, and no fact tried by a jury shall be otherwise reexamined in any court of the United States than according to the rules of the common law.

Amendment 7. If a sum of money larger than $20 is disputed, the people involved may insist on a jury trial. However, in actual practice, cases do not reach federal courts unless much larger sums are involved.

Amendment 8. Bails, Fines, Punishments (1791)

Excessive bail shall not be required, nor excessive fines imposed, nor cruel and unusual punishments inflicted.

Amendment 8. The Eighth Amendment continues an enumeration of the rights of the accused. Before a criminal trial, the accused may be released from jail on payment to the court of a sum of money called bail. Bail is returned if the person comes to trial as ordered. Neither the amount of bail set nor the punishment inflicted should be excessively severe. The Supreme Court has the final say in deciding just what is "excessive," "cruel," and "unusual" in any case.

Amendment 9. Powers Reserved to the People (1791)

The enumeration in the Constitution, of certain rights, shall not be construed to deny or disparage others retained by the people.

Amendment 10. Powers Reserved to the States (1791)

The powers not delegated to the United States by the Constitution, nor prohibited by it to the states, are reserved to the states respectively, or to the people.

Amendment 11. Suits Against States (1798)

The judicial power of the United States shall not be construed to extend to any suit in law or equity, commenced or prosecuted against one of the United States, by citizens of another state, or by citizens or subjects of any foreign state.

Amendment 12. Electing the President and Vice-President (1804)

The electors shall meet in their respective states, and vote by ballot for President and Vice-President, one of whom, at least, shall not be an inhabitant of the same state with themselves; they shall name in their ballots the person voted for as President, and in distinct ballots the person voted for as Vice-President, and they shall make distinct lists of all persons voted for as President, and of all persons voted for as Vice-President, and of the number of votes for each, which lists they shall sign and certify, and transmit, sealed, to the seat of government of the United States, directed to the President of the Senate; the President of the Senate shall, in the presence of the Senate and House of Representatives, open all the certificates and the votes shall then be counted; the person having the greatest number of votes for President shall be the President, if such number be a majority of the whole number of electors appointed; and if no person have such majority, then from the persons having the highest numbers not exceeding three on the list of those voted for as President, the House of Representatives shall choose immediately, by ballot, the President. But in choosing the President, the votes shall be taken

Amendment 9. This means that the rights listed in the Constitution are not necessarily the only rights that exist. Other rights shall not be denied to the people, simply because they are not enumerated in the Constitution.

Amendment 10. In the same vein as the previous amendment, the Tenth Amendment stipulates that those powers not extended to the federal government are reserved to the states or the people.

Amendment 11. A state cannot be sued in any courts other than the courts of that state. This amendment overrules a Supreme Court decision (*Chisholm* v. *Georgia*, 1793) that allowed two citizens of South Carolina to sue Georgia in a federal court.

Amendment 12. This amendment nullifies Article 2, Section 1, Clause 3. At first the electors voted for President and Vice-President without specifying which person they wanted for each office. After the election of 1796, in which the people elected a Federalist President and Republican Vice-President, and the election of 1800, which was a tie, the 12th Amendment was passed to require each elector to cast two ballots—one for President, one for Vice-President. Electors are nominated by the political parties and elected by the people. Each state has as many electors as it has senators and representatives in Congress. The party with the most *popular* votes—that is, votes from the people of the state—gets to cast all the state's electoral votes for its candidates. The electoral votes are counted by the president of the Senate in the presence of the two houses of Congress. Each candidate for both President and Vice-President must receive a majority of electoral votes to be elected.

An interesting sidenote to the election process is that political parties are not mentioned in the Constitution—the framers considered them unnecessary. In practice, however, the 12th Amendment works best when there is some organization to serve as a filter, selecting candidates and arranging tickets. Political parties have served this function.

by states, the representation from each state having one vote; a quorum for this purpose shall consist of a member or members from two-thirds of the states, and a majority of all the states shall be necessary to a choice. [And if the House of Representatives shall not choose a President whenever the right of choice shall devolve upon them, before the fourth day of March next following, then the Vice-President shall act as President, as in the case of the death or other constitutional disability of the President.] The person having the greatest number of votes as Vice-President, shall be the Vice-President, if such number be a majority of the whole number of electors appointed, and if no person have a majority, then, from the two highest numbers on the list, the Senate shall choose the Vice-President; a quorum for the purpose shall consist of two-thirds of the whole number of Senators, and a majority of the whole number shall be necessary to a choice. But no person constitutionally ineligible to the office of President shall be eligible to that of Vice-President of the United States.

Amendment 13. Abolition of Slavery (1865)

Section 1. Neither slavery nor involuntary servitude, except as a punishment for crime whereof the party shall have been duly convicted, shall exist within the United States, or any place subject to their jurisdiction.

Section 2. Congress shall have power to enforce this article by appropriate legislation.

Amendment 14. Citizenship (1868)

Section 1. Citizenship defined. All persons born or naturalized in the United States and subject to the jurisdiction thereof, are citizens of the United States and of the state wherein they reside. No state shall make or enforce any law which shall abridge the privileges or immunities of citizens of the United States; nor shall any state deprive any person of life, liberty, or property, without due process of law; nor deny to any person within its jurisdiction the equal protection of the laws.

Amendment 13. The 13th, 14th, and 15th Amendments were passed after the Civil War. The 13th Amendment abolishes slavery and gives Congress the right to enforce this order.

Section 1. The main purpose of this amendment was to give Blacks equal rights. The first sentence, by definition, gives Black Americans citizenship. The second sentence prohibits the states from interfering with any citizen's right to equal protection under the law or with the right of due process of law. In recent years the Supreme Court has interpreted the phrase "due process" to mean that the states had to respect the judicial rights guaranteed by the Bill of Rights.

Section 2. Apportionment of Representatives. Representatives shall be apportioned among the several states according to their respective numbers, counting the whole number of persons in each state, [excluding Indians not taxed]. But when the right to vote at any election for the choice of electors for President and Vice-President of the United States, Representatives in Congress, the executive and judicial officers of a state, or the members of the legislature thereof, is denied to any of the male inhabitants of such state, [being twenty-one years of age] and citizens of the United States, or in any way abridged, except for participation in rebellion, or other crime, the basis of representation therein shall be reduced in the proportion which the number of such male citizens shall bear to the whole number of male citizens [twenty-one years of age] in such state.

Section 3. Disability for engaging in insurrection. No person shall be a Senator or Representative in Congress, or elector of President and Vice-President, or hold any office, civil or military, under the United States, or under any state, who, having previously taken an oath, as a member of Congress, or as an officer of the United States, or as a member of any state legislature, or as an executive or judicial officer of any state, to support the Constitution of the United States, shall have engaged in insurrection or rebellion against the same, or given aid or comfort to the enemies thereof. But Congress may, by vote of two-thirds of each house, remove such disability.

Section 4. Public debt. The validity of the public debt of the United States, authorized by law, including debts incurred for payment of pensions and bounties for services in suppressing insurrection or rebellion, shall not be questioned. But neither the United States nor any state shall assume or pay any debt or obligation incurred in aid of insurrection or rebellion against the United States [or any claim for the loss or emancipation of any slave]; but all such debts, obligations, and claims shall be held illegal and void.

Section 5. Enforcement. The Congress shall have power to enforce, by appropriate legislation, the provisions of this article.

Section 2. This section nullifies the three-fifths compromise and declares every man over the age of 21 to be entitled to one vote. Notice that Indians and women are still excluded. This section further provides for a punishment against any state preventing its eligible citizens from voting. This penalty has never been imposed.

Section 3. This section was designed to punish the leaders of the Confederacy for breaking their oaths to support the Constitution. Many southern leaders were excluded from public office by this amendment, but by 1872 most were permitted to return to public life. In 1898 all the Confederates were pardoned.

Section 4. This section dealt a harsh financial blow to the South. The war debt of the Union is declared valid; the war debt of the Confederacy is declared void. There would be no reimbursement on Confederate bonds and no payment for the loss of slaves.

Amendment 15. Right to Vote (1870)

Section 1. The right of citizens of the United States to vote shall not be denied or abridged by the United States or any state on account of race, color, or previous condition of servitude.

Section 2. The Congress shall have power to enforce this article by appropriate legislation.

Amendment 15. This amendment prohibits federal or state governments from preventing any citizen from voting because of "race, color, or previous condition of servitude." It was designed to guarantee voting rights to Black American men.

Amendment 16. Income Tax (1913)

The Congress shall have power to lay and collect taxes on incomes, from whatever source derived, without apportionment among the several states, and without regard to any census or enumeration.

Amendment 16. This amendment permits Congress to tax individual incomes without basing the tax on state populations. This is now the major source of revenue for the federal government.

Amendment 17. Electing Senators (1913)

Section 1. Method of election. The Senate of the United States shall be composed of two Senators from each state, elected by the people thereof, for six years; and each Senator shall have one vote. The electors in each state shall have the qualifications requisite for electors of the most numerous branch of the state legislatures.

Section 2. Filling vacancies. When vacancies happen in the representation of any state in the Senate, the executive authority of such state shall issue writs of election to fill such vacancies: *Provided* that the legislature of any state may empower the executive thereof to make temporary appointments until the people fill the vacancies by election as the legislature may direct.

[**Section 3. Not retroactive.** This amendment shall not be so construed as to affect the election or term of any Senator chosen before it becomes valid as part of the Constitution.]

Amendment 17. This amendment gives the people the right to elect their senators directly. Before this, senators were elected by the state legislatures. If a senator dies or leaves office during his or her term of office, the governor of the state can either order an election for a successor or appoint a temporary successor.

Amendment 18. Prohibition (1919)

[**Section 1.** After one year from the ratification of this article the manufacture, sale, or

Amendment 18. This amendment forbade the manufacture, sale, and shipment of alcoholic beverages. It was repealed by the 21st Amendment.

transportation of intoxicating liquors within, the importation thereof into, or the exportation thereof from, the United States and all territory subject to the jurisdiction thereof for beverage purposes is hereby prohibited.

Section 2. The Congress and the several states shall have concurrent power to enforce this article by appropriate legislation.

Section 3. This article shall be inoperative unless it shall have been ratified as an amendment to the Constitution by the legislatures of the several states, as provided in the Constitution, within seven years from the date of the submission hereof to the states by the Congress.]

Amendment 19. Women's Suffrage (1920)

Section 1. The right of citizens of the United States to vote shall not be denied or abridged by the United States or by any state on account of sex.

Section 2. Congress shall have power to enforce this article by appropriate legislation.

Amendment 19. This amendment gives women the right to vote.

Amendment 20. "Lame Duck" Amendment (1933)

Section 1. Beginning of terms. The terms of the President and Vice-President shall end at noon on the 20th day of January, and the terms of Senators and Representatives at noon on the 3rd day of January, of the years in which such terms would have ended if this article had not been ratified; and the terms of their successors shall then begin.

Section 2. Beginning of Congressional sessions. The Congress shall assemble at least once in every year, and such meeting shall begin at noon on the third day of January, unless they shall by law appoint a different day.

Amendment 20. This amendment moves the President's inaugural day from March 4 to January 20. Members of Congress take office on January 3 instead of the following December. The date of congressional sessions was also moved to January. Previously, Congress convened in December. Transportation and communication were so slow when the Constitution was written that it would have been almost impossible for officials elected in November to reach the capital in time. Hence newly elected representatives did not "sit" until the next congressional session began, 13 months later. The expression "lame duck" was used to refer to the defeated candidate still serving during the period between the election and inauguration.

Section 3. Presidential succession. If at the time fixed for the beginning of the term of the President, the President-elect shall have died, the Vice-President-elect shall become President. If a President shall not have been chosen before the time fixed for the beginning of his term, or if the President-elect shall have failed to qualify, then the Vice-President-elect shall act as President until a President shall have qualified; and the Congress may by law provide for the case wherein neither a President-elect nor a Vice-President-elect shall have qualified, declaring who shall then act as President, or the manner in which one who is to act shall be selected, and such person shall act accordingly until a President or Vice-President shall have qualified.

Section 4. Filling Presidential vacancy. The Congress may by law provide for the case of the death of any of the persons from whom the House of Representatives may choose a President whenever the right of choice shall have devolved upon them, and for the case of the death of any of the persons from whom the Senate may choose a Vice-President whenever the right of choice shall have devolved upon them.

[**Section 5. Effective date.** Sections 1 and 2 shall take effect on the 15th day of October following the ratification of this article.

Section 6. Time limit for ratification. This article shall be inoperative unless it shall have been ratified as an amendment to the Constitution by the legislatures of three-fourths of the several states within the seven years from the date of its submission.]

Amendment 21. Repeal of Prohibition (1933)

Amendment 21.   This repeals the 18th Amendment.

Section 1. The eighteenth article of amendment to the Constitution of the United States is hereby repealed.

Section 2. The transportation or importation into any state, territory, or possession of the

237

United States for delivery or use therein of intoxicating liquors, in violation of the laws thereof, is hereby prohibited.

[**Section 3.** This article shall be inoperative unless it shall have been ratified as an amendment to the Constitution by conventions in the several states, as provided in the Constitution, within seven years from the date of the submission hereof to the states by the Congress.]

Amendment 22. Two-Term Limit for Presidents (1951)

Section 1. No person shall be elected to the office of the President more than twice, and no person who has held the office of President, or acted as President, for more than two years of a term to which some other person was elected President shall be elected to the office of the President more than once. [But this Article shall not apply to any person holding the office of President when this Article was proposed by the Congress, and shall not prevent any person who may be holding the office of President, or acting as President, during the term within which this Article becomes operative from holding the office of President or acting as President during the remainder of such term.]

[**Section 2.** This Article shall be inoperative unless it shall have been ratified as an amendment to the Constitution by the legislatures of three-fourths of the several states within seven years from the date of its submission to the states by the Congress.]

Amendment 22. This amendment was passed because many feared that President Franklin D. Roosevelt's four terms had set a dangerous precedent. Prior to his election to a third term in 1940, Presidents had followed the tradition of serving no more than two terms.

Amendment 23. Presidential Electors for District of Columbia (1961)

Section 1. The District constituting the seat of Government of the United States shall appoint in such manner as the Congress may direct:

A number of electors of President and Vice-President equal to the whole number of Senators and Representatives in Congress to

Amendment 23. This amendment gives the residents of Washington, D.C., three members in the electoral college and hence the right to vote for President and Vice-President.

which the District would be entitled if it were a state, but in no event more than the least populous state; they shall be in addition to those appointed by the states, but they shall be considered, for the purposes of the election of President and Vice-President, to be electors appointed by a state; and they shall meet in the District and perfom such duties as provided by the twelfth article of amendment.

Section 2. The Congress shall have power to enforce this article by appropriate legislation.

Amendment 24. Poll Taxes (1964)

Section 1. The right of citizens of the United States to vote in any primary or other election for President or Vice-President, for electors for President or Vice-President, or for Senator or Representative in Congress, shall not be denied or abridged by the United States or any state by reason of failure to pay any poll tax or other tax.

Section 2. The Congress shall have the power to enforce this article by appropriate legislation.

Amendment 24. When this amendment was passed, five southern states still used the poll tax as a means of discouraging Blacks from voting. This amendment applies only to national elections.

Amendment 25. Presidential Disability and Succession (1967)

1. In case of the removal of the President from office or his death or resignation, the Vice-President shall become President.

2. Whenever there is a vacancy in the office of the Vice-President, the President shall nominate a Vice-President who shall take the office upon confirmation by a majority vote of both houses of Congress.

3. Whenever the President transmits to the President pro tempore of the Senate and the Speaker of the House of Representatives his written declaration that he is unable to discharge the powers and duties of his office, and until he transmits to them a written declaration to the contrary, such powers and duties shall be discharged by the Vice-President as Acting President.

Amendment 25. This amendment clarifies Article 2, Section 1, Clause 6. The Vice-President becomes President when the President dies, resigns, or is removed from office. The new President then nominates a new Vice-President, who must be approved by a majority of Congress. If a President is unable to perform the duties of the office, Congress must be informed of this fact in writing by the President or by the Vice-President and a majority of the cabinet. In this case, the Vice-President performs as acting President until the elected President is once again able to function.

This amendment was first used in a case where presidential disability was not a factor. In 1973 Vice-President Spiro T. Agnew resigned; President Richard M. Nixon filled his office, according to Section 2 of this amendment, naming Gerald R. Ford, a member of the House of Representatives, as the new Vice-President. Mr. Ford was approved by a majority in both houses of Congress. In 1974 Nixon became the first President in history to resign from office. Ford, in succeeding Nixon, became the first President not elected to that office or the vice-presidency. For the vice-presidential vacancy, Ford appointed Nelson A. Rockefeller, who was then approved by both houses of Congress.

4. Whenever the Vice-President and a majority of either the principal officers of the executive departments or of such other body as Congress may by law provide, transmit to the President pro tempore of the Senate and the Speaker of the House of Representatives their written declaration that the President is unable to discharge the powers and duties of his office, the Vice-President shall immediately assume the powers and duties of the office as Acting President.

Thereafter, when the President transmits to the President pro tempore of the Senate and the Speaker of the House of Representatives his written declaration that no inability exists, he shall resume the powers and duties of his office unless the Vice-President and a majority of either the principal officers of the executive department or of such other body as Congress may by law provide, transmit within four days to the President pro tempore of the Senate and the Speaker of the House of Representatives their written declaration that the President is unable to discharge the powers and duties of his office. Thereupon Congress shall decide the issue, assembling within 48 hours for that purpose if not in session. If the Congress, within 21 days after receipt of the latter written declaration, or, if Congress is not in session, within 21 days after Congress is required to assemble, determines by two-thirds vote of both houses that the President is unable to discharge the powers and duties of his office, the Vice-President shall continue to discharge the same as Acting President; otherwise, the President shall assume the powers and duties of his office.

Amendment 26. Voting Age Lowered to 18 (1971)

Amendment 26. This amendment lowers the minimum voting age to 18.

Section 1. The right of citizens of the United States, who are 18 years of age or older, to vote shall not be denied or abridged by the United States or any state on account of age.

Section 2. The Congress shall have the power to enforce this article by appropriate legislation.

PUTTING IT ALL TOGETHER

UNDERSTANDING THE MAIN IDEAS

1. How did the delegates to the Constitutional Convention find a way to organize the 13 states into one whole nation?
2. How did the delegates find a way that would not force any part of the area to give up its way of living?
3. How did the delegates find a way that could guarantee that everyone would be heard and everyone would be represented in the decisions of a nation?
4. How did the delegates try to find a way that would last through the years to come?
5. How did they try to make their plan of governing strong enough to make decisions for all the states, yet representative enough to take care of all the variety, and flexible enough to change when necessary?

ACTIVITIES

1. Use your school or local library for this activity. Find a book on one of the Founding Fathers. As you read, what happens to your understanding of the Constitution itself? Put your findings into a one page book report.
2. Make an outline map of the original 13 states. On the map, label each state and show the date it ratified the Constitution.
3. Show the Bill of Rights to any two people you know. Ask them to choose the one that they think is the most important. Ask them to explain their choice. Are their reasons the same reasons of the people who wrote the Constitution?
4. In class, choose any of the amendments to the Constitution. Prepare to debate the proposition: Resolved that "The X Amendment is more important than the elastic clause." Before you choose sides, be sure your team has a long list of arguments, both pro and con. Spend enough time discussing the points you plan to make with your team. Then present the debate to your class.

BOOKS TO READ

Fisher, Dorothy C., *Our Independence and the Constitution* (New York: Random House, Inc., 1974).

Morris, Richard B., *First Book of the Constitution* (New York: Watts Publishing Co., 1958).

Orrmont, Arthur, *The Amazing Alexander Hamilton* (New York: Julian Messner, Inc., 1964).

Sanderlin, George, *A Hoop to the Barrel: The Making of the American Constitution* (New York: Coward, McCann and Geoghegan, Inc., 1974).

chapter 10
One Purpose For All?

1798–1802

1. DECIDING WHAT IS BEST FOR AMERICA
2. WAR IN EUROPE—POLITICS AT HOME
3. THE PRESIDENTS AND THE PEOPLE

INTRODUCTION

To plan a nation was one task. To be a nation was another. And to act like an nation was a third. First of all, the states had to fill the new national jobs. Elections for Congress were held in January and February of 1789. In April the electors for President and Vice-President met in New York, the temporary capital. On April 6, it was announced that George Washington had been the unanimous choice for President. John Adams was chosen Vice-President. On the 16th of April, Washington left his home in Mount Vernon for New York.

The picture of Washington traveling to his inauguration is one of the most delightful close-up views in American history. He was met at the edge of each town by an honor guard and escorted

	1789	1790	1791	1792	
Who?	George Washington	Samuel Slater	Alexander Hamilton	Issac Shelby	
What?	inaugurated first president of United States	builds the first spinning machinery	submits a bill on U.S. bank	becomes the 1st governor of the new state	
Where?	in New York, New York	in Rhode Island	in Philadelphia	of Kentucky	

through streets all filled with excited people. Guns boomed salutes. Church bells rang. Town officials made formal speeches. By the time Washington got to the New Jersey shore he was met by a barge decorated with flowers and rowed by 13 ship's captains. When the barge landed in New York City, girls in white robes spread flowers in Washington's path as a 15-gun salute was fired. For the people of this brand new nation, George Washington was the United States of America.

The picture from farther away is the picture of the new nation itself. It is hard to draw a picture of a new nation. This one did not have ceremonies like a European kingdom. Its officials did not wear special costumes. In fact, its first President went to his inauguration wearing a brown suit made by a textile mill in Hartford, Connecticut. But the new nation, the United States, did have representatives elected by the people and a printed document called the Constitution. It had been founded on the consent of the people. The Constitution represented both America's past and its hopes for the future. Now that Americans had a new nation, they had to prove that the union they had created could protect liberty and give the people the added power they had been promised.

For the first 15 years after Washington's inauguration in April 1789, Americans had to make the government work. As you read this chapter, think about these questions.

1. What actions did the national or federal government take?
2. Did a powerful, active federal government help or hurt the states?
3. How did the nation organize itself to make decisions?

1793	1794	1797	1798	1801
Genêt, a Frenchman	Monongahela Valley farmers	John Adams	"XYZ" French agents	Thomas Jefferson
recruits American soldiers for France	angry over federal tax, start Whiskey Rebellion	becomes President	demand a bribe from Americans	inaugurated as third President
in Washington D.C.	in western Pennsylvania	in Philadelphia	in France	in Washington D.C.

This picture shows Washington arriving at his inauguration in New York.

1. DECIDING WHAT IS BEST FOR AMERICA

Acting like a nation was not easy for a country with so many differences and a long history of acting according to what was best for each state or even part of a state. Washington, Adams, and the rest of the leaders of the new nation wanted very much for the United States to act like a strong nation. These leaders held two beliefs in common. They believed that the United States had a mission to show the world that people could govern themselves well. They also believed that Americans had only one chance to do this right.

The President and his Cabinet

1. What was the President's Cabinet?

Washington gathered around him the best men he knew. He did not try to narrow the choice simply to those who thought alike or came from one part of the country. He wanted people with a variety of ideas. To be sure that each job was done with special knowledge, he had special advisers for special tasks of the government. Each adviser was given the simple title of "Secretary," just as Washington and the others had decided that he should be called, simply,

The leaders knew what they wanted for the new nation. Not everyone was as sure as the leadership.

"Mr. President." For secretary of war, Washington chose General Henry Knox of Massachusetts. For attorney general, or the lawyer for the government, he chose Edmund Randolph of Virginia. For secretary of state, in charge of foreign affairs, he chose Thomas Jefferson. For secretary of the treasury he chose Alexander Hamilton of New York.

The President first met with these advisers individually. After a time, Washington invited them to meet as a group. These advisers became known as the President's Cabinet.

Deciding How to Act

What else could President Washington do on his own? He could and did decide what a President ought to be—and ought not to be. If the President were too informal, he would be at the mercy of every person who wanted a favor. If the President were too formal, he would look as if he thought he was a king.

To dignify the office of President, Washington rode a great white horse, with a leopardskin saddle cloth banded in gold. His servants were dressed in *livery*, or uniform, and wore powdered wigs. His carriage was drawn through the streets of New York by six matching cream-colored horses.

But Washington was restrained in his relations with Congress. He did not believe the President should offer ideas for laws. Nor would

The Cabinet was a group of presidential advisers, or secretaries, for special tasks of the government. It included a secretary of war, attorney general, secretary of state, and secretary of the treasury.

2. How did Washington believe a President should act?

1) Washington thought a President should be dignified and command respect, but should avoid the display and formality of a monarch. 2) He believed that only Congress, as representatives of the people, should create new laws, and that a President should not offer suggestions. 3) He believed that the President should not veto a bill unless he thought it was against the Constitution.

Washington is pictured here with his Cabinet. From left to right: Edmund Randolph, Henry Knox, Alexander Hamilton, and Thomas Jefferson. Why did Washington choose people who disagreed with one another for his Cabinet?

245

he veto a bill unless he thought it was against the Constitution. Only Congress, as the representative of the people, should create new laws, Washington believed.

Congress Begins Its Work

3. *What were the first acts of Congress?*

1) Congress sent 12 amendments to the states; the states ratified 10 of them, which became the Bill of Rights. 2) Congress passed the Judiciary Act, which established a Supreme Court with a Chief justice and five associate justices, plus three regional, or circuit, courts and thirteen federal district courts.

The first action the Congress took was to plan for the Bill of Rights. Suggestions for amendments were gathered from the states. Twelve of these were approved by Congress and then sent to the states for ratification. The states agreed to 10 amendments, and these were added to the Constitution in 1791.

With the Judiciary Act of 1789 Congress also created a plan for federal courts. The act set up a Supreme Court with a chief justice and five associate justices. Three regional or *circuit courts* and 13 federal district courts were also set up. John Jay, the foreign minister and co-author of *The Federalist Papers*, was named first Chief Justice of the Supreme Court by Washington.

Alexander Hamilton and His Plans

4. *How did Hamilton plan to get capital for manufacturing?*

Hamilton planned to get capital with which to encourage manufacturing by 1) taxing the sale of goods (excise taxes) and the sale of foreign goods (tariffs) 2) forming the Bank of the United States and selling shares.

After the Bill of Rights and the Judiciary Act, Congress did not have a clear idea of what to do next, but Alexander Hamilton did. He was a brilliant planner and only 34 years old when he became Washington's chief adviser. Hamilton had a clear, precise vision of a strong, powerful United States of America. In his view a powerful nation was one that could pay its bills and help its citizens lead more comfortable lives. A powerful nation was also one that

This check was written by Thomas Pinckney, the minister to Great Britain, in 1792. Notice that it is drawn on the Bank of the United States.

other nations would want to trade with and would be afraid to fight.

Between 1790 and 1791 Alexander Hamilton presented the Congress with a complete set of his plans for the United States. The purpose of Hamilton's plans was to make it worthwhile for all the states to cooperate with the federal government. A second purpose was to collect within the federal government enough wealth to help pay people to go into manufacturing. A strong country needed *capital*. An independent country needed to produce and sell more than it had to buy from foreign nations.

Hamilton planned to use one of the powers given to the federal government by the Constitution—the right to raise and collect taxes. If the new government had money, it could pay or assume the war debts of poorer states and pay money owed to wealthy Americans and foreigners. One way to raise money was to tax. Two kinds of taxes could be used by the government. They were a tax on the sale of goods, or *excise* taxes, and a tax on foreign goods, or tariffs. Another way to raise money was to form a bank and sell shares. This new Bank of the United States would be a partnership between the private shareholders and the government. For its part the government would keep the tax money, or federal treasury, deposited in the same bank. This meant that the treasury of the United States and the bank were one organization. The bank shares, the deposits, and the new taxes together would form the capital. Then the government could spend capital to help private manufacturers get a start. Hamilton's plan was a web of ideas, each connected to the other. Either the Congress would go along with most of them or none of it would work.

Hamilton looked forward to a nation very different from the one that existed in 1789. He saw a nation of manufacturers who sold to American farmers and to customers all over Europe. To reach that vision, he was willing to take actions that would help to bring it about—excise taxes, tariffs, a partnership between the people with money and the new government.

Hamilton's plan was a work of genius. He showed Americans how to pool their resources to build a strong nation out of 13 separate states. But the plan required the United States to pay a price. The people with money were going to become richer. Those with little money would find themselves in a worse situation.

Hamilton did not mind that the separation between the rich and the poor was going to become greater. He believed that the poor, uneducated people could not play equal parts in the government with those who were talented, trained, and successful. The people of talent, whom he dared to call "the best," ought to run the government, he said.

Alexander Hamilton, shown here, disagreed with Jefferson about the purposes of government. How were their disagreements helpful for the country?

Objections to the plan were not economic. The plan would aid the richer citizens and encourage competition in trade and manufacture.

Jefferson Disagrees

5. *Why would Hamilton's plan further separate the rich from the poor?*

1) The rich would make profits from manufacturing. 2) The poor would be taxed as well as the rich, but they would not benefit from the success of the manufacturers.

6. *Why did Jefferson disagree with Hamilton's plan?*

1) There were already differences between the rich and the poor. 2) He didn't want Americans to leave farming for trade and manufacture. 3) He thought that freedom was more important than security.

7. *How did Jefferson and Hamilton each view the Constitution?*

1) Jefferson, a strict constructionist, opposed the Bank of the United States as unconstitutional, since establishing a bank was not one of the listed powers of Congress. 3) Hamilton argued for a loose interpretation of the Constitution, saying it was a sketch to be filled in, a blueprint.

1) Washington supported Hamilton's financial plan, and in February of 1790 signed the bill chartering the Bank of the United States. 2) American credit was restored, capital was available for investment, and the rich did make money and support Hamilton in other matters of policy.

8. *What were the results of the argument?*

Jefferson objected to Hamilton's plan. He felt that there were already too many differences between rich and poor. Hamilton's plan was clearly designed to link the rich and their wealth to the future success of the country. Also, Jefferson did not want Americans to leave farming for trade and manufacture. Let Europeans compete in business. Americans should each own land and stay at peace with one another.

Hamilton's unkind words about "the people" made it even harder for Jefferson to listen to him. If there were to be a choice between security and freedom, Jefferson would certainly choose freedom. Hamilton chose the security and strength of a nation in which the people who already had individual power would become richer because they supported the government.

Two Views of the Constitution

Jefferson wrote a long paper in which he opposed the Bank of the United States as unconstitutional. He thought it was unfair to the people who were not rich. He used the Tenth Amendment to support his argument. According to this amendment powers not specifically given to Congress were reserved to the states or to the people. Since establishing a bank was not one of the listed powers of Congress, it was reserved to the states or the people. By staying so close to the exact wording, Jefferson used a strict constructionist method of interpreting the Constitution.

This was an argument Hamilton enjoyed answering. It was difficult to answer Jefferson's charges that the bank would make the rich richer. That, after all, was the idea. But the argument on the Constitution was easier. In a long written response to Jefferson, Hamilton argued that the Constitution was not a finished, detailed daily calendar of how Congress should vote. He argued for a loose construction or interpretation of the Constitution. He said that the Constitution was a sketch to be filled in, or a blueprint. If Jefferson was looking for a constitutional clause for every law, then he should look at Article I, Section 8, which states that Congress "shall have all power to enact laws necessary and proper for carrying into effect the foregoing powers." The bank was necessary to build trade and sound credit, and these powers were definitely listed.

Both men's arguments were supported by the Constitution. But Washington favored Hamilton's plan for giving the new nation credit abroad, a way of printing money, and a way of paying its bills. In February of 1790 Washington signed the bill chartering the Bank of the United States. The bank was a great success. American credit was restored. Capital was available for investment.

The rich did make money, and they supported Hamilton in other matters of policy, just as he planned.

A Fair Trade

Hamilton had to bargain to get Congress to approve his plan for having the federal government pay the state debts. The states that had debts to pay off were delighted to turn them over to the federal government. But the states like Virginia, which had paid their debts, were hard to convince. Why should they pay taxes to help the states in debt? Jefferson and Madison met Hamilton over a private dinner and made an agreement. They would make sure the Virginia delegation to Congress would vote for the "assumption of state debts," if Hamilton would promise that the capital of the United States would be located on the banks of the Potomac River. That is what happened, much to the distress of Philadelphia, which had hoped it would be chosen as the site of the new capital. Philadelphia was made the temporary capital for ten years while the new capital city was being built.

9. Why was the nation's capital moved?

Hamilton promised Jefferson and Madison that the capital would be moved to the Potomac River if Virginia would vote to have the national government take over the debts of the States.

The Questions and the Sides Change

At the time of the ratification of the Constitution, both Hamilton and Jefferson had been on the same side. They both believed a strong union was needed. But Hamilton wanted the union in order to collect capital, make investments, tax the citizens, and help private business. Jefferson wanted a strong union to bind the people together, and to keep them from being controlled by people like

10. What effect did the ratification have on the nation's leaders?

Leaders divided into groups according to their individual interests. The east coast merchants who sided with Hamilton called themselves Federalists; the western farmers who sided with Jefferson were called anti-Federalists, or Republicans.

Edward Savage painted this picture showing George and Martha Washington with their two children. They are looking over the plans for the new capital city.

249

SURVEYOR OF THE CAPITAL

Once the decision was made to locate the new capital of the United States on the banks of the Potomac, the land there had to be surveyed. One of the chief surveyors was a free Black named Benjamin Banneker. Using his skills as a mathematician, Banneker set the location of the District of Columbia. He also laid out many of the District's streets.

Born to free Black parents in 1831, Banneker was able to get an education. When he left school, he worked on his father's farm until a Quaker friend and neighbor lent him some books on astronomy. Banneker became very interested in the subject. He built his own telescope, and with it was able to make an accurate prediction of an eclipse. His considerable ability as a mathematician led him to be named a member of the commission to survey the new national capital in 1789.

In addition to his work as an astronomer and surveyor, Banneker published an almanac. His almanac was almost as widely read as Benjamin Franklin's. In 1791 Banneker sent the first copy of his almanac, along with a letter protesting the system of slavery, to Thomas Jefferson, then Secretary of State. Banneker also proposed a league of nations to achieve peace, and was against capital punishment. In these views Banneker was ahead of his time. He died in 1806.

Benjamin Banneker was a mathematician, astronomer, and surveyor. Besides helping to survey Washington, D.C., he wrote an almanac in the 1790's.

the British king. He wanted a strong union based on what government was not allowed to do. Jefferson trusted the people and mistrusted government. Hamilton mistrusted the people and trusted the government, as long as the wealthy people were in partnership with it.

Although Hamilton won Washington over to his side, he did not win everyone. There were leaders in the nation who trusted the people. There were people who wanted to follow a leader who had their interests in mind. Leaders in the federal government and in the states began to choose sides. The east coast merchants tended to side with Hamilton. The western farmers sided with Jefferson. The Union was not dividing over state lines. People divided into groups according to what was best for themselves. These were *factions*, or special-interest groups. The factions clustered around Hamilton and Jefferson. Hamilton's friends and followers began to call themselves Federalists while Jefferson's supporters called themselves anti-Federalists or Republicans. As time went on the arguments that separated the Federalists and the Republicans became clearer.

Which do you trust the most—the people or the government? Why?

The first years of the new government proved that a powerful federal government could help some of the people more than others. Jefferson disliked this. But Hamilton argued that in the long run, the Bank of the United States and higher taxes would not only help merchants, manufacturers, and investors, but they would also help the whole nation. Hamilton's plan would create an environment in which business could grow. The poor would be able to find jobs in the new businesses.

The Election of 1792

In 1792, Washington would have liked to retire from the presidency, but the nation was too divided. Jefferson's group did not have enough strength to capture the vice-presidency from John Adams as they had hoped. They did, however, win the most seats in the House of Representatives. So during the next four years, Washington and Hamilton had to struggle for every representative's vote in Congress.

Representation was no longer being used simply to guarantee freedom. By 1792, representation had become a way of helping one group over another. Jefferson began to receive support from two sources: those who wanted freedom from government, and those who wanted more help from government for their special interest. Jefferson wanted more influence in government. And he accepted followers of both kinds.

11. What was the effect of the election of 1792?

Jefferson's supporters won most seats in the House, so Washington and Hamilton had to struggle for every representative's vote during the next four years.

Checking the facts

1. What was Washington's view of the presidency?
2. Why were Hamilton and Jefferson in conflict?
3. How did the conflict between the Hamilton and Jefferson followers affect politics in the United States?

2. WAR IN EUROPE—POLITICS AT HOME

Americans began to take sides over another situation much farther from home. A revolution had broken out in France in 1789, the same year Washington became President and the new United States government was formed. Within four years the king of France, Louis XVI, had been beheaded. The other nations of Europe had gone to war against the French. Europeans wanted to make sure that revolutionary ideas did not spread.

A continuing issue—Should the United States help all people who want freedom?

A continuing issue—Should the United States take the side of any important trading nation?

The French rebels sent out a call for help to all who loved liberty. They expected the Americans whom they had helped in the Revolution to return the favor. In the alliance of 1778 the Americans had promised not to go to war, but to protect the French colonies in the West Indies, if they were attacked. Now, however, the Americans had more to lose. Since their trade with Great Britain was increasing, they did not want to get involved in a war with France against Britain.

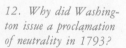

12. Why did Washington issue a proclamation of neutrality in 1793?

1) France was having a revolution. Other European nations went to war against France to keep revolutionary ideas from spreading. 2) Americans wanted to keep up trade with both sides, although both England and France declared that trade with the other side would be an act of war.

Americans did have favorites in that war. Jefferson and the other Republicans stood with the French Revolution. They thought the United States ought to help the new French government. Hamilton and the Federalists were on the side of the solid British government and the orderly continuation of their trade. The best policy for the Americans was not to take sides but to sell to both sides. However, the French and the British let it be known that trade with the other side would be considered an act of war. And that included the important trade with the French West Indies. President Washington did not think that Americans should become involved in European wars. He issued a proclamation of neutrality in 1793.

Citizen Genêt

Instead of waiting for the Americans to help, the French took action on their own. In 1793, the French sent a special agent, named Citizen Genêt (zhe-NAY), to the United States to recruit privateers and arrange for volunteer armies. Genêt was enormously popular. He began to recruit Americans without the approval of President Washington or the Congress. He was ordered to stop his activities by the President. Some Americans formed groups in support of France. Among them were the back-country Scotch-Irish, who still wanted to be left alone by the national government. Others were shipowners and traders who could profit from attacking Spanish lands in Florida in the name of helping France. Still others, like Jefferson, wanted to spread liberty to other people.

Trouble with England

The British also made it difficult for Americans to remain neutral. They began to capture American ships on the high seas and take sailors from them. Because American sailors were forced or pressed into the service of the British, this practice was known as *impressment*. Americans protested but there was little they could do to stop the British navy. In 1793 and 1794, the British captured 600 United States ships. The new nation was challenged. But should it go to war? Hamilton did not want to fight the British because their trade was too important. Being angry at the British was a problem because British trade was taxed and helped fill the

Citizen Genêt is shown here with Washington and Jefferson. Why did some Americans respond to Citizen Genêt's call?

United States treasury. Successful merchants also paid tax dollars. In addition, other people were angry at the British because they still occupied the forts in the Northwest.

Jay's Treaty

In 1794, Washington sent Chief Justice John Jay to London to try to settle differences between the two countries peacefully. The British were too strong for America to fight. Perhaps they could be persuaded to leave America alone. In November of 1794 Jay signed a treaty with the British. The main point, or *concession*, won by the Americans was the British withdrawal from the forts in the American West, which they had continued to occupy since the Revolution. The British also agreed to allow a limited amount of American trade with the British West Indies. But otherwise, they refused to give in. The United States was not allowed to trade as a neutral with Britain's enemies. Jay's Treaty was not the victory of a little republic over the great empire that many Americans wanted. But in spite of the disappointment, Washington had no choice but to ask the Senate to ratify the treaty.

Pinckney's Treaty

One unexpected outcome of Jay's Treaty was its effect on the Spanish. They became frightened of a new alliance between the United States and Britain. In a treaty negotiated by Thomas Pinckney in 1795, Spain finally gave the United States the right to navigate the Mississippi and deposit riverboat cargo at New Orleans for transfer to oceangoing ships. Pinckney's Treaty was a popular treaty. But Jay's Treaty was not. Jefferson's friends tried to tell the people that the Jay Treaty was a slap in the face.

The Western Frontier

The western frontier was still a problem. Native Americans fought the continuing spread of settlement. But the Native Americans in the Northwest Territory were defeated by General "Mad Anthony" Wayne. In the Treaty of Greenville in 1795, the Native Americans gave up all claim to the Northwest Territory. It was now safe to move onto that new land. New land meant opportunity. People gave the government credit for Wayne's victory.

The Whiskey Rebellion

The Federalists seemed so successful to the people that Jefferson had a hard time convincing Americans that such a strong government could become dangerous. Jefferson was afraid of strong government. He wanted more political power for his group.

John Jay served as Washington's minister to France. How did Jay's Treaty keep the United States from going to war with Great Britain?

13. Why was Pinckney's Treaty popular, whereas Jay's was not?

Both treaties won concessions for the United States, but Jay's failed to allow the United States to trade as a neutral with Britain's enemies.

14. What did the Treaty of Greenville mean for Americans?

The Native Americans gave up all claims to the Northwest Territory, and it was now safe to move onto that new land.

15. How did the results of the Whiskey Rebellion help Hamilton's cause?

Land meant opportunity for many Americans. Foreign nations and Native Americans were seen as keeping traders and settlers from moving westward and using the Mississippi River.
What do you think? Can an active government that does not consult the people be a danger?

1) Washington sent militia to deal with whiskey distillers who resisted paying the excise tax. 2) Only a few rebels were there, but the nation was relieved that the government had kept people obedient to the law. 3) Jefferson's political power shrank, and he lost in his bid for the presidency.

The Federalists continued to have success, even when they took action to control those who opposed the government. In western Pennsylvania, farmers made their grain into whiskey. Whiskey sold well and jugs of whiskey can be transported to market easier than loads of grain. Hamilton had convinced Washington and Congress to tax whiskey in 1791. This was an excise tax, designed to raise money for the government. The farmers resented the new tax. By 1794, they had armed themselves and were prepared to resist, just as they had done during Shays' Rebellion in 1786. Washington sent more than 12,000 troops (voluntary militia) to put down the rebellion. The Constitution gave him this right as Commander-in-Chief of the army. The troops were led by Hamilton and Henry Lee. When the army got to western Pennsylvania, they found few rebels. Two or three were put in jail for a short time. Still, Hamilton managed to work the defeat of the Whiskey Rebellion to his advantage. The reaction in the nation was one of relief that the government had kept people obedient to the law. Jefferson watched in dismay. He saw his opportunity for political power shrink. Two years later he lost the presidency to the Federalist, John Adams.

General "Mad Anthony" Wayne is shown here after the battle of Fallen Timbers. Why did government troops fight with the Native Americans?

This painting by Frederick Kemmelmeyer was to help Americans remember George Washington as President. What made him a great President?

Washington's Farewell

Washington was glad to leave office in 1796. He did not like being attacked in the press. Nor did he like the way in which the United States was becoming involved in the affairs of foreign nations. He also disliked the differences of opinion that had become such a dividing force in the new nation. In his Farewell Address, which was not spoken but, rather, printed in several newspapers, Washington advised the United States not to enter into any permanent alliances with foreign countries. He also warned against factions and explained the need for strong government as he saw it: "Liberty itself will find in such a government with powers properly distributed and adjusted, its surest guarantee." People should live within the laws, Washington said, and thereby keep the "peaceful enjoyment of the rights of person and property."

16. What was Washington's concern for the nation?

1) He did not like the way the United States was becoming involved in the affairs of other nations.
2) He felt that the differences of opinion had become a dividing force in the nation.

Washington remembered the weakness of the Articles. How can you tell if your government is strong or weak?

The Election of 1796

17. *How did the election of 1796 divide the nation further?*

The presidency and vice-presidency—the two top offices in the land—went to the heads of two opposing factions.

By 1796 both the Federalists and Republicans held secret meetings to decide who their candidates would be. The Republicans chose Jefferson as their candidate for President, and Aaron Burr, a Senator from New York, as the candidate for Vice-President. John Adams was the Federalist choice for President, and Thomas Pinckney, his running-mate.

The Republicans managed to organize a successful campaign in Pennsylvania. There were no Federalist electors from Pennsylvania at all. But the Virginia electors threw their votes away by voting for Sam Adams, who did not have a chance to win. The electors from New England did not want to vote for a southern candidate like Jefferson. The result was that John Adams, the Federalist candidate, received 71 votes to Jefferson's 68. Since the second highest candidate automatically became Vice-President, no matter how much he disagreed with the President, the two top offices in the land went to the two heads of the opposing factions.

Regions and Politics

There was still a debate over what the government should do. In 1796, eight years after the Constitution was ratified, the states seemed less important than the regions of the nation. Each region was determined to stand up for what was best for it. The farmers, and the merchants, and people interested in becoming manufacturers disagreed on trade and tax laws. With Washington gone from the presidency, and Adams and Jefferson both in office, what kind of organization would hold the nation together? How would one group in Congress ever be able to gather enough votes to make any decisions?

Checking the facts

1. Why did France expect help from America?
2. What problems did the central government have in the western frontier?

3. THE PRESIDENTS AND THE PEOPLE

No one really knew in 1789 what the relationship of the President would be to the people. Washington was their adored military hero. But there were no rules about keeping a civilian President in touch with the people. During the time a President was in office, how much information should be given to the people? How much criticism of the government must the President take? What could or should be done about criticism of the President or the government if it seemed to threaten their ability to act?

Washington had worried a great deal about all of these questions. He chose to keep the position of President somewhat apart from the people. When the House of Representatives asked for a copy of what had been said in secret treaty talks, Washington said no. He said that the Constitution required the Senate, not the House, to "advise and consent" on treaties. He felt that if the people trusted him, they would not need to know or ask about private talks. Washington thought the request from the House was an attack on his honor. If the people did not trust him, he said, they could impeach him. He believed a President should be judged on the results of his actions.

John Adams felt the same as Washington. He believed that the President should do what seemed best to him. If the people did not like it, they could vote him out in the next election. The American press felt free to say what they pleased about government officials. Adams and Jefferson were both attacked in the public press often. Adams did not like it. He did not care a great deal about popularity, but he felt name-calling was wrong.

18. How did Washington and Adams agree on the presidency?

1) They both believed that the President should do what seemed best. 2) The people could vote the President out in the next election if they didn't like the President's actions.

Trouble with France—The XYZ Affair

Adams became popular because of the way he handled the French in 1797 and 1798. No sooner had the Jay and Pinckney treaties been signed than the French began to attack American ships. The important question before Adams' administration was what to do about France. In 1797 Adams tried to stop worse trouble by sending three people, Charles Pinckney, John Marshall, and Elbridge Gerry, to France to negotiate a settlement without war. The French foreign minister, Talleyrand, did not think too highly of the United States. He sent three Frenchmen, later nicknamed X, Y, and Z by Adams, to meet the Americans. They demanded payment, a *bribe*, as the price of settlement.

The Americans refused. President Adams was furious about the French attempt at bribery. The United States had been insulted. In April 1798, the President told the story of the bribe to Congress. The people were outraged. "Millions for defense, but not one cent for tribute" became the cry of many. John Adams became a public hero overnight. The Congress began to plan for war. A Department of the Navy was created and money set aside, or *appropriated*, for 40 warships and a much bigger army. The nation looked as if it

John Adams became the second President of the United States. Why did Adams disagree with Jefferson, his Vice-President?

How is public opinion about foreign affairs formed? How much should the people be told?

257

19. *What was the result of the XYZ Affair?*

1) A Department of the Navy was created, and money was appropriated for 40 warships and a much bigger army. 2) Washington came out of retirement to head the army with Hamilton second in command. 3) American privateers began to attack French ships on the high seas.

really wanted to go to war against France. Washington came out of retirement to head the army. Hamilton was made second in command. On the high seas American privateers began to attack French ships. John Adams could have made himself very popular by leading the United States into war against France. But he knew that there were only 3,500 Americans in uniform and the chance of defeating the French was slim. What he did was to agree that the United States should build up its army and a navy. He and other Federalists also used the threat of war to try to silence the Republicans.

The Alien and Sedition Acts

Adams asked: How could the nation defend itself against other nations if the country was full of foreigners? How could the nation pull together if the newspapers carried attacks on the President and his policies? The Constitution was no help in answering either of these questions.

20. *Why were the Alien and Sedition acts passed?*

1) Adams and the Federalists claimed that the laws would ensure loyalty to the government in time of war. 2) In reality, the acts were used to stop open criticism of the government and to delay the naturalization of aliens, many of whom voted Republican when they became citizens.

Over the summer of 1798 Adams and his followers in Congress passed a group of laws. These laws were to make sure everyone was loyal to the government in case of war. The Naturalization Act extended the time that it took a foreigner to become a citizen from 5 to 14 years. Since many foreign immigrants became Republicans, this act was meant to keep them from voting for a longer period of time. The Alien Enemies Act was directed against foreign immigrants, or *aliens*, who had not yet become citizens. It gave the President the power to force any foreign-born alien considered "dangerous to the peace and safety of the United States" to leave the country.

The Sedition Act, also passed in the summer of 1798, made it a crime to stand in the way of any law or to start a riot. This was understandable. But the law also made it illegal to write or speak any "false" criticism of government officials. The officials should decide for themselves whether the criticism was false.

Adams and the other Federalists defended the Sedition Act. They said that all governments needed protection against people who refused to obey the law. But in reality, the Sedition Act was used to stop open criticism of the government. Republican newspaper publishers were fined and jailed.

The Virginia and Kentucky Resolutions

21. *How did Jefferson and Madison justify their activities?*

Jefferson and Madison argued that in a government by the people, open discussion is the only way the people can learn about new ideas or other ways of taking action. Rule by the people, or *democracy*, needs to give information to the people and get their opinions. Information to the people's representatives is not enough. Jefferson and Madison said in public that the Alien and Sedition Acts attacked the First Amendment, which guaranteed free speech. But how could they draw attention to their views? They went to the Virginia and Kentucky state legislatures and got them to pass resolutions cancelling, or *nullifying*, the Alien and Sedition Acts.

According to Jefferson and Madison, when the federal government passed laws that went beyond the powers the states had given it, the states could refuse to recognize the laws.

How could the states get away with such resolutions? Were not federal laws supreme under the Constitution? Jefferson and Madison based their protest on the idea that the nation was formed by an agreement among the states. This was the states' rights, or *compact*, theory of the Constitution.

According to it, the states had given the federal government some powers, but when the federal government passed laws that went beyond those powers, the states could refuse to recognize the laws. They could cancel, or declare *null* and *void*, unconstitutional acts of Congress. Some people feared that the Union could break up over this question.

The Federalists in Trouble

The question of states' rights was not settled. But the situation in Europe changed. Early in 1799, the French army under Napoleon Bonaparte was trapped in Egypt. England, Russia, and Austria attacked the French in Europe. Now war against the United States seemed unwise. When Adams heard that the French might make peace, he had a serious decision to make. It was the year before the presidential election. The possibility of war against France had been the reason for most of his policies and for what little popularity he had. If he called off the war, it would be better for the country. But he would no doubt lose the election. The Jeffersonians would say that the Alien and Sedition Acts had been passed just to silence them.

22. How did Adams put his nation's best interests first?

France wanted to make peace with the United States. Adams called off the war even though he knew he would lose the election because of the Jeffersonians' opposition to the Alien and Sedition Acts.

Adams did a brave thing. He made peace with France. The outcome of this action was as he had expected. He lost the election of 1800 to Jefferson. A show-down had not come on the question of what states could do about laws they did not like. But Jefferson and Madison were satisfied that they had made their public protest about the misuse of government power and the need to keep the people informed.

Jefferson Creates a Majority

If elected, Jefferson planned to use his term as President to bring the nation together. He wanted to do away with factions. In a nation of differences this was not easy to do. But Jefferson understood how to organize the American people. He built local groups

23. What trend did Jefferson set in American politics?

Jefferson was a skilled political organizer. Why is it important to organize the voters?

259

1) Jefferson recognized that there could not be a political party to represent each group. 2) He got a combination of individuals and groups with different interests—a coalition—to work together to get votes.

of followers all over the country. It was their job to know the people and get them to support electors and representatives to Congress who favored Jefferson's point of view.

Jefferson thought that people did not have to live alike or have the same economic interests to join together and win elections. People must work together to get the votes. This combination of individuals and groups with different interests was a *coalition*. Jefferson created such a coalition between his planter friends in the South and the Sons of St. Tammany in New York City. These were Irish immigrants who as newcomers did not have much power in New York State. Jefferson offered them and their leader, Aaron Burr, his support in return for their votes.

Jefferson taught people how to work together politically, even if they were very different in other ways. American political parties have done this ever since. In a nation the size of an empire with all the differences among Americans, it was not possible to have a political party to represent every group. There would be hundreds of parties and not one with a majority. Jefferson found a practical, political way of bringing factions together.

The Election of 1800

In 1800 Jefferson chose Burr as his running-mate. They ran against Adams and Charles Pinckney again. This time the Republicans won. But there was a tie in the electoral college. Both Jefferson and Burr received the same number of votes. Although Burr was supposed to be the vice-presidential candidate, he refused to step down. Finally the House chose Jefferson as President, and Burr became Vice-President.

The Constitution had to be amended to prevent this situation from happening again. The Twelfth Amendment, in 1804, provided for separate balloting for President and Vice-President. In a little more than ten years, the American way of governing had grown. And the Constitution had grown with it.

Jefferson as President

Jefferson was determined to stay close to the people. He also wanted to keep his majority in the nation. What would he do as President? All he had as a model were the actions of Washington and Adams. In the 12 years of their presidencies, Jefferson had opposed them most of the time.

The first thing Jefferson found out is that a new President cannot undo everything that has gone before. Too much had been built,

Jefferson designed and built his home in Monticello, Virginia. He filled it with many of his inventions, including a dumbwaiter.

even in that short period of time. The Bank of the United States was working. To cancel it was impossible, and unwise. Thanks to Hamilton, the credit of the nation was improving all the time.

Jefferson and the Federalist Officeholders

Unfortunately for Jefferson, Adams had filled many jobs in the government with Federalists. There were few jobs left to which Jefferson could appoint his supporters. They wanted to come to Washington, the new capital city, and help Jefferson run the government his way.

Marbury v. Madison

Many Federalists were left in the government—for life. Among them was the Chief Justice of the Supreme Court, John Marshall. In the 34 years he held that office, Marshall wrote opinions and led the vote for a strong federal government. While Jefferson was President, the first major case before the Supreme Court came up. Jefferson and his secretary of state, James Madison, had decided not to carry out Adams' last minute job-filling, particularly in the appointment of judges. It was an involved case. A Justice of the Peace named Marbury sued Madison because he was not made a judge, although he knew Adams had signed the papers. Marbury sued to have the papers delivered. And he lost. What happened to Marbury was unimportant compared to John Marshall's statement that the Supreme Court did not have the power to help Marbury. The method Marbury used to complain was unconstitutional, said Marshall.

The Supreme Court declared that the Constitution had not been interpreted properly! Who said the Supreme Court could say what the Constitution meant? Who said the Supreme Court could decide if action by government was constitutional? This was called the power of *judicial review*. In 1803 Marshall made an important change in the way America was to be governed when he said the Supreme Court could decide if a law was constitutional.

Marshall, like the other brilliant thinkers during the first years of government, made a lasting contribution. From then on, when laws were passed that a person believed to be unconstitutional, a person could appeal directly to the Supreme Court of the United States for a decision. Since court justices were appointed for life, the threat of not being re-elected could not be used as pressure on them. Thus the Supreme Court became the major protector of the people against unconstitutional use of power by lawmakers. Little by little, and day by day, the American system based on the blueprint of the Constitution was built.

John Marshall was named Chief Justice of the Supreme Court by John Adams. Why was the Supreme Court's decision about judicial review important?

24. What problems did Jefferson encounter as President?

1) Jefferson could not reverse the policies of previous Presidents to which he had always been opposed. The Bank of the United States was working and the nation's credit was improving, so he could not cancel it. 2) Adams had filled government jobs with Federalists. Jefferson was not able to find jobs for all his supporters who wanted to come and help him run the government.

In what way does the Supreme Court protect the people from the Congress?

261

Changing Power the American Way

President Thomas Jefferson was enormously popular. He was as informal in his manner as Washington and Adams had been formal. He spoke with the same feeling for the beauty of the English language that he had used so effectively in writing the Declaration of Independence 25 years before. He knew how to work with his cabinet and the Congress. It was said that he knew each member of Congress personally.

25. *What contribution did Jefferson make to the election process?*

1) This was the first time that a new party, with a new viewpoint, had been chosen by the American people. 2) There was a peaceful transfer of power, free of riots in the streets and of attacks on the new government by defeated leaders.

In his Inaugural Address on March 4, 1801, Jefferson had recognized that this was the first time that a new party and a new point of view had been chosen by the American people. There were no riots in the streets by the losers or attacks by the new government on the defeated leaders. The peaceful transfer of power was to become a symbol of the American way to govern. Jefferson said in his speech that others might not understand the American freedom to criticize each other during an election. But that once the votes had been counted, Americans "all will, of course, arrange themselves under the will of law and unite in common efforts for the common good."

Margaret Bayard Smith, the wife of a newspaper publisher in Washington, also commented. After watching the inauguration, she wrote a letter to her sister: "I have this morning witnessed one of the most interesting scenes a free people can ever witness, the changes of administration, which in every government in every age have most generally been epochs of confusions, villainy, and bloodshed, in this our happy country take place without any species of . . . disorder. This day one of the most amiable and worthy men has taken that seat to which he was called by the voice of his country."

Checking the facts

1. What circumstances brought Jefferson to the presidency?
2. What major changes took place during the Jefferson presidency?
3. Why did Adams believe that the Alien and Sedition Acts were needed?
4. How were the results of the treaties signed by Jay and Pinckney different?

How does each of the three branches of government represent you?

Look at the newspaper. How many nations do not have "peaceful transfer of power"?

PUTTING IT ALL TOGETHER

UNDERSTANDING THE MAIN IDEAS

1. What actions did the national or federal government take?
2. Did a powerful, active federal government help or hurt the states?
3. How did the nation organize itself to make decisions?

ACTIVITIES

1. In class discuss the following question: "It is better for a President to use the power of the office than it is to be too afraid to use it." Use the information you have gathered in this chapter to support your views. Have any recent events influenced your thinking?
2. Read the editorial page of your local newspaper. Locate an article on the presidency. Do the writers think that the President today is using enough power? Do they think the President is using too much power? What do the writers look at in the President's behavior in order to make their judgment? Do you agree with them? Present your findings in a brief written report in which you outline the main ideas presented in the editorial.
3. Look at a recent almanac in your home or school library. What states have the Presidents come from? What conclusions can you draw from the information?
4. How did a recent President come to be nominated by the party? What experience did the President have in politics? in other fields? What kind of education did the President have? Place your information in a well-written outline.

BOOKS TO READ

Chidsey, Donald Barr, *Mr. Hamilton and Mr. Jefferson* (New York: Nelson Publishers, Inc., 1975).

Coy, Harold, *First Book of Presidents* (New York: Watts Publishing Co., 1973).

Holland, Janice, *They Build a City* (New York: Charles Scribner's Sons, Inc., 1968).

Lisitzky, Gene, *Thomas Jefferson* (New York: Viking Press, Inc., 1933).

chapter 11
Problems For Representation

1803–1817

1. LOOKING WEST AND USING POWER
2. JEFFERSON'S SECOND TERM
3. GROWING STRONG AND DIFFERENT
4. WAR AGAINST GREAT BRITAIN

INTRODUCTION

As a planter, writer, philosopher, diplomat, and politician, Thomas Jefferson was one of the most talented people ever to be elected to the presidency. What would he do now that he had the power to carry out his deep feelings for the rights of the people? It so happened that the great events of Jefferson's presidency were not the result of his ideas on democracy. Instead they were the result of a great opportunity for the United States that came from Europe. Jefferson had the chance to add land to the nation—land for the nation of farmers that he so believed in. To get that land, Jefferson used power and took action in precisely the way he had feared Presidents would act. He was praised and loved for his action, and he liked it himself.

The story of the years of Jefferson's presidency and the Presidents who followed him is closely tied to the land in the West and to the development of the nation in the East. Political leaders had to

	1803	1805	1807	1811	
Who?	President Jefferson	Lieutenant Zebulon M. Pike	Commodore Barron	Tecumseh's Indian Confederacy	
What?	buys Louisiana	explores new territory	refuses to let the British search his ship	is attacked and defeated	
Where?	and adds acres to the American West	in Colorado and New Mexico	and is fired on three miles from Norfolk, Virginia	at Tippecanoe, Indiana territory	

All Presidents, even a genius like Jefferson, must deal with the practical growth and changes in the nation.

Look at the map on page 268 and remind yourselves about the Mississippi and the importance of New Orleans.

figure out how the differences among regions of the nation could be expressed and represented. As you read about the early part of the 1800's, think about these questions:

1. How did the West fit into the total picture of the nation?
2. How might the different regions be tied together?
3. What foreign policy did American leaders think was best for the regions of the nation?

1. LOOKING WEST AND USING POWER

In 1803 the people of the United States and their President, Thomas Jefferson, had one goal in mind about the West. They needed to be able to use the port at New Orleans. (See map, page 268.) If Americans could not use the port at New Orleans, then people could not live successfully west of the Appalachians. They depended on the Mississippi and the use of the port at New Orleans. Trade was the way their surplus grain could be used to buy the other kinds of goods they were determined to have. Pinckney's treaty with Spain had given the United States the right to use the Mississippi and New Orleans. But by 1803, this right was threatened by the French.

1. Why did Americans need use of the port at New Orleans?

The people west of the Appalachians used the Mississippi River to get their surplus grain to New Orleans, where they could trade.

Napoleon and the American West

The Americans found out that in a secret treaty signed in 1800, the Spanish had given all of the territory of Louisiana, including New Orleans, back to the French. Jefferson was alarmed. The French were now under the leadership of the greatest military genius of Europe, Napoleon, and Jefferson did not trust Napoleon. He was right to be concerned. Napoleon had a plan to establish triangular trade between France and the French West Indies, and

2. How did Jefferson decide to handle the French threat?

He decided to try to buy New Orleans, West Florida, or other Mississippi River land on which a port could be built.

1812	1814	1815	1817	1818
James Madison	Francis Cabot Lowell	Andrew Jackson	Clinton deWitt	Andrew Jackson
asks for a Declaration of War	completes spinning and weaving mill	defeats the British	finances the Erie Canal	leads an expeditionary force
against England	in Lowell, Massachusetts	at New Orleans, Louisiana	from Albany to Buffalo	to Florida

Recall that modern nations gained their strength through surpluses and trade. Just growing enough to feed oneself does not pay for improvements and control.

the very fertile land of the Louisiana Territory. He wanted to create a powerful French Empire. Jefferson was afraid that such an empire would not only interfere with United States trade, but also cause trouble for the United States with the Native Americans west of the Mississippi River. Jefferson believed that it might be necessary to fight the French for control of the Mississippi. But then the United States would need the help of the British navy. Tying the nation to Britain in order to stop France was not a pleasant thought. Therefore, Jefferson ordered the minister to France, Robert Livingston, to offer to buy New Orleans and West Florida, or other land near the mouth of the Mississippi, on which a new port city could be built.

3. What information would have saved the United States some money?

Jefferson didn't know that the French army had been destroyed by yellow fever in Santo Domingo.

Luckily for Jefferson and the United States, other events changed France's plans. Napoleon would not put his plan for North America into effect without Santo Domingo. However, the native population, under the leadership of Toussaint L'Ouverture, had revolted and set up their own government. Napoleon sent 20,000 troops to the island of Santo Domingo to put down the revolt. But the fight to regain that island failed. The French finally won the battle, but an epidemic of yellow fever destroyed the French army.

Jefferson did not know that Napoleon's army was dying in Santo Domingo when he decided to up the price the United States would pay for New Orleans. James Monroe, Jefferson's friend, was sent to join Livingston in France. The offer to Napoleon was $10 million for New Orleans and West Florida. If Napoleon refused, Monroe was to begin conversations with the British about taking action against the French.

The Louisiana Purchase

4. Why did Napoleon accept the offer?

He needed money and troops for a war with England.

It took Napoleon just seven days after getting the news about his army in Santo Domingo to give up all of his plans for North America. His decision had little to do with the United States, however. Napoleon was about to go to war with England again, and he needed money and troops for this war. So the United States' offer of money came at a moment when France needed it. Livingston was startled when the French offered to sell all of Louisiana to the United States. He also was relieved to see Monroe, who arrived that week. The timing could not have been better! Together they made the French an offer of $15 million. The offer was accepted. (See map, page 268.)

5. What did the United States gain?

It gained territory amounting to a third of the continent and the 50,000 new citizens who lived there.

The Americans did not know what they had bought. The French did not know what they had sold. When Livingston asked about boundaries of Louisiana, the French minister, Talleyrand, replied, "I can give you no direction. You have made a noble bargain for yourselves, and I suppose you will make the most of it."

266

This painting hangs in the United States Capitol. It shows Livingston and Monroe negotiating with the French for Louisiana. Why was France ready to sell and the United States ready to buy the land? How did each nation get what it wanted from the deal?

The Louisiana Purchase was a triumph for Jefferson. However some people argued that it was unconstitutional for a President to go out and buy a third of a continent and automatically acquire for the nation 50,000 new citizens to protect!

Jefferson, on the other hand, claimed that the power to govern territory given the President in the Constitution meant that he also had the right to acquire it. The attempt to make a lasting political statement to cover the act was impossible and unnecessary. And the Senate upheld Jefferson's action when it ratified the treaty with France in October of 1803. The nation was pleased with itself.

The Louisiana Purchase was a tribute to Hamilton as well as Jefferson. When France accepted United States bonds as payment, it was a statement that the nations of Europe trusted the credit and the economic future of the United States. The United States bonds could be sold for gold or for the money or goods of other nations. In 15 years the United States had become a good credit risk.

6. How could Hamilton take some of the credit for the purchase?

Hamilton's financial planning had made the nation a good credit risk. France accepted United States bonds as payment for Louisiana.

Exploring the Louisiana Territory

Thomas Jefferson did not stop at the purchase of Louisiana. He wanted to know what was out there. Exactly what plants and animals were found there? What was the quality of the soil and the length of the growing season? How much of the land could be used for farming? What tribes of Native Americans lived there, and would they cause trouble?

7. What information did Jefferson want on the Louisiana Territory?

Rivers were the easiest route because their destination was clearer. Explorers knew that rivers would eventually empty into the sea.

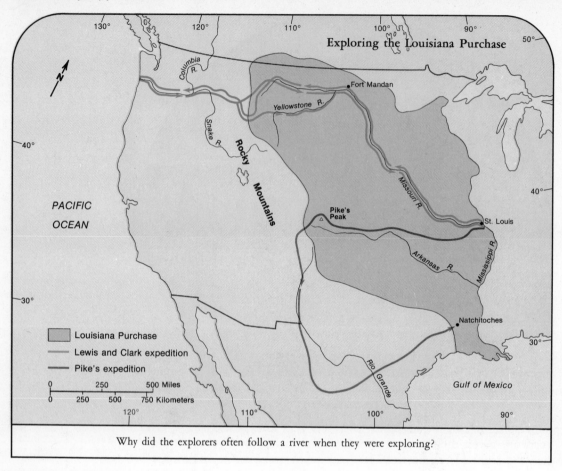

Exploring the Louisiana Purchase

- Louisiana Purchase
- Lewis and Clark expedition
- Pike's expedition

PACIFIC OCEAN

Gulf of Mexico

Why did the explorers often follow a river when they were exploring?

He wanted facts about 1) the land itself—its plants and animals, its soil, the length of the growing season; 2) Native American tribes— where they were, and whether they would cause trouble; 3) the western boundary, because the nation was competing with England for the fur trade in the Oregon country.

8. How did Jefferson plan the exploration?

He got $2,500 from Congress and hired Lewis and Clark to lead an expedition.

Jefferson was not as concerned about the western boundary of Louisiana. He knew the Spanish had lands along the west coast. But he did not worry about Spain. Spain's power in the world was on the way downhill. Jefferson also wanted the land explored all the way to the Pacific Ocean because the United States and England were competing for the fur trade in an area called the Oregon Country.

Jefferson asked Congress for $2,500 to support the exploration of the new territory. Then he hired his own private secretary to lead it. Meriwether Lewis was a Virginian who had served in the army in the West. Lewis, in turn, chose a fellow officer, William Clark, the brother of George Rogers Clark, the hero of the Revolutionary War in the West, to go with him. These men were loyal to Jefferson. They got their instructions directly from him. They were told to send Jefferson detailed reports on what they found.

Jefferson's relationship with Lewis and Clark was another use of presidential power.

Jefferson, the national political leader and man of vision, wanted to know how close the western edge of the territory was to the Pacific Ocean. The Spanish and the Native Americans were not part of his vision of the territory. He sent a message with Lewis and Clark to the Native Americans who lived in Spanish territory. The United States would protect them. However, he did not offer to leave them alone.

Lewis and Clark planned carefully. They hired 48 men, all experienced in living in the wilderness. They spent the winter of 1803–1804 training for the trip, and then they started out from St. Louis in the spring. In six months they had followed the Missouri River into what is now North Dakota. There they built a small settlement, Fort Mandan, and spent the winter. Jefferson was delighted to receive boxes of specimens of plant life and detailed reports on what they had seen.

The expedition set out again in the spring of 1805. The most serious problem ahead of them was getting through the Rocky Mountains. But fortunately they had a Shoshone woman, Sacajawea (sac-uh-juh-WEE-uh), and her French-Canadian husband as guides. With their two guides, the expedition was able to cross the Rockies. Lewis and Clark recorded their excitement at reaching the *Continental Divide*, or ridge, at the top of the mountains from which water flows east to the Mississippi and west to the Pacific. They

9. Why was the trip a success?

1) Lewis and Clark hired 48 men experienced in wilderness living. They spent the winter of 1803-1804 training for the trip. 2) They hired a Shoshone woman, Sacajawea, and her French-Canadian husband to guide them through the Rocky Mountains. 3) They got all the information Jefferson wanted.

Sacajawea, a Shoshone woman, guided Lewis and Clark through the Louisiana Territory.

This painting shows Lewis and Clark, on the far right, meeting the Flathead tribe. Why did Jefferson send the expedition?

reached the Pacific by November, the beginning of their second winter. The plan was to go home by ship. But they waited six months for one without any luck. So they had to walk home. The trip back to St. Louis took almost another six months. They did not arrive there until the fall of 1806.

After Lewis and Clark's return, detailed maps and journals were published. Americans were thrilled by these reports of the trip. Jefferson was particularly pleased with the stories of the friendly Native Americans Lewis and Clark had met and with the two grizzly bear cubs they brought him as a gift.

10. What happened after Lewis and Clark returned from exploring the new territory?

1) Other explorers set out, including Zebulon Pike who explored the Colorado area. 2) Not many settlers followed, but the fur trade increased. 3) Most people settled near the mouth of the Mississippi. By 1812 there were enough people there for Louisiana to be able to join the Union.

After Lewis and Clark, other explorers were sent out West. In 1805 a lieutenant in the United States army, Zebulon Pike, followed the Mississippi north, explored the Colorado area, and described the mountain peak that is now named Pikes Peak. Pike also traveled south and west to Santa Fe and the northern Rio Grande River.

No flood of settlers followed the explorers. Fur traders from St. Louis did go to the Northwest. And by 1808, a steady supply of furs was beginning to appear back in the East. But most people tended to settle in the area near the mouth of the Mississippi. This area had been the original reason for the interest in the West. And by 1812 enough people lived there for the state of Louisiana to join the union. The state was but a small part of the total area, however.

The United States had a future in the West. But as that possibility became clear, it was also obvious that the people in the older part

What place did the Native Americans have in any of these explorations and plans?

of the nation would want to extend their ways of life to the West. And people who lived in the northern cities, the southern plantations, and the frontier farms led very different lives. Whose West was it going to be?

Checking the facts

1. Why was Napoleon willing to sell the Louisiana Territory?
2. What was the importance of the Louisiana Purchase?
3. What did the Lewis and Clark expedition accomplish?

2. JEFFERSON'S SECOND TERM

Jefferson had achieved much during his first term in office. His second term (1804 to 1808), however, was marked by unusual events that divided the people. His former Vice-President, Aaron Burr, was involved in these events. Jefferson never forgave Burr for allowing his vice-presidential electoral votes to be counted as presidential votes in 1800. After the election, Jefferson ignored Burr and refused to support him for reelection in 1804. Furious, Burr began to plan his revenge. Twice he plotted with others to form a separate nation out of a part of the United States.

The first attempt was in 1804, and it included members of the Federalist party in New England. They used the argument that the new western territory would soon send representatives to Congress who were farmers. The farmers would outnumber New England's merchant vote in Congress. Before it was too late, they said, New England should form its own confederacy. They offered support to Burr who encouraged them. But they plot fell through, and Burr was attacked in the press, particularly by Alexander Hamilton. Burr then challenged Hamilton to a duel in which the latter was killed. The brilliant Hamilton died at the age of 47.

Burr's Conspiracy and Trial

Three years later, in 1807, Burr again plotted to make a nation out of the western territory of the United States. He asked the British for money for this purpose. But when they refused, he joined forces with the governor of Louisiana, James Wilkinson. With about 70 men, they moved toward New Orleans. Then James

11. How did Jefferson make an enemy of Burr?

1) Jefferson never forgave Burr for allowing his vice-presidential electoral votes to be counted as presidential ones in 1800. 2) He ignored Burr and refused to support him for reelection in 1804.

12. Why did Burr kill Hamilton?

1) Hamilton attacked Burr in the press after Burr tried to form a separate nation of New England. 2) Burr challenged him to a duel.

13. How did Burr's political life come to an end?

Burr was tried for treason for plotting to set up a new nation in the West. Although acquitted, he never returned to politics.

Burr played on the differences in the nation. In his view a region could just pull out and set up a new nation.

271

Aaron Burr was almost elected President in 1800. Later he was tried for conspiracy.

14. What resulted from the war with the Barbary pirates?

1) United States payments to the Arabs were lowered. 2) American sailors gained experience in naval warfare.

15. Why did Britain take hostile action toward the United States?

1) Britain and France were at war. They were trying to keep supplies from getting to each other. 2) The United States was selling to both sides. 3) Britain began seizing American ships that were trading with France and the West Indies.

Wilkinson betrayed Burr to the President. Burr tried to escape to the Spanish in Florida. But he was captured and tried for treason. The trial was a disaster. Jefferson meddled in it by offering aid to anyone who would testify against Burr. Chief Justice Marshall, acting as judge in the Circuit Court, was angry at Jefferson and deliberately tried to help Burr. The trial bogged down. Burr was declared not guilty, but he never again returned to political life. The rest of Jefferson's time in office was spent worrying about events that began in Europe.

War with the Barbary Pirates

As the United States' trade abroad increased, the pressure to copy the powerful European nations grew greater. Jefferson wanted the United States to stand up for its rights among other nations. National reputation and honor were important, he said.

The first situation that presented itself involved the Arab states of North Africa. These states demanded tribute, or bribes, from any ships that sailed the western end of the Mediterranean Sea. All nations gave in to these Barbary pirates, as they were called. But the United States was the first to decide that the practice was outrageous. In 1801 Jefferson sent American ships to fight the pirates. (See map, page 273.) The Americans fought well and were praised throughout Europe. Lieutenant Stephen Decatur was one of the best fighters. He captured two ships and boarded another. The fighting finally came to an end in 1805. The results of the war were lower payments to the Arabs and a good deal of experience in naval warfare for American sailors.

War in Western Europe

Jefferson also had to worry about the war that had broken out again in Europe in 1803. Napoleon was determined to conquer Europe, and by 1807 most of western Europe, except for England, lay in his power. The two nations, France and Britain, were at a stalemate, unable to attack each other. So they tried to starve each other out by preventing supplies from getting to each other.

For a while, war meant more business for American traders. American ships carried produce from the French West Indies back to the United States and then reloaded it onto other ships bound for France. This trade was very profitable.

Between 1803 and 1806, profits on this trade more than quadrupled. In one year, Americans had shipped 47 million pounds (21.15 million kilograms) of coffee from the islands to Europe. But in 1805, the British began to seize American ships that were trading with France and the West Indies.

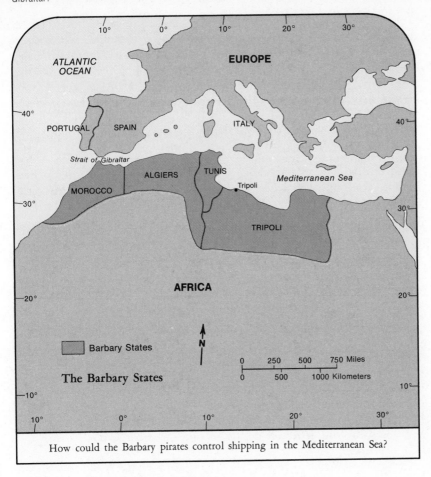

The Barbary States

How could the Barbary pirates control shipping in the Mediterranean Sea?

The *Chesapeake-Leopard* Affair

The British moved with force. They seized hundreds of American ships and took several thousand seamen off the ships—claiming they were British citizens. In 1807, the British ship *Leopard* fired on the American ship *Chesapeake* when the American commodore, James Barron, refused to allow his ship to be boarded and searched. Three Americans were killed, and 18 were wounded. The Americans also were forced to give up four of their sailors to the British. For Jefferson this was more evidence that the United States had been insulted.

The American Embargo

Jefferson decided to punish the British by cutting off trade with them. When this measure failed to have the desired effect, Jefferson called for a total *embargo*. No American ships were to go to any port anywhere. Jefferson thought this was a way to stay neutral,

16. What were the effects of the Embargo Act of 1807?

Notice the idea of boycott again. Why did the idea of an embargo appeal to some Americans in 1807?

273

1) American sales abroad dropped 80 percent in one year. 2) American ability to buy goods in Europe dropped 50 percent. 3) Prices of American goods went up. 4) Sailors were out of jobs, and merchants went out of business. 5) Jefferson became unpopular, and left office realizing that Americans often cared more for their own success than the nation's honor.

protect the few ships the United States had, and cause both France and Great Britain to give in. He waited for the time when they would have to allow the United States to trade with them. But the Embargo Act, passed in 1807, was a huge public failure. In one year, American sales abroad dropped 80 percent. Also, the American ability to buy goods from Europe dropped over 50 percent. Prices of American goods went up because of the shortage of both food and manufactured goods. Sailors were out of jobs, and merchants went out of business.

New Englanders in particular were furious with Jefferson. When he left office in 1808, the embargo law was changed to apply only to France and Great Britain.

Jefferson left office realizing that Americans often looked to their own success more than to the nation's honor. Also, what was good for the merchants of New England might not be what was needed or wanted by the farmers or the people now beginning to move onto the frontiers of the western territory. How these regional special interests would make themselves felt was not yet clear.

Checking the facts

1. What actions did Jefferson take during his second term in office that divided the people?
2. What was Burr's conspiracy?
3. Why did Jefferson decide to put an embargo on British trade?

1) Americans had confidence in the nation's future. 2) They wanted to produce more goods faster and at lower cost. For this they needed new tools and resources. 3) They wanted improvements that would provide more comforts and make them less dependent on fair weather, nearby markets, and crude homemade goods. 3) Competing in manufacturing with Great Britain, had become a goal of Americans.

17. Why were the Americans ready for the development of new technology?

3. GROWING STRONG AND DIFFERENT

The early years of the 1800's were years of tremendous growth. More people began to farm the land, and more people also began to start banks and other private businesses in towns and cities. Americans had begun to believe in their future together. They had confidence in the federal government's ability to protect them from the Native Americans and to stand up to foreign nations. In this atmosphere of protection, people felt free to pursue the American values of individual opportunity and control over the environment.

New Inventions

It was a creative period for inventors. People were trying to find ways to produce more goods faster and cheaper. They knew that

The people who were in a position to participate in building the nation were living at a time of great opportunity.

TIME LINES

In social studies you study events in the past that happened at different times. The past is both what happened before you were born and what went on last year. One reason that people study the past is that it sometimes gives them clues to what is happening in the present. As you read about the past struggles of labor unions, wars, or human suffering, you get a sense of how and what people went through to solve their problems. As you read, it is important to be able to put events of the past in order. Putting events in order is called *chronology.*

How can you show chronology? A helpful tool is to put the information in a time line. A time line can be used to do three things. It can tell when something happened. It can tell how many things happened at the same time. It can help to put the events in the order in which they occurred. Why is a time line a useful social studies tool? Because knowing the order in which events took place can help you find out why some events influence other events.

In some ways a time line is like a map. They both use a scale. In a map the scale is distance. In a time line the scale is time. For example, look at the time line of the Westward Movement shown here. The years 1790 to 1850 are covered. Look at the time line with three questions in mind. What is happening? Where is it happening? How did the events of one time influence later events? For example, look at the entry for the Louisiana Purchase on the time line. What other events were occurring at the same time? What happened later on?

Select a time period or a subject from your reading. Make your own time line. How did making a time line help you understand events of history?

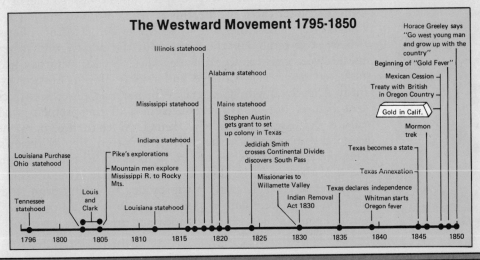

The Westward Movement 1795-1850

Americans wanted the kinds of inventions that would give them more comfort and make them less dependent on fair weather, nearby markets, and fairly crude homemade goods. Americans, therefore, were interested in new tools and new methods of using natural resources. The combined use of tools and resources is called technology. Americans of the nineteenth century were eager for new technology.

Often inventions, or improvements, came about because the British would buy more of a raw material such as cotton. Or they could happen because the British were manufacturing something that Americans wanted to do for themselves, such as spinning thread by machine. Being a partner in British trade was a great help to Americans who wanted to sell raw materials. And competing with Britain in manufactured goods also became a goal of confident Americans.

The Cotton Gin

The British made cotton cloth. They built their first mill, or factory, for cotton cloth in 1770. Most of the raw cotton they used came from Egypt. But some also came from the United States. The long, silk cotton that made the smoothest cloth could be grown on the islands off the coast of South Carolina and Georgia. Nowhere else in the South had the long hot growing season necessary for that kind of cotton. In other places, another kind of cotton could be grown. However, it had green seeds that were very difficult to remove, and, in the course of removing them, the cotton fibers often broke. The task of taking out the seeds from one pound (.45 kilograms) of cotton took one person a whole day.

Southerners wished for a way to speed up the task so that it would be profitable for them to ship this type of cotton to England. Many planters were experimenting with varieties of cotton plants and with ways of removing the seeds. But the person who solved the problem was a visitor to the South. In 1793 Eli Whitney had just graduated from Yale College and taken a job as a tutor with a family near Savannah, Georgia. Whitney had never seen a cotton plant before, but he became interested in the problem when he heard it discussed one night at dinner. Within three days, he had designed a machine that he called the cotton gin. Whitney's machine made it possible for one slave to clean 50 times the amount of cotton that could be done by hand in a day. One of Whitney's classmates from Yale put up the money to manufacture the gin, and soon there were cotton gins of various sizes all over the Deep South. People stole Whitney's idea and built their own machines without paying him.

1) Egyptian cotton fibers were long and made the smoothest cloth. 2) Most American cotton was hard to clean.

18. Why did England buy most of its raw cotton from Egypt?

The cotton gin turned cotton production into a very profitable industry. The slaves were able to pick more cotton because the gin did the separating, as shown here.

Why do some inventions become instant successes?

What does this chart show about the power of an invention? What does it show about the spread of a successful way of life? Note that cotton is measured in bales.

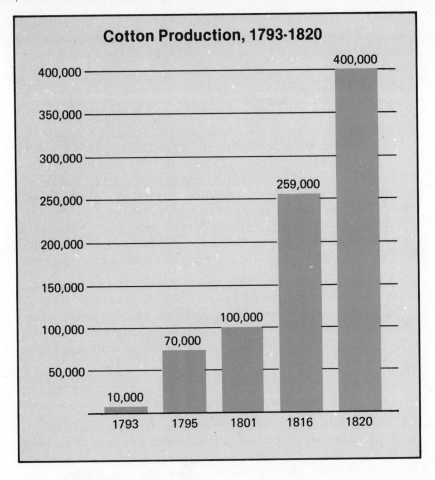

Cotton Production, 1793-1820

Year	Production
1793	10,000
1795	70,000
1801	100,000
1816	259,000
1820	400,000

Cotton growing spread wherever there were 200 days without frost and 24 inches (60 centimeters) of rain. Georgia and South Carolina almost gave up indigo and rice for cotton. Even southern Virginia began to produce cotton.

Links to the North

Cotton helped not only the South. There were important links to the North as well. Northern merchants bought cotton from the southern planters and took it abroad in their ships. The ships and their cotton cargo were insured by northern insurance companies. And the shipbuilders expanded their businesses with credit from northern banks.

Cotton plantations needed more and more slaves. To feed the larger population on plantations, planters had to buy corn and hogs from

1) In the North, it helped merchants who bought southern cotton and shipped it abroad. This brought more business for insurance companies and created a demand for ships. Shipbuilders expanded by borrowing, which in turn helped the banks. 2) In the West, it benefited farmers, who supplied cotton plantations with corn and hogs.

19. What other groups benefited from increased cotton production?

In what ways was cotton good for all parts of the United States?

277

the independent farmers in the West. Cotton, and the profits it made in England, created more jobs and increased the amount of goods and services people could buy throughout the United States.

Cotton and Slavery

20. How did cotton production affect slavery?

It increased the need for slaves, halting the back-to-Africa movement and other efforts at abolition.

Cotton also interfered with the effort to do away with slavery. One idea had been to colonize the Blacks in a back-to-Africa movement. A Black Quaker from Massachusetts, Paul Cuffe, paid for the relocation of 38 Blacks to Sierra Leone. And the American Colonization Society, founded in 1817, bought land in Africa and started the nation of Liberia, which was named for liberty. About 12,000 Blacks were willing to go to this totally foreign area. But the experiment was a disaster. Almost half of those who went died in the early years from tropical diseases to which they had no immunity. And cotton ended the colonization movement at this time.

Slaves were imported until 1808 when the Constitution banned the slave trade. Afterward, some overseas trade in slaves was carried on illegally. But most slaves were bought in lots, or parcels, from plantations or sellers in Virginia. The busiest slave markets were in Richmond, Virginia, on the east coast, and in Natchez, Mississippi, on the Mississippi River.

Northern Manufacture

21. How did Samuel Slater help manufacturing in the American North?

1) In England Slater memorized all the measurements and necessary details to make and repair textile machines. 2) With Moses Brown's money, he built a duplicate of an English thread-making factory at Pawtucket, Rhode Island, in 1790.

The British cotton mills were the envy of the New England merchants. If only they knew how to build those machines, they could invest their money from trade and begin to manufacture their own cotton cloth. But the British machines and the methods were guarded by *patents*. It was illegal to take either drawings of the machines or parts of them out of the country. Skilled workers were not allowed to leave the country either.

A major breakthrough for the United States came when Samuel Slater arrived from England in 1789. He could not only make and repair textile machines, but he had memorized all the measurements and necessary details. Slater was an ambitious man. He came to the United States to make money from his knowledge of the British methods. Hired by a Rhode Island merchant named Moses Brown, Slater built a duplicate of an English thread-making factory at Pawtucket, Rhode Island, in 1790.

With the help of the British inventions, Mr. Slater's memory, Mr. Brown's money, and everyone's desire to get rich, the United States began its history of manufacturing. But this new way of business grew very slowly. The thread made in the factory was sold in Brown's store and also was given out to individuals who wove it into cloth at home.

Soon spinning mills began to be built at a faster rate in New England. The narrow rivers with their natural falls were just right for producing the needed power to turn the machines. Owners opened branches of their mills. By 1800 there were seven. By 1815 there were 213. Most of the work was done by children. They were paid little, but the families at first seemed pleased at the opportunity for added income.

Because they were starting from scratch, even the merchants who had money to spend built one factory at a time. It also took time for people to get used to the idea of working in a factory rather than at home. And since spinning mills had to be built near waterfalls for power, it also took time for people to decide to move there. Living near a factory was a new idea.

Large Factories

The first large factory was built near Boston on the Charles River at Waltham, Massachusetts, in 1813. At this factory, all the operations from spinning thread to weaving cloth were taken care of. Since there were no hand looms that could keep up with the speed of the spinning jennies which produced the thread, the owner, Francis Cabot Lowell, studied British mills and designed his own power loom.

Lowell had invested $300,000 in his first factory. Ten years later, he and a group of partners set up a corporation worth twice that much. Within three years, a town named Lowell had grown up around the textile mills started in Massachusetts by Lowell and his partners. The corporation built dormitories for the young women, known as Lowell girls, who came to work there. Shops were also part of this complete company town.

Small Businesses

In spite of the textile mills, most finished goods were not produced in factories. There were made in shops attached to people's houses. They were sold either by the maker or by a *wholesaler* who bought the work of several craftmakers and then took them by wagon to nearby villages and towns. Hats, shoes, clocks, pencils, pottery, and even pianos were made and distributed in this way. Some back-country areas, such as Ohio, also had their clusters of crafts which were distributed in a network around them.

The people in these areas did not know that the factory system had come to America. They lived and thought within the narrow boundaries of their walks or horse-drawn carriage rides. There they learned their craft, practiced it at home, and sold their work to their neighbors.

Notice that, close up, people's lives changed slowly. Handcrafts were sold to a new buyer—a wholesaler.

22. Why were new spinning mills built in New England?

1) The narrow rivers with natural falls provided the needed power to turn the machines. 2) The money for building factories was there.

23. How did Lowell, Massachusetts, develop?

1) Lowell built several large mills that housed all textile operations, from spinning thread to weaving cloth. He developed a power loom, which sped up production. 2) His corporation built dormitories for the young women who came there to work. 3) Shops were also built. 4) A town developed around the mills.

24. How were finished goods produced and distributed to buyers?

1) Goods were made in shops attached to people's houses. 2) The maker sold the goods either directly or to a wholesaler, who bought the work of several and distributed it by wagon to nearby villages and towns.

The Northeast began to produce cotton in large factories such as the one shown here. Who worked in the factories? What kinds of jobs did the workers do?

Although new factories were being built, factories were slow in developing in the United States. Of course, there were those like Jefferson who could imagine the nation stretching all the way to the Pacific Ocean. The merchants with money could see themselves as far as five to ten years into their next investment. But by 1820 most people were still doing handwork. Training was still through the apprentice system in which a young person worked with a master to learn a trade.

Changes in Work

25. Why did pride in the quality of work become less important?

1) There was pressure for greater production, because there were more people who wanted more goods. 2) Merchants began dividing up the work. When workers didn't complete the whole job, they took less pride in it.

Over a period of time, people began to take a different view of their work. The first thing a handworker would notice was the pressure for greater production. The wholesaler-merchant who carried the goods from town to town needed more goods for the expanding markets. And for the most part, the merchant wanted more goods rather than better ones. This was the first major change in the way of producing. Merchants would divide up the work of making hats or shoes by giving different jobs to different people. The feet of knitted stockings were made by one person; the legs were made by someone else! Division of labor was faster and cheaper. But the pride in the quality of work became less important as workers did only part of the job.

What were the signs of change in a handworker's life?

By breaking up the task into small jobs, factories could hire less skilled labor. The first factory workers were women and children who were glad to contribute to the family income. There was such a shortage of labor in the United States at that time that men had no trouble finding work in farming, shipping, and skilled trades. Even male immigrants off the ships did not have to go to work for low wages in the new factories. When the spinning mills advertised for workers, they had to assure their readers that they were not taking men off the farms.

Frequently men moved into the western territory first to clear the land, build a cabin, and plant the first crops. It was often a year or more before they could send for their families. In the meantime, the women and children supported themselves by working at the local spinning factory or they worked at home making cards to untangle and separate the raw cotton.

The Network Grows

The beginnings of machine production, and the beginnings of marketing networks, would not have produced much change in people's lives if they could not get the goods to markets. Also, the purchase of the western lands and the control the United States had won over the Mississippi River would have made little difference if people could not get across the land or travel up the rivers against the current.

The early 1800's were also the time of the invention and development of roads, canals, and steamboats. And these, too, developed slowly. It took a long time to build roads. Rocks and trees had to be cleared, drainage ditches had to be built, and the roads had to be carefully sloped, or graded, so that they would not wash away in the first storm. Then the roads had to be covered with gravel, and bridges made of stone or wood had to be built.

Turnpikes

Building roads was expensive because workers in the United States, who were often immigrants, were paid more than those in Europe. The road construction companies had to borrow the money from the banks to hire the crews and get the work done. They made their money by charging travelers who used the road. At checkpoints along the road, they placed a wooden stake, or pike, with a hinged pole that stretched across the road. The roads themselves were referred to as *turnpikes*, or pikes. The first of the turnpikes had been built in Washington's time. This was the Lancaster Pike, which led through Pennsylvania from Philadelphia to Lancaster. (See map, page 287.)

26. Why were women and children generally the factory workers?

1) Breaking up the task into small jobs required less skilled labor. 2) Because women and children were unskilled, they were paid low wages. 3) Even though wages were low, they contributed to the family income. 4) Now that their wives and children could support themselves, men could go to the western territory to clear and settle the land before sending for their families.

27. What was needed to expand the marketing network into the new western lands?

1) People needed ways to get goods across land to rivers and then go up the rivers against the current. 2) The development of roads, canals, and steamboats became necessary.

28. How did construction companies meet the high costs of constructing roads?

1) The companies borrowed money from banks. 2) When the roads were built, they charged travelers for the use of the roads. 3) Travelers were stopped by a pike with a hinged pole that stretched across the road at each checkpoint where they had to pay.

281

This picture shows the National Road. Notice the conestoga wagon on the right. How did the National Road encourage migration?

29. *Why was a government subsidy necessary to build a road?*

1) It took a long time to build a road and to establish the road as a business route. 2) The road company often went bankrupt before it could earn back its original investment.

Towns and states were anxious to have roads, and they often contributed tax money to the turnpike companies by buying stock in them. This was called a government support, or *subsidy*. Government help was necessary because it took a long time for a road to be built, and then it took more time before people had a reason to use the turnpike for regular business trips.

In a sense, the road was a gamble on future business. Business always came. But it often took so long that the road company had lost its money, or became bankrupt, before it replaced its original investment or made a profit. The profit was needed to find other road-building projects.

There was no national plan regulating the building of interstate roads, their locations, the distribution of federal money, or the rights of states to control parts of the roads.

30. *Why was there little interstate road building?*

New York was one state which invested in road building. A road from Albany all the way to Lake Erie was finished by 1812. The cost of such a road was about $13,000 per mile (1.6 kilometers)! By the 1820's, New York had almost 4,000 miles (6,400 kilometers) of well-built roads.

The federal government was slow to enter road building, although between 1811 and 1818 it did complete the National Road from Cumberland, Maryland to Wheeling in the western part of Virginia. That road took over seven years to build. One problem was that every time a road crossed a state boundary, there was trouble about who got the most federal money and who controlled what

How are turnpikes and freeways financed today?

part of the road. The government never developed a national plan listing which kinds of roads in which kinds of locations would be built first. Constant rivalry among the states meant little road building between states, or *interstate*.

Merchants could not take anything that was too heavy or that might spoil on the roads that were built. Heavy loads took too long and, therefore, cost too much to send by wagon. One historian has estimated that if a farmer sent oats by wagon from Buffalo to New York City, the horses that drew the wagon would have eaten the oats long before the trip was over. Roads were best for carrying items such as clothing, tools, books, and coffee.

31. What defect did the roads have?

Merchants could not transport anything that was too heavy or that might spoil, because the trip took too long.

River Traffic

The best way to send heavy freight was by ocean-going ship from Boston, New York, or Philadelphia to the nearest mouth of a river and then by riverboat to the growing river cities. This method was much cheaper than by road. But the problem was how to travel up the river against the current. Oarsmen could try to row a boat upstream, but a better source of power was needed.

A steamship could go up or down a river and didn't need wind. What was the steamship's source of power?

32. What did the invention of the steamboat do for the marketing system?
1) Steamboats brought the Northwest Territory into the national market system. 2) Farmers there planted more crops and sold the surplus in New Orleans by floating it down the Mississippi on barges and rafts. 2) Then they sold the rafts as lumber. 3) They bought manufactured goods and returned home by steamboat.

Steamboats

The person Jefferson sent to France to buy Louisiana from Napoleon was also the one who paid for, or financed, the first steamboat in the United States. Robert Livingston met the artist and engineer, Robert Fulton, while they were both in France. They talked about the importance of the Mississippi River and the city of New Orleans. Then when Fulton returned to the United States in 1807, he built a steamboat, the *Clermont*. It was 142 feet (4,260 centimeters) long, 18 feet (540 centimeters) wide, and took up, or drew, only 7 feet (210 centimeters) of water. These dimensions were important because rivers were often shallow and narrow. What Fulton had done was to put together several other inventions—a boiler to make steam, the steam engine, paddle wheels from the mills and the hull of a ship. In 1807 the *Clermont* made its first voyage up the Hudson River from New York to Albany. Other people could easily copy Fulton's boat, and they did.

The steamboat made possible real development of the lands of the old Northwest Territory. Now the farmers could plant more and sell their surplus crops in New Orleans. That city and other cities along the Ohio and the Mississippi rivers, such as Cincinnati, Pittsburgh, St. Louis, Louisville, and Memphis grew. New Orleans became the entertainment, as well as the shipping center for the old West. After the harvest, farmers could float their crops down river on barges and rafts. In New Orleans they sold their crops, and they also sold the rafts for lumber. They bought souvenirs and other items from the shops of New Orleans, which carried manufactured goods from the eastern cities and from Europe as well. Then the farmers returned home by steamboat. Thanks to the steamboat, they were now part of the buying and selling, or *market*, system of the rest of the nation that was east of the mountains.

33. What did the building of canals do for the marketing system?

1) Canals allowed produce to go directly to cities or rivers that flowed to the Atlantic instead of to the Gulf of Mexico. 2) Horses on the bank pulling barges through canals could pull much greater loads than they could on roads.

However, steamboats could only go where the rivers went. Because the only connection from the West to the East was through New Orleans, merchants with money began to plan to build rivers or canals. With canals they could take their produce directly to cities or rivers that flowed to the Atlantic instead of to the Gulf of Mexico. The produce was carried on barges, which were pulled by horses walking alongside the canals, on towpaths. The smoothness of the water meant that horses could pull much greater loads on canals than they could on roads.

The Erie Canal

34. Why was the Erie Canal such a success?

The most successful idea for a canal came from DeWitt Clinton of New York. He had the vision of a canal that would connect the Great Lakes to New York City! In 1810 Clinton traveled through the state and planned a canal. It would start in Buffalo on Lake

Erie and follow the Mohawk River Valley that cuts through the Appalachian Mountains to Albany. He chose people to build the canal who were good engineers and good organizers. One of them, Canvass White, went to England to observe their canal system. He studied the locks the English built to close off the falls in the canal and fill the section with water so that the barges would rise to the next level. Then he returned to America and designed better locks. White also invented a waterproof cement made from local limestone. Inventions were needed in an America that wanted to grow. Inventors, designers, planners and builders were considered valuable people in a nation of great resources and vast distances.

Begun in 1817 and completed in 1825, the Erie Canal was an enormous success. New York City became the major port of the United States. And other cities along the canal, such as Buffalo, Rochester, and Syracuse, also grew.

Other states built canals, but none was able to compete with New York for the east-west traffic. Pennsylvania tried, but the landscape was so mountainous that it was difficult to build a good canal. The

1) The Erie Canal was well designed, and connected the Great Lakes with New York City. 2) New York City became the major port of the United States. 3) Other major cities—Buffalo, Rochester, and Syracuse—grew up along the canal.

The Erie Canal cost $7 million and took eight years to build. What were the advantages of canals over roads?

people who lived on the western lands beyond the Appalachians also built their own network of canals to connect the Ohio River with the Great Lakes. These were not completed, however, until the next decades—in the 1830's and 1840's—and were never as successful as the Erie.

Government Helps

35. How did some states help manufacturing and trade?

1) Some states helped in the building of roads and canals. 2) Some lowered taxes for people who would invest their own money in factories.

Without the help of government investment, the building of roads and canals, or internal improvements as they were called then, would have been delayed. Those states that did not help business did not get the improvements. They lost trade to those states that did. Some states also levied lower taxes for people who would invest their own money in factories. Vermont, New York, and Ohio helped to build their textile, iron, and glass industries by encouraging business investors with lower taxes.

Interstate Commerce

36. What two Supreme Court decisions were important in deciding United States policy about interstate commerce?

1) In *Gibbons* v. *Ogden*, Marshall ruled that no state could give a monopoly of commerce on an interstate waterway. 2) In *McCullock* v. *Maryland*, Marshall ruled that state governments may not interfere with the business of interstate or federally licensed banks.

States' investments in improvements were important, but if commerce was to grow, it had to cross state boundaries without difficulty. Here the Supreme Court and Chief Justice John Marshall made a lasting contribution between 1819 and 1824. In 1824 in a case in which the owner of one steamboat company was permitted by New York State to take all of the business between New Jersey and New York City, Marshall ruled that no state could control all trade or give a monopoly of commerce on an interstate waterway. With this case, known as *Gibbons* v. *Ogden,* John Marshall used the interstate commerce clause of the Constitution as a powerful force for the development of business across state lines.

Marshall also spoke out in several cases that strengthened private property. In the Dartmouth College case of 1819, he declared that contracts were untouchable—even by the state government that had licensed a business in the first place. In the case of *McCulloch* v. *Maryland* in 1819, he ruled that state governments may not interfere with the business of interstate or federally licensed banks. Marshall, like Hamilton before him, believed in the system of private property aided by government. In this way the nation could become bigger and stronger than the states that had originally created it.

The West, the Sections, and the Business Network

37. What had the United States accomplished in one generation?

The Louisiana Purchase opened up enormous possibilities in the minds of the American people. But bringing that land into the American system of buying and selling took many steps. New

States helped encourage investment so that they could have the jobs and the improved standard of living.

Today we still use laws and taxes to encourage investment. Can you give an example?

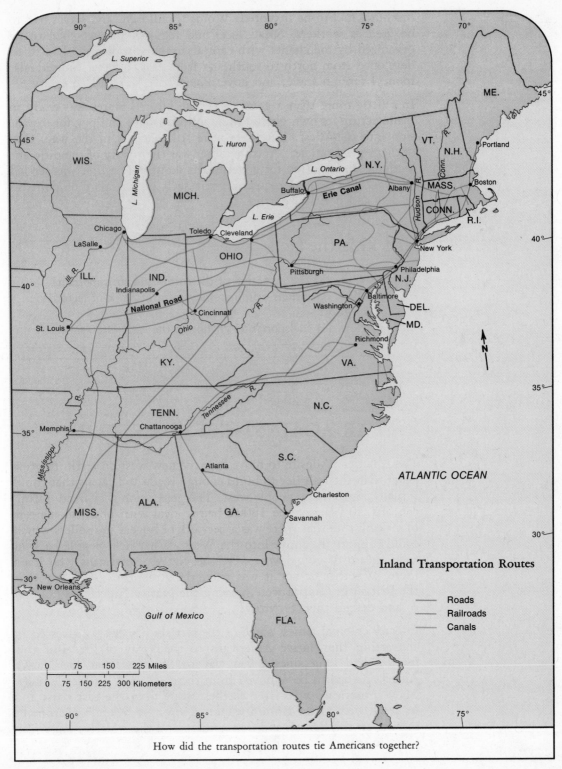

Inland Transportation Routes

Roads
Railroads
Canals

How did the transportation routes tie Americans together?

New transportation routes allowed goods to travel east and west as well as north and south.
This developed into an interdependent system.

287

The nation was ready to manufacture its own goods, trade with Europe, and pay for expansion into the West.

machines had to be invented. Women, children, and slaves had to be used as workers. Small local and regional markets had to be organized by merchants with capital, and transportation had to be developed from north to south and from east to west. Individuals, money, foreign trade, and government help were all necessary.

In a little more than a generation, the United States was ready to manufacture its own goods, trade with Europe, and pay for expansion into the West. But there were still barriers in the way. One of them was England. And the other was the rivalry of the different sections of the nation for government money. The first was settled by war. The second required great skill on the part of political leaders and political parties.

Checking the facts

1. Why was the invention of the cotton gin so important?
2. What conditions were necessary for a network of factories to grow?
3. How did transportation change in the early 1800's?

4. WAR AGAINST GREAT BRITAIN

38. What was needed to settle the new territory in the West?

1) More roads and canals were needed to enable people to move west. 2) A network of buyers and sellers was needed to support the move west. 3) The settlers wanted Native Americans removed from areas of White settlement.

The Americans' desire to move into the new western territory grew faster than their ability to build enough roads and canals that could actually move many people west. The generation that lived during the first 20 years of the 1800's had to deal with practical matters of making sure that there was a network of buyers and sellers which could support the move into the West. What held people back in their dream of going west were the Native Americans who lived there. Whether or not it was true, the Americans were sure that the British in Canada were helping the Native Americans hold on to and defend their territory.

In early colonial times, some of the settlers had been interested in converting the Native Americans to their way of life. But this interest had long since given way to the view that the Native Americans had to be removed from the areas of White settlement. Those Americans who lived farthest away from the east coast and its trade with Great Britain wanted a stronger federal government to take on the British and defeat them and their Native American allies in war.

Notice that the Native Americans did not have a part in the picture of the future drawn by White traders.

Madison as President

James Madison, trusted framer of the Constitution and master of compromise, had succeeded Jefferson to the presidency in 1808. But Madison found himself unable to make compromises among the three groups putting pressure on the United States: the Americans who wanted war, the British, and the French. Madison was lured by Napoleon into thinking that the French would leave American ships alone. So Madison closed United States ports to British shipping. But this action did not help the United States. The French continued to attack American ships while the British also stepped up their attacks on American ships and their *impressment* of seamen. Fooled by Napoleon, Madison was in a difficult position at home. He was afraid of being caught between the growing differences of the westerners and the people of New England. The West wanted war with Britain, but the New England merchants, whose best supplier and customer was Great Britain, did not want war. Madison could not please both sections.

39. Why was Madison in a difficult position?

1) Napoleon lured Madison into thinking that the French would leave American ships alone, so Madison closed United States ports only to British shipping. 2) Instead, the French continued to attack American shipping while the British stepped up their attacks. 3) The West wanted war with Britain, but New England merchants didn't.

Tecumseh and the Battle of Tippecanoe

Madison was not sure what to do. But others took events into their own hands. The Shawnee chief, Tecumseh, and his fanatic brother, known as the Prophet, lived on the Wabash River near the mouth of the Tippecanoe River. Tecumseh felt pushed by the American General William Henry Harrison who had been made governor of the Indiana Territory. Harrison took land from the Native Americans in any way he could. So Tecumseh moved to form a confederacy of all the tribes east of the Mississippi River.

Considering the differences among eastern tribes, Tecumseh's move was a well organized and highly political idea. The Americans had treated all the Native American tribes as if they were one enemy. Therefore, the Native Americans could use that common treatment as a way of making a united stand against the White settlers. Tecumseh traveled from Wisconsin to Florida talking to other tribes. His brother preached the importance of living like Native Americans and not taking on the White culture. The two brothers were able to organize thousands of Native Americans.

This picture shows Tecumseh's one-eyed brother, who was called The Prophet. Why did he and other Native Americans join into a confederation?

When the word got out that the Native Americans were planning to drive the Whites off their land, General Harrison decided to attack first. Tecumseh was away, and the Prophet proved to be a poor organizer for war. The Native Americans were defeated at Tippecanoe in November 1811. After the battle, the westerners cried even louder for war against Great Britain. They did not believe that the Native Americans could have organized for war without British aid.

There were more differences among Native Americans than there were similarities. Why did they join together?

War Fever

40. *How did Madison finally decide on a course of action?*

1) The young "war hawks" in Congress wanted the nation to stand up to Great Britain once and for all.
2) Madison promised to send Congress a war message before the November election if the war hawks would support his reelection in 1812.

War fever spread for a number of reasons. Some westerners thought that in a war with Great Britain the United States could conquer Canada. Other western farmers thought they would have better luck selling their produce abroad if the British were not harming their merchant ships. But the strongest support for war came from a group of young Congressmen who thought that America's honor was at stake. The nation should stand up to Great Britain once and for all. These war hawks had been elected to Congress in 1810. They included Henry Clay of Kentucky, who was elected Speaker of the House of Representatives, and John C. Calhoun of South Carolina, who was a member of the House Committee on Foreign Affairs. His job was to make sure that Congress raised the money needed for war.

What was Madison to do? He made a political deal with the young war hawks. If they would support his reelection to the presidency in 1812, he would promise to send Congress a war message before the November election. War was indeed declared in June 1812, but not by a very large majority. The representatives of many of the people in New England and the Middle States, such as New York and New Jersey, thought the war was a poor idea.

Early Victories at Sea

41. *What accounted for the early American victories at sea?*

1) The navy scored some victories before the British navy was organized to fight.
2) The American navy had three warships that were faster and had more guns than those in the British navy.

The Americans were able to score a few naval victories on the Atlantic early in the war before the mighty British navy was organized to fight. Americans did not have much of a navy, nor had they taken the time to plan and build one. Most of the navy was made up of several hundred privateers with cannons lashed to their decks. But the United States did have three warships, the *United States,* the *President,* and the *Constitution,* that were faster and had more guns than those in the British navy. Each of these ships was able to capture or destroy the British ships with which it did battle. In one encounter, the *Constitution* took so much fire that it was nicknamed Old Ironsides.

The War on Land

42. *What lesson did the Americans learn early in the war?*

1) The Americans were not prepared for war. 2) The British did not wait in Canada; they attacked Detroit and Fort Dearborn. 3) The Native Americans viewed the war as a fight to the finish.

If the United States navy was small, so was its army. Congress asked for a volunteer army of 25,000, but only 5,000 volunteers signed up to fight. Clay's own state of Kentucky supplied just 400 soldiers for the war he had supported so strongly. With this small and poorly trained force, the Americans planned to launch a three-pronged drive into Canada. The first push was across the Detroit River at the Canadian shore. But Tecumseh and his Native Americans interfered. The British then attacked Detroit, and in July of

They wiped out the population of Fort Dearborn.

From the locations of the fighting, can you tell what Americans wanted out of the War of 1812?

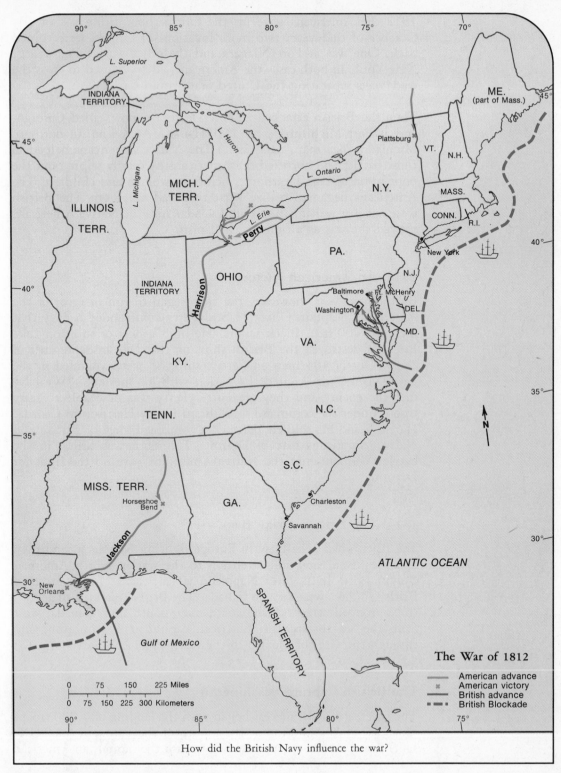

L. Superior

INDIANA TERRITORY

L. Huron

MICH. TERR.

L. Michigan

ILLINOIS TERR.

INDIANA TERRITORY

OHIO

L. Erie

Perry

Harrison

L. Ontario

N.Y.

PA.

N.J.

New York

Plattsburg

VT.

N.H.

MASS.

CONN.

R.I.

ME. (part of Mass.)

KY.

VA.

Baltimore

Ft. McHenry

Washington

DEL.

MD.

TENN.

N.C.

S.C.

MISS. TERR.

Horseshoe Bend

Jackson

GA.

Charleston

Savannah

New Orleans

ATLANTIC OCEAN

SPANISH TERRITORY

Gulf of Mexico

0 75 150 225 Miles

0 75 150 225 300 Kilometers

The War of 1812

— American advance
✕ American victory
— British advance
- - - British Blockade

90° 85° 80° 75° 70°

45°

45°

40°

40°

35°

35°

30°

30°

N

How did the British Navy influence the war?

The British blockaded the entire coast.

291

1812 the Americans gave up the fort without firing a shot. By October of that year, two more invasions of Canada were turned back. One was at Fort Niagara and the other was at Plattsburg, New York. In both cases the American soldiers refused to cross the waterways separating the United States from Canada!

Then the British attacked at Fort Dearborn, now called Chicago, and at Fort Michilimackinac (MISH-il-i-MACK-i-no) in northern Michigan. (See map, page 291.) The Native Americans helped in those battles and horrified the Americans by totally wiping out the population of Fort Dearborn, including women and children. The Americans began to realize what they had taken on. The British were not just waiting quietly in Canada. And the Native Americans viewed the war as a fight to the finish.

1813: An American Victory

43. How did the war change for the Americans in 1813?
1) Captain Perry built a fleet of ships on Lake Erie and destroyed the British ships there. 2) Perry ferried Harrison's troops over to Canada, where they defeated a combined force of British and Native Americans east of Detroit.

By the next year, however, the tide began to run in favor of the Americans. Captain Oliver Hazard Perry commanded a navy that included 400 free, Black sailors. He built a fleet of ships on Lake Erie and destroyed the British ships on that lake in September of 1813. Out of 103 men on Perry's ship, 85 were wounded in the battle. But Perry excited the nation with his message, "We have met the enemy and they are ours." Perry was now able to ferry troops under the command of William Henry Harrison to Canada. Harrison and his soldiers defeated a combined force of British and Native Americans east of Detroit. Tecumseh was killed in the battle. Without him the Native Americans gave up the fight for Detroit.

1814: The British Strike Back

44. Why were the British able to capture Washington in 1814?

1) The British sent 14,000 soldiers to Canada after defeating Napoleon in Europe. 2) They landed 4,000 troops southeast of Washington. 3) Madison had no plan to defend Washington. The 5,000 troops he did send ran when the British fired their new rocket guns into the air.

The British had been busy in Europe fighting Napoleon, and they had not given their full attention to the war in North America. But in April 1814, after Napoleon was defeated, 14,000 trained British soldiers were sent to Canada. The British planned their own three-pronged attack. They would move south from Canada, west from the sea toward the American capital at Washington, and through the Gulf of Mexico to the territory of Louisiana.

The British Capture Washington

The greatest British success began with the landing of 4,000 troops southeast of Washington at the mouth of the Patuxent (pa-TUX-sant) River. As the troops marched toward the capital, an American army of almost 5,000 met them. But when the British fired their new rocket guns into the air, the Americans ran.

President Madison had made no plan to defend Washington. No one thought the British could get that far. According to one story, Madison borrowed a pair of dueling pistols and went out in a carriage to look at the war. When he realized how close the British were, he and his wife, the popular Dolley Madison, had to leave the city. She was able to save a portrait of Washington by the famous American painter, Gilbert Stuart. She also saved a wagon full of important papers, the silver dishes used at the White House, and her parrot.

The British invaded the city. When they reached the White House, they found that dinner had been prepared for a party of 40 people. The British soldiers sat down and ate the President's dinner, drank his wines, and "finished by setting fire to the house which had so liberally entertained them," one soldier reported. The city, and the bridge leading to it, were burned. The British admiral rode through the town carrying the President's hat and a cushion from Mrs. Madison's chair.

The British burned Washington, D.C., during the War of 1812. When they arrived at the White House, the china was still on the table. Why was Washington burned?

Francis Scott Key watched the British attack on Fort McHenry, near Baltimore. Key was inspired to write a poem, which later became the national anthem.

After capturing Washington, the British headed for Baltimore, where they attacked Fort McHenry during the night. The Americans held the fort. Francis Scott Key, a prisoner on one of the British warships, wrote a poem about the battle he had seen.

45. How did Francis Scott Key come to write "The Star-Spangled Banner"?

"The Star-Spangled Banner"

The British then headed for Baltimore. On the night of September 13, 1814, the British fired on Fort McHenry at the mouth of the river. The 1,000 soldiers in the fort held out all night, and when the British came close enough, they returned their fire. By the next morning, fresh troops had arrived, and the British had to retreat toward their ships in Chesapeake Bay. That memorable night, a lawyer from Washington, named Francis Scott Key, was a prisoner on one of the British warships. He watched for signs of the battle for Fort McHenry. When morning came and the American flag was still flying, he wrote a poem about it:

Many national anthems are war songs. Why?

"And the rockets' red glare, the bombs bursting in air,
Gave proof through the night that our flag was still
there."

A printer in Baltimore set the poem in type, and copies were distributed to the happy crowds. They sang it to the tune of an old English song

American Victory at Lake Champlain

The burning of Washington caused the Americans to fight harder. Even as the British were leaving Washington for Baltimore, the Americans were scoring an important victory much farther north. The main British army coming south from Montreal had been stopped in a battle at Plattsburg on Lake Champlain. Some 11,000 British troops had been defeated by 3,500 Americans and a small fleet of boats.

46. *Why were the peace talks ready to begin?*

1) The Americans defeated the main British army at Plattsburg, on Lake Champlain. 2) The British no longer needed to stop American trade because Napoleon had been defeated. 3) The Native Americans had been badly beaten in the war.

Peace Talks Begin

While the fighting was still going on, British and American diplomats met at Ghent, Belgium, in the summer of 1814 to talk about the terms of peace. The British no longer needed to stop American trade because Napoleon had been defeated. Also, the Native Americans had been badly beaten in the war. Thus the reasons for the war had disappeared, and peace was sure. But the British deliberately delayed the meetings with the delegation from the United States, headed by John Quincy Adams, minister to Russia and son of President John Adams.

The Hartford Convention

While the talks dragged on, a group of Federalists in New England called a meeting in Hartford, Connecticut, in December of 1814. The purpose was to take New England out of the United States! Most of the New England states had not supported the war. And although their ships did business throughout the fighting, New Englanders were angry that the West had pushed the country into war. The Hartford Convention did not quite get to the point of leaving the Union, or *secession*. But it did take a public stand against the war—just as the news of the peace treaty arrived. This further damaged the Federalist party. They were ridiculed in cartoons in the public press, and they could never put enough votes together again to make a difference.

47. *What damaged the Federalist party?*

1) A group of New England Federalists met in Hartford, Connecticut, to take the region out of the Union. The merchants were angry that the West had pushed them into war. 2) Before they could take action, news of the peace treaty arrived. The party was ridiculed in cartoons in the press.

As the war became more popular, the political power of the Federalists died. Why?

The War of 1812 was an emotional war. So the peace treaty was an emotional victory.

The Peace of Ghent

48. *What were the terms of the peace treaty?*

1) The seas were open to all ships. 2) Landholdings on both sides remained what they had been before the war.

The treaty that the United States and England signed in December 1814 did little except to say that the seas were open to all ships. Landholdings on both sides remained what they had been before the war. And the British did not apologize for impressing seamen. But the treaty and the war were thought of by many Americans as a victory. To have fought the mighty British to a standstill was an achievement. American honor had been saved. And trade with Great Britain could start up again.

The Battle of New Orleans

49. *How did the United States benefit from the battle of New Orleans?*

1) The victory, with so few lives lost, boosted American morale. 2) Eventually, the United States was able to negotiate some of the boundaries with Great Britain.

The Americans won their greatest victory two weeks after the treaty was signed. Late in November 1814, the British sent over 50 ships from the island of Jamaica to New Orleans. Two days before Christmas, word reached the American general, Andrew Jackson, that the British had landed along the coast and were coming overland to the city instead of sailing up the river. Jackson did not wait for

Black riflemen fought with Andrew Jackson and helped defeat the British at the battle of New Orleans.

the British to attack in the morning. At 7:30 that night he led his troops, including a whole division of Black soldiers, in a surprise attack. Then he withdrew to set up a line of defense. The defense line was an earthen wall. With the river on one side and a swamp on the other, the British had no place to attack except in front of that protective barrier.

The British waited two weeks. During that time Jackson's patrols attacked British sentries each night. Finally the British attacked head on. The British had 5,300 redcoats pitted against 4,500 American militia. Jackson had arranged his soldiers in three rows. When the first row fired, they dropped down to reload, then the second line fired, and then the third line. Thus the British faced a continuing line of fire. Of the British, 2,036 were killed or wounded, including their general. As for the Americans, eight of their soldiers were killed, and 13 were wounded.

The battle of New Orleans boosted American morale and made Andrew Jackson a national hero. And in the next few years, Americans were able to settle by negotiation some of the boundaries of the United States. They agreed with the British that the border with Canada was to be unarmed. This border became the longest unarmed border in history.

Florida

When James Monroe became President in 1816, he sent Jackson into Florida to fight the Seminole Indians. Jackson also captured two poorly defended Spanish forts, which embarrassed the Spanish government. Then in 1819, John Quincy Adams was able to negotiate a treaty in which the United States acquired Florida, and the western boundary of the American territory was set at the line formed by the Sabine, Red, and Arkansas rivers.

50. What was Adams able to negotiate for the United States?

1) Adams acquired Florida from Spain. 2) He got Russia to sign a treaty giving up its interest in fishing rights and land in the northwestern part of the North American continent.

The United States in a World Setting

Adams was a superb negotiator. He was involved in one other act of foreign policy that temporarily settled the United States' relations with the rest of the world. In 1823 Adams was able to get the Russians to sign a treaty in which they gave up their interest in fishing rights and land in the northwestern part of the continent.

The Monroe Doctrine

When the leaders of the government of the United States looked at a map of the world, they saw the United States as a trading partner of Europe. They also saw the two American continents in

What makes a good negotiator? Do you know one? Have you ever been represented by a negotiator?

297

a closely related way. In the first years after the War of 1812, the United States wanted to help the newly independent countries in Latin America. Between 1810 and 1822 all of the colonies on the mainland of South America successfully rebelled against Spain. They set up independent countries. The governments of these new countries were weak. Some of the Spanish officials wanted to take advantage of the weak governments and make them colonies again. French leaders had the same idea. They thought they could go into Latin America and set up French colonies there.

51. Why did the United States think it could protect Latin America?

1) Monroe knew that Britain didn't want Spain and France to gain more power by taking over the new weak Latin American governments. 2) He knew that Britain would use its navy to keep Spain and France away from Latin America. 3) Monroe's promise of protection was therefore supported by the powerful British navy.

The Americans and the British wanted to keep Latin America free so they could trade with the new countries. On the recommendation of the new British foreign minister, George Canning, President Monroe decided to speak up against European interference across the Atlantic. Monroe could afford to sound strong and determined. He knew the British would use their ships to keep Spain from reconquering Latin America. In a message to Congress, Monroe stated his policy, later called the Monroe Doctrine. He said that the United States would not meddle in European affairs—and that no other power should interfere in the *Western Hemisphere.* In 1823 the United States felt that it was recognized as a full-fledged nation. However, it was still new and not very powerful. The Monroe Doctrine was a helpful link to the future because the American promise of protection to Latin America was supported by the powerful British navy.

With relations with other countries settled, Americans could turn to other matters. The War of 1812 left many Americans with a sense of power—and an additional desire to expand. Americans living in the East saw the land as if it were waiting to be developed. They ignored the Native Americans living on it. They began to extend their eastern networks of buyers and sellers into the western lands. The people who moved West looked forward to more produce, more trade with easterners, and more votes for their part of the nation in Congress.

Checking the facts

1. Why did some Americans want war with Great Britain?
2. Why were the Americans able to fight the British to a standstill?
3. What was the importance of the treaty with Great Britain and the battle of New Orleans?

Notice that the values of liberty, opportunity, and control had not changed. The stage was much, much bigger now.

PUTTING IT ALL TOGETHER

UNDERSTANDING THE MAIN IDEAS

1. How did the West fit into the total picture of the nation?
2. How might the different regions be tied together?
3. What foreign policy did American leaders think was best for the regions of the nation?

ACTIVITIES

1. How does representation work in your state? Do certain geographical sections often vote together in the state legislature? What political parties represent which areas of the state? To find this information, ask your teacher to help you write a letter to your representative in the state legislature.
2. Draw a voting map of your state. Show which parties are strong in which areas. Choose one vote (on school aid or water conservation) and show how each district voted. Can you explain why? Ask your teacher or school librarian to help you locate information to be used on your map.
3. What are the major goods sold in your state? How far away are they sold? What is the oldest road in your state? When was it built? Who paid for it? You may be able to find this information in an almanac or in a recent encyclopedia. Place your findings in a portfolio of facts on your state.
4. Look at the map of transportation routes on page 287. Then locate a map of the United States showing present-day roads. How many present-day roads follow older, earlier routes? Which transportation routes are no longer used? How did geography influence the location of early roads? How has it influenced present-day road builders?

BOOKS TO READ

Adams, Samuel H., *The Erie Canal* (New York: Landmark Books, 1951).

Guillet, E., and M., *The Pathfinders of North America* (New York: St. Martin's Press, Inc., 1973).

Nolan, Jeannette C., *Soldier, Statesman, and Defendant: Aaron Burr* (New York: Julian Messner, Inc., 1972).

Tucker, Glenn, *Tecumseh: Vision of Glory* (New York: Atheneum Publications, 1973).

chapter 12
Representing Regions

1816–1836

1. REPRESENTATION AND COMPROMISE
2. A LEADER FOR THE PEOPLE
3. JACKSON: THE PRESIDENT IN PRACTICE

INTRODUCTION

The War of 1812, sometimes called the Second War for Independence, added a feeling of pride and power to the recognition of how different the regions, or sections, of America were. Americans and the differences that separated them were now clustered into regions. The inventions of the cotton gin and the spinning jenny had made plantation life in the Deep South and factory life in New England the patterns of the future for Americans in the 1800's. Questions to think about in the period after the War of 1812 are:

1. What did Americans do about the representation of their differences?
2. Where did Americans find the leadership to manage those differences?
3. On what policies could Americans agree?

	1819	1820	1821	1823	
Who?	U.S. Congress	Henry Clay and John C. Calhoun	Stephen Austin	James Monroe	
What?	buys land from Spain	negotiate the Missouri Compromise	leads American settlers	issues Monroe Doctrine	
Where?	in Florida	in Washington D.C.	to Texas	in regard to Latin America	

1. REPRESENTATION AND COMPROMISE

The period immediately after the War of 1812 is sometimes called the Era of Good Feelings. During this short period, Madison and Monroe were able to settle some of the boundaries of the United States. They were also able to tell the world that the welfare of the continent of North America was to be the sole concern of the United States. The western hemisphere was not to be influenced by other nations.

At home, Congress turned to the kinds of policies that only the national government could handle—international trade, banking, and the sale of the western lands. In these three matters, the votes in Congress showed that people in the different regions were looking out for their own best interests. But for a few years there was enough agreement to get a majority vote.

The Tariff of 1816

In 1816 there was some support for tariffs in every section of the country, but not for national reasons. New England merchants did not favor a tariff. To them, high tariffs on foreign goods meant less trade. But other people in New England and in the middle states were not merchants. They had begun to manufacture goods during the war when English goods were not available. And these people did not like the fact that Great Britain sold $113 million worth of goods in the United States in the year 1815 alone. That figure was up from just $12 million in 1814, the last year of the war. To ironworkers, hat makers, and especially textile manufacturers this was money they might have made from the sale of their products in the United States. They wanted a tariff that would protect American industry by making foreign goods more expensive.

Even some southerners supported the tariff in 1816 because they hoped they would be able to build textile mills in the South near

1. How was this an era of good feelings?

1) Some of the boundaries of the United States were settled. 2) The world was informed that the United States would look after the Western Hemisphere. 3) There was enough agreement among the people for Congress to handle international trade, banking, and the sale of the western lands.

2. Why was the tariff of 1816 passed?

1) There was support for the tariff from every section of the country.
2) Manufacturing had increased in New England and the middle states during the war. 3) Some southerners wanted textile mills in the South, near where the cotton grew.
4) Western farmers believed that when easterners had more factories, they would do less farming. They would need to buy more food from the West.

1826	1829	1830	1831	1833
Thomas Jefferson, and John Adams	Andrew Jackson	Robert Hayne and Daniel Webster	Nat Turner	Women students
die on July 4, 4 hours apart	is inaugurated President	debate the nature of the Constitution	leads a slave revolt	admitted to first co-ed school
in Monticello, Va. and Quincy, Mass.	in Washington, D.C.	in U.S. Senate	in Virginia	in Oberlin, Ohio

Notice the problem that is caused when a nation has both traders and manufacturers.

where the cotton grew. The western farmers had the idea that if the easterners built more factories, they would do less farming. And less farming meant easterners would have to buy their wheat, corn, and hogs from the West.

So the tariff was passed in 1816 on the needs of the northern manufacturers and the hopes of the South and West. The leaders of the bill in Congress came from all sections. John C. Calhoun from South Carolina and Henry Clay from Kentucky supported the tariff along with the New Englanders. The support of the South and the West would not last long. But for the moment, self-interest and common interest were one.

The Second Bank of the United States

3. Why was the second Bank of the United States needed?

More reserves were needed to cover the money state banks had loaned out during the war.

Self-interest and common interest merged on the question of a second Bank of the United States. A second Bank of the United States was voted in partly because the state banks that had existed during the War of 1812 had loaned out more money than they should have. When depositors tried to take their money out of the

These craftspeople are making wheels. What did people need wheels for in the early 1820's?

Notice the issues in today's news where self-interest and common interest could be the same thing. Name one.

banks, they discovered there were not enough reserves to cover everyone's deposits. Support for the second bank came from all sides, but not because everyone in the nation favored power for the federal government.

The Panic of 1819

By 1818, however, people who had supported the bank turned against it because the managers had issued too much paper money for the amount of gold and silver, or *specie*, in their reserve supply. People in different regions also argued over the price of western land. Westerners wanted cheaper prices. Eastern speculators wanted to make as much money from the sales as possible. Poor management of the Bank of the United States and speculation in the sale of western lands were two causes of panic in 1819. Another cause came from abroad. The Europeans stopped buying western produce because they had now recovered from war. The farmers could not pay back the money they had borrowed from the banks to buy new land. The banks did not have enough money coming in to pay depositors. And the people from the North who were depositors could not get their money out of the banks. There was a run on the banks as everyone tried to withdraw funds. Banks closed. Businesses could not sell to people who had no money. Businesses closed down. People who were out of work could not buy food. Farmers could not sell their crops. The Era of Good Feelings was marred by the first nationwide *depression*.

The depression lasted three years. During this time, people became more concerned about their own well-being and less interested in tariffs, banks, land sales, or canals and roads that would help some other part of the nation.

The Missouri Compromise

In the midst of the depression and the rivalry between the sections of the nation, Congress was faced with an extremely important decision. Another part of the Louisiana Territory wished to become a state. It had fulfilled all the requirements. There were more than the necessary 60,000 settlers. The new state of Missouri was part of the traffic on the Arkansas, Missouri, and Mississippi rivers. Many of Missouri's settlers had come from slave-owning areas and had brought their slaves with them.

Congressmen James Tallmadge of New York introduced an amendment to the Missouri statehood bill that prohibited "the further introduction of slavery." Tallmadge's amendment also said that any Black slave born after Missouri became a state should be freed on becoming 25 years old. What Tallmadge said seemed right to many

4. What changed the Era of Good Feelings into a depression?

1) Poor management of the Bank of the United States, speculation in the sale of western land, and loss of the European markets for the western farmers caused the banks to be short of funds. 2) Depositors couldn't get their money; banks closed; businesses closed down.

5. Why were there differences of opinion over the amendment to the Missouri statehood bill?

The Northwest Ordinance had forbidden slavery in those states north of the Ohio and east of the Mississippi, but Missouri wanted to be admitted as a slave state.

When are citizens the least selfish—when times are wonderful, when times are terrible, or somewhere in between?

303

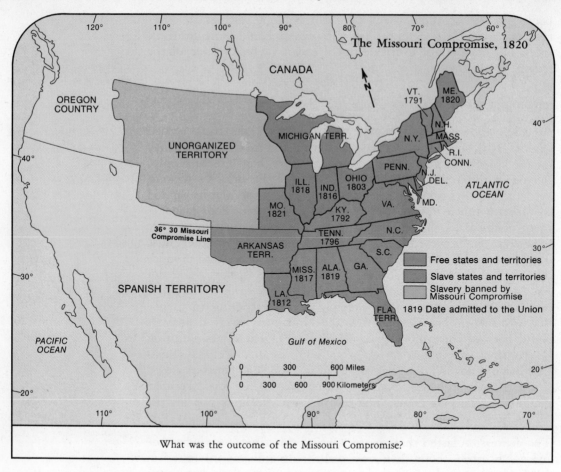

The unorganized territory would not be allowed to have slaves. Missouri entered as a slave state. Slavery was abolished in Washington, D.C.

The Missouri Compromise, 1820

CANADA

OREGON COUNTRY

UNORGANIZED TERRITORY

VT. 1791
ME. 1820
N.H.
MASS.
R.I.
CONN.
N.Y.
PENN.
N.J.
DEL.
MD.
ATLANTIC OCEAN

MICHIGAN TERR.

ILL. 1818
IND. 1816
OHIO 1803
VA.

MO. 1821
KY. 1792
TENN. 1796
N.C.

36° 30 Missouri Compromise Line

ARKANSAS TERR.
S.C.
GA.
MISS. 1817
ALA. 1819

SPANISH TERRITORY

LA. 1812

FLA. TERR.

PACIFIC OCEAN

Gulf of Mexico

Free states and territories
Slave states and territories
Slavery banned by Missouri Compromise
1819 Date admitted to the Union

0   300   600 Miles
0   300   600   900 Kilometers

What was the outcome of the Missouri Compromise?

people. After all, the Northwest Ordinance had forbidden slavery in those states north of the Ohio and east of the Mississippi. And Missouri was north of the Ohio.

Congress had not expected this issue to arise. Slavery was certainly considered wrong by many people. But whether a state allowed slavery or not had been left to each state. And since cotton had become such a successful crop, slavery was discussed less and less. When the House of Representatives voted on Tallmadge's amendment, the vote split on sectional, or regional, lines. Southerners voted against it. Northerners voted for it. But the North was able to carry the vote because the population of the northern states had increased with the arrival of immigrants from Europe after the War of 1812. Now northerners were in the majority in the House of Representatives.

In the Senate, however, the states were equally divided. With 11 slave states and 11 free states, there was no way for the Tallmadge

6. Why did the North carry the vote in the House of Representatives?

The North had a majority in the House because European immigrants after the war had increased the population of the northern states.

7. Why didn't the northerners want Missouri to enter the Union as a slave state?

From the map can you tell why Missouri was ready for statehood and why its settlers owned slaves?
Missouri was new territory. Thus slavery had to be considered by the Congress.

amendment to pass. Northerners were not going to let slavery enter territory they expected to be open to them. They did not want their free labor to compete with slave labor. In addition, the Constitution allowed three-fifths of the slaves to be counted for purposes of representation. This would mean that the southern, or slave-owning states, would have more representatives in the House than the North. And in the Senate, there would be 12 slave states to 11 free states.

1) They didn't want their free labor to compete with slave labor. 2) Since ³/₅ of the slaves were counted for representation, the slave-owning states would have more representatives in the House and outnumber the free states in the Senate.

A group of northerners offered a middle-of-the-road compromise. With the help of Henry Clay, the bill passed the House and was accepted by the Senate. Missouri would be allowed to have slavery because slavery already existed there. But no further introduction of slavery would be allowed north of Missouri's southern border, the 36° 30′ latitude. To keep the balance in the Senate, the state of Maine would be admitted to the union as a free state. The count in the Senate would then be 12 free and 12 slave states. Was the Missouri Compromise of 1820 a solution, or was it a recognition that the slave question had no answer?

8. How was a compromise reached?

1) Missouri would be allowed to keep slavery. 2) There would be no further introduction of slavery north of Missouri's southern border, the 36° 30′ latitude. 3) Maine would enter the Union as a free state to keep the balance in the Senate.

In what ways were the sections of the country competing over Missouri? Why was compromise possible?

This painting by Samuel F. B. Morse shows the House of Representatives in the 1820's. Many national issues were debated in the House of Representatives.

People throughout the nation were frightened. Slavery had existed for 200 years in North America and for the entire 31 years of the United States. But it had never divided the nation before. Now only the art of compromise and the skill of a few members of Congress had been able to patch over for the time the differences that existed over the issue of slavery. From his home in Monticello, Thomas Jefferson wrote that the debate "like a fire bell in the night, awakened and filled me with terror."

Henry Clay's American System

9. What was Henry Clay's plan for the United States?

1) Each part of the United States could supply the others with produce or goods. 2) Tariffs would protect manufacturers. 3) Roads and canals to connect the West to the East would be improved. 4) Southern trade with Europe would bring money into the nation through the sale of cotton.

Was it possible to find any policy on which all Americans could agree? People could not agree on single policies, such as tariffs or internal improvements. But Henry Clay grouped policies together as he helped bills become laws. Clay reasoned that each part of the United States could help to make the whole nation less dependent on trade with foreign nations. The United States was big enough so that each part could supply the others with produce or goods. And the laws of Congress could help each of the sections. Clay supported tariffs for the manufacturers. A new tariff was passed in 1824. He also favored internal improvements—roads and canals to connect the West to the East—and southern trade with Europe to bring money into the nation through the sale of cotton. In Clay's American System, the nation would be strong, rich, and independent because every need would be met within its borders. Clay believed that the sections would support his system because it included what they wanted for themselves.

But the sections did not want to be just part of the nation. Each wanted to be the leader in the Congress. Each felt its way of living was better than the rest. And each wanted to have the most say in how tax money was spent. This meant getting a majority of votes. To achieve such a majority would take special leadership that could point out Americans' strengths and what they had in common. Somehow their differences had to be overcome by common action or a common feeling.

Who could lead all the Americans? Who could help them overlook their differences? Several leaders within the Republican party wanted to try.

Henry Clay played a role in national government for over 40 years. He is shown here in 1824.

Checking the facts

1. Why was an American System for developing a national interest needed?
2. Why did slavery become an issue in Congress?

What do you think was so important and exciting about Clay's American system?

2. A LEADER FOR THE PEOPLE

The Missouri Compromise of 1820 was put together by people who recognized the seriousness of the split in the nation. The competition for votes in Congress was real. Americans did not want their representatives to vote for what was best for the country. Instead they wanted them to vote for what was best for their particular interest.

More Voters

Americans were excited by the success of the nation. And many people wanted to play a more active part in government. At the state level, conventions were held during the 1820's to study the state constitutions and revise them if necessary. Now that more people from different backgrounds were involved in new kinds of jobs and businesses, the old idea that a man had to own much property before he could vote seemed outdated. Property qualifications for voting belonged to a time when wealth was measured

10. Who were the voters in the 1820's?

1) In all states but three, all White males could vote.
2) All states still excluded women, Blacks, and Native Americans from the vote.

In the West, the number of voters grew as the population grew. How did newspapers help people know about the whole country?

only in land. Now all states but three did away with the previous property-owning restrictions on voting. Virginia, Florida, and Louisiana still required voters to be taxpayers. And all of the states still excluded women, Blacks, and Native Americans from the vote.

More Power to the Voters

11. How did the westerners get more voters to participate in elections?

1) Western states began to allow the voters to vote directly for the electors who selected the President and Vice-President; state legislatures had been selecting them. 3) Electors began announcing in advance which presidential candidate they supported; voters were then almost voting directly for the President.

With greater differences in the population and greater participation in voting, the next question was more equal representation. The people who lived west of the Appalachians were anxious to have more influence in the government. This was hard to achieve. The older states had most of the wealth and most of the population. So no matter which way the voters were counted for representation, the East seemed to have a greater voice than the newer states west of the Appalachians.

But at the national level, the westerners pushed for more voter participation. In the 1820's and 1830's, states allowed the voters to vote directly for the electors who selected the President and Vice-President instead of leaving the choice to the state legislatures. Gradually, the electors began to announce in advance which presidential candidate each would support. The voters then could almost vote directly for the President. These changes in who could vote and what they could vote for meant more rule by the people, or more democracy.

Choosing the President

12. How had the methods of selecting party candidates changed?

1) In Jefferson's day, they were chosen in a congressional caucus. 2) By the late 1820's, they were chosen at a national convention, where the different groups could compromise.

Times had changed since Jefferson's day when party candidates were chosen by the leaders of Congress in a secret meeting, or *caucus*. At that time, the next person in a line of known, powerful leaders became President. The Virginians had supplied Washington, Jefferson, Madison, and Monroe in this way. And the Adams family from Massachusetts had produced the other of the first five Presidents in the first 40 years of the nation's history.

Jefferson had been the first to organize people at the local and state level. The people he organized got out the vote for the party's candidates. But it was not until the late 1820's that the same system was applied to the national elections. With so many different groups wanting to be represented on the national level, each had to send representatives to a national party convention. At the convention, the different groups could make their peace with each other and select candidates whom they knew had the support of most of the people of their party.

13. How did national conventions operate?

The competition to become a delegate to the convention was great because the delegates actually chose the candidates. And people

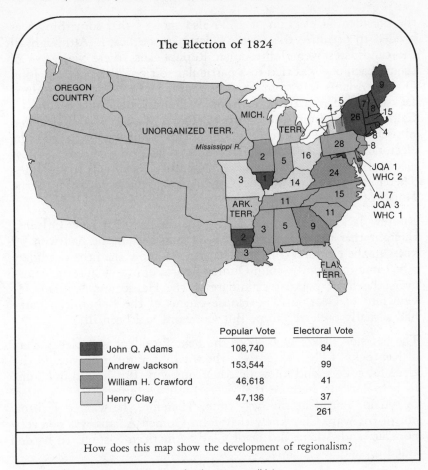

The Election of 1824

		Popular Vote	Electoral Vote
■	John Q. Adams	108,740	84
■	Andrew Jackson	153,544	99
■	William H. Crawford	46,618	41
▫	Henry Clay	47,136	37
			261

How does this map show the development of regionalism?

The states in one region tended to vote for the same candidate.

1) The Credentials Committee decided who the proper delegates were. 2) The delegates chose the candidates. 3) The Resolutions Committee decided what issues the party would speak out on.

competed to become members of the committee to decide who the proper delegates were—the Credentials Committee. Another important committee assignment was the one that decided what issues the party would speak out on—the Resolutions Committee.

Anyone who wanted to win had to reach the people. Citizens of the United States had long experience in running their state governments and deciding on such things as taxes, banks, canals, roads, licenses for business, and schools. Now they wanted to feel part of their national system. They looked to their political parties for a way to participate. Politics—the art of getting the job of governing done—was about to become the politics of the people.

The Election of 1824

The presidential election of the year 1824 was in some ways like the Era of Good Feelings. The Federalist party had disappeared, and the nation had one major party to look to for leadership. But

14. What set of circumstances gave John Quincy Adams the presidency?

Party conventions today still give power to decide to credentials and resolutions committees.

309

1) Five men from the same party ran for the presidency —Adams, Clay, Crawford, Calhoun, and Jackson. 2) Jackson received the most electoral votes, but not a majority. 3) The decision then went to the House of Representatives; Clay gave his support to Adams, who supported his American System.

the presidential election of 1824 also showed that something was needed to organize the people's desire to be heard. Although all the candidates were Jeffersonian Republicans, there were five of them. Each one was tied to a particular section of the nation. John Quincy Adams was from New England, Henry Clay and Andrew Jackson were from the West, and William Crawford and John C. Calhoun were from the South. Calhoun withdrew and declared himself the candidate for Vice-President. Thus four men split the electoral college vote. Although Andrew Jackson received the most electoral votes, he did not have a majority. (See map, page 309.) Therefore, according to the Constitution, the vote went to the House of Representatives.

Andrew Jackson of Tennessee, hero of the battle of New Orleans, thought that the House should elect him because he had won 99 votes in the electoral college. That was 15 more than the candidate who came in second—John Quincy Adams of Massachusetts. However, the most popular candidate in the House was William H. Crawford of Georgia. The House caucus of the Republican party had actually preferred him. But Crawford had been ill.

The decision maker who chose the next President was Henry Clay of Kentucky. Clay had received the smallest number of votes in the electoral college and knew he could not win. But he did not want to help Jackson because they were both westerners. Clay wanted to run for President the next time. Therefore, he wanted Jackson out of the way. Clay knew that John Quincy Adams was not very popular, and Adams did favor Clay's American System, so he decided to support Adams.

All of the candidates in 1824 were from the same party. There was not enough party organization to prevent the four-way split. When it was announced that the House had voted for Adams, Jackson was very angry. And when Adams chose Clay for the best post in the Cabinet, secretary of state, Jackson let everyone know that he believed Adams and Clay had made a deal for their two offices. "Corrupt bargain" was the charge Jackson made. Adams spent his entire four-year term trying to deny it.

John Quincy Adams—His View and His Method

15. *What was Adams' plan for a strong national government?*

John Quincy Adams had the respect of most people for being highly intellectual, a hard worker, and a careful planner. But he was as strict with everyone else as he was with himself. The image the nation received of him was one of a cold person without charm or personality.

Adams studied the problems of each of the sections of the nation. He tried to develop programs that would solve these problems. His plan was for a strong national government which would take total responsibility. Adams truly believed that government should come *from* the consent of the governed *to* the people who knew best what to do. And those leaders should take action *for* the benefit of the people. Adams would not think of asking the people what they thought ought to be done. Nor would he travel to explain his policies to them. He refused to accept invitations to cattle fairs and other local events. He said openly that these activities were a waste of a President's time.

Adams' program called for the federal government to increase tariffs gradually as manufacturers grew. Federal taxes also would be used to build public roads and other internal improvements. They would be used to build a great national university in Washington, to pay for scientific and geographic explorations, and to pay for promoting literature and the elegant arts. It was a master plan for the entire country. All the people and their representatives had to do was to give up their sectional feelings, pay their taxes, and trust the President—that same President who would not leave the White House to talk to them.

Adams did not understand the way the sections felt nor the new kind of participation in conventions and other forms of politics the people had come to expect. In fact, when his Cabinet urged Adams not to present more programs than Congress would pass, he told Congress to go ahead and act without worrying about the people they represented. When Andrew Jackson saw the speech, he made sure that the people heard what Adams thought of them. Adams did not see the great gap between his federally planned, paid for, and managed program and Henry Clay's individual bills for each section of the nation.

A New Tariff

Any political leader who would like to lead the whole United States had a problem with the tariff bill. And it was no different for Adams in 1828.

A new tariff bill was promoted by members of Congress from farming districts in the North and the West. These districts produced raw wool, hemp for rope, flax for linen, fur, and liquor. Therefore, the House committee recommended to the House high tariffs on these products. Thus Americans would find it cheaper to buy the home-grown rather then European products. However, the tariffs would cause the American prices to go up as well.

Manufacturers of woolen goods in New England did not wish to pay higher prices for raw wool, American or foreign. Their representatives in Congress objected on their behalf. The southerners

This is a portrait of John Quincy Adams. How does he impress you?

1) He believed that government should come, from the consent of the governed, to the people who know best what to do, the leaders. 2) Federal taxes would pay for public roads and other internal improvements, a national university in Washington, scientific and geographic explorations, and the promoting of literature and the "elegant arts."

16. Why was there no agreement on the new proposed tariff bill?

1) Farming districts in the North and West wanted wool, hemp, flax, fur, and liquor protected. 2) Prices would go up. 3) Manufacturers in New England would have to pay more for wool. 4) Other nations would raise their tariffs, and the South would have to pay more for foreign manufactured goods.

who sold raw materials to England and Europe did not want a tariff at all. Because the other nations could and probably would raise their tariffs to get even, the South would then have to pay higher prices for all the manufactured goods it bought from abroad.

Calhoun's Doctrine

17. *Why was Calhoun opposed to the tariff of 1828?*

1) He noted that what was good for the North was not good for the South. 2) He believed that the people of each state had to decide what was best for them.

The Tariff of 1828 forced two men who wanted to become leaders of the whole nation to line up with just one part of it. Daniel Webster, the fiery speaker from Massachusetts, earlier had opposed tariffs on behalf of New England's merchants. Now he came out in favor of the tariff on behalf of New England's manufacturers who made finished products other than wool.

But John C. Calhoun, Vice-President under Adams and leader of the South Carolina representatives, decided as he watched the tariff pass that what was good for the North was not good for the South. Calhoun wrote an essay called *The South Carolina Exposition and Protest.* In it he said that the tariff was not only unfair, it was unconstitutional! He said that a state could turn down, or nullify, a law passed by Congress, if the people of the state believed that the law was against the Constitution. Calhoun's Doctrine of Nullification was a sign that the differences among sections of the United States were getting in the way of the idea of one nation in which people worked together for the common good. Calhoun felt the people of each state had to decide what was best for them.

The Question of National Leadership

18. *Why was it difficult to be a national leader during these times?*

1) Americans no longer looked to the national government for guarantees of freedom or for power for the whole nation. 2) Americans wanted to use the vote in Congress to get most of the national tax dollars for their sections.

How could any one person or any one policy represent everyone? This was especially difficult as more and more people were becoming active in government and were thinking about themselves first. The old values of individualism and opportunity were now becoming pressures on the representatives in Congress. Americans no longer looked to the national government for guarantees of freedom as they had in the Revolution, or for power for the whole nation as they had during the framing of the Constitution. By the time of the 1820's, Americans wanted to use the vote in Congress to get most of the national tax dollars for their sections. Webster and Calhoun had been national figures during the War of 1812. Now they found it hard to be national figures while defending or promoting one section of the nation over the others.

Andrew Jackson—A Different Appeal

19. *What made Jackson a winner?*

One person in this period knew how to reach all the people. He and his political advisers also knew how to organize both a political

List some special interests today and some common or national interest, for example, on energy policy.

party and the federal government. Andrew Jackson was the first modern President in many ways. He won the election in 1828 by an enormous majority of 178 to 83 in the electoral college.

Adams lost his bid for a second term, just as his father had. He won the same New England states that had supported his father, but Jackson won all the states that had supported Jefferson in the election of 1800 and the new western states as well. Jackson's party was a new party formed out of the old Republicans. At first they called themselves Democratic Republicans. And then after Jackson's election, they simply called themselves Democrats. Several state political leaders, in particular Martin Van Buren of New York, had put together for Jackson a national party that could deliver the votes. These men also managed to appeal to enough voters to take over both houses of Congress.

The Democrats presented themselves as believers in the people. That was how Jackson saw himself, and that was how the people saw him. He was a striking personality and a war hero. His soldiers in the War of 1812 had nicknamed him Old Hickory, the toughest title they could think of. He had a crop of snow-white hair, a scar on his cheek made by a British sword in the Revolution, a bullet from an old duel in his chest, and another in the bone of his left arm.

Jackson was thought of as one of the people because he believed in their right to make decisions for themselves. He also believed in as little government as possible. He was not, however, a common man. He was a lawyer, a judge, and a wealthy owner of a cotton plantation with slaves. But he was very proud of the United States and able to get his message across to the people. How did Jackson manage questions about the tariff during the campaign? He took the advice of Senator Thomas Hart Benton of Missouri and did not say anything about such difficult issues. Jackson was the first President to be presented to the people as their nationwide candidate. He was simply a winner.

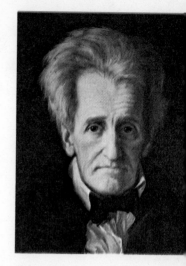

How does this picture of Andrew Jackson compare with the one of John Quincy Adams on page 311?

1) The Democratic party became a strong national party with enough votes to take over both houses of Congress and elect Jackson to the presidency. 2) Jackson didn't say anything about difficult issues during the campaign so that he wouldn't offend any of the sections.

Checking the facts

1. How did John Quincy Adams get elected?
2. How did Andrew Jackson avoid being defeated a second time?
3. How did Calhoun's Doctrine of Nullification point out differences among the regions of the United States?

What would make you think a candidate is a winner *and* a representative of what is best for the nation?

3. JACKSON:
THE PRESIDENT IN PRACTICE

20. *What changes did the Jackson administration bring to the presidency?*

1) Jackson consulted his "Kitchen Cabinet" more than the Cabinet. 2) He removed about 20 percent of all top officials who had not supported his election.

Jackson's inauguration day was certainly the people's celebration. His followers mobbed him as he rode to the White House. Later they held a party in the White House that the nation would never forget. People danced on the tables, tore down the curtains, and climbed over the chairs with their muddy boots. Jackson himself had to flee out the back door. Finally, the happy mob was lured outside by tubs of punch, which someone was clever enough to put on the White House lawn.

To The Winners—Everything

Jackson ran the government from the White House fireside with a group of close friends who were not all elected officers. They were jokingly referred to as his Kitchen Cabinet. But in reality they were closer to him than the Cabinet. In particular, they advised him on the use of his power to appoint all federal officeholders and judges.

Jackson used this presidential power more than it had been used before. He removed the top officials who had not supported his election. In all, he replaced about 20 percent of the officeholders. The angry opposition watched as experienced government people, or *civil servants,* were dismissed. They said that Jackson treated political opposition like the enemy in a war. "To the victor belongs the spoils." That was exactly the way Jackson saw it.

Political parties since Jackson's time also have used the *spoils system* to fill government jobs. This system, also called *patronage,* is an important part of a democracy. While appointed officials need to agree with the newly elected one, they also should be skilled, experienced, and honest.

The Veto

21. *How did Jackson use the veto?*

1) He refused to sign bills he didn't like; other Presidents had used the veto only on constitutional questions. 2) He was the first to use the pocket veto. When a bill was passed near the end of a session, he used the allotted 10 days to think about it; the bill was automatically vetoed if Congress had adjourned by then.

Andrew Jackson had a definite opinion on every bill Congress sent him. He expressed his opinion by refusing to sign bills he did not like. His use of the veto was new in the United States. Other Presidents had used it only on constitutional questions. But Jackson believed he knew what the people wanted. He represented their best interests. And if Congress disagreed, he simply said no. He was also the first to use the pocket veto. When Congress sent the President many bills that passed near the end of a session, Jackson used the allotted time of ten days to think about the bill. If the Congress had adjourned by the end of that time, the bill automatically was vetoed.

How important do you think it is for the people to feel close to the President?

Can you argue both for and against the spoils system?

The Sections Argue Again

Jackson could not avoid the continuing distrust of the North and the South for each other. He tried to take a calm position in most of the disagreements. When he had to speak up about the tariff, he said he supported a slight lowering of it. When asked about internal improvements, he said he was in favor of the federal government paying only for those roads and canals that went through more than one state. Thus he vetoed the Maysville road bill, which would have used federal funds to build a road within Kentucky.

Jackson clearly disagreed with Adams on the spending of federal money. He believed that most projects should be carried out by the states. But the power of states had definite limits in Jackson's thinking. For him the Union was more important than any single state. Jackson was very patriotic. When he said the *United* States he meant it.

The Webster-Hayne Debate

In 1830 an argument broke out in the Senate over the price of western land. Senator Foot of Connecticut began by saying that the government land in the West should not be sold too rapidly. Senator Benton of Missouri charged that Foot was part of a plot to keep New England's workers from moving west. Senator Hayne of South Carolina supported Benton and said that the South and the West should form an alliance to force low tariffs and cheaper prices for land through the Congress. Daniel Webster defended the Northeast. Hayne became angry and began to preach Calhoun's Doctrine of Nullification, which said that states have the right to declare a law passed by Congress null and void.

At this point, Daniel Webster rose to give one of the most popular and instantly famous speeches ever delivered in Congress. Webster was clearly out to attack Calhoun, the Vice-President. He spoke of love of country and warned of the danger of chaos and bloody civil war if the states nullified every law passed by Congress that they did not like. Webster's words were quoted all over the land:

> "When my eyes shall be turned to behold for the last
> time the sun in the heavens, may I not see him
> shining on the broken and dishonored fragments of a
> once glorious Union. . . . Let their last feeble and
> lingering glance rather behold the glorious ensign
> [flag] of the Republic, now known and honored
> throughout the earth . . . bearing for its
> motto . . . dear to every true American heart, Liberty
> and Union, now and forever, one and inseparable!"

22. How did Jackson disagree with Adams?

1) They disagreed over the spending of federal money. 2) Jackson believed most projects should be carried out by the states but that state power had definite limits.

23. What was the source of disagreement between Webster and Hayne?

1) Senators from the Northwest thought that government land in the West should not be sold too rapidly. 2) Senators from the South and West wanted low tariffs and cheaper prices for the land. 3) Hayne supported the South and West, and claimed states had the right to declare a law passed by Congress null and void. 4) Webster supported the Northeast and warned of the danger of civil war if states nullified every law passed by Congress that they didn't like.

When do you feel most patriotic? When do you think about membership in the whole country?

Daniel Webster, standing at the right, is shown debating in the Senate. Seated to the left at a desk is Calhoun. These two men represented different political views. Webster defended the Union and Calhoun stood for states' rights.

Jackson and Calhoun

24. Why did Jackson name Van Buren as his choice for the presidency?

1) Van Buren had helped Jackson get elected by forming the Democratic party. 2) Calhoun, the other possible candidate, disagreed with Jackson on the need for a strong national government.

Calhoun had wanted very much to be President, but the issues of the time caused him to side more and more with a states' rights position. How else could the South protect itself from a majority in Congress that might some day turn against cotton, slavery, and the liberty of southerners to lead their own lives? For Calhoun the issue was liberty as well as the preservation of the South. For Jackson the issue was union, although he came from the South and believed in slavery.

The conflict between the two men came out into the open at a dinner given by the southern states to honor Jefferson's birthday on April 15, 1830. At the dinner, the guests made many speeches and toasts about states' rights. Then the President of the United States rose to give a toast. He raised his glass, stared at Calhoun, and said, "Our Federal Union: It must be preserved!"

Calhoun offered the next toast: "The Union, next to our liberty, most dear!" Jackson and Calhoun were equally interested in the future of the nation. They were rivals who agreed with each other on almost every other point. And they were two leaders who examined the hardest issue the nation had to face. This was an issue

Should people be free to hurt others?
Should people be required to put national interests ahead of their own?

that had existed from the day the first slave ship landed. These two men came face to face with the need to make a choice. They chose differently. Another generation would pass before the rest of the nation faced the question again—and dared to answer it. As for Jackson and Calhoun, they broke openly with each other shortly after the Jefferson Day dinner. Instead of Calhoun, Jackson named Van Buren as his choice for the presidency.

The Nullification Crisis

The planters of South Carolina and Georgia were still upset about the tariff of 1828. A new, lower tariff was passed in 1832, but it did not lower the rates enough to convince the southerners that the rest of Congress really wanted to help them.

In addition, the Whites of the South were frightened by a series of slave revolts. In 1822 Denmark Vesey had led a revolt in Charleston. Then in 1831 the slave Nat Turner had led an attack on White homes in Virginia. About 160 Whites and Blacks were killed before Turner was captured and put to death. Southerners worried that the northern majority in Congress would use the revolts as an excuse to abolish slavery. They were afraid the tariff was just the beginning of trouble for them.

In 1833 the South Carolina legislature called a special convention to nullify the tariff laws. They also set aside money to raise an army and buy weapons. South Carolina was prepared to leave, or *secede from*, the Union if the national government tried to force it to obey the tariff laws. Jackson wanted Congress to lower the tariff so that only nullification would be left as an issue with South Carolina. He also asked Congress to pass a force bill, giving him the right to use force against the state. Ten days before the deadline, South Carolina withdrew its nullification law. South Carolina had been unable to get other southern states to stand with it. In addition, Henry Clay had worked out a compromise with Calhoun. Calhoun had resigned as Vice-President to represent South Carolina in the Senate. In exchange for a gradual lowering of the tariff over the next ten years. Calhoun had agreed to urge the state to repeal the nullification law.

The tariff was not a big enough issue to destroy the Union. With the lowering of the tariff, Calhoun felt that a major point had been won. But some people in South Carolina were not so hopeful. They began to look to the other southern states for support in the future.

Jackson and the Bank of the United States

Jackson disliked all banks, but he particularly disliked the Bank of the United States and its president, Nicholas Biddle. To Jackson,

25. How was the nullification crisis resolved?

1) Worried over the tariff and the slave revolt, South Carolina prepared to secede from the Union if forced to obey the tariff laws. 2) Clay worked out a compromise. In exchange for a gradual lowering of the tariff over the next ten years, Calhoun urged the state to repeal its nullification law.

26. How did Jackson's actions cause an economic panic?

1) Jackson opposed the Bank of the United States because it did not give equal treatment to the common people. 2) To embarrass Jackson, Clay brought up a bill to recharter the bank before the bill was due. 3) Jackson vetoed the bill and removed all government funds from the bank and deposited them in state banks around the country. 4) The state banks went wild lending money at low rates to people who wanted to buy land. 5) Jackson ordered all land payments to be made in gold and silver. The banks called in their loans, causing a run on the banks.

the bank stood for special privileges for important people. He felt it did not give equal treatment to the common people. No bank did. And he disliked the bank's policy of printing paper money. Most of the people who liked gold and silver instead of paper money were people who favored the rich and the Bank of the United States. But Jackson, in his own special way, was against the Bank of the United States for the same reason the rich people were for it.

Jackson's enemy, Henry Clay, brought up a bill to recharter the Bank of the United States several years before it was due just to embarrass Jackson. But Jackson was popular. In 1832 he was re-elected easily over Clay. And since Jackson did not believe in strong central banking, he vetoed the bank bill. He also removed all the government funds from the Bank of the United States and had them deposited in state banks around the country. They were called Jackson's pet banks.

The state banks went wild lending money at low rates to people who wanted to buy land. When the lending seemed to be out of hand, Jackson suddenly switched policies and ordered all land payments to be made in gold and silver. He caused a run on the banks. The banks called in their loans. In 1837 Jackson left for his successor, Martin Van Buren, the inheritance of one of the worst panics the nation had seen. Jackson had vetoed the Bank of the United States because he was against one bank having too much power. But he found that many banks could cause problems also.

Native Americans—The End of an Era

27. How had contact with European-Americans affected Native Americans?

It became difficult for Native Americans to survive as separate tribal cultures. Tribes competed. One group would trade away tribal lands without telling the others. Agreements were made that ignored the way Indians used land and organized their families.

Jackson also had to make the final decision on the fate of the Native Americans of the Southeast. In the 225 years that the Native American tribes had lived in contact with the European-Americans, it had been difficult for the Native Americans to survive as separate cultures. Once the Native Americans began to depend on the White people's trade, the different tribes competed for that business. Tribes often disbanded. One group would trade away tribal lands without telling the others. This only increased the misunderstanding between Whites and Native Americans. The Whites never knew who represented the tribe. And when Whites did make treaties, they often destroyed the Native American culture in the process. One such agreement between the Creek tribe and the state of Mississippi ignored the way the Native Americans used land and organized their families. The treaty said that all chiefs and heads of families were to keep homesteads even though the lands were given over to the state.

28. Why did Jackson think the Removal Bill of 1835 was humane and just?

In 1832 the state of Georgia took over the Cherokee territory. Under Georgia law, the Native Americans had no legal standing.

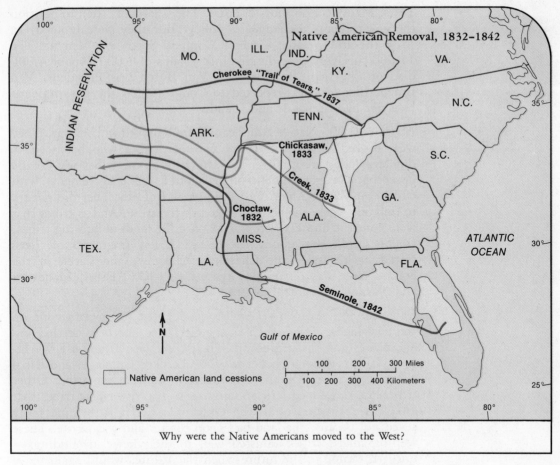

Native American Removal, 1832–1842

Cherokee "Trail of Tears," 1837

INDIAN RESERVATION

MO. ILL. IND. KY. VA.

N.C.

ARK. TENN.

Chickasaw, 1833

S.C.

Creek, 1833

Choctaw, 1832 ALA. GA.

MISS.

TEX. LA. FLA.

ATLANTIC OCEAN

Seminole, 1842

Gulf of Mexico

N

Native American land cessions

0   100   200   300 Miles
0   100   200   300   400 Kilometers

Why were the Native Americans moved to the West?

The Native Americans were moved west so the settlers could use the land for growing crops.

But they appealed to the Supreme Court of the United States. In *Worcester* v. *Georgia,* the Court ruled that Georgia had no power over the Cherokees because they were a "domestic, independent nation" under the rule of Congress. However, the Georgians took the land away from the Cherokee and the neighboring Creek tribe anyway because they had discovered gold on it. In 1835 Congress passed the Removal Bill setting aside land in the Oklahoma Territory for these southeastern tribes. They would have to move west of the Mississippi. Jackson signed the bill. He argued that people would continue to take Indian lands. He was sure that the Native Americans would realize the "humanity and justice" of the Removal Bill. (See map, above.)

He claimed that people would continue to take Indian lands, and the bill provided for a territory of their own in Oklahoma.

The Trail of Tears

By 1836 what was left of the powerful Creek tribe, about 2,000 people, started west along what became known as the Trail of

29. *What were the results of the removal process for the Native Americans?*

What did Jackson and the other people who designed the Removal Act believe about Native Americans and their land?

Why would Native Americans appeal to the Supreme Court? Whose law did they turn to? Why?

1) About 100,000 Native Americans were removed; 4,000 of 15,000 Cherokees died on the trip. 2) Tribal structure was upset. 3) Trouble broke out when nomadic hunters were moved onto lands of farming tribes. 4) The five major tribes that settled in the Oklahoma Territory were fairly successful because the land had good timber and was fertile.

Tears. Many had no shoes or coats. The Cherokees tried to petition the government to change its policy. But they were ignored. In 1838 the army, under General Winfield Scott, was sent in. The 15,000 survivors were divided into groups of 1,000. About 4,000 died on the trip. By this time Van Buren was President. Van Buren, like Jackson, reported to Congress that the government's behavior had been just and friendly.

About 100,000 Native Americans were removed in this way. They were moved into the territory of other tribes who belonged to different language groups. The structure of the tribes was totally upset because government officials often made agreements with whichever Native Americans could speak English. They did not try to find out where the person ranked in the tribe. And as tribes that were nomadic hunters were moved onto the lands of farming tribes, trouble broke out among the tribes. A few fragments of tribes stayed back east—some Cherokee, Choctaw, and Creek in the South, some Passamaquoddy (pass-a-mah-KWAD-ee), Mohegan, and Narragansett in the North.

Still, some of the Native Americans adapted to *reservation* life on the new lands. Tribes such as the Cherokee had been settled and organized from the beginning. Their chief, Sequoyah (si-KWAH-yuh), had made an alphabet for the Cherokee language, and tribal newspapers were printed to inform and educate the tribe. Other tribes also developed written languages. The five major tribes that established themselves in the Oklahoma Territory became fairly successful because the land had good timber and was fertile. These well-organized tribes adjusted well to their new surroundings—until that time in the future when the Whites would again move west.

Another National Party Forms

30. Why was the Whig party formed?

1) They formed in opposition to the Democratic party by collecting all the people from each section who didn't like "King Andrew." 2) Like the Democrats, they were trying to control sectional rivalries in order to win.

In the election of 1828, the nation had united behind Jackson. His party had won because it had support in every section of the nation. Shortly after the election, the people who disliked Jackson applied the lessons of 1828 and formed another political party. It, too, was a national party that collected all the people from each section who were against Jackson.

By the middle of the 1800's, the idea of a political party was to get out the vote and win. In so doing the United States had developed two national parties, one in and one out of office. Both were trying to appeal to everyone. Thus they were able to control the rivalries of the sections. The new party took the British title of Whig. The Whigs were the party that had opposed too much power by the king of England. In the United States, the Whigs declared themselves against the rule of King Andrew. They were

This painting, called "The Trail of Tears," shows the Cherokees on their forced move to territory west of the Mississippi River.

not able to settle on a candidate to run against Van Buren in 1836. But by 1840, they, too, had found a popular general, William Henry Harrison. They, too, had a well-organized national party.

Representation of the People—A National Question

The United States had increased in size and variety. Its citizens continued to value liberty, opportunity, and control over the land. The carefully constructed system of representation worked to give the nation leadership and unity to develop its resources. By the middle of the 1800's, the country was producing enough food to feed all of its people. Also, inventions in transportation and manufacture helped to make each section of the nation more prosperous.

Prosperity and opportunity caused many Americans to want to use representation for their own benefit. People in the different sections talked about equal opportunity, but they usually meant opportunity within the way of life they knew best.

Leaders tried to represent and lead the entire nation. But as the power of each section grew, this task became more and more difficult. The popular Jackson and his well-organized party were able to hold the nation together at election time. But issues that involved spending the taxpayers' money made it clear that the North and the South had different needs. Yet both sections were a part of America's success. And both looked to the West for expanded opportunity for individuals.

Checking the facts

1. What changes did Jackson make in the presidency?
2. How did Jackson and Calhoun differ on states' rights?
3. How was the Native American question resolved?

Representation is the only way such variety could operate under freedom. How can a leader represent the whole nation and those who voted for him or her?

PUTTING IT ALL TOGETHER

UNDERSTANDING THE MAIN IDEAS

1. What did Americans do about the representation of their differences?
2. Where did Americans find the leadership to manage those differences?
3. On what policies could the Americans agree?

ACTIVITIES

1. Ask two adults who is or was their favorite political candidate. What do they remember about him or her before the election? What do they remember about the candidate after the election? If there was a change, what brought it about?
2. How does one get to be a party worker in your area? Interview a precinct delegate and/or a local party committee person to find out. Report on your findings to the class.
3. Draw a voting map of your own area. Locate your congressional district, your state senate and state house district, your ward and precinct. Then find out the people who are active in party politics in your neighborhood. Who represents you?
4. Imagine that you are campaign manager for Andrew Jackson. What kinds of strategies would you use to get your candidate elected? How would they differ if you were running a campaign today? Describe your plans in a brief essay.

BOOKS TO READ

Clark, Electa, *Cherokee Chief; The Life of John Ross* (New York: Macmillan, Inc., 1970).

Miller, Douglas T., *Then Was the Future: The North in the Age of Jackson, 1815–1850* (New York: Alfred A. Knopf, Inc., 1973).

Oates, Stephen B., *Fires of Jubilee, Nat Turner's Fierce Rebellion* (New York: Harper and Row, 1975).

Remini, Robert, *The Revolutionary Age of Andrew Jackson* (New York: Harper and Row, 1976).

REVIEWING THE UNIT

BUILDING VOCABULARY

The following is a list of some of the vocabulary words in Unit 2:

sovereignty	tariff	subsidy
federalism	impressment	specie
compromise	concession	caucus
bicameral	democracy	spoils system
treason	coalition	secede
capital	continental divide	reservation
excise	embargo	

1. Pick out one or two of the words listed above and write a short paragraph on one of the following topics: a. The decisions made by the delegates to the Philadelphia Convention regarding the national and state governments, b. The structure of the national legislature, and c. Tax systems proposed by Alexander Hamilton to help raise money for the new government.

BUILDING SOCIAL STUDIES SKILLS

1. Turn to the maps on the pages given here. Then complete the following activities:
   a. Page 268—Write a sentence explaining why the Louisiana Purchase was so important to expansion in the United States.
   b. Page 291—Find the three routes which the British planned to use when they attacked the United States during the War of 1812. List the routes.
   c. Page 319—The Removal Bill of 1835 forced the Cherokee Indians of the South to move west of the Mississippi River to the Oklahoma Territory. Using the scale on the map, find the length, in miles and kilometers, of the "Trail of Tears."

BUILDING WRITING SKILLS

1. The Missouri Compromise of 1820 was an important attempt to please both the free states in the North and the slave states in the South. List the three important elements of this compromise. Then imagine that you had been voting on this bill. Would you have considered it a lasting solution to the differences between the people who owned slaves and those who disagreed with slavery? Write a short paragraph explaining why you said yes or no.

The Americans discovered that with the liberty they had under the Articles of Confederation the states agreed on very little. The Congress of the Confederation had no power to tax, and the states had little desire to contribute.

The convention that was called in Philadelpia in 1787 had the task of designing a way of government. The new government had to represent all of the differences among the states and still be able to make decisions for the good of everyone. It also needed enough power to carry its decisions into action.

Creating the Constitution

The Constitution was built on the colonists' English heritage. The most important guarantee of the people's liberty was a strong two-house legislature and a bill of rights. Government was forbidden to interfere with the natural rights of the people.

The Constitution was drawn up by practical men who knew how important it was to compromise. Compromise was particularly important in two areas of permanent differences. One was the power of small states and large states. The other was the question of deciding how to count the slaves for purposes of determining a state's population.

The Presidency

The role of President was not thoroughly described in the Constitution. But the details were filled in by the practical actions of Washington, Adams, and Jefferson. John Marshall, the Chief Justice, also filled in the picture of the federal government. With his decision, he gave it more power over the states. Marshall also made clearer the role of the Supreme Court when he declared that it had the power of judicial review. A successful plan for the nation's economy came from Alexander Hamilton, then Secretary of the Treasury. As he and Jefferson disagreed, two factions clustered around them: Hamilton and the Federalists, and Jefferson and the Republicans.

When Jefferson became President, he used much more power than he had expected. The purchase of Louisiana gave the nation enormous amounts of land.

Economic Change

While France and Britain fought, the states began to consider their own trading needs and to pressure the government to help each section. The question of which section to aid became another division between Republicans and Federalists.

Inventions such as the cotton gin and the spinning jenny changed the way people worked. Merchants in the North began to extend their selling areas and become organizers of handworkers. As roads and canals were built and steamboats were introduced on the rivers, the areas that could buy and sell to each other were slowly increased. Cotton began to take over as the major crop in the South. All areas of the nation looked to the new western land as a possible supplier and customer.

National Pride and Regional Competition

The War of 1812, the settlement of Russian claims in the Far West, and the Monroe Doctrine gave Americans a great sense of pride and power. None of these was a special victory. But the War of 1812 did put problems with Native Americans in the West temporarily to rest. After the war each section of the nation tried to get its representatives in Congress to pass favorable bank, tariff, and land laws. The Compromise of 1820 was formal recognition that there were two permanent sides and that slavery was not an issue on which the two sides could compromise.

People and Party Politics

The 1820's saw a continuation of Jefferson's plans to bring more voters to the polls and to have more people participate in the political process. The people, however, began to be more concerned about their own sections.

Americans would follow the political leadership of a strong and appealing personality. Andrew Jackson was popular because the people believed he represented what they wished to be. His actual policies and decisions were not all wise. He stood up against John C. Calhoun's attempt to let states nullify federal laws.

A major question was left unanswered, however. How would the growth of strong economic sections and the new political party deal with the unresolved issue of who would control the West—the slave South or the free North?

AMERICA IS...

EXPANSION AND INDIVIDUALISM

UNIT THREE

What did you do today? What are you going to do tomorrow? What do you want to be when you grow up? How old were you when people began to ask you questions like these? At one time in America only boys were asked these questions. Now girls and boys hear them as soon as they can listen—and certainly long before they are able to make up an answer. Americans are expected to be "do-ers." They learn early to look forward to favorable results.

It is no wonder that Americans soon learn to say "I'd like some more of that." "More" is an important word to Americans. America is a nation that expects that there will be more. Americans are frustrated, angry, or confused when someone says, "There isn't any more." Whether it is oil, or fresh water, or clean air—people find it hard to believe that they are going to run out of anything.

If you look at the advertisements on television and in popular magazines, you will see that they are aimed at people who have money to spend and choices to make. Advertising is often blamed for making people want to buy things they never would have bought. But advertising experts say that the most successful advertisements are ones that can link new products to old values. Many ads are linked to the idea of "more." When a company says in an advertisement that "progress" is their main business, they want the public to look kindly upon them. They want people to choose their brand over other companies' products. Some companies tell the customer that their products create more fun, more beauty, and more friends. Others promise more status, more responsibility, and more power. If you compare ads aimed at people of different incomes and different ages, you will find that the products and the prices differ. But the message and the values are the same.

Ads for educational toys promise parents that their children will improve in skills, knowledge, muscle control, and vocabulary by playing with the toys. Parents buy these toys, because they want their children to get ahead. Where is ahead? Ahead is beyond where you are now. It is beyond the boundaries that you know. That edge of what you know is called the frontier. Americans have always pushed to get beyond the frontier. Americans, perhaps more than other people, expect that there is more beyond the limits. In medicine, people talk openly about the research that will cure disease. People hope to find new ways to use the resources they have for energy and to discover new resources for the future. In the exploration of space, people walked on the moon and expect to be able to travel far beyond it. Some people worry about the expense of research aimed at simply finding out more. But it is impossible to keep Americans from taking the next step—or at least wanting to do so.

Americans worry about inequality. There are times when they do not have enough money or do not have a choice. They know that some people have a great deal more of both than others. But all Americans hope to be able to make choices. Immigrants to America from very poor countries had not been here very long before they wanted and expected more.

For whom do people want more? In New England, the Puritans wanted more so that their community could serve as a model for other communities. The European settlers in other parts of the country wanted more for themselves at the beginning. Then they learned to think of themselves as Virginians or Pennsylvanians. They saw themselves as part of a society with certain leaders and certain ways of governing and making a living. By the time of the Revolution, John Adams and Thomas Jefferson saw Americans as part of the dream of a great nation. It was not a nation of equals, but a nation of free people. Some were leaders and others were followers. Some were rich and others poor. But all had a share in a future in which there would be more for everyone.

By the middle decades of the 1800's people began to think of themselves as individuals with an equal right to participation in government and an equal chance to get more. New inventions, new methods of transportation, capital investment in trading and manufacturing, and the new lands in the West all provided opportunities. These were not part of a national effort but were opportunities for individuals in America to have more.

By 1830, new values had been added to the early ones of variety among people, liberty, opportunity, control, and representation. Now Americans were concerned with expansion and individualism and equality. "More" was the password in the 1830's and 1840's.

chapter 13
Greater Growth — Stronger Ties

1836–1850

1. REGIONAL AMERICA: NEW ENGLAND AND THE ATLANTIC STATES
2. REGIONAL AMERICA: THE NEW WEST
3. THE SOUTH AT MID-CENTURY

INTRODUCTION

Andrew Jackson was the symbol of individual achievement. In spite of his problems with the banks, people thought of him as a model. He could take action. He could look out for himself. He had been a success in battle, in his work, and in his political career. He believed that other people should have a chance to be successful. Americans liked his style.

In the mid-1800's people believed in themselves. They expected to look out for themselves. They expected their representatives to look out for them, too. That was what representation meant to them. Individuals saw work as their own effort for their own results. The owners of the mills, farms, and plantations took great personal risks. The people who worked for them also took risks. The conditions they worked under were their personal risk. They were willing to risk moving to new places and taking new jobs in order to fulfill their particular dreams.

	1833	1837	1841	1842	
Who?	Anti-Slavery Society	Elijah P. Lovejoy	Dorothea Dix	51,342 Irish immigrants	
What?	opens a school for Black children	an abolitionist editor is murdered	asks the legislature to provide care for the insane	arrive in the United States	
Where?	in Philadelphia	at Alton, Ill.	in Massachusetts	from Ireland	

The period from 1830 to 1850 was a time of spectacular expansion and progress in America. More and more goods and services were bought and sold. That was one kind of expansion. Links were formed between people within each region in order to produce and transport goods and services efficiently. That was another kind of expansion. Each section supplied additional goods to every other section. That was a third kind of expansion. Then there was the West. It created more opportunity for all three kinds of expansion—for those easterners who got there first and organized it their way.

During this period of expansion and individualism some people were caught in other people's progress. Factory workers and road and canal builders often worked under terrible conditions. Slaves were trapped, and Native Americans were pushed aside without a thought to their future. Women were ignored, except as a source of cheap labor. Anyone who was willing to go along with the big push was welcome. The competition was rough and the pace was rapid. Those who stopped to worry aloud about the people who were hurt in the process had few serious listeners. As you read about this period of expansion and individualism, think about these questions:

1. In what ways did the American system expand to take in so much new land and so many new people?
2. How did people learn to live in the new cities?
3. What happened to Blacks and women in this period?

1. REGIONAL AMERICA: NEW ENGLAND AND THE ATLANTIC STATES

By 1836 the economy of each section had become more specialized. Over a generation people had started new businesses using the new

1844	1845	1846	1847	1848
Samuel Morse	Edgar Allen Poe	Elias Howe	The Mormons	Lucretia Mott and Elizabeth Cady Stanton
puts his telegraph into operation	publishes The Raven and other poems	invents the sewing machine	trek	call a womens' rights convention
between Washington, D.C. and Baltimore	in New York	in Cambridge, Massachusetts	to Salt Lake City, Utah	in Seneca Falls, New York

Notice the changes in New England's manufacturing and factory system.

Make a chart or diagram that shows all of the parts of this new manufacturing system.

inventions. In New England the spinning mills had been joined by textile factories or mills where cloth was woven. Little by little families had become used to working in the factories. The younger people had grown up working in the factories and mills.

Work was becoming more specialized in order to speed up production. Work was seen more as a way to make money, and less as a skilled task in which the worker took personal pride. More products were sold by contracts to major buyers and less by the individual craft worker to neighbors in the area.

The Change to Manufacturing

1. How had the Americans moved into the world of manufacturing?

1) They had all the ingredients to begin manufacturing. 2) They had the raw materials. 3) They had the streams and coal mines to provide power for the machines. 4) They had a great number of people for laborers and consumers. 5) They had the capital for investment. 6) They had the transportation system to bring raw materials for the factories and to take them out to customers.

The northeastern and middle Atlantic states had all the ingredients of a manufacturing center. In the period from 1830 to 1850 these ingredients were combined. Rivers and coal mines provided the power to run the machines. The people who had been traders and merchants could apply their know-how to run manufacturing businesses. The great number of people living in the area provided both workers and customers. The North had banks and wealthy individuals with cash who could lend money to start new businesses.

Most of the products made in the new factories were made from agricultural goods. Therefore efficient transportation was necessary to get the grain to the flour mills and the liquor distilleries, the leather to the shoe factories, the cotton and the wool to the textile mills, and from there to the clothing factories. Transportation made much of the growth possible. Raw materials from the farms were brought to the cities by boat, barge, and road. Grain and hides came along the Erie Canal, and raw cotton came by ship to the Atlantic ports.

These women are shown binding books in the mid-1800's.

This picture shows an early locomotive and passenger cars. In these earliest trains, the stagecoaches were on rails. How would you describe the experience of riding on a train at this time?

The United States began to move into manufacturing in a step-by-step fashion. First, its raw materials were sold to foreign countries. Then, they were turned into manufactured goods at home. This took about 100 years from the time of the British navigation acts, which guaranteed protected markets in the British Empire. America's wealth had grown. But the change had not happened totally by luck or overnight. Each generation created the changes and had to adjust to them.

Railroads

In the 1830's and 1840's the newest form of transportation, the railroad, was introduced. Wheeled vehicles riding on rails had been used for about 15 years, but they were drawn by horses. Two inventions made it possible to carry heavy freight. They were the steam engine for power and the traction wheel which prevented slipping back and made it possible to stop.

With trains, manufactured goods from the cities could be sent to a larger area in a shorter amount of time. Each city that had a railroad tended to think of itself as the center of a web of business. There were no planned connections from one manufacturing city to another. In fact, the cities competed with one another, and each was quite jealous of its own local territory. Some of the local railroads deliberately designed their tracks so that the width between them, or *gauge*, was different from that of the next city.

2. What did the introduction of the railroad do for cities?

1) Each city became a center of a web of business, sending manufactured goods out to a larger area in a shorter amount of time.
2) Cities competed with each other.

Notice that manufacturing in England first became profitable in foreign trade. This indicates one advantage of an empire.
Railroading took half a generation to catch on.

In the excitement over new forms of travel, there was little concern for people who could not afford to travel.

Canals

3. Why did some consider riding on an Erie Canal boat entertainment?

It was a very difficult way of traveling. The bridges were very low; sometimes passengers had to bend double if seated, and sometimes they had to lie flat on their backs.

Americans, and a number of visitors from England and Europe, were delighted by the chance to travel. Riding on the Erie Canal boats was thought of as great entertainment. (See map, page 287.) There were three different classes of travel. One New Yorker described his first-class trip between Schenectady and Buffalo in 1836 with complete details:

> "These boats have three horses, go at a quicker rate, and have preference in going through the locks, carry no freight, are built extremely light, and have quite genteel men for their captains. . . . The bridges on the canal are very low. Every bridge makes us bend double if seated on anything, and in many cases you have to lie on your back. The man at the helm gives the word to the passengers: 'Bridge.' In general it affords amusement to the passengers who soon imitate the cry and vary it with a command such as, 'All Jackson men bow down.' After such commands we find few aristocrats."

Success on the High Seas

4. Why was New York a major trade center?

1) New York shippers owned the fastest sailing ships in the world. 2) The city had a long coast with good harbors for ports.

Despite the new factories, foreign trade was still a major source of income for Americans. Because of this trade cities like New York continued to prosper. Unlike Boston, New York did not yet have the great supply of immigrant labor that would make manufacturing possible. But New York was the home of the fastest sailing ships in the world. Fifty-two ships sailed regularly between New York and Europe by 1845. Many more sailed up and down the Atlantic coastline of the United States. The long coast with good harbors for ports provided a natural market for shipping.

Whaling

5. Why did the United States have such a large whaling fleet?

1) Whale oil was the world's major source of fuel for light. It provided a good profit-making business. 2) The adventure and money made was part of the American feeling of expansion and opportunity.

As New York became the center for trade, the other sailing towns of New Bedford, Massachusetts, and Providence, Rhode Island, put their energies into the profit-making business of whaling. Whale oil was the world's major source of fuel for light before the first oil field was discovered in 1859. Whaling flourished from 1830 to 1860. The island of Nantucket off the Massachusetts coast became the most important whaling port in the world.

The whaling fleet of the United States numbered over 700 ships at its peak. Captains took their ships as far away as New Zealand or the Bering Sea. It was fairly common for a whaling ship to be gone three to four years at a time. Whaling offered an exciting life

Cities were the centers of excitement because of their function as centers for trade and travel.

This is a detail of a painting by John E. C. Peterson. It shows one of the ships of the famous Black Ball Line. This shipping line was set up in 1817 and made regular trips across the Atlantic Ocean.

for the sailors. It was a chance to test the future with their physical strength. The adventure and money made in whaling was part of the American feeling of expansion and opportunity.

Clipper Ships and Steamships

In the early 1850's the design of ships was improved. Clipper ships cut the sailing time around Cape Horn in South America to San Francisco, California, from a five or six-month trip to a three-month trip. These ships were so streamlined they could not carry bulky cargo. But they were able to bring back tea from Hong Kong in the Far East, and this trade was very profitable.

The clipper ships did not last long. Their best days were also the beginning days of the steamships. At first steamships were used on the rivers, because they could not carry enough coal for the whole transatlantic trip. In the beginning steamships carried only mail, passengers, and small items of first-class freight. But they had the ability to move in any kind of weather, without wind, and against the wind, as they must on the return voyage. They were worth the slightly slower speed.

6. Why did the steamship replace the clipper ship?

Steamships were slower, but they could carry more cargo and move in any weather.

7. *What changes did the steamship bring about?*

1) The cheap transportation costs made the prices of imported goods cheaper than American goods. 2) European immigrants could afford to travel on the American ships on the return trips.

It was no wonder that the American manufacturers, especially in the New England and the middle states, wanted higher tariffs. The transportation costs for European goods were cheap on the efficient steamships. Therefore, the prices of imported goods were lower than those of American products.

The British fleet of modern ships was more desirable than the American one. But the American wooden steamships did well carrying American cotton and Canadian lumber to Europe and bringing back manufactured goods. They also brought back immigrants from Europe. These people were crowded into converted cargo space, and many became ill. But without cheap transportation, the European poor could not have come to America at all.

Urban Living for Women Factory Workers

8. *How did the mills keep the women workers on the job?*

1) They put social and economic pressure on the women. 2) If a woman left the mill before a year was out, she was blacklisted.

The earliest years in the spinning mills were exciting for the young farm women who came in answer to the factories advertising. For an unmarried woman to go to the city and live on her own had seemed a wonderful opportunity. She could live in a comfortable boardinghouse with a friendly atmosphere.

But within ten years, life had changed for the mill workers. With more mills, each competed with the others and tried to keep down costs. All the mill would pay to the boardinghouses was $1.25 per week, which was deducted from the pay of each worker. The mills refused to pay more, so the boardinghouses had to crowd six to eight women in a room to make any profit at all.

The mills used every possible method to keep young women on the job, including social pressure at the boardinghouse. The rules of one house said:

> "Each is to have her place at the table during meals.
> The two who have worked the greatest length of time
> in the factory are to sit each side of the head of the
> table. All new hands will of course take their seats
> lower down, according to the length of time they have
> been there."

In addition to social pressure there was economic pressure. If a woman left the mill before a year was out, she was refused an honorable discharge and no one else in the area would hire her. She was *blacklisted* in every mill village.

Women Strike

9. *How did women workers organize?*

Mills had not been in existence long before women began to protest the working conditions and long hours. Protests and *turn outs,* or

Women mill workers
of the 1800's are shown
on strike.

strikes, were frequent. The women took action although their contracts stated that any time spent in union activities would be deducted from their pay.

The women at the Lowell mill went out on strike in 1834 when the mill announced that it was going to cut their wages. Each woman pledged to give up $5.00, or about a month's pay, if she went back to work before the others did. The company organized the community, pressuring the women to return to work. Church sermons told them that they should be grateful for their jobs. The company quickly began to recruit other farm women to come and replace them. The newspapers spoke out against the strike. Finally the women went back to work. Their wages were cut, and their leaders were fired. But the women organized a Factory Girls Association and kept up their protest.

1) After the Lowell strike in 1834, the women organized a Factory Girls' Association and kept up their protest. 2) The craft unions formed the first national union, the National Trades' Union.

Early Unions

Sometimes men supported the women workers. Beginning in the 1700's skilled workers had organized into craft unions. The different trades formed city-wide unions, and by 1834 they formed the first national union, the National Trades' Union. Where women made up a large part of the work force, men often were on their side. But in work such as printing and bookbinding where women were a small part of the business, the men organized to "drive the women out."

Notice how complicated women's place in society was. Some women had the courage and belief to act in strikes for better working conditions. Other women believed they should stay at home and not work.

335

Political Action

10. *What made the mill workers' demand for a shorter work day valid?*

In 1840, President Van Buren signed an order stating that people who worked for the federal government would have a ten-hour day.

In order to cut costs, the mills bought new machines that could do the work faster. But the pay of the workers was the same as it had been 20 years before when the mills first opened. Mill workers worked a 75-hour week. They wanted to work fewer hours but they were afraid of losing their jobs. When their union fell apart during the panic of 1837, they did not dare start up another one. Instead they began to petition the state legislature for a ten-hour work day. One of their popular songs carried the message, too:

"But if I still must wend my way,
Uncheered by hope's sweet song,
God grant that, in the mills, the day
May be but ten hours long."

A leader for political action in this struggle was Sarah Bagley. During the 1840's she went from town to town, pressuring the state legislature to hold public hearings on working conditions. She also wrote articles for the woman's paper, the *Lowell Offering*. The organization she formed had as its slogan "Try Again," which was all the mill workers could do.

But the petitions for shorter hours did not work. The owners of the mills had too much power and the women needed the jobs. The only hope was the news in 1840 that President Van Buren had signed an order stating that people who worked for the federal government would have the ten-hour day. But privately owned industry was slow to follow.

John McCloskey, the son of Irish immigrants, became the first American cardinal of the Catholic Church.

Irish Immigrants

The late 1840's saw a change in the working picture. Factory owners found a cheaper source of labor than unmarried New England farm women. When a potato famine hit Ireland, immigrants from that country began to pour into the New England area. They were peasants from the farms who were faced with starvation. They could not go to the South because slaves did the unskilled work there.

There had always been a steady flow of immigrants to America. From the time of the Declaration of Independence to the period just before Jackson's election in 1828, about one million people had arrived. But in the ten years from 1840 to 1850 almost 2 million came, and in the next ten years another 2.5 million came. Forty percent of this number were Irish. In fact, one quarter of the total population of Ireland came to the United States in these years!

Open immigration to the United States was always a major reason for the success of new business.

Family Contracts

The Irish came in family groups and went to work in family groups. In the mill towns they replaced the protesting mill women, who either took jobs as sales clerks or went home.

The Irish families signed contracts for a year at a time. One contract signed by the Slater mill, in Rhode Island, showed how the whole family was employed:

> "Agreed with Abel Dudley for himself and family to work one year from the last day of March past. Mary and Caroline have the privilege of going to school two months each, one at a time. Amos (who was too young to go to school) is to work when they are out."

If families did not work when they said they would, they lost the house which they rented from the factory.

The family system was used throughout Rhode Island, Connecticut, Massachusetts, Pennsylvania, New York State, Virginia, Maryland, and the Middle West. More than half of all mill workers in the United States worked under the family system.

A Permanent Class of Poor Workers

The workers continued to try to get state laws passed for better hours. But when laws were passed as in Pennsylvania in 1848, the owners simply lowered the wages. They wanted to expand. For those with money to invest, the 1840's were good years. But a permanent class of poor workers was developing in the eastern cities. The immigrants and their children could not take advantage of America's expansion. Their lives stood in great contrast to the lives of those who did benefit from the prosperous years of the 1840's.

Machines and Jobs

The invention of new machines like the sewing machine created more jobs for unskilled workers. The American sewing machine was invented by Elias Howe in 1846. It was improved in 1851 when Isaac Singer invented a foot treadle to replace the hand wheel. It revolutionized the shoe business and the clothing business. Skilled hand tailors were put out of business as unskilled immigrant workers took over.

The sewing machine made it possible for one person to do as much work in one day as 12 people sewing by hand for 10 hours. It was

11. What effect did the Irish family contract plan have on the factory working force?

1) They replaced the protesting women workers.
2) More than half of all mill workers in the United States worked under this plan.
3) They became a permanent class of poor workers.

12. What effect did the sewing machine have on the labor force?

1) Skilled hand tailors were put out of business as unskilled immigrant workers took over. 2) Workers had to produce more work in an hour for the same pay.

Poor immigrants could work in America in the mid–1800's, but as a group they could no longer catch up to those with capital.

American Inventors 1775-1850

YEAR	INVENTOR	INVENTION
1775	David Bushnell	Submarine
1787	John Fitch	First American steamboat
1793	Eli Whitney	Cotton gin
1802	Oliver Evans	Steam engine
1827	Joseph Henry	Insulated wire used in telegraph
1830	Peter Cooper	First American locomotive
1831	Cyrus McCormick	Reaper
1835	Samuel Colt	Repeating pistol
1836	Hiram and John Pitt	Thresher
1837	John Deere	Steel plow
1839	Charles Goodyear	Vulcanization of rubber
1840	Norbert Rillieux	Vacuum evaporator for refining sugar
1844	Samuel Morse	Telegraph
1846	John Roebling	Suspension bridges
1846	Elias Howe	Sewing machine

invented just as the Irish immigration hit its peak. Jobs were scarce and people competed for them. Men and women had to work faster to keep up with the machines. Although they produced more work in an hour, they received the same pay.

Other Jobs for Unskilled Workers

13. Why did the Irish get mostly unskilled jobs?

1) They were willing to work for lower wages. 2) The better jobs went to American-born workers, except when the Irish were priests, doctors, and lawyers serving other Irish immigrants.

Irish women who could not find work in clothing and shoe factories became domestic servants. Over 2,000 Irish women became domestic servants in Boston. Earlier housewives had taken care of their own work or had paid farm women high wages. But Irish women needed work so desperately that they created a new domestic service in Boston.

When the Irish came to Boston, they settled in poorer sections, or *slums*. Their arrival created a demand for better housing for others. Boston merchants built fine new homes on Beacon Hill and in the Back Bay area. The boom in house building did provide some jobs

Notice how poor Irish labor changed the lives and the place of residence of more established Bostonians.

for the Irish. But most of the better jobs went to American-born workers.

The commercial community of America was native-born. Some 90 percent of the merchants, 86 percent of the shipping agents, and even 88 percent of the clerks had been born in America. The Irish who did manage to have a profession usually served other Irish immigrants. People preferred priests and doctors and lawyers from their homeland. These were people they felt they could trust.

New Businesses

The supply of cheap Irish labor caused Boston to become an industrial city. People with capital deliberately moved to Boston to start new businesses there. Among the new businesses were the Chickering Piano Company and the Mason and Hamlin Organ Company. They employed over 1,000 workers. Donald McKay moved his shipyards to east Boston in 1845. And in ten years, over 1,000 men worked at shipbuilding.

14. What changes did the Irish immigrants bring to Boston?

1) Businesses started in Boston because of the supply of cheap Irish labor.
2) Boston became an industrial city.

The people who benefited the most were native-born Americans. They were the owners—the people with capital. And they made the profits. But some Irish and Germans went into the clothing business, and an Irishman named John Donnelly started outdoor billboard advertising.

Women's Rights

Trying to help working women was difficult, since both men and women workers had so little power and needed their jobs so badly. But in 1848 at Seneca Falls, New York, a public effort was made to call attention to the problems of women who worked as well as those who did not. Originally planned for women only, the convention eventually was open to the public.

This photograph shows Elizabeth Cady Stanton. She helped organize the first women's rights convention at Seneca Falls, New York. What was the goal of this meeting?

Three hundred people came, including 40 men. Among them was Frederick Douglass, the ex-slave and antislavery leader. The main concerns of the meeting were economic. One was that in New York State married women had few property rights. Husbands could also spend their wives' earnings as they wished.

Another concern was that women were not welcomed into apprenticeships. They could work as helpers, doing low-skilled work in print shops and the bookbinder and shoe businesses. But they were not allowed to enter the crafts and get the training to advance themselves.

A resolution for women's vote, or *suffrage,* was passed at the convention. But it did not pass unanimously as did the other resolutions. The delegates reached unanimous agreement on all the other

In a time of boom, like the mid-1800's, the most benefit goes to those who have extra money (capital) to invest.

Lucretia Mott was a Quaker minister, an abolitionist, and an organizer for women's rights.

Frederick Douglass escaped slavery by disguising himself as a sailor on a ship bound for New York.

issues. The main speaker was Elizabeth Cady Stanton. Lucretia Mott, an antislavery leader and lecturer, was another organizer. She had founded the Philadelphia Anti-Slavery Society in 1833 and had opened a school for Black children. Mott said that "the speedy success of our cause depends upon the . . . untiring efforts of both men and women for securing to women an equal participation with men in the various trades, professions, and commerce."

The Abolition Movement

The antislavery, or *abolition*, movement did not attract many factory owners or workers. Northern factories bought from the South and sold to the South. The two regions grew stronger from this arrangement. Southern plantation owners let it be known that any factory whose owner or workers supported the abolition movement or helped runaway slaves would lose their business. The factory owners also frightened the workers by telling them that if slaves were freed, they would come north and take their jobs. Many Irish immigrants were afraid of the competition from free Blacks.

Some workers, however, did help. But the main leadership of the movement came from the Quakers and the non-slave Black population. A newspaper publisher in Boston, William Lloyd Garrison, was one of the important leaders. In 1831, he published the first issue of a paper called *The Liberator*. In it, Garrison demanded immediate and total freeing of all slaves. He wrote: "I will not excuse—I will not retreat a single inch—*and I will be heard*!" Mobs burned his newspaper in Boston. When news came of a Virginia slave revolt led by Nat Turner, Garrison and the northern abolitionists were blamed.

The most tragic story of all was that of Elijah Lovejoy of Alton, Illinois. He was a minister and ran a printing press. When in 1837 he declared slavery to be a sin against God, the people in his town threw his press into the river and killed him. They paraded his body through the streets while people stood by and applauded.

Many Blacks were involved in abolition groups. There were more than 50 such groups in 1830, before Garrison began to speak out. The most powerful of the Black abolitionists was Frederick Douglass, an ex-slave who escaped from Maryland in 1838. Douglass had learned to read and write and had learned a trade. By 1845 he was a well-known speaker for the Massachusetts Anti-Slavery Society and had published his autobiography. In his book, Douglass gave a detailed account of life as a slave. He spoke out not only for freedom but for full equality for Blacks. His views on freedom were more popular than his view on equality. But Douglass was an impressive speaker for Black rights and an impressive representative of what Blacks could become if given the opportunities others had.

People's views on opportunities for Blacks differed depending on their jobs and locations; many more people were antislavery than were for equality. What is the difference between being anti-slavery and being against equality?

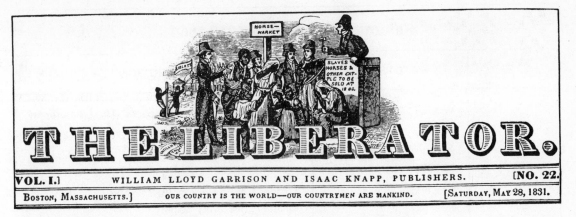

This picture shows the name of the paper founded by the abolitionist, William Lloyd Garrison. Garrison also supported the women's rights movement.

Women were also active in the antislavery movement. Sarah and Angelina Grimké (GRIM-key) and Lucy Stone became important abolitionist speakers. The Grimké sisters had grown up in the South and their family had owned slaves. They moved to Philadelphia as adults, however, and became Quakers.

Other Reform Movements

Abolitionists were not the only people who wanted to improve society between 1830 and 1850. Other reformers were concerned with the plight of the unskilled urban poor. They realized how lonely it was for the old and sick to live in the growing cities of strangers. They spoke out against the individualism which caused people to watch out for themselves and to forget about helping others.

There were many reform movements from 1830 to 1850. They were not organized into a single group. Each reform movement attacked what its members felt was the worst problem in society. Several groups formed ideal communities. The best known was Brook Farm, started in Massachusetts in 1841. At Brook Farm each member was supposed to do the jobs that pleased him or her most, and everyone was paid either equally or according to the job. People who did the unpleasant jobs were paid more. Brook Farm failed after six years, and other groups did not last long either.

A number of people started new organizations to help others. Horace Mann worked to improve the quality of public education, and set up the first school to train teachers. Thomas Gallaudet (gal-ah-DET) established special schools for the deaf. Samuel Gridley Howe

Like Frederick Douglass, Sojourner Truth wrote about life as a slave. She spoke out for women's rights, also.

Notice that individualism and expansion separated the newcomers from the more established Americans. Those who had more, organized to help for those who had less.

341

What is the time period of the reforms included on the chart? What are some of the reforms?
How did the reforms change the way Americans lived?

Reformers in America, 1810-1860

AREA	REFORMER	CONTRIBUTION
Abolition	William Lloyd Garrison	Sets up an anti-slavery newspaper, *The Liberator* in 1831
	American Anti-Slavery Society	Established as a national organization in 1832, in Philadelphia
	Frederick Douglass	Escapes from slavery in 1838 and writes and speaks for the Anti-Slavery Society
	Dred Scott	Sues for his freedom after he has been a resident of a free state
	Harriet Tubman	Conducts slaves to freedom on the underground railroad between 1849 and 1860
	Elijah Lovejoy	A minister in Alton, Illinois who was killed for his anti-slavery activities in 1859
Women's Rights	Mary Lyon	Establishes Mt. Holyoke as the first women's college in the United States in 1836
	Sarah and Angelina Grimké	The first women to speak to audiences of both men and women
	Supporters of Married Women's Property Laws	Between 1830 and 1850 most states pass laws recognizing the right of married women to hold land
	Elizabeth Cady Stanton Lucretia Mott	Call a Women's Rights Convention in Seneca Falls, New York in 1848
Social Service	Thomas Gallaudet	Establishes the first school for the deaf in Hartford, Connecticut in 1817
	Samuel Gridley Howe	Establishes a school for the blind in 1832
	Dorothea Dix	Begins work with the insane in 1841
Education	Deans of Oberlin University	Allow their school to be the first to admit women and Blacks in 1835
	Emma Willard	Establishes the Troy Female Seminary in Troy, New York; the first school opened for girls with public money

did the same for the blind. Special institutions were also set up to reeducate criminals and improve conditions for the insane, the poor, and the orphans. The people who started these institutions were the first to believe in curing social ills rather than just punishing or isolating people. Among them was Dorothea Dix, who was well-known for her work on behalf of the insane. Dix surveyed jails, prisons, and poorhouses in Massachusetts. She presented her findings to the state legislature in 1843. She pointed out that insanity was an illness and that victims should be in hospitals, not jails. As a result of her work, special hospitals were built in several states.

Some people believed liquor was the main cause of social problems. They preached self-control, or *temperance*. Their organization, the American Temperance Union, tried to get a law passed that made the drinking of liquor illegal.

Each of these reform movements believed that human beings could solve all their problems, if they thought clearly and scientifically, organized carefully, and carried out their plans in a detailed way. Reformers approached the problems of people with the same belief in themselves and the same energy shown by the builders of railroads and factories. From the middle of the 1800's on, reform movements grew as business and cities grew.

Individualism in Literature

The spirit of individualism also showed itself in the literature of American writers. The first original American literary group met, talked, and published in Boston during the second quarter of the 1800's. Ralph Waldo Emerson was the leader of the group, which also included his writer friend, Henry David Thoreau.

Emerson wanted Americans to think creatively and produce works of art on their own. He and Thoreau agreed that the new machines were a terrible danger to the spirit of each individual. Thoreau so objected to the new machine age that he spent two years living as simply as he could in a cabin by Walden Pond outside Concord, Massachusetts. In his book, *Walden,* he described how he saw life itself and the natural beauty around him. He also wrote how he hated factories and railroads.

The 1840's and 1850's produced other major American writers. Nathaniel Hawthorne wrote short stories and novels. Edgar Allen Poe wrote mystery tales and short stories. Walt Whitman experimented with new forms of poetry in which he celebrated the power of the individual and the greatness of America. Margaret Fuller edited a literary magazine called *The Dial*. She also wrote *Women in the Nineteenth Century*. This work dealt with American feminism.

15. What were the goals of Emerson's literary group?

It wanted Americans to think creatively and produce works of art on their own. Emerson and Thoreau agreed that the new machines were a terrible danger to the spirit of the individual.

Volunteer reform groups have always been popular in America. Can you name some that are active today? The great number of important writers writing about the need for reform in this period shows that they were acting and reacting to some of the same events.

343

Checking the facts

1. How did the development of transportation affect the New England and Atlantic states?
2. What effect did the wave of Irish immigration have upon labor and industry?
3. What social and labor reforms were attempted during this period?

2. REGIONAL AMERICA: THE NEW WEST

16. How were railroads built in the new West?

City governments were permitted by the state legislatures to invest tax dollars in railroad building.

The years from 1830 to 1850 were important years of growth for the river cities of the West. City governments, like the one in St. Louis, Missouri were permitted by the state legislatures to invest tax dollars in railroad building. The Missouri-Pacific Railroad was started by the city government with voter approval. These railroads, like the ones on the eastern side of the Allegheny Mountains, did not connect city to city, nor east to west. Crossing the mountains was still a terrible engineering problem.

17. Why were there so many differences in population?

1) Each immigrant group was represented as people moved west to buy cheap government land. 2) Families could start a new life if they could afford the price of transportation.

Differences in the population of western cities were striking. Every immigrant group was represented as people moved west to buy cheap government land. The sale of the former Native American lands provided great opportunities for other Americans. The father of a family might go west, if the family could afford the price of transportation. Then the rest of the family could join him later. In this way families were able to start over again. Newcomers arrived continually in the western cities. How did all of the different groups live in one place?

Cincinnati: A Case Study

18. What group became the wealthy people of Cincinnati?

The earliest settlers became the "first families." They owned the best land and the key businesses. Their descendants became the upper classes.

From census records and real estate lists, historians have been able to draw a picture of how the people who came to one river city lived. Population maps of Cincinnati, Ohio in the middle 1800's show where people lived after they settled down. Much had to do with the time that people arrived. The earliest settlers became the "first families." Although they had to go through the difficulties of founding a new community, the survivors became the owners of the best land and the key businesses. Their descendants became the upper class.

In Cincinnati the homes and churches of these wealthy people with capital to invest were located along one street. These people sup-

Why would city governments invest in private railroad companies?

What do you need to know to make this map useful to you?

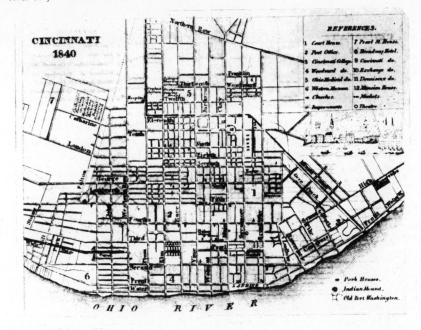

This is a map showing Cincinnati, Ohio, in 1850. What can you locate on this map?

ported the anti-Jackson Whig party and were the builders of roads and canals. They owned steamboats and were bankers and investors in the railroad.

Immigrant groups who came later lived in other parts of the city. The Germans, who worked as skilled tradesworkers or laborers, built their homes and churches on the east side of the canal. The Irish group settled near the Ohio River. (See the map above.) The Jews were divided into two groups. Those who came before 1848 had lived first in eastern American cities. They settled in the eastern part of Cincinnati, while those who came in 1848 and 1849 settled on the west side of town. Each group had a separate synagogue, but they shared one burial ground.

19. What immigrant groups came later?

The Germans, Irish, and Jews.

In the year 1850, Cincinnati had a population of 115,000 people. Only 3,300 of the people were Jews. But Christianity was not a way of uniting people. In the newer river communities, each new group started its own church. The Catholics and Protestants in Cincinnati built different churches, depending on national origin and also on race. For example, the Catholics built 17 churches. Seven of them were known as German churches. Of the seven Baptist churches, two were for Blacks. Of the 14 Methodist churches, three were for Germans. People of different social classes also went to different churches, depending on the neighborhoods they lived in. Neighborhoods were divided by the size of houses and the amount of property each had.

20. Why wasn't Christianity a way of uniting people?

Catholics and Protestants built churches on the basis of the national origin, race, and social class of the congregations.

Churches and synagogues were social centers. Notice that people wanted to belong to a church that used their native language or whose members came originally from their native country.

Education in Cincinnati

21. What educational opportunities were there in Cincinnati?

1) White and Black children went to segregated public schools financed by the state and the city. 2) There were free night classes for working people. 3) The city had a parochial school system and 50 private schools. 4) The system of higher education included three colleges, one law school, four medical colleges, five business colleges, and five theological colleges.

The state of Ohio and the city shared the cost of the public school system. Over 12,000 White children and 1,000 Black children went to segregated public schools. The Catholics had a separate *parochial* school system with almost 5,000 children. There were 50 private schools. The system of higher education included three colleges, one law school, four medical colleges, five business colleges, and five colleges for training ministers, or *theological* schools. The city also provided free night classes at the public schools for working people who had not been educated. Education was important in the river cities like Cincinnati.

Despite Cincinnati's educated population, not everyone who came to the city was impressed with it. The Englishwoman, Frances Trollope, was one such person. She came to the United States in 1827 to found a large department store in Cincinnati. The store failed, but her book about America was a great success. However, many Americans were furious, because she wrote with such sharp detail and humor. In her account of Cincinnati, she said:

> "It is a city of extraordinary size and importance when it is remembered that 30 years ago the (native) forest occupied the ground where it stands. Every month appears to extends its limits and its wealth. . . . During nearly two years that I lived in Cincinnati I neither saw a beggar, nor a man of sufficient fortune to permit his stopping his efforts to increase it. . . . Every bee in the hive is in search of money. Neither art, science, learning, or pleasure can [lure them away]. . . . In America that polish which removes the coarser and rougher parts of our nature is unknown and undreamed of."

Blacks in Cincinnati

22. What rights did the Blacks have in the city of Cincinnati?

Blacks in Cincinnati were never slaves. And since the city was the largest inland city and one of the earliest to develop in the West, many Blacks first learned about urban life in Cincinnati. At the end of the War of 1812, there were 410 Blacks in a city of 9,602. By 1848, there were 3,237 out of a total of 115,538. Therefore, the Black population stayed within 2 to 3 percent of the total. The state of Ohio passed "Black Laws" in 1804 and 1807 that allowed only free Blacks to enter the state. They had to post a $500 bond guaranteeing both their good behavior and the skills to support themselves.

From the beginning, Blacks had to live in a separate part of town. However, conditions there were reported to be good. In this section

What values would you expect to find in a town built by newcomers looking for a second chance?

were Black schools, churches, and businesses. Within the Black section of town there were definite class distinctions.

For the first 25 years Blacks were tolerated in Cincinnati, but could only get low-paying unskilled jobs. In the next 15-year period race riots broke out between Blacks and the Irish. Then upper class Whites came to the defense of the Black community, and a new business offered the Blacks a chance to improve their situation. Blacks who were skilled and had an education could get good jobs on the upper decks of the steamboats. The unskilled could get jobs on the lower decks or as workers on the banks, or *levees*, of the river. The Blacks who worked on the upper decks of the steamboats were able to save money, and go into business for themselves.

The river cities like Cincinnati were an important step in the spread of city life from east to west. These cities sold their goods to Europe. But their cultural ties were with the eastern cities, from which their founders had come.

1) Ohio passed "Black Laws" that allowed only free Blacks to enter the state. 2) Blacks had to post a $500 bond guaranteeing both their good behavior and their ability to support themselves. 3) They had to live in a separate part of town. 4) After 25 years, during which Blacks could get only low-paying, unskilled jobs, riots broke out between Blacks and Irish. Some upper-class Whites came to the defense of Blacks. Skilled Blacks with good jobs on steamboats were able to save money and start businesses.

The Lake Cities of the Middle West

As Americans moved west they planned their cities along with their farms. Many Americans went west to be city-dwellers and go into trading businesses. Others hoped to open shops and provide services to the growing population. Farmers needed a nearby town where they could sell their crops and purchase manufactured goods from the East. The people who went west wanted comfort, control over their futures, and the money that more land could bring. The West meant near or greater opportunities, and cities were needed in every area of the westward expansion.

Cities grew along the trading frontier. River cities such as St. Louis and Cincinnati were that frontier in the 1820's. They had established the north-south trade to the Mississippi and from there to the ocean. The next group of cities, chartered in the 1830's, became the new trading centers on the Great Lakes. These were the cities of Buffalo, Cleveland, Chicago, Detroit, and Milwaukee. The population of each of these cities grew at a rapid rate. Each city followed a pattern of growth similar to that of the Atlantic seacoast cities in 1800 and the river cities in the 1820's. By 1850 the lake cities had gone through this same process of development.

23. How were the trading centers on the Great Lakes like the other cities?

Their pattern of growth was similar. By 1850 they had gone through the same process of development as the seacoast and river cities.

City Laws

By reading the laws passed by people in cities and by noticing the order in which they passed them, it is possible to tell a great deal about people's customs and what they cared about. The first laws city people passed were for safety. They had to do with fire prevention. Health protection was also a concern. Immigrants were

24. What types of city laws were needed?

Why did these cities grow independently of each other? Use the map to identify who they traded with.

1) Safety laws, especially for prevention of fires and the spread of disease. 2) Regulations to keep city life orderly. 3) Laws to regulate trade, so that no merchant got a monopoly.

quarantined to make sure that they did not bring new diseases into the community. Rules were set about draining stagnant water and about locating and maintaining slaughterhouses for cattle.

People in cities also passed regulations to keep city life orderly. Close living required less noise and slower driving speeds for horse-drawn vehicles. Cities were concerned about things like trash and snow that blocked the sidewalks. Children were not to play ball in the street.

These laws tried to make life in close quarters more convenient for everyone. They show why people who move from the farm to the city often have trouble adjusting to problems of sanitation, trash disposal, and medical care. For example, in Cleveland in 1836, the city government ordered that the streets were to be swept twice a month by the owners or occupants of property, that horses were not to be driven on sidewalks, and that wooden signs were not to stick out more than three feet (0.9 meter) from the building toward the street. The uncontrolled spread of disease, or *epidemic*, was a constant cause of fear. In Milwaukee physicians had to make an official report on contagious disease and all causes of death. In Buffalo, graves had to be at least five feet (1.5 meters) deep. Even annoyances were carefully spelled out. For instance, in one city no musical instruments were to be played on Sunday.

City laws also dealt with trade. Cities tried to keep people from getting too much of the trade, or a monopoly. All sellers had to do business in licensed market stalls. In this way they were forced to compete with other sellers in the next stalls. The market places had to be kept clean. No dogs, horseshoe tossing, or unacceptable language were allowed in the market. Also, merchants were not allowed to buy produce and keep it off the market in order to force the price up. Weights and measures were supervised, and products, such as food, firewood, and fodder for animals, on which the survival of the community depended, were carefully regulated.

Competing for Settlers

25. Why did Chicago get more settlers than Milwaukee?

1) Chicago was farther south and had easier access to the river system. 2) The railroads being built around Chicago also gave it an advantage.

Cities competed with each other by sending out advertising to eastern cities. They told how wonderful their city was and warned the reader about diseases in the other places! Chicago and Milwaukee in particular were in competition. But Chicago won because it was farther south and had easier access to the river system. The railroads being built around Chicago also gave it an advantage.

The growth of trade from 1830 to 1850 depended on the plank roads and railroads that were built in a web or network around each city. The idea was not to link up one city to the other. Instead it was to bring the surrounding area into a tight web of trade and

If you had money to invest in 1830, what might cause you to invest it in a lake city like Chicago?

support. The lake cities planned to manufacture their own goods but it would be another 20 years before they could make sizeable profits.

Volunteer Organizations

How did these new cities get the services they needed? Everyone had to pitch in and donate part of their time for almost no pay. There were not enough people with money who could be taxed, and without taxes people could not be hired to clean the streets. Thus in 1847 Chicago passed a law which said that all men would have to help repair the streets three days a year at 50 cents a day.

The police and fire departments were also volunteers. Anyone who refused to serve in the bucket line was fined, and insurance companies offered yearly prizes to the best fire brigade. Benefit concerts and subscription dinners to which tickets were sold helped to raise money for equipment.

During the winter when ice stopped the lake traffic, the unemployed required aid. Women's organizations raised money to provide fuel and food for them, and soup kitchens were set up by private groups. Cultural services such as libraries, theaters, colleges, and public parks were also managed and paid for by volunteer organizations.

What do you think about parties and lotteries to raise money for community services?

26. Why were volunteer organizations needed?

Volunteers raised funds and donated their labor for the good of the community. There was not enough tax money to pay for such services as police protection, street cleaning, fire fighting, and feeding the unemployed, or to provide libraries, theaters, colleges, and parks.

In this picture, Cincinnati volunteer firefighters try to put out a fire in a theater.

The people of these cities were not more community-minded than the competitive individualists of other places. The appeal was not to community feeling, but rather to the needs of individuals. The cities had become large enough to require cooperation. As cities grew, laws and social organizations were necessary to make living pleasant, safe, and profitable. The motives behind these laws and organizations were the same ones that had sent people to cities in the first place: personal success, comfort, and control.

Checking the facts

1. How did the settlers of Cincinnati regard opportunity, religion, education, and race?
2. What did the cities of Buffalo, Cleveland, Chicago, Detroit, and Milwaukee have in common?

3. THE SOUTH AT MID-CENTURY

27. How did slave trading become big business?

The section of the nation that changed the least in the 1830's was the South. This period saw a steady rise in demand for cotton in both the Northeast and in England. As cotton was planted in the extremely fertile soil of Mississippi and Alabama, production rose.

Cotton was such an important crop in the South that it was called "King Cotton." This picture shows slaves picking cotton.

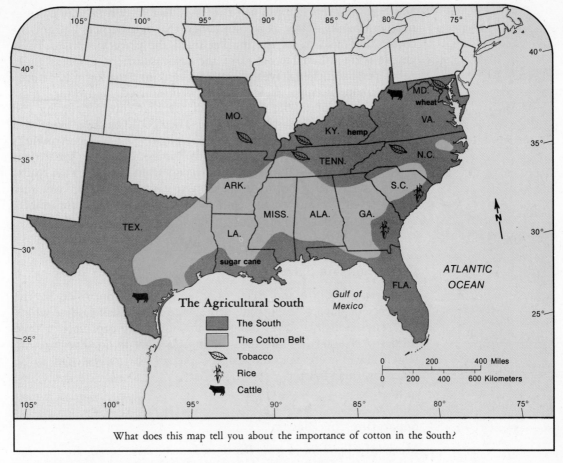

The Agricultural South

- The South
- The Cotton Belt
- Tobacco
- Rice
- Cattle

MD. wheat
VA.
KY. hemp
TENN.
N.C.
S.C.
GA.
MISS.
ALA.
LA.
sugar cane
TEX.
ARK.
MO.
FLA.
Gulf of Mexico
ATLANTIC OCEAN

What does this map tell you about the importance of cotton in the South?

The map shows how much of the land in the South was actually involved in cotton production.

The value of slaves grew with the value of cotton. Thus the subject of slavery was discussed in terms of money rather than in moral terms. By 1850 the price of a strong field hand had tripled to about $1,500.

The Southern Economy

Slave-trading within the United States became big business as owners in the upper South sold slaves to people in the states who could afford to pay the highest prices. As slaves became more expensive, the slave traders also rented slaves to people who needed extra help at harvest time. But the smaller farmers found themselves priced out of the slave market. By 1850 only 250 people owned 200 or more slaves. It was not efficient to use slaves on small farms. The small farmers grew food crops, and if they had a few slaves they worked with them in the fields.

1) The value of slaves rose as the value of cotton rose. 2) Owners in the upper South sold slaves to those who could afford to pay the highest prices. 3) Owners also rented slaves to small farmers who needed extra help at harvest time.

The slave, or cotton, system was the life-style of the most powerful southerners. Could anyone have changed it?

351

28. Why were the southern planters dependent upon the northerners?

1) Southerners were doing so well planting and producing cotton that they left banking, marketing, manufacturing, and the development of transportation to the North.

Southern planters complained that they had to borrow money from northern banks. They also complained that northerners bought the cotton and held it off the market until the price went up. These people were called factors. But the same southern planters could never persuade themselves to go into banking, marketing, or even textile manufacture. A few mills were started. However, most southerners kept to the same way of life that cotton growing and slavery had made possible for them. They could make a great deal of money by raising cotton. (See map, page 351.) It was America's biggest and most profitable export to Europe. Also, the great river system of the Mississippi kept southerners from noticing that roads, canals, and finally railroads were more flexible ways of reaching new parts of the nation. Success made life in the South comfortable. All other decisions were related to it.

Restrictions on Slaves

29. What restrictions were placed on the Blacks?

1) Slaves could not make contracts or own property. 2) Free Blacks in southern cities were totally segregated from Whites. 3) But churches were separated because Blacks preferred it that way. Churches were centers for most independent Black thought, activities, and leadership.

The lives of White and Black southerners were controlled by the existence of slavery. Each state had laws, called Black Codes, which put restrictions on slaves. They could not make contracts or own property. These rules also told the master what to do. Every action which slaves were not allowed to take for themselves had to be taken by their master.

Separating the Blacks

Much of city life in the South was also structured around the relationship of Whites and Blacks. The free Blacks who lived in the cities created more and more problems for the Whites. Their presence made slavery more obvious as a set of rules and regulations. Also, White people in the cities were embarrassed at not being able to tell the slaves from the free Blacks.

To solve these problems the White population made rule after rule separating all Blacks from all Whites in public places. Blacks had to sit in separate sections in theaters, attend separate schools, and use separate hospitals, jails, and poorhouses. They had to pay for their own schools. Blacks were not allowed in gardens and public parks, unless they had a card identifying them as nursemaids to White children. They had to live in housing that was separated, or *segregated,* by blocks rather than by whole sections of town. This was because the trading area with the cotton exchange and the shops formed the center of southern towns. The wealthiest and oldest White families tended to live near that center. Free Blacks had to find their housing on the outside edge of wherever the Whites lived at the time.

Explain in your own words how segregation happened in the cities.

EDUCATION FOR THE DEAF

Before 1817 no free schools for the deaf existed in America. In that year the first such school was established in Hartford, Connecticut, by Thomas Hopkins Gallaudet.

Born in Philadelphia in 1787, Gallaudet moved with his family to Hartford when he was 13. He attended Yale College, and somewhat later, Andover Theological Seminary. But when ill health prevented him from becoming a minister, Gallaudet turned his energies in another direction. He met a deaf child named Alice Cogswell, and tried to teach her the names of various objects. Gallaudet had read articles on the education of the deaf. He persuaded Alice's father to get her a regular teacher. Mr. Cogswell was so impressed with Gallaudet's interest and concern with the problems of educating deaf people that he and a group of friends raised money to send Gallaudet to Europe so that he could study the methods used in schools there.

Gallaudet spent several months studying at a special school for deaf mutes in Paris. He returned to America in 1816 with a Frenchman named Laurent Clerc (CLERK), who was a teacher at the school in Paris. Together the two men were able to raise enough money to found their own school for deaf children. Gallaudet served as principal of this school until 1830. During this time he trained many people who later became heads of other schools for the deaf.

Sophia Fowler, one of Gallaudet's first pupils at the school, became his wife shortly after she graduated. Their two sons, Thomas and Amos, shared their parents' concern for the deaf. Thomas became a well-known minister to the deaf, and Amos set up a school for the deaf in Washington, D.C. Eventually this school became Gallaudet College, named in honor of Amos' father. On the grounds of the college stands a monument to Thomas Gallaudet, erected by the deaf people of the United States in memory of his work for them.

Although best known for his role in the education of the deaf, Gallaudet also supported education for Blacks and for women. He died in 1851.

Slavery in the cities was weaker because the free Blacks were concentrated there. Segregation by color became the way the southern Whites could preserve their society.

Only the churches were separated because the Blacks wanted it that way. The masters often preferred to have the slaves go to church with the masters' families on Sunday and sit in a separate part of the church. But as the southern cities grew, free Blacks had their

RAFFLE

Mr. Joseph Jennings respectfully informs his friends and the public that, at the request of many acquaintances, he has been induced to purchase from Mr. Osborne, of Missouri, the celebrated

DARK BAY HORSE, "STAR,"

Aged five years, square trotter and warranted sound; with a new light Trotting Buggy and Harness; also, the dark, about

MULATTO GIRL, "SARAH,"

Aged about twenty years, general house servant, valued at *nine hundred dollars*, and guaranteed, and

Will be Raffled for

At 4 o'clock P. M., February first, at the selection hotel of the subscribers. The above is as represented, and those persons who may wish to engage in the usual practice of raffling, will, I assure them, be perfectly satisfied with their destiny in this affair.
The whole is valued at its just worth, fifteen hundred dollars; fifteen hundred

CHANCES AT ONE DOLLAR EACH.

The Raffle will be conducted by gentlemen selected by the interested subscribers present. Five nights will be allowed to complete the Raffle. BOTH OF THE ABOVE DESCRIBED CAN BE SEEN AT MY STORE, No. 78 Common St., second c or from Camp, at from 9 o'clock A. M. to 3 P. M. Highest throw to take the first choice; the lowest throw the remaining prize, and the fortunate winners will pay twenty dollars each for the s'vubments furnished on the occasion.
N. B. No chances recognized unless paid f r previous to the commencement.

JOSEPH JENNINGS.

This poster advertises items to be raffled: a horse and a slave. What does this tell you about slavery?

own congregations. And city slaves preferred them. In this way the churches became the one self-segregated part of the lives of southern Blacks. They were the center of most independent Black thought, activities, and leadership.

Regional Growth

Southern cities were simply trading centers until the movement west and the war for the Mexican territory gave the South a goal for expansion. Then southern cities grew as the movement of cotton and slavery westward caused a great increase in trade. Southern investment in railroads was also a major part of this development.

The regional growth of the United States from the election of Martin Van Buren in 1836 to 1850 was made up of a great burst of individualism and capital investment. Those who could acquire capital to buy land, invest in factories, or in the development of cities and railroads prospered. Americans wanted to move farther and build faster than any other country. They wanted more. A great many people achieved this goal. Part of the reason why capital investments were so successful was the availability of a vast supply of cheap labor. First came women and children from the farms, then whole families of Irish and German immigrants, and a growing number of Black slaves. Americans knew there were problems, and some tried to get at the causes of these problems. But, on the whole, most of the immigrants who came to America during these years did not turn back. There still seemed to be more opportunity in America.

The nation developed regionally. As regions became wealthier, they became more specialized and more dependent on one another. The middle western cities were similar to the cities of the East, but the South remained different. All of the regions were caught up in the exciting news that came from Texas.

Checking the facts

1. How was the South different from the other regions at mid-century?
2. What was life like for Blacks in the South at mid-century?
3. Why was cotton so important for the growth of the economy of the South?

Make a chart or diagram that summarizes regional growth. Notice how all the events interconnect.

PUTTING IT ALL TOGETHER

UNDERSTANDING THE MAIN IDEAS

1. In what ways did the American system expand to take in so much new land and so many new people?
2. How did people learn to live in the new cities?
3. What happened to Blacks and women in this period?

ACTIVITIES

1. Choose one industry (not a company) in your area and trace its beginnings. Who was its founder? Why did it start in your area? Was there any competition? If so, when did it begin? How many people are employed? Did it grow steadily or suddenly? Why? For this activity, you may want to ask your teacher's help in contacting someone from the industry. You could start by writing a letter of introduction in which you state your purpose. Many industries provide brochures with the kind of information you are looking for.
2. With a classmate, find out about the history of any one public service in your area. This could be the police or fire department, the library, or the hospital. Include your findings in a short written report. You can probably locate this information in your nearest library.
3. What is the history of settlers and neighborhoods in your town or city? Which group of settlers came first? Were the neighborhoods settled by any one ethnic group? Were they affected by employment? by size of house and property? Write a neighborhood history and illustrate it with a timeline.
4. Interview an older person in your community. This could be a grandparent, neighbor, or family friend. What does he or she remember about changes in the neighborhood? Before you start your interview, prepare a list of questions you want answered. Be sure to introduce yourself and state your purpose before you ask your questions.

BOOKS TO READ

Bontemps, Arna, *Frederick Douglass: Slave, Fighter, Freeman* (New York: Alfred A Knopf, Inc., 1974).

Douglass, Frederick, *Life and Times of Frederick Douglass*, Barbara Ritchie, editor (New York: Thomas Y. Crowell, 1966).

Faber, Doris, *Oh Lizzie: The Life of Elizabeth Cady Stanton* (Wooster, Ohio: Lathrop Publishers, 1972).

Kromer, Helen, *The Amistad Revolt, 1839: The Slave Uprising Aboard the Spanish Schooner* (New York: Watts Publishing Co., 1973).

Tamarin, Alfred, *Voyaging to Cathay: Americans in the China Trade* (New York: Viking Press, 1976).

chapter 14
Many Cultures—One Destiny

1836–1850

1. SPAIN, NEW MEXICO, AND TEXAS
2. APPEALING TO THE PUBLIC

INTRODUCTION

The continent of North America in 1836 contained many ways of living. Within the English-American culture of the United States were regional differences based on geography, technology, and economic growth. In addition, there were the minority cultures of new European immigrants, Black slaves, and a small number of Native Americans. West of the United States were Native American and Spanish-Mexican cultures which had developed separately. Events in Mexico in the 1820's and 1830's had a great impact on all the others, east and west. The Spanish-Mexican development had followed the pattern of tight government control and government support of the Roman Catholic church. The Spanish pattern had come to the New World with Columbus and Cortés, and its values had not changed. The English-American pattern was very different. Americans had a tradition of representative government. They also allowed people of different religions to worship as they pleased. The colonies of both England and Spain had grown up in

	1836	1837	1838	1841	
Who?	William B. Travis and Davy Crockett	During Van Buren's Presidency	Frederick Douglass	John Tyler	
What?	are killed in an attack by Santa Anna	the first depression closes banks	escapes from slavery and	becomes President when William Henry Harrison dies	
Where?	at the Alamo, San Antonio, Texas	in Philadelphia and New York	lectures for the Anti-Slavery Society in Massachusetts	in Washington, D.C.	

the traditions of government, family, and religion of the home countries. And when these two very different cultures met 300 years later, there was trouble. As you read about the period from 1836 to 1850 in the West think about these questions.

1. In what form did the American cultures arrive in the West?
2. What was the form of the Spanish-Mexican culture?
3. What were the results of the meeting of the two cultures for the Americans, the Mexicans, and for the Native Americans of the Southwest?

1. SPAIN, NEW MEXICO, AND TEXAS

What was life like for Spanish Americans? It was as much like life in Spain as possible, with change permitted only when necessary. In Spanish America the king's stand-in was the viceroy, and viceroys were changed often to keep the soldiers and the priests loyal to the king in Spain.

The Northern Provinces

In the 300 years of Spanish rule, the pattern had stayed the same. The purpose of the colonies was still mining gold and silver. The land to the north of those mines—the provinces of New Mexico, Texas, and California—was looked upon by the Spanish government as a *buffer,* or protection against invasion of the mining area. In the northern provinces the Spanish soldiers built forts or presidios, priests established missions, and a few civilians made their homes. The soldiers and civilians were encouraged by the priests to settle down and marry Native Americans from peaceful tribes. Some settlements gave an extra margin of safety from hostile Apache and

1. Why were the northern provinces established as a buffer zone?

1) The buffer zone protected the Spanish mines against invasion. 2) Some settlements and *presidios* gave an extra margin of safety from the Indians and the Russians.

1842	1843	1845	1846	1849
Secretary of State Daniel Webster	First wagon trains of settlers	John L. O'Sullivan	Americans	The 49ers
concludes Webster Ashburton Treaty	leave St. Louis, Missouri	introduces the term "manifest destiny"	overthrow the Mexican government	seek gold
settling boundary disputes between Canada and the U.S.	for Oregon	in regard to Texas	in California	in California

357

Father Junipero Serra founded many missions in California. This one is the mission of San Carlos Borromeo in Carmel.

2. Why were there few people in the northern provinces?

1) Farming was necessary to keep the village and its mission alive, but much of the land suffered from lack of water. 2) Spain did little to settle its colonies in North America. It had no policy of letting discontented people leave Spain and settle elsewhere.

Comanche Plains Indians to the north and the Russians, who had an eye on the land south of their territory in Alaska. The whole area, however, was sparsely populated.

The Spanish taught the Native Americans their language, the Catholic religion, and agriculture. No private property was allowed, however. The mission priest was like the head of the family—representing both the king and the pope. The mission and its surrounding village established Spanish-style life which was closely tied to family and to the church. Farming was necessary to keep the village and its mission alive. The villages were far too distant from the main provinces of Mexico to receive supplies or food. The population of about 25,000 was spread over large areas of land. And much of the land of New Mexico, West Texas, and California suffered from lack of water.

Spain did little to settle its colonies in North America. The Spanish had no policy such as the English had of letting discontented people leave the country and settle elsewhere. They insisted on absolute loyalty and control. Thus by the early 1800's, there were not enough permanent residents to ward off any attack by a strong army of French or Americans. But after the Louisiana Purchase of 1803, the French were out of the picture, and the Spanish did not worry too much about the United States.

Recall any differences between the Spanish west and the English east.

The Spaniards and their Native American friends in New Mexico did come into contact with American explorers and the mountain men or fur trappers from up north. Zebulon Pike, who had explored Colorado, was one of them. (See map, page 268.) The Spanish were not very happy about the arrival of non-Spaniards. Trade with them was strictly forbidden.

A New Nation With New Policies

In 1821, just one year after the United States had made its North-South compromise about Missouri, the Spanish province of Mexico staged a successful revolution against the Spanish government. An independent nation of Mexico was established. The new nation changed the policies regarding the lands of the northern provinces.

Mexico welcomed settlers from the southern United States. They called these settlers "Anglos." Many nationalities were represented in the United States, but to the Spanish-Americans in Mexico, the way of life of Americans was English, or "Anglo."

In 1821 a large land grant was given to the family of Moses Austin by the governor of Texas. Texas was now a province of the new nation of Mexico. The government of Mexico knew that the northern provinces had always needed more settlers. There was good farm land in east Texas, near Mississippi. Settlement by Anglos would protect the Mexican population to the south from unfriendly Native Americans.

The Mexican government also allowed American traders and trappers to come to Mexican territory. Almost immediately wagon trains began to leave from Missouri. The first group was led by William Becknell. He and his party traveled across the plains and the Cimarron Desert and came to Santa Fe, the capital of New Mexico. The route they followed became known as the Santa Fe Trail.

The town of Santa Fe was not large. It had only 3,000 inhabitants. But it was the main trading center for the 40,000 people who lived in the province of New Mexico. These people were delighted with the opportunity to trade gold, silver, and furs for the manufactured goods of the United States, particularly, cotton cloth, tools, and knives.

In the meantime more American settlers came into Texas. By 1830 there were 20,000 Anglos in Texas. They had brought about 2,000 slaves with them. Because the land was ideal for growing cotton, Southerners moved west, just as northerners had feared they would.

3. What encouraged the Americans to move into Mexico's northernmost provinces?

1) Mexico had become independent after a successful revolution against the Spanish government. 2) Mexico welcomed settlers from the southern United States. 3) Mexico encouraged American traders and trappers who could trade American manufactured goods for gold, silver, and furs. 4) The land was ideal for growing cotton.

Stephen Austin carried out his father's plans to colonize Texas. Why did he want to separate Texas from Mexico?

Conflict in Texas

4. What were the sources of conflict between the Anglos and the Mexicans in Texas?

1) The Anglos saw no reason to change their culture or to learn the Spanish language. 2) Mexican law said that immigrants had to be Catholic, but most Anglos were Protestant. 3) The Mexicans passed a law against slavery. The Anglos freed their slaves, but then signed them to lifetime contracts as indentured servants.

Soon, serious problems existed between the Anglos and the Spanish in Texas. The Anglos brought their own culture with them and expected to keep it. In the United States, people expected regions— and even groups within regions—to be different. But this was not the Spanish way, or the Mexican way. The Mexicans expected the Anglos to be Roman Catholic. In fact, Mexican law said that all immigrants had to be Catholic. Anglos did not understand this. Throughout the history of the United States, people of different religions had existed side by side. Also, most of the Anglos were Protestant.

The Anglos did not speak Spanish and showed no interest in giving up their culture for the Spanish-Mexican one. The Mexican government did not like slavery and passed a law against it. The Anglos freed their slaves, but then signed Blacks up for lifetime contracts as indentured servants. After ten years of conflict between the two cultures, the Mexicans decided to change their policy toward settlers by discouraging new immigrants.

New Restrictions

5. How did the Mexican government attempt to get control of Texas?

1) It announced that no new immigrants could enter Texas. 2) It tried to enforce restrictions on Anglos already living there.

In 1830 the Mexican government cancelled its earlier policy and announced that no new immigrants could enter Texas. The Mexicans also tried to enforce restrictions on the Anglos already living in Texas. But it was too late. The Texans from the American South had no intention of obeying the laws of the Mexican government. Armed fights broke out between the Mexican authorities and the Anglos whenever they happened to meet in that huge and almost empty land.

Americans in California

6. Why did Josiah Gregg take 100 wagons of cargo on a 10-week trip to California?

Settlers were moving there and he could make a big profit on his goods.

Meanwhile, several hundred Americans began to move into California. The trade on the Santa Fe Trail grew. In 1831 Josiah Gregg took 100 wagons with cargo worth $200,000. According to Gregg, the people in his caravan included "men from every class and grade of society, with a little sprinkling of the softer sex." Each type of traveler dressed differently:

> "The most fashionable prairie dress is the frock [coat] of the city-bred merchant furnished with a multitude of pockets. . . .Then there is the backwoodsman with his wool or leather hunting shirt—the farmer with his blue jean coat—the wagoner with his flannel sleeve vest—beside an assortment of other costumes that go to fill up the picture."

The Alamo is at the junction of the territory claimed by Texas and the Republic of Texas. It is about 100 miles (160 kilometers) from the Nueces River. It is 155 miles (248 kilometers) from the Gulf of Mexico.

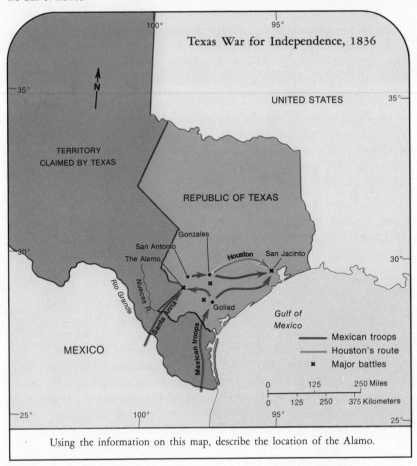

Texas War for Independence, 1836

UNITED STATES

TERRITORY CLAIMED BY TEXAS

REPUBLIC OF TEXAS

Gonzales

San Antonio

The Alamo

Houston

San Jacinto

Rio Grande

Nueces R.

Santa Anna

Goliad

Mexican troops

Gulf of Mexico

MEXICO

——— Mexican troops
——— Houston's route
✕ Major battles

0   125   250 Miles
0   125   250   375 Kilometers

Using the information on this map, describe the location of the Alamo.

Why did the fighting occur where it did?

Each type of traveler also carried a different kind of gun. Guns were necessary to protect against attacks by the Pawnee and Comanche Indians. The trip on the Santa Fe Trail was dangerous and long. The one-way trip took ten weeks. But it was considered well worth it. (See map, page 367.)

War for Independence

A few years after Gregg and his party went to California, trouble between the Anglos and Mexicans in Texas came to a head. The Anglos would not act as the Mexicans wished. And they angered the Mexicans by demanding the self-government and civil rights that their English-American heritage had taught them to expect. (See map, above.)

In 1834 General Antonio Lopez de Santa Anna declared himself president and put Mexico under military rule. That was the final blow to the Americans. A year later fighting broke out between

7. *Why did Santa Anna bring an army into Texas?*

The Anglos angered the Mexicans by demanding self-government and civil rights. General Santa Anna declared himself president and put Mexico under military rule.

361

the Anglos and the Mexican officials in Texas. Americans from across the border came in to help the settlers fight. In 1836, Santa Anna marched an army of 6,000 north to fight the Anglo settlers. The Mexicans considered the Anglos rebels, but after 15 years of living in Texas, the Anglos considered themselves Americans and free settlers of Texas.

8. What was the importance of the Alamo?

1) One hundred eighty-seven Americans held out against the 6,000 Mexicans for two weeks. 2) After the massacre, the Americans knew that no peaceable settlement could be expected. 3) The battle became a rallying cry for the Texans.

Santa Anna moved into the city of San Antonio in February 1836. There he found a small group of 187 Americans under the command of Colonel William Barret Travis. Travis and his men refused to surrender and held out bravely for almost two weeks in an old Spanish mission called the Alamo.

On March 2, 1836, the Texan Anglos declared their independence from Mexico. Their leader was Sam Houston, who had been a congressman, governor of Tennessee, and an Indian fighter. But Houston and his men were unable to save the Alamo. Colonel Travis sent a message to Houston on March 3, 1836:

> "The power of Santa Anna is to be met here or in the settlements; we had better meet them here, than to suffer a war of desolation to rage in our settlements. . . .Their threats have had no influence on me or my men, but to make all fight with desperation, and that high-souled courage which characterizes the patriot who is willing to die in defense of his country's liberty and his own honor. . . . The bearer of this will give your honor . . . . a statement more in detail should he escape through the enemy's lines. God and Texas!— Victory or Death!"

This painting shows the fighting at the Alamo. Davy Crockett is using his rifle as a club. Why did "Remember the Alamo" become a rallying cry for the Texans?

Three days later the Mexicans attacked. The Texans were totally outnumbered but Santa Anna refused to spare their lives. Every defender of the Alamo was killed, including the famous Indian fighter Davy Crockett of Tennessee and Jim Bowie, the inventor of the Bowie knife. The bodies of the Texans were burned. Now the rest of the Texans led by Sam Houston were ready to fight on under the battle cry, "Remember the Alamo!"

Even some Mexicans thought Santa Anna had gone too far. One of his soldiers, writing about the battle some 13 years later, said:

> "In our opinion the blood of our soldiers as well as that of the enemy was shed in vain. . . . what could the wretches do, being surrounded by 5,000 men, without proper means of resisting, no possibility of retreating. . . . The massacre of the Alamo convinced the rebels that no peaceable settlement could be expected, and that they must conquer, or die, or abandon the fruits of ten years of sweat and labor, together with their fondest hopes for the future."

Susana Dickinson was a survivor of the battle at the Alamo. She nursed the wounded during the fighting. Later she wrote about what had happened.

Sam Houston agreed. He first retreated with his army until he found a place where he could make a stand. Then on April 21, 1836, his army attacked the Mexican army at the San Jacinto River. They were victorious, and the Mexicans were driven out of Texas. In October, Sam Houston was elected President of the Republic of Texas.

One month later the Texans, using their Anglo practice of voting under majority rule, voted to join or be *annexed* to the United States. But President Andrew Jackson was afraid that such action would involve the United States in a war with Mexico. He and others also feared that the North-South compromise over western land would come apart if Texas were admitted to the Union. Jackson on his last day as President finally recognized Texas as a new foreign nation.

Jackson's successor, Martin Van Buren, took no action on annexation, either. The Lone Star flag flew over Texas for nine years. During this time, the Republic of Texas established its own cotton trade with England.

The United States government and the three major sections of the nation looked at Texas with mixed feeling. They were happy about the chance to expand but also feared that, as Jefferson had warned, the slavery issue would tear Americans apart. The "fire bell in the night" was about to ring again.

9. Why did the Lone Star flag fly over Texas for nine years?

Although Texas had voted to be annexed to the United States, Jackson and his successor took no action, fearing both a war with Mexico and sectional conflict over the slavery issue.

1. What changes did the independent Mexican government bring about?
2. What circumstances led up to the battle of the Alamo?
3. Why was there a delay in annexing Texas?

2. APPEALING TO THE PUBLIC

Jackson and Van Buren did not try to bring Texas into the Union because they knew that the North and South were divided on the question of annexation. Texas was cotton country. The North did not want another slave state, while the South did. Representatives to Congress from Texas would vote with the South on tariffs, banks, roads, and canals. The Democrats, under the leadership of Jackson and Van Buren, were trying to be a national party. And so were their opponents, the Whigs. They had learned from Jackson that in order to win elections, a party had to represent every area of the nation. And they knew that no matter what stand they took on Texas, they would lose the votes of one of the sections.

The Campaign and Election of 1840

10. How did the Whigs win the election of 1840?

1) They nominated Harrison, the hero of the War of 1812.
2) They falsely advertised Harrison as a "common man," born in a log cabin, and a tough frontier fighter who drank hard cider.
3) They made sure Harrison said nothing about the difficult issues of the day.
4) They chose John Tyler, who supported the states' rights position, to balance the ticket.

The Whigs copied Jackson's style, wherever possible. They chose their party name so that it would remind Americans of the Whigs, or the patriots who ran the American Revolution. They hoped that Van Buren would remind the voters of the Tories, or people who had sympathized with the English. They found a military hero for a candidate, called him a man of the people, and made sure he did not say anything about the difficult issues of the day.

The Whigs chose William Henry Harrison, the general who had fought the Native Americans at the Battle of Tippecanoe just before the War of 1812. They did not choose Henry Clay, who had hoped for their nomination. Clay was heartbroken, angry, and felt betrayed. As for Harrison, he was old and had done very little for the nation since the war. And he was not a "common man." He lived in a beautiful white mansion in Ohio, which he called "The Log Cabin" in memory of a cabin that had once stood on that property. But the Whigs knew how to sell Harrison to the people. They knew that he was more appealing than Henry Clay and his complicated solutions to problems.

The Whig party told the public that Harrison had been born in a log cabin and was a tough frontiersman who drank hard cider.

How can a political party and its candidate win without pretending that every problem can be easily solved?

For his part, Harrison followed the instructions of his campaign manager, Nicholas Biddle, who hated Jackson and Van Buren because of the bank fight. Biddle reportedly said, "Let no committee, no convention, no town meeting ever get from Harrison a single word about what he thinks now, or what he will do hereafter." And Harrison was superb at keeping quiet.

The Whigs ran a noisy, active campaign filled with attention-getting stunts. In some cities they built 40-foot (12-meter) log cabins, where they gave away hard cider. They rolled a huge paper ball from city to city and took it to Washington, chanting, "As rolls the ball Van's reign doth fall."

Their campaign slogan was "Tippecanoe and Tyler, too." John Tyler, the Whigs' vice-presidential candidate, was a Virginian, who supported the states' rights position. Tyler believed states came before the federal government. The Whigs had chosen him to "balance the ticket." Tyler could get votes from the old Southeast but would be relatively harmless. The Whig strategy worked. They won by a huge margin.

John Tyler—President by Mistake

But something totally unexpected happened to the Whig's grand plan. Harrison had been President for only four weeks when he went out in an early morning rain, caught a cold—and died! In April 1841 John Tyler became President of the United States. He was the first person to become President in this way.

11. Why were Tyler's four years in office marked by no action?

1) He was in disagreement with both parties. 2) Every member of his Cabinet resigned except Daniel Webster, the secretary of state. 3) Tyler couldn't get the sections of the nation to agree, so no important or lasting laws were passed.

The ball shown here was part of William Henry Harrison's campaign for the presidency. How do candidates gain attention today?

Settlements between nations happen when negotiators are skilled enough to focus on areas of agreement without causing embarrassment to either side.

Tyler's four years in office found him in disagreement with both parties. He was against the national bank that the Whigs wanted. He vetoed his own party's bill. Every member of his Cabinet resigned—except Daniel Webster, the secretary of state. Besides the bank, tariff and land sales were still issues. Since the sections of the nation could not agree, no important or lasting laws were passed.

Settling the Northern Boundary

12. What circumstances led to the treaty with Great Britain?

1) Americans and Canadians were in conflict in the Maine area over timber. 2) The Americans were doing little to stop illegal slave ships, so the British began stopping and searching American ships out of the British West Indies.

The only major achievement of Tyler's unhappy administration was a treaty with Great Britain over the boundary between Maine and Canada. The Canadians had cut timber in what the residents of Aristook County, Maine, believed was United States territory. As a result, the Americans and Canadians in that northern area had been on the verge of war for four years.

In addition, relations between the United States and the British were strained over the slave trade. Both the British and the Americans had outlawed the slave trade, but in 1833 the British had also freed all the slaves in their portion of the West Indies. But while the American government did little to stop the illegal slave ships that continued to arrive, the British took their antislavery position seriously. They began to stop and search American ships. There was increasing trouble.

Finally, in 1842 the British had a new prime minister, Sir Robert Peel, who wanted to settle differences with the Americans peacefully. Lord Ashburton was made minister to the United States. He was a British banker whose company had invested a great deal of capital in the United States.

13. What were the results of the Webster-Ashburton treaty?

1) A peaceful border was established from the Great Lakes to Lake of the Woods, Minnesota. 2) The United States received 6,500 square miles of disputed territory rich in iron ore. 3) The British continued to buy American products and invest in American business and transportation.

Webster and Ashburton not only settled the Maine border but also arranged for a peaceful border all the way from the Great Lakes to Lake of the Woods, Minnesota. This was a great achievement. Trouble between the two nations was avoided. The United States received 6,500 square miles (16,900 square kilometers) of disputed territory—land that later became famous for its iron ore. The Webster-Ashburton Treaty was ratified by the Senate in August 1842. Afterwards, the British continued to buy American food products and invest in American business and transportation.

Tyler and Texas

14. Why was the treaty to annex Texas defeated?

1) Both parties claimed that annexing Texas would bring war with Mexico. 2) Tyler

As a southerner, Tyler was anxious to annex Texas to the United States. When Webster, the New Englander, resigned as secretary of state in 1843, Tyler appointed a fellow Virginian, Abel Upshur, to negotiate a treaty of annexation that would be ratified by the Senate. When Upshur died suddenly, Tyler made John C. Calhoun

Indicate, on the map, the region where the question of slavery was settled.

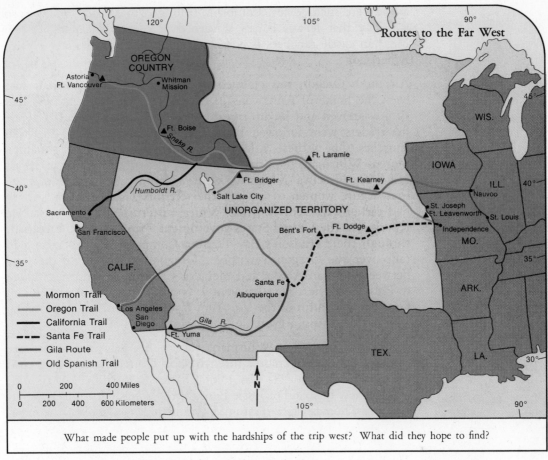

Routes to the Far West

OREGON COUNTRY

Astoria
Ft. Vancouver
Whitman Mission
Ft. Boise
Snake R.
Humboldt R.
Ft. Bridger
Salt Lake City
Sacramento
San Francisco
CALIF.
Los Angeles
San Diego
Ft. Yuma
Gila R.
Albuquerque
Santa Fe
Bent's Fort
Ft. Dodge
Ft. Laramie
Ft. Kearney
St. Joseph
Ft. Leavenworth
Independence
St. Louis
Nauvoo
Salt Lake City

WIS.
IOWA
ILL.
MO.
ARK.
TEX.
LA.

UNORGANIZED TERRITORY

Mormon Trail
Oregon Trail
California Trail
Santa Fe Trail
Gila Route
Old Spanish Trail

0   200   400 Miles
0   200   400   600 Kilometers

N

120°   105°   90°
45°   45°
40°   40°
35°   35°
                        30°
105°   90°

What made people put up with the hardships of the trip west? What did they hope to find?

Answers will vary. They may include gold, land, trade, furs, or adventure.

secretary of state. This was too much for the senators from the North and West. Calhoun represented the slaveowning South to them. They did not trust him. As the presidential election of 1844 approached, both major parties came out against the treaty to annex Texas. They said it would probably cause a war with Mexico. When the treaty was voted down, 35 to 16, the Texans were angry and embarrassed. But the British were delighted. Their cotton trade with Texas could continue, without any questions about high tariffs on their manufactured goods. The British could hardly believe the Americans were so divided among themselves that they would miss such an opportunity for expansion. But sections were thinking of themselves first and were afraid to lose representation in Congress. Was there any national pride and excitement left?

California and Oregon

There was national pride and excitement, but it concerned places where slavery was not a question. California and Oregon in the Far

appointed Calhoun, a southerner, secretary of state, and neither the North or West trusted him.
3) Americans still couldn't agree on the slavery issue.

15. Why were the British so delighted with the results?

They could continue to buy cotton from Texas without paying the high American tariffs.

16. How did Americans become interested in the Oregon Territory?

1) In 1842 Marcus Whitman returned from there and reported a rumor that the British, through their Hudson's Bay Trading Company, were planning to take over the Oregon Territory. 2) In New York, Whitman published articles about Oregon, causing a great deal of excitement. 3) Charles and Jesse Frémont wrote a popular book about their explorations of the major mountain passes of the Rockies.

West were such places. California belonged to Mexico, but was so far away that it was hardly governed or controlled at all. A few Mexican cattle ranchers lived there, along with priests and Native Americans.

Although Oregon was claimed by the British in Canada, it had been the home of Americans in the fur-trading business who had simply arrived and set up communities (See map, page 371.) The fur traders were followed by missionaries from several Christian churches. One of these, a doctor and Congregational minister named Marcus Whitman, took the first wagon across the Rockies in 1836. His wife, Narcissa Whitman, went with him. She was one of the first White women to go into the territory that Lewis and Clark had earlier explored. In 1842 Whitman returned to the East. He reported to the United States government a rumor that the British, through their Hudson's Bay Trading Company, were planning to take over the Oregon Territory. "Oregon" meant all of the land between Russian Alaska and Mexican California. Whitman talked to President Tyler. He then went to New York and spoke to Horace Greeley, the editor of the *New York Tribune.* Articles about Oregon appeared, causing a great deal of excitement.

About the time that Whitman was on his way east across the Rockies, a young explorer hired by the United States Army had set out to go west. He was John Charles Frémont, 29 years old, and the new husband of Jessie Benton, the daughter of the Missouri senator, Thomas Hart Benton. Frémont had the help of the expe-

The Whitman mission in Washington became a stopping-off point on the Oregon Trail. The Whitmans trained Native Americans in agriculture.

How important were the Whitmans to the settling of the Oregon Country?

Follow the Oregon Trail on the map on page 367. Notice the geographical reasons why this was the route west.

rienced scout, Kit Carson. They explored and recorded the major mountain passes of the Rockies. When Frémont returned home, he and Jessie wrote a book about his trip. Like the articles about Oregon, it was enormously popular. Both Whitman and Frémont had a great deal to do with the fact that the next year in 1843, some 1,000 pioneers headed west along the Oregon Trail (See map, page 367.)

The Oregon Trail began at the western border of Missouri—outside Independence, where the Santa Fe Trail also began. The trail to Oregon then followed the Kansas, Little Blue, and Platte rivers past Fort Laramie to the Rockies. The Platte River was hated by the travelers because it was muddy and seemed to be "six miles wide and six inches deep." The trail crossed the Continental Divide at South Pass, then turned south to Fort Bridger in Mexican Territory. From there the route ran north and west, following the Snake River Valley and the Columbia River to the British fort of Vancouver. The Oregon Trail brought settlers to the Willamette Valley, with its fertile soil for farming.

In Oregon, the American Fur Company actually hired several hundred trappers and traders, who worked the mountain area and traded with the Native Americans. The Indians met regularly with the Americans and traded furs for guns, ammunition, bear traps, blankets, and colorful scarves.

The Far West was appealing to both independent American farmers and those Americans who dreamed of foreign trade through its three great harbors—San Diego and San Francisco in California and Puget Sound in the Oregon Territory. The fact that these ports and the land around them were Mexican and British did not bother Americans. They saw their future extending from coast to coast. The only stumbling block was Texas, because the North and the Old Northwest did not want to lose voting power to the cotton and slave culture of the South.

The Election of 1844—Texas Again

The southern states gathered behind Calhoun's leadership and declared that the United States deserved Texas. Calhoun said it was backward of Congress not to let those Americans in the Republic of Texas add to America's wealth and strength. He forced the Democratic party to take a stand in favor of Texas.

The Democratic National Convention had a hard time finding a known candidate for President who had not already lost popularity over the issue of Texas. Finally, they chose an unknown, or as a last minute winner is called, a *dark horse* candidate—James K. Polk of Tennessee. The convention was held in Baltimore. The news

17. Why did the Oregon Trail follow so many river bends?

Rivers were natural passes through the Rockies.

18. Why was the Far West appealing to Americans?

The Far West had 1) fertile farmland; 2) fur-bearing animals to be trapped in the mountains or traded from the Native Americans; 3) three great harbors—San Diego, San Francisco, and Puget Sound—for future foreign trade.

19. How did the Texas statehood issue decide the election?

1) Calhoun forced the Democrats to take a stand in favor of annexing Texas. 2) The Whigs nominated Clay, who refused to take a position on the issue. 3) A group of Whigs who wanted a much stronger stand against slavery chose their own candidate. They took enough votes from Clay for him to lose the election.

Calhoun's stand on slavery kept him from having a national following on other issues.

that the Democrats had decided to push for expansion into both Texas and Oregon was flashed to Washington by the new magnetic telegraph, invented by Samuel F. B. Morse.

Since annexation of Texas was now a campaign issue, to come out against it would have meant sure political defeat. But Henry Clay, the Whig candidate, did not know how to explain his years of refusing to talk about Texas. Clay made a public statement that was neither for or against annexation. Another northern group which wanted a much stronger stand against slavery broke off from the Whigs and ran a separate, or third-party, candidate. They took enough votes from Clay in New York State for him to lose New York by 36 electoral votes. The Democrats and their candidate Polk won a close election, 141 to 134. The election of 1844 showed that the issues of slavery and expansion were a dangerous combination in politics.

Tyler asked Congress for a two-thirds vote to admit Texas to the Union. This was just three days before he left the White House.

This action deprived Polk of the glory that his election had really brought about. Texas became a state in December of 1845. But unlike the other states, which had not been separate nations to begin with, Texas kept the ownership of its public lands and paid off its own debts.

Oregon Brings Votes

20. Why did the British decide to settle with the United States at the 49th parallel?

1) The 49th parallel gave Britain more land than did the Americans' original demand for a border at 54°40'. 2) Americans said it was their "manifest destiny" to settle the whole continent, and by 1845 some 5,000 Americans had moved to Oregon. Britain knew it couldn't hold Oregon with only 750 British citizens living there.

During Polk's campaign for the presidency, one of his supporters coined the slogan "Fifty-four, forty or fight!" These numbers represented the latitude line of the Alaskan border, and the appeal to the voters was obvious. A vote for Polk meant that the United States was going to take the Canadian ports on the Pacific and the Oregon fur trade.

Once Polk was elected, he let the British who claimed that territory know that he would actually settle for half of the Oregon Territory. The border would be the 49th parallel.

At first, the British rejected the idea. Then Polk asked the Congress to insist on the whole area, instead of just the southern half. One Congressman picked up a popular phrase and said, "It is our manifest destiny to spread over this whole continent." That term "manifest destiny" meant that Americans had no choice but to settle everywhere and fill in the continent.

The British began to change their minds. They were startled by the number of American farmers pouring into the Willamette Valley. By 1845, 5,000 people had followed Marcus Whitman and John Frémont's advice. And in all that time, only 750 British

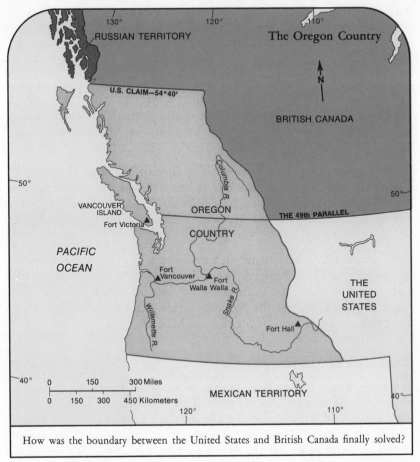

The Oregon Country

130° 120° 110°

RUSSIAN TERRITORY

BRITISH CANADA

U.S. CLAIM—54°40'

50°

VANCOUVER ISLAND

Fort Victoria

OREGON

COUNTRY

THE 49th PARALLEL

50°

PACIFIC OCEAN

Columbia R.

Fort Vancouver

Fort Walla Walla

Snake R.

THE UNITED STATES

Willamette R.

Fort Hall

40°

0   150   300 Miles
0   150   300   450 Kilometers

MEXICAN TERRITORY

40°

120° 110°

How was the boundary between the United States and British Canada finally solved?

A treaty divided the Oregon Country at the 49th parallel. The northern section was under British control, and the southern section was under United States' control.

citizens were living in Oregon north of the Columbia River. The British knew they could never hold on to all of Oregon, so they offered to settle with Polk on the 49th parallel. The treaty was ratified in June 1846. In the treaty, Vancouver Island was left to the British. Both nations kept the use of the Strait of Juan de Fuca, which was the connection from the Pacific Ocean to Puget Sound. The British were allowed to use the Columbia River. It was a very peaceful settlement, although some Americans would have preferred "Fifty-four, forty" and a good fight.

War Spirit—Mexico

President Polk was annoyed that Tyler had made the headlines by annexing Texas just two weeks before Polk's inauguration. But as President he had even greater plans. He wanted all of northern Mexico—especially California. He was willing to buy it, cause a revolution from within, or, if necessary, send out an army and take

21. What circumstances led to the Mexican War?

371

1) Polk wanted the rest of northern Mexico, especially California, for the United States. 2) General Zachary Taylor and 4,000 soldiers waited on the northern shore of the Rio Grande; Ambassador John Slidell went secretly to make a deal with Mexico. 3) The Mexican government was overthrown, and the new leaders would not negotiate with Slidell. 4) The Mexicans attacked, and Congress declared war on May 13, 1846.

it. Polk made two moves at once. He sent General Zachary Taylor and 4,000 soldiers to the northern shore of the Rio Grande River. He also sent an ambassador, John Slidell, on a secret mission to Mexico to try to make a deal with the Mexican government.

Slidell brought an offer. The United States would cancel the $2 million that Mexico owed Americans, if the Mexicans would recognize the annexation of Texas and accept the Rio Grande as the border between the two nations. In addition, the United States would pay $30 million for New Mexico and California.

Slidell's offer came at a bad time. The current Mexican government was being challenged in Mexico. When the word got out that the government was even talking to Slidell, there was a revolt and a new government. The new Mexican leaders would not negotiate at all.

Polk decided to resort to his other strategy. Taylor and his army, including the Texas Rangers, were lined up across the river. A war had to begin. The Mexicans made it easy by attacking first. For the American Congress the Mexican attack was all that was needed. Congress declared war on Mexico on May 13, 1846.

Planning the Mexican War

22. What problem did Polk have in planning his war strategy?

1) He needed a general from his own party, one who could win that large territory using as few troops as possible. 2) His two best generals were Whigs, who could become heroes to voters in the next presidential election.

Winning a few battles and taking most of northern Mexico were two different tasks. The Mexican Territory was huge, and there were few roads. How could the United States take the territory and use as few troops as possible? This required planning. The master planner or strategist for the Mexican War was the President him-

In 1843 many travelers headed for Oregon. The trip was difficult and dangerous. Why did people move west?

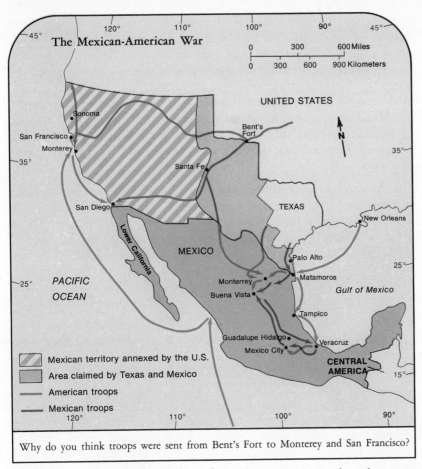

The Mexican-American War

Why do you think troops were sent from Bent's Fort to Monterey and San Francisco?

self. Polk knew every detail, from how many mules the army bought to which soldiers were promoted from corporal to sergeant.

Polk had a hard time, however, finding a good general who belonged to his Democratic party. Polk did not want to create a war hero for the opposition to run for the presidency in the next election. But he had no choice, for both of his generals were Whigs— Zachary Taylor and Winfield Scott. Taylor was loved by the soldiers in the army and was a good field commander. They called him "Old Rough and Ready." And Whig politicians came to him on the battlefield to tell him that they had great plans for his political future as soon as the war was won.

The American Strategy

Polk's plan for the war had three parts. (See map, above.) First, the Mexicans would have to be driven from Texas. Part of the army would attack central Mexico from the Gulf; another part would take California and New Mexico. This was Zachary Taylor's re-

23. Why were the Americans successful in part one of Polk's strategy?

Why does it help to know the strategy of the war and the politics at home?

1) They had an efficient supply system. 2) They had newer and better weapons.

sponsibility. He defeated the Mexicans in a battle at Resaca de la Palma, (re-SA-ka day lah PAL-ma) and then moved west across 500 miles (800 kilometers) of land that was almost desert. When the Americans reached the fortified town of Monterrey in Mexico, they attacked. In three days, after hand-to-hand fighting in the streets of the town, the Mexicans fell back. After the defeat at Monterrey, the Mexicans under Santa Anna raised a new army, 15,000 strong. In February of 1847 they met Taylor at a mountain pass near the village of Buena Vista (BWAY-nah VEES-tah). The battle lasted two days.

The Americans were able to win at Buena Vista because of their efficient supply system. In order to travel a long distance, Taylor's army had to have food, water, clothing, and ammunition. These supplies followed his army and were available when he needed them. The Americans also had new and better weapons—Colt revolving pistols and long-range howitzers or cannons. The Mexicans were still using smooth copper cannon balls that could be seen coming and could be dodged as they bounced across the battlefield.

24. What made part two of the plan work?

1) Californians aroused by Frémont staged a revolt. 2) The coast was attacked by Commodore John Sloat. 3) The army under General Stephen Kearney crossed the Rockies and took Santa Fe, going on to San Diego and Los Angeles.

Part two of Polk's plan was to conquer California. The year 1846 was the year that California fell. Polk had said he would take it by starting a revolution or by using the United States army or the navy. As it happened, the Americans did all three. American settlers in the Sacramento Valley, stirred up by John Frémont, staged a revolt. And a navy squadron under Commodore John Sloat captured Monterey in California, as well as San Francisco, and then moved south and attacked again. Another army under General Stephen Kearney crossed the Rockies from Fort Leavenworth and took Santa Fe. Kearney and some of his soldiers then went on to San Diego and Los Angeles to complete the conquest of those towns. In less than nine months, the United States had actually taken most of Mexico north of the capital city.

25. How did General Scott prove himself to be an excellent leader in part three of the plan?

1) Scott managed the first amphibious military operation in American history, landing at Vera Cruz. 2) He outmaneuvered the Mexicans waiting for them at the major roadway to the central plateau of Mexico, taking 3,000 prisoners and much equipment. 3) He knew how to wait for supplies and to keep his troops under control.

Part three of Polk's plan was an attack on the heart of Mexico, Mexico City. The Americans landed at Veracruz, a port on the Gulf of Mexico. This sea-and-land, or *amphibious,* operation was the first in American military history. The army that landed at Veracruz was under the leadership of General Winfield Scott. While Zachary Taylor was easygoing, Scott was precise and proper. The soldiers nicknamed him. "Old Fuss and Feathers." But Scott had trained the army well. And he planned the invasion of Mexico with very great care. The Americans took Veracruz, a city of 10,000, with very few American losses. Then Scott outmaneuvered the Mexicans waiting for the Americans at the major roadway to the central plateau of Mexico. The Americans took 3,000 prisoners and a great deal of equipment. Winfield Scott knew how to wait for supplies and how to keep his troops under control. He wanted no revenge upon the civilian population, and there was none.

In the battle for Mexico City, Scott's army lost 1,000 soldiers, compared to the Mexicans, who had 4,000 casualties and 3,000 taken prisoner. The Mexicans fought bravely and well. But Scott's army was managed in expert style. As Polk had feared, Scott was building a brilliant reputation for himself. On September 17, 1847, the Mexican forces under Santa Anna surrendered to Scott.

The Americans React to the War

The Mexican War was popular in the West. But the farther away one got from the frontier, the less people cared and the more they complained. This was especially true in the Northeast. The people who opposed the war were members of abolitionist groups. They believed that taking more southern territory was an invitation to more slavery. There was an organized peace movement, and some of the best-known writers of the period were part of it.

26. Why were some people opposed to the war?

Abolitionists believed that taking more southern territory was an invitation to more slavery.

The peace group offered a $500 prize for the best essay on the Mexican War issue. The most popular writing was done by James Russell Lowell, who wrote poetry and prose—supposedly the work of two characters, Hosea Biglow and Birdofredom Sawin, that he made up. Birdofredom wrote that "getting ninepunce a day for killin' folks comes kind o' low fer murder." And in the Biglow Papers, a popular poem read:

What was the importance of the peace group? What did they hope to achieve?

Kearney's army is shown passing through San Felipe, New Mexico. This army traveled from Fort Leavenworth, Kansas, to Santa Fe and on to San Diego in six months. Can you trace Kearney's journey on the map on page 373?

"Ez fer war, I call it murder—
There you hev it plain an' flat;
I don't want to go no furder
Than my Testyment fer that;
God hez sed so plump an' fairly,
It's ez long ez it is broad,
An' you've gut to git up airly
Ef you want to take in God."

Thoreau Speaks for the Individual

27. What basic question did Thoreau raise in American political thought?

What should a person do when he or she truly believes that the legal representatives of the majority are morally wrong?

The writer Henry David Thoreau did not join any of the antiwar organizations, but he protested against the war by refusing to pay taxes. He said that taxes were supporting the army. He was arrested in 1846 for his refusal to pay taxes. In 1848 he wrote an essay called "Civil Disobedience" in which he stated that he believed in majority rule but that an individual's own conscience was always more important than the law. That was the meaning of free speech and rule by the people. He said that democracy becomes tyranny when it denies the right of the individual to be responsible for what she or he believes to be correct. Thoreau's argument is one of the most famous in American political philosophy. He raised the question of what a person should do when he or she truly believes that the legal representatives of the majority are morally wrong. This question would occupy a central position in American thought in both the North and South in the years to come.

The Debate in Congress

28. What issues regarding the Mexican territory concerned the American Congress?

1) Had the Americans started a war on territory that legally belonged to Mexico?
2) Should slavery be permitted there? 3) Should people from all states, slave or free, be permitted to settle there? 4) Should the Missouri Compromise line extend all the way to the Pacific? 5) Should the settlers themselves decide whether their state would be slave or free?

Congress also discussed whether the Mexican War was worth the cost in dollars and in people. A representative from Illinois, Abraham Lincoln, wondered if the Americans had not started the war on territory that legally belonged to Mexico. And David Wilmot of Pennsylvania introduced an amendment to a bill that would provide money for the war. The amendment, or *rider*, to the bill said that slavery should not be allowed in any part of the territory which might be acquired from Mexico. The Wilmot Proviso, as it was called, passed the House, where the populous North was in control. But, as might have been expected, it was defeated in the Senate, where the South had an equal vote with the North.

In February 1847, John C. Calhoun, once again a senator from South Carolina, introduced a set of resolutions. They said that all new territories belonged to the whole nation, and therefore the people of all the states, slave or free, ought to have equal right to settle there. Calhoun suggested that if one group of Americans wanted slavery, then the government should protect them from being hurt or forced in any way by those who disagreed. Calhoun

What is the difference between saying "the majority decision is not good for me" and saying "the majority decision is wrong"?

was talking about the rights of people who were not in the majority and with whom the majority disagreed. This idea of protecting a minority got nowhere in the House of Representatives. It was obvious that the North-South split over slavery would have to be kept out of the discussion about the Mexican War. Perhaps the territory taken from Mexico could simply be admitted by treaty without any rules or laws about slavery. After all, it would take years to settle the Far West. Maybe the slave question would just die out quietly as the Americans moved closer to the Rocky Mountains and into territory where cotton could not be grown. Some people hoped that the movement westward would take years and years, by which time slavery might die out.

Congress also discussed whether or not to extend the Missouri Compromise line all the way to the Pacific. This would give the North and South an equal amount of territory in the West. But most of the western land was not "slave land." It was mountainous and did not have enough rainfall.

Lewis Cass of Michigan suggested that the whole question of slavery be left out of the discussion about the territory won from Mexico.

Slavery and its spread were important factors in the decision to admit Texas to the Union. How does this engraving show the injustices of slavery?

Cass believed that whoever wanted to should go west. When there were enough settlers in a territory to qualify for statehood, then those who lived in the state could vote whether slavery was to be allowed or not. The right to make this decision belonged to those who claimed, or *squatted* on, the land. Thus the people of the territories should have squatters' rights. The more formal term was *popular sovereignty*, or letting the people decide for themselves by majority rule.

The Treaty to End the War

29. What happened to the Mexicans who remained in the United States?

The Anglos took over, and the Mexican way of life was no longer respected.

There were few leaders left in Mexico to negotiate a treaty with the victorious United States. But on February 2, 1848, the United States and Mexico signed the Treaty of Guadalupe Hidalgo (gwa-da-LOO-pay ee-DAHL-go). The United States borders now included the Rio Grande River and the Pacific Ocean! In return, Mexico received $15 million and had all other debts to Americans cancelled. Mexicans were allowed to remain where they were and become American citizens if they wished, or they could move south and sell their property without having to pay taxes on it. They were to have all the rights of all American citizens, including protection from the Native Americans. The treaty showed no mercy to the Native Americans by either side.

Mexican-Americans later complained that although the treaty was a fair one, the only right they were actually granted was the right to practice their own religion. They did not feel that they were protected in finding jobs, keeping land, or being elected to office. The Anglos took over, and the Mexican way of life was no longer respected.

A Future in the Land

30. What was needed to fill the western lands with settlers?

1) Transportation was needed, as crossing the Rockies by wagon train was a difficult and dangerous way to travel. 2) A motive was needed, other than farming, to draw settlers to the West.

The new western land was on everyone's mind. Some day, far in the future, Americans believed, it would be filled by settlers from back east. But two factors were missing. One was transportation. Crossing the Rockies by wagon train was a difficult and dangerous way to travel. In the winter of 1846, a party of settlers led by the Donner family was trapped in a snowstorm on the way to California. Only half of the party lived through the ordeal. Few people wanted to risk their lives in this way.

Also, there could be no great settlement of the West without a major reason or motive for going. Farming was a reason, but farmland took time to develop. And farming was not everyone's idea of a good reason for leaving home, family, and friends on a very dangerous journey across the mountains.

Gold

On January 24, 1848, James W. Marshall was finishing building a sawmill for John A. Sutter on the South Fork of the American River in California. As he took water out of the river for his building purposes, he happened to examine it and saw—gold! The news of gold spread first in California. When the word reached the eastern cities, the President made a speech about it and the newspapers carried the story in headlines. People poured out of the East. Now they had a reason.

31. How did people react to the discovery of gold?

Some 80,000 newcomers came to California in 1849— 55,000 by land and about 25,000 by sea.

Towns along the Mississippi River were crowded with travelers on their way west. St. Louis became an important city, and St. Joseph, Missouri, became the place to buy equipment before heading on the trail to the gold fields.

How many ways can drastic change occur?

This painting shows San Francisco just before the gold rush. How do you think the discovery of gold will change San Francisco?

People also tried to get to California by sea. Some of these tried to cross the Isthmus of Panama, the narrow strip of land between the Atlantic and the Pacific, and board a ship on the other side. Some went around Cape Horn. Ships came all the way from Europe, Australia, and South America. When they got to San Francisco, they lost their crews, because the sailors stayed to look for gold. People said that there were ships riding at anchor with only a cat left on board.

The gold rush changed the population picture out west. Towns in California lost their entire populations to the gold mines. Some 80,000 newcomers came to California. In 1849, 55,000 came by land, and about 25,000 by sea. Within two years of the finding of gold, the population of California had grown from 15,000 to 93,000. By 1852 the state had more than a quarter of a million people. Most of these people lived in northern California. Many found gold, but many more found hardship. The people who came thought that their gamble would pay off. This was expansion at its peak. Each individual was out for himself or herself.

Expansion, Individualism, and Votes

When Congress met to discuss how to make western lands into states, the debate was no longer only about cotton and slavery in Texas. Gold and thousands of people in California were added to cotton and slavery. Once again, the issue was representation. If all that land became states with voters, how would they vote on tariffs, banks, canals, and now railroads? When the majority ruled, who would be in the majority? If, as Calhoun had warned, there was a permanent minority, what kind of future would there be for them?

Checking the facts

1. Why did the Webster-Ashburton Treaty become necessary? What were the provisions?
2. Why was the treaty with Britain over the Oregon Territory necessary? What were the provisions?
3. How did Texas finally become a state?
4. How did Americans react to the Mexican War?
5. How did the gold rush affect the West?

How did the expansion of the nation change the issue of who represents whom? What happened to the issue of slavery?

PUTTING IT ALL TOGETHER

UNDERSTANDING THE MAIN IDEAS

1. In what form did the American cultures arrive in the West?
2. What was the form of the Spanish-Mexican culture?
3. What were the results of the meeting of the two cultures for the Americans, the Mexicans, and for the Native Americans of the Southwest?

ACTIVITIES

1. This is an activity that requires some research in your school or local library. Ask your librarian for a book about explorers who crossed the Rocky Mountains. Read an account of their experiences crossing the Rockies. In that account, how much was motive? How much was bravery? How much was luck? Prepare a brief book review in which you answer these questions.
2. Find some picture books on Santa Fe, New Mexico. What kinds of things do you see in these pictures? What impressions do you have of Santa Fe? Incorporate your findings in a one page essay.
3. On a current map of the United States, study the boundaries of the states west of the Mississippi River. Which state boundaries are formed by natural barriers, rivers, and/or mountains? Which ones were formed by treaty? How can you tell?
4. Look at a current map of the state of California. Where was the gold found? Where are the ports located? What are the names of towns and cities in the north and south? What are the differences in the kinds of place names? Give an oral report to the class, using a map if possible.

BOOKS TO READ

Bauer, Helen, *California Rancho Days* (Garden City: Doubleday and Co., Inc., 1967).

Chamber, M. C., *Boy Heroes of Chapultepec* (New York: Holt, Rinehart and Winston, Publishers, 1970).

De Trevino, Elizabeth B., *Juarez: Man of Law* (New York: Farrar, Straus and Giroux, 1974).

Hoyt, Edwin P., *John Tyler* (New York: Abelard Press, 1970).

Meltzer, Milton, *Bound for the Rio Grande: The Mexican Struggle, 1845–1850* (New York: Alfred A. Knopf, Inc., 1974).

Young, Robert and Young, Jan, *Fifty-Four Forty or Fight: The Story of the Oregon Territory* (New York: Julian Messner, Inc., 1967).

chapter 15
The Nation at Mid-Century

1850

1. GOLD AND COMPROMISE
2. THE CULTURES OF THE WEST

INTRODUCTION

The combination of land, gold, and a flood of people hit the nation with such force in such a short period of time that all attempts to hide the issues of slavery and sectional rivalry were out of the question. Gold was discovered in California in January 1848, and the war with Mexico was officially ended in February of that year. A new President was elected in November, and by 1849 the debate was on. The states now had to face the fact that the Union could not always represent the special interests of each of them. Those northerners who were in the majority reminded the others that expansion brought power to the nation as a whole. The southerners found comfort only in maintaining an equal vote in the Senate and government protection for their way of life. There was no protection for Mexicans and Native Americans, however. The questions Americans discussed were not new. But the size of the nation was.

1850

Who?	Henry Clay	California legislature petitions for	Millard Fillmore	Secretary of State, John M. Clayton	
What?	figures out how to settle sectional differences	admission to the union as a non-slave state	becomes President	negotiates a treaty with Great Britain over ship canal routes	
Where?	between the North and South	in Congress	in Washington, D.C.	across the Central American isthmus	

How can the nation as a whole be doing well when some of its people are in very difficult situations?

As you read, think about these questions to bring this period into focus:

1. How did the national government try to represent the unexpected results of expansion? Was it possible for the differences of a whole continent to be represented by that same federal government?
2. How could the desire of individuals to live as they please exist at the same time as their desire to benefit from the wealth of each section?
3. In the midst of the congressional debate about political unity, what happened to the mixture of the cultures of the Anglos and the Spanish-Americans?

1. GOLD AND COMPROMISE

The Election of 1848

In the middle of the debate about the West and the rush to California, another presidential election took place. Polk had been right. He had so managed the war that he had made heroes out of his generals. The Whigs ran Zachary Taylor—and won. The campaign was carried on much like the 1840 campaign for "Tippecanoe and Tyler, too." It featured pictures of the battles of Buena Vista and Monterrey and very few answers to questions by the candidate. Taylor seemed to have no opinions, so it was easy for him to be silent. He had never voted before in his life.

The Democrats split their vote. The main branch of the party ran Lewis Cass of Michigan. Cass had promoted the idea of letting the people of a state decide for themselves about slavery. His stand caused the northerners who were definitely antislavery to form a

1. How did Taylor win the election of 1848?

1) He was a Mexican War hero. 2) He was silent on the issues. 3) An antislavery group formed the Free Soil party, splitting the Democratic vote.

	Nathaniel Hawthorne	The population	The Congress	315,334 immigrants	Horace Mann
	publishes The Scarlet Letter	reaches 23,000,000	eliminates slave trade	arrive from foreign countries	recommends tax supported schools
	in Massachusetts	in the United States	in Washington, D.C.	to the United States	in Massachusetts

San Francisco after the gold rush was a boom town. Building construction could not keep up with the large number of newcomers.

separate, or Free Soil, party. This group had decided that slavery was a question of right and wrong—a moral question. They ran Van Buren. Although Van Buren was coming to the end of a very active political career, he wanted to lend his name to the cause of stopping the spread of slavery.

The campaign was a dull one, because most people did not want to face the real issues. Also, the candidates were all quite uninspiring. The Free Soil party took about 10 percent of the vote. Taylor won the election of 1848. But the vote was very close and not split along North-South lines. Taylor carried 8 of the 15 slave states, and Cass carried 7 of the 17 free ones. The country was not prepared to take a final stand on the slavery question.

California Forces the Issue

2. Why was the Great Compromiser, Henry Clay, called upon again?

1) Clay was thought able to solve the national conflict over California Statehood. 2) California was ready to apply for statehood within less than two years of the first gold strike. 3) California drew up a constitution that outlawed slavery. Congress could no longer avoid the issue.

The population of California grew so fast that the area was ready to apply for statehood within less than two years of the first gold strike. The Californians drew up a constitution which outlawed slavery. There were no slaves in California and little likelihood of any being brought in. When California forced the issue, Congress could no longer avoid it. President Taylor was no help in the search for a lasting solution. Besides, northerners did not trust him, because he himself owned a plantation and slaves. The leadership in Congress turned to the Great Compromiser, Henry Clay. Clay was over 70 years old and ill, but he, better than anyone else, was able to figure out a package of laws with something for everyone. He called it his Omnibus Bill, because he hoped it would be able to appeal to everyone.

The Compromise of 1850

Clay knew that the fears of the South were real. If California entered as a free state, the balance between North and South in the Senate would be gone. Southerners also feared that the southern vote in Congress would sooner or later be overrun by votes from other free states formed out of the rest of the Mexican territory. But California was already a free state. Its people had already voted. The United States government could not force a new state to buy slaves.

Clay used his old formula of giving every section something. He relied on the hope that each section would have enough concern for the whole nation to give the others something, too. The nation needed Henry Clay. He rose for the last time to provide the kind of practical answers combined with national vision for which he had become so famous.

The compromise of 1850 gave the North two victories and one promise. California would be a free state. The District of Columbia would never again have slave-trading. And the rest of the Mexican

3. What solutions did the Compromise of 1850 provide?

1) The rest of the Mexican territory would be divided into two possible future states, Utah and New Mexico. Northern gains: 2) California would be a free state, 3) The District of Columbia would never again have slave-trading. Southern gains: 4) Texas had entered as a slave state, so the count in the Senate was still even. 5) The federal government would enforce a new and more strict fugitive Slave Law requiring northern states to return fugitive slaves.

This painting shows fugitive slaves trying to escape. What did the Fugitive Slave Law do to keep escaped slaves from remaining free?

List the reasons why the Fugitive Slave Law was important.

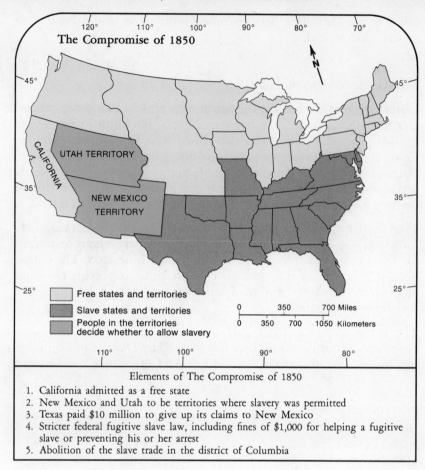

The Compromise of 1850

CALIFORNIA

UTAH TERRITORY

NEW MEXICO TERRITORY

Free states and territories

Slave states and territories

People in the territories decide whether to allow slavery

0   350   700 Miles
0   350   700   1050 Kilometers

Elements of The Compromise of 1850

1. California admitted as a free state
2. New Mexico and Utah to be territories where slavery was permitted
3. Texas paid $10 million to give up its claims to New Mexico
4. Stricter federal fugitive slave law, including fines of $1,000 for helping a fugitive slave or preventing his or her arrest
5. Abolition of the slave trade in the district of Columbia

territory would be divided into two possible future states, Utah and New Mexico. The people in each area would make their own decisions about slavery. However, both would probably become free states because of their geography.

The South was also given two victories. Texas had entered as a slave state, so the count in the Senate was still even. And the federal government would enforce a new and more strict Fugitive Slave Law. All *fugitive,* or runaway, slaves must be returned to their owners. Northern states which harbored fugitive slaves would have to obey. This was the first time that the federal government acted to protect slavery where it already existed.

Clay, Calhoun, and Webster

The debate was a debate of giants. For the last time the statesmen of the War of 1812 appeared on the floor of the Senate to show the nation what the real issues were. Clay, Calhoun, and Webster were great leaders and brave men. All three had missed the presidency because they had spoken out on the issues and dared to be unpopular with some voters. In their final debate, they once again made clear what values lay behind their decisions.

John C. Calhoun looked like a ghost. He sat wrapped in a huge cape and listened while the speech he had written was read for him by Senator James Mason of Virginia. In it Calhoun spoke against Clay's compromise because it did not guarantee equality for the South and its slave system. The compromise might look fair in 1850, but it would not be long before the western states had a larger population and, together with the northern states, would outnumber the southern ones. And a minority which can never be part of a majority vote lives under tyranny. Calhoun felt that the United States should guarantee the South an equal vote—whether or not the population or the number of states was equal. He also suggested a constitutional amendment to restore and preserve the balance between North and South. Unless this was done, the minority would forever be at the mercy of the majority, and the slave South would be doomed.

Calhoun was right about the future. But he left no choice for the nation except to give up the system of representation by majority rule. Otherwise, Calhoun felt that the South had no choice but to leave, or secede from the Union. "Let the states agree to separate and part in peace," he said. Calhoun knew that in the future under the Constitution there could be only one winner. That meant that a great many Americans, the southerners, were going to lose.

Daniel Webster agreed with Calhoun that there was no way for the nation to stay together unless one section gave in. But to Webster the idea of the North and the South separating was unthinkable. He knew that many people among his supporters in New England would be glad to see the South go. They did not want Webster and their other representatives to support the Compromise, because they did not want to protect slavery. However, Webster spoke out for what he believed was best for the country, even though the voters who had sent him to Congress disagreed.

Webster, too, was old and ill. He rose for the last time to support Clay's proposal. He spoke out against Calhoun. There was no such thing as "peaceable secession," he said. The Union must be preserved. "Where is the flag of the republic to remain?" he asked.

Clay, Calhoun, and Webster knew the facts. They knew the price of decisionmaking. And they knew that the issue of slavery had now become a national moral issue. In the midst of the debate, President Taylor, the southerner, died. The new President, Millard Fillmore, came from Buffalo, New York. He was able to bring northern senators to support each of the bills of the Compromise.

4. What was Calhoun's concern about the Compromise?

1) The compromise seemed fair in 1850, but it wouldn't be long before the combined western and northern states would outnumber the southern ones in population. 2) Calhoun believed that a minority which can never be a part of a majority lives under tyranny.

5. What was Calhoun's solution for the South?
1) He suggested a constitutional amendment to maintain a balance between North and South. 2) The nation had to give up the system of representation by majority rule, or the South would secede.

6. How did Webster show his great courage?

1) Webster risked conflict with voters in New England who didn't want him to support the compromise because it protected slavery. 2) Webster agreed with Calhoun that one section would need to give in. 3) The idea of the North and South separating was unthinkable to him. 4) He supported the Compromise, despite the effect of this position on his political career.

7. What helped the Compromise to pass?

How much help do you think the winner or the majority should give to those who cannot be a majority? Give an example.

387

1) President Taylor died during the debate. His successor, Fillmore, was a northerner, and won support from northern senators for each part of the Compromise.
2) Only four senators voted for every part of the bill.
3) Illinois senator Stephen A. Douglas led the fight to get the bill passed.

The States in 1850
(with dates of their admission to the Union)

FREE STATES	SLAVE STATES
Pennsylvania 1787 New Jersey 1787 Connecticut 1788 Massachusetts 1788 New Hampshire 1788 New York 1788 Rhode Island 1790 Vermont 1791 Ohio 1803 Indiana 1816 Illinois 1818 Maine 1820 Michigan 1837 Iowa 1846 Wisconsin 1848 California 1850	Delaware 1787 Georgia 1788 Maryland 1788 South Carolina 1788 Virginia 1788 North Carolina 1789 Kentucky 1792 Tennessee 1796 Louisiana 1812 Mississippi 1817 Alabama 1819 Missouri 1821 Arkansas 1836 Florida 1845 Texas 1845
16 Free States	15 Slave States

The Compromise of 1850 passed, piece by piece. Each member of Congress voted for the parts that pleased his section of the nation, and each part received enough votes to pass. Only four senators voted for every part of the bill.

A young senator from Illinois, Stephen A. Douglas, led the fight to get the bill passed. But other younger men looked to the future, when one side or another would win. The great leaders who had labored for a lifetime to lead and hold the nation together were dying. Calhoun died less than four weeks after his speech. His last words were, "The South. The poor South." Webster also died within two years, knowing he was hated by the people of New England.

Who would lead the nation? The Congress was exhausted. Stephen Douglas vowed that he would never make another speech about slavery as long as he lived. Everyone hoped that the settlement of the West would take attention away from the slavery question.

The way in which the Compromise of 1850 was put together has been the way most difficult policies are put into law. It was put together piece by piece; each section of the law had a different coalition of support.

Checking the facts

1. What were the provisions under the Compromise of 1850?
2. What was Calhoun's response to the Compromise?
3. What was Webster's response to the Compromise?

2. THE CULTURES OF THE WEST

Other events in the United States had little to do with slavery and Congress. The Anglo population of the West had conquered the native population of Mexicans. The mixture of cultures made great changes in the lives of both groups.

California

As a result of the gold rush, the Mexican population was now a small minority in California. In fact, the towns were now run by Easterners, who called themselves the "true Americans." People of Latin-American background were often thought of and spoken of as inferior. They were called "foreigners." In the town of Sonora, a riot occurred when the miners attempted to drive out the Latins.

The people from the East were out to "Americanize" the West. In the first constitution for the state of California, it was necessary to include legal protection for those of Spanish descent, even though they owned the territory two years before. All laws were to be published in both English and Spanish so that everyone could understand them. But the power was to be in Anglo hands.

During the first few years of the gold rush, California was mostly an all-male society. The wild days of the frontier mining towns soon took on old-fashioned, settled ways of living. Eastern families were anxious to settle down and create towns like the ones they left behind. The California frontier attracted many educated people who came because of the gold. Lawyers, doctors, teachers, university professors, ministers, and businesspeople came. They did not necessarily practice their professions in California. As one woman wrote home, "Everyone must do something; it matters but very little what it is. If they stick to it, they are bound to make money."

The California frontier also attracted many Chinese. They worked in the gold and silver mines of the West and stayed to help build the railroads.

1) The eastern majority, brought by the gold rush, thought of California's Mexican population as inferior and "foreigners."
2) A riot occurred in Sonora when the miners tried to drive out the Latins.

8. Why was it necessary for the California state constitution to provide legal protection for those of Spanish descent?

This picture is called "The Independent Gold Hunter on His Way to California." How does it show the hopes and dreams of the people who set off to California?

In what year did the largest number of Irish come to the United States? How many Irish came to the United States in 1846?

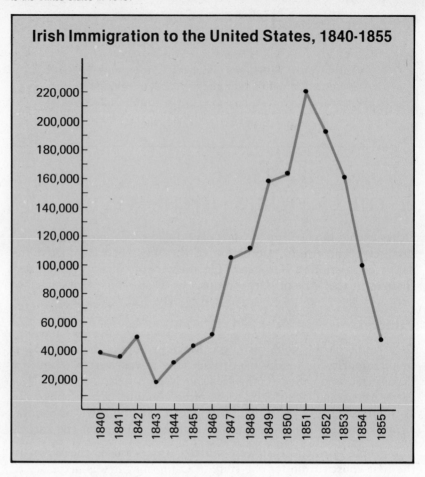

Irish Immigration to the United States, 1840-1855

220,000
200,000
180,000
160,000
140,000
120,000
100,000
80,000
60,000
40,000
20,000

1840 1841 1842 1843 1844 1845 1846 1847 1848 1849 1850 1851 1852 1853 1854 1855

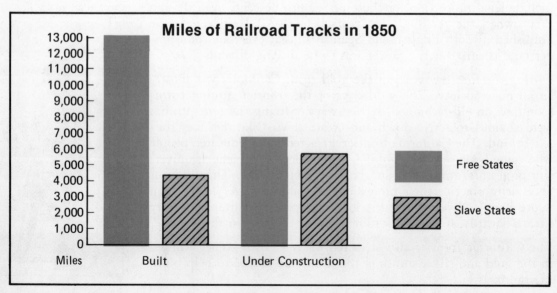

Miles of Railroad Tracks in 1850

13,000
12,000
11,000
10,000
9,000
8,000
7,000
6,000
5,000
4,000
3,000
2,000
1,000
0

Miles   Built   Under Construction

Free States

Slave States

How much can you tell about the nation from each graph? How much can you tell by putting the graphs together?

Which section of the country had the most miles of railroad tracks in 1850? What are the advantages of having railroads in a region?

How could you describe the increase in cotton production? Why did slavery increase with cotton production?

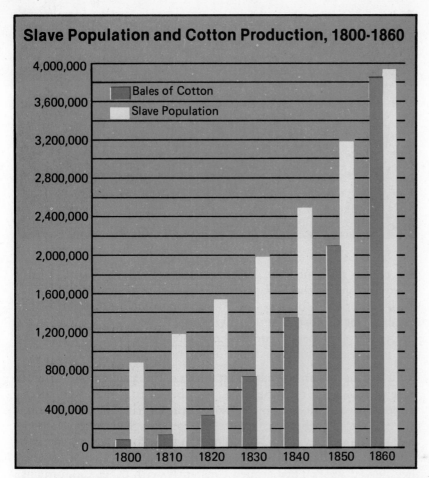

Slave Population and Cotton Production, 1800-1860

Legend:
- Bales of Cotton
- Slave Population

y-axis values: 0, 400,000, 800,000, 1,200,000, 1,600,000, 2,000,000, 2,400,000, 2,800,000, 3,200,000, 3,600,000, 4,000,000

x-axis values: 1800, 1810, 1820, 1830, 1840, 1850, 1860

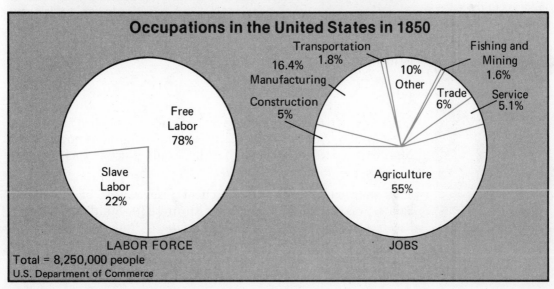

Occupations in the United States in 1850

LABOR FORCE
- Free Labor 78%
- Slave Labor 22%

JOBS
- Agriculture 55%
- Manufacturing 16.4%
- 10% Other
- Trade 6%
- Service 5.1%
- Construction 5%
- Transportation 1.8%
- Fishing and Mining 1.6%

Total = 8,250,000 people
U.S. Department of Commerce

What kinds of jobs did most Americans have in 1850?

Immigrants from China came to the West Coast during the gold rush. These prospectors are working the Auburn Ravine. Chinese labor was also important in building the railroads.

9. *What different views were held on education?*
1) In California, the missionaries had established the first schools; but as more settlers came, Californians began to disagree about the purpose of education.
2) Some people wanted only schools for miners, farmers, and cattle ranchers. 3) In San Francisco, they wanted tax-supported universities, libraries and theaters. 4) Horace Mann wanted tax supported education.
Brigham Young led the Mormons to the valley of the Great Salt Lake in 1847.

One of the signs of hope for the future was the widespread push for education. In the East, Horace Mann recommended public education supported by taxes as a way of preventing disaster for the rest of society. Most Americans viewed education as a way to make sure that young people would hold jobs, vote sensibly, and take part in the effort for individual opportunity and equality.

In California the missionaries established the first schools. But as more people came into the state, they began to disagree about the purpose of education. Some of the people in San Francisco wanted universities and libraries, and to put on the Shakespearean plays that were so popular in New York and Boston. They wanted to show that they had lost nothing of the advantages of the East when they moved west. They argued constantly with other Californians. And there were other people who had come only for wealth and cared for little else. They did not want taxes to go for what they called upper-class culture. They wanted schools for miners and farmers and cattle ranchers.

Utah

Gold was not the reason that settlers came to another area of the West which later became a state. A religious group known as the Mormons settled in Utah so that they could practice their religion in peace.

The Mormon Church, or Church of Jesus Christ of Latter-Day Saints, was founded by Joseph Smith in 1830. Smith said that he had received special messages, or *revelations*, from God. They enabled him to find a set of golden tablets with unknown writing on them. Smith translated the writing and published it as the Book of Mormon.

Note that in every society, education is based on the traditional values of the culture. Why?
What is the purpose of education in a society made up of people from many cultures?

CHARTS AND GRAPHS

There are many ways in which information can be reported efficiently and quickly. This is important today because of the many kinds of information available to people. Think of the kinds of information you might want to know about. Some examples might be athletic records, exam scores, geographical information, and scientific information.

One way a large amount of information can be presented at one time is in a picture. Advertising uses pictures all the time to convey a series of messages to the public. However, not all information can be shown in a picture. Another way of presenting the information has to be found. One way is to make a chart or a graph. Turn to page 390. Locate the bar graph. This graph shows how many miles (kilometers) of railroad tracks have been built and how many miles (kilometers) were under construction during a specific time in America's history. It is easy to read. The graph allows us to compare the miles (kilometers) of railroad track in the free states and slave states. A bar graph tends to show what happened in one time period. What time period is shown in this graph?

Now turn to the line graph on page 390. It shows Irish immigration to the United States. The higher the line the more people emigrated. By using this kind of graph one can get a general idea of the differences for each year. Look more carefully at the lines and then check the graph to find out the years shown. To read the number of immigrants put a ruler or straight edge from the year to the number. A line graph makes it possible to see the changes in something very easily. What changes do you see?

Look at the pie chart on page 391. A pie chart shows a percentage. The whole circle is equal to 100 percent. The circle is divided into wedges. Each wedge equals a percentage. Half the pie equals 50 percent. The whole circle shown in this chart is 100 percent of the working people of the United States in 1850. It is divided into two sections. The larger section equals free workers. The smaller section equals slaves.

Now look at the graph at the top of page 391. What does it tell you? Can you identify the type of graph shown? Is it a bar graph or a line graph? How much of the information can you translate into another kind of graph or chart?

Thousands of people joined Smith's new church. They believed that they were God's chosen people. This belief was one of the reasons why they were persecuted by other people. The Mormons moved from New York to Ohio, Michigan, Illinois, and Missouri. In Missouri, Smith was killed. Non-Mormons, and some of the Mormons as well, had become angry when he began to preach that

10. Why did the Mormons go to Utah?

America continues to appeal to people because they can develop as individuals. How is this a strength? When can it cause problems?

393

1) The members of Smith's new church believed that they were God's chosen people. 2) Wherever they went, they were persecuted for this belief and for Smith's statement that a Mormon man could have more than one wife. 3) Smith was killed in Missouri; Brigham Young led them out west.

Mormon men could have more than one wife. Smith was arrested, put in prison, and then dragged from prison and murdered.

The new leader of the Mormons, Brigham Young, led them out of Missouri and into the deserts of the West. In 1847 they arrived at the edge of the Great Salt Lake in Utah. The Mormons built a city there and went to work irrigating the dry lands. The Mormon state, which was given the name of Deseret, became very successful as a stopping-off place for settlers on their way to California.

New Mexico

11. What happened to the Latin culture in New Mexico?

Life continued in the Spanish style. The eastern settlers learned to build houses suited to the climate and to center their social life around family and home.

In New Mexico life continued in the Spanish style. The settlers did not come in such numbers that they ignored the language and customs of the people already there. They learned to build their houses from the red earth, or adobe. Adobe lasted in the climate of New Mexico. Houses were built, in the Spanish style, around a patio or courtyard. The rooms opened on the patio, giving the house more air and privacy from the road. Social life centered around the family and the home.

Anglos did not come in droves, because there was no gold in New Mexico. Those who came as traders tended to take on the comfortable, quiet life of the Spanish-Americans who lived there. And today, New Mexicans of Latin heritage still refer to themselves as Spanish-Americans.

Texas

12. What was life like for the Mexicans in Texas?

1) They often lost titles to their land. 2) They couldn't get jobs in the cotton country; landowners had brought slaves to work there. 3) Urban Mexicans were often forced to live in shacks on the edge of town, making a living selling to the Anglos. 4) Family life and the language spoken at home continued to be Spanish. 5) Anglo and Mexican populations stayed separate, with the Anglo majority in control of jobs and elections.

In Texas there was competition between the Mexicans, who had title or claims to land, and the Anglos, who came from the southern states to plant cotton on large estates. Special courts tried to sort the conflicting land claims. The results were often in favor of the Anglos.

Urban Mexicans in Texas lived very differently from those who lived in the country or in the towns nearer the Rio Grande and the Mexican border. In the Anglo cities the Mexicans were often forced to live in shacks on the edge of the town. They made a living selling to the Anglos. Their family life and the language spoken at home continued to be Spanish, but their way of making a living was at the mercy of the Anglos. Mexicans had little chance to make a living in the cotton country, because the landowners brought their slaves with them.

The cultures of the Anglos and Mexican-Americans did not blend in California and Texas. They tended to live side by side, with the Anglos in control of the jobs and the elections. New Mexico was different, but it did not have the wealth of either cotton-growing

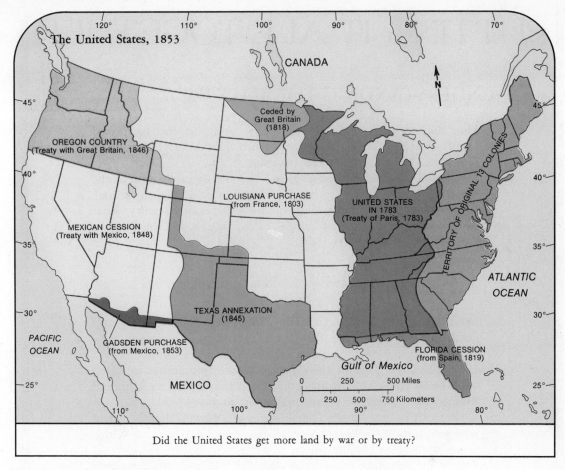

The United States, 1853

CANADA

Ceded by Great Britain (1818)

OREGON COUNTRY (Treaty with Great Britain, 1846)

LOUISIANA PURCHASE (from France, 1803)

UNITED STATES IN 1783 (Treaty of Paris, 1783)

TERRITORY OF ORIGINAL 13 COLONIES

MEXICAN CESSION (Treaty with Mexico, 1848)

ATLANTIC OCEAN

PACIFIC OCEAN

GADSDEN PURCHASE (from Mexico, 1853)

TEXAS ANNEXATION (1845)

FLORIDA CESSION (from Spain, 1819)

Gulf of Mexico

MEXICO

0   250   500 Miles
0   250   500   750 Kilometers

Did the United States get more land by war or by treaty?

The United States got more land through treaties.

Texas or gold-rush California. In these western lands the majority ruled. And the majority was Anglo and as Eastern as possible.

"More" had been the password to expansion. A great number of Americans had achieved more in this short time period than in any part of America's history. Now the nation was free to continue its growth. Some people hoped that the problems of minority rights would disappear over a long, slow development of the West.

Checking the facts

1. How did the movement of the Anglo population westward affect the lives of the Mexicans?
2. How did the Anglos regard education?

Why could it be said in the 1850's that the nation had grown both in size and in its regard for the individual?

Why could it be said in the 1850's that the nation was not fulfilling the hopes of everyone?

PUTTING IT ALL TOGETHER

UNDERSTANDING THE MAIN IDEAS

1. How did the national government try to represent the unexpected results of expansion? Could the differences of a whole continent be represented by the same federal government?
2. How could the desire of individuals to live as they please exist at the same time as their desire to benefit from the wealth of each section?
3. In the midst of the congressional debate about political unity, what happened to the mixture of cultures of the Anglos and the Spanish-Americans?

ACTIVITIES

1. Read a biography of Clay, Calhoun, or Webster. Then write an essay on the subject: One Brand of Political Leadership. In the essay, comment on the major political decisions in the person's career.
2. Look at the front page of a newspaper. What compromises are being made today on the subject of energy? On pollution? On equal rights? Present your findings in a brief oral report to your class.
3. Draw a cartoon map of the United States as a New Englander would have seen it in 1850. Draw one as a Texan would have seen it. Which places would have the most detail?
4. Debate the following question in class: Do you believe a conquered culture can ever survive without change? Why or why not? Give examples to support your view.

BOOKS TO READ

Chu, Daniel, *Passage to the Golden Gate: A History of the Chinese in America to 1910* (Garden City: Doubleday and Co., Inc., 1967).

John, Annabel and Edgar, *Wilderness Bridge* (New York: Harper and Row, 1968).

Latham, F. B., *The Law or the Gun* (New York: American Book Publishing, Inc., 1965).

Politi, Leo, *The Mission Bell* (New York: Charles Scribners Sons, Inc., 1970).

Wilkie, Catherine E., *The Man Who Wouldn't Give Up* (New York: Julian Messner, Inc., 1970).

REVIEWING THE UNIT

BUILDING VOCABULARY

The following is a list of some of the vocabulary words in Unit Three:

suffrage	rider	abolition
annex	fugitive	dark horse

1. Choose the correct vocabulary word above and write on one of the following topics: a. The work of Elizabeth Cady Stanton and Lucretia Mott, b. The Texas War for Independence, c. Frederick Douglass.

BUILDING SOCIAL STUDIES SKILLS

1. Turn to the maps on the pages given here. Then complete the following activities:
   a. Page 371—In 1846 President Polk made an agreement with the British which gave the United States half of the Oregon Territory. The northern border was the 49th Parallel. In 1844 Polk introduced the slogan "Fifty-four forty or fight!" for use during the campaign. When the British seemed willing to settle peacefully for half the territory, the United States agreed. Using the scale on the map, calculate how much land both the United States and Britain gained in the agreement.
   b. Page 367—The Oregon Trail and the Santa Fe Trail began in the same place. Locate that place on the map.
   c. Page 373—In the Mexican War the American army landed at Veracruz. Find Veracruz on the map. Write a sentence explaining why this was called an "amphibious" operation.

BUILDING WRITING SKILLS

1. During the potato famine in Ireland, one quarter of Ireland's population came to the United States. How did New Englanders treat the new immigrants? How has power shifted since then? Answer these questions in an essay.
2. What rights did factory workers have in the 1800's? Write a paragraph in which you answer this question.
3. At one time the United States had the largest whaling fleet in the world. What country does today? Compare and contrast the whaling industry of the 1800's with the whaling industry today. Comment on the ships used today and the methods of catching, processing, and marketing the whales. Incorporate your comments in a well-organized essay. Arrange the information you plan to use in an outline before you begin to write.

In the short span of half a generation, the United States had continued its development from a trading nation into a trading and manufacturing nation. The nation grew around its towns and cities. And they grew where there was coal and water power. Raw materials came into towns, and manufactured goods went out from them. The movement of goods depended on the kind of transportation that was available. Roads, canals, and railroads now formed a system of transportation east of the Appalachian Mountains. Each city was the center of its own trading system.

The American Economy Becomes Regional

The Northeast and Middle Atlantic area grew into a region that specialized in manufacturing. They used farm products—cotton from the South and grain and cattle from the old Northwest.

The old Northwest itself was made up at first of trading cities. These cities were tied to the river traffic that followed the Mississippi to New Orleans. The cities of the Great Lakes grew up during these years, since their trade was also part of the Mississippi connection. They sold goods to Europe. And they sold goods to the East by using the Erie Canal.

In the South, cotton became king, and the plantation way of life moved west into the Louisiana Territory. The southerners were the first to go west beyond the Mississippi, even to the point of settling within the Mexican province of Texas. Slavery increased with cotton growing. Slavery was now a matter of money for the southerners. The question of right and wrong was no longer discussed openly in the South. On the high seas, the United States sent its whaling fleet and its sailing ships around the world.

Reformers Look at the Results of Expansion

Reformers were concerned about slavery in the South and the unfair working conditions in the mills and factories of the North. Expansion and competition were possible for those who could get together enough capital to invest or who had enough money to travel and start a farm.

Opportunity and Hardship

The years of growth in manufacturing meant jobs for farm women and children. It meant jobs for the Irish and German immigrants who came in great numbers to the United States. But these workers found that long hours, low pay, and poor working conditions were the price of opportunity. Although they welcomed the chance to have jobs, they also began to organize themselves and put pressure on the owners for improvements. They especially wanted shorter hours. To emphasize their demands, they organized strikes. There was more opportunity for those who had come first than for those who arrived later.

The West

The Mexican revolution against Spain caused the Mexican government to welcome American settlement and trade. By the time the Mexicans realized that the highly organized ways of the southern Americans differed greatly from the life of local, scattered Mexican farmers, it was too late. Anglo culture replaced Mexican culture, except in the trading towns of New Mexico. In Texas, cotton plantations and slavery took over. In California, the gold rush of 1849 brought a variety of people from the East who were interested in wealth.

The Politics of the Midcentury Expansion

Politics moved on two levels. The political parties ran candidates and campaigns that appealed to the pride of the nation in its expansion and its power. The Presidents were war heroes from the War of 1812 and the Mexican War. And each of the major parties had supporters in each of the three regions of the nation. A new party movement was just beginning in the North based on the feelings against slavery. Although any of these parties could take votes from other candidates, they could not win for themselves.

When the old leadership of the Senate—Clay and Webster—put together the Compromise of 1850, they hoped that the competition for the West would take many years. Slavery might die out during that time. But the warning of Calhoun was clear. The future of the South depended on the willingness of the growing northern majority to protect the special way of life of the minority in the South. The compromise was a delicate one at best. Everyone hoped for a long breathing period before the majority–minority issue would come up again over slavery.

AMERICA IS... MAJORITY RULE, MINORITY RIGHTS

UNIT FOUR

"Raise your hand. How many want to play baseball?"

How old were you the first time you raised your hand, and someone in the group quietly and seriously counted the hands and then announced what everyone was going to do? It probably happened the first time you were allowed to go out and play with other children. You learned at that moment that it is easier to get your way when more people agree with you than disagree. You learned that outside your home, decisions often are made by a show of hands. This method of making decisions is based on two important beliefs. One is that every single person should be heard. The other is that what most people want is more fair than what only a few want. The majority rules.

Majority rule by law shows up in your life every time you stop for a traffic light, go to school, get a vaccination at the doctor's office, and pay sales tax on the records and books that you buy. If you are in a hurry, you must still stop at the light. If you would rather sleep in on a weekday, you cannot. On school days, you must get up. As a citizen, you must do what the majority of society wants. You may not like vaccinations, but you must get one so that you will not give contagious, preventable disease to others. You may not like paying a little extra when you buy a book or record, but these sales taxes are one way that your state gets money for public schools and road repairs.

Majority rule can be a matter of custom or habit. "Why do I have to wear shoes on the train?" Majority rule does not bother people when jobs are available, prices are not too high, and when everyone follows the same customs and has the same values and the same taste in spending their money.

Action by the Minority

If you are in the minority, and a belief that is very important to you is at stake, what can you do about it? You can try to convince other people that yours is a better point of view. One of the advantages of living in a country that guarantees free speech, free press, and the right to call meetings is that minorities can try to become a majority. This has worked time and again in American history. People do sell ideas to each other, and people's ideas do change.

Sometimes people's ideas change because they gain more information and discover important facts they had not known before. Sometimes people change their minds because they find out that the change would be helpful to them, too. It is in their interest to change. Some people change their minds because they come to believe that their earlier point of view was wrong. Morally, they now hold a different opinion and they are willing to say so in public. Some people only change when they can make a trade with someone else. "I'll do what you want this time—if you'll do the same for me on something else." This is an element of compromise. You may not like some compromises. But compromises are important because they sometimes achieve solutions. These solutions are agreed upon by the greatest number of people, the *majority*.

However, sometimes you cannot get what you want by majority rule. Perhaps what you want is too expensive, or too dangerous, or too selfish. Perhaps what you want is really better and more fair for some people. But if not enough people care, the majority will not help you. This is very frustrating if the position of the minority is morally right. In that case, the majority has to be persuaded to do what is right.

What else can people who belong to a minority do besides persuade? If they disobey the law then, like Thoreau, they have to be willing to go to jail. To break the law in protest and then hide or run away is an action that destroys the idea of majority rule and the idea of rule by law. People who break the law must take the legal consequences of their action for government by the people to exist. Otherwise, laws and guarantees of rights will not be there when they want the majority on their side on some other question. People who do not like a law or ruling by a judge and simply break it are saying that law is only useful for the majority. Their action denies all the rights built into America's Constitution and its history.

To be in the minority is very difficult. But to be in the minority when the majority is morally wrong is even worse. Every time citizens of a democracy find themselves in the minority, they have to decide how to become a majority or how to protest and still keep the system that guarantees government by the people.

These questions of how to keep representative government under majority rule and how to guarantee minority rights became the most important questions for Americans in 1850. At that time, the minority in the South wanted its legal rights and its guaranteed protection. But this minority knew that it would never be part of a voting majority again. And, worst of all, some of the southern minority knew that their position was morally wrong. How could the American nation do what was legal and what was right?

chapter 16
Technology Brings Change
1848–1861

1. RAILROADS, RESOURCES, AND PEOPLE
2. NATIONAL POWER AND MINORITY FEARS
3. NATIONAL LEADERSHIP

INTRODUCTION

When Congress passed the laws that made up the Compromise of 1850, it hoped many years would pass before the North and the South had to face each other again. With all of the land in the Northwest and the Southwest, each section of the nation should have room enough to develop its own special brand of wealth without competition.

But Congress has not counted on one factor. The railroad, by its very existence, speeded up the settlement of the West. With the end of the Mexican War, and the availability of all that land, came new inventions in the construction of trains and track. There are times in history when technology seems to have a life of its own. There was no way to tell the railroad to slow up its development. These inventions made it easier for the railroads to cross the mountains. Once railroads could cross the mountain ranges, they could not be stopped. The railroads did, however, have to cross public

	1848	1849	1852	1853	
Who?	Americans	Zachary Taylor	Harriet Beecher Stowe	James Gadsden	
What?	find gold	becomes the twelfth President	publishes Uncle Tom's Cabin	purchases territory for the United States	
Where?	at Sutter's Saw Mill in California	of the United States	in the United States	from Mexico	

or government-owned land. Therefore, Congress had to answer the question of where to build the railroads. And the North and South faced each other again over this question.

The period in America's history from 1848 to 1861 was a period of enormous change. As you read about it, think about these questions:

1. How did the railroads affect the development of natural resources in the United States?
2. What effect did the railroad have on where and how people lived in the North, South, and West?
3. What effect did the added power and wealth of the United States have on its relations with foreign nations?
4. What leadership was able to help a divided nation?

1. RAILROADS, RESOURCES, AND PEOPLE

When the Mexican War ended in 1848, the United States had about 6,000 miles (9,600 kilometers) of railroad track. Almost all of it was east of the Appalachian Mountains. This was more track than in all the continent of Europe. But it did not form a connected railroad system in the United States. The railroad builders had seen their profits coming from the supply of farm goods to the cities and the sale of manufactured goods to the farm areas. Each city was connected to the surrounding area by lines, but the cities were connected to each other only by waterways—rivers or canals.

As soon as the Mexican War was over, the railroad builders saw the future of their profits differently. Instead of building railroads where cities already existed, they could now build railroads into the vast empty western land and let the cities grow up alongside

1. How did the idea of railroad building change?

1853	1858	1859	1860	1861
Commodore Matthew Perry	Lincoln and Douglas	John Brown	Pony Express riders	Abraham Lincoln
opens trade	debate on slavery	raids the government arsenal	carry mail	becomes the sixteenth President
with Japan	in seven cities in Illinois	at Harpers Ferry, Virginia	across the United States	of the United States

403

Instead of building only where cities already existed, railroad companies could now build through the vast, empty western land and let the cities grow up alongside the railroads.

2. *What inventions made the railroad safer?*

1) Flexible wooden cross ties attached to iron rails made the tracks stronger and safer and the ride smoother. 2) The pilot wheel, placed in front of the drive wheel, enabled the train to go around bends and travel long distances. 3) The heating of water for steam by burning coal reduced the danger of forest fires along the train route. 4) The telegraph made it possible for dispatchers to send out trains on schedule and to warn them of conditions on the track.

the railroads. At the same time that their view of the future changed, the technical problems of how to take a railroad across mountains and rough land, or *terrain*, were solved.

Engineering Solutions

Rough terrain caused the trains to vibrate on the tracks. And since the tracks were wooden rails held down by U-shaped iron straps, the vibration caused the straps to break. When the straps broke, the rails would fall out of line. But with the invention of iron rails that could be attached with spikes to wooden crossties, this problem was solved. The rails no longer broke away from the ties. The ride was smoother because the wooden ties were quite flexible. Flexible ties were important because the road bed under the tracks followed the hills and valleys of the land. The ties acted as a spring, or shock absorber, between the train and the road bed.

To enable trains to go around curves, a new type of wheel had to be invented. The large steam-powered drive wheels could not guide the train around a bend. But when pilot wheels were added ahead of the drive wheels, trains could travel long distances and go around bends.

The first engines, or locomotives, were driven by steam. This meant the train carried a supply of wood and water for a boiler. The water was heated by burning the wood. Often the sparks from the burning wood caused forest fires along the train route. When coal was introduced at this time, the danger of fire was reduced and so was the space needed to carry fuel. Also, the cost of coal was cheaper than firewood cut to size.

The people who built and ran the trains needed to be able to communicate over long distances. The railroad companies were among the first to use the telegraph. Sending out the trains on a schedule and warning them of conditions ahead on the track was the work of dispatchers. By 1851 most trains were controlled this way. Signals at crossroads and train stations were still worked by hand. But with the invention of standard signals, a train could be told whether to proceed, slow down, or stop. The first wooden signals were like the signal flags used by the army and navy.

Railroad Builders

3. *Why was the Erie Railway a competitor of the Erie Canal?*

Like the canal, the railway connected New York City with the Great Lakes.

Within four years after the end of the Mexican War, the amount of track in the United States had doubled. And it doubled again within the next three years. Railroad companies connected the Atlantic coastal cities to the Mississippi Valley. By 1851 the Erie Railway was the longest in the world. It had 537 miles (859.9

Notice how and why the telegraph and the railroads developed together.

kilometers) of track that ran from the Hudson River just north of New York City to the town of Dunkirk on Lake Erie. Within less than a generation, the Erie Canal had its biggest competitor.

In 1852 the Baltimore and Ohio Railroad completed its dream. The title of the railroad itself was an expression of confidence in the engineers. Between Baltimore and the Ohio River were mountains. And when the famous B & O reached the city of Wheeling, West Virginia, people were very excited.

In 1853 a banker made a big breakthrough in railroading. Erastus Corning saw that the networks of railroads around each city would and should be connected to each other. He built the connecting links among eight separate, short railroads. His New York Central line connected Buffalo on the Great Lakes to Albany on the Hudson River. Corning was known not only as a banker and investor but also as a person who was truly interested in railroading. He supervised the building of the lines, the purchasing of the best track, and the scheduling of the trains for efficient service.

In the 1850's, all sections of the nation were interested in building railroads. The Pennsylvania Railroad finished its line across the mountains from Philadelphia to Pittsburgh by 1858. West of the mountains, Ohio and Illinois each laid more than 2,000 miles (3,200 kilometers) of track. Even Wisconsin had nearly 900 miles (1,430 kilometers) of track. The South still relied heavily on the Mississippi River for its traffic. But some of the individual southern cities built railroads. The town of Jackson, Mississippi, was connected with Vicksburg to the west on the river and with New Orleans to the south. A railroad was built linking Montgomery, Alabama, with the neighboring farm lands and with the cotton trading center of Atlanta, Georgia. The extent of the railroads provides a clear picture for the way the South saw itself. It was a separate economic region based on the Mississippi River and the port of New Orleans.

One of the most interesting developments in railroad building centered around Chicago, Illinois. In 1850 not one railroad line had reached Chicago. But, by 1855, 2,200 miles (3,520 kilometers) of track ended there. The plan of the Chicago railroad builders was to connect Chicago on Lake Michigan with St. Louis on the Mississippi River and St. Joseph on the Missouri River. The Illinois Central Railroad would make Chicago the market town for the farms in the northern Mississippi Valley. Produce from this valley no longer would have to travel south to New Orleans and then on ocean-going ships to New York. Instead, it could come to Chicago by train. From there it could go by ship on the Great Lakes to the Erie Canal, or by train to Columbus, Pittsburgh, Philadelphia, and Baltimore. (See map, page 406.)

With the invention of refrigerated railroad cars in the 1840's, fresh food could be carried great distances without spoiling.

4. Why wasn't there much railroad building in the South?

The South was a separate economic region based on the Mississippi River and the port of New Orleans.

5. What would the Illinois Central Railroad finally accomplish?

1) The Illinois Central enabled produce from the upper Mississippi Valley to come to Chicago by train. It could then get to New York by ship on the Great Lakes and the Erie Canal, or to Columbus, Pittsburgh, Philadelphia, and Baltimore by train. 2) The Illinois Central also connected Chicago and Mobile, Alabama, on the Gulf of Mexico.

What is the value of people who can think up new ideas and ways of making them practical?

405

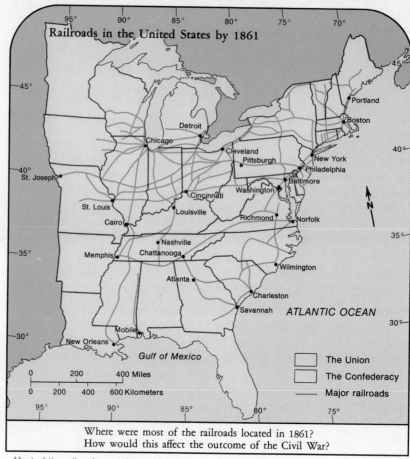

Railroads in the United States by 1861

The Union
The Confederacy
Major railroads

Where were most of the railroads located in 1861?
How would this affect the outcome of the Civil War?

Most of the railroads were located in the North in 1861. The North, therefore, had better transportation of supplies, equipment, and soldiers. This contributed to its victory over the South.

A railroad from Chicago to Mobile, Alabama, on the Gulf of Mexico, also was planned. The Congress gave the states along the route federal land. The states gave the Illinois Central 2½ million acres (one million hectares) of land in a 200-mile (320-kilometer) long strip. Some of the land was for the track itself. Some of it was farm land that the railroad company could sell. In this way, the company could raise the money to pay the construction costs and be assured from the beginning that the railroad would succeed.

The north-south connection from Chicago to Mobile was the only railroad the South was interested in, but this line was not completed until after the 1850's. Private southern investors would not put their money into a rail system connecting the East to the West. The South was doing so well growing cotton and transporting it on the rivers that it did not have to think about changing patterns of trade and transportation.

How did railroads affect the regional differences in the United States?

Paying for the Railroads

Most railroads were paid for by private investors who bought stock in the companies. Farmers who hoped their farms would be connected to eastern cities by a nearby railroad mortgaged their farms and used the borrowed money to buy railroad stock. People who owned stores or had trading businesses in small towns also bought stock. They hoped that a railroad would go through their town and that the town would grow into a wealthy city. No one had to pay for the stock all at one time. The railroad builders asked people for installment payments as the track was laid. The roads were so successful that the first piece of track made enough money from freight charges to pay for the next track to be laid.

6. How did the railroads get money to build their lines?

The railroads permitted investors to buy their stock on the installment plan, providing capital for further construction.

Railroads and Agriculture

The early 1850's were boom years for agriculture. Farmers needed customers and transportation from their farms for their produce. The railroads made it possible for farmers who did not live near rivers or lakes to sell their produce to faraway cities—even to cities in Europe. Railroads also made it possible for more people to become farmers because more land could be reached. The railroad companies sold their land cheaply and advertised widely to get farmers to move west.

7. What did the railroad do for agriculture?

1) Farmers who lived away from rivers or lakes could now sell their produce to faraway cities. 2) Railroads sold their land cheaply and advertised to get farmers to move west.

This was just the beginning of a chain reaction of events. Now that land was cheap and there was so much of it available to transportation, there was a shortage of people to work on it. Wages of farm hands and profits of farm owners went up. But the shortage of workers was serious. Now a new technological change occurred. Machinery that could do the work of many farmhands was invented in this period. In 1839 John Deere invented the steel plow. The new plow made it easier for farmers to clear away the tough grass of the prairies. In the beginning Deere could turn out ten plows a year in his own shop. Deere's plow was in such demand that he could afford to build a factory. In 1857 alone, he sold 10,000 plows.

8. How did technology help to solve the labor shortage problem?

1) In 1839 John Deere invented the steel plow, which made it easier to clear away the tough prairie grass. 2) In 1831 Cyrus McCormick developed a horse-drawn mechanical reaper, enabling 2 people to do the work of 14.

With Deere's plow, farmers could plant new lands. But harvesting the crops was a problem. The season was too short between the full growth of the crop and the onset of winter weather. Crops that were ready to be harvested would spoil if left in the fields too long. But another inventor solved this problem. In 1831 Cyrus Hall McCormick developed a horse-drawn mechanical reaper. It bent the grain against a cutting blade and then placed the cut grain on a platform. One person drove the horse while another man raked the wheat into rows. Two men could now do the work of 14.

"WESTWARD THE COURSE OF EMPIRE TAKES ITS WAY" WITH McCORMICK REAPERS IN THE VAN.

McCormick's reaper helped America become the largest grain-producing country in the world. What is this advertisement saying?

McCormick made a wise business decision. His reaper was ready for factory production just at the end of the Mexican War. This was five or six years before the major success of the railroads. But McCormick bet on the Illinois Central, and he built his factory in Chicago. The manufacturers let the farmers pay for the machines with monthly payments—on the installment plan. Competition and credit were part of the agricultural success of the Midwest. Wheat production went up 75 percent in the 1850's.

Railroads and the Cities

9. What did railroads do for business?

Railroads created new business. They needed money for investments and to pay good business managers. They needed parts made of iron and coal to heat the boilers. Railroads bought $15 million worth of iron and steel in the year 1860 alone. This was about half of all the iron and steel that was produced in the United States. Railroads also needed places where they could pick up their parts and drop off their cargo. These places were the railroad cities.

408

The sale of surpluses to foreign countries was one of the reasons for America's success. List the causes for America's great wheat productions.

Henry Clay would have been thrilled by his American System now—at least the northern and northwestern part of it. Cattle transported on the hoof in the railroad cars provided two thirds of the meat eaten in New York City. And since prices for shipping were low, even Europeans could afford to buy American wheat. There was a demand for wheat in Europe because a war broke out in Europe at the same time that the European crops failed. The Crimean War, which took place from 1853 to 1856, gave the American farmers and their railroads new customers. More farmers could move to Illinois, Wisconsin, and Indiana to grow wheat to sell abroad.

As the 1850's progressed, the farming picture changed. More machinery meant that farmers needed bigger farms to sell enough crops to pay for the machines and make a profit. The small frontier farmer had to sell out to those who had more money and more land. As the land filled up, new land became more scarce and more

1) Railroads bought about half the iron and steel produced in the United States. 2) Cities grew in places where railroads picked up parts and delivered cargo. 3) Railroads transported cattle to cities for meat. 4) Since rates for shipping were low, Europeans could afford to buy American wheat, thus bringing new customers for American farmers.

10. How did the farming picture change?

1) More machinery meant that farmers needed bigger farms to sell enough crops to pay for the machines and make a profit. 2) New land became more scarce and more expensive.

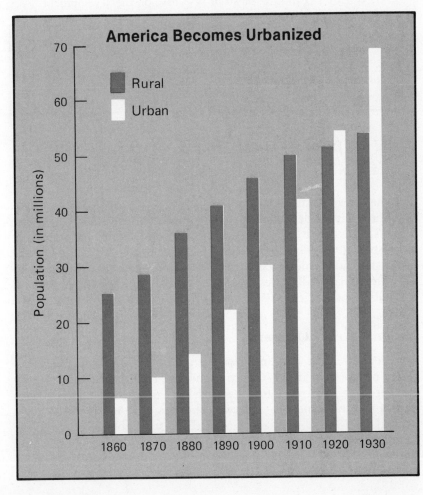

America Becomes Urbanized

Rural
Urban

Population (in millions)

Why is the change in farming so important? Why did cities grow during the same period that farms became bigger and more mechanical?

expensive. As the railroads brought manufactured goods from the cities, farmers began to want more and more of them. Farming became bigger and more mechanical. Farmers became more like manufacturers and merchants in their way of living.

But most important of all, the network of transportation between the North and the West was established. It had happend so fast that the South had hardly noticed what had occurred. But by the end of the 1850's northern cities were linked to each other and to the farmlands of the West. Which came first? The city? The West? The desire for land? The farm machinery? The railroad? The capital to invest? That would be hard to say. But the ten years after the Mexican War had changed America forever.

Checking the facts

1. What effect did the Mexican War have on the development of the West?
2. What made the development of the north and west railroad network possible?
3. Why didn't the South develop an extensive system of railroads in the 1850's?

2. NATIONAL POWER AND MINORITY FEARS

The majority of Americans in the 1850's found much to be proud of. And that pride began to show in their relations with other nations. Now that California was opened up, Americans were very interested in the Pacific Ocean. Easterners wanted to get there faster, and westerners wanted to sell to the East more efficiently. The entire United States began to think of trade with Asia as profitable and exciting.

National Power Overseas

11. How did the United States attempt to gain national power overseas?

One year after the beginning of the gold rush, the American Secretary of State, John M. Clayton, and the British Minister, Henry Bulwer, signed a treaty for a two-nation canal across the narrowest part of Central America. The two countries were not ready to build a canal in 1850, but they wanted the rest of the world to know that any such quick way from the Atlantic to the Pacific would belong to them. No thought was given to any future reaction by the native people of Panama.

For the majority, American power was exciting and helpful.

American imagination extended to the other side of the Pacific—Japan. In 1852 President Fillmore sent Commodore Matthew Perry, brother of the hero of the War of 1812, with four steam-propelled ships, to persuade the Japanese to open their ports to American trade. On July 8, 1853, Perry entered the harbor of Yedo Bay, and he refused to leave until he could give a note from the American President to the Japanese emperor. He left the note, sailed home, and returned in February 1854, to receive the answer. This time he had seven ships and the Japanese greeted him warmly. Six Japanese ports were opened to American trade by 1858.

An attempt by the United States to buy Cuba from Spain in a secret deal was less successful. In 1853 the American ministers met with the British and the French in Ostend, Belgium, to plan an approach to the Spanish government. Word leaked out about the "Ostend Manifesto." Northerners in Congress decided that it was an attempt by a southern-dominated administration to get more slave territory. They protested loudly against the manifesto, and the attempt to buy Cuba had to be abandoned.

1) In 1850 the United States and Great Britain signed a treaty for a two-nation canal across the narrowest part of Central America.
2) Commodore Perry sailed to Japan, and six Japanese ports were opened to American trade in 1858. 3) In 1853 Americans tried unsuccessfully to make a secret deal to buy Cuba from Spain.

This picture shows the Japanese giving a banquet for Perry and his men.

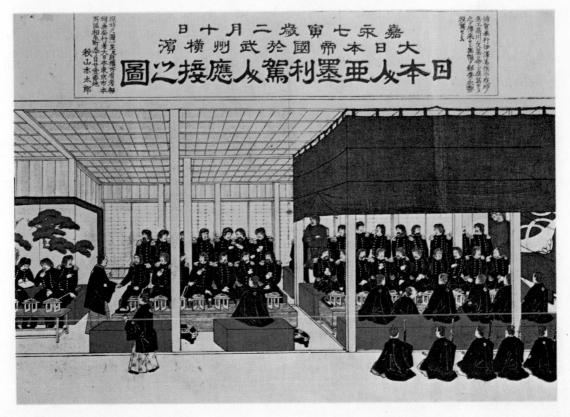

Politics and the Railroad

12. Why did General Scott lose the 1852 election?

The Whigs were divided along northern and southern lines, and Scott was unable to bring them together.

13. Why did Douglas want to bring Nebraska into the nation as a territory?

1) Douglas was a director of the Illinois Central and wanted to make money. 2) A transcontinental line from Chicago through Nebraska would make Chicago a great railroad terminal. 3) Douglas and his friends hoped to get rich by buying Nebraska land and selling it at a profit.

14. Why did Douglas want his railroad built before the one from Mobile to Sante Fe?

Douglas knew that Congress would not spend money on land for more than one railroad at a time.

15. How did Douglas win southern support for his railroad?

1) Douglas asked Congress to repeal the Missouri Compromise of 1820, under which Nebraska would join the Union as a free state. 2) He proposed dividing the territory into Kansas and Nebraska and permitting each to decide if it would be slave or free. 3) The Kansas-Nebraska Bill became law in 1854.

In the presidential election of 1852, both parties supported the Compromise of 1850. But the Whigs were split along northern and southern lines. They ran the popular General Winfield Scott for President. However, Scott was unable to bring the party together, and he won very few states. The Democrats won the election with an unknown, Franklin Pierce, of New Hampshire.

Another Democrat had wanted his party's nomination in 1852, and he looked for it in 1856. Stephen Douglas of Illinois, aged 38, hoped to use his popularity in managing the Compromise of 1850 to become President. However, Douglas was also director of the Illinois Central Railroad and had a particular interest in the success of that railroad. As a buyer, or *speculator*, in the land over which the rails ran, he wanted to make a profit. His plan was to bring Nebraska into the nation as a territory. This would give Douglas' railroad the chance to build a transcontinental line from Chicago through Nebraska. Chicago would boom as a great railroad terminal. And Douglas and his friends could get rich by buying up Nebraska land and selling it later at a higher price. But a northern railroad would not win Douglas southern votes.

The southerners wanted a railroad from Mobile and New Orleans through to Texas and Santa Fe, New Mexico. A slice of land that had belonged to Mexico had been bought by the United States. It was named for the United States minister to Mexico, James Gadsden. The Gadsden Purchase gave a clear right of way over the new land for a transcontinental railroad. Douglas did not mind the idea of a southern railroad. But he wanted his railroad out of Chicago first. He knew that Congress would not spend money on land for more than one railroad at a time. So he had to win southern support some other way.

In order to persuade the southerners to let the east-west railroad go through the North, Douglas changed the bill on the Nebraska territory. The territory would be divided into two parts—Kansas and Nebraska. When each was ready to become a state, the people of each part would decide for themselves whether their state should be slave or free. (See map, page 413.)

Since the northern, or Nebraska, part of the territory was supposed to be free under the line drawn in 1820, Douglas asked Congress to repeal the Missouri Compromise of 1820. The South was delighted. They hoped to fill the territory with slaveholders and slavery sympathizers. As for the northerners, they could not get enough votes in Congress to stop the repeal. The Kansas-Nebraska Bill became law in 1854 with President Pierce's approval.

Recall that Madison had said that the great number of factions would make it necessary and possible for American leaders to think about the whole nation.

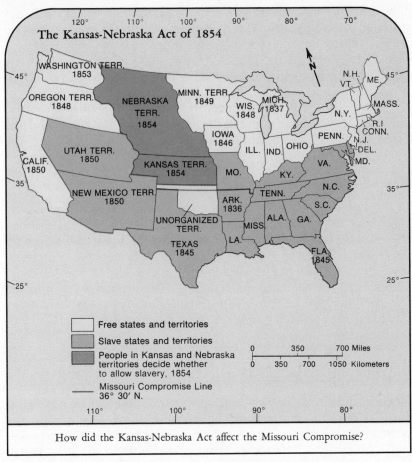

The Kansas-Nebraska Act of 1854

Free states and territories

Slave states and territories

People in Kansas and Nebraska territories decide whether to allow slavery, 1854

Missouri Compromise Line 36° 30′ N.

0   350   700 Miles

0   350   700   1050 Kilometers

How did the Kansas-Nebraska Act affect the Missouri Compromise?

The Kansas-Nebraska Act repealed the Missouri Compromise by permitting slavery north of the Missouri Compromise line, between Missouri and the Rocky Mountains.

Bleeding Kansas

Douglas did not give clear leadership on the question of slavery in the territories. He never said whether slavery was right or wrong. And he never said whether the idea of the people voting on slavery was to be done before or after the population entered the territory. And so as soon as the Kansas-Nebraska Bill passed, a competition began. Thousands from the North and the South poured into the area. They hoped to become a majority before the vote was taken. Not many of the southerners who came actually owned slaves, but they were loyal to the South. New Englanders, backed by the abolitionists, formed a New England Emigrant Society to send antislavery people into the territories. This news caused proslavery people from Missouri to rush in. In fact, the day the election for the territorial assembly was held, a large group of proslavery men came into Kansas—just to vote.

16. Why was everyone at fault in the Kansas bloodshed?

1) Northerners from the East had used Kansas as a testing ground for abolition.
2) Southerners in Missouri had come in illegally to vote, so that Kansas could become a slave state.

Was there any other way to settle the Kansas question? What was the problem with this kind of majority rule?

This picture shows people from the South on their way to Kansas to vote for slavery. What conflicts resulted when they were met by abolitionists?

John Brown, an antislavery activist, announced he would kill anyone who allowed slavery. With Brown were his four sons and two friends. These seven men shot and murdered five members of a proslavery family. Although later Brown was proved to be mentally ill, the bloodshed had started. And it spread. By the end of 1856, some 200 people had died. Everyone was at fault. Northerners from the East had used Kansas as a testing ground for abolition. Southerners in Missouri had come in illegally to vote. And the President, Franklin Pierce, had been on the side of the South.

Politics and Popular Sovereignty

In the Congress, Charles Sumner of Massachusetts spoke with passion about the crime that was committed in Kansas. He demanded that Kansas be brought in as a free state. In his speech, Sumner also insulted Senator Andrew Butler. Butler's nephew, Congressman Brooks, then attacked Sumner in the Senate with a cane. Sumner fell to the floor unconscious. The whole incident made Sumner a hero in the North and convinced many people that Douglas' idea of popular sovereignty may have sounded fair, but, in reality, it was impossible.

The Republican Party

What would the antislavery northerners do? Some formed a political party that came out strongly against extending slavery into the territories. This group met for the first time in Ripon, Wisconsin, and took the old Jeffersonian name of Republican for their party. Many northern Whigs joined the new party since their party had died out. The new party did very well. Thirty congressmen joined its ranks. By July of 1854, the party held a national convention at Jackson, Michigan, and another in Saratoga Springs, New York. In the next congressional election, the Republicans were able to elect one of their members as speaker of the House. That election was a symbol of what was happening in American politics. Candidates no longer could sit on the fence or try to please both North and South. The divisions were clear. The Republican candidate had been a worker in a northern textile mill. The man he beat for the job of Speaker was the owner of 1,100 slaves.

The Republicans had found a popular position. The Old South could do as it pleased. But the new lands had to be free.

17. *What was the importance of electing a Republican as speaker of the House?*

The Republican candidate had been a worker in a northern textile mill, while the man he beat was the owner of 1,100 slaves.

18. *What stand did the Republicans take in the 1856 election?*

The Election of 1856

Stephen Douglas did not care if people voted for or against slavery. He wanted to keep the country united and build his railroad to the

When does a party help the country by not taking a stand on an issue and when does a party help the country by taking a firm stand?

The Development of the Two-Party System

DATE	HAMILTONIANS (Nationalists)	JEFFERSONIANS (States' Rights)
c. 1791	Federalists	Republicans
c. 1820	Republicans "Era of Good Feelings"	
1824–1825	National Republicans	Democratic-Republicans
1834	Whigs	Democrats (Jacksonian)
	Free-Soil Democrats	Southern Democrats
1854	Republicans	Democrats
Present	Republicans	Democrats

West. But other people recognized that popular sovereignty was not the solution to the problem of slavery.

In 1856 the Republicans almost had a presidential victory. For a party that was only two years old, this was remarkable. The Republicans had a fine candidate in John Charles Frémont from California, and they had a wonderful bonus in the candidate's wife, Jessie Benton Frémont. The Frémonts campaigned hard. For the first time, a major candidate said out loud that slavery was immoral. And northerners and midwesterners responded. Frémont's supporters included college professors, ministers, poets, and many young people. The Republican campaign song was:

> Arise, arise, ye braves
> And let our war cry be
> Free Speech, Free Press, Free Soil, Free Man
> Fre-mont and victory!

The Democrats got a great deal of help from wealthy northerners. They were afraid that Frémont's position would cause the South to

1) They were afraid that Frémont's position would cause the South to secede from the Union and this would hurt banking and trade. 2) Buchanan, the Democratic candidate, thought that slavery was wrong, but he didn't believe anything could be done about it.

19. Why did wealthy northerners help the Democrats?

Notice that in this country the two parties have often had the same platform. In a big country with such variety, it is hard for an extreme group to become a majority.

How do you feel about candidates who take a strong moral stand on difficult issues?

secede from the Union, and this would hurt banking and trade. Even Jessie Frémont's father, the famous Missouri senator, supported the Democratic candidate, James Buchanan of Pennsylvania. Buchanan believed that slavery was wrong, but he did not believe anything could be done about it.

20. How did Buchanan win?

The Know-Nothings, a third party that was anti-Catholic and anti-immigrant, took away just enough votes from the Republicans to allow Buchanan to win.

A third party, calling themselves Know Nothings, also ran a candidate. Their stand, or *platform*, was anti-Catholic and anti-immigrant. They took away just enough votes to give the election to Buchanan, even though fewer than half of the voters had supported him.

Buchanan had had a long career in government, including the State Department. Some hoped he would be able to hold the country together. Others called him a "doughface," the name given to a northerner who supported the South and slavery. His major distinction seemed to be that he was the only bachelor President of the United States.

Uncle Tom's Cabin

21. What did the book Uncle Tom's Cabin accomplish?

It made people think about slaves as individuals.

The abolitionists had been hard at work throughout the 1840's and 1850's. Some abolitionists wrote books. The most popular of these was Harriet Beecher Stowe's *Uncle Tom's Cabin,* published in 1851. Stowe was the daughter of the president of a college for ministers in Cincinnati. She knew little of the South and was not a professional author. But she was so upset by the idea of the Fugitive Slave Act (see page 386) that she wrote a novel against slavery. However, she was careful to show that not all southern White people were evil. In fact, the villain, Simon Legree, the overseer of slaves, was a northerner working in the South. The book made people think about slaves as individuals. Readers became emotionally involved with the characters. *Uncle Tom's Cabin* sold 10,000

Why are novels, movies, and plays so powerful in reaching people and influencing their thinking? Which ones have affected you the most?

Members of the Underground Railroad in Indiana help runaway slaves.

copies in one week and 300,000 in a year. It was translated into many languages and read by millions of people. The story was acted out in theaters all over the world.

The Underground Railroad

Abolitionists also were active in the Underground Railroad. This was not a real railroad, but rather a chain of houses and hideaways extending all the way from border states, such as Kentucky and Maryland, to Canada. Bands, or "trains," of runaway slaves were led by men and women "conductors" from one hiding place, or "station," to another until they reached safety. The Underground Railroad helped somewhere between 40,000 and 100,000 slaves to escape to the North and to Canada. A number of free Blacks also went to Canada for fear that they would be mistaken for runaway slaves under the Fugitive Slave Act. This law won many more northerners over to an active position against slavery. Under the Fugitive Slave Act, a slave catcher only had to state that a Black was his slave in order to take him or her back from the North to the South. The law was a threat to the rights of Blacks everywhere, and northerners reacted strongly to Congress telling them that they had to take personal action against Black people.

Harriet Tubman, a Black woman, made two trips to the South each year to bring slaves North with her on the Underground Railroad. She disguised herself in order to get by the slave catchers who put a price on her head. In the summers, she worked as a cook to make money to finance those trips. In 1858 she became a lecturer, and she told her story to other people. Her lectures, and those of other abolitionists such as Frederick Douglass, the Grimké sisters, Lucretia Mott, and William Lloyd Garrison made more people realize that slavery was wrong. Some Americans were using their liberty to hurt the liberty of others.

But the American way to handle minority rights was by majority rule. The Black minority did not have a vote. As for the White southern minority, it felt that it had every constitutional right to its point of view—whether or not slavery was morally wrong. And in the Congress, some individual southerners were very powerful.

Harriet Tubman, an Underground Railroad "conductor," led fleeing slaves to freedom. What qualities did she have that helped her do this job?

22. What did abolitionists such as Harriet Tubman and Frederick Douglass accomplish?

1) They brought slaves North through the Underground Railroad. 2) They made more people realize that slavery was wrong.

Checking the facts

1. How did the Compromise of 1850 come to be repealed?
2. Why was the Republican party formed?
3. What actions were the abolitionists taking during this time in American history?

In your opinion, does a minority have as much right to be wrong as does the majority?

417

3. NATIONAL LEADERSHIP

Was there to be any national leadership at all? Would anyone be able to take action that would satisfy the South's need for protection, the North's growing feelings against slavery, and the West's push for settlement?

The Dred Scott Decision

23. Why did the Dred Scott decision bring more northerners to the antislavery cause?

The Supreme Court ruled that slaves were private property guaranteed by the Bill of Rights. It seemed that the Supreme Court was using the Bill of Rights to keep human beings in slavery.

In March of 1857 the Supreme Court took action. A slave named Dred Scott sued in the courts for his freedom on the grounds that he had lived in free territory. The abolitionists of the nation hoped for some leadership on the issue of slavery in the territories. President Buchanan had told the nation that the Court would offer help. But in the court decision, written by Chief Justice Roger Taney, the Supreme Court supported slavery. The Court ruled that although Dred Scott had been taken into free territory by his master, he was a slave under the laws of the state where he had lived before, and he must remain one. Slaves were private property guaranteed by the Bill of Rights. And no law of Congress, such as the Missouri Compromise, could take away a man's property—even if the property was another human being. According to the Court, Dred Scott was a slave wherever he lived. There could be no free territory. Therefore, according to the Dred Scott decision, the Missouri Compromise was unconstitutional.

The Dred Scott decision was complicated to understand. But northerners got one general message. The Supreme Court was using the Bill of Rights to keep human beings in slavery. Thousands more in the North joined the antislavery cause.

The President and Kansas

24. Why did Congress reject the Kansas state constitution?

Since the Free Soil people refused to attend the convention, the constitution did not represent the will of the majority.

Buchanan also failed to provide leadership. In Kansas a group of proslavery people got together in convention to draft a state constitution. The Free Soil people refused to attend the convention. As a result the new constitution, known as the Lecompton Constitution, allowed slavery in Kansas. Although the constitution did not represent the will of the majority, Buchanan backed it. Congress, however, rejected the constitution and Buchanan's leadership as well.

Douglas—and Abraham Lincoln

25. How did Abraham Lincoln regard the slavery issue?

The only leader left seemed to be Stephen Douglas. Yet his plan for popular sovereignty had caused riots and bloodshed, and it did not get at the heart of the problems between the abolitionists and the South. In 1858 Douglas was up for reelection to the Senate

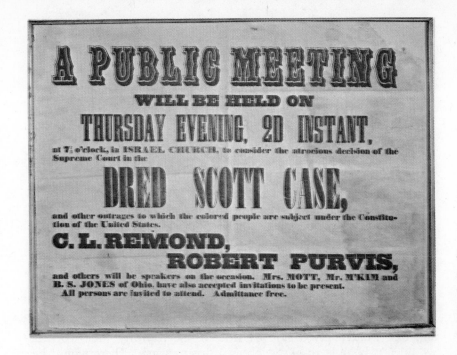

A PUBLIC MEETING

WILL BE HELD ON

THURSDAY EVENING, 2D INSTANT,

at 7½ o'clock, in ISRAEL CHURCH, to consider the atrocious decision of the Supreme Court in the

DRED SCOTT CASE,

and other outrages to which the colored people are subject under the Constitution of the United States.

C. L. REMOND,
ROBERT PURVIS,

and others will be speakers on the occasion. Mrs. MOTT, Mr. M'KIM and B. S. JONES of Ohio, have also accepted invitations to be present.
All persons are invited to attend.   Admittance free.

This poster appeared after the Dred Scott decision. It tells of a meeting by Black abolitionists to speak out against the decision.

from Illinois. Running against him for the Republican party was a young lawyer who had been in Congress for two years. Abraham Lincoln was a loyal party worker, a lawyer for owners of businesses in Springfield, and a *lobbyist* on behalf of the railroads. He was an abolitionist. He did not believe in doing away with slavery in the South. But he did not believe that popular sovereignty would work to settle the problems of the territories.

The senatorial election in Illinois became a national event because the two men, Douglas and Lincoln, were such dramatic opposites. Both were also enormously popular. They debated each other in all the major cities of Illinois so that all the people could come to hear them and decide how to vote. One member of the audience, Gustave Koerner, reported how each of the candidates looked and what effect each had on his audience:

> "Douglas was fighting for his political life. No greater
> contrast could be imagined than the one between
> Lincoln and Douglas. The latter was really a little
> giant physically . . . while Lincoln, when standing
> erect, towered to six feet four inches (1.9 meters).
> Lincoln, awkward in posture and leaning a little
> forward, stood calm . . . He addressed his hearers in a
> somewhat familiar yet very earnest way with a clear,
> distinct, and far-reaching voice, generally well
> controlled, but sometimes expressive of sadness,

1) He thought it was morally wrong. 2) He didn't believe in doing away with slavery in the South. 3) He didn't want slavery extended into the new territories. 4) He felt that if slaves and free workers lived side by side in one territory, free workers would not be able to get a job at a decent wage, and this would lead to riots.

Notice the details of Lincoln's stand on slavery. Why is it important to take a stand?

> though at times he could assume a most humorous, and even comical look. . . . Douglas, powerful as was his speech, never showed anything like genius. There came from Lincoln occasionally flashes of genius and burning words. . . . Douglas was immensely talented; Lincoln was original. But what made Lincoln so vastly more effective in this contest was that even the slowest hearer could see at once that Douglas spoke for himself, and Lincoln for his cause."

In a speech before the Republican convention that nominated him, Lincoln had pinned the issue down.

> "A house divided against itself cannot stand. . . . I believe this government cannot endure permanently half slave and half free. . . . I do not expect the house to fall; but I do expect it will cease to be divided. It will become all one thing, or all the other."

Lincoln made people look carefully at popular sovereignty. If slaves and free workers lived side by side in one territory, free workers would not be able to get a job at a decent wage. There would be riots. Lincoln forced Douglas to admit that only police power could protect the slaves and their owners from the free people in a free land. And Lincoln made it clear that he believed slavery was morally wrong. Lincoln thought that southerners were trapped into their system . . . that someday slavery would wither away. But it should never be extended into new territories.

26. How did the debates ruin Douglas' chances for the presidency in 1860?

1) Lincoln pointed out that the Dred Scott decision made it possible for people with slaves to move to a territory which did not allow slavery. 2) Douglas argued that, in spite of the Dred Scott decision, people in a territory could bar slavery by refusing to enact the slave codes necessary to support the system.

As Lincoln debated Douglas at Freeport, he pointed out the contradiction between the idea of popular sovereignty and the Dred Scott decision. The Supreme Court had ruled that the government had no power over slavery in the territories. People with slaves could bring them into new territories. How then could people in a territory vote on whether or not to allow slavery? In his reply, known as the Freeport Doctrine, Douglas argued that in spite of the Dred Scott decision, the people in a territory could bar slavery. They could do this by refusing to enact a body of laws, or slave codes, necessary to support the system.

Douglas' stand made many southerners angry. He won the senatorial election, but his chances for the presidency in 1860 were ruined by the debates. At the same time, the debates exposed Abraham Lincoln to the public. By the time they were over, Lincoln was known throughout the nation.

"Honest Abe"

27. How did Lincoln feel about the Union?

Lincoln was indeed "Honest Abe," as his friends and followers at home called him. He hated slavery. But he could not lie by saying

Notice how realistic Lincoln was.

that a simple vote would take away the problem. And he repeated over and over again that no difference among people in a vast and varied nation must ever be allowed to destroy the Union. The Union was formed to provide strength and guarantee liberty. Now it was going to have to face the problem that had existed since the 1600's. And while facing it—not lying about it nor running away from it—Americans would have to pledge their loyalty to a nation that was bigger than the sum of its parts.

Lincoln called for more than an American system and more than a compromise among differences. He called for loyalty to something bigger—the Union. What Lincoln said was not new. But when he said it and how he said it made all the difference. His argument for union took the spotlight off the idea of political compromises about the West. And the South feared his voice and his courage.

Economic Rivalry

The years when Lincoln became known nationally were years of continued expansion: more machines, more strikes, more trade, more cities. And this expansion provided more reasons for separation between the North and the South.

The South also was interested in building cities and railroads. It wanted to catch up with the North. In the 1850's some southerners tried unsuccessfully to do this. Several people tried to boost southern cities. J.D.B. DeBow promoted Norfolk, Virginia, as the southern city to challenge the port of New York. Norfolk had mild weather, a good harbor, and was located about midway between North and South. But Richmond, Virginia, was not happy about DeBow's plans for Norfolk. And New Orleans certainly did not want to see Atlantic trade centering on eastern ports. Over a long period of 100 years northern cities always had competed with each other. But competition was difficult for southerners because they had waited until the 1850's to take railroad systems and urban trading centers seriously. By that time the northern connections had grown naturally. By that late date the South would have to coordinate its efforts as a region. But no American cities, or governments at any level, had even been able to do away with competition for trade and manufacturing.

Not until the 1850's did the South realize that it must have manufacturing in order to build urban centers. Trade alone was not enough. Newspapers in Mobile and Richmond published editorials explaining that the South could not be independent from the North without its own industry. The first southern industries were textile mills. As the soil in the eastern states wore out, the cotton plantations moved west. To compensate for this wasted land, Georgia made an effort to set up cotton cloth factories. By 1848 Georgia boasted 32 of these mills. Virginians built flour mills and tobacco

This picture shows Abraham Lincoln as a young man.

1) No difference among people in a vast and varied nation should ever be allowed to destroy the Union. 2) The Union was formed to provide strength and guarantee liberty.

factories. Richmond was number one in tobacco by 1860, with 52 manufacturing businesses. Richmond and other southern cities in the 1850's developed at the same time as the newer cities of the Midwest. But they developed so much later than New York, Boston, and Philadelphia that they could not compete seriously with the latter cities. New York City had long had its connection to the West through the Erie Canal, and now it had the railroad. New York was the trading center of the nation. The South could not close a generation gap in one decade. It could not become independent of northern banks and factors. Its financial ties were in the North, and southerners who could afford it bought northern goods. The North also benefited most from the clipper ships and their trade. And the discovery of oil in Pennsylvania in 1859 helped the North. With the switch in fuel from wood and coal to oil, machines could run more smoothly. This was one more reason the South could not move quickly enough to catch up to the North.

John Brown Again

28. How did John Brown become a hero for the abolitionists?

1) He and an army of 18 captured the United States armory at Harper's Ferry, Virginia. Brown hoped that all the slaves would rise up in revolt and join him. 2) The United States Army, under Robert E. Lee, retook the building, and Brown was taken prisoner. 3) Brown was publicly tried, convicted of murder and treason by the state of Virginia, and sentenced to death. This made him a hero to some people.

The question of the South's economic independence was less an issue in the news than the antislavery question. Economic development takes a long time and is seldom dramatic. Abolitionist activity was more spectacular. In October of 1859, the fanatic John Brown collected an army of 18 people, and he captured the *armory* of the United States at Harper's Ferry, Virginia. Brown believed that his action would cause all the slaves to rise up in revolt and join him. Instead, the United States Army, under Colonel Robert E. Lee, took the building from Brown and his army. Ten of Brown's men died, and Brown himself was taken prisoner. He was given a fair trial and then convicted of murder and treason by the state of Virginia. He was sentenced to death by hanging. Brown's death made him a hero for the abolitionists.

Plays, stories, and songs were written about him. A line from one of these was: "John Brown's body lies a moulderin' in the grave— but his truth goes marching on."

The Election of 1860

29. How did Lincoln win the election of 1860?

In the Deep South, people had begun to talk of leaving the Union if they were not allowed to live as they pleased. The legislature of Alabama voted to secede if a Republican were elected President. The Democrats met in April 1860 in Charleston, South Carolina. When Stephen Douglas would not promise to let slavery exist in the territories, the party split. The northern Democrats nominated Douglas. The southern Democrats left the party and nominated John Breckinridge of Kentucky.

The political parties could not contain the results of expansion.

Lincoln's Republican Party offered the majority in the North and West just what they wanted. Yes. The northern states voted Republican and the southern states voted Democratic. The vote predicts the approximate division of the nation into the Union and Confederacy.

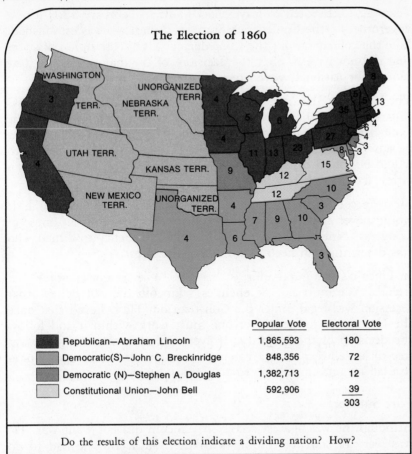

The Election of 1860

WASHINGTON TERR. 3
UTAH TERR.
CALIFORNIA 4
NEW MEXICO TERR.
UNORGANIZED TERR.
NEBRASKA TERR.
KANSAS TERR.
UNORGANIZED TERR. 4
9
4
6
4
7
11
13
5
5
6
4
12
9
8
10
3
4
28
27
35
15
12
10
3
13
6
4
4
3
3
8
3

		Popular Vote	Electoral Vote
■	Republican—Abraham Lincoln	1,865,593	180
■	Democratic(S)—John C. Breckinridge	848,356	72
■	Democratic (N)—Stephen A. Douglas	1,382,713	12
■	Constitutional Union—John Bell	592,906	39
			303

Do the results of this election indicate a dividing nation? How?

1) The northern and southern Democrats split, nominating Douglas and Breckinridge. 2) The Republicans ran Lincoln and a party platform including everything the North and West wanted, including no slavery in the territories. 3) The Constitutional Union Party ran Bell of Tennessee. 4) Lincoln took all the Northern states, which had the most electoral votes.

In Chicago the Republicans chose Abraham Lincoln on the third ballot. Lincoln himself was not at the convention. But his supporters kept the meeting lively with their cheering from the gallery. The Republican platform included everything the North and West wanted—cheap land for the farmers, a high tariff for manufacturers, federal aid for a railroad to the Pacific, unrestricted immigration so that new workers could enter the country, and no slavery in the territories.

A fourth party, called the Constitutional Union party, also ran a candidate, John Bell of Tennessee. With the vote split among so many candidates no one could win a popular majority. But Lincoln took all the northern states, which had the most people, and, therefore, the most electoral votes. (See map, above.)

The South Secedes

With Lincoln's election, the South Carolina legislature voted for secession. Within three months, the lower South from Georgia to

30. Why did some southerners favor secession?

1) Slavery and cotton was profitable. 2) The South would never again be a part of the majority in either house of Congress. 3) They had lost the presidency to a man who was determined to keep slaves out of the West.

Texas also had voted to leave the Union. In February 1861 a new government—the Confederate States of America—was established. Like the confederation, the Confederacy was a loose union of states that did not have to obey the decisions of the majority in a strong central, or national, government.

The states of Alabama, Tennessee, North Carolina, and Arkansas did not join right away. But they warned Lincoln to leave the Confederacy alone. Some southerners were in favor of secession because of slavery and cotton. Some favored it because the South would be forced to become more independent and develop its own cities, factories, banks, and shipping.

Most agreed with the argument that whatever the South did, it would never again be part of a majority of votes in either house of Congress. Now southerners had lost the presidency to a man who was determined to keep slaves out of the West.

31. Why was Lincoln opposed to secession?

He believed that secession was not legal under the Constitution. Once the Union was formed, everyone must work within it and follow the decision of the majority.

In Lincoln's inaugural address, he said, "We are not enemies, but friends. We must not be enemies." Lincoln did not believe that secession was legal under the Constitution. He believed that once the Union was formed, everyone must work within it and follow the decision of the majority. If every unhappy voter or state was free to leave every time a vote was lost, there would be no Union to plan for and no loyalty to a common future.

Fort Sumter

32. How did the war begin?

The army of the Confederacy opened fire on the United States Army post at Fort Sumter, South Carolina, on April 12, 1861.

Although he was against secession, Lincoln did not want war. He was wary of starting trouble with the South. But he had to do something about the American army posts in the South, especially the one at Fort Sumter in Charleston harbor. Removing the soldiers from these posts would mean that he recognized the South's right to secede. But sending reinforcements might start a war.

Lincoln decided on a middle course. He would send supplies to Fort Sumter. But before the supply ships arrived, the army of the Confederacy opened fire on the fort on April 12, 1861. Events then moved rapidly. The North was angry. Lincoln called for 75,000 volunteers and the war started.

Checking the facts

1. What made it possible for Lincoln to be elected President?
2. Why did the election of 1860 bring about the breakup of the Union?
3. What was Lincoln's attitude about secession?

Why are people so interested in fixing the blame for the first shot fired at Fort Sumter?

PUTTING IT ALL TOGETHER

UNDERSTANDING THE MAIN IDEAS

1. How did the railroad affect the development of natural resources in the United States?
2. What effect did the railroad have on where and how people lived in the North, South, and West?
3. What effect did the added power and wealth of the United States have on its relations with foreign nations?
4. What leadership was able to help a divided nation?

ACTIVITIES

1. When were railroads built in your state? What towns were helped by them? Are railroads or roads most important now in your state? With gas and oil shortages, are there new plans for railroads? You can use your local or school library to find the information. Prepare a map of railroads that pass through your state.
2. Read one of the speeches of Abraham Lincoln. You will probably be able to find it in a book of famous speeches. Ask your teacher or school librarian for help in finding this type of book. Analyze the order of the sentences, the choice of words, the rhythm, and the tone, as well as the ideas presented. Why is it a good speech?
3. Find a book of political cartoons and photographs of Abraham Lincoln. Using this evidence, what conclusions can you draw about why he is such a famous President? Incorporate your findings in a written report or oral presentation to your class.

BOOKS TO READ

Bany, James P., *Bloody Kansas, 1854–1865* (New York: Watts Publishing Co., 1972).

Cook, Fred J., *The Demagogues* (New York: Macmillan, 1972).

Coolidge, Olivia, *The Apprenticeship of Abraham Lincoln* (New York: Charles Scribner's Sons, Inc., 1974).

Corder, Eric, *Prelude to the Civil War* (New York: Macmillan, 1970).

Goldston, Robert, *The Coming of the Civil War* (New York: Macmillan, 1972).

Petry, Ann, *Harriet Tubman, Conductor on the Underground Railroad* (New York: Macmillan, 1968).

chapter 17
War and Peace: For What?

1861–1876

1. WAR FOR UNION OR
   PROTECTION?
2. REBUILDING—FOR WHOM?

INTRODUCTION

Lincoln, like Calhoun before him, understood exactly what was at
stake. Majority rule had to be preserved for the health of the Union.
Minority rights had to be preserved for the liberty of individuals.
When the two were in conflict in 1850, Calhoun had chosen minority rights, even though the minority were slaveholders. Lincoln
in his time chose majority rule, even though it meant civil war.
Both men were aware of the price to be paid for taking one side
or the other. Both men suffered the agony of making decisions that
could not be reversed. Both were attacked as if they had not seen
all sides to the question. And both took their responsibility as
leaders seriously, because they believed that the United States could
still serve as an example of self-government to the rest of the world.

	1861	1862	1863	1861-1865	
Who?	General Beauregard of the Confederacy	Blacks	Union and Confederate soldiers	Clara Barton	
What?	leads an attack on the federal garrison	organize into Union regiments	fight a battle	supervises nurses on the battlefield	
Where?	at Fort Sumter in South Carolina	in the North	at Gettysburg in Pennsylvania	behind Union lines	

As you read about the period of the Civil War and the years of rebuilding, or reconstruction, after it, think about these questions.

1. What did a war between the states achieve?
2. How did the North, South, and West develop during and after the war?
3. How much did political leadership achieve for Blacks and Native Americans when the war was over?

1. WAR FOR UNION OR PROTECTION?

The South believed it had the right to secede. Since the states made the Union in the first place, the states could unmake it. In a way, the South was turning to the Declaration of Independence when it said that the governed in the South no longer consented to the United States government. The southern strategy in the war, therefore, was not to conquer the North at all, but to defend the borders of its new nation, the Confederate States of America. (See map, page 428.)

The Confederacy

The Confederate States of America was set up in Richmond, Virginia. Its president was Jefferson Davis. Davis was a graduate of West Point, the United States military academy, and was the owner of a successful plantation. He had preferred that the South not secede, but had joined the Confederates because he believed that Lincoln would not let the South make its own decisions. Davis would rather have been a soldier in the field than an administrator in an office. He had trouble running his new country, partly because the Confederacy gave so much power to the individual states.

1. Why was the South in the war?

1) The South believed that, since the states made the Union in the first place, the states could unmake it. 2) Its strategy was not to conquer the North but to defend the borders of its new nation, the Confederate States of America.

2. Why was Davis having trouble running his new country?

The Confederacy gave so much power to the individual states that it was almost impossible for Davis to raise taxes, run an army, and keep it supplied.

1865	1867	1868	1869	1876
General Robert E. Lee of the Confederate army	Local members of the Ku Klux Klan	President Andrew Johnson	Ulysses S. Grant, the former Union general	The Sioux Indians
surrenders to General Grant	are formally organized	is impeached by a vote of the House of Representatives	becomes the eighteenth President	defeat General Custer
at Appomattox Court House in Virginia	at Nashville, Tennessee	in Washington, D.C.	of the United States	at the Little Big Horn in Montana

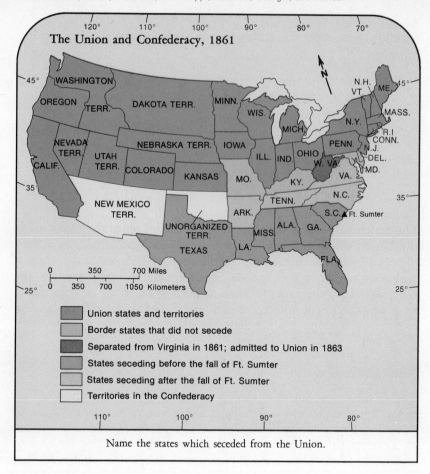

What ties were broken by the Civil War?

The states that seceded from the Union were Virginia, Arkansas, Tennessee, North Carolina, South Carolina, Texas, Louisiana, Mississippi, Alabama, Georgia, and Florida.

The Union and Confederacy, 1861

Union states and territories

Border states that did not secede

Separated from Virginia in 1861; admitted to Union in 1863

States seceding before the fall of Ft. Sumter

States seceding after the fall of Ft. Sumter

Territories in the Confederacy

Name the states which seceded from the Union.

It was almost impossible for Davis to raise taxes, run an army, and keep it properly supplied.

3. What advantages did the South have?

1) The South did not have problems of supply and transportation. 2) The Confederate general, Robert E. Lee, was the best soldier and leader of troops on the continent.

The South did not expect northern merchants and textile mill owners to support a war that would cost them so much money. The southerners also had an advantage. They were able to stay home and defend themselves. They would not have problems of supply and transportation.

The Confederacy's most important advantage was its general. Robert E. Lee was the best soldier and leader of troops on the entire continent. He could have led either the Union or Confederate army. He had hoped Virginia would not secede. But when his home state joined the Confederacy, Lee went with it.

The Union Army

4. What did bringing the South back into the Union mean?

The northern army had a different purpose. From Lincoln's point of view, the South had to be brought back into the Union. This meant that the Union army would have to march through the South and occupy it. The rebel leaders must be captured, and the new Confederate government disbanded.

The North had a number of advantages over the South. One of these was population. There were over 20 million Americans in the North, compared to 9 million in the South. Also, the southern population was more than one-third slave, and no southern army was going to give guns to the Blacks. The North had the factories and the railroads to supply its army. It also had a navy to blockade the southern ports so that they could not receive aid from their European trading partners. Both armies had more untrained volunteers than they could handle. And they did not have the time to develop well-trained field troops. Each state was responsible for recruiting soldiers. Volunteers joined up to fight alongside their neighbors.

1) The rebel leaders had to be captured. 2) The Confederate government had to be disbanded.

5. What advantages did the North have?

1) The North had 11 million more people. 2) Three million people in the South were slaves who could not carry guns. 3) The North had factories and railroads to supply its army. 4) It had a navy to blockade the southern ports from their European trading partners.

This picture shows New York's Seventh Regiment parading down Broadway on April 19, 1861. What emotions are being displayed by the people?

The Battle of Bull Run

6. How did Lincoln's strategy backfire at Bull Run?

1) The Union army was to capture the Confederate government at Richmond, and then find and easily defeat the rest of the Confederate army.
2) Jackson put his troops on a hill and waited for the Union troops to advance. The Union army was forced to retreat to Washington.

The capital cities of the Confederacy and the Union were only 110 miles (176 kilometers) apart. The first battle of the Civil War was fought between them. The Union sent out an army of 30,000 from Washington to capture Richmond and break up the Confederate government. Then, Lincoln thought, it would be easy to search the South for the rest of the Confederate army and finish the job quickly. But it did not turn out that way. Crossing the Potomac River, the Union army met a Confederate force at Bull Run, or Manassas Junction, on July 21, 1861. (See map, page 431.) The Confederate army was as large as the Union one. The Confederate general, Thomas Jackson, took his troops back to a hill that could be easily defended, and then stood there "like a stone wall." As the Union troops advanced, Jackson gave the signal, which was followed by a blood-curdling "rebel yell" from the southern army. Southerners fired their guns at point blank range, and then they charged with bayonets. The northerners retreated to Washington.

7. What steps did Lincoln take after Bull Run?

1) Lincoln chose George McClellan as his new general. McClellan insisted on more supplies before attempting a massive attack on the South.
2) Factories and shops all over the North were put to work. Women were used as workers because so many men were in the army.

The Battle of Bull Run was a shock to the Union cause. Northerners had been so sure of victory that a good many people had packed picnic baskets and come out from Washington to watch the battle. But luckily for the North, "Stonewall" Jackson did not follow the army back to Washington. The southern strategy was to defend its territory, not to conquer. Lincoln, however, had to find a new general and a new battle plan. He chose George McClellan, who was 34 years old. McClellan insisted on more supplies for the army before he attempted a massive attack on the South. Factories and shops all over the North were put to work making guns, ammunition, wagons, shoes, and uniforms. With so many men going into the army, women took on many of the jobs in the factories. Women like Clara Barton in the North and Phoebe Levy Pember in the South organized relief societies and hospitals to care for the wounded soldiers. This turned into one of the major jobs of both sides during the war.

War in the West

8. Why was the battle at Shiloh such a terrible one?

In two days, more Americans died than in all the battles of the Revolution, the War of 1812, and the Mexican War combined.

While support for the army was building in the East, the Union army in the West invaded Tennessee from Illinois. Their general, Ulysses S. Grant, used armored gunboats on the rivers and captured two southern forts, Henry and Donelson. Grant took 14,000 prisoners in all.

But then the Confederates under General Albert Johnston stopped Grant's invasion by a surprise attack at Shiloh in April, 1862. The South won the first day of that terrible battle. The North won the next. But in two days, more Americans died than in all the battles of the Revolution, the War of 1812, and the Mexican War.

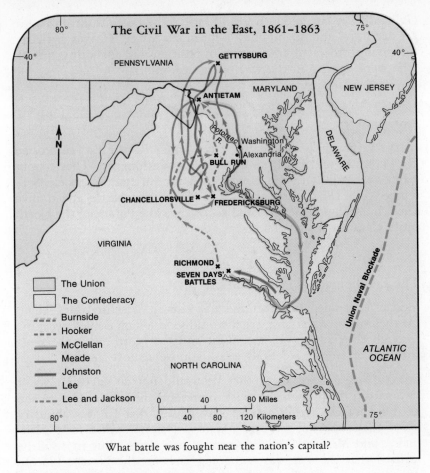

The Civil War in the East, 1861–1863

80°   75°

40°   40°

PENNSYLVANIA   GETTYSBURG

MARYLAND   NEW JERSEY

ANTIETAM

DELAWARE

Potomac R.

Washington

Alexandria

BULL RUN

CHANCELLORSVILLE   FREDERICKSBURG

VIRGINIA

RICHMOND

SEVEN DAYS' BATTLES

Union Naval Blockade

ATLANTIC OCEAN

The Union

The Confederacy

- - - - Burnside
– – – Hooker
———— McClellan
———— Meade
———— Johnston
———— Lee
- - - - Lee and Jackson

NORTH CAROLINA

0   40   80 Miles
0   40   80   120 Kilometers

80°   75°

What battle was fought near the nation's capital?

The battle of Bull Run was fought near the nation's capital.

The Battle for Richmond

When McClellan was ready for his attack on the South, he decided to approach Richmond by sea. This seemed like a good plan. Already in the first battle of ironclad warships the northern ship, the *Monitor,* had turned its guns, which were set in a revolving tower or turret, on the southern ship *Merrimac*. Although there was no real victor, the battle proved that the new technology was successful on water as well as on land. McClellan almost had a great victory near Richmond. But he refused to chase the Confederate army and either capture or destroy it. McClellan and the other generals of both the North and South had been trained in old-fashioned warfare at West Point. The idea was to win battles until the political leaders made peace.

The President Takes Over

But Lincoln knew this war was different. This war was a war against

9. What kept McClellan from a great victory near Richmond?

McClellan almost had a great victory, but he refused to chase the Confederate army and either capture or destroy it.

10. How did Lincoln justify his actions?

431

He knew that the entire South, including civilians, had to be defeated, and he had to act in a hurry.

civilians. The entire South would have to be taken. Lincoln had to act in a hurry and he did not ask for much advice. He was criticized for giving orders to silence the opposition and for jailing people who were getting in the way of the war effort.

Antietam

11. Why did Lee retreat across the Potomac?

The South's strategy was to defend its borders rather than to conquer the North.

In the meantime Confederate forces under Robert E. Lee crossed the Potomac, and began to advance on Washington. They fought a bloody battle with the Union army at Antietam Creek on September 17, 1862. (See map, page 431.) The battle ended in a draw, but because Lee retreated back across the Potomac, the North could claim a victory of sorts.

The Emancipation Proclamation

12. Why did Lincoln issue the Emancipation Proclamation?

1) The working people in the North wanted Lincoln to take a stand against slavery.
2) Many runaway slaves were joining the Union army.
3) Lincoln knew that if he freed slaves in the Confederate states, many might desert their owners and join the Union army, or at least help the North by rioting against the southerners.

Lincoln continued to direct the war himself. He fired McClellan. He then planned a strategy that would send Union armies sweeping through the South from the West and the North. But the most startling of Lincoln's actions was his move against slavery.

Lincoln had said all along that he would not do anything about slavery until he thought he must to preserve the Union. One reason he did not take action against slavery was that he was afraid of losing the support of the border states—Delaware, Maryland, Kentucky, and Missouri. All these states had slaves. But in 1862 he realized that the war was not going well for the North. Lincoln was also afraid that England and France might decide to help the South. As yet England and France had not taken sides. But the cotton trade with the South was important to them, and Lincoln feared this might lead them to enter the war on the side of the Confederacy. Furthermore, the working people of the North were angry at Lincoln because he had not taken a firm stand against slavery. By this time, runaway slaves were joining the Union army. They were known as *contrabands*. They were not allowed to be actual fighters, but they did work as cooks, scouts, and spies. Lincoln knew that if he freed the slaves in the Confederate states, many more might desert their masters and join the Union army or at least help the North by rioting against the southerners.

For these reasons, Lincoln issued his Emancipation Proclamation on January 1, 1863. It was not a law but a presidential statement. It only freed the slaves in those states that were "in rebellion." These states of course did not recognize Lincoln's authority. So the Proclamation had little immediate effect on slaves. It was, however, a major step in the history of American freedom.

Black soldiers recruited for the Union army fought bravely at the storming of Fort Wagner, South Carolina. Over 200 Blacks were killed in the fighting.

Draft Riots

Some of the recent immigrants to the United States did not like the fact that they were being drafted into the northern army to help free Blacks, who could then come north and take their jobs. Riots against the draft broke out in several cities. The worst was in New York, where the mob attacked the houses and shops of Blacks.

Slowly the attitudes of many people toward Blacks began to change. Blacks were recruited for the army. They were often assigned chores around camp and, until 1864, they were paid less than White soldiers. They had separate regiments and White officers, but their bravery helped to convince a great many northern Whites of the loyalty of Blacks to the United States. Twenty-one Blacks received the Congressional Medal of Honor for outstanding heroism during the Civil War.

13. Why did northern immigrants oppose the draft?

They didn't want to fight in a war to free Blacks who could then come North and take their jobs.

14. How did the Blacks change people's attitudes?

Their bravery in battle showed their loyalty to the United States.

Notice how the questions of jobs and race are linked. In what ways are they separate questions?

Southern Victories

The Union army was not able to follow up on its victory at Antietam. When Union forces pushed into Virginia in the winter of 1862, they were defeated by Robert E. Lee first at Fredericksburg, and later at Chancellorsville in May 1863. (See map, page 431.) The latter battle was an important victory for Lee, but many Confederate soldiers were killed, among them "Stonewall" Jackson.

Lee knew that these victories should be followed by an attack across the Pennsylvania border into northern territory. His sense of timing was correct. The northerners were becoming tired of losing. The southern army could not go on forever without supplies. In addition, there was word that the Union army in the West was moving in on the Confederate supply center at Vicksburg. If Lee were to invade the north, this was the moment.

15. Why was it necessary for Lee to change strategy and attack in northern territory?

1) Lee had defeated the North at both Fredericksburg and Chancellorsville, and the North was tired of losing. 2) There was word that the Union army in the West was moving in on the Confederate supply center at Vicksburg.

Lee at Gettysburg

The site for the important battle was not exactly chosen. In late June 1863, the southern army had stopped in Gettysburg, Pennsylvania, to look for some boots and saddles. (See map, page 431.) When they ran into a Union force, both armies sent for help and a major battle was soon under way. The Union army took its place on Cemetery Ridge and the Confederate army on Seminary Ridge. General Pickett led a southern charge of 15,000 soldiers across the plain between the two armies. But most of Pickett's soldiers were killed by northern artillery fire. Lee suffered his first great defeat.

The year 1863 was a turning point in the war. The North began to win. Grant took Vicksburg and cut the South off from the West and the Mississippi River. Grant also took Chattanooga, Tennessee, which was the railroad center of the South. (See map, page 436.) Shipping, supplies, and cotton were now in northern hands.

16. Why was the year 1863 a turning point in the war?

1) Lee suffered his first major defeat at Gettysburg. 2) Grant took Vicksburg, cutting the South off from the West and the Mississippi River. 3) Grant took Chattanooga, the railroad center of the South, putting shipping, supplies, and cotton in northern control.

The Gettysburg Address

The year 1863 is also remembered for the speech Lincoln gave at Gettysburg. In November, four months after the battle, he came to dedicate a cemetery for the Union dead. The Gettysburg Address is only ten sentences long. It ends with Lincoln's reminder to both North and South that the war was being fought for the preservation of a very special nation. He said:

> "We here highly resolve that these dead shall not have died in vain—that this nation, under God, shall have a new birth of freedom—and that government of the people, by the people, for the people, shall not perish from the earth."

17. What was the purpose of Lincoln's address at Gettysburg?

It was to honor those who died there and to remind both North and South that the war was being fought to preserve a very special nation.

Many Americans believe that by acting together, there is more freedom for each individual.

General Lee, left, and Stonewall Jackson met for the last time on May 2, 1863. That evening, Jackson was accidentally shot by his own soldiers and died.

1864—Northern Success

By 1864 the North had scored both a military victory and an economic one. While the war went on, the Congress—now a northern legislature—passed the Republican platform of 1860 into law. The Homestead Act of 1862 gave western lands to people who would settle on them for five years. The Morrill Act in that same year gave states land to support agricultural colleges. This was a major change in the view of higher education as well as a new use for government aid. Higher tariffs protected manufacturers. Land

18. How were the North and West tied together?

Notice how active Congress can be when all of the voters agree on what ought to be done.

1) They were tied together by a series of new laws. The Homestead Act distributed western lands. 2) The Morrill Act gave states land for agricultural colleges. 3) Higher tariffs protected manufacturers. 4) Land and money were set aside for a transcontinental railroad. 5) A banking act gave every state the same currency.

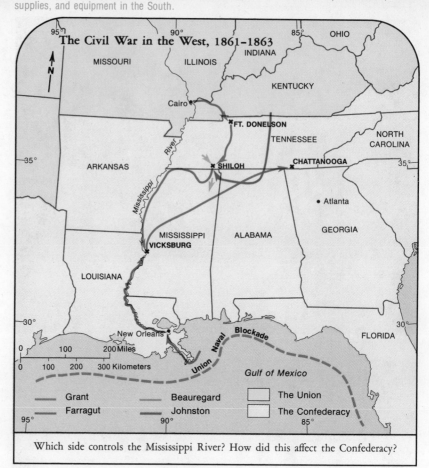

The Civil War in the West, 1861–1863

Which side controls the Mississippi River? How did this affect the Confederacy?

Describe the changes in the war that are symbolized on this map.

and money were set aside by Congress to build the transcontinental railway that had been everyone's dream. A banking act gave every state in the United States the same currency. The North and West were tied to each other by each of these laws.

19. Why was the South running out of supplies?

1) The South didn't have enough factories to produce the goods it needed. 2) It couldn't get supplies from Europe, as the North had blockaded their ports.

As for the South it was running out of supplies. The South did not have enough factories to produce the goods it needed. A successful northern blockade of southern ports meant that the South could not get supplies from Europe either. Although there was no real business boom in the North, supplies were turned out steadily.

Grant in Command

20. How were Lincoln and Grant in agreement?

After Vicksburg, General Grant was made head of the Union armies. Lincoln finally had a general who realized that it was not enough to win battles. Lincoln and Grant agreed that the South had to be taken back into the Union. Grant moved south to attack

436

Lee at Richmond. He also sent General William Tecumseh Sherman to march from Tennessee through Georgia to Atlanta. Grant lost 60,000 soldiers in a month. But he believed that the only way to beat the Confederates was through repeated attack.

They agreed that the southern states had to rejoin the Union, and that the only way to beat them was through repeated attack.

The Election of 1864 and Sherman's March

Lincoln was nominated for a second term in June 1864, but he expected to lose the election. His running mate was Andrew Johnson, a supporter of the war from Tennessee. People in Lincoln's own party, who wanted to punish the South after the war, became angry with Lincoln when he vetoed their plan. These Republicans, known as Radicals, considered running their own candidate. The antislavery people were impatient with the costly war. And the Democrats ran General McClellan with the idea that a quick settlement with the South would be better than all the killing.

Lincoln seemed trapped between the two points of view when Sherman marched through Georgia into Atlanta and finally all the way to the Atlantic. Sherman was not just fighting armies. Sherman fought southerners. His soldiers burned the houses and the crops as they went. The South's ability to grow food and cotton in that area was ruined. The destruction of Georgia was heartbreaking to southerners, but was considered good news to the northern effort. Sherman's success brought Lincoln a reelection victory in November 1864.

21. How did Lincoln get reelected in 1864?

1) Lincoln expected to lose, because he was trapped between those who wanted to punish the South and those who were impatient with the costly war and wanted a quick settlement.
2) Sherman's total destruction of Georgia brought Lincoln a reelection victory.

The End of the War

In spite of the terrible cost of the war to both sides, Lincoln looked forward to bringing the nation back together again. In his second inaugural address he said:

> "With malice toward none; with charity for all; with firmness in the right as God gives us to see the right, let us strive on to finish the work we are in; to bind up the nation's wounds; to care for him who shall have borne the battle, and for his widow and his orphan—to do all which may achieve and cherish a just, and a lasting peace, among ourselves and with all nations."

22. How did Lincoln plan to bring the nation together again?

1) He urged the nation to bear no malice. 2) He asked the people to have charity for all, and to care for the soldiers, widows, and orphans of both North and South. 3) He called for a just and lasting peace.

Lee's Surrender at Appomattox

One month after Lincoln's second term began, Grant and an army of 115,000 finally succeeded in taking Richmond. By this time Lee had less than 30,000 soldiers with him. He tried to retreat

23. How did Lincoln show lack of malice at Appomattox?

Lincoln's speeches are excellent examples of the power of carefully chosen thoughts written with style.

The Confederate soldiers were required only to put down their guns. They could keep their horses and return immediately to their homes.

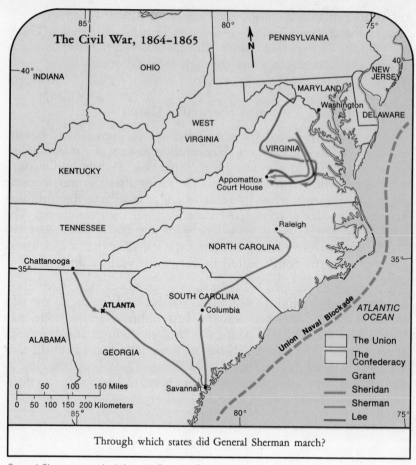

The Civil War, 1864–1865

Through which states did General Sherman march?

General Sherman marched through Georgia, South Carolina, and North Carolina.

west to join the Confederate army fighting Sherman in South Carolina. Grant cut him off. (See map, above.) Lee had to surrender. On April 9, 1865, at Appomattox Court House, Lee appeared in an elegant light gray uniform, carrying a jeweled sword. He rode through the lines of Grant's army and then surrendered. Grant followed Lincoln's orders. The Confederate soldiers were only required to put down their guns. They could keep their horses and return immediately to their homes.

24. What had to be done now that the war was over?

1) The railroads had to be rebuilt and the fields restored in the South. 2) The Blacks had to be brought into a working society.

Now it was time to begin the work of repairing the nation and making representative government work again. The war had not made that task any easier. Some 600,000 people had died in the war. Two-thirds of the South's railroads had been destroyed. The crops and the fields had been burned, and also the cotton stored for shipment. Slavery was over. But the South was ruined and the Blacks had to be brought into a working society. Lincoln's job of showing the nation how to turn to peace "with malice toward none" had just started.

Lincoln believed deeply that majority rule was the best way for a free people to do what was right.

ON OBSERVING

Have you and one of your friends gone to a movie or a ballgame and later, when you discussed it, discovered that your friend described some events that happened and you did not remember seeing them? Or you might have done the same thing and your friend did not remember ever seeing what you saw? Then you would argue over what really happened. What you have experienced is very basic to people everywhere—you do not always see the same thing as others even when you are in the same place at the same time. The reason for this is not because of differences in eyesight or in the ability to remember. The reason is that seeing is more than just identifying what is "seen." You also *interpret* what you see as you are seeing it. Why is this so?

There are many reasons for the differences in people's interpretations of events they have seen. One is that people have different feelings about what they are seeing. Some may be frightened by an event. Others may find the same event exciting. Also, some people may pay closer attention to what is going on around them. How many times have you let your mind wander during class only to miss some important information? Lastly, you may not have enough understanding of what is going on. Take a few minutes to imagine yourself as a visitor from another planet. On this visit you see a baseball game. How would you explain it to someone (tell just what you've seen)? How would you interpret it for someone (explain what is going on)? Now do you understand the difference between seeing and interpreting?

Why are observational skills important? You observe events, things, and people every day of your life. It is through observation that you learn much about what is going on in the world. It is through observation that you even learn how to act. Have you ever been in a new situation and you did not know how to act? What did you do? You probably watched what other people did and then you did the same thing. This is called *observational learning*. Think of some examples of observational learning and share them with your fellow students.

Why is observation important in the social studies and history? Much of the knowledge you have of the past comes from the observations of others. For example, much of the information about a soldier's life during the Civil War comes from somebody's first-hand account of his own experiences. Journalists and historians of the time also observed and wrote what they saw. What they wrote about the Civil War was their interpretation of what they said they saw. As a student of history, you have questions to ask of such material. For example, who else saw the same thing? What did they say happened? Did all observers agree? To get a sense of differences in what people see, try to get some of your classmates to observe the same events you do. Compare your observations.

Lincoln's Assassination

25. What did Lincoln's assassination mean for the nation?

The nation would have to put itself together without the person who had the faith that majority rule in America could provide minority rights.

On April 14, 1865, just five days after Lee's surrender, President Lincoln was killed. He had gone to Ford's Theater in Washington to see a play called *Our American Cousin*. During the performance a half-crazed actor, John Wilkes Booth, who belonged to a group of pro-slavery fanatics shot Lincoln. Booth fled from the theater, but was later found, and killed. Lincoln died the next day. The nation would have to put itself together without the person who had the faith that majority rule in America could provide minority rights.

Checking the facts

1. How did the South and North differ in the way they conducted the war?
2. What advantages did the North have over the South in the war?
3. What were the results of the Civil War?

2. REBUILDING—FOR WHOM?

26. Why wasn't the North helping the South to rebuild?

1) Northerners were fighting among themselves over how to punish the South. 2) A northern Republican group wanted Blacks advanced rapidly to equal status with other American citizens. They competed with southerners for the loyalty of Blacks.

The fighting was over. Many of the South's new cities and railroads had been destroyed. The slaves were freed. What could be done? The choices might have been to help the ex-slaves; to rebuild the houses, businesses, railroads, and farms of the South; to invest in new industry to help the South become less dependent on cheap Black labor. These were all possible actions that the victors of the North might have taken.

What the victors actually did was to fight among themselves about how much punishment the South should receive for having seceded from the Union. They also competed with the White southerners for the loyalty of the Blacks. The southern Whites wanted the Blacks to stay in the jobs they had held as slaves and gradually to learn new skills. A group of northerners wanted the Blacks advanced rapidly to equal status with other American citizens. These northern Radicals also wanted the new Black citizens to vote Republican, the party of the Emancipation Proclamation.

Lincoln's Plan for Reconstruction

27. What did Johnson consider to be the reconstruction of the South?

No one seemed as worried as Lincoln with helping the Whites in the South get back on their feet. They had suffered terribly and Lincoln had said the North would help them. The new President,

What does it take for majority rule to provide minority rights?
Neither Northerners nor Southerners expected peaceful, fair majority rule for all.

This photograph of Charleston, South Carolina, shows the destruction suffered by many cities in the South.

Andrew Johnson, followed Lincoln's plan for letting the southerners back into the Union quickly and easily. Andrew Johnson pardoned, or granted *amnesty* to, the states in which 10 percent of the citizens took a loyalty oath to the United States. The only southerners who were not pardoned were Confederate government officials, army officers, former representatives to Congress, and those who had held a good deal of property. To rejoin the Union the southern states also had to ratify the Thirteenth Amendment, which freed all slaves. By the time Congress opened in December, 1865, President Johnson thought he had completed the reconstruction of the South. All the southern states had ratified the Thirteenth Amendment, and they had elected new senators and members of the House of Representatives.

1) Johnson granted amnesty to the states in which 10 percent of the citizens took a loyalty oath to the United States. 2) To join the Union, the southern states had to ratify the Thirteenth Amendment, which freed all slaves. 3) The southern states could then elect new senators and members of the House of Representatives.

The Radical View

The northern Radicals in Congress had no intention of being easy on the South. They would not seat the representatives elected to Congress by the post-war southern states. One of their leaders was Thaddeus Stevens of Pennsylvania. He wanted every southerner punished. If "Old Thad Stevens," as he was called, had his way, the plantations of the South would be divided into 40-acre (16 hectare) farms and sold to former slaves for $10 an acre (2/5 hectare). If White southerners wanted to leave the country, Stevens would have been happy to send northern settlers to fill up the South and give it northern attitudes. Stevens was certain that the South had not changed its feelings when it surrendered at Appomattox.

28. *What views did the Radicals hold about Reconstruction?*

1) Thaddeus Stevens of Pennsylvania wanted to divide the plantations and sell them to former slaves. If this plan caused White southerners to leave the country, he wanted northerners to populate the South and give it northern attitudes. 2) Charles Sumner

The Radicals wanted to end the postwar split by making life in the South similar to life in the North.

441

of Massachusetts wanted Blacks treated fairly and felt they should participate in their state governments.

Charles Sumner of Massachusetts was another important Radical in Congress. You will remember that he was the senator who was beaten on the floor of the Senate before the Civil War. Sumner wanted Blacks treated fairly and felt they should participate in their state governments.

Black Codes

29. How did the Black Codes restrict the former slaves?

1) The laws gave Blacks certain legal rights, but did not give them freedom to leave farming and domestic service or to move out of the South. 2) In some states, they actually put Blacks back into a permanent working situation, calling it "wage labor" instead of slavery.

The Congress was not happy that the South reelected their old Confederate leadership to the legislature in Washington. They also had no liking for the Black Codes that were being passed in southern states. These laws were an improvement on slavery. They gave Blacks certain legal rights, but did not give them freedom to leave farming and domestic service or to move out of the South. Southerners admitted slavery was over, but they could not think of a community in which slaves were freed overnight. The Black Codes restricted the freedom of Blacks and tried to set rules for ways in which the two races could live in the same community. In some states the codes actually put Blacks back into a permanent working situation. They got around the Thirteenth Amendment by calling the system "wage labor" instead of "slavery."

The Freedmen's Bureau

30. What acts did Congress pass over Johnson's veto?

The Freedmen's Bureau was established under the reconstruction program to help former slaves.

Congress passed Reconstruction Acts of its own. In 1866 the Congress passed a law extending the power of a government agency called the Freedmen's Bureau. The Bureau was to help freed Blacks find jobs and housing, and get an education. It was also given the power to aid Blacks when their rights were threatened. Johnson vetoed the law about the Freedmen's Bureau, saying that these matters should be left to the states. But Congress managed to get it passed over his veto with a two-thirds vote. In 1866, Congress also managed to pass a Civil Rights Act over Johnson's veto. The Civil Rights Act made Blacks citizens and gave them all the rights of United States citizens. It was aimed against the Black Codes, which deprived Blacks of certain civil rights.

Stevens and his followers in Congress were called Radical Reconstructionists. They wanted to use this moment in history to rebuild the South by law. But they found that many northern states which opposed Black Codes still did not believe that Blacks should have the same rights in court or the right to vote. Three years after the end of the war, Blacks were refused the vote in Wisconsin, Minnesota, Connecticut, Nebraska, New Jersey, Ohio, Michigan, and Pennsylvania.

The Radicals felt that it was not enough to give Blacks the same rights as Whites. Blacks needed special protection from the local

Notice that protection is not the same as participation in government.

For Lincoln, the main purpose of the war was to rebuild the Union. For the radicals, the war was to destroy old southern power.

The Confederate States' Readmission to the Union

STATE	READMISSION
Tennessee	1866
Alabama	1868
Arkansas	1868
Florida	1868
Louisiana	1868
North Carolina	1868
South Carolina	1868
Georgia	1870*
Mississippi	1870
Texas	1870
Virginia	1870

*Georgia had been readmitted to the Union in 1868, but after failing to comply with the terms of the Reconstruction Acts it was returned to military rule until 1870.

1) Congress gave power to the Freedman's Bureau, which helped Blacks find jobs and get an education, and which aided them when their rights were threatened. 2) It passed the Civil Rights Act, which made all Blacks citizens and gave them all the rights of citizenship.

Whites who would try to keep them away from the polls, good jobs, and good land. In June 1866, the Radicals in Congress managed to pass the Fourteenth Amendment. Like the Civil Rights Act, this amendment made Blacks citizens of the United States. The amendment guaranteed that states must give every citizen the same rights in court and the same method of treatment—called "due process of law." Finally, the amendment made it illegal for former officials of the Confederate government and high-ranking army officers to hold federal or state office. President Johnson dared to come out against the amendment. And when it passed, he was publicly humiliated.

The congressional election of 1866 showed that more and more people sided with the Radicals in Congress than with the President. It was a great victory for the Radicals against the President and the first laws passed by the new Congress were aimed at limiting the President's power. The Command of the Army Act required that the President issue all orders to the army through the General of the Army, Ulysses S. Grant, who was believed to be a Radical. The Tenure of Office Act prohibited the President from removing appointed officials without the consent of the Senate.

At the same time, Congress began to change the South with a military government. In a series of acts passed between March 1867 and March 1868, Congress did away with the governments established in the South under Lincoln's and Johnson's plans. The South

31. What did the Radical Congress elected in 1866 do?

1) Congress passed laws aimed at limiting the President's power. The Command of the Army Act required that the President issue all orders through the General of the Army. The Tenure of Office Act prohibited the President from removing appointed officials without the consent of the Senate. 2) Congress began to change the South with a military government. The

What conditions did the southern states have to satisfy before they could be readmitted to the Union?
Notice the power of a Congress that does not have any opposition within it.

South was divided into five military districts, each under the control of a Union general who ruled by military law.

was divided into five military districts, each under the control of a Union general, ruling by military law. Also, the majority of the people in a state had to take an oath of past loyalty, and all of the states had to ratify the Fourteenth Amendment.

Johnson's Impeachment

32. What were the grounds for Johnson's impeachment?

He had dismissed his secretary of state without consulting the Senate.

The Reconstruction Acts were passed over Johnson's veto. By March 1868 Congress was ready to take final action against the President himself. Johnson was accused of wrong-doing when he dismissed his secretary of war without consulting the Senate. This was *impeachment*. But when Johnson came to trial before the Senate and the Chief Justice of the Supreme Court in May 1868, he was *acquitted* by one vote. But he was also dishonored. No President had ever been impeached.

The Election of 1868 and the Fifteenth Amendment

33. Why was the Fifteenth Amendment to the Constitution passed?

1) The decisive popular votes that elected Grant came from southern Blacks who had registered under the Reconstruction Acts. 2) A law guaranteeing suffrage to all was needed.

In 1868 General Ulysses S. Grant was the Republican party's choice. He won handily with a large electoral vote. But his popular majority was less. The deciding popular votes came from southern Blacks who had been registered under the Reconstruction Laws. This gave the Radicals their next idea. Blacks must vote. And since the states could not be trusted to make that decision, there must be another amendment to the Constitution. The Fifteenth Amendment, guaranteeing suffrage to all regardless of race, was passed by Congress in 1869 and ratified in 1870.

34. What did the carpetbaggers do?

1) Carpetbaggers were northern Republicans who ran the daily government activities of the South. 2) They saw that Blacks remembered to vote Republican. 3) They set up public schools for Blacks and provided more rights for women and better codes of criminal law. 4) Some made other Whites feel humiliated, and many were corrupt.

The Republicans needed the Black voters. Without them their party would be a minority party in the nation. So they sent northerners to the South to make sure the Blacks remembered to vote for the party that freed them. These northerners who actually ran the daily activities of the reconstructed governments in the South were called *carpetbaggers*. Their southern friends were known as *scalawags*. They did good work setting up public schools for Blacks, providing for more rights for women, and better codes of criminal law. But they also made other Whites feel humiliated. Also, many of them were corrupt. However, the Republican party held together as a result of their work. In 1867 figures show that in the reconstructed states, 703,000 Blacks could vote compared to 627,000 Whites.

35. What did Black voting power mean?

Some Blacks did hold office at the local, state, and national levels of government.

But Black voting power did not mean Black rule during Reconstruction. Most of the top positions in the South were held by Whites. Nevertheless, some Blacks did hold office at the local, state, and national levels. P.B.S. Pinchback served as lieutenant governor and later governor of Louisiana. Then he was elected to the House of Representatives, and then to the Senate. Hiram Revels

This cartoon shows President Grant riding in a large carpetbag carried by the South. How do you interpret this cartoon?

of Mississippi and Blanche K. Bruce of Virginia were other Blacks who were elected to the Senate.

White Responses to Reconstruction

When the Radical reconstruction would not allow White southern leaders to take part in their government, some former Southern leaders joined secret societies to keep the Blacks from going to vote. The Ku Klux Klan and other organizations were determined to keep the South from changing at any cost.

Even southerners who hated the Klan resented northern interference in their way of life. Both northern Radicals and White southerners seemed to have forgotten what Lincoln had hoped the war would accomplish. There were no good feelings left. The South had lost the war and was now being punished. The North had won the war

36. How did southern Whites react to Reconstruction?

1) Some leaders joined secret societies, such as the Ku Klux Klan, to keep the Blacks from going to vote. 2) Even those who hated the Klan resented northern interference in their way of life.

The Radicals sincerely thought it was possible to pass laws and thus require change. The laws helped, but what else was needed?

and was now trying to create a new political world by constitutional amendment and by careful control of the Black vote. The Radicals were trying to give the Blacks equality. But in so doing they also tried to strengthen their own position politically—and this was resented.

The End of Reconstruction

37. What sign was there that the end of Reconstruction was near?

1) The Blacks were afraid to vote in spite of the Force Acts of 1870–1871. 2) White Democrats began to take over the governments of most of the southern states.

In 1870-71 Congress passed the Force Acts to stop southern Whites from keeping Blacks from the polls. The Force Acts helped for a while, but soon Blacks were afraid to vote again. At the same time White Democrats began to take over the governments of most of the southern states.

President Grant

38. Why did the Democrats begin a comeback?

1) Some of Grant's friends were so corrupt that liberal Republicans began to vote for anti-Grant candidates. 2) The split in the party gave more power to the Democrats.

Grant was the people's choice for President again in the election of 1872. He was popular because he was a military hero, but he offered no help to rebuild the South, and no help to the Blacks. Grant loved the power and the rich friends that being President brought him. Some of Grant's friends were so corrupt that liberal Republicans began to vote for anti-Grant candidates. The split in the Republican party gave more power to the Democrats. The latter party began its comeback on the national level, as well as in the South.

The Election of 1876

39. How did Rutherford B. Hayes become President of the United States?

The two parties made a deal. In the Compromise of 1877, Hayes agreed to remove federal troops from the South and let the states run their own affairs if the Democrats would support his presidency.

In the election of 1876 the Democrats got all the electoral votes of the southern states from which northern carpetbaggers had been sent home. But in three southern states, Florida, South Carolina, and Louisiana, the people who counted the ballots tried to prove that the Democrats had lost. Congress had to appoint an election commission. To keep it fair, the commission's members were equally divided between the two parties with one judge who belonged to neither one. This impartial judge became ill at the last minute and his replacement cast the tie-breaking vote for his own party—the Republicans.

The Democrats and their candidate, Samuel Tilden, said the election had been stolen. The Republicans said that Blacks had been kept from voting by force. There seemed to be evidence that both charges were true. The result was that the two parties made a deal called the Compromise of 1877. Rutherford B. Hayes, the Republican, agreed to remove federal troops from the South and let the states run their own lives, if the Democrats would support his presidency.

Why is it important to understand how political parties and elections work?

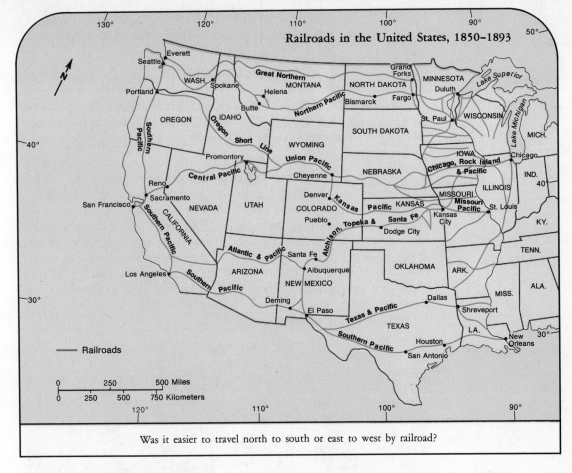

Railroads in the United States, 1850–1893

Was it easier to travel north to south or east to west by railroad?

It is easiest to travel east-west by railroad.

Left out of the compromise were the four million ex-slaves. They had the Fourteenth and Fifteenth Amendments on their side. But enforcing them was another question. The states would not take that responsibility. And the federal government had just made a deal to let the states and their White leadership do as they pleased.

National Growth in the 1870's

What had been achieved? The war had prevented the break-up of the nation. But the war and reconstruction had destroyed the economic power of the South. The reconstruction period had given the Blacks extra support followed by a Compromise in which they did not figure. Blacks had civil rights on paper, but were afraid to vote. Voting was supervised by southern Whites who did not know how to live in a society of mixed races—all of them equal. They made sure that Blacks and Whites were segregated on trains, in

40. What had been achieved since the Civil War ended?

447

Why do the races get along better with each other when there are jobs?

It has been said that people of different groups seem to work together better than they play together. Do you agree? Why or why not?

1) The Union had been preserved, but the war and Reconstruction had destroyed the economic power of the South. 2) The Blacks had rights but were unable to exercise them. 3) In 1867, the United States had bought Alaska from Russia for $7,200,000. 4) In 1869 the transcontinental railroad was completed. 5) Homesteaders went west; a frontier of cities grew up along the railroad.

schools, and in other public places. The North was also segregated, but it did not have as many Blacks as the South. And it had more jobs.

The nation continued to grow. In 1867 the Russians made a surprise offer to sell Alaska to the United States. Secretary of State William Seward agreed to the price of $7,200,000. The purchase of Alaska was ridiculed as "Seward's Folly." No one believed that Alaska was worth two cents an acre (2/5 hectare).

In 1869 the *transcontinental* railroad connecting the Northeast to the West was completed by two railroad companies, the Union Pacific and the Central Pacific. (See map, page 447.) Both operated under government land grants of 23 million acres (9.2 million hectares) and easy government loans of $64 million. A gold-headed spike was driven into the railroad tie at Promontory Point, Utah, to mark the completion of the transcontinental railroad. Its completion finished the hope of the South to compete with the North for generations. The railroad had taken 20,000 workers three years to build. Many of the workers were Chinese. It was 1,775 miles (2,840 kilometers) long.

Chinese, Irish, Mexicans, and Native Americans worked together to lay the tracks for the transcontinental railroad.

After the war many people went west, where free land was available to homesteaders. A whole new frontier of cities—this time they were railroad cities—grew up. They followed the earlier patterns of city growth. New cities like Billings, Montana were places where cattle and wheat were brought before being sent to other parts of the country. The railroads brought new cities into being.

Native Americans Fight Back

As the plains filled with settlers, the Native Americans were pushed out again. This time something different happened. The tribes who had little in common began to unite to fight the settlers. The Plains Indians appointed war chiefs, and since they were now always at war, those chiefs became powerful. In response to the slaughter of the buffalo by Whites, the coming of the train that split the herd, and the constant warfare, the western tribes developed a new kind of organization. They were ready for war under a great chief.

41. *What brought the western Native American tribes together?*

1) Native Americans were pushed off their land. 2) Whites were slaughtering the buffalo. 3) The coming of the train split the buffalo herd. 4) The tribes were fighting against the White settlers.

In its plan for Native American reservations, the United States Department of Interior had tried to give each tribe both land and money. But after the Civil War, soldiers and settlers went west for land and came into conflict with Native Americans. Some tribes gave up. The Pawnee did not fight. They accepted a reservation. (See map, page 465.) "Better to turn around and lead a new life." Many became scouts for the Whites.

But the real buffalo hunters did not give in. They organized as best they could for war. The Sioux and their leader Red Cloud chose to fight. Finally Red Cloud had to accept a reservation in the Black Hills of South Dakota. (See map, page 465.)

42. *What happened to the remaining western Native American tribes?*

1) The Pawnee did not fight and accepted a reservation. Many became scouts for the Whites. 2) Red Cloud and the Sioux chose to fight but had to accept a reservation in the Black Hills of South Dakota. 3) The Sioux led by Sitting Bull and Crazy Horse left the reservation when prospectors came there looking for gold. They defeated Custer at Little Big Horn River but were finally forced to surrender. 4) The Nez Percé, under Chief Joseph, refused to give up their lands in the Pacific Northwest and accept reservation life. Joseph tried to lead his people to safety in Canada but was persued by the army and forced to surrender.

By the 1870's the United States government had stopped seeing Indians as hostile enemies. They stopped signing treaties as if the Indians were foreigners. Indians were then considered Native Americans. As Americans they were no longer to be isolated but to be educated like other new Americans. In spite of this new policy, the Indians were disappointed. Settlers from the East continued to come onto their land.

When gold was discovered in the Black Hills in 1874, prospectors began to move into the Sioux reservation. Angry bands of Sioux, led by Sitting Bull and Crazy Horse, left the reservation. Then in the summer of 1875 the government sent three armies after the Sioux to bring them back. One of the armies under General George Custer tried to surprise a Sioux camp on the Little Big Horn River in southeastern Montana. The Sioux and Cheyenne surrounded the army and killed all of them, including Custer, at the Battle of Little Big Horn. This battle took place in June of 1876. However, the Sioux were finally forced to surrender.

Notice that the Indians of the plains in the era after the Civil War were not all members of the same tribe.

In the Pacific Northwest the Nez Percé (nez-PER-say), under their leader, Chief Joseph, also held out against the government of the United States. They refused to give up their lands and accept reservation life. As a result fighting broke out between the Nez Percé and the White settlers in 1877. Chief Joseph tried to lead his people to safety in Canada, but he was pursued by the army. Finally, he had to surrender. "My heart is sick and sad. From where the sun now stands I will fight no more forever," he said.

43. Why didn't American attempts to change the Native American culture succeed?

Americans tried to make Native Americans farmers, but they were hunting tribes, and farming was a threat to their way of life.

The meeting of the Native American and White cultures never seemed to work. When the Board of Indian Affairs offered land to Native Americans of the Plains, they expected them to farm it. But these tribes were hunters. Farming was a threat to their way of life. White Americans could not understand the Indians. To them, owning land was a dream come true. Still, the Board of Indian Affairs tried to teach the Native Americans to be farmers. They built schools for them, and gave the Native Americans cattle in the hope that they would become cowhands. These attempts to change the culture of the Native Americans did not work.

More Expansion

44. How did America expand or change in each of its regions?

1) The West was filling up with cowhands and miners. 2) In the East, bankers and investors were fighting for control of the railroad and control of candidates for public office. 3) Northern manufacturing, transportation, and banking continued to grow strong.

America expanded in every way. The West filled up with cowhands riding herd on cattle, and miners who came when silver was discovered in Nevada's Comstock Lode in June 1859. Meanwhile in the East, bankers and investors in stocks fought each other for control of the railroad and control of candidates for public office. Some people became wealthy buying stock in railroad companies and selling it to others at much higher prices. Often prices were higher than the real value of the stock. Jay Gould, Jim Fisk, and Cornelius Vanderbilt became controllers of railroads and gamblers on the price of gold. Some said they managed business empires from their offices on Wall Street in New York.

How different can a minority culture be? What does it gain? What does it lose?

There seemed to be no way to stop the powerful in business and in government. But the cartoonists of the day and some newspaper people began to pay attention to what they did and inform the public. Thomas Nast, who drew cartoons for *Harper's Weekly*, was most famous for his exposure in 1871 of Tammany Hall and its leader, "Boss" William Marcy Tweed. This was the organization that controlled jobs and money in New York City.

When the United States celebrated its 100th birthday, the Centennial, in 1876, there was much pride in all that expansion had accomplished. There was pride in individual achievement. There was a growing awareness that the manufacturing, transportation, and banking industries of the North were very strong.

During and after the Civil War, Susan B. Anthony dedicated her life to organizing women in their fight to get the vote.

Uneven Progress

The South was badly beaten in the Civil War. Blacks and Native Americans were being "placed" in society where the powerful Whites wanted them.

Working men and women were organizing for their own good into unions. Also, some women began to talk about getting the vote and even running for office. Now that former slaves were voting in some places and had their own constitutional amendment, the women began to be interested in politics as a way of having a voice. Wyoming women got the vote in 1869. But Susan B. Anthony of Rochester, New York, was fined for voting in 1872.

The West seemed more able to accept change. But western workers were not happy with the Chinese laborers brought in to work for little money on the railroads.

The Majority Grows

The majority forces that were moving to connect the separate regions in the United States were forces that believed in liberty, opportunity, representation, expansion, and individualism for those who could compete. Now they added another characteristic—bigness. Why should a business or a movement or an idea remain small? It became the American way to be big.

Checking the facts

1. What were the important events of the Reconstruction period? Why were they important?
2. What was life like for the Blacks after the Civil War?
3. How did the completion of the transcontinental railroad affect the Native Americans?

PUTTING IT ALL TOGETHER

UNDERSTANDING THE MAIN IDEAS

1. What did a war between the states achieve?
2. How did the North, South, and West develop during and after the war?
3. How much did political leadership achieve for Blacks and Native Americans when the war was over?

ACTIVITIES

1. The Civil War was the first war to be photographed on the battlefield. Find a book of the photographs of Mathew Brady. Look at his photographs. Note that people could now see pictures of fighting, death, and destruction. What difference did this make in their attitudes toward the war? How do you feel about television coverage of wars and riots? What effect do you think it has?
2. Choose any group that is asking for civil rights today. How are its members making their demands known? Are they using the press, the vote, or the courts? Are they using all three? Or are they waiting for the majority of people to change their attitudes? What are the advantages and disadvantages of each method?
3. Read about the organizations of Native Americans today. How do they feel about these words: Indians? Tribe? Rights? Ownership of property? What changes have they made in their native culture in order to get what they want under majority rule? Present an oral report of your findings to your class.
4. Look at a map of Navajo territory today. What is the history of that land? What are the Navajos doing about selling natural resources and keeping their old culture? Who is helping them? Why? Prepare a brief essay in which you comment on these questions.

BOOKS TO READ

Drisko, Carol, and Edgar Toppin, *Unfinished March* (Garden City: Doubleday and Co., Inc., 1975).

Green, Margaret, *President of the Confederacy: Jefferson Davis* (New York: Julian Messner, Inc., 1963).

Katz, William Loren, *Reconstruction and National Growth* (New York: Watts Publishing Co., 1974).

Noble, Iris, *Susan B. Anthony* (New York: Julian Messner, Inc., 1975).

Place, Marian T., *Retreat to the Bear Paw: The Story of the Nez Percé* (New York: Four Winds Press, 1969).

Wyatt, Edgar, *Geronimo, the Last Apache War Chief* (New York: Whittlesey Publishing Co., 1952).

REVIEWING THE UNIT

BUILDING VOCABULARY

The following is a list of some of the vocabulary words in Unit Four:

speculator	armory	acquit	amnesty
terrain	contrabands	scalawags	

1. Use the related vocabulary words above in writing on one of the following topics: a. runaway slaves during the Civil War, b. groups working in the South during Reconstruction, c. the military strategy of the Union and Confederate generals.

BUILDING SOCIAL STUDIES SKILLS

Turn to the maps on the pages given here. Then complete the following activities:

1. Page 406—Where were most of the railroads located in 1861? What was the importance of the railroads during the Civil War?
2. Pages 431, 436, and 438—Locate the major Civil War battles by looking at the maps on these pages. List the battles and the generals for each side. Where were the battles fought? In Confederate or Union territory?

BUILDING WRITING SKILLS

Southern leaders believed that they were following the principles of the Declaration of Independence when their states seceded from the Union and formed the Confederate States of America. Do you believe that secession was a good way to handle differences between members of the Union? Write a paragraph explaining why or why not.

At the end of the Reconstruction period, many changes had taken place in American life. Write a brief paragraph on one of the following two changes:

1. The southern Blacks had achieved equal rights under the law. However, because they were afraid to exercise their rights, Blacks had little influence in local, state, and national government. How does that compare with today?
2. The Native Americans out West had been placed on reservations, where they were expected to change from a hunting culture to a farming or ranching culture. They resisted the change then. Have the Native Americans adjusted to that change today?

Railroads

After the Mexican War the railroad industry solved many engineering problems. Railroads could now cross mountains. All sections of the nation built railroads. They were often financed by local governments, farmers, and tradespeople. Only the South did not invest in connecting rail lines from east to west.

Railroads made more land available for agriculture. The boom in land caused a shortage of labor. Farm machinery made agriculture into big business. Cities such as Chicago grew up around the railroads and factories.

To The Pacific

Americans looked west to the Pacific Ocean for many reasons. They had plans with the British to build a canal across Central America. American businesses wanted to open trade with Japan.

The North and South were rivals over the building of a transcontinental railroad. They competed for voters in the new Kansas and Nebraska territories. Riots broke out.

Antislavery

The antislavery northerners began to demand political leadership. The Republican party was formed in 1854. It began to have immediate success in the North. Abolitionists gained attention by helping Blacks escape slavery through the Underground Railroad.

Debate was carried on throughout the country about slavery in the territories. The Supreme Court supported slavery in the Dred Scott decision. In his debates with Stephen Douglas, Abraham Lincoln showed the nation that slavery and free labor could not exist side by side. Southern cities could not become centers of trade and manufacture fast enough to compete with the North. When Lincoln was elected in 1860, southern states seceded from the Union. Lincoln could not permit the Union to be dissolved by any state.

The Civil War

The southern states fought the Civil War for the preservation of their rights and freedom to decide for themselves. They fought to protect their new Confederacy. Lincoln had to persuade his generals and the northern public to take the Civil War into the South. Lincoln knew that the southern territory had to be occupied and every Confederate defeated. The battles of the Civil War were fought from coast to coast.

Not until 1863 did Lincoln act against slavery in an effort to weaken the South. Later that year General Robert E. Lee of the Confederacy attempted to carry the war into the North at the battle of Gettysburg. The southern army suffered its first great defeat. Ulysses S. Grant successfully carried out Lincoln's war strategy, and with the help of William Sherman's march through Georgia, brought the Union to victory in 1865.

Reconstruction

Lincoln's assassination in April 1865 brought an end to any hope for charitable reconstruction in the South. President Andrew Johnson's plan for reconstruction was defeated by congressional radical Republicans. The radical Republicans wanted the South to pay for its role in the war. They also wanted to change the Southern way of life by constitutional amendment. Finally, they hoped to get southern Blacks to vote Republican.

In the election of 1876, it became clear that southern Whites would not allow ex-slaves to hold political power. In the competition for southern support, the two major parties made a deal. In the Compromise of 1877, the Republicans won the presidency for Rutherford B. Hayes, and the White Democrats regained control of voting in the South.

More Growth

By the 1870's the purchase of Alaska and the completion of the transcontinental railroad had added to America's resources. The Native Americans of the Plains were forced either to accept reservation life and American education or to fight. In either case, they lost their status as separate nations.

In this period women worked to be allowed to vote. Workers organized to be heard in their work places. But power went to those bankers and investors who could connect the growing cities of the East to mining and transportation centers in the West. The stage was set for transcontinental business.

AMERICA IS... **BIG**

Imagine that you are driving through an unfamiliar state in the United States. Suddenly your car radio reports, "Warning to all drivers: Beware of icy roads." Too late. The car in front of you skids. To avoid a crash, you head for the drainage ditch.

Within an hour you have faced the facts. The repairs on your car will take about 24 hours to complete so you look for a motel.

There are several motels, and the signs outside are ones you've seen often. You go in to register at one that you have seen advertised many times on television and in magazines. This chain of motels has toll-free phone numbers to make reservations "in more than 40 cities." It is something of a relief to think that many people must have found these motels satisfactory or there would not be so many of them. You sign the register at the motel. Luckily you have enough cash to pay for the room in advance. A man and woman ahead of you at the desk used a credit card from a banking group. They were able to charge their room on the card.

To save money you decide to go out and find a restaurant. Anyway, a cheeseburger and a milkshake seems more like home than the more expensive food in the motel dining room. On the way out of the motel you remember that you need a comb, toothbrush and toothpaste, and something for the headache that this trip has already caused you. There is a drugstore across the street, and you quickly find both the brand of toothpaste you like and the headache remedy that promises to ease the symptoms in 20 minutes. You

feel safe with familiar products which you know have passed government testing. After supper, you find a telephone and call home long distance. It is a real relief to know how easy it is to call from one part of the country to another—and reverse the charges.

Afterwards you go to the local movie. The film must be a popular one across the country. People are already lining up to see it in this town, just the way they are in yours.

On the way back to the motel you pick up a local newspaper to get the weather map and the local TV channel numbers for the late night network shows. One of the good things about being stuck in a motel is having an excuse to lie in bed and watch color TV. The network channels here carry the same late night shows as at home. The weather map in the newspaper carries the weather forecast from the National Weather Bureau. It looks like better driving weather tomorrow.

And so it is. By mid-morning your car has been fixed. Imagine the parts for a seven-year-old car being available so far from home! The mechanics at the garage say they had no trouble fixing it. They see cars like yours often.

Before leaving town you fill up the car with gasoline. The price of gas is different, but the type of gas you need, with the right octane level, is available. On the way out of town you watch carefully for the Interstate Highway sign that is marked on your road map. The highway entrance sign is that welcome green color. You are on your way.

The United States is about 3,000 miles (4,800 kilometers) from west to east, on this continent alone. Is there any place your car might have stopped in which you might have found only unfamiliar surroundings? In a nation that is as big as an ancient empire of many nations, how is it possible that wherever you go you find so much that is the same?

America is big—big in geographical area and big in the way most Americans live. Few countries in the world have both the enormous size of the United States and the ease with which Americans move across the land.

It is true that different parts of the country have different accents and some different customs. Many of these accents and customs started with the earliest native inhabitants and the earliest settlers. But, compared to many nations, what is more surprising than the variety is the number of similarities in the way Americans live.

The period in our history in which activities and life-styles became big enough to be nationwide is the subject of our study. *When* and *how* and *why* did America become the nation of "bigness"?

chapter 18
Organizing Nationwide

1880–1899

1. BIG ORGANIZATIONS IN THE WEST
2. THE BEEF INDUSTRY: A CASE STUDY
3. OTHER BUSINESSES ORGANIZE NATIONWIDE

INTRODUCTION

By 1880 the West had been conquered and the transcontinental railway had made the link between coasts. The southerners, the Mexicans, and the Native Americans now had to adjust to the development within the nation. Between Canada and Central America the land and the people were all part of one nation. The end of the nineteenth century was a period of expansion with more land to be used for mining, ranching, and farming. Throughout the nation the links that bound the people together tightened because the new railroads connected the cities.

The arrival of the railroads changed the lives of Americans. Now, even isolated places in the country could be reached by rail. Railroads carried news to people separated from each other by great distances. They also carried goods across the nation. The railroads eventually helped create new towns and new businesses.

	1881	1881	1885	1885	
Who?	Booker T. Washington	President James A. Garfield	Grover Cleveland	The people of France	
What?	opens Tuskegee Institute for Blacks	is assinated by Charles Guiteau	a Democrat from New York, becomes President	give the Statue of Liberty to the American people	
Where?	in Alabama	in a railroad station in Washington, D.C.	of the United States	to stand in New York Harbor	

The expansion of industry and its connection with networks like railroads, shipping, and distribution centers meant the growth of big organization.

As you read this chapter, think about the following questions:

1. How did mining, cattle raising, and farming in the West develop in the last 20 years of the nineteenth century?
2. What connections did ranchers and farmers in the West have to the rest of the nation?
3. How did business organizations and business people tie the entire nation together?
4. How did bigness in business cause new kinds of organization and new kinds of jobs?

1. BIG ORGANIZATIONS IN THE WEST

After the Civil War, miners came into the areas of the Great Plains and Rocky Mountains. Gold and silver were discovered in Nevada, Colorado, Wyoming, Montana, Idaho, and the Dakotas. And mining towns like Virginia City, Nevada, Denver, Colorado, and Helena, Montana, grew up. (See map, page 460.)

But by the 1880's the big push into the gold and silver country had almost ended. In fact, the mines in Colorado and those in the Sioux country of the Black Hills of the Dakotas were under the control of large corporations. Extracting gold and silver from deep veins in the rock needed expensive equipment. Only big companies could afford it. Much of the stock in these companies was owned by people in large cities who had never seen a mine.

The existence of the mines, however, had made a great difference to life in the West. Other settlers followed the prospectors. Mining towns had doctors, lawyers, ministers, storekeepers, school teachers, and newspaper editors. Since people in the towns had to eat, the towns were soon surrounded by farms and by cattle ranches.

1. How did mining affect the West?

1) Many mines came under the control of large corporations. Only they could afford the expensive equipment required for extracting gold and silver from deep veins in the rock. 2) Settlers followed the prospectors. Soon towns developed, surrounded by farms and cattle ranches.

1890	1891	1895	1898	1899
Two hundred Sioux	Populist	The Italian scientist, Guglielmo Marconi	American soldiers, led by Theodore Roosevelt	Secretary of State John Hays
are killed by the U.S. cavalry	organize a national political party	develops the wireless telegraph for use	capture San Juan Hill	develops the Open-Door Policy
at the Battle of Wounded Knee in South Dakota	in the United States	throughout the world	in Cuba	regarding U.S. relations with China

459

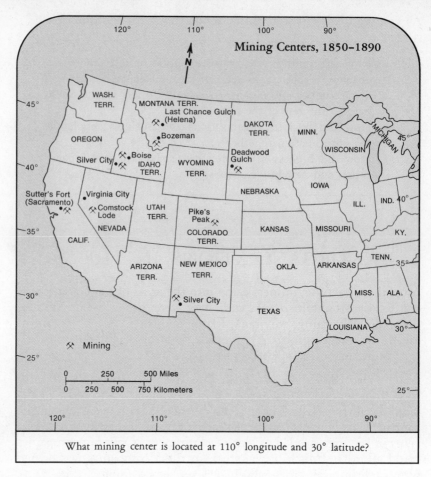

Mining Centers, 1850–1890

What mining center is located at 110° longitude and 30° latitude?

Silver City in New Mexico territory is located at 110° longitude, 30° latitude.

Billings, Montana

2. How did Billings, Montana, develop?

1) The Northern Pacific Railroad and a land developer, Herman Clark, planned and built Billings together. 2) They advertised for residents as far east as St. Paul, Chicago, and New York. 3) By the time the railroad reached Billings one year later, in 1882, there was a city ready for it. 4) All around it cattle ranches grew up, providing a network for buying and selling.

If the railroad came through a town, then it grew to be a city. Some cities were planned to be part of the development of the railroad. Billings, Montana was an example of a city that was built by a combination of the railroad and a land developer. In fact the land developer, Herman Clark, named the city after Frederick Billings, the former president of the Northern Pacific Railroad. The plans for the city were laid out in 1881 at a site high enough to be safe from the flood waters of the Yellowstone River and close to the government survey line—which would give the town and the railroad more land in one place than was usually allowed. The streets were laid out, parks were planned, and building lots and farm land were set aside in advance. Then land was advertised to residents as far east as St. Paul, Chicago, and New York.

By the time the railroad reached Billings one year later, in 1882, there was a city ready for it. A bank was organized to help people

Americans enjoyed making big plans for the future.

who wanted to go into the cattle business. All around it cattle ranches grew up. Billings became a trading center. Jobs in Billings centered on railroad repairs, building and road construction, and entertainment for the people who came to town. Billings had saloons, pool halls, dance halls, and skating rinks. By 1883, there was an opera house for traveling companies such as the Boston Comic Opera Company. The town had a brass band, a German Orchestral Band, McKee's Italian Band, and a military band from the army's Fort Custer. By 1884 the Gazette Publishing Company had bought the rights, or *franchise,* of the Associated Press and could issue a morning newspaper with national news coming in by telegraph from long distances.

Mining had started the movement of people into the western plains. But mining was not all that kept the area going. Farms and cattle ranches grew up around the cities, and railroads connected them. The West, too, became a network.

Farming Grows Big

The settlement of the plains came in two stages. After the Civil War, farmers also flocked to the West to take advantage of the government's offer of land. But the land was difficult to farm. The soil did not hold water well, and there was little timber to use for building fences or houses. The first settlers who moved onto the prairies had to build their houses out of chunks of the land, or *sod.* These sod houses were plastered on the inside and the walls were about two feet (60 centimeters) thick at the bottom. Land that was tough enough to be used for building blocks was almost impossible to cultivate without machinery.

3. What difficulties did the first settlers have in farming on the prairie?

1) The land was impossible to cultivate without machinery. 2) The soil did not hold water well. 3) There was no timber to build houses or fences. 4) Poor climate, insects, and fires were also problems.

Think about the result of national telegraphed news. Every point of view could be spread nationally.

The Shores family were homesteaders in Nebraska in 1887. Their sod houses are shown in the background.

The first plains settlers found themselves at the mercy of the climate as well as the soil. Much of the Great Plains lay beyond good rainfall. West of the 98th meridian, lack of rain was a serious problem. In addition, there were winter blizzards, spring floods, grasshoppers which destroyed the crops, and prairie fires.

4. Why did large farming businesses buy out the first settlers?

Large farm businesses could buy machinery to break up prairie sod, put up fencing to keep out cattle, build houses for farm families and workers, and ship grain to market by rail at favorable rates.

By the 1880's the settlers who had come to the plains in the first stage had to sell their land. The price of that difficult land had gone up because of the demand for it. Unable to afford farms of their own, many of the early settlers had become farm laborers on other people's farms. At best, they could be renters, or *tenant farmers*, on land owned by large farming businesses. Some of these farms were called "bonanza" farms but they were really estates. They were owned by land developers who could afford the machinery to break up the sod on the prairie, put up the fencing to keep out the cattle, and build houses for the farm families and workers.

The large farms could afford to pay to get the grain to market. They had so much produce to sell that they could demand a better price from the railroads for transporting it. In spite of the difficulty of cultivating the land, by the late 1880's four out of five of the leading wheat-producing states were west of the Mississippi River. Kansas and Nebraska became important corn-growing areas.

No Plan for Conservation

5. Why were the estate builders concerned about conservation?

They knew it would help protect their capital investment in the land and machinery.

In the 1880's and 1890's the settlement of the plains and the West was not controlled. People knew about conserving resources but few cared. In those parts of the Far West, such as the Sierra Nevadas where there were forests, speculators in lumber were free to do as they pleased. Trees were cut without a thought of replacing them. On the farms of the plains, the estate builders tried to persuade their tenants to use scientific methods of farming—proper rotation of crops, weed-killers, setting aside land for pastures, the planting of alfalfa and clover, and the use of lime to replenish the soil. The owners knew that conservation would help protect their capital investment in the land and machinery.

The Cattle Industry

6. Why did the cattle corporations begin buying up large tracts of land?

1) Cattle corporations needed to own land along a stream so that the cattle could have water. 2) But, competition for water was great.

Miners, railroad builders, farmers, and cattle ranchers were all active in developing the West at the same time. The years after the Civil War were also the years in which the Texas longhorn cattle were driven on the long drive from Texas to the end of the railroad lines in Missouri and Kansas. Cow towns like Abilene, Wichita, and Dodge City in Kansas grew up along the route.

By 1880 the cattle had been brought to the northern plains and allowed to graze on open grassland. This was called open-range

Notice the factors used to describe settlements in the early years—soil, rain, fire. In the 1880's competition, money, and machines were the descriptive words for settlements.

This picture was painted by Charles Russell. It shows cowboys gathered around the campfire after a long day of herding cattle. Why do you think the title of this painting is "Laugh Kills Lonesome"?

ranching. A cattle rancher only needed to own a few acres (hectares) of land along a stream, so that the cattle could have water. The grazing land was public land.

However, competition for the water was great. In order to get water, rich cattle barons or groups of investors in cattle *corporations* began to buy up large tracts of land. The Nebraska Land and Cattle Company was owned by British investors. The Union Cattle Company in Wyoming was worth over $3 million.

Barbed Wire Fences

These big cattle businesses competed for land with the developers of large farming estates. Sheep-raisers also wanted the same land. Many people began to fence in the land with a new kind of fence. This was barbed wire fence, invented in 1874 by Joseph Glidden, a farmer in Illinois. It had sharp barbs at the joints and at the top. Barbed wire was used by ranchers against other ranchers, by farmers against cattle ranchers, and by sheep-raisers against cattle ranchers.

7. *What did the invention of barbed wire fences do for cattle ranching?*

Ranchers could raise cattle under controlled conditions and prevent their loss in blizzards on the open range.

The text shows the development of the system in which the cowboy existed.

Competition for bigness was based on the old shared values of liberty, opportunity, and control over land and water.

Once the cattle were fenced in, then food had to be brought to the animals in bad weather. Much of the open range had become divided into giant pastures, owned by large businesses. The final days of the open cattle business came in 1886 when the cattle became trapped in a blizzard. Nearly 90 percent of the cattle on the open range died that winter. After that, ranchers raised cattle only under controlled conditions. Cattle were bred for meat and were fed hay in the winter. Water was supplied by wells powered by windmills. Cattle ranching, too, was now a big business.

Western Land and Indian Policy

8. *Why was the General Allotment Act passed?*

1) White western settlers wanted the land that had been given to Native Americans. 2) Reformers believed the reservation system had failed. 3) The Commissioner of Indian Affairs and religious missionaries thought that if Native Americans were given individual parcels of land, they could be absorbed into American society, much as immigrants were.

The executive secretary of the Indian Rights Association wrote in 1892: "The Indian and the White man have changed places. We, the White men, are no longer few in number. The Indian is no longer to be feared. He numbers about 250,000 souls; we 60,000,000." The Indian rights group recognized that western White settlers now wanted the land which had been given to the Native Americans for reservations. At the same time, reformers felt that the reservation system had failed. They believed that if Native Americans were given individual parcels of land, then they could be absorbed into American society much as the immigrants were. The government's policy was to allot land to individual Indians who would settle on it permanently. The Commissioner of Indian Affairs and the religious missionaries who often served as government agents to the Indians were in favor of helping the Indians take on the White culture. As a result, the General Allotment Act, or the Dawes Act, was passed by Congress in 1887. The law authorized the breaking up of tribal reservations. The land was to be divided among the members of the tribe. Each head of a family could get 160 acres (64 hectares), and each adult single person 80 acres (32 hectares). The government kept legal ownership of the land for 25 years, but after that time the Native Americans became the legal owners. They also became citizens of the United States. The remaining reservation lands would go to the non-Native American settlers. "The Indians are to be individualized and dealt with one by one," said the Commissioner. "The American Indian is to become the Indian American."

9. *What groups were opposed to the general allotment?*

Land-grabbers and reformers both thought that removal of Indians from reservations and allotment of land to individuals was the best policy. If it were not possible to protect Indian culture, then it was better to *assimilate* individual Indians into the White way of life. The voices against this action belonged to those estate-owners who wanted to buy up large sections of the reservations. In addition a small group of anthropologists led by Lewis H. Morgan also opposed breaking up the Indians' land. Morgan wrote that the Indians

In what ways was the government's Native American policy in keeping with traditional American values?

In what ways were the American legal system and land ownership customs difficult for the Native Americans to adopt?

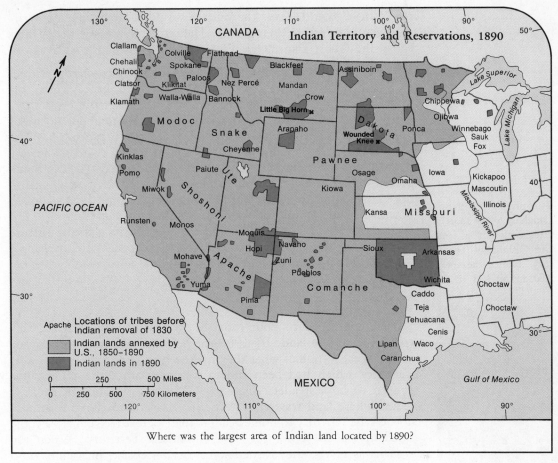

Indian Territory and Reservations, 1890

Apache — Locations of tribes before Indian removal of 1830

Indian lands annexed by U.S., 1850–1890

Indian lands in 1890

Where was the largest area of Indian land located by 1890?

By 1890 the largest area of Native American land was located in Oklahoma.

would not be able to adjust to the White way of buying and selling private property. He believed that many Indians would sell their land to estate-owners and then spend the money. Morgan predicted that without tribal support the Native Americans would end up in poverty—lost in the White people's world.

Indians on Reservations

Allotment was not forced on the tribes of the Southwest. But tribes in other parts of the West did not fare as well. The government agents were so afraid of trouble that they supervised any religious movements or ceremonies that they felt would get out of hand. One of the most tragic incidents happened on the Pine Ridge Reservation of South Dakota in 1890. There the agents tried to prevent the Ghost Dance. The Ghost Dance was part of a religion practiced by many western tribes, but especially by the Sioux at Pine Ridge. The Native Americans looked forward to a time when

1) Estate owners who wanted to buy up large sections of the reservations opposed the act. 2) Anthropologists led by Lewis H. Morgan believed that many Indians would sell their land to estate owners, and end up in poverty. up in poverty.

10. What brought about the battle at Wounded Knee?

1) Government agents, afraid the religious ceremonies might get out of hand, supervised them closely. 2) The agents brought in the army to stop the Ghost Dance by the Sioux at Pine Ridge.

What kind of tribal support do you think would have helped the Native Americans?

465

the Whites would leave, the buffalo would return, and dead warriors would rise from their graves. The ceremony, which the Whites called the Ghost Dance, was meant to bring this time back again.

When the army was sent in to stop the Ghost Dance at Pine Ridge, many Sioux fled from the reservations. In the fighting which followed, Sitting Bull, the leader of the Ghost Dancing, was shot. Then a fierce battle was fought at Wounded Knee about 20 miles (32 kilometers) from the reservation. (See map, page 465.) The army rounded up a band of 340 Sioux, of which two thirds were women and children. When the soldiers demanded that the Sioux give up their guns, the trouble began. Exactly what happened is not known. But the result was that many of the Sioux were gunned down. About 30 soldiers were also killed in the fighting. The United States was only able to add the West to its national culture and economy at a great cost to the Native Americans. Many people were concerned, but no one seemed to know what to do.

The West at the Turn of the Century

Settlers continued to pour into the West and Native Americans continued to lose land. By 1900 the holdings of Native Americans in the West were half what they had been in 1887. The Oklahoma Territory which had been Indian Territory since the 1830's was opened to homesteaders in 1889. Oklahoma was one of the last places where land was still cheap. No sooner had the government opened the territory to homesteaders than a great race began. People lined up on the borders of the Oklahoma Territory. When the signal was given, they rushed across on horseback, in wagons, and on special trains to get land.

The race for Oklahoma took place in 1889. By the next year the United States Census Bureau reported that the American frontier was gone. Much of the land that had been almost empty before was now taken over by big mining companies, big farms, and cattle ranches.

This photograph shows Oklahoma City shortly after settlers raced into the Oklahoma Territory. Notice the tents that are pitched.

Checking the facts

1. Why was the railroad a lifeline to those who settled in the West?
2. How did farming grow big?
3. What was the policy regarding the Native Americans in the western lands?

The American value of liberty allows people to move. This may cause unfair results.

Can you think of a way of settling Oklahoma that would have been fair to all yet still would have allowed individuals the freedom to move?

FANNIE FARMER

Fannie Merrit Farmer published a cookbook in 1896 and became famous. It was a very American cookbook, in that it brought a businesslike attitude to the art of preparing food. For it was Fannie Farmer who wrote the first cookbook based on scientific principles—exact measurements and good nutrition. Before Fannie Farmer's time, cooks used to follow recipes that called for a "handful" or a "pinch" of a certain ingredient. The results of such recipes could prove to be very unreliable. Fannie Farmer changed all this by inventing the level teaspoonful. This meant that cooks throughout the nation could use the same directions and achieve exactly the same results. Three million copies of her cookbook in 11 editions were published.

Fannie Farmer's achievement is a story of personal bravery and unusual talent. When Fannie was 16 years old she suffered a stroke that left her partly paralyzed for life. For many people this would have meant the end of any chance for a useful life. But Fannie would not be stopped. She took a job as a mother's helper. Then her older sister discovered a teacher-training school that would take students who did not have a high school diploma. Fannie took the two-year course at the Boston Cooking School and then stayed on to become assistant to the principal. One year later, when the principal died, young Fannie took the job.

In 1902 she opened her own school called Miss Farmer's School of Cookery. Fannie gave demonstration lectures twice a week on the newest methods of cooking and meal planning. She also held several kinds of classes, one for hospital dieticians and cooks, one to teach people how to do the marketing, and one for women of middle- and upper-class homes who needed to know how to manage their staffs and plan their households. She also held classes for the immigrant Irish girls of Boston. For three or four dollars she would teach them enough in two weeks so they could get jobs as cooks. She also taught them how to set a table, how to serve, and how to present themselves in public.

By the end of her life, Fannie Farmer was lecturing in a wheelchair. But she lived long enough to see new appliances invented that helped make cooking more scientific. Some of these new inventions were the gas oven, the icemaker, and the thermostat. The new inventions also helped to free women from some of the hard labor of running a home.

2. THE BEEF INDUSTRY: A CASE STUDY

11. Why was getting meat from the West to eastern markets expensive?

Transportation was expensive: cattle had to be driven from Texas to the railroad terminal; only so many would fit into a boxcar, which cost $1,000 to use. 2) Slaughterers, wholesalers, and butchers all added to the final cost.

People in the larger urban centers in the East bought large amounts of food made from produce that grew in the West. The railroads were the way of linking the western food to eastern customers. The cattle and the grain were shipped east, processed into food products—meat, cereals, flour, and whisky—and sold.

But transporting the goods was expensive, especially in the meat industry. Cattle had to be driven (on foot) from Texas to the western terminal of the railroad. Only so much beef could be sent live in a single railroad boxcar and every step of the way added more to the cost of the final product. To begin with, the railroad collected $1,000 for the use of each boxcar. Then the slaughterers at the eastern centers of Brighton (near Boston), and Albany and Buffalo in New York collected their fees. Next the beef carcasses were sold to dealers called wholesalers. The wholesalers took the meat to local town butchers who cut it up and sold it in markets or delivered it to customers. Although the cattle came from far away, the meat-selling business was still local. Meat from the West was sold in the same way as the cattle grown on farmland near the town.

Thinking Nationwide

12. Why did Swift move his business west?

1) Swift knew he could sell more meat if he could lower the price. To do that, he would have to lower his expenses. 2) His plan was to slaughter and trim the meat as far west as possible so that he would not have to pay freight on the inedible parts of cattle (about 400 lbs. each) or pay for feeding the cattle for 1,000 miles.

One man had an idea that was as big as the distance the cattle traveled. His name was Gustavus F. Swift. Since he was a teenager he had been in the meat delivery business supplying homes in Cape Cod, Massachusetts. Swift realized that he could sell much more meat if he could sell it at a lower price. In order to lower the price to the customer he would have to lower his own expenses. Swift's idea was to buy his meat closer to its source. In this way he could cut down the payments to the wholesalers.

Swift moved his business west, following the railroad from the customer toward the source of the cattle. His plan was to slaughter and trim the meat as far west as possible, so that he would not have to pay railroad shipping costs on the inedible parts of the cattle. A 1,000 pound (450 kilograms) steer was worth only 600 pounds (270 kilograms) of meat. Why pay freight on 400 pounds (180 kilograms) of excess weight? In addition, Swift calculated the savings on not having to feed the cattle for all those miles (kilometers). He also knew that cattle lost a great deal of weight on the long railroad trip. Slaughtering the cattle farther west meant more meat from each steer.

Swift moved from Cape Cod to Brighton, from Brighton to Albany, then to Buffalo, and finally to Chicago in 1875. Chicago was the first railroad stop from the western cattle range to the East. (See

Why are these centers located where they are? Think back to what you know about networks of buying and selling.

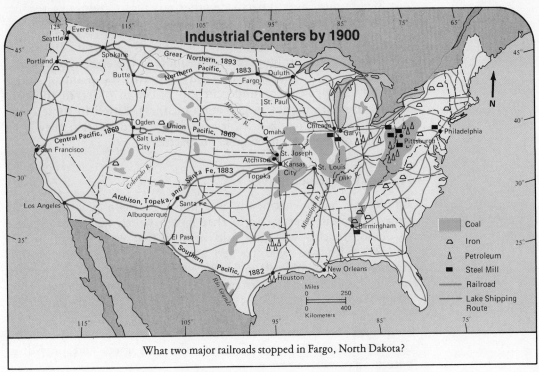

Industrial Centers by 1900

What two major railroads stopped in Fargo, North Dakota?

The Great Northern Railroad and the Northern Pacific Railroad stopped at Fargo, North Dakota.

map, above.) Swift went into the beef business in Chicago. There were others already in business there, such as Morris and Armour, but they were primarily in the pork business. And they sold their products to local markets. They thought Swift was out of his mind to try to sell fresh beef and, worse yet, to try to sell it to customers 1,000 miles (1,600 kilometers) away!

Building Nationwide

Swift first had to find a way to sell slaughtered meat to eastern markets on a year-round basis. Eastern butchers might sign up to be sales agents for Swift meats in the wintertime. But most meat-packers closed down in the summer. To sell meat from 1,000 miles (1,600 kilometers) away in the hot summer months was unthinkable. Swift could not afford to shut down his business in the summer, so he made a major decision. He had heard about a new invention—refrigerated railroad cars. In 1878 Swift was the first to use those cars in large numbers to guarantee the freshness of his meat.

Swift's next problem was the opposition of local butchers in eastern cities. They formed groups to try to stop him from selling meat more cheaply than they did. The butchers' plan was to refuse to

13. How did Swift keep his business going in the summer?

Swift refrigerated railroad cars to guarantee the freshness of meat.

14. What did Swift do when local butchers boycotted his meat?

Which of Swift's actions do you think was the most important?

He put his own employees into business in the eastern towns and sold meat as cheaply as necessary, even to the point of losing money.

buy Swift's meat and to persuade other butchers to refuse to become Swift's agents.

Their refusal to buy, or boycott, was a serious threat. But Swift often put his own employees into business in the eastern towns and sold the meat as cheaply as necessary, even to the point of losing money. The practice of undercutting prices in order to compete was a common practice in getting a business started in those days. When the others realized Swift was determined to stay, they gave in. Some of them even became his partners.

National Representatives

15. How did Swift make sure that business was being done by his own standards?

1) He established "branch houses" in major cities. Each branch had a cold-storage plant and its own marketing organization. 2) He put his brother in charge of the eastern end of the business. 3) He traveled to every branch, and he demanded weekly reports and monthly accounts.

Employing people nationally was not a common practice at this time, but Swift learned early that it was worth the extra expense to do so. In this way he could be sure that each person he did business with was well trained and efficient, cared about high standards, and would sell in Swift's own way. Swift put his younger brother in charge of the eastern, selling, end of the business. They established their employees in "branch houses" in major cities. Each branch house would have a cold-storage plant, designed by Swift and run by his rules. Each would have its own marketing organization in charge of finding new customers and providing personal customer service.

Swift took no chances on something going wrong. He traveled to every branch. He demanded weekly reports and monthly accounts. As Swift meats were advertised and became more popular, it became difficult to supply meat to all the branch houses in the growing organization. Swift added meat-packing plants near the stockyards where the live cattle were sold. He looked west continually and set up slaughterhouses and packing plants that would be closer to the supply of cattle and close to each new major city. Swift's method of cutting expenses by cutting transportation costs was working. He opened a plant in Kansas City in 1888, one in Omaha, Nebraska, in 1890, and another in East St. Louis, Illinois, in 1892.

Swift's Business Grows

16. What did Swift do to expand his business?

1) Swift borrowed money to finance business. He thought of uses for the leftovers of slaughtering—glue, hides, sausage, pickled and smoked meats, and oil. 3) He added lamb, mutton, pork, poultry, eggs, and dairy products to make a "full line."

Swift borrowed money and expanded his business so rapidly that his competitors could not catch up. He knew it was only a matter of time before others would organize their businesses the same way. He wanted to capture all the customers he could before the others got started. He moved into St. Joseph, Missouri, in 1896, and then into South St. Paul, Minnesota, and into Sioux City, Iowa. By 1903 he had 7,000 employees and sales of $160 million a year.

Swift found ways of using the leftovers, or by-products, of slaughtering. He sold glue, hides, sausage, pickled and smoked meats, and oil. Using leftovers was another way of making more profits. Swift had to keep all the branch houses busy, so he expanded into other areas of meat and livestock production. He added lamb, mutton, pork, poultry, eggs, and other dairy products to make a "full line." If his agents were selling beef, they might as well sell all these other items to the same customers. The Swift label became famous throughout the nation and across the Atlantic.

Managing Nationwide

The most difficult part of running such a large business was knowing what was happening in so many locations at so many stages of the process. Swift needed to know if any stage of production or distribution was taking too long or using too many people. He needed to know how many people were working overtime to produce a particular product. Paying too many people for too many hours meant that the meat products cost Swift & Co. too much money. If Swift had to raise his prices to the customers, they might buy meat from someone else.

In order to produce the best possible goods and service for the least possible cost, Swift set standards for each part of the process. In order to know what standards it was possible for people to carry out, Swift needed information on a regular basis. In this way, he could compare one time period with another and one branch house with another. The telegraph lines were kept busy with information from the branches and directions from the home office.

Within 20 years Swift had developed an organization that included every step of the manufacturing and delivery process. This type of organization is called *vertical* because the operation goes from the bottom up in a straight line from raw material to finished product to final delivery.

marketing   (distributing to branch houses, advertising, selling to retail customers)
processing   (slaughtering, cutting into usable pieces, creating by-products)
purchasing   (buying the cattle)

Swift's accounting department watched over all of the steps. Many of the employees became specialists in one part of the business—unlike Swift himself, who had known all parts. Working in such a big business organization was quite different from the small partnerships that had been the way of doing business less than 20 years earlier.

Large organizations such as Swift's made the owners of smaller companies unhappy. Competing was difficult because the big vertical organization, if it was well run, could buy large quantities of

17. How was Swift's vertical organization managed?

1) Standards were set for each operation.
2) Telegraphic communication was established. 3) The accounting department watched over all three steps —purchasing, processing, and marketing. 4) Many employees became specialists in one area.

18. What did Congress do to protect smaller companies and businesses?

Companies can often operate more efficiently by becoming bigger. Sometimes bigger businesses are unfair to smaller ones. Do you think a business should be stopped from growing bigger? Why and when? Why not?

1) Congress passed laws to protect small companies from unfair pricing and unfair service policies. 2) It set up a commission to report on the activities of the large businesses that crossed state lines.

supplies cheaper and never run out. There was so much public concern about the influence of big corporations that laws were passed by Congress to protect smaller businesses from unfair competition and consumers from unfair pricing and unfair service policies. Congress also set up a commission on corporations to report on the activities of the large businesses that crossed state lines. In a 1905 report on meatpackers, the Commission commented that Swift and Company kept the highest standards by careful supervision of all its employees nationwide.

Checking the facts

1. What changes did Swift make in supplying meat to customers throughout the nation?
2. How did Swift come up with the idea of a nationwide big business?
3. How did Swift's big business affect other businesses?

3. OTHER BUSINESSES ORGANIZE NATIONWIDE

Other companies, like Swift, followed the new way of organizing their businesses nationwide. They, too, moved to form organizations which could own the raw materials, the processing and packaging factory, and the distributing and selling operations. They, too, cut their costs by cutting the profits made by others at each step along the way. They, too, made sure that there would be supplies for every step of the process.

The United Fruit Company used a nationwide distributing and selling organization to introduce bananas brought all the way from Central America. United Fruit actually persuaded the American public to like bananas and to include them in their diet.

Organizing the Sales

Methods of national marketing were not only applied to foods. Singer Sewing Machines were sold in branch offices all over America and in foreign countries by people employed by the Singer Company. This was a new way of organizing the sales of a manufactured product. Before this time, factories signed up with independent agents who represented many different companies and many different products. These "manufacturers' agents" traveled from customer to customer and town to town selling from their long list of manufactured products.

Do you think this picture would make a good advertisement for sewing machines? Why or why not?

Was it wrong to advertise bananas? Was it necessary to do so?

Singer branches or centers displayed the machines and demonstrated them. If a machine needed service, the center that sold it would repair it. If the customers could not pay for a sewing machine all at one time, the Singer center would allow the bill to be paid in installments over a longer period of time. This was called *credit*. Before this, a customer would have to borrow money from a bank and take the cash to the store to buy the goods. The bank charged interest for letting the person use its money. Singer provided the same kind of credit so that the customer did not need to borrow from a bank.

Many manufacturers became famous in this way from 1880 to 1900. James B. Duke introduced machine-made cigarettes to the tobacco industry. This was a new idea that had to be sold to smokers who made their own cigarettes. Duke organized a national marketing business in New York City, the nation's trade and communication center.

Spreading the Word

New products and new ideas for using familiar products had to be sold to people through advertising. No new way of eating, buying, working, or relaxing was automatically successful. People's fears had to be quieted, and their interest had to be awakened.

In the beginning advertising was "keeping the name before the people." Recognizing a name or a brand was important when a customer could buy several products for the same use. Some of the earliest advertisements were for "home remedy" medicines.

The first time a business used advertising to sell nationwide, it was not just to keep the name before the public, but to tell the public about a new product. Two brothers brought several hundred cracker factories together into one business. Each of the owners received shares, or stock, in the combined corporation, which they then named the National Biscuit Company. National would buy the flour mills near the grain fields, and high grade flour would be supplied to the cracker factories. Each cracker factory would mix the batter and bake crackers in the same way. These crackers would then be packaged, labeled, and distributed across the country. Households across the nation could buy family-sized packages of crackers with the Nabisco label.

Here was a vertical organization designed to get crackers into every home. However, they needed a package that would be appealing, and a sign, or label, that would serve as a common trademark. They went to an advertising agency, N.W. Ayer and Son, for a national promotion idea. Ayer thought up a name, "U-Needa-Biscuit" and a trademark, a boy in a slicker raincoat. The National

Inventions, such as this camera, led to the growth of big business organizations.

19. Why was it important for a business to advertise nationwide?

1) Advertising introduced new products to new customers. 2) It created a national market.

Biscuit Company was the first to pay $1 million for advertising. The biscuit account was the beginning of big advertising to match big business.

The American advertising industry in which specialists are hired by a manufacturer-distributor is as old as nationwide business itself. One of the first businesses to use advertising to introduce a new idea was a maker of substitute foods. These were products that people had never eaten before. Mr. C. W. Post had been cured of an illness by a Doctor Kellogg of Battle Creek, Michigan, who used substitute coffee and cereal. Post opened a factory in Battle Creek and made his own brand of substitute coffee, Postum, and a dry cereal, Grape Nuts. Kellogg was furious that Post was making money from his idea. Kellogg set up a rival company which made corn flakes. Both businesses did well, especially because they advertised. The founder of modern advertising, Albert Lasker, wrote about them. He said:

> "Kellogg was successful—and Post was successful. All of a sudden, in 1902 or 1903, a boom in cereal foods was born—a boom comparable to a real estate boom. People came from all over the country and started cereal food factories in Battle Creek. At one time, I believe, there were 24 of them."

It's Hard to Stay Small

Many companies, such as Kellogg's and Post's, were successful in growing into nationwide, vertically organized businesses. These businesses were so efficient that it became difficult for other businesses to stay small and still make a profit.

It was difficult, for example, for a small business to be successful if it was involved in just one step of the total process. For example, a meat-packing plant that did not have branch houses could not have as many steady customers as Swift and Company. Such a business might have more meat on hand than it could sell. It would have to drop its price and, perhaps, lose money. If meatpackers wanted to find more steady customers, they would have to do what Swift did. They would have to set up branches that would be required to sell their brand of meat. The other action they could take, and many did, was to sell their meat-packing plant to Swift or another large company and become part of the larger organization of that company.

Not only the producers but many of the retailers also had to join the big companies. Local butchers who tried to buy meat only from local farmers found that some days there was not enough local meat

20. What difficulties did small businesses have in competing with nation-wide vertically organized businesses?

1) If a small business had too many supplies on hand, it would have to drop its price and perhaps lose money. 2) If it didn't have enough supplies on hand, it would lose customers to the large company that did.

This painting shows the various stages involved in pork-packing in a plant in Chicago. What jobs do meat packers do today?

to supply all of their customers. Their regular customers would then go to Swift or another large meat supplier. The larger business that uses meat from all over the country would always have a steady supply. Local butchers often found that they were better off joining an organization like Swift's and selling the products of a large producer.

Businesses in America got bigger when smaller businesses joined the bigger ones. But this was not the only way that businesses became bigger. The other way was to try and win customers away from other large companies. Before 1880, many companies operated in only one area or region of the nation. When a large company decided to move into a new territory, it had to win business away from small, local producers and sellers. By 1880 it also had to win the new business away from other large companies working in the same territory.

21. How did businesses get bigger?

1) Smaller businesses joined the bigger ones. 2) Large companies expanded into new territories, where they competed with small, local producers and sellers and often with other large companies in the same area.

Mergers

Owners of some competing businesses often got together and decided that they could make more profits if they were not lowering prices in order to fight each other. They looked for a way to join businesses together and keep them all operating. One popular method of getting businesses together to make bigger businesses was to join them at the level of top management. Each company would buy shares in the other companies. Then all the shares in all the companies were put under the control of one committee or board of trustees. The trustees could then decide that one company could have all the business in one state and another company would have another state as its special territory. At the end of the year they would put all the profits together and divide them equally. This was called *pooling*. Putting businesses together into one organization was called a *merger*. Mergers of separate businesses under one board of trustees were called *trusts*.

22. How was a business organized into a trust?

1) Separate businesses merged. Each company bought shares in the other companies. 2) All shares in all companies were controlled by one board of trustees. 3) All profits were pooled at the end of the year and divided equally.

A new industry creates jobs as well as doing away with some old ones. Is that right from your point of view?

Organization has been important from the beginnings of life on the American continent. Why is it important for a citizen to know how organization happened and how it works?

Mergers grew out of two needs. Some mergers grew out of the need to have steady sources of supply. Others grew out of the need to have control over the other end of the process, or the distribution and sales of goods.

Andrew Carnegie

23. What did Carnegie add to the vertically organized business?

1) Carnegie bought the mines that supplied the coal and iron for his steel, instead of buying these materials from others. 2) He bought ships and a railroad to carry the ore to his steel mills, instead of paying others to transport it.

Among those businesses that bought the stock of their suppliers were those which produced semi-finished goods. For example, Andrew Carnegie had built a business which produced steel beams and sheets of steel. Steel was made by melting iron ore. The heat to melt the ore came from burning coal. Carnegie wanted to protect his business from a competitor who might control the supply of coal and iron. Just as Swift moved his business closer to the source of the meat supply, so in 1896 Carnegie bought iron mines in the Mesabi Range of Minnesota and coal mines in Pennsylvania. Carnegie also bought the ships that carried the ore from Minnesota through the Great Lakes to Erie, Pennsylvania. Then he and his partner, Henry Frick, bought and rebuilt a railroad to bring the iron from Lake Erie and the coal from other parts of Pennsylvania to their steel mills in Pittsburgh.

24. Why was Carnegie successful?

1) His ability impressed people, so they lent him money. 2) He watched for newer and better methods of producing iron and steel products. 3) He chose the right people to supervise the work and to sell his products.

The story of Andrew Carnegie's success is a famous one in American business history. He had come from Scotland as a boy and had worked hard in a textile mill and as a telegraph operator sending Morse Code. He so impressed the people he worked for that they lent him money to buy stock in a railroad. From that first entrance into ownership in the railroad, Carnegie moved into iron and steel manufacturing. Carnegie was always watching out for newer and better methods of producing iron and steel products. He also had a knack for choosing the right people to supervise the work, and for selling his own products. These abilities contributed very much to his success.

25. What influence did Carnegie feel that his United States Steel Corporation had?

1) He said that since the nation could now make the world's cheapest steel, it could lead the world in manufacturing.

It all boiled down to being able to build an efficient organization that could afford to sell for lower prices than its competitors. By 1901 he had merged his various steel-making organizations into the great United States Steel Corporation. Carnegie spent the rest of his life writing about business and money, and giving away huge sums of money to schools, public libraries, and an organization to promote peace. By 1902, Carnegie wrote with enthusiasm about the influence of his huge corporation:

> "The influence of our steel-making capacity upon
> development at home must be marvelous. The nation
> that makes the cheapest steel has the other nations at
> its feet so far as manufacturing in most of its branches
> is concerned. The cheapest steel means the cheapest
> ships, the cheapest machinery, the cheapest thousand

Businesses need surpluses. How can you make sure that you will get them when needed? How did Carnegie solve this problem?

Why was there such a jump in the production of pig iron and steel between 1880 and 1890?

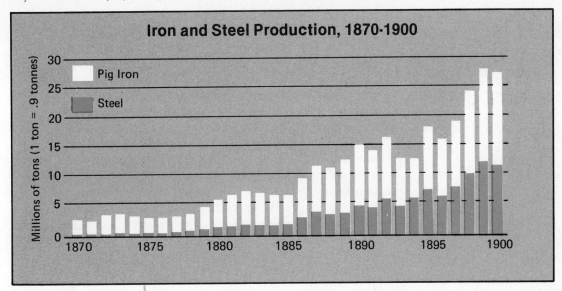

Iron and Steel Production, 1870-1900

Millions of tons (1 ton = .9 tonnes)

Pig Iron

Steel

and one articles of which steel is the base. We are on the eve of a development of the manufacturing powers of the republic such as the world has never seen. . . ."

Oil

Other corporations decided to get control of all the stages in the process of their business—from raw materials to selling to the customer. One of the most famous of these was the Standard Oil Company. This business was begun by John D. Rockefeller when he borrowed money to buy one oil refinery.

The refineries were the middle step in the oil producing and distributing process. Crude oil from the oil wells must be cleaned, or *refined*, before it can be sold to customers in the form of lubricants or fuel. Rockefeller's original idea was to buy up other refineries. He acquired a firm hold on the refining business by lowering his prices to the point that his competitors had no choice but to sell out to him. When his business was the only one left, he then raised the prices. By 1882 Standard Oil was a huge trust made up of many refineries.

In 1887 Rockefeller realized that the oil wells of Pennsylvania, where he originally had obtained his supply, were producing less. But new oil sources had been discovered in Indiana. To be sure that there was a steady supply of oil to its refineries, Standard Oil bought some of these Indiana oil wells. In 1899, Rockefeller explained to a committee of the federal government why big business was better:

26. How did Rockefeller develop Standard Oil into a huge trust?

1) Rockefeller lowered his oil-refining prices until his competitors were forced to sell out to him. 2) When his refineries were the only ones left, he raised the prices.

27. Why did Rockefeller think that big business was better?

Did Carnegie have a right to be proud of the steel-producing ability of the United States? How important was it?

From afar we talk about vertical organization. Notice, however, that each kind of industry is different. Why is it important to know each major industry up close?

1) Big business could use its volume of business, and the best and cheapest methods of manufacturing, to offer the products more cheaply. 2) It hired the best superintendents and workers and paid the best salaries. 3) It could spend the money to develop by-products and introduce them to the public.

"The success of the Standard is due to its policy of making the volume of its business large through the merits and cheapness of its products. It has spared no expense in utilizing the best and cheapest methods of manufacture. It has sought the best superintendents and workers and paid the best wages. It has not hesitated to sacrifice old machinery and old plants for new and better ones. It has placed its factories at the points where they could supply markets at the least expense. It has not only sought markets for its principal products, but for all possible by-products, sparing no expense in introducing them to the public. It has had faith in American oil. It has brought together millions of dollars for the purpose of making it what it is, and for holding its markets against the competition of Russia and all the countries which are producers of oil and competitors against American oil. . . .

Much that one person cannot do alone two can do together. Once admitting the fact that cooperation, or, what is the same thing, combination, is necessary on a small scale, the limit depends solely upon the necessities of business."

An Age of Inventions

28. How was Edison different from a scientist?

Edison's standard of success was the "silver dollar." If people bought an invention, this proved it was useful.

Just as industries got bigger and bigger, so scientists and inventors put all of their efforts into developing new devices. The most famous inventor of this period was Thomas Alva Edison. He was interested in inventions which were useful to many people. Edison never referred to himself as a scientist:

"That's wrong! I'm not a scientist. I'm an inventor.
. . . [Scientists don't] work for money . . . But I do.
I measure everything I do by the size of a silver dollar.
If it doesn't come up to that standard then I know it's no good."

Checking the facts

1. How did the advertising business change during this expansion period?
2. Why did businesses have difficulty in remaining small?
3. What are the advantages and disadvantages of big business to the consumer?

Edison's work was always in a practical, business framework. He actually thought up the idea of public lighting of an entire area.

PUTTING IT ALL TOGETHER

UNDERSTANDING THE MAIN IDEAS

1. How did mining, cattle raising, and farming in the West develop during the last 20 years of the nineteenth century?
2. What connections did ranchers and farmers in the West have to the rest of the nation?
3. How did business organizations tie the entire nation together?
4. How did bigness in business cause the rise of new kinds of organizations and new kinds of jobs?

ACTIVITIES

1. Read a biography of Singer or Rockefeller. How did they begin their big businesses? What was so unusual about their ideas? Include your findings in a brief book report.
2. Write an essay on one of the following topics: "The Advantages of a Business Becoming Nationwide," or "Advertising Tells a Great Deal About the Customer."
3. Do some research on a branch of a nationally advertised store near where you live. Which services are supplied by the national company to your local store? Which services does your store handle on its own? With whom does the local manager meet? You may want to work with a fellow classmate in this activity. Arrange to contact the store manager or public relations department, either in writing or by telephone. Explain your purpose. Arrange an interview or request some written information. Make an oral report to the class when you have completed the activity.
4. Draw an outline map of the United States. On the map show how the local store researched in the previous activity connects to its national network. Display this information on the map by inventing a key and symbols.

BOOKS TO READ

Cather, Willa, *My Antonia* (Boston: Houghton Mifflin and Co., 1926).

Hogg, Garry, *Union Pacific: The Building of the First Continental Railroad* (New York: Walker and Co., 1969).

John, Dorothy M., *Buffalo Woman* (New York: Dodd, Mead and Co., 1977).

North, Sterling, *Young Thomas Edison* (Boston: Houghton Mifflin and Co., 1958).

Weisberger, Bernard, *Captains of Industry* (New York: American Heritage Library, 1966).

chapter 19
Cities and Big Business

1890–1911

1. CITIES HELP BIG BUSINESS
2. THE WEALTHY IN CITIES
3. LIVING IN INDUSTRIAL
   CITIES: IMMIGRANTS
4. SCHOOLS—FOR WHOM AND
   FOR WHAT PURPOSE?
5. THE NEW MODERN MIDDLE
   CLASS

INTRODUCTION

When America became a modern nation, the lives of Americans changed. The changes were very different for people who lived in big cities compared to people who lived in farming areas. Within the cities, too, the changes were different. Life was different for the very rich who ran the large corporations and the banks compared to the newly arrived immigrants. It was even different for the second-generation immigrants who still lived in their old neighborhoods in the cities.

Historians have learned about the many ways people lived during the years when the United States organized nationwide. They learned from statistics about who held certain jobs or what they bought with their money. They have also learned from the houses people built and the letters and diaries they wrote. In these written accounts people often told how they spent their free time, what

	1892	1893	1897	1898	
Who?	President Benjamin Harrison	Grover Cleveland	William McKinley	American troops	
What?	opens the Crow Indian reservation to settlement	becomes President a second time	becomes the twenty-fifth President	fight in the Spanish-American War	
Where?	in Montana	of the United States	of the United States	in the Carribean and the Philippines	

Notice that the arrival of new immigrants and new businesses plus bigness made for new kinds of variety. The old values are in a fast-changing setting.

they thought about their work, and whether they intended to stay where they were or to move. As you look at the ways in which people lived in this period of bigness, try to answer these questions:

1. Why were cities so important at the turn of the century?
2. What caused the differences among city people in the United States?
3. Which Americans were grouped together within cities because of the new ways of life? Which were separated from each other? How did these groupings happen? Why did they happen?

1. CITIES HELP BIG BUSINESS

The new factories and businesses were located in cities where large numbers of workers lived within a trolley ride of the factory. Cities were also the stopping places for the railroad or for river traffic. This was important for steady supplies of raw materials and easy shipment of finished goods to other marketplaces.

Cities as Customers

Cities themselves became big customers. Therefore they helped businesses grow. You may recall that in the 1870's and 1880's when the railroads were expanding, the railroads were the largest buyers of steel, copper, power machinery, and explosives. In the 1890's, however, the major building of new railroads was finished. Now the building of cities was expanding. As people moved to the cities for jobs in factories, the city governments used the taxpayers' money to buy street lighting, telegraph lines, telephones, heating systems, power plants for electricity, coal, street cars and trolleys.

1. How did cities help big business?

1) New factories and businesses were located in cities, where workers could easily get to work. 2) More people came to the cities because more jobs were created. 3) Building and businesses expanded to meet city people's needs.

1899-1902	1901	1901	1904	1911
Filipino	Cherokee, Creek, Choctaw, Chickasaw, and Seminole Indians	President William McKinley	Puerto Ricans, under an order from the Supreme Court	Twenty thousand U.S. troops
rebels lead a revolt against American occupation forces	are granted citizenship	is assasinated	are not to be denied admission	are sent to protect Americans
in the Philippines	in Oklahoma	in Buffalo, New York	to the Continental United States	during a revolution in Mexico

The amount of building construction is a sure sign of growth. Can you make a diagram of how cities made jobs and jobs made cities?

481

Notice how industries are linked to each other. As the nation grew in technical expertise, it became more interdependent.

They also needed materials to build roads, sewers, and large buildings. To keep up with these needs, steel companies, like Andrew Carnegie's, shifted from making rails to making steel for large buildings.

Attractions of City Life

2. How could a newcomer see the drama that was New York City?

One way was to ride an elevated train and look through people's windows.

People were very conscious of how different city life was from life on small towns and farms. A city had many strange attractions for the newcomer. The elevated train on Third Avenue in New York City was famous. It ran on tracks two or three stories above street level. A novel by William Dean Howells described what could be seen from this train:

> "It was better than the theater . . . to see those people [in nearby houses] through their windows: a family party of work-folk at a late tea, some of the men in their shirt-sleeves; a woman sewing by a lamp; a mother laying her child in its cradle; a man with his head fallen on his hands upon a table; a girl and her boyfriend leaning over the window-sill together. . . .What drama!"

"The Bowery at Night, 1895," was painted by Louis Sonntag. It shows the elevated train and trolley cars of New York City.

The growth of a national sport with national rules, like baseball, shows how well the network of communication worked.

The Trolleys

One reason that cities were such exciting places to live was that there was so much to see and do right near home. City living appealed to Americans' desire to keep busy.

For the first time sight-seeing was possible for Americans who could not afford to own expensive horses and carriages. Now a person could ride in a public trolley or a horse-drawn cab just by buying a ticket or paying a fare. Another attraction of the big city was the night life. Cities now had electric lights. This meant that trolleys, theaters, and dance halls could stay open after dark. In 1888 one New Yorker recalled a trolley party: "For a very small expense a car could be lit from one end to the other in a perfect blaze of multi-colored lights, producing at once a carnival spirit that was quite irresistible."

3. Why did city living appeal to Americans' desire to keep busy?

1) They could afford to ride in a trolley or a horse-drawn cab to see the sights. 2) The invention of electric lights made night trips possible.

Bigness in Sports

There was a ready-made crowd of city people looking for entertainment. This provided a push for great growth in the spectator sports—baseball, football, boxing, and car-racing. By the late 1800's, many major cities had privately owned baseball teams. They traveled by railroad and played games against other teams in other cities. Public baseball had been played as early as 1845. Yet it was in this boom period that baseball teams grew in number and the game gained in popularity.

This was a time of inventions and baseball saw more than a few. The kid-glove mitt, the catcher's wire mask and shinguards, as well as the standardized ball were invented and came into regular use during this time. By 1900, baseball was played by the same rules and with the same equipment in every major city.

Other sports, too, caught on with the public. Boxing stars traveled from city to city for their matches. Their fame traveled ahead of them by telegraph. Articles about them appeared in the newspapers and magazines.

4. What accounted for the growth of spectator sports?

1) City people wanted entertainment. 2) The railroad enabled teams to play against teams in other cities. 3) The sports and their stars were kept before the public through the telegraph, newspapers, and magazines.

The Theater

Every large city had its playhouses and traveling groups of actors who brought live theater to every part of America. What the public wanted to see was often hard to guess. Americans came from many backgrounds and there was no such thing as "one American taste for the arts." Many of the most popular plays were by English authors. American minstrel shows and plays by Shakespeare were often presented in the same town on the same night. Otis Skinner, the Shakespearean actor, and Buffalo Bill Cody and his Wild West Show were known to play Lincoln, Nebraska, at the same time.

5. How did the theater reflect the variety found in America?

It reflected the wide range of popular tastes. There might be a minstrel show, a play by Shakespeare, and a Wild West show playing in a city at the same time.

483

Where does your favorite entertainment come from? Is it local or national?

Phineas T. Barnum and James A. Bailey organized a famous circus. One of the stars of the circus was Jumbo, an elephant who drew huge crowds of city people.

The big cities were all filled with variety. This variety was often found within each city block. In Chicago each business of any size had its own impressive buildings. They often had new plate-glass windows and were designed as the novelist Theodore Dreiser said, "to make a gulf between poverty and success seem both wide and deep." Each of these cities, however, had its own features which made it special. San Francisco, for example, was a mixture of Mexican and Anglo cultures. Other special features of the city were its mild climate and steep hills.

New Ways of Communicating

6. Why did Samuel Clemens see the invention of the automatic typesetter to be the most important invention?

He was a printer and an author, and the new process made it possible for more people to buy printed matter.

Which came first? The size and life-styles of the population in the cities or the inventions which were a part of that life-style? It is hard to know which came first, because the big-city boom and the businesses and inventions appeared in such rapid succession.

For example, so many people living in one large location caused a need for new and bigger ways of communicating information. City people provided an eager market for newspapers and magazines. The newspaper business made profits from advertisers who welcomed ways of reaching as many people as possible through the "mass media." It is no surprise that the development of improved typesetting and printing machinery came about during the same

Are differences in wealth more or less noticeable in cities?

time in which the need for information was shared by so many people. The automatic typesetting machine was a thrill for Samuel Clemens. He was a printer better known as the author Mark Twain. In 1890 he wrote to a friend and described what it was like to see the machinery that made big business in words possible:

> "All the other wonderful inventions of the human
> brain sink pretty early into commonplace contrasted
> with this . . . mechanical miracle. Telephones,
> telegraphs, locomotives, cotton gins, sewing
> machines, . . . calculators, . . . looms, perfecting
> presses—all mere toys, simple things!
> The . . . typesetter marches alone and far in the lead
> of human inventions."

Cities Are Centers

At the turn of the century, Americans who lived in cities felt the excitement of the new age of bigness. The increased wealth, comfort, and control that some Americans had achieved was obvious in the city.

Checking the facts

1. What kinds of entertainment did big cities offer? What made them possible?
2. What made new ways of communicating possible?
3. What was one author's impression of the new elevated trains in New York City? What was special about them?

2. THE WEALTHY IN CITIES

Studies of life in modern American cities show who had power and what people cared about. They also show the relationship between owners and workers and between old-timers and newcomers to America.

Business Leaders and Their Beliefs

Who were the people who held many of the high positions in business and banking? One well-known study shows that they were all men. Most of them came from families who had been in America

7. What did it take to hold a high position in business or in banking?

1) Bankers and business leaders were men, usually from families who had been in America for at least four generations. 2) They were usually of English descent. 3) Half of them were college-educated.

In what ways are modern cities a symbol of older American values?

485

Cornelius Vanderbilt was a wealthy railroad tycoon. This is the billiard room in his summer house. It cost $3 million to build in 1895.

for at least four generations. Many of them came from families of English descent dating back to the earliest colonial days.

These particular business leaders not only came from the same kinds of families. They also shared a similar educational experience. Half of them went to college before going into business. These college-trained men ended up with better jobs.

The way some of these people lived reflected the way they felt about being American in modern times. They believed in hard work. They continued to go to their offices long after they had become rich enough to retire. They also believed in spending money on themselves and their families. Spending money showed the world how successful a person had been at his work.

Many wealthy business people used their money to build and decorate houses. These were not just big houses, but very big houses. They were not just handsome houses, but houses that would cause people to stop and stare. Wealthy American business people wanted their houses to become symbols of American beliefs and American success. They wanted everyone to know from looking at their houses that American success meant the power to use great wealth in any way they liked.

Wealthy business leaders were trying to preserve bigness, liberty, and control. Some did not worry about the other people who lived in these same cities and could barely afford housing at all. They were not the least bit embarrassed about the differences between the rich and the poor. They even believed that the differences in the way they lived were both natural and good.

The Separation of Rich and Poor

The wealthy owners of the giant businesses—people like Andrew Carnegie, John D. Rockefeller and J.P. Morgan—were well aware that they had become separated from other Americans. They knew that their interests, activities, and even their daily contacts brought them closer to other wealthy business people across the nation than to the workers in their own mills, railroads, and factories. Andrew Carnegie saw the dangers in this situation:

> "The price we Americans pay is great. We bring
> together thousands of workers in the factory and in the
> mine about whom the employer can know little or
> nothing. . . . All dealings between employer and
> employee are at an end. Rigid classes are formed and,
> as usual, not knowing each other breeds distrust. . . .
> There is often trouble between the employer and the
> employed, between rich and poor."

The separation in modern times of owners from managers and managers from workers and workers from the poor was partly brought on by the new ways of organizing. How?

Carnegie knew that some people had more skill than others at some things. He knew that some were born richer or became so. What do you think these people owe the rest of the nation? What do you owe?

Power to do Good

Carnegie and others believed there was a good side to the fact that a few people had become so rich. They thought it was better for America if the most qualified people had the money and the power. They could then use their money and power to make the best decisions for everyone. Carnegie was sometimes asked, "How can we know who are the best people?" He would answer that the best people are the ones who have won in the competition for mergers, customers, and profits. Carnegie knew that the competition for power hurt many people. But to him and to others like him, the result was worth it. He said, "Competition is hard on the individual . . . but it makes sure the survival of the fittest."

In Carnegie's view, people who became rich had a duty to society. Rich people must give the money they made back to the whole society in the form of gifts that most individuals could never afford—colleges, public libraries, concert halls, hospitals, public parks, and swimming pools. Carnegie's own favorite gift to the people was a library, open to the public. To him, a public library was a place where any boy or girl, no matter how poor, could learn from all the great minds that had lived before. Carnegie gave a library to his native town in Scotland. He gave over $5 million to build public libraries all around the city of New York. He gave Pittsburgh a large central library building and eight branch libraries. In his lifetime Carnegie and the Carnegie Corporation gave a total of almost $44 million for the building of libraries.

One part of Carnegie's idea was that the people should also have to make a contribution to these libraries. He, therefore, insisted that the town or the college where one of his libraries was located should buy the books and pay for the librarians. He thought the rich ought to make big *capital gifts* to the community. Other members of the community should then work to match the gift with their own support. The idea of gift-giving by the rich to other people was a way of showing their love for human beings. It was called by its Greek name, *philanthropy.*

By the turn of the century there was a definite style of living among the very rich. It was quite the same in every large city. A belief in the survival of the fittest, a habit of spending money lavishly, and the practices of philanthropy went hand in hand.

8. How did Carnegie defend wealth in the hands of the few?

1) Carnegie said that only the most qualified people became rich, and that these people would use their money and power wisely to make the best decisions for everyone 2) He believed that the rich had a duty to society.

9. Why did Carnegie feel that people should also have to make contributions to libraries?

He believed people should match large capital contributions with the kind of support they could afford, such as the buying of books and payment of librarians' salaries.

Checking the facts

1. What was meant by the "survival of the fittest"?
2. Why did the wealthy practice philanthropy?

It takes large amounts of money at one time to build or start one big project. How many ways are people in your community paying for big projects?

3. LIVING IN INDUSTRIAL CITIES: IMMIGRANTS

New York: The Largest Immigrant City

10. Why did immigrants live where they did?

1) Immigrants lived where work could be found—in the central business, factory, and dock sections of the biggest cities. 2) It took time for them to save enough money to buy better housing outside the cities.

Big cities were an important part of modern America. Cities were the places where work could be found. In the cities jobs were the key to the future. A great many of the workers in the big cities were foreign-born or the children of immigrants. Between 1880 and 1910, 8½ million southern and eastern Europeans came to America looking for jobs. In one year, 1907, over half a million Italians and Russians arrived. They lived where the work was—in the central business, factory, and dock sections of the biggest cities. Others like them also had to live close to their jobs in the same neighborhood. Where were the families who had been in America longer? They had saved enough money to buy better housing and had moved out of the cities. People who could afford to ride the trolley to work and afford better housing lived as far from the factories as possible. Therefore, the new immigrant working families had only each other to know and rely on. Housing and the new electric trolleys had separated them from other Americans.

Worker Neighborhoods

11. Why did immigrants from the same country cluster in neighborhoods?

1) Immigrants often had the address of someone from their native village. 2) They moved in with relatives, friends, or friends of friends. 3) They retained their native language, food, and customs in their neighborhoods.

The worker neighborhoods of the cities were often divided into smaller sections. They were made up of families who came from the same country in Europe. There were clusters of city blocks which were either almost entirely Polish, or Italian, or Russian. These little neighborhoods of immigrants from a particular country became centers of daily living for many new Americans. These neighborhoods were like islands within the giant city. Whatever people needed was supplied right there.

Immigrants arriving at Ellis Island in New York presented their papers to immigration officials. Later they were examined by health officials.

488

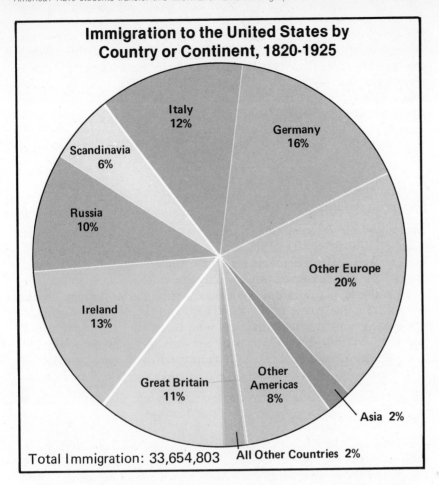

Immigration to the United States by Country or Continent, 1820-1925

Italy 12%

Germany 16%

Scandinavia 6%

Russia 10%

Other Europe 20%

Ireland 13%

Great Britain 11%

Other Americas 8%

Asia 2%

Total Immigration: 33,654,803

All Other Countries 2%

Where else would a newcomer go, except to old friends of the family in Europe or to those who spoke the same language, ate the same food, and went to the same place of worship? Often when newcomers arrived in America, they only had the address of someone from their native village or church or synagogue. These newest arrivals simply moved in with relatives, friends, or friends of friends.

Sweatshops: The First Jobs

Newcomers were given a room to sleep in and the chance to learn a trade. And the trades requiring the least skills were the "needle trades"—making clothes. Owners or contractors from larger businesses squeezed all they could out of the immigrant workers. The owners were called "sweaters," and the rooms the poor lived and worked in were called "sweatshops." The sweater's own room was often the shop. The beds or cots were moved during the day to make room for the sewing machines.

12. What effect did the sweatshops have on immigrants?

1) The shop was often the worker's own room.
2) Women with small children worked at home.
3) Because these women would take any wages offered, the pay of others who could go out to work

How did people who were starting life in America without money get a job?

Chinese immigrants had their own neighborhoods in the large cities. Both New York and San Francisco had large Chinese communities.

was lowered.
4) Children were kept out of school to work.

13. How did the Americans deal with the Chinese immigrants?

In 1882 Congress passed the Chinese Exclusion Act, which limited the number of Chinese immigrants and denied American citizenship to Chinese born in China.

It often took more than a generation for immigrants to move out of this condition, because the pay was low. There were three times the number of women as men in some of the sweatshops. Children were kept out of school so that they could earn pennies in the sweat shops. In that way the family could survive. Women were grateful that they could do some of this sewing in their own apartments while taking care of their small children. They would take any wages offered. This lowered the rate for others who would go out to work.

Newcomers and Old-timers

Although the different *ethnic* groups took care of their own, the older groups did not treat the newcomers any better than they had been treated. Advertisements for jobs once had said, "No Irish need apply." Now they carried other group names. The Irish had become the landlords of the slum buildings where newer groups lived. Blacks were the worst off of all. They were kept out of even the low-paying jobs by the employers who hired the immigrants first and then by the immigrants who got jobs for their own families and friends. Slum landlords of all groups refused to rent to Blacks, or rented only certain blocks of certain neighborhoods to Blacks.

The Chinese

The Chinese who came to the West Coast also had difficulty. They came to work in the mines and on the transcontinental railroad. But when these jobs were over, American workers began to worry that the Chinese would take their jobs away from them. They started an anti-Chinese campaign. It was especially strong in San Francisco. The result was the Chinese Exclusion Act, passed in 1882. This act set a limit, or *quota,* on the number of Chinese who could immigrate to the United States. It also denied American citizenship to Chinese born in China. The act remained in force until World War II.

The Muckrakers

14. What purpose did the Muckrakers serve?

1) They focused on the struggle of the poor in the cities. 2) They hoped that by raking up and exposing problems they would get other people and governments to do something to help.

A number of professional writers focused on the struggle of the poor in the cities. They wrote detailed accounts of daily life in the slums. They hoped to rake up and expose the problems and, thereby, get other people and the governments to do something to help. One of the best known of these *muckrakers* was Jacob A. Riis. In his book *How the Other Half Lives,* he described how each new group that entered America suffered but survived by controlling one local business or trade for itself:

Today there are ads on television to buy American products and support American workers. How old is this idea? What would have happened if no one in Europe had bought American products?

"Sunday, Women Drying Their Hair" was painted by John Sloan in 1912. Immigrant women worked hard and found little time for leisure.

"The Italian garbage collector of our time is fast graduating into exclusive control of the corner fruit stands, while his . . . boy monopolizes the boot-blacking industry in which a few years ago he was an intruder. The Irish hod carrier in the second generation has become a bricklayer, if not the representative of his ward, while the Chinese worker is in almost exclusive possession of the laundry business. The reason is obvious. The poorest immigrant comes here with the purpose and ambition to better himself and, given half a chance, might be reasonably expected to make the most of it."

Riis answered the charge that the poor created the bad conditions under which they lived. The muckrakers reminded their readers that the poor could not be judged without judging the system in America which caused urban newcomers so much suffering.

Where They Lived

Many of the immigrants who came to America around the early 1900's were from poor farms and small villages in Europe. Some of them went to farming areas in America. But in order to buy a

15. Why did only a few immigrants go to the farming communities?

What can you learn from the two kinds of sources on this page—the quote from the muckraker and the painting?

1) They were poor and unable to buy a farm.
2) There were few people in isolated rural areas to help them. 3) They had friends, relatives, and familiar social activities in the city.

farm they had to borrow money, and it was hard for strangers to get credit. Once they bought the farm they had no one to help them. There were no social activities to remind them of home. Having more space was not enough. The farms were isolated and poor. At least in the cities the immigrants had friends, activities, and the hope that one job might lead to a better one.

Housing in the City

16. What were the features of tenement housing and why were tenements built?

1) They were close together, and several stories high.
2) They housed many people in one building. 3) They had one front door to save money. 4) They had an air shaft up the center of the building for ventilation.
5) They were designed to house as many people as possible, using the smallest possible amount of land.

Housing was a terrible problem in a crowded modern city. Housing close enough to the factories, shops and docks, was needed for the thousands of immigrants who must walk to work. These people could afford very little rent. So houses were designed and built to get as many people as possible onto the smallest amount of land.

From 1880 to 1920, the years of the great immigrations from Eastern Europe, builders in New York City put up structures that were six or seven stories high. Each floor had three or four apartments. The lots were 25 feet (7.50 meters) wide. They ran 100 feet (30 meters) deep. They used the smallest amount of street-front space possible.

As early as 1903, more than two-thirds of New York City's population of 3½ million people lived in these *tenements*. Each tenement contained more than a hundred people. They led a miserably crowded life. The tenements had an air shaft which ran up the center of the building. Half the rooms in the building faced on this air shaft. But the air shaft was only open at the top. Instead of being a source of fresh air, the shaft was a trap for stale air. When a fire broke out in the rooms on lower levels, the draft of hot air was drawn through the shaft and rapidly spread the fire to the apartments above.

Were tenements an advantage in any way? In other cities with more land (like Philadelphia), row houses were built.

Immigrant families often lived in over-crowded apartments in tenements.

Adjusting Meant Helping Each Other

The people who left Russia, Poland, Greece, Lithuania, and Italy for the United States in the early 1900's realized that the life they would find in America would be much different from anything they knew. That is why they came. They wanted to try something new. The tales of the great new American businesses and their huge new factories in the growing cities meant jobs and opportunity. These were changes that they wanted. To have those opportunities they had to learn to live in cities, in crowded housing, and near strangers. That was not easy.

To make life easier they learned to help each other. They organized themselves into groups. Together they could look out for each other. They tried to make their entry into the working and social life of America less painful. Their neighborhood newspapers were written in their native languages. They published lists of families in need. They told people where to take clothes and furniture to help the needy. There were notices in the editorial pages and in news columns about how to apply for a job and how American workers were supposed to act. There were ads for classes in English which would help families learn the new language.

The new immigrants were friendly toward anyone who spoke their language or belonged to their church or synagogue. Before coming to America, friends and families were often in the same or nearby villages. They did not know people in other towns. They thought of and identified themselves by name and by village. Once in America they began to think of themselves as Italian or as Jewish. The common language gave them a sense of belonging. For the first time in their lives people from all over Italy and Sicily began to think of themselves as Italians. This happened while they were trying to become Americans. It was the first step in reaching out beyond their own relatives to people who were strangers.

This tie to strangers through language and religion was also experienced by Eastern European Jews. They used a common language, called Yiddish. Many European Jews who had to live in separate Jewish sections of towns spoke Yiddish as well as the national language of their home country. Yiddish was a street language. It consisted of several German dialects and added words from Polish and Russian. Yiddish was written in Hebrew letters. This meant that immigrant Jews from different places could use Yiddish to speak and write to each other. In the strange new city life, Yiddish allowed Eastern European Jews to feel more comfortable while learning about new jobs, new customs, new neighbors, and new neighborhoods.

17. What purposes did the native language newspapers serve?

1) They gave immigrants information about English classes and about jobs and how to get them. 2) They published notices about families in need and told how to provide help.

18. What happened to immigrants as a result of living in ethnic neighborhoods?

They began to think of themselves as belonging to a larger group than a family or village—a group united by language and customs.

19. How did Yiddish unite the Jewish immigrants?

Yiddish let them communicate with other Jews regardless of the countries from which they came.

Notice that Jewish neighbors had their religion and Yiddish in common, although in other ways they were totally foreign to each other. What holds neighborhoods together?

493

Parents and Children

20. *How did the immigrant children become different from their parents?*

The children spoke English and learned American customs in school and in city streets.

The immigrant parents who had decided to live in America expected to learn new jobs and live among strangers. They did not realize in how many other ways their lives would change. They became worried that their children were learning new rules of behavior from the other families in this new mixture of city life. They often felt that their children were no longer under their control. The adults often stayed at home. They became friendly with people who were as much like themselves as possible. The children, however, met children from other backgrounds in school or at play on the city streets. These children talked and played differently.

Many stories of immigrant families describe the arguments between the older and younger generations. As they met children from other backgrounds the children of immigrants decided that their parents' language, food, and rules for entertainment were strange. One child of immigrant parents wrote:

This immigrant Jewish boy is wearing a prayer shawl. He probably speaks both Yiddish and English.

"At the age of five I knew Yiddish better than English. I attended my first day of kindergarten as if it were a visit to a new country. The teacher asked the children to identify various common objects. When my turn came she held up a fork and without hesitation, I called out its Yiddish name, a 'goopel.' The whole class burst out laughing at me. That afternoon I told my parents I had made up my mind never to speak Yiddish to them again, though I would not give any reasons."

Children could wander down the street and out of their immigrant neighborhood into another. There was an Irish section, an Italian section, and a Russian Jewish one. The children made jokes about each other. Sometimes fights broke out. But even the fights proved to the children of the tight little neighborhoods that there were other ways to live.

In the crowded misery of a new industrial city, only the idea of the future made poor people feel better. It was an old American value dating from the earliest colonial times. The immigrants were willing to endure present suffering. After all, life would be better for their children. The early American values of control over one's life and the chance to make it better were some of the reasons why the thousands of immigrants came to America. They suffered the hardships of living in the crowded cities because at least in America they were free to try to get ahead.

Even with job shortages, people still move to America's cities from other nations and from farms. Why?

I HEAR AMERICA TALKING

If America spoke, what would it speak? In what language would you hear America talking? More than 25 million Americans today are *bilingual*; they speak two languages. Most of these people are not recent immigrants. They use one language in their homes and communities—with their families, in local stores, and in churches and clubs—and speak English on their jobs or in public meetings.

In the United States, English gives you the widest possible audience of listeners. You can speak to other Americans. You can speak to people in far away countries. Many people consider English the national language of the United States. However, the Constitution of the United States names no official national language. In early America, people tolerated many languages. They kept their native language, and learned English. They used their native language in their religion, social activities, and often for local government and newspapers. Public schools in large cities of America held bilingual classes. Only in the late nineteenth century did efforts begin to replace these languages with English.

In schools, teachers gave more and more attention to defining standard or correct English. Schools worked to establish this kind of English as necessary for all professional and government functions. Factories offered English classes at night for workers. People began to use standard English as a symbol of hard work, self-improvement, and success. This standard language came to be a national symbol of unity.

People talked about differences in the speaking and writing styles of others. Different ways of pronouncing words, putting them together in sentences, and naming things were called *dialects*. A Southerner working in a northern city found that people did not like the way he or she talked. Black, Irish, German, and Italian speakers learned that, in order to be understood, they had to change their ways of speaking when they talked to their bosses. Regional, ethnic, and social differences in language became ways people sorted out their friends and fellow professionals. Everywhere there were strong pressures telling speakers of different languages and dialects to give up their ways of talking and to speak only standard English.

Yet in spite of these pressures, many people kept their native languages as well as their regional and social dialects of English. That is why today so many Americans born in the United States are bilingual. Their families and communities have kept the pattern of using one language at home and another in public situations. Today, as in the nineteenth century, some public schools have bilingual classes where students have an opportunity to use their native tongue, as well as the English language.

From afar, the language of America is standard English. Up close, we notice great differences. What languages do people whom you know speak?

An American Language?

1) Foreign-born children were grouped by native language, so that it could be used as a basis for comparison with English. 2) After five months many students had learned enough English to enter regular classes.

School administrators and teachers were worried about how to teach the American language and customs to so many immigrant children at one time. For example, in Boston one out of three children was foreign-born. In Philadelphia it was one out of four. Four out of five New Yorkers were either foreign-born or the children of those who were. Because of the housing situation, most of the immigrants' children who spoke a European language went to the same schools. For example, in 1905 there were 38 elementary schools on the East Side of Manhattan that held a total of 65,000 students. Ninety-five percent of those students were Jewish. Teachers debated whether the foreign-born should be taught in a group or whether they should be separated and put into classes with American-born children.

The policy before 1903 was to put immigrant children into classes with much younger American-born children. When their English improved, the immigrant children were allowed to go to class with children their own age. However, the great number of children from different language backgrounds caused the schools to try a new plan. In 1904 foreign-born children were placed in special language classes. In this way English could be taught as a second language to students who all shared the first language. The native language could then be used as a basis for comparison with English. After five months many students had learned enough English to enter regular classes.

Immigrants and the Public Schools

1) She had the schools teach American government, grooming, manners, and ways of speaking to people. 2) She organized parent groups in the schools and sponsored lectures on practical subjects. 3) She placed nurses in public schools as a way of delivering health care to every family.

One of the New York City District School Superintendents, Julia Richman, saw the public school as a service to the whole immigrant family. Through the school, the family could learn the information and customs that would help it become part of American life. Richman changed the subject matter from memorized history of the United States to what she called practical civics. In civics, the immigrants could learn the real workings of the American government. In the schools in her district, students also had to follow strict rules about grooming, manners and proper ways of speaking to people.

Julia Richman knew how important it was to involve parents in the children's education. She organized parent groups. The schools sponsored lectures on practical subjects such as: *How to Prevent Illness in Children, First Aid to the Injured, Trade Unions—Why They Came and What They Do, The Street Cleaning Department.* Lectures were also given on American history, music, and art.

What do you think every American citizen should have to know about this nation? Why? Do people who live in a democracy have to know more or less than those who live in a dictatorship?

Many immigrant children learned English in public school classes like this one. In what other ways did the public schools help immigrant children adapt to American life?

Nurses were placed in the public schools, as a way of giving health care to every family. Children had regular eye examinations in school. Some schools had public baths because the facilities in the tenements were so poor.

To both parents and children the public schools were a way of becoming part of the United States. But in doing so, children had to give up some of their closeness to parents and grandparents. This was a high price. It was not possible to stay in one ethnic or religious neighborhood forever. It was not possible to work and vote or to help others and be helped without speaking English and without learning the new culture and customs of America.

23. What price did immigrants pay for becoming a part of the United States?

They gave up some of their closeness to relatives as they learned the new language, culture, and customs.

Trying to Improve

The crowded slum neighborhoods continued to exist. But the people who lived in them were not the same families year after year. For example, in the Italian sections of Chicago, half of the families

Many of the city schools had very large classes with 45–55 children, or more. What kinds of behavior are required if every student is to learn in a very large class?

Business and socializing took place on streets in immigrant neighborhoods. Why do you think it was important for immigrants to help each other?

changed housing each year. However, Italians continued to make up between 50 and 75 percent of the population in those sections. Those who learned better skills and got better jobs could rent better housing.

24. How did the immigrants work to improve their lives?

1) They handled their own banking needs by depositing or borrowing money from some neighborhood grocers or saloonkeepers. 2) They formed neighborhood clubs called "mutual benefit" organizations, which collected dues on which members could draw when they were ill or out of work. 3) Social events were usually neighborhood affairs sponsored by the church or synagogue.

Immigrants worked to improve their own lives and those of other newcomers in several ways. People needed to deposit money in a safe place and also send it to relatives in Europe. Owners of neighborhood grocery stores tried to provide that service. Very few people had enough money to loan to others. Few people would lend money to those who owned no property and had no savings. The immigrant grocery store became a sort of bank. These "banks" required no credit references. Any new neighbor who wanted to buy and send a steamship ticket to a relative in Italy could go to one of these "banks." The "banker" charged him or her a fee for the service. The banks operated without any government rules or controls for a number of years. When controls were set up to prevent cheating a customer, they were not very strict controls. The success of the system depended on trust between neighbors.

What do newcomers in a giant city do when they are sick? How do they find a doctor? How do they pay for a serious illness? Groups

If no one has a great deal of money to start a business, people can chip in and start one together. What causes people to trust each other enough to work together in this way?

of neighbors set up mutual-benefit organizations. They got together with people who came from their native country. Separate small clubs of Italians merged into one larger organization called the Sons of Italy. Several Polish groups formed the Polish National Alliance. The dues paid by each member formed a fund. Members could draw on it when they were ill and out of work. They could ask for money to help pay doctor bills and funeral expenses. These organizations gave people a sense of belonging that they had lost when they left their native land. They gave them help at a time when other Americans did not know or care about them.

Social events were usually neighborhood affairs. The synagogues and churches served as centers of activity and help. Parties and celebrations were often organized around religious holy days.

Social workers in settlement houses also helped the new immigrants to improve their lives. They held English classes, sewing classes for women, and political and social clubs for men. The social workers sponsored neighborhood theater groups and summer camps, such as the Fresh Air Camps. City children could go to these camps for two weeks in the summer. The camps were in the mountains and at lakes. The social workers often arranged for rural families to take the city children for a summer holiday. They also set up free employment agencies. People from the neighborhoods could now find out about jobs without having to travel around the city.

Immigrant groups also worked to improve their lives through the local city political organization. The city was divided into wards which were under the control of the city government. The mayor's office and the big city-wide jobs were often in the hands of earlier arrivals, the Irish-Americans. But the newcomer Italians could get control over the ward and jobs like sanitation and street repair by working for the election of the Irish. And the Irish ward leaders, in turn, gave day-to-day ward control to the various Italian American politicians.

The various organizations the immigrants developed to help themselves were fair when the people were fair. But when people accepted bribes or worked for criminals, the organizations could also get caught up in crime. Crime was one of the problems of people living in the crowded slums.

Not every immigrant used every aid available. Some ignored all of the associations. But the immigrants believed in the future, and they used jobs and education to survive the early days of slum living. They had to see themselves as part of the America that valued opportunity, control, and liberty. They had to remember what they left in Europe and why they came to America. Many of them made their daily lives better by helping each other.

25. What services did the settlement houses provide for the new immigrants?

1) They provided English classes for all, sewing classes for women, political and social clubs for men, and theater groups. 2) They sponsored Fresh Air Camps in the country for children. 3) They set up free employment agencies.

26. What is meant by ward politics?

A ward is a division of a city government. Immigrant groups often gained control of city jobs within the ward by working to elect ward leaders who would do them favors in return.

27. What immigrants benefited from the various associations?

1) Those who believed in change used the associations to help them survive. 2) The associations helped them get jobs and education. 3) Immigrants saw themselves as part of the America that valued opportunity, control, and liberty.

How do you think children can be helped not to choose the criminal way? What makes some people turn down an offer to make money illegally?

Checking the facts

1. List the features of life for new immigrants to America.
2. What evidence is there that large cities cared about the new immigrants?
3. What were some of the ways in which immigrant children were exposed to new ways of living in the cities?

4. SCHOOLS—FOR WHOM AND FOR WHAT PURPOSE?

28. What was the status of education and equal opportunity during this period?

1) Only the rich could go to college. Most people were considered lucky if they finished the eighth grade, although the number of people graduating from high school was growing. 2) Most boys went to work in their early teens to help support their families. Girls went to work if their family needed the money. 3) Educators were concerned about social changes resulting from industrialization and urban life. Debate focused on what should be taught and what the purpose of education was.

Americans recognized the changes that modern industrial life had brought. They worried about how people starting out generations apart could have the same opportunities. They worried about the differences in jobs which made differences in who people knew and what they knew.

Most people were considered lucky if they finished the eighth grade. However, the number of people graduating from high school was growing. More skills and knowledge were becoming available to city children who did not have to work on family farms.

Before and during this period college was a possibility only for the wealthy. Most boys had to go to work in their early teens in order to help support their families. Most girls were not expected to go on to college. They went to work if the family needed the money, or stayed at home if the family could afford it.

In 1897 the National Education Association (NEA) asked several important educators to speak about education and equal opportunity in industrial America. The discussion over education showed how concerned Americans were about the changes that industrialization and urban life had brought. Some felt school courses should match the new business opportunities. Others felt that the traditional courses of study, such as Latin and Shakespeare, should not only be kept but should also be offered to more people. The debate focused on what should be taught and, most important of all, what should be the purpose of education.

Commercial Courses

29. What stand did Thurber take at the NEA convention in 1897?

Thurber argued that if commercial courses were offered as electives, boys and girls might stay in school to

One speaker at the NEA meeting of 1897, Charles Thurber, was concerned about dropouts. He felt that boys tended to drop out of school to get a job. If commercial courses were offered as electives, then boys as well as girls might stay in school and learn to read and write and study literature, history, and mathematics. In addition, school could inspire in them "a spirit of commercial ambition and confidence."

Everyone knows that there are differences in skill, talent, and opportunities that children are exposed to before they reach school age. What do you think school should or can do about those differences? What should the individual do?

John Dewey

Not everyone in American education agreed that a business society required business courses in school. One of the greatest educators and philosophers in America, John Dewey, wrote and spoke on the purpose of education. Dewey was worried that Americans were not thinking about what he felt was the most important goal for citizens in a democracy—developing the ability to make moral decisions. Dewey believed that American schools and courses could be organized so that children would learn to behave in a more ethical or moral way. In this manner they would develop their individuality and still be contributing members of the society.

Jane Addams

One of the best-known speakers at the National Education Association meeting in 1897 was Jane Addams, a leader in the field of social work. She had founded an organization to help poor immigrants living in Chicago. Her neighborhood *settlement house* was called Hull House. Its programs were designed to help individual families find housing, jobs, health care, cultural activities, and recreation.

Jane Addams believed in John Dewey's ideals of the educated citizen. She also believed that there was a serious gap between wealthy children and newly arrived immigrants. She described how much better it would be "if all the children should be taught to use equally and to honor equally both their heads and hands. . . . It would then be of little importance to themselves or to others whether the child finally served the commonwealth in the factory or in the legislature."

Jane Addams was an important reformer who helped slum dwellers in Chicago. She founded Hull House in 1889.

learn to read, write, study literature, history, and mathematics.

30. What did Addams add to Dewey's ideals of the educated citizen?

Addams believed that all children, whether wealthy or immigrant, "should be taught to use equally and to honor equally both their heads and hands."

Modern America

Change had come to American business and to the life of every American. Some of the change was welcomed. But many people felt helpless to correct the problems that bigness had made worse.

Checking the facts

1. Compare John Dewey's view of education with that of Jane Addams'. How did they differ? How did they agree?
2. How would both Dewey and Addams disagree with Charles Thurber's view on education?
3. Who was able to go to college during this time period?
4. What was the general attitude about education for women at this time?

5. THE NEW MODERN MIDDLE CLASS

One result of the age of technology and industrial organization was that people came to believe in technical skills and big organizations as the best ways to attack problems. Modern industrial life in America helped to create a whole new generation of specialists. Corporate businesses needed specialists. And people like doctors, lawyers, and teachers became specialists.

Specialists and Professionals

People who did these jobs began to organize and got to know each other throughout their states and the nation. They began to see themselves not just as members of their local communities, but as members of national professions. These professions and their organizations shared certain ways of thinking and behaving. They believed that technical information and skills caused the spectacular growth in American production and the dramatic changes in American living. They thought that what they did required special scientific training. They created organizations which set scientific standards for membership in their professions. These organizations became important links in uniting Americans.

The American Medical Association, founded in 1847, suddenly took a great leap in membership. It became important for doctors to be regarded as specialists with advanced training. In 1900 only 8,400 doctors were members. By 1910 there were 70,000 members. And ten years after that, two out of every three doctors in the nation had joined the A.M.A. They got together and set admission standards for medical schools. They made sure that state legislatures passed laws requiring specific kinds of training and examinations before a person could practice medicine. This was a scientific and technological age. And medicine was looked upon as a set of scientific principles and rules.

Public Health

A new branch of medicine called Public Health was formed. By the early 1900's, most large cities had their own departments of health. In New York State, under the leadership of Dr. Herman Biggs, standards were established for purifying water and milk. Methods of isolating, or *quarantining,* the sick were required by state law. If a child came down with measles, the public health official would visit the house. A notice would be posted on the front door that no one in the house could leave, and no one outside the house could enter. This was the best way to keep diseases from spreading at a time when there were few vaccines and few effective medicines.

---

31. Why did specialists create professional organizations?

1) They wanted to get to know each other. 2) They saw their skills as special—requiring special scientific training and specific standards for membership in their professions.

32. What influence did the American Medical Association have on its profession?

1) The A.M.A. set admission standards for medical schools. 2) It saw that state legislatures passed laws requiring specific kinds of training and examinations before a person could practice medicine.

33. How did Public Health medicine differ from private practice?

1) Public health departments established health standards to help control disease. 2) Public health doctors and nurses were paid from taxes. 3) They provided free medical care. 4) They did research to eliminate diseases that caused epidemics.

New inventions and careful scientific controls had helped to create whole new businesses that gave people the control over the environment that they had always wanted. Name some of those controls (like heating and air conditioning) in your life.

Public health departments provided medical services to school children and to adults who could not pay for private medical service. Public health doctors and nurses were paid from taxes. The effect of this new branch of medicine was dramatic. Out of every 1,000 births in 1885, 273 babies had died. By 1915, that figure had been cut by two thirds.

Doctors also became involved in tracking down the causes of diseases that had created epidemics. The control of mosquitoes, lice, and ticks made it possible for government and medicine to control malaria, yellow fever, typhus, and Rocky Mountain spotted fever. In Panama, between 1904 and 1906, Colonel William Gorgas used the scientific findings of Dr. Walter Reed to wipe out yellow fever. This was a disease carried by mosquitoes.

Specialists and Professional Institutions

Lawyers, too, began to see themselves as specialists. By 1916, the lawyer's organization, the American Bar Association, had set up chapters in the 48 states. The bar association got the state legislatures to pass laws requiring state examinations. They were then administered by the state's bar association. The bar association, like the A.M.A., tried to make sure that every member of the profession had certain basic knowledge and met the same standards of technical skill.

34. What did the American Bar Association do for its profession?

The Bar Association got laws passed requiring state examinations, to ensure that every lawyer met the same standards of basic knowledge and technical skill.

Jobs in law and medicine were becoming professions. As other jobs became specialized, a pattern emerged. First, people joined together to define what they did in their jobs. Then they formed a professional association. And finally they required specific academic training for others to become members of that association. Businesses formed the National Association of Manufacturers. Businesses were looking for managers who had talent and experience in one step or another of the giant operations. They wanted specialists in purchasing, or marketing, or selling, or production supervision, or engineering, or cost control. How could a person learn how to be a manager in such complicated businesses? One answer was the creation of the nation's first college of business. The Wharton School of the University of Pennsylvania was founded in 1881. Wharton began teaching its first college courses on how to keep track of costs, or *accounting,* only two years later.

35. What pattern emerged that other professions followed?

1) People joined together to define what they did in their jobs. 2) Then they formed a professional association. 3) They required specific academic training for other members. 4) New colleges were formed to teach the courses, such as schools for accounting, journalism, social work, and education.

Newspapers began to set standards for reporting the news. And colleges of journalism were set up at a number of universities. Social workers first formed the National Federation of Settlements in 1911. Then they set up complete professional schools at the University of Chicago and at Harvard. Education also came to be seen as a technical field. In the past, people learned to teach by teaching. But in the early 1900's colleges began to offer majors in

36. What changes were seen in education in the early 1900's?

At the university nearest to where you live, how many professional graduate schools are there?

503

1) Education became a technical field with standards established by the states. 2) Laws were passed requiring children to go to school and take required courses. 3) The number of teachers and students rose dramatically.

This is a physics class at Cornell University. A college education became necessary for men and women who wished to become specialists.

education. State agencies were established to set standards for training teachers. The movement to make teaching a scientific or technical subject was caused by the vast numbers of children in the big cities who needed to be taught. A school system with a set sequence of courses that would be required of everyone in a city came to be accepted during this period. The eight years of required education were seen as a ladder which everyone must climb. Laws were passed requiring children to go to school and take the required courses. In the years from 1890 to 1910 the number of teachers and students quadrupled. In the ten years from 1910 to 1920 the number doubled again.

37. What did the National Education Association hope to achieve for the profession?

By 1911 there were requirements for special teacher training in 42 states. Teaching was considered a national profession. The teachers worked together from city to city through the National Education Association. The association worked to raise teachers' salaries and to guarantee that teaching was kept out of local politics. The idea that experienced teachers should be protected from being fired by local politicians brought about the *tenure system.* In many cities the school boards which directed the school systems were elected on a non-political or non-partisan basis.

Who runs the schools in your area? Who pays for them? Who decides what should be taught and what must be learned for graduation?

The training of teachers was particularly common in the cities. Rural teachers, however, were usually not able to get this training because of a lack of transportation and also of tax money. A great difference developed between city schools and country schools.

1) It worked to raise teachers' salaries. 2) It helped separate teaching from ward politics by establishing the tenure system and by electing school board members on a non-partisan basis. 3) It worked to give children the same standard of education regardless of where they lived.

Farmers were able to increase their production by using the new machinery that was invented in the late nineteenth century. Mail-order catalogs such as this one made it possible for farming people in rural areas to buy machinery and other items which were not available in their communities.

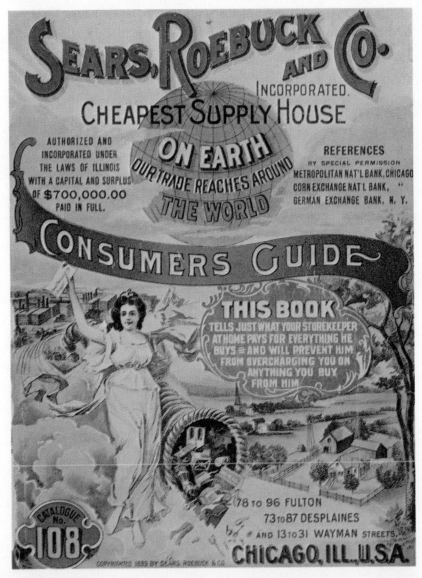

Today we sometimes have farm surpluses but no one to buy them. Was it a good idea to advertise machinery that some farmers could not afford to buy or that would later cause surpluses?

505

Some nations that do not allow freedom of choice will not let some farmers become wealthier than others by purchasing land and borrowing money to buy machines. Why was that not the American way?

38. How did farmers use new technology?

1) Farmers formed marketing cooperatives to run their combined selling as one large business operation.
2) Agents from state colleges, state government, and the American Farm Bureau Federation traveled from farm to farm demonstrating new scientific methods.

Farmers were also caught up in the new scientific and technical movements. The well-to-do farmers who owned huge commercial farms prided themselves on scientific farming. They also saw themselves as business people. They talked and wrote about borrowing money to expand their businesses and about scientific management of farming businesses. Farmers established organizations called *marketing cooperatives* for selling their products. Through the cooperatives, farmers could sell their produce at higher prices and run their combined selling as one large business operation.

State colleges of agriculture and state departments of agriculture helped farmers become more scientific about producing. They also helped them become more businesslike in their methods. Farmers formed organizations and set up agents who traveled from farm to farm demonstrating scientific farming. By 1919 the American Farm Bureau Federation had become a national organization of the most powerful agricultural business people in the North and in the South.

39. What were the features of this new social class?

1) Professionals regarded one another as qualified specialists. 2) They had a network of national connections through their organizations. 3) They believed in national organization to preserve America's progress and in national problem-solving to improve what they saw as the American way of life.

People in every professional field formed a new social class. They were well-educated and active in their communities. They saw themselves as being modern and scientific. They viewed each other as qualified specialists. Their connections to each other were professional rather than ethnic or religious.

These job-related or occupational organizations created the kind of national network that Andrew Carnegie and other business owners had established. The United States at the turn of the century was becoming a nation of organizations and a nation of specialists.

Americans not only specialized and organized, but they believed in it. Americans believed in technical training and in organizations. Organizations could make plans, collect money, and bring people together to solve problems. This new middle class of specialists believed in national organization to preserve America's progress. They believed in national problem solving to improve what they saw as the American way of life.

Checking the facts

1. What goals and requirements did the organizations of specialists all have in common?
2. What would belonging to a national professional organization do for the individual specialist?
3. How did organizations of specialists help improve American life?

Farmers' cooperatives are like mutual-benefit societies. What cooperatives are there in your area?

PUTTING IT ALL TOGETHER

UNDERSTANDING THE MAIN IDEAS

1. Why were cities so important at the turn of the century?
2. What caused the differences among city people in the United States?
3. Which Americans were grouped together within cities because of the new ways of life? Which were separated from each other? How did these groupings happen? Why did they happen?

ACTIVITIES

1. Write an essay expressing your point of view on big city life. What are the advantages and disadvantages of big city life? Incorporate information you have gathered from your reading in your essay.
2. Read about one of the wealthy corporation owners at the turn of the century. Ask your teacher or librarian to help you find a biography of one of these individuals. In what ways was the person a help to the nation? Would you describe the person as a "robber baron"? Why or why not? Make your answers to these questions the main focus of a brief book report.
3. The following is a research and mapping activity. Read about one of the states between the Mississippi River and the Rocky Mountains. When and where were farmers, miners, or cattle ranchers in that area? Look for this information in an encyclopedia or a similar resource book. Create a key and symbols for your findings in each of these categories. Then locate the information on an outline map of the United States.
4. Stage a debate on the following topic. Resolved: that all American children should have the same education since they all have an equal vote.

BOOKS TO READ

Brooks, Charlotte, ed., *The Outnumbered: Stories, Essays, and Poems About Minority Groups by America's Leading Writers* (New York: Dell Publishing Co., Inc., 1967).

Hoag, Edwin, *American Cities: Their Historical and Social Development* (New York: J.B. Lippincott, Co., 1969).

Meigs, Cornelia Lynde, *Jane Addams: Pioneer for Social Justice* (Boston: Little, Brown and Co., 1970).

National Committee on Urban Growth Policy, *The New City* (New York: Praeger Publishers, 1969).

chapter 20
Action on a Bigger Scale

1886–1899

1. WORKERS HELP THEMSELVES
2. WORKING WOMEN ORGANIZE
3. OTHER PROBLEMS, LITTLE HELP
4. AMERICA EXPANDS OVERSEAS: BIGNESS IN FOREIGN POLICY

INTRODUCTION

Other people besides muckrakers, philosophers, and social workers believed that something needed to be done to correct the problems caused by big businesses and big cities. The period at the turn of the century saw workers and farmers begin to strengthen their organizations. They were not very successful, but they did go on record in favor of better lives for the poorer people. And they did begin putting pressure on government to think about ways of making the American economic system fairer. Action taken by government at home was limited, but action taken overseas was much bolder. America spread its influence to a variety of areas in the world in the late nineteenth century. These places were Hawaii, the Far East, and the Caribbean. Americans were looking for ways in which to gain a position in the world that would match their

	1886	1889	1890	1891	
Who?	Samuel Gompers	Jane Addams	The chief of the Sioux, Sitting Bull	Andrew Carnegie	
What?	is elected the first President the A.F.L.	founds Hull House	is killed by U.S. soldiers	gives money to build Carnegie Hall for the performing arts	
Where?	in Columbus, Ohio	in Chicago	in South Dakota	in New York City	

Getting together is a way for workers, voters, and others to be heard. Name the organizations that appear in your newspapers.

prosperity and technological skill. As you read this chapter, you may find it helpful to think about these questions:

1. What made working men and women and farmers organize in the late nineteenth century?
2. How successful were they? What problems did they have?
3. What did government do? What reasons did leaders have for the action they took and for the action they refused to take?

1. WORKERS HELP THEMSELVES

The trade union movement had grown along with the industrial corporations. By the turn of the century over 3 million people worked in industry. Their success depended on their skills. But even that success was limited, because every time they went out on strike, some of them lost their jobs. The owners were getting more powerful rather than less so. Workers would have to try something else besides craft unions if they were ever to have enough strength to stand up to the owners and win.

1. What did the workers need?

Workers needed something besides craft unions to have enough strength to win anything from the owners.

Knights of Labor

An organization called the Knights of Labor had been founded in 1869, but for over ten years its activities had remained secret. In the 1880's, however, one of its leaders, Terence Powderly, decided that the Knights should be a publicly known group and should invite both skilled and unskilled workers from industries all over the nation to become members. The idea of cutting across crafts for membership was new. And the Knights welcomed women and Blacks into their union.

2. Why did many workers join the Knights of Labor?

1892	1893	1894	1896	1898
Steel workers on strike	American women	Workers, angry with layoffs and wage cuts	James B. Connolly	American ships under the command of Dewey
protest a wage cut and violence breaks out	are granted the right to vote	call a strike with the help of the American Railway Union	becomes the first American champion	destroy the Spanish fleet
at the Carnegie Steel Mill in Homestead, Pennsylvania	in Colorado	at the Pullman Company near Chicago	in the Olympic Games in Greece	at Manila in the Philippines

What did workers have to gain by forming bigger unions of different kinds of workers? What did skilled craft workers have to lose by joining bigger unions?

1) The Knights of Labor welcomed both skilled and unskilled workers, including women and Blacks, from industries across the nation. 2) They promoted the welfare of workers so that someday they would become managers and owners of businesses. 3) They led a few successful strikes against some of the western railroads.

The Haymarket Riot took place in Chicago in May 1886. This picture was done from sketches made by two eyewitnesses.

The goal of the Knights was not new. They wanted to promote the welfare of workers so that someday they could become managers and then owners themselves. The Knights became popular as they led a few successful strikes against some of the western railroads. By 1886 they had 700,000 members. But their success made the owners more strict.

The Haymarket Riot

3. Why did workers leave the Knights of Labor?

The Knights of Labor were blamed for a bomb that killed 7 police officers and wounded 70 people at a protest meeting during the McCormick strike in Chicago, although several anarchists were convicted of the crime.

In 1886 the Knights organized a strike of 80,000 workers against the McCormick Harvesting Machine Company in Chicago. They were trying to win the eight-hour day for the workers there. But when a striker was killed in a fight with company police, a group of political radicals known as *anarchists* called a protest meeting at Haymarket Square. Police came to break up the meeting and someone threw a bomb into the crowd. Seven policemen were killed and 70 other people were wounded. Several of the radicals were tried, convicted, and sentenced to death. But many people blamed the Knights of Labor even though they were not involved in the bombing. Members began to resign from the union and the organization never recovered.

American Federation of Labor

4. What were the goals of the American Federation of Labor?

A new organization made up of craft unions from all over the nation had been formed in 1881. Its membership was more limited than the Knights. But it had strong leadership and a new idea. By joining together, workers from different skilled trades could fight for the kind of practical goals they all had in common. They wanted better pay. They wanted workers to stop competing among themselves and agree to take the same pay. Then all the workers in that same kind of job could work together to put pressure on the managers to give everyone the same raise. They worked in the same way for shorter working hours, better working conditions, and laws to protect workers with dangerous jobs. This new organization of skilled trade unions was called the American Federation of Labor. Its president was Samuel Gompers of the Cigar-Makers Union. Gompers realized how important it was to have a large, loyal union membership. Only then would there be enough dues to pay for a strike. And a strike was the workers' most important weapon—as long as the members struck together. During Gompers' 34 years of leadership, the A. F. of L. grew steadily from 150,000 members in 1886 to more than a million dues-paying members in 1901.

1) The AFL wanted better pay, shorter working hours, better working conditions, and laws to protect workers from dangerous jobs. 2) It wanted workers in the same job to take the same pay so that they could put pressure on the managers to give everyone the same raise. 3) It wanted a large membership, which would enable it to organize effective labor strikes.

The Homestead Strike

Many strikes occurred during the first 15 years of the A. F. of L. Many of them were violent. Sometimes the strikers destroyed company property. The corporations often employed non-union or *scab* labor during strikes. The Carnegie Steel Company hired private guards to protect the strikebreakers at the Homestead, Pennsylvania, steel plant near Pittsburgh. In this strike in 1892, some of the workers attacked the guards and killed seven of them. But the corporation held out against the strikers and the union organization was almost destroyed in the steel industry.

5. How was scab labor protected during the strikes?

1) Some corporations hired private guards for protection. 2) In other cases of labor violence, the federal government sent the army to keep order.

In other cases of labor violence the federal government sent the army to keep order. The government was particularly concerned about railroad strikes which could hurt businesses across the nation. As early as 1877 President Rutherford B. Hayes had sent the army to stop railroad strikes in four states.

The Pullman Strike

The most famous strike was at the Pullman Palace Car factory outside Chicago in 1894. Pullman had cut wages but refused to lower rents in the town he had built for his workers. Supported by the American Railway Union and its leader, Eugene V. Debs, the workers at Pullman went on strike. Railroads all over the country were affected. Finally President Grover Cleveland sent troops to the Pullman factory to stop the violence there. The federal courts also issued an order, or *injunction*, against the strike. When Eugene Debs refused to obey the order, he was sent to jail, and the strike ended soon after.

6. How did the federal government end the Pullman strike?

The federal courts issued an injunction against the strike and jailed the union's leader, Eugene Debs, when he refused to obey the order.

Neither business nor labor knew what to do to manage the rapid growth of businesses and cities. Most people were excited by the

7. What did Samuel Gompers voice for the first time?

Gompers stated that workers were a group, or class, who deserved recognition and rights within the American system.

new opportunities and very worried about the ups and downs of business and the treatment of many workers. There were no solutions to unemployment in depressions, to machines taking away jobs, to the hiring of cheaper immigrant labor and firing of older workers. However, big unions came into being to try to match the power of big business. Gompers explained why workers had to organize on a large scale in a letter to the judge who ordered the Pullman strike to stop. In the letter he said:

"You recognize that the industrial forces set in motion by steam and electricity have changed the structure of our civilization. You also admit that a system has grown up where the earnings of the individual have passed from his control into that of representative combinations and trusts . . . . You say that labor cannot afford to attack capital. Let me remind you that labor has no quarrel with capital, as such. It is merely the possessors of capital who refuse to give to labor the recognition, the right, the justice which is the laborer's right, with whom we contend."

The idea of workers as a group or class within the American system was stated openly for the first time. It was to remain a basic idea of the American labor unions. The workers were building their own national professional organization.

Checking the facts

1. How were the Knights of Labor different from the craft unions?
2. What contributions did Samuel Gompers make to the labor movement?
3. How did businesses react to the major strikes of workers during the late 1800's?

2. WORKING WOMEN ORGANIZE

8. *Why did women workers attempt to organize on a large scale?*

Women were paid even less than men.

In 1910 one out of every four women in the United States worked outside the home. These women workers had a special problem. Like male workers they were underpaid. But they were paid even less than the men were.

The first women to organize on a large scale were those in the clothing industry in New York and Chicago. They were followed

Notice both the national and the up-close view of labor, plus the change from workers' seeing themselves as individuals to their seeing themselves as an organized group in a system of organized groups.

by workers in the textile mills in New England, Pennsylvania, and the South. Women joined the regular craft unions with the men. They also tried to organize a league of women workers. The first meeting of women took place in 1903 in Boston. An announcement was made at the convention of the A. F. of L. that a meeting of working women would be held.

The National Women's Trade Union League

The idea of a women's league of workers was approved by Samuel Gompers, the President of the A. F. of L. But he and the men did little to help the women organize. The person who called the Boston meeting was Mary Kenney O'Sullivan. She herself worked in a Chicago book bindery. She and her husband, an editor of labor newspapers, worked together to organize a national union of working women.

The first organizational meeting included women workers and the men who headed the unions which had large numbers of women workers. Those unions were the International Ladies Garment Workers Union, the Retail Clerks, the Amalgamated (United) Meatcutters, the Shoe Workers, the United Garment Workers, and the Textile Workers. The Boston meeting of 1903 ended with the formation of the National Women's Trade Union League. Its first officers were Mary Kehew, President, and Jane Addams of Hull House, Vice-President.

In the beginning, the National Women's Trade Union League had to have help from people with money and connections in politics and business. Women who had money and social power worked with this new league. They made sure that it had funds for paying organizers. Money was also needed to provide bail when women were arrested for going on strike. These *allies*, as they were called, were helpful in the early years of the league. The first board of directors of the National Women's Trade Union League had more women on it who were political and social reformers and social workers than it had working women. But by 1907, the board had a majority of working women, which was in keeping with the league's constitution.

9. Why were women with money and social power needed in the league?

Money was needed for paying organizers and for bail when striking women were arrested.

Women Speak Out

Women workers in industrial cities were proud and relieved to have an organization of their own. The League found meeting rooms which could also serve as social centers for their members. These were good places to hand out notices of meetings. Women also stood outside churches and synagogues. They passed out leaflets telling the women how to report bosses who broke the state labor

10. How did the women workers benefit from having their own organization?

1) Members met in places that also served them as social centers. 2) They got information on state labor laws, on hours and safety, and on how to report violations. 3) They had health clinics set up just for women.

laws on hours and safety. They even held meetings on street corners to reach women who did not have the courage to go to meetings. One organizer recalled what happened:

> "We had the best sort of attention then. You don't have to send out notices. You just take a platform along, put up a banner and begin to talk. While someone is speaking, others go round and distribute circulars among the girls and ask questions. These circulars are in Yiddish, Italian, and English and we vary them. The last one we got was on getting married. . . . It is helpful in time of strike to hold street meetings . . . we . . . talk to the scabs when they come out of the factories. . . . It gives tremendous courage to the union girls to have us talk there. . . . I think these street meetings are something we can all get courage out of. We make great friends with the policemen in New York. Miss O'Reilly has already converted one policeman."

One league committee worked on health problems of women. It helped set up clinics where women could see women doctors. In Chicago, the city government took over these clinics once they had been set up by the women's labor league.

What Women Hoped to Achieve

11. What did women workers hope to achieve?

1) They wanted self-government in the shop, good working conditions, a living wage, and equal opportunity with boys and men in trades and technical training, with equal pay for the same work. 2) They wanted to be represented on important committees and to let the public know the purposes of their movements.

Women were clear about what they hoped to achieve. The goals of the National Women's Trade Union League were:

> "To encourage self—government in the workshop. To develop leadership among the women workers, inspiring them with a sense of personal responsibility for the conditions under which they work. To insure the protection of the younger girls in their efforts for better working conditions and a living wage. To secure for girls and women equal opportunity with boys and men in trades and technical training, and pay on the basis of occupation and not on the basis of sex. To secure the representation of women on industrial committees and government boards and committees. To interpret to the public generally the aims and purposes of the trade union movement."

For this last purpose of providing information, the League published a handbook that described working conditions for women in the textile mills.

The women organizers had a difficult job. Many working women were immigrants who still remembered their hard lives in Europe. It was not easy convincing these women that they ought to risk their new jobs to make life better for workers everywhere. When Margaret Drier Robins became president of the National Women's Trade Union League, she realized the need to have more organizers. In 1914, she worked to set up schools to train union women to become leaders. Forty-four women studied for one year, combining classroom work with practical organizing. These women went on to leadership positions in their own local unions.

12. Why were labor organizers required?

1) The organizers encouraged immigrants, who were afraid of losing their jobs, to join a labor organization.
2) Organizers often became leaders in local unions.

The Shirtwaist Strike

When the workers shared their first major strike, they realized how much power they had. The first important strike was in the shirtwaist (blouse) industry. In the early years of the 1900's the style of shirtwaists and skirts for women had become very popular. Some 500 shirtwaist factories were operating in New York City in 1909. In these factories, workers were on their own. They were sure of jobs only in the time of year when shirtwaists were in season. Employees had to pay for their sewing needles. They paid an extra fee for electricity for their sewing machines. They also had to rent boxes to sit on and a locker for their coats. If work was damaged, they paid for it. If they were late, they paid a fine.

13. What conditions led to the first major strike in the shirtwaist industry?

1) The work was seasonal.
2) Workers paid for their own needles, electricity, seats, and lockers. 3) They paid for damaged work and were fined when late. 4) The Triangle Shirtwaist Company fired 150 women who had joined the industry union, and hired non-union workers to replace them.

In May 1912, 15,000 women marched down Fifth Avenue in New York City. Poor as well as wealthy women carried signs. What were they demanding?

The owners did not want their workers to join larger, national unions because these unions had more money to support workers if they went out on strike. So, many of the workers were members of company unions. A company union could discuss working conditions with the bosses. But it could not raise enough money to go on strike.

The trouble began when the Triangle Shirtwaist Company fired 150 women who had joined the International Ladies Garment Workers Union. The 150 women who were locked out of their jobs then picketed the company. The company hired non-union workers to replace them.

Support for Strikers

14. What effect did the strike have on others?

1) Five hundred shirtwaist factories were picketed.
2) Bail money was raised when strikers were jailed.
3) The National Association for the Protection of Colored Women discouraged poor Black women from replacing the striking workers.

Other unions in New York saw the opportunity to boost the union movement and help the women strikers at the same time. A mass meeting was held and Samuel Gompers spoke. Other strikers spoke too, in both Yiddish and English. A teenage girl, Clara Lemlich, called for a general strike and the idea caught on. "Thousands left the factories from every side, all of them walking toward Union Square," it was reported. "I can see the young people, mostly women, walking down the street and not caring what might happen." What happened was that the women were arrested and taken to workhouses on Blackwell's Island for a two-week sentence of scrubbing floors.

The shirtwaist union had hoped for support. And they received more support than anyone expected. Some 20,000 workers left their jobs. Picket lines were set up in front of all 500 shirtwaist factories. Twenty-four meetings were held in New York City to raise bail money for the workers who had been arrested. Each meeting was held in Italian, Yiddish, and English.

Help also came from rich society women who worked as allies and held meetings both to raise money and to get newspapers to feature the strike. Working women were sent to Washington, Boston, Buffalo, Philadelphia, and other cities. They spread the word about the shirtwaist strike and asked for money from other workers. They raised $50,000.

Three of the wealthiest women in New York City, Anne Morgan, Mrs. O.H.P. Belmont, and Mrs. Henry Morgenthau held a rally. They rented a huge hall called the Hippodrome, and sold seats to all their wealthy friends. The garment workers filled the rest of the hall. Many people came but only $300 was raised. In addition, support for the strike came from a number of Black workers. The National Association for the Protection of Colored Women helped keep the factories from hiring poor Black women to replace strikers.

From the story of this strike, what can you tell about the layers of New York society and the ways in which they were and were not connected?

Both men and women worked in the shirtwaist and clothing factories. What kinds of working conditions are shown in this picture?

Results of the Strike

The strike ended in many factories in December 1909. Some workers were disappointed. They wanted to hold out longer—until the shirtwaist companies would agree to hire only union labor (a *closed shop*). But the companies offered workers shorter hours (52 hours a week) and four paid holidays a year. They also agreed to distribute the work during the off season. In that way each worker would have some pay and not be laid off. For the first time, employers agreed to buy needles and pay for electricity. Most of the women went back to work, willing to settle for better terms. Once they got what they wanted from the strike, many left the union.

There was a tragic after-note to the strike. On March 25, 1911, a fire swept through the Triangle Shirtwaist Company in New York City. Over 100 workers died in the fire, most of them women. It was only after this tragedy that the city of New York established a new strict building code and revised the labor laws.

Workers Across the Nation

During this same period men and women worked for better hours and safer working conditions in the mills and mining towns across the nation. Women and children were hired for new textile mills. In the Southwest, immigrant Mexicans were hired to work on the railroads and on ranches and farms. These workers were not organized, but social workers and other reformers were beginning to speak up about the hours and working and living conditions among the Mexican laborers. The Mexican workers were often brought across the border by employers. They would work for less than the local American-born workers.

In what way could this picture be labeled "opportunity"? In what way could it be called "suffering"?
Why would Mexicans agree to work under such conditions? Why does this still go on in some parts of the nation? How can it be stopped?

15. What effect did the strike have on the shirtwaist workers?

1) They didn't get a closed shop 2) They did get shorter hours, four paid holidays a year, some work during the off-season, and free needles and electricity. 3) Many left the union now that they had better working conditions.

16. What was the effect of the Triangle Shirtwaist Company fire?

New York City established a new strict building code and revised the labor laws.

17. Why was there little help from government in solving the problems of the workers?

1) States competed with each other for factory locations and jobs. They didn't want factories moving to other states because of their laws. 2) Federal government did not intervene, because the

517

HOW TO LEARN AND REMEMBER

You have just read a chapter on reform in America. You probably have spent some time studying the material in this chapter. But there will be times when you will not have the book around to look up certain facts. At such times you'll have to trust your memory. There are many reasons why it is important to train yourself to keep information in your mind:

    to help you understand other related material,

    to tell others about what you read,

    to help you on tests,

    to give you a broader understanding of the history of the United States.

The following is a set of suggestions to help you to learn and remember what you have just read.

First, you must realize that this is a job you have to do yourself. Thus the first thing you have to do is to make decisions about what you read.

Decision 1. What Is the Major Theme of the Chapter?

Every chapter has some theme. A theme is the idea to which everything in the chapter is tied. What is the theme of this chapter? Write it down.

Decision 2. List the Main Ideas That Relate to the Theme.

A main idea is an idea that is not as big as the theme but relates to many events and many people. In this chapter each section has one main idea. In Section 1, Workers Help Themselves, the main idea is that workers began to organize labor unions and strikes to improve their wages and working conditions.

Write down the main ideas of the chapter in a reasonable order of sequence. Keep this list in your notebook.

Now compare your list of main ideas with someone else's. Do your lists agree? If they don't agree, discuss your ideas with that person.

Decision 3. Make Sure You Have Listed All the Main Ideas.

At this stage check the chapter to make certain that your list of main ideas is complete. Notice how you have remembered many of them just by careful reading. Correct your list by adding or by taking out those that do not belong. If you left some out, try to figure out why.

You should now have a complete list of important ideas that you have checked out. Your next task is to search for facts.

Decision 4. What Facts Support Each Main Idea?

Main ideas are built on facts. A fact refers to something that is true or really happened. For example, in Section 1, Workers Help Themselves, the following are facts:
1. The American Federation of Labor was founded in 1881.
2. The American Federation of Labor organized strikes to get better pay and working conditions for their members.

There are many facts in this chapter. Write down the facts for each main idea. List the facts that are related to each of your main ideas under your statement of the idea. Do not look back to the chapter. Just list the facts.

After you have completed your list, use the chapter to check for the following:

A list of all the facts along with each idea.

A list of the facts that you have left out. List them in a separate column.

Decision 5. Review Your Main Ideas with Related Facts.

After you have reread your lists, discuss the main ideas and facts with someone in your class. Have your classmate ask you questions about what you read. Check your answers to these questions.

Decision 6. How Many of the Themes and Main Ideas Are Generalizations about All People Everywhere at Any Time?

What you are learning about Americans may be true about Americans in the early twentieth century, people everywhere in the early twentieth century, or Americans at all times.

Think about what you have learned. In what ways are the themes and ideas tied to a certain time, place, and people?

In what ways do the themes and ideas go far beyond the time and place that you have just studied?

courts decided that these were matters for the states to decide. 3) Working conditions and child labor could not be regulated on a nationwide basis unless laws about them were passed by Congress.

The first 10 or 12 years of the twentieth century was a time of growing concern and the beginnings of organization among workers. A great number of people needed jobs. Yet, because of the large number of immigrants, it was difficult for a national union to build support and keep the organization strong between strikes.

Workers in modern industrial America were both excited about their opportunities and unhappy in their working conditions. Many workers were not able to look far beyond their daily problems. But some did look ahead, and they helped the other workers to organize. But a national organization was not going to be a gift from the owners nor a popular, spontaneous movement of the workers.

Checking the facts

1. How did the National Women's Trade Union League get organized?
2. What were the goals of the League?
3. What were the results of the women workers' first major strike?

3. OTHER PROBLEMS, LITTLE HELP

This young boy had to operate a thread machine instead of going to school. Why was it important to eliminate child labor?

The problems of the workers and the slum dwellers were not considered to be problems for the federal government. Many state legislatures, on the other hand, did try to pass laws limiting working hours to ten hours a day and preventing young children from being kept out of school to work in factories. Some states passed laws forbidding sweatshops in small apartments. They also passed laws requiring better plumbing, safer fire escapes, and better fireproofing of buildings.

These state laws ran into trouble with people who were afraid they would lose the benefits of big business. If business had to hire more workers or pay them more in one state than in another, they might just close up a factory and move it to another state. States competed with each other for factory locations and jobs. If a state had factories, it could count on other investments in transportation and building. No state felt it could afford to lose out on business because its laws favored workers more than those of other states.

The people who opposed the state laws sued in the courts. The courts regularly decided that these were matters for states to decide under their powers "to make safe the daily lives of people." These were the "police powers" of the states described in the Constitution.

States still compete for businesses. What do they do today to get or keep industry?

Business was nationwide. But until Congress passed laws about working conditions and child labor, these things could not be regulated on a nationwide basis. Railroads which crossed state lines were regulated at this time, but the ways in which businesses treated their employees were not.

Political Leaders and Parties

Changes happened so rapidly at the turn of the century that it was difficult for anyone to try to decide on a plan of action. Businesses acted on their own. Labor unions worked to organize themselves. The poor immigrants were pleased to have new opportunities, but at the same time, suffered from both the living and working conditions. Some of the American-born children of immigrants who were growing up in the slums became criminals. Teenage gangs appeared for the first time as a part of big city life.

Leadership in the Cities

As cities became crowded and some neighborhoods became dangerous, the rich families left them. Trolleys and trains made it possible for the people who could afford it to live farther away from the city. Those families who moved to the *suburbs* left behind their positions of leadership in the community.

When the older families left, the children of the immigrants who had come before the Civil War became the new leaders. Many of these were Irish–Americans. They ran the cities through the neighborhoods. They recognized that the poor immigrants needed help. These neighborhood, or *ward*, leaders provided person-to-person help in return for votes on election day. They helped in many small ways. They found jobs, gave away food, provided entertainment for the children, and got medical aid for old people. If a member of the family got into trouble, the ward leader would help by talking to the police or to the judge.

Because the ward leaders could command votes, they became part of a network of power in the city. They would see to it that their people voted for the city officials who in turn would give the ward leader favors. Some of these favors were licenses to sell liquor and licenses for street peddlers. The licenses were given to friends who promised to give the ward leader a share of the profits. In this way, some of the ward leaders became rich and powerful. The connections between local businesses, local party politics, and the city government were strong.

The political leaders who controlled the party candidates throughout a big city were known as *bosses*. They did not necessarily hold political office themselves. But by using their connections they

18. What changes were taking place in the cities at the turn of the century?

1) Labor unions worked to organize workers.
2) Teenage gangs appeared for the first time. 3) Trolleys and trains made it possible for the people who could afford it to live farther from the city, leaving behind their positions of leadership.
4) Children of immigrants became community leaders.

19. How did the ward leaders operate?

1) They ran the cities through the neighborhoods. 2) They provided person-to-person help in return for votes on Election Day. 3) They saw to it that their people voted for the city officials who in turn gave the ward leaders favors, making some of them rich and powerful.

Can you argue for and against this use of political power in the cities?

This Granger poster illustrates the kind of rural life its members hoped to achieve. What was the Grange's main demand?

20. What did the Grange accomplish for the farmers?

1) The Grange first helped individual farmers to manage their farms better. 2) Then it tried to get protection for farmers through federal control of activities and rates of railroads.

21. Why was the Interstate Commerce Act a change in the actions of government?

1) Before the act, the government had helped big businesses become more successful. 2) Now the federal government was taking on the job of watchdog and regulator of business.

could guarantee the election of almost anyone they wanted. Many of them used their power to see that business contracts in the city went to those who would give them *kickbacks*. In this illegal way people such as William Marcy "Boss" Tweed and Richard Croker of New York City came to have enormous personal power and cost the taxpayers millions of dollars.

Honest citizens became afraid to run for office. The *machine* and the boss had such control that people who wanted to fight them had to have an organization of their own. Such an organization also had to reach every ward and every block and "get out the vote" on election day.

Farmers Organize

While older immigrant groups were organizing for power in the cities, farmers were also forming their own organizations. The first farm organization was the National Grange of the Patrons of Husbandry, founded in 1867. At first the Grange tried to help individual farmers manage their farms better. But later it turned to political action. Through the Grange, farmers tried to get the federal government to protect them by controlling the activities and the rates of the giant railroad companies. The Grange had managed to get the state governments and the Congress to realize how unfair big railroads had been to farmers. What the railroads had done was to charge lower rates for freight on longer distances where more than one railroad company competed. The short runs which had no competition charged higher prices. Farmer-customers who said they would take their business elsewhere, found that the new railroad and the old one simply pooled their earnings. These railroads split the profits at the end of the year. State governments were helpless because the railroads traveled through so many states. A state could only control a railroad within its own borders.

The Interstate Commerce Act

Finally members of the Grange went to their Congressmen and demanded action to control railroads and their pricing policies. Congress could, under the Constitution, "regulate commerce between the states." The report of a Senate committee recommended that an agency of the executive branch be established to set and enforce equal treatment for all railroad customers. The Grange thought it had won its battle when the Interstate Commerce Commission was established by a law of Congress in 1887.

This was an important change in the actions of government. Before that time the government had helped businesses such as railroads to be more successful. The government, you recall, had given land

In what way are the Grange and the labor unions part of being big in America?

to those railroads and loaned them money up through the 1880's. But now the federal government was taking on the job of watchdog and regulator of business. Businesses had become too large for farmers or state organizations to try to control them. So in 1887 the federal government took on the additional role of regulator of the economy.

The Sherman Antitrust Act

Two years later Congress passed another law designed to control big business. Since the formation of the Standard Oil Trust in 1879, many other businesses had also formed large combinations or trusts. The Sherman Antitrust Act of 1890 made trusts illegal.

Big business caused big results. Among these results were bigger protests and bigger government agencies to take bigger action. Farmers were not against business. But they felt helpless against the railroad trusts. But a new era had begun. A Senate report described it:

> "Through the absence of national legislation the railroads have been left to work out their own salvation. The practical results of their efforts have not been encouraging . . . ."

In spite of these two major laws which were supposed to regulate business, railroads actually continued to charge as they pleased and businesses continued to merge when they wanted to. The Interstate Commerce Act of 1887 and the Sherman Antitrust Act of 1890 had sounded as if they would protect smaller farmers and business people. In truth, however, no law works simply by being passed. A President has to direct his legal aid, the attorney general, to sue businesses in court, if they do not act according to the law. Between 1896 and 1904 few law suits were started by the government. When the smaller companies or farm organizations sued, the courts usually decided in favor of the big businesses.

Political Parties

The shift to big business in cities and on farms was the major cause of change in the way people lived in America in the last 25 years of the 1800's. And people at the time were aware of this fact. The corporations and their officers were often better known than the political parties and their candidates. Even winning candidates for the presidency could not capture the public's imagination the way the changing life-styles had. Attention was on the new jobs, the new inventions, the new ways of buying and selling, the new millionaires, and the new problems of immigrants and cities.

22. What was needed to make the Interstate Commerce Act and the Sherman Antitrust Act effective?

The President needed to direct his attorney general to sue businesses in court if they violated the laws.

23. How did the political parties lose their influence on Americans?

Today the Sherman Antitrust Act is often used by the federal government to keep businesses from becoming too big. How does government mirror the mood of the voters?

1) Attention was on the new jobs, inventions, ways of buying and selling, millionaires, and the problems of immigrants and cities. 2) The political parties after the Civil War had trouble organizing, as they had been badly hurt by their stand for or against slavery. 3) The problems the business boom had created were so new that the Republicans and Democrats chose not to try to come up with solutions.

Political parties after the Civil War had trouble organizing. The political parties which had done so much to hold the nation together before the war had been badly hurt by their stand for or against slavery. When the Civil War was over, the Republican party held the presidency but could not get the support of both the South and the North. The Republicans' appeal to the new Black voters in the South made it difficult for them to win White southern votes. As a result, the Democrats controlled the South after the Civil War. But there were more voters in Republican New England. In national elections, the vote between the North and South was so close that both parties tried to win the states with the most voters that were in the middle. These were New York in the East, and Ohio, Indiana, and Illinois in the Midwest.

Candidates in political campaigns did not take strong stands on issues. Most Americans were pleased with the results of the business boom, but also worried about the problems it had created. These problems were so new that Republicans and Democrats alike chose not to try to come up with solutions. They were glad not to have to debate about trusts, railroads, and cities.

Campaigns and Candidates

Sometimes parties without strong opinions on issues can win with popular candidates—but not in this period. The Republicans won most of the elections, but no Republican was elected to a second term until 1900. The Democrats had one winning candidate, Grover Cleveland, who had two terms, but they were split by the election of a Republican between his two terms.

Neither of the two major parties was united on the questions of the day. Taxes on foreign-made products to make them more expensive than American-made ones were supported by some people for some products, but not for others. Everyone agreed that these taxes or tariffs should not be too high. The trouble was that every member of Congress voted for less protection for the products made in someone else's state. Neither party recommended a nationwide policy.

Government Workers

There were people in both parties who misused the right to appoint political supporters to office. Jobs in the executive branch of the federal government, as in all levels of government, went to the people who worked for and helped pay for the political campaigns of the winning candidates. The spoils system and patronage meant that the people who were to carry out laws directed at protecting the helpless were in agreement with those who already had the power. They did not need to share power.

There was a move to change this situation by giving examinations for government, or *civil service*, jobs. The people who scored the highest on these civil service examinations would get the jobs. In 1881 Chester A. Arthur had become President when James A. Garfield was assassinated by a disappointed office seeker. In 1883 a civil service reform act, known as the Pendleton Act, was passed with Arthur's support. This act set up a civil service commission which would administer competitive examinations to people seeking certain government positions. The act also made it illegal for the party in power to ask for campaign contributions from government officials.

Like the other reform laws, the Pendleton Civil Service Act was a small beginning. Few people wanted to risk hurting the big boom which had brought so much wealth to the nation and so many jobs to the people. Americans were both pleased with the results of bigness and afraid of it, at the same time. The executive branch of the federal government had increased greatly during this period. In 1871 there had been 53,000 government appointees. By 1900 there were 250,000.

Cleveland and Harrison

In the election of 1884, the Republicans did not rally behind the President, Chester A. Arthur. Instead they nominated James G. Blaine as their candidate for President. The Democrats chose Grover Cleveland of New York as their candidate. After a rough campaign on both sides, Cleveland finally won. As President, Cleveland continued the attack on the spoils system begun during Arthur's administration. But his efforts to get a lower tariff cost him the election in 1888. In that election, Cleveland lost to the Republican candidate, Benjamin Harrison, the grandson of the hero of the Battle of Tippecanoe.

Money: Silver or Gold

The one issue that attracted some excitement in the nation never became an important issue in either major party or for any elected President. The issue was how to control the money supply. The people who were most worried about there being enough money were those who borrowed it. These were the farmers.

They wanted the government to issue more money so that each dollar would actually be worth less. Since farmers had to borrow money, they did not worry that the amount of goods and services that money would buy might also shrink. They wanted *cheap* or *soft money* that would be backed up in the treasury by plentiful silver or just printed on paper (*greenbacks*) without gold or silver behind it.

Before becoming President, Grover Cleveland was a lawyer, mayor, and governor. How did these jobs help to prepare him for the presidency?

24. Why wasn't Grover Cleveland reelected to the presidency?

1) Cleveland attacked the spoils system. 2) He tried to get a lower tariff.

25. How did farmers and bankers disagree on the money supply?

1) Farmers, who had to repay loans, wanted "soft" money, backed in the treasury by plentiful silver or without gold or silver behind it. 2) Bankers wanted money to be worth as much when it was repaid as when they loaned it, so they wanted "hard" money, backed by gold.

The bankers in the cities who loaned the farmers money wanted the money to be worth as much in buying or purchasing power when it was repaid as when they loaned it. They wanted *hard money* backed in the government's treasury by bars of gold.

The People's Party

26. How did the People's party propose to reform government?

1) Party members wanted a graduated income tax.
2) They wanted the government to own the railroads and telegraph, since these were monopolies.
3) They wanted citizens to be able to put candidates and issues on the ballot without political party approval, and to recall politicians who had broken the law.

The farmers formed a new organization called the Farmers' Alliance. They tried to get the two major parties to follow their cheap money policies. With colorful leaders like Mary Elizabeth Lease, "Sockless Jerry" Simpson of Kansas, and "Pitchfork Ben" Tillman of South Carolina, the farmers were fairly successful in some state elections in farm states. In order to try to become nationally powerful they formed the People's party with the industrial workers of the Knights of Labor. They ran a candidate, James B. Weaver of Iowa, in the election of 1892. The Democrats ran Cleveland, and the Republicans ran Harrison. Cleveland received the most votes, Harrison came in second, and Weaver came in third. Most voters were afraid of the money issue.

The platform adopted by the People's, or Populist, party at its convention in Omaha, Nebraska, showed that its leaders recognized

This cartoon is called "A Party of Patches." How does it poke fun at the Populists?

526

how widespread were the effects of the new bigness on the life of the nation. These reformers wanted an income tax that would go up in percentage for people with more money—a graduated income tax. They wanted the government to own the railroads and the telegraph since they were monopolies anyway. They wanted citizens to be able to put candidates and issues on the ballot without political party approval. They also thought that elected office-holders should be recalled after their election if the voters thought they had broken the law. These widespread attacks on the new way of life and the people who controlled it were the first organized political efforts to take action.

The Election of 1896

Finally in 1896 the Populists managed to get the Democratic party to run a candidate and adopt the platform of cheap money in the form of plentiful or "free" silver. The candidate was a brilliant public speaker and a native of a farm state, William Jennings Bryan of Nebraska. At the Democratic convention in Chicago, Bryan thrilled those Democrats who supported free silver with a speech, later known as the Cross of Gold Speech. Turning to the Democrats who favored gold over silver, Bryan declared, "You shall not press down upon the brow of labor this crown of thorns. You shall not crucify mankind upon a cross of gold."

However, the Democratic party split on the silver issue. Although Bryan tried hard and did well in the popular vote, enough Democrats voted for the Republican candidate William McKinley to make him President in 1896. In addition, there was a great deal of big business money behind McKinley's carefully run campaign. Voters by the thousands were brought to his house in Canton, Ohio, by special railroad cars to hear him speak from his front porch. But this was not a campaign of rich against poor or old families against newcomers. Many workers voted for McKinley and immigrants split for the two candidates. McKinley appealed to a broader group than did Bryan. Bryan's stand on cheap money was pleasing to farmers. But other people in the country did not think that free silver was the solution to the farmers' problems.

Plessy v. Ferguson

Every part of the federal government under McKinley seemed to accept the nation's problems as if it were unnecessary to solve them. In the Supreme Court case of *Plessy* v. *Ferguson* in 1896, the Court ruled that keeping Blacks separated from Whites in railroad carriages was all right as long as the two groups had equal facilities. "Separate but equal" was the Court's phrase. There was no attempt to face the fact that forced segregation was a way of keeping Blacks from making their own choices about schools, housing, and jobs.

27. Why did McKinley defeat Bryan in the presidential election of 1896?

Bryan's stand on cheap money appealed to farmers, but other people in the country did not think "free" silver was the solution to the farmers' problems.

28. What was meant by "separate but equal"?

Separating Blacks from Whites was legal as long as the two groups had equal facilities.

What American values were behind *Plessy* v. *Ferguson*? Which were left out?

527

McKinley represented the bright and powerful side of America's future. He was President during the expansion of the American economic boom outside its continental borders.

Checking the facts

1. How did the political machines operate in the large cities?
2. How did the federal government take on the role of regulator of industry?
3. Why did government civil service examinations become necessary?
4. For what issues were the national political parties failing to propose solutions?

4. AMERICA EXPANDS OVERSEAS: BIGNESS IN FOREIGN POLICY

29. Why did the United States export more goods than it imported?

Other nations found American products useful, and cheaper than their own goods.

American industry and American farms had produced so much that they began selling to foreign markets in the 1880's. These exports grew until they amounted to over a billion dollars a year in sales during the 1800's. Americans also bought foods from other nations. These imports also grew in value yearly.

By 1898 America sold more manufactured goods abroad than it bought from those countries. American products were popular partly because they were useful and partly because they were cheap. Buyers abroad often bought American goods instead of those produced in their own country because they could cut costs that way.

Most Americans were anxious to sell abroad. Both industrialists and labor unions supported exports. Besides, Americans, like the older empire builders of Europe, especially in England, believed that it was better for the rest of the world to share in the superiority of Anglo-American technology, as well as in Anglo-American culture and religion.

The peoples of Africa and Latin America were seen by the conquerors and empire builders of the late nineteenth century as inferior. They were viewed as Indians had been when they were pushed onto reservations.

30. Why did Americans become interested in the Pacific?

England and France had controlled most of Africa and a great deal of Asia. Therefore the Americans turned their interest to the Pacific. As Americans moved west across the continent they wanted to open trade with the Far East. Trade with the Chinese was begun in 1844 and with the Japanese in 1858.

What were the United States' connections to foreign nations at this time?

Hawaii

The Hawaiian Islands were important stop-overs for American ships on the way to China and Japan. (See map, page 530.) The United States established a naval base at Pearl Harbor in 1887. In Hawaii there were a number of American settlers. Descendants of these pre-Civil War American missionary families had become sugar planters. They became the most powerful people in the sugar exporting trade. They received favors from the American government. Hawaiian sugar was allowed into American markets without the tariff others had to pay. When American sugar producers objected, Americans living in Hawaii began to take action to have Hawaii become a territory or possession of the United States. In 1893 American settlers and American marines took action. They complained that American lives and property were in danger in Hawaii. They seized the government of Hawaii and deposed Queen Liliuokalani (Le-LEE-oo-oh-ka-LAH-nee.)

But when the Americans in Hawaii sent a delegation to the United States to sign a treaty making Hawaii an official United States territory, President Cleveland refused to sign, because he objected to the use of armed force. The debate in the United States over Hawaii went on for over four years, as American sugar planters continued to oppose annexation.

The Hawaiian Islands were finally voted in by the American Senate when the country went to war in the Pacific against Spain. The reason given was that the naval base at Pearl Harbor and others acquired by the United States on Midway and the Samoan Islands would need protection during a war. (See map, page 530.)

Spain and the United States

For a generation Americans had looked south of their borders for expansion and control of trade. There was competition between the French and the Americans over who would build a canal across the narrow stretch of land called the Isthmus of Panama. A canal there would make it possible for ships to travel from the Atlantic Ocean right through to the Pacific Ocean without going around the tip of South America.

In the 1880's the American Presidents talked openly about control and power in Latin America. The talk was formal and friendly at a Pan American Conference held in Washington in 1889–1890. When one of those countries did not act favorably toward the United States, however, the President almost asked Congress for a declaration of war.

How far the American government should go in trying to establish its power in Latin America was never made a clear, planned policy.

Queen Liliuokalani was the last reigning queen of the Hawaiian Islands. She was overthrown in a revolution supported by sugar planters and the United States minister to Hawaii.

1) Americans wanted to trade with the Far East. 2) England and France controlled most of Africa and much of Asia, but the Pacific area was not tied to an empire.

31. How did the United States regard Latin America?

1) Americans wanted to expand and control trade in Latin America. 2) The United States government had no clear policy for establishing power in Latin America; but the United States wanted to provide leadership for both North and South America.

Why is it important to know what the rest of the world is doing at any moment?

529

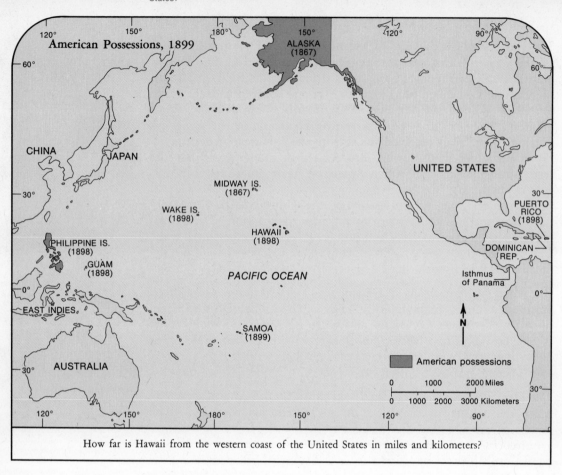

American Possessions, 1899

ALASKA
(1867)

CHINA

JAPAN

UNITED STATES

MIDWAY IS.
(1867)

WAKE IS.
(1898)

HAWAII
(1898)

PHILIPPINE IS.
(1898)

GUAM
(1898)

PACIFIC OCEAN

PUERTO
RICO
(1898)

DOMINICAN
REP.

Isthmus
of Panama

N

EAST INDIES

SAMOA
(1899)

AUSTRALIA

American possessions

0   1000   2000 Miles

0   1000   2000   3000 Kilometers

How far is Hawaii from the western coast of the United States in miles and kilometers?

American businesses traded in these countries. And whenever crises arose, the American government would take advantage of them to make America more powerful.

Revolt in Cuba

32. Why did Congress vote to help the Cubans revolt against Spain?

1) A private letter from the Spanish minister in Washington criticizing President McKinley was published. This and the blowing up of the American warship Maine in Havana harbor angered Americans.
2) The newspapers used these two incidents to arouse the American public against Spain.

One of these crises was the revolt of Cubans against the Spanish in 1894. Only 90 miles (144 kilometers) from the American mainland, Cuba had interested Americans for half a century. (See map, page 532.) Public opinion in the United States was on the side of the Cubans, but President McKinley was wary of taking on a war with Spain. Americans who had invested money in Cuban sugar plantations wanted to send an army to help the rebels. However, other business people agreed with President McKinley that trade with Spain was more important than aid to Cuba.

For two years, McKinley was able to keep the country from going to war to help Cuba. But the publication of a private letter from

How did trade get the United States involved outside its borders? Without trade what happened to the United States?

the Spanish minister in Washington criticizing McKinley and the blowing up of the American warship *Maine* in Havana harbor were too much for the expansion-minded Americans. Newspapers such as Joseph Pulitzer's *New York World* and William Randolph Hearst's *New York Journal* also used every possible chance to arouse Americans to war. Spectacular headlines on colored paper told the reading public to "Remember the Maine." No one could really blame the Spanish for the ship. But everyone seemed willing to do so anyway. The style of writing and the content of the Hearst and Pulitzer newspapers came to be known as "yellow journalism."

McKinley could no longer hold back the Congress. It voted to recognize Cuba as an independent country and send the army and navy to drive the Spanish out. Congress also voted that the United States wanted no part of Cuban territory. Spain then declared war on the United States in April of 1898.

The Spanish-American War

The first battle against the Spanish was almost half way around the world from Cuba in the Philippine Islands. The American Assistant Secretary of the Navy, Theodore Roosevelt, had already sent a message to Commodore George Dewey. It ordered him to attack the Spanish base at Manila in the Philippines, if war were declared. (See map, page 530.) Dewey was ready. One week after the declaration of war he entered Manila Bay and destroyed the Spanish ships. McKinley then sent an army and more ships to do battle. By the middle of August, the Philippines had fallen to the United States. The Americans were helped by native Filipinos who hoped to be independent.

The entire Spanish-American War lasted only three months. The United States had a small regular army of 23,000 soldiers to which were added 280,000 volunteers. Most of the army units sent to Cuba were poorly trained and poorly equipped. One of the few effective units in Cuba was the "Rough Riders" under Theodore Roosevelt. He was a lieutenant colonel and led a charge up San Juan Hill. The Americans sent the army to shut off the city of Santiago and the navy to blockade the harbor. The Spanish fleet had to run the blockade and was destroyed in a four-hour battle. Other American troops occupied the Spanish-held island of Puerto Rico. Thus when the war ended in August of 1898, the United States was in control of Puerto Rico and the Pacific island of Guam in addition to Cuba and the Philippines. (See map, page 530.) Within three months' time, the Americans had become a colonial power. The 300-year-old Spanish Empire had been too feeble to fight back.

33. How did the United States become a colonial power in three months?

1) Commodore George Dewey destroyed the Spanish ships in Manila Bay, and Filipinos, hoping for independence, helped the American army capture the Philippines. 2) The American army shut off the city of Santiago, Cuba, and the navy blockaded the harbor. The Spanish fleet was destroyed in a four-hour battle. 3) At the end of the three-month war, in 1898, the United States controlled Puerto Rico, the Pacific island of Guam, the Philippines, and Cuba.

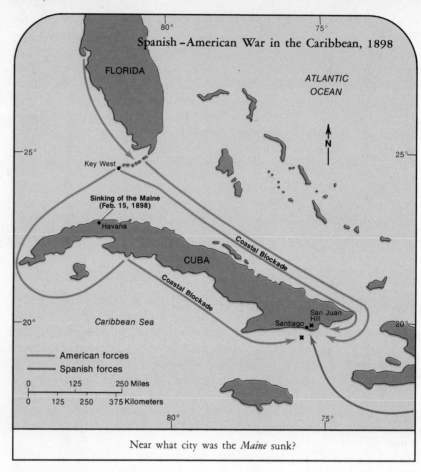

Spanish–American War in the Caribbean, 1898

FLORIDA

ATLANTIC OCEAN

Key West

Sinking of the Maine (Feb. 15, 1898)

Havana

Coastal Blockade

CUBA

Coastal Blockade

Caribbean Sea

San Juan Hill

Santiago

—— American forces
—— Spanish forces

| 0 | 125 | 250 Miles |
| 0 | 125 | 250 | 375 Kilometers |

Near what city was the *Maine* sunk?

The *Maine* was sunk near Havana, Cuba.

Objections to Colonies: How to Rule?

34. What were the re-actions to the United States as an empire?

1) Some Americans insisted that the Constitution did not permit colonies. 2) These Americans argued that a nation begun in the revolutionary spirit of the Declaration of Independence should never take over the lives of other people without their consent. 3) The Filipinos fought for three more years in an attempt to gain their freedom from the United States. 4) On the whole, however, the American public went wild over the victory.

Some very important Americans from a wide variety of fields thought that acquiring colonies was going too far. Andrew Carnegie, Samuel Gompers, Mark Twain, Jane Addams, and some Republicans and Democrats agreed that the American Constitution would not permit colonies. They also said that a nation begun in the revolutionary spirit of the Declaration of Independence should never take over the lives of other people without their consent.

The Filipinos certainly did not consent. They fought a hard and bloody revolution against the Americans. Their leader, Emilio Aguinaldo (AH-gwe-NAL-doe), was the same one who had just helped the Americans against the Spanish. It took 70,000 American soldiers and three more years of fighting to stop the Philippine revolt. McKinley was reelected in the middle of those war years. He made the decisions to fight to win. When the war was over, he sent William Howard Taft to the Philippines to establish a government in which Filipinos would take part.

532

Locate the Philippines on a world map. How does the Philippines' location help to explain why that nation was involved in the affairs of bigger nations?

Cuba was in a shambles, and the United States government decided that the Cubans needed direction more than they needed freedom. By 1900 Cuba did have its own government with the promise never to take action in foreign affairs without American approval. A United States naval base was established at Guantánamo Bay.

On the whole, however, the American public went wild over the victory. It seemed a fitting climax to the era of bigness. The United States was the last western nation to have an empire. Although it was not a very big empire, other nations would now have to think of the United States as a world power.

The Open Door Policy

In its new role as a world power the United States was ready to make a new statement of foreign policy. This statement had to do with trade rather than new territory, and it was aimed at China rather than Latin America. Russia, Japan, England, France, and Germany were already competing for trade with the Chinese, and the United States did not want to be left out. In the fall of 1899 Secretary of State John Hay sent letters to all of the countries interested in China. In the letters he asked that these countries agree to keep all "treaty ports" open, and also guarantee equal trading rights for everyone. Each country replied that it would agree if the others did. Nevertheless, Hay announced that the Open Door Policy was now in force.

In 1900 a Chinese secret society, called the Boxers, attacked western traders. The United States joined other nations in putting down the Boxer Rebellion. The Chinese government was charged a large amount of money to repay the westerners. America used its share to provide scholarships for Chinese students to study in the United States. The importance of this event was that trade with the West was kept open.

The United States at the Turn of the Century

The United States seemed strong at the turn of the century, but the American people were aware that there were great gaps between American big power and the Americans who needed help. Somehow there had to be a way to put bigness, the need for reform, and the desire for world power together.

35. How did the United States keep trade open with China?

1) The United States got all countries interested in China to agree to keep all "treaty ports" open and also to guarantee equal trading rights to all. 2) When China was forced to pay damages to western governments after the Boxer Rebellion, the United States used its share to provide scholarships for Chinese students to study in the United States.

Checking the facts

1. How did the United States acquire Hawaii?
2. What were the results of the war with Spain?

Why is it important to know the background of American actions with foreign nations? How many reasons can you think of?

PUTTING IT ALL TOGETHER

UNDERSTANDING THE MAIN IDEAS

1. What made working men and women and farmers organize?
2. How successful were they? What problems did they have?
3. What did government do? What reasons did leaders have for the action they took and for the action they refused to take?

ACTIVITIES

1. Read a biography of one of the early labor leaders. When and how did he or she get started? How long did it take before the organization had success? Answer these questions in a brief book report.
2. Look at your local newspaper for information about farmers today. What do they want from state government? What do they want from the federal government? Who might oppose them? Deliver an oral report to your class on your findings.
3. Read about newspaper publishers Pulitzer and Hearst at the time of the Spanish-American War. How were they important at the time of this war? Write a brief essay on the importance of newspapers then and now.
4. Use a world map in your classroom or a globe for this activity. Keep a tally of the places in the world that are mentioned in the news. Keep this list for one week. How many places are on your list at the end of the week? Locate them on the map or globe.

BOOKS TO READ

Brau, M.M., *Island in the Crossroads: The History of Puerto Rico* (Garden City: Doubleday and Co., 1968).

Conroy, Robert, *Battle of Manila Bay* (New York: Macmillan Publishing Co., Inc., 1968).

Haskins, Jim, *The Long Struggle: The Story of American Labor* (Philadelphia: Westminster Press, 1976).

Hoyt, Edwin P., *William McKinley* (Chicago: Reilly and Lee Co., 1967).

Noble, Iris, *Labor's Advocate: Eugene V. Debs* (New York: Julian Messner, Inc., 1966).

REVIEWING THE UNIT

BUILDING VOCABULARY

The following is a list of some of the vocabulary words in Unit Five:

tenant farmer	quota
corporation	tenement
assimilate	settlement house
boycott	marketing cooperative
merger	scab
trust	injunction
philanthropy	closed shop
ethnic	ward

Choose any three of the vocabulary words above and write a short paragraph on one of the following topics: a. the rise of big business, b. immigrant life in the cities, c. the growth of the union movement.

BUILDING SOCIAL STUDIES SKILLS

Turn to the maps on the pages given here. Then complete the following activities:

1. Page 465—This map shows what happened to the lands occupied by Native Americans in the 1800's. In 1887 the General Allotment Act, or Dawes Act, was passed. This act took away the reservations which had been given to some Native American tribes. Instead, individual Native Americans were to be given parcels of land. The purpose of the act was to help assimilate Native Americans into the White culture of the United States. Do you think the Dawes Act was a good idea? Why or why not?

2. Page 532—This map shows the Spanish-American War in the Caribbean in 1898. When the United States took control of Cuba and Puerto Rico, an important change took place in America's role as a world power. In what way did this change make United States foreign policy similar to those of the European nations?

BUILDING WRITING SKILLS

Using the information in Unit Five, list eight ways in which immigrants to the United States were assimilated into American life.

From 1870 to 1900 the United States became an industrial nation. By 1900, individuals had been linked together by large businesses and organizations, by the growth of cities, and by new technology such as the railroad and the telegraph. All of these networks operated nationwide. The new organizations created permanent connections among Americans. They have therefore become part of America's institutions. These institutions changed the way in which most people lived. Whether or not individuals liked the changes, the changes made life in America "modern."

Business Had Changed

Businesses in 1900 were bigger in many ways than they had been in 1870. Because businesses sold shares, they had more money to invest in building more machines and bigger factories. Bigger factories meant that more workers could be hired. Since modern factories could hold more machinery, manufacturers could produce more goods faster and more cheaply than could smaller factories. Business could continue to invest and grow as long as they could get raw materials when they needed them and sell the finished products to a larger number of people.

Workers Had Changed

By 1900, workers in manufacturing and transportation noticed important changes in their places of work. They no longer knew the owners of the businesses for which they worked. The people they dealt with were the managers, who could seldom make decisions that mattered most to the workers. Decisions about how much to pay a worker or how many hours a person should work were often made at corporate headquarters.

Pay, hours, and working conditions were tied to the national picture of costs, sales, and profits.

Farming Had Changed

By 1900, cities, machinery, and a nationwide system of railroads made a difference in corporations that manufactured goods. They also changed farming. In the years after the Civil War, farmers planted as much as they and their farmhands could harvest. By 1900, farmers who could afford to buy new machines for planting and harvesting turned farming into a big business. Those farmers who had enough money, or could borrow enough, were like the big corporations. They could invest in land and seed. They could harvest more crops and sell them to more customers. And they found more customers among the people who moved to the cities and had to buy food instead of growing it themselves.

The Population Had Changed

During the boom years of the Industrial Revolution, thousands of Europeans came to the United States. Most newcomers settled in the larger cities. Those who were skilled in using tools and machines were able to find jobs in expanding industries. But those who came from farms on which all work had been done by hand had no experience and skills that could help them get the factory jobs they needed.

A Power in the World

By 1900 the United States was a powerful, modern industrial society. It had begun to extend its power and influence beyond its borders. Americans were pleased that their victory in the Spanish-American War had made it possible to trade freely whenever they wished, anywhere in the Western Hemisphere. American businesses, protected by the United States government, could influence the decisions of governments in Latin America.

Politics in 1900

William McKinley won his second term as President in 1900 because most Americans were pleased with the prosperity that industry had brought and with the nation's new power to extend that industry overseas. Americans in the early twentieth century accepted the changes in their lives. But some were not happy about them. People such as Jacob Riis and Jane Addams tried to call attention to the terrible living conditions of the poor in the city slums. Most voters ignored the reformers who wanted help given to the urban poor. The only reformer who was popular enough to make reform a national issue was Theodore Roosevelt. He was a hero of the Spanish-American War. To keep Roosevelt quiet and out of the public eye, Republican leaders gave him the least noticeable political job, that of Vice-President of the United States. How long would the Republican plan to keep Roosevelt quiet last?

AMERICA IS... # TRYING TO PRESERVE, TRYING TO IMPROVE

UNIT SIX

In every town in America today people are talking about an important question—How can America be improved so that more people can have the chance to enjoy what makes America special? America is special because it combines such things as variety, liberty, opportunity, conservation, representation, expansion, bigness, majority rule, and minority rights. Most Americans approve of these features. They would like to preserve these special benefits.

All around, you see and hear about people who are trying to improve and preserve this nation. Listen to the conversations among adults whom you know. Look at your newspaper. Turn on your radio or television to a news or a talk show. You will hear how different people think America ought to be improved and preserved. As you listen, begin to think about your opinions.

What Do People Think About Variety and Shared Values?

America had a variety of people from the very beginning. There was a variety of Native Americans and colonists. Even today there is a variety of immigrants. Having a variety of people also means that Americans have different customs and experiences. But in spite of those differences, Americans share a surprising number of values.

What Do Americans Think About Liberty?

Americans like the freedom, or liberty, to make choices for themselves. They want to preserve the liberty to choose their jobs, their representatives in government, and where they will live. But as you listen, you will also hear Americans wishing that they had even more liberty—to do what they want to do when they want to do it and with the people whom they choose. How much liberty do *you* think a person should have?

What Do Americans Think About Opportunity and Representation?

Americans value opportunity and representation. Americans know that there are more opportunities for people who speak and write easily, who know how to meet people, and who know how the world around them works.

Representation in local and state and federal governments is a right of all Americans. But Americans do not often agree on what their

representatives ought to decide. Should there by any requirements for being heard? Should all people get an equal hearing? What do *you* think?

What Do Americans Think About Expansion and Bigness?

Americans value expansion and bigness. American businesses need to try new ideas and to sell to new customers. Americans wonder how they can expand and let organizations grow without losing their right to be represented when decisions are made. How can America expand without using up its natural resources? Americans are also asking whose money should pay for expansion. Should businesses expand only within the country, or should they expand in other countries as well? How can the United States cooperate with other countries to attain a common goal?

What Do Americans Think About Majority Rule?

Americans value majority rule. In this nation decisions are still made by counting how many people are in favor of an idea and how many are not. Americans believe that the people and ideas that receive the most support are the ones that something should be done about.

Americans value minority rights too. They are looking for ways to use majority rule to help minorities get equal opportunities. What ideas have *you* heard for getting the majority of people to help minorities?

Free to Preserve: Free to Improve

This unit is the story of Americans in the twentieth century. Why do Americans today need to learn about the plans that have been debated and tried since 1900?

It is important to know how plans developed. By understanding who was involved, what steps they took, and in what order they took them, it is possible to learn how to build on past strengths.

As the story of twentieth-century America—trying to preserve and trying to improve—is replayed, think about the following questions as you read. Which are the correct goals for America? Which are the correct ways of reaching those goals? What should Americans do to preserve what is special about America? What should Americans do to help improve America? In the future what will Americans do with their freedom? How will Americans find solutions to the problems currently facing them?

chapter 21
Reform in Modern America

1900–1910

1. PROGRESSIVES TAKE ACTION
2. THEODORE ROOSEVELT: A REFORMER AS PRESIDENT
3. GOVERNMENT ACTION AT HOME
4. AMERICAN BELIEFS IN ACTION ABROAD

INTRODUCTION

At the beginning of the twentieth century, Americans were proud of the industrial improvements that had become part of their everyday lives. But most Americans were also aware of city slums and dangerous working conditions in factories.

Improvements and inventions brought Americans what they had always wanted—more control over their environment. Improvements were part of a new nationwide system. People from coast to coast had more control than ever before in history. The growth of business had created thousands of jobs. No other country had work for so many newcomers.

However, by the beginning of the twentieth century, big businesses had merged into trusts. And the trusts were making it harder to correct bad working conditions in mines, mills, and factories. The owners were far away from the workers, and the managers were concerned with keeping costs low. The labor unions could not get

	1900	1901	1903	1904	
Who?	The Boxers, Chinese rebels	Theodore Roosevelt, a hero of the Spanish-American War	The Wright Brothers	Ida Tarbell	
What?	fight against foreigners, including Americans	becomes the twenty-sixth President	complete the first airplane flight	publishes an expose of the Standard Oil Company	
Where?	in China	of the United States	at Kitty Hawk, North Carolina	in the United States	

In what way was modern America a land of both progress and problems?

big business to listen to the workers. Women and children had even fewer ways of being heard because the early labor unions were run for and by men in the skilled trades.

In this period Americans solved problems by using science and technology. Perhaps scientific management could also be used to solve the problems that the city and the factory had brought. Some reformers who held jobs in government thought that scientific government could correct the problems of the nation. They said that government could reform the American system. These government reformers believed that the American system was basically good. It had, after all, brought progress. These reformers were called Progressives.

More and more Americans came to agree with the Progressive political leaders. People began to ask very important questions, first at the local and state levels of government and then at the national level. As you read this chapter, think about the following questions:

1. What worked well in the American system in the early 1900's?
2. What needed to be reformed in the American system in the early 1900's?
3. What did government do to make the American system work better?

1. PROGRESSIVES TAKE ACTION

The Progressives believed that the nation's troubles came from the use of power by selfish people for unjust or corrupt purposes. To the Progressives the way to cure the problems of the poor, the farmers, women, and children was to prevent powerful people from misusing their power.

1. What did Progressives believe was needed to reform the American system?

1904-1905	1907	1909	1909	1901-1914
The Russians and Japanese	Japan and the United States	William Howard Taft	Black Americans	American engineers and medical officers
oppose each other in the Russian-Japanese War	agree to limit Japanese laborers from emigrating	becomes the twenty-seventh President	establish the National Association for the Advancement of Colored People (NAACP)	supervise work on the Panama Canal
in Manchuria	to the United States	of the United States	in the United States	in Central America

Do you agree with the Progressives' view about powerful selfish people? Why are some people neither selfish nor corrupt, although they have power?

541

What can we do today to make sure everyone can and does vote?

Name some government regulations designed to force people and businesses to be fair and honest with each other.

Good people were needed in the government to pass laws that would protect workers (including women and children), small businesses, and farmers.

How could these powerful, corrupt people be stopped? The Progressive reformers believed in working for reform in two ways. The first was making sure that all Americans could vote to elect good people to the government. The second was to get representatives to pass laws to ensure that employers would be fair to their workers. They could work for special rules to protect working women and children. Through laws and regulations small businesses and farmers could be protected from unfair action by bigger businesses and railroads.

These political reformers treated government in the same way that other reformers had treated medicine, law, education, and social work. Among the best known Progressive reformers were Robert M. La Follette, governor of Wisconsin, Sam "Golden Rule" Jones, mayor of Toledo, Ohio, Tom L. Johnson, mayor of Cleveland, Ohio, and Charles Evan Hughes, governor of New York. These Progressive political leaders began to use government to reform American life.

Getting Citizens Involved

2. How did reformers work to help citizens to use their voting rights?

Reformers convinced some states to 1) use secret ballots, 2) use primary elections so that voters could select the party candidates, 3) give women the right to vote, 4) use the initiative, whereby voters could get propositions on the ballot by signing petitions, and the referendum, whereby voters had the right to approve of a law passed by the legislature, 5) elect U.S. senators rather than have them appointed by the legislatures, 6) use the recall process, which gave the voters the right to remove an elected official from office before his or her term expired.

Many Progressive reforms aimed at helping citizens to use their voting rights without fear. Some citizens needed protection from their bosses. They needed protection from powerful people in their political parties who told them how to vote. Reform governors such as La Follette of Wisconsin worked to get the secret ballot. The secret ballot, developed in Australia, included the names of all the candidates on a single piece of paper printed by the states. Voters could mark their choices in private. Reformers also worked for elections in which the voters enrolled in a political party could vote

Many women supported reform causes even though they were not able to vote. Here women are campaigning for female suffrage.

542

by secret ballot for the person they want to be the party's candidate in the next election. These were primary elections. They allowed more citizens to choose candidates for general elections. They also kept party bosses from choosing friends to run for office.

Reformers also worked for the election of senators directly by the people rather than by a vote of the state legislature. Following the lead of some western states (see chart, page 544), the Progressives supported giving the vote to women. In Oregon and other western states, voters could present ideas for laws directly to the state legislatures. They did this by signing their names to a list that was attached to a proposal for a law. When the state legislators received the proposal, they were bound by law to debate it. This process was called the *initiative*. When a proposed law was referred to the people by the state legislature for a vote of approval or disapproval, it was called a *referendum*. The *recall* process gave voters the right to remove elected officials before their terms were completed. If 25 percent of the voters wanted to do this, they presented a petition to the legislature. Then a special election was held. People voted to keep or to remove the official from office.

Reformers Manage the Cities

During this same period, particularly in the Midwest and in the South, Progressives worked to get specialists into city government. In several cities they set up commissions of elected officials to plan for and run the city. Often they hired city managers, who were not tied to any political party. The job of the city manager included cleaning up slums, providing public health services, and improving city housing. All of these projects were to be carried out as if the city were a well-run big business.

When the Progressives controlled the cities, elections for city commissions were often held citywide, instead of ward by ward. In this way threats against voters by neighborhood bosses could be avoided. Voters in city elections could vote for the best candidate, no matter what party the voters belonged to. Citywide elections were considered "cleaner," freer elections.

3. What changes did the reformers want in the cities?

1) They wanted specialists, who were not tied to political parties and were free to carry out necessary reforms, to run city governments.
2) They wanted nonpartisan, citywide elections.

Reformers Use the Power of the States

Several of the reform governors were very successful in winning voters over to their ideas. With the support of local voters, they could pressure the state legislatures to pass reform laws. Governors Robert La Follette of Wisconsin, Albert Cummins of Iowa, and Hiram Johnson of California got laws passed against the formation of trusts in their states.

4. What success did the reformers have in using the power of the states?

How is your local government organized? Does it work well to represent everyone? Are elections areawide or by ward.

543

Why did women get the vote in the West before they got it in the East?

Why was it easier to get state laws to protect farmers against unfair railroad practices than national laws? What is needed to get a national law?

With the support of the voters, some reform governors pressured their legislatures to 1) pass laws against the formation of trusts, 2) set railroad rates.

STATES THAT GAVE THE RIGHT TO VOTE TO WOMEN BEFORE 1920	
Year	State
1890	WYOMING
1893	COLORADO
1896	UTAH
1896	IDAHO
1910	WASHINGTON
1911	CALIFORNIA
1912	ARIZONA
1912	KANSAS
1912	OREGON
1914	MONTANA
1914	NEVADA
1917	NEW YORK
1918	NEBRASKA
1918	NORTH DAKOTA
1918	RHODE ISLAND
1919	INDIANA
1919	IOWA
1919	MAINE
1919	MINNESOTA
1919	MISSOURI
1919	OHIO
1919	TENNESSEE
1919	WISCONSIN

August 26, 1920, the Nineteenth Amendment became part of the Constitution of the United States

Some state governments passed laws to regulate the railroads. That meant that the states could tell the railroads that ran within their borders that all customers had to be charged the same rates. It became illegal for the railroads to charge different rates to different shippers. This reform helped the small farmers who used the railroads. Sometimes state governments set the rates that railroads were allowed to charge.

New Experts in Government

5. How would government commissions, which the reformers wanted, work?

1) Experts would be hired by elected officials. 2) Each commission would oversee one area of public industry. 3) They would report to the legislature on their progress in making businesses act fairly.

Reformers wanted the government to be a source of expert information. And so they worked to set up government agencies, or commissions, made up of specialists. The people in these agencies were not elected. They were hired by the elected officials. It was each agency's job to oversee one area of the nation's public industries, such as the railroads or the electric companies.

The agencies were supposed to report to the state legislatures about their progress in making businesses act fairly. Governor La Follette of Wisconsin worked to set up a railroad commission in his state.

Today there are thousands of government agencies. What problems does that create for elected representatives and for the voters?

What can a citizen do who objects to a regulatory agency's decision?

The commission was made up of engineers, accountants, and others. Their job was to set rules for the railroads. Governor Johnson of California worked to set up an industrial welfare commission in his state. The job of this commission was to set maximum hours and minimum wages to protect working women and children.

New Experts in Business

The state agencies, or commissions, were making rules for businesses. These businesses wanted their ideas represented in government. And so they had to work with government experts. This need created a new set of jobs in the world of business. Businesses hired people to work with government agencies. Their job was to tell agencies and lawmakers what kinds of laws would be best for their businesses. They were not allowed onto the floor of the House or the Senate. Therefore, they talked to legislators in the outer lobbies of the state capitol buildings. Thus they became known as lobbyists.

There were specialists in different areas of American life who worked for the government, or for the "public interest." And now there were specialists working for private interests such as the New York Life Insurance Company and the American Medical Association.

Many Kinds of State Laws to Regulate and Reform

Reformers at the state level of government got laws passed to make taxes fairer and to make sure that everyone paid them. Laws were also passed to protect forests and to provide clean water to the public. Conservation of these natural resources was very important

6. Why were lobbyists needed?

Businesses believed that they needed representatives to work with lawmakers to pass laws that would be best for them.

7. What kinds of laws were passed in some states to improve life for Americans?

1) Taxes were made fairer. 2) Forests were protected, and clean water was provided. 3) Workers who were hurt on the job were compensated. 4) The working hours of children and the work performed by them were regulated. 5) The hours, working conditions, and wages of women were regulated.

This photograph, showing children at work in a vegetable cannery, was presented to the National Child Labor Commission. What was its purpose?

545

to people living in the West and in the South. Laws to make companies pay, or *compensate,* workers who were hurt on the job were also passed by progressive states. Wisconsin was among the first to set up a commission to get workers' compensation laws passed.

Progressive reformers were concerned about working children and women. They passed laws to limit the working hours of children. They also restricted the kinds of work that children were allowed to do. They regulated the hours and wages of working women. These laws did not mean that women were to be paid the same wages as men. That idea did not even occur to many reformers. Reformers believed that working women needed special protection such as shorter hours and better working conditions.

There were debates in state legislatures about what needed improvement in American life. Legislators agreed that improvement was needed in businesses that treated customers unfairly. Certainly people who cheated their employees or their customers were doing wrong. People who took advantage of the poor in the cities also needed to be regulated.

Power in the States Was Not Enough

8. Why did the Progressives feel that the national government should become involved in the reform movement?

1) There was disagreement within the states about what reforms were needed. 2) Big national businesses could not be watched over easily by the legislatures.

There was so much discontent that not enough improvements could be made at the state level of government. When state legislatures passed laws to regulate life in the cities, there was often an outcry from city people. Many people in the cities believed that farmers and people in small towns were telling them what to do. In state senates representation was by geographical area, not by population. Voters in farm areas and towns were therefore likely to have more representation. And so small towns or rural areas were often seen by cities as places where powerful strangers were trying to run the cities and the lives of city people.

Big national businesses could not be watched over easily by separate state legislatures. A railroad that moved through many states could change its rates from state to state. A business whose home office and license came from one state did not have to obey the laws of every state in which it did business. This was very true if the laws of the different states in which a business operated were not the same.

Because business, labor, and many of the specialists were linked nationally, reformers in government also wanted reform to be nationwide. The Progressives and many others began to think that national government could be organized to act as a regulator, rule maker, and reformer. This was a new thought. Was there any one person who could make it happen? And if there were, how could it be done?

Notice the shift since 1900 in attitudes about women. Where do you see the American values of liberty, opportunity, and control in women's struggle for equality?

Checking the facts

1. What job do lobbyists do?
2. What are the initiative, the referendum, and recall?
3. What areas of American life did state government change?

2. THEODORE ROOSEVELT: A REFORMER AS PRESIDENT

In September 1901 the person who became President was a Progressive reformer who looked beyond his home state. He had ideas on what to do about America's problems. And now he had power. That person was Theodore Roosevelt.

The Background of the New President

What made Theodore Roosevelt believe that he could help the nation? After all, he was only 43 years old when Leon Czolgosz (CHOL-gosh) shot and killed President William McKinley. Theodore Roosevelt was the youngest President in America's history.

In spite of his youth, Roosevelt had a great deal of experience. He was well-known and popular. He became known as a reformer when he was a member of the New York State Assembly. Later he became a commissioner of civil service under two Presidents, police commissioner of New York City, and assistant secretary of the navy. Roosevelt became known to most people as a hero of the Spanish-American War. By 1898 he was governor of the state of New York. As governor he fought against the New York City machine and its powerful "Boss" Platt. Partly to get Roosevelt out of New York, Platt and others urged the Republican party to run him for Vice-President.

9. What qualifications did Roosevelt have to be President?

1) He had experience in local, state, and federal governments. 2) He was well-educated, popular, and a well-known reformer.

Roosevelt was a Popular President

Roosevelt appealed to many people. Well-educated, wealthy easterners liked him because he was a Harvard graduate and came from an old New York family. Westerners also liked him. He had lived on a ranch in South Dakota, had written western history, and had led the Rough Riders in the Spanish-American War. Southerners liked him because his uncles had fought for the South in the Civil War.

Roosevelt was a lively person who made news. Americans liked to think of him as "the typical American." It was more likely that he

10. Why did Americans think of Roosevelt as the "typical American"?

He combined characteristics that they admired—love of publicity, sports, action, people, and power.

This cartoon appeared in a magazine just before Congress was to debate the Sherman Antitrust Bill. What point is this cartoon making?

was one of a kind. He combined characteristics that Americans admired. He loved sports, action, people, publicity, and power. The American people were excited about their new President and his reform ideas.

The Republican party leaders were shocked. They had backed Roosevelt for the vice-presidency to please his followers and to keep him quiet. Now with McKinley dead the party and the nation had as its leader an active, outspoken politician. Roosevelt was known across the country as one who cared about the people.

Roosevelt's Ideas

11. What evidence was there that Roosevelt would be a fair reformer?

He judged organizations not by their size, but by their actions. Was their behavior good, moral, and ethical? He was against those businesses that broke the law, treated their workers badly, and cheated their customers.

Roosevelt believed that there was nothing basically wrong with the new industrial corporations and the new inventions. These changes made it possible for Americans to produce more, buy more, and sell more, both in the United States and overseas.

Roosevelt also believed that there was nothing wrong with businesses being big. Nor did he want small businesses to be kept from becoming big. What was wrong was that some big businesses were run by people who broke the law. These people treated their workers badly and cheated their customers. Roosevelt did not believe that government was evil because it was big. He was angry that some politicians took bribes. For example, some jobs to build government buildings were given to construction companies that paid politicians money to get the jobs. Roosevelt was angry that some politicians stole or used the taxpayers' money for their own benefit. He believed that corrupt acts by big businesses and politicians should be punished because they hurt other Americans.

Roosevelt judged most people and organizations by their actions. Were their actions good, moral, and ethical? Or were they evil,

Why are the President's beliefs about people important?
Roosevelt's plan for government action required punishment for wrong action. How does government prevent wrong action from taking place?

immoral, and unethical? How do you punish business organizations? How do you punish trusts? Roosevelt had an answer. He said that the federal government should make laws and regulations. He was the first President to believe that the government could and should act against those who used power to hurt Americans.

Roosevelt in Action

Roosevelt had three and a half years of McKinley's term to serve before he could run for the presidency on his own. He used that time to compaign for his favorite projects and to speak out against trusts. However, he was not against all trusts—only those that misused their power. During his term of office, more trusts were formed than ever before.

Roosevelt wanted to take action on problems that affected all the people. For example, when the hard coal (anthracite) miners went on strike in 1902, there was danger of a coal shortage. The strike was therefore not in the national interest. Roosevelt brought representatives of the miners and the mine owners together at the White House. If they did not reach an agreement, he said, he would have the government take over the mines and use the army to mine the coal. The owners and the miners agreed that a committee representing both sides—an *arbitration committee*—would settle the dispute. The miners won a 10 percent rise in wages. But they were still not allowed to have a union represent them.

12. How did Roosevelt show that he was concerned about problems that affected all people?

1) He opposed trusts that abused their power, even though more trusts than ever were formed during his term of office. 2) He got representatives of the miners and of the mine owners to reach an agreement by threatening to use the army to mine the coal.

The United Mine Workers was founded in 1890 to help better the lives of coal miners. This is a detail of a 1902 membership certificate.

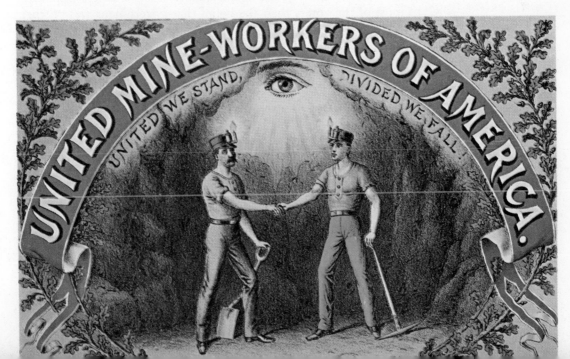

Roosevelt had no easy answers to questions such as how much power owners should have or what rights workers should have. He believed that as these questions came up, the President and the federal government should support actions and decisions that were best for the whole country.

Action Across State Borders

13. How did Roosevelt use the power of the national government to take action when problems arose?

1) He created the Department of Commerce and Labor to collect information about unfair action by an industry that operated within a state or across state boundaries. 2) He took the Northern Securities Company to court for charging unfair rates and for preventing other railroads from doing business.

Roosevelt believed that it was the government's job to watch over all parts of the nation and to offer solutions or take needed action when problems arose. He asked Congress to create the Department of Commerce and Labor to watch for problems in those two areas. A group within the department was to collect information about unfair action by any industry that operated within a state or across state boundaries. Businesses were not pleased with this new area of control by the President. Roosevelt convinced Congress to pass the law anyway.

Before the election of 1902 the federal government announced that it was going to take a huge railroad trust to court. The government wanted to break up the trust for having violated the Sherman Antitrust Act. The Northern Securities Company was accused of charging its customers unfair rates and of keeping other railroads from doing business. Many people were shocked that the President would fight a giant industry like the railroads—especially when it got much of its money from the powerful banker J. P. Morgan. Others were delighted and excited that Roosevelt dared to speak and act against such a large trust. In 1904 the Supreme Court ruled that the Northern Securities Company had to be divided. The fact that Roosevelt did not act against many trusts was less important to most of the voters than the belief that government was on their side.

The President in the News

14. How did Roosevelt get his message across to Americans that he cared?

1) He created news on Sunday when very little was happening. 2) He made the Monday morning headlines and was the subject of many cartoons.

The public's belief in the government was important to Theodore Roosevelt. The modern industrial way of life of the early twentieth century caused most people to feel cut off from the power to make decisions. They believed that they needed someone more powerful than their representatives in Congress to represent them. Theodore Roosevelt understood the need of the American people for a visible, active, caring President.

But how could even the most concerned President get the message across to all the people in America that he cared? Roosevelt knew that the newspapers of the country were read by many people. Even those who were not well educated looked at the front page of a daily paper. The President of the United States is news. Roosevelt knew this. "The White House is a bully pulpit," he said. It was a good place from which to talk to the people. Roosevelt also knew that very little happened on Sundays in the United States. It was the traditional day of worship and family relaxation. Because of the lack of news on Sundays, Monday morning newspapers were often very dull reading.

Roosevelt was skilled at making big news stories or so-called personal-interest stories happen on Sunday. Then he could be the subject of many Monday morning headlines.

One popular writer, Mark Sullivan, described Roosevelt's delight in using cartoons.

> "At any zesty word from Roosevelt, cartoons filled the air like autumn leaves in a high wind. . . . About the time Roosevelt became an important figure in American life, there had been invented a photoengraving process which permitted the making of a chemically etched zinc block (instead of hand-carved wood blocks) within a few minutes of the artist's pen drawing. Thus cartoonists were able to make their drawings within an hour of receiving the current news, and thus the newspapers were able to present them to the public a few hours later."

Leadership and Reform

Theodore Roosevelt knew how to use the presidency to call attention to new ideas. He also knew how to use reform as a way of calling attention to his leadership. Because of his style he was able to spread his belief that problems should be solved nationally by the national government. This was a new kind of President, calling for a new kind of government action to make the modern American way of life better.

15. Why was Roosevelt a new kind of President?

He knew how to use the presidency to call attention to new ideas. Because of his style, he was able to spread his belief that problems should be solved nationally by the national government.

Checking the facts

1. Theodore Roosevelt was known as "the trust buster." Is that an accurate label? Explain your answer.
2. What was Roosevelt's view of big corporations?
3. How did Roosevelt use newspapers to make contact with the American people?

Today some people still believe problems must be solved nationally. Others think problems can be solved locally. In your opinion, does it depend on the problem or is one way better than the other?

551

3. GOVERNMENT ACTION AT HOME

In 1904, when Roosevelt had completed McKinley's term of office, old-fashioned Republicans leaders had enough talk and action about reform. They wanted to nominate McKinley's friend and campaign manager Mark Hanna to run in the election of 1904. But Hanna died. There were no other challengers to the popular "Teddy" Roosevelt. Roosevelt defeated a conservative Democrat. He was elected to a four-year term of his own. During those four years he showed what he thought government should and could do both to preserve and to improve upon the strengths of the United States.

The Trusts

16. Why was it necessary for the Justice Department to bring lawsuits against some trusts?

1) Congress failed to give the federal government the power to set rules to prevent bad business practices.
2) Some trusts failed to reform themselves.

In the years from 1904 to 1907, newspapers and magazines were full of attacks on trusts—the Standard Oil Trust, the beef trust, the railroad trust, and the sugar trust. In 1907 there was a financial panic. Prices on the stock market dropped and businesses failed. The panic of 1907 showed that business had borrowed too much. Banks had loaned too much. And businesses had to lay off or fire workers because there were fewer customers with money to buy goods and services. There seemed to be a need for rules.

Roosevelt tried to get Congress to give the federal government the power to set rules by which all interstate businesses would operate. He thought that government could then prevent bad business practices rather than only punishing them. He said to Congress: "Our laws have failed in enforcing the performance of duty by the owner toward the man who works for him, by the corporation toward the investor, the wage earner, and the general public."

But Congress would not give the federal government that power. Some trusts would not reform themselves. And so Roosevelt had to fight those trusts by means of lawsuits brought by the attorney general in the Justice Department. One famous lawsuit was brought against the Standard Oil Trust. The oil companies in the trust were forced to break up into smaller companies because the trust had too much control of the oil industry.

Roosevelt did not attack every trust. Nor did lawsuits keep new combinations of businesses from forming. Roosevelt's most important success was a law regulating interstate railroads.

The Railroads

17. What were the provisions of the Hepburn Act?

After the Interstate Commerce Act of 1887 became law, 800 railroads combined into six huge railroad systems. Three out of every four miles (6.4 kilometers) of railroad track were controlled by the

Panics made people distrust banks and other businesses.

owners of the six railroad trusts: Vanderbilt, Morgan-Belmont, Harriman, Cassatt, Gould, and Hill. These railroads charged lower rates to their favorite customers or gave back some of the money in *rebates* at the end of the year.

At first Roosevelt was only able to get Congress to gather information about, or investigate, the railroads. People from all over the country came to Washington. They told Congress what the railroads had done to them. Congress then agreed that a law was needed to force railroads to act fairly.

The law that Congress passed in 1906 was called the Hepburn Act. It gave the Interstate Commerce Commission the power to decide what railroads should charge. Railroads would have 30 days to do what they were told. If they objected, they could ask the courts to decide.

Government Acts for the People

For the first time in America's history, a majority of the representatives of the people considered it necessary to interfere with private business decisions. This decision was a large change for government and for business. Just as railroad tracks built by separate companies were connected to one another, so the railroad companies combined their managements. In fact, big railroad systems were probably more efficient. But if big business was necessary, limiting its power also seemed necessary. There was a public interest, and Congress now openly represented it.

Food and Drugs

Upton Sinclair was among the writers who tried to show that businesses were acting irresponsibly. Sinclair felt that nothing could be done to make American business act fairly. He believed that the idea of private ownership of business should be given up. Sinclair and others like him were Socialists. They thought businesses should be owned and regulated by the workers and other citizens through their government.

Sinclair wrote a novel called *The Jungle.* It was about the meat-packing industry. The book was published in 1906. It exposed the unsanitary and unsafe working conditions in the slaughterhouses and processing plants. The power of the press worked well. The government investigated the meat-packing industry and reported the following conditions:

> "Meat scraps were found being shoveled into containers
> from dirty floors, where they were left to lie until
> again shoveled into barrels or into machines for

1) It gave the Interstate Commerce Commission the power to decide what railroads should charge.
2) The railroads had 30 days to comply or to seek redress from the courts.

18. How did Congress justify regulating the railroads?

Limiting the power of business was necessary in the public interest.

What does this picture tell you about the response of some businesses to the Pure Food and Drug Act?

Notice the order in which regulation happened: 1) Business, 2) networks of business, by nationwide systems with national management, 3) state attempts to punish or control, 4) national regulations, with courts' regulating congressional laws.

chopping. These floors, it must be noted, were in most cases damp and soggy, and the employees spit upon them at will. In a word, we saw meat shoveled from filthy wooden floors, piled on tables rarely washed, and pushed from room to room in rotten boxcarts. Where comment was made to floor superintendents about these matters, it was always the reply that this meat would afterwards be cooked, and that this sterilization would prevent any danger from its use. Even this, it may be pointed out in passing, is not wholly true. A very considerable portion of the meat so handled is sent out as smoked products and in the form of sausages, which are prepared to be eaten without being cooked. . . ."

Roosevelt joined the investigators and spoke out against the meat-packing industry. He promised a "drastic" law to regulate it. The law, called the Pure Food and Drug Act, set up a commission that had the right to inspect the meat packers. The meat inspectors were paid out of taxes.

Forests and National Parks

19. What were Roosevelt's beliefs about the nation's natural resources?

During Roosevelt's presidency the government acted for the first time to preserve the nation's natural resources. Theodore Roosevelt

SOME OF THE MUCKRAKERS			
Authors	Titles of Their Works and Dates		Evils They Exposed
Ray Stannard Baker	Following the Color Line	1908	racial discrimination
	The Railroads on Trial	1906	railroad corruption
Thomas W. Lawson	Frenzied Finance	1905	insurance and stock manipulation
Gustavus Myers	History of the Great American Fortunes	1910	fortunes made by corruption and exploitation
David Graham Phillips	The Treason of the Senate	1906	senators representing banking and corporate interests
John Spargo	The Bitter Cry of the Children	1906	hardships of child labor
Lincoln Steffens	The Shame of the Cities	1904	city corruption due to corrupt political bosses
	The Struggle for Self-Government	1906	
Ida M. Tarbell	The History of the Standard Oil Company	1904	unfair business practices of a major corporation

loved outdoor life. He valued the wilderness areas of the nation. He tried to get public support for protecting these lands as part of the national treasure.

Roosevelt believed in conservation. He used his power to set aside 150 million acres (60 million hectares) of government forest land. The big lumber companies of the West did not object to this plan as much as the small ones did. The big companies had to plant new trees every year and cut carefully in order to stay in business. The small, independent loggers cared less about replanting. They wanted the freedom to cut trees wherever and whenever it was easiest and cheapest to do so.

Roosevelt used the conservation issue to speak out against those who would use up the resources of the nation because they owned the land. He was one of the first to explain that private ownership of natural resources did not mean that the public should have no say in how the resources were used.

Protecting the People

Theodore Roosevelt believed that more government regulation was necessary to protect the public from the misuse of power by some of the people. During the panic in 1907, Roosevelt was convinced that many people were hurt by poor business practices in industries and banks. In his view, privately owned businesses could not control activities in their own and others' businesses. Roosevelt believed that something more had to be done. He believed the federal government could do the job.

1) He believed that the wilderness should be protected because it formed part of the national treasure.
2) He believed that private ownership did not mean that the public should have no say in how resources were used.

Checking the facts

1. Why was it necessary for government to interfere with business?
2. What practices of the meat-packing industry were attacked by Upton Sinclair?
3. What was Roosevelt's stand on conservation?

4. AMERICAN BELIEFS IN ACTION ABROAD

In his years as President from 1901 to 1908, Roosevelt changed the government's way of behaving abroad as well as at home. His beliefs guided his dealings with foreign governments.

How much liberty, opportunity, and control do you think people should have? Only as much as the least-responsible person can handle? Or a great deal, unless and until individuals prove they can't handle the freedom and the power?

555

What Roosevelt Believed

20. How did government and business leaders view the world in the early 1900's?

1) Roosevelt believed that good nations, like the United States, were democratic and scientific. 2) Many American leaders looked at the rest of the world as sources of trade and profit. 3) They wanted to show the rest of the world how powerful the United States was.

Roosevelt believed that there were good and bad nations, just as there were good and bad trusts. Good nations, he believed, were democratic and scientific like the United States.

The United States was not the only nation that believed that to be modern was to be better. During the early twentieth century all the industrially powerful nations of Europe believed that Africa, Asia, and Latin America were inferior and in need of protection. Industrialized meant civilized to these modern nations. Helping others to become more like Europe had been the belief behind much of the empire building carried out by England, France, and others in the seventeenth and eighteenth centuries.

Roosevelt and other leaders in government, business, and banking knew little about promoting American business in other nations. Secretary of State John Hay, railroad millionaire E. H. Harriman, and the powerful banker J. P. Morgan looked at the world with their own points of view. Could the United States trade there? Could we run a railroad there? Could we make a profit by investing in their raw materials? These were the questions that America's leaders wanted answered.

These government and business leaders wanted to let the industrialized world know that the United States was powerful. They did not want other powerful countries to ignore the United States. That the world looked different to the people of Africa, Asia, and Latin America was not known to Americans, nor did they seem to care. It seemed only natural to many Americans that the President of the United States would want to show the world how powerful the country was.

Showing the World: But How and Where?

21. What problems did Roosevelt have in showing the world how powerful the United States was?

1) Roosevelt wanted the United States to achieve power without being burdened by the responsibility of maintaining colonies. 2) He wanted to prove the power of the United States and have that power noticed without involving the country in costly wars that could not be won.

If the United States was to be thought of as a power around the world, it had to be seen. One way to be seen was to send ships to foreign ports. Theodore Roosevelt believed in a strong navy. This was a belief that he shared with many leaders of government in the early 1900's.

Under Roosevelt Congress voted to spend tax dollars to build ships. New American battleships and four new armored cruisers were built between 1902 and 1905. By 1906 the American navy was second only to England's in might. The United States had more ships than did France, Germany, Russia, and Japan.

However, the United States had no wars to fight. Without successful wars there seemed to be little a newly rich nation could do to become noticed as a world power. This was a problem for

Roosevelt. The powerful nations at the beginning of the twentieth century all had colonies somewhere in the world. England, France, and Germany had taken most of the land in Africa around the Mediterranean Sea and in South Asia. Latin America did not seem to be worth colonizing. And Asia was too far away. Besides, Roosevelt wanted power for the United States without setting up colonies abroad.

Roosevelt searched for means other than colonizing to prove that the United States was a world power. He wanted to find ways that would not involve the country in costly wars that could not be won. Whatever he did would involve Central and South America and East Asia. Roosevelt looked for ways to take action and to have that action noticed.

Policy in Action: The Panama Canal

One of the first places where the United States took action and was noticed was in Central America. The need for a canal had been of special interest to the American government ever since the Spanish-American War. During that war the battleship *Oregon* had taken 71 days to get from the Atlantic Ocean to the Pacific Ocean by sailing around Cape Horn at the southern tip of South America. What was needed was a waterway cut through Central America at either the narrowest or easiest point for construction purposes. A canal would make it possible for the United States to move its navy from ocean to ocean quickly.

By 1901, when Theodore Roosevelt became President, the question was not whether a canal should be built; it was, which route was the best? Two possible routes were being considered. One was across 170 miles (272 kilometers) of fairly high and dry land in the nation of Nicaragua. If this route was chosen, the problem of cutting through high ground would be great. However, there was the advantage that the route could use existing lakes and rivers as part of the canal.

Another route was one that had already been tried by a private French company years before. That company had been given the right to build a canal through the province of Panama, then a part of the nation of Colombia. The French company stopped working on the canal in 1889 after losing $260 million and the lives of thousands of workers. The Panama route was closer to sea level than was the one in Nicaragua. It was, therefore, easier to dig. However, the location was infested with mosquitoes that caused yellow fever and malaria.

There were a number of people interested in the Panama route. However, they were not thinking about the difficulty of building

22. What advantages did a canal route through Colombia have over one through Nicaragua?

A canal route through Colombia was closer to sea level than was the one in Nicaragua and was therefore easier to dig.

23. How did American business and government cooperate in building the canal?

Why is it important to know the geography of Central America?

557

This cartoon shows Theodore Roosevelt swinging a big stick at Latin Americans and Europeans. What was the cartoonist trying to say?

1) Bankers exchanged stock with the French company and invested the money to build the canal. 2) American lawyers made the legal arrangements. 3) Congress authorized the canal route and agreed to pay $40 million to the French company. 4) Roosevelt offered the Colombian government $10 million in cash and $25,000 a year rent. In return American ships could use the canal, and the United States would control 300 square miles of Colombian territory forever.

a canal. They were a group of American lawyers and investors. They had business connections with representatives of both the old French company and the Republican party in the United States. These American investors formed a company called the Panama Canal Company. They were prepared to exchange stock with the French company. Wall Street bankers would invest their money to build the canal. And American lawyers would make the legal arrangements. All that these business people and lawyers needed was the government's approval to build an American canal across the Isthmus of Panama. (See map, page 530.) Which government's approval? Not that of the Colombian government, but that of the Congress of the United States. In June 1902 Congress authorized the canal route and agreed to pay $40 million to the private French company that had received the right to build a canal from Colombia over 12 years before.

This was the moment that Roosevelt had been waiting for. Without a war and with the backing of American businesses and bankers, he could take public action. Roosevelt offered the government of Colombia $10 million in cash and a rent of $250,000 a year for the use of the canal by American ships. In return the United States would have control of 300 square miles (780 square kilometers) of Colombia. For how long? Forever.

Why was it important to Roosevelt that the businesses and bankers wanted a canal? What traditional American values did the canal appeal to?

Panama Becomes Independent

The Colombian government said no to Roosevelt's plan. It was then that Roosevelt's view of nonindustrialized nations came to the surface. He called the Colombians bandits and blackmailers. To show them that they should be grateful to the United States and recognize its power, Roosevelt planned to land troops and occupy the Isthmus of Panama.

Instead, a group of Panamanians who wanted to break away from Colombia and form a separate nation met in New York. It has been said that the Republic of Panama was created at the Waldorf Astoria Hotel in New York City on October 14, 1903. Money was supplied to the Panamanian rebels. Three weeks later, when the rebels took over the army posts of the Colombians in Panama, the United States had a warship in the harbor.

Roosevelt knew that the United States would not have to go to war over Panama. But he wanted the world to know that when the United States wanted something for its own good, nothing would be allowed to stop it. The new President of Panama shouted, "President Roosevelt has made good. . . . Long live President Roosevelt." It took only 76 minutes for the United States secretary of state to recognize the new nation of Panama. In one week a treaty was signed. This treaty gave the United States the right to run the Canal Zone, the territory through which the canal was to be built. The $10 million went to the new nation of Panama instead of to Colombia. The $40 million for the French company went to the Wall Street bankers, J. P. Morgan and Company, who did not reveal to whom the money was given. And Roosevelt never asked.

The Building of the Canal

The actual digging of the canal began in 1904. It was a scientific and engineering triumph for Americans. Roosevelt took a personal interest in the progress of the canal. In 1908 the privately owned engineering company had trouble getting the job done. And so Roosevelt sent in an army engineer, George W. Goethals, to run the canal-building project. Roosevelt went to Panama to observe the building of the canal, which surprised many people. No American President in office had ever left the territory of the United States. The building of the canal was the kind of publicity that the President wanted for the United States. The canal showed American power and authority in the Western Hemisphere. And it did this without an expensive war and without loss of life. Roosevelt said, "Some people say that I caused rebellion in Panama. I did not have to cause it; I simply lifted my foot."

24. How was the nation of Panama formed?

1) Americans supplied money to Panamanian rebels who took over Colombian army posts. 2) The United States had a warship in the harbor to support the new nation of Panama.

25. How was the building of the canal regarded?

1) It was a scientific and engineering triumph for the United States. 2) It generated the kind of publicity that the President wanted, for it showed American power and authority in the Western Hemisphere. 3) The Panama action did not win the United States many friends in Central and South America.

The canal was a brilliant achievement of American science and technology. It excited Americans.

559

The entire Panama action helped to put the United States into the group of nations that did as they pleased. Roosevelt liked to quote a West African proverb, "Speak softly, but carry a big stick." This was his idea of how the United States should become a better known and more powerful nation. But the Panama action did not win the United States many friends in the rest of Central and South America. Among these least powerful nations, the treatment of Colombia was not an example of speaking softly. Nor was it forgotten by many people.

Managing the Affairs of Venezuela and the Dominican Republic

26. How did Roosevelt tell other nations to leave the Western Hemisphere to the United States?

1) When European ships fired on Venezuelan ships and ports, Roosevelt demanded that disagreements be settled by a third party—the United States. 2) When the Dominican Republic could not repay $40 million that it had borrowed from European investors, the United States took charge of its customs, giving 55 percent of the duties on imports toward paying its bills.

During these same early years of Roosevelt's presidency, he reminded the nations of Europe that the United States was in charge of keeping the peace in the Western Hemisphere. In 1902 the German and the English governments sent ships to blockade the ports of Venezuela. The head of Venezuela refused to pay back debts owed to German and English investors. No Latin American ruler, in Roosevelt's view, could be taken seriously.

When the European ships fired on Venezuelan boats and ports, Roosevelt spoke up and demanded that the disagreement be settled by a third party. Obviously, that third party was the United States. The other nations actually did not mind as long as the United States kept those countries from rebellions. European nations and the United States had lent money to governments and businesses in Latin America. They did not want local wars to destroy property or to prevent repayment of debts.

Another case of American involvement in Latin America happened in 1903. This time the nation was the Dominican Republic in the Caribbean Sea. (See map, page 530.) The government of that island nation could not pay back $40 million that it had borrowed from European investors. There was pressure from European governments to use force to get the Dominican Republic to pay back the money.

President Roosevelt did not want other nations involved in Latin America. And he also believed that nations, no matter how small, should pay their debts. What action could the United States take that would be "right"? He did not want to make an American colony out of the Dominican Republic. In Roosevelt's words, "I have about the same desire to annex it as a gorged boa constrictor might have to swallow a porcupine wrong-end-to."

What Roosevelt did was to set up a way for the United States to make sure that the Dominican Republic kept its records carefully and paid its debts. The United States government took charge of the customs of that country. Customs is the point where taxes are collected on goods entering or leaving a country. When the customs taxes, or *duties*, were collected, 55 percent of all taxes on imports were to go toward paying bills. After the bills were paid, then the government of the Dominican Republic would be allowed to have the rest.

A Plan Becomes a Policy: The Roosevelt Corollary

The United States developed a plan to make itself the caretaker of the Western Hemisphere. Some called it being the "policeman" of the Western Hemisphere. In a speech to Congress in December 1904, Roosevelt made a formal statement of policy. He had learned from the canal dealings and the experiences with Venezuela, the Dominican Republic, and others. He believed that he could state what the United States government would do to keep Latin American governments under United States control. This policy statement made it plain that the United States wished to be considered a world power by other world powers.

27. What made the Roosevelt Corollary to the Monroe Doctrine believable to other nations?

Through his actions in Panama, Venezuela, and the Dominican Republic, Roosevelt showed that he intended to make the United States a world power.

The policy was known as the Roosevelt Corollary to the Monroe Doctrine of 1823. According to this corollary, or addition, the United States would use "international police powers" whenever it thought that Latin American nations were guilty of wrongdoing. This policy pleased American investors. It particularly pleased those who had put money into Cuban sugar and Latin American mines. But it frightened many Latin American rulers. These rulers were afraid that their nations would become colonies of the United States.

East Asia—More Words Than Policy

The Western Hemisphere was the easiest region for the United States to influence. The other nations of the hemisphere were not as rich and were not as industralized as was the United States. Also European nations were glad to have the United States keep the peace and protect their investments in the Americas for them. There was no competition for power.

28. Why was the United States having difficulty gaining influence in East Asia?

1) It was 7,000 miles away, too far for Americans to fight a war. 2) Other nations had established trade with China and didn't want to share their profits. 3) American business would not risk investing in China because China was in a period of trouble.

East Asia was different. The Pacific Ocean's width of 7,000 miles (11,200 kilometers) made it diffcult for Americans to fight a war or supply a navy in Asia. Besides, England, Germany, France, Spain, and Portugal had been in China a long time. These nations had no intention of allowing the United States to share in the profits of the China trade.

Foreign policy means a general rule for a nation's behavior in the future as well as the present. Who made American foreign policy when Teddy Roosevelt was President?

561

Roosevelt wanted to do something in East Asia to make America even more powerful. He could not get American businesses and bankers to risk investing in China even though all nations dreamed of selling to the Chinese. Selling to China was considered good business because there were so many millions of Chinese. China was going through a time of trouble. Some Chinese wanted to become like the modern Europeans. Others wanted to keep their traditions. In spite of Roosevelt's desire to do something important in China, he could get no help from business leaders in America.

Because American business was afraid of investing in China, whatever action the United States took would have to be political. Action had to be something that the United States government and the President could do on their own. An event occurred that gave Roosevelt just the chance he wanted.

The Russo–Japanese War

29. What were the results of Roosevelt's attempt as a peacemaker?

1) He got Japan and Russia to end their war over Manchuria. Japan was given the right to move into Korea, Russia was protected from having to pay a great deal of money to Japan. 2) Roosevelt won the Nobel Peace Prize, but both nations resented the United States. 3) He worried whether the Philippines were secure against Japan, and so he sent the United States navy around the world to demonstrate its power.

In 1905 the Russians and the Japanese, two major powers in East Asia, went to war over the control of Manchuria on the Asian mainland. The Japanese wrecked the Russian fleet and won several battles on land. The war looked as if it might drag on. But the Japanese did not want a long war. And so the Japanese government asked President Roosevelt to help it make peace with Russia. As peacemaker, Roosevelt could show the world that the United States could be an influence even in Asia. He could also reinforce the Open-Door Policy in Asia. And the United States did not need to go to war to do so.

The peace conference was held in Portsmouth, New Hampshire. As a result of the peace settlement, Japan was given the right to move into Korea as well as into islands in the Pacific off the coast of Russia. Russia was protected by the peace treaty from having to pay a great deal of money to Japan. For his part as peacemaker, Roosevelt won the Nobel Peace Prize.

The treaty ending the war between Russia and Japan did not make America's situation in Asia secure. Neither the Russians nor the Japanese thought that the treaty was helpful. In the long run, both nations resented the United States. Roosevelt worried that the United States would not be able to protect the Philippine Islands from attack in case Japan decide to spread its power in Asia.

Roosevelt decided to send the United States navy on an around-the-world tour to impress other nations with American power. He especially wanted to impress Japan, which was upset with what it believed was United States interference in its prizes of war.

Many Japanese came to the United States and settled in California. They suffered discrimination and segregation in schools and on jobs.

Race and Foreign Policy

Around 1905 and earlier many Japanese came to the United States to work. Racial discrimination against Japanese living in California made the situation between Japan and the United States worse. In the San Francisco school system, Oriental children were put into separate schools. The Japanese in the United States were angry about their mistreatment. Immigrants from Japan worked for little money. They were thought of as cheap labor and were thought to cause low wages for others who wanted jobs. This tension between two groups—Whites and Orientals—in California affected the nation's foreign policy. Theodore Roosevelt decided that it was time for the United States government to take action to resolve the problem. But how could this be done? Problems within state school systems were supposed to be solved by the individual states. The federal government did not have the authority to make such rules for the states.

30. *Why did Roosevelt enter the dispute over schooling for Japanese American immigrants? How was it resolved?*

1) The tension created affected foreign policy. 2) Roosevelt entered into a gentlemen's agreement with Japan. He would not allow laws to be passed against Orientals if Japan would not give passports to workers who wanted to come to the United States.

The fear of immigrants as cheap labor had been seen before in the United States. When? Where? Race had made a difference again to White Americans. Now, however, the President tried to stop racial trouble. Why?

563

For the President of the United States to become involved in a problem within a city school system was unusual. But Roosevelt knew that the Japanese government would see the problem of the San Francisco schools as a problem of relations between the United States and Japan. And foreign affairs and foreign policy were the President's job.

Besides, it gave Roosevelt a chance to make an agreement with the Japanese. The President promised not to allow laws to be passed against Orientals. In return the Japanese agreed not to give passports to workers who wanted to come to the United States. This agreement was known as the "Gentleman's Agreement" of 1907. It was not put into writing, although a formal agreement on trade was signed. Even though relations between the two countries were patched up by presidential action, the feeling between the United States and Japan remained unpleasant.

The Result of Government Action Abroad

Theodore Roosevelt was able to show the world that the United States should be viewed as a world power. The point had been made through the kinds of action that he took in Panama, in Latin America, and in East Asia. He had managed to achieve a reputation for the United States without getting the nation involved in wars that it was unable to fight.

In the first decade of the twentieth century, Theodore Roosevelt used his personality and his view of the United States to put the nation on the world stage. The United States wanted freedom to trade, respect for and from other nations, and control of the Western Hemisphere. Roosevelt achieved those goals. When he left office in the winter of 1909, he was assured that the American system included the rest of the world. It was clear that the United States would play bigger parts on the world stage.

Checking the facts

1. Why was building the Panama Canal important to President Roosevelt?
2. What concerns made American business leaders want to see the United States take a more active role in world affairs?
3. What was the Roosevelt Corollary?

In what ways do you believe that Theodore Roosevelt changed America?

PUTTING IT ALL TOGETHER

UNDERSTANDING THE MAIN IDEAS

1. What worked well in the American system in the early 1900's?
2. What needed to be reformed in the American system in the early 1900's?
3. What did government do to make the American system work better?
4. What did government do to help other countries solve their problems and still help America?

ACTIVITIES

1. Read a biography of one of the Progressive reformers. How did this person help to improve American life? Was there any part of this person's career that might inspire people today? Place your findings in a brief book report.
2. Make a chart of the reforms made during Theodore Roosevelt's presidency. The chart should list at least five reforms, the people or groups against the reform, and the people or groups in favor of the reform.
3. During Theodore Roosevelt's presidency, America was involved overseas. In a paragraph, answer one of the following questions: Why did the United States want a canal? Why did the United States want to get involved in East Asia?
4. Write to a government agency to find out what kinds of jobs are done there and what kinds of education and experience are needed for those jobs.
5. Does your state have the initiative and the referendum? When were they voted in? When were they most recently used?
6. For one week, one group of students should make a list of all the government action mentioned on the front page of the local newspaper. Another group should make a list of the government action mentioned in the nightly news. Compare the two lists. What was on both lists? Which mentioned the most national, state, and local news?
7. Collect a series of political cartoons from your local newspaper or from a national news magazine. Which one of the cartoons makes the point without using too many words?

BOOKS TO READ

Carter, Samuel, *The Incredible Great White Fleet* (New York: Macmillan Publishing Co., 1971).

Chu, Daniel, and Samuel Chu, *Passage to the Golden Gate: A History of the Chinese in the United States to 1910* (Garden City: Doubleday and Co., Inc., 1970).

Garraty, John A., *Theodore Roosevelt: The Strenuous Life* (New York: American Heritage Publishers, 1971).

chapter 22
Should Government Do More?

1910–1918

1. SOME GROUPS WERE STILL UNHAPPY
2. LAWS WITHOUT PRESIDENTIAL LEADERSHIP
3. WILSON TAKES OVER
4. NEW LEADERSHIP OVERSEAS

INTRODUCTION

Theodore Roosevelt spoke up louder for reform than did most political leaders. He tried to give everyone a "square deal." But some people were disappointed because he did not do more.

During Roosevelt's presidency, and those of the two Presidents who came after him, reformers were asking for greater change. How would the nation's new political leaders respond to their demands? As you read this chapter, think about the following questions:

1. How much action should national government take to solve problems in America and abroad?
2. How much power does a President have? How much power should a President use?
3. What should Congress do? Should it act on its own or wait for the President to act?

	1911	1912	1913	1914	
Who?	Chinese revolutionaries	Woodrow Wilson	150,000 garment workers	American workers	
What?	set up a republic	is elected the twenty-eighth President	go out on strike	work on assembly lines	
Where?	in China	of the United States	in New York City	at Ford auto plants	

Leaders often try to use phrases that will catch on in popular speech and symbolize their policies. Do you think it is important for a leader to be a phrasemaker?

1. SOME GROUPS WERE STILL UNHAPPY

Industrial Workers of the World

In 1905, workers from a small group of radical unions formed the Industrial Workers of the World (IWW), nicknamed the Wobblies. They wanted to call attention to the lack of power among workers. The IWW taught many unskilled workers the importance of belonging to unions. They organized unskilled farm workers in the West. Then, turning to direct action, they led several strikes by industrial workers in the East. The Wobblies never gained a great deal of support, although they received a good deal of newspaper publicity. They were unpopular with many Americans because some of their members were against both organized religion and government. The Wobblies were so extreme that they wanted no government at all. They preferred to have government by workers' committees.

1. Why did the Wobblies remain a small radical group?

They were unpopular with many Americans because some of their members were against organized religion and any form of government.

Roosevelt and Debs

Roosevelt had shortened working hours to eight hours a day and raised the pay of government workers. He did this by signing a presidential order. But he did not push Congress to pass laws that would protect women and children who worked in interstate businesses. Although he was against monopolies, Roosevelt was not against other big businesses. But some political leaders were. The labor leader Eugene V. Debs became a *socialist* after he was arrested for refusing to end the Pullman strike in 1894. At that time he was head of the American Railway Union (ARU). He led those who believed that big business made many evils possible. Debs ran for the presidency as the candidate of the Socialist party from 1900 to 1920. While serving a jail term, Debs received more than 900,000 votes as a candidate on the Socialist ticket.

2. On what issues did Debs and Roosevelt disagree?

They disagreed on the effect of big business.

	1914	1915	1916	1917	1918
	The armies of European nations	German submarines	General John J. Pershing	American soldiers	Over 100,000 American soldiers
	are engaged in World War I	sink the Lusitania	leads soldiers in pursuit of Pancho Villa	take part in the fighting in World War I	are killed in the battle of the Argonne Forest
	in Europe and the Middle East	near Ireland	in Mexico	in France	in northern France

Why is it important to know candidates' political and economic beliefs?

567

In 1908 the IWW held a rally with other socialist organizations. What other organizations do you see in this picture?

3. *What did Lincoln Steffens learn about how people with money control people in local government?*

1) The tax assessor padded the voting list with the names of dead dogs, children, and nonexistent persons. 2) The police were at the ballot box to see that repeaters were permitted to vote on names that the police had supplied.

Corrupt City Machines

Other critics who were not socialists published articles about the two organizations they believed were responsible for pushing people around—big business and corrupt city government. Most Progressives did not wish to change the whole system. They each paid attention to one part of the system that they believed was not working or was run by dishonest people.

Lincoln Steffens wrote about political machines. He traveled to St. Louis, Philadelphia, Pittsburgh, Minneapolis, and Cleveland. In each of these studies he showed how people with money controlled people in local government. They got their power by exchanging money for personal favors. Therefore, most people could not influence local government because they did not have enough money. Steffens published his findings in a book called *The Shame of the Cities:*

> "The machine controls the whole process of voting, and practices fraud at every stage. The [tax] assessor's list is the voting list, and the assessor is the machine's man. . . . The assessor pads the list with the names of dead dogs, children, and non-existent persons. . . .
>
> "The repeating [voting more than once] is done boldly, for the machine controls the election officers,

What can citizens do to keep a political machine from getting control of politics in an area? What can they do to stop a machine from controlling the vote? Why is it hard to stop one?

often choosing them from among the fraudulent names. . . . The police are at the [ballot] box and they are there to see that the machine's orders are obeyed and that repeaters are permitted to vote on the names they, the police, have supplied. . . ."

Forgotten People

Neither the President nor most of the reformers included Blacks or Native Americans among the people whom they were working to help. There were, however, some White people and a few Black leaders who worked outside government to call people's attention to the problems of Blacks. Segregation in the South was upheld by Jim Crow laws, which assigned Blacks special seats on streetcars and kept Blacks out of White hotels and restaurants. In the North, Blacks also experienced discrimination. Many White workers in the North were afraid that Blacks would compete with them for jobs. By the early 1900's, they had convinced most labor unions not to admit Blacks.

In this period two Black educators wrote and spoke out to help Blacks. These two disagreed with each other about what Blacks could do to help themselves. Both men became well-known leaders.

Booker T. Washington, the president of Tuskegee Institute, was the most powerful Black in America from 1895 to 1915. He was a friend and an adviser to Presidents Roosevelt and Taft and was greatly admired by Andrew Carnegie and other business leaders. In his book, *Up From Slavery,* published in 1901, he told how Blacks had progressed from slavery to citizenship in just one generation. He believed that because White people had all the power, they would have to make most of the changes. He did not think Blacks would be allowed to do more than manual labor jobs. He expected Blacks to keep to themselves socially. Washington believed that industrial education was the only way Blacks could get ahead in American society. The program at Tuskegee reflected his views. His students, who were Black, were trained for industrial and agricultural jobs involving manual labor.

Washington never made a direct public attack on the Jim Crow laws. He was able, however, to raise money from Whites for his institute.

The other outspoken Black educator was William Edward Burghardt Du Bois (DOO-boys). In 1903 he began to speak out against Booker T. Washington's ideas. Du Bois was a graduate of Harvard. He believed that Washington was "leading the way backward." He disagreed with Washington on what Blacks could do to help themselves. He believed that political or governmental rights were the

Booker T. Washington was a Black educator who organized a school for Blacks at Tuskegee Institute in Alabama in 1881.

What action against racism can be taken through government? What action can be taken outside of government?

569

key to changing the position of Blacks in America. He also disagreed on what kind of education Blacks should have. In his view, the most talented 10 percent of the Black population should receive the same college education that the best White colleges were giving to their students.

Blacks who read both Booker T. Washington's and Du Bois' writings were forced to choose sides. In his book of essays, *The Souls of Black Folk,* Du Bois stated:

> "Self-respect is worth more than land and houses. . . .
> So far as Mr. Washington preaches thrift, patience,
> and industrial training for the masses we must hold up
> his hands and work with him. . . . But so far as he
> apologizes for injustices, North or South, does not
> rightly value the privilege and duty of voting . . . and
> opposes the higher training and ambition of our
> brighter minds—so far as he, the South, or the nation,
> does this—we must . . . firmly oppose him."

In 1905, with other Blacks such as William Monroe Trotter, a Harvard graduate and the editor of the *Boston Guardian,* Du Bois formed the Niagara Movement. The Niagara Movement called for ending discrimination based on race and color.

4. Why did Du Bois and others form the NAACP?

They wanted to end discrimination in public life.

In 1909, Du Bois joined forces with other Blacks, such as Ida Wells Barnett, the Reverend Francis J. Grimké, and Bishop Alexander Walters, and with Whites, such as Oswald Garrison Villard, Jane Addams, Mary E. Woolley, Rabbi Stephen S. Wise, and the Reverend John Haynes Holmes. They formed the National Association for the Advancement of Colored People (NAACP). The purpose of the NAACP was to end discrimination in public life.

But aid to Blacks was not seen as government's responsibility. Government leaders did not think of passing laws about prejudice against groups of people. Most of the legislation was concerned with businesses and workers. And people in politics debated about how much the President ought to do.

Checking the facts

1. What had Roosevelt failed to do for all workers?
2. How did Lincoln Steffens find the big city political machines to be alike?
3. How did Booker T. Washington and W.E.B. Du Bois differ in their opinions of how to help Blacks?

Why did the NAACP have both Black and White founders?

2. LAWS WITHOUT PRESIDENTIAL LEADERSHIP

Many reformers wished that Theodore Roosevelt had done more in the area of reform. However, they agreed with the rest of the nation that a great deal was accomplished. Roosevelt put a spotlight on the idea that there is a national or public interest greater than the interests of all the groups in the nation. He brought up the issue of how much reform should be done by the national government through the courts and through laws. He supported the idea that government should regulate and control private organizations for the good of the nation. He wanted government to protect the people who had little power.

Taft Becomes President

When Roosevelt left office in March 1909, he picked his Secretary of War, William Howard Taft, as his successor. Roosevelt believed that Taft would carry out his policies of reform at home. He also hoped that Taft would maintain an active leadership in the Western Hemisphere.

William Howard Taft won easily over the Democratic candidate, William Jennings Bryan. Taft was an experienced administrator. He had been a judge and the governor of the Philippines.

What Taft did not know, however, was how to hold the country together when so many people had so many ideas on how to change it. Some members of Taft's own Republican party argued that some of the changes people wanted would destroy the system that had made America so rich and powerful.

To carry on Roosevelt's program would require great personality and the ability to act clearly and calmly. Taft, unfortunately, did not have the charm, the public image, or the sense of how far to push for action. Although he got more reform laws passed by Congress than Roosevelt had, he lost the public feeling that the person at the head of the government knew what to do. Under Taft the nation lost a sense of togetherness. Without that feeling, people began to fight each other over whose ideas were best.

A Variety of Government Action

President Taft did not have a program of his own. He was satisfied to follow Theodore Roosevelt's ideas, but he did not want to push them himself. He was so afraid that he might take too much power into his own hands, that he left most of the leadership to the lawmakers in the House and Senate.

This is a campaign poster for Taft in 1908. How did Taft's personality differ from Theodore Roosevelt's?

Does a President today require charisma to stay popular? What makes people feel secure about the President?

5. *What Progressive laws did Congress pass?*

1) The Mann-Elkins Act of 1910 gave the Interstate Commerce Commission the power to prevent railroads from raising their rates without government permission. 2) Congress divided the Department of Commerce and Labor into two executive departments, for each required individual attention from the government. 3) A Bureau of Mines was established to watch over that important part of the economy. 4) A children's bureau was established. 5) The Post Office began a savings bank and was authorized to handle packages. 6) Alaska got a territorial government, and New Mexico and Arizona became states in 1912.

Congress passed laws that put into practice the Progressive ideas of Theodore Roosevelt. The list of major laws is long and varied. In 1910 the Interstate Commerce Commission was given the power to prevent the railroads from raising their rates until the government said that it was all right to do so. This change was recommended by Taft in the Mann-Elkins Act.

In the field of government organization, Congress divided the Department of Commerce and Labor into two executive departments. They believed that business and labor required individual attention from the government. Business and labor had become so separate in their activities that government needed two agencies to regulate them. A Bureau of Mines was established to watch over that important part of the economy. Problems of children, especially the children of the working poor, were to be handled by the new Children's Bureau. Julia Lathrop, from Hull House, was made its first chief.

New government services were begun. A savings bank was to be operated by the Post Office. The Post Office was authorized to handle packages (parcel post) as well as letters. The banks and the express companies had not wanted the government to provide these services. They believed that government competition would force them to lower their rates.

Amendments to the Constitution

6. *What amendments were added to the Constitution?*

1) The Sixteenth Amendment gave the federal government the right to tax yearly incomes directly. 2) The Seventeenth Amendment allowed citizens to vote directly for their senators.

In Taft's term of office, two amendments to the Constitution were proposed by Congress. The Sixteenth Amendment was a change in the way the United States taxed and collected money earned by its citizens. Under this amendment, the federal government could tax yearly incomes directly without going to the state governments. Wages and salaries were now considered part of the national interest. They were another source of revenue for the nation.

The Seventeenth Amendment allowed citizens to vote directly for their United States senators. Up to that time, state legislatures had chosen senators, and the party in power in the states had often rewarded their loyal party members with those important federal offices.

The President Is Unpopular

7. *How did Taft become unpopular?*

Taft encouraged his attorney general to break up trusts by accusing them of not obeying the Sherman Antitrust Act. The most famous action was brought against Standard Oil for having bought the Tennessee Coal and Iron Company. Some of Theodore Roosevelt's followers were angry at Taft. The former President had promised to leave Standard Oil alone. This was done as a favor to the banker who had helped Roosevelt by providing credit during the bank panic of 1907.

Taft also lost the support of many citizens and of several lawmakers when he promised to lower the tariff. The reformers in the House of Representatives insisted on a bill that would greatly lower the tariff. But many business and farming groups insisted that the Senate support amendments to the bill that would keep or raise the tariff on their particular products—wool, steel, tobacco, cotton. The tariff that was passed favored these groups.

Theodore Roosevelt had refused to take a stand either for or against a tariff when he was President. As a politician, he knew that tariffs always lose friends. When the Payne-Aldrich Tariff passed both houses of Congress, President Taft was in a difficult situation. Whether he signed the bill or vetoed it, he would anger some people. What he did was to anger everyone. He signed the bill into law. Then he made a speech declaring it the best tariff the nation had ever had.

Taft suffered from being compared with Theodore Roosevelt. But it was generally agreed that he made things worse for himself. On the campaign trail, he refused to greet the public. His military aide noted the following reaction to Taft's campaign style:

> "Jimmie Sloan, the secret service man, whispered to me: 'What an opportunity he is missing! For God's sake, captain, get him to lift his hat when the people yell, for if he don't they will stop yelling when he will want them most.' "

1) During his administration, a suit was brought against the Standard Oil trust, angering some of Roosevelt's followers. 2) He signed the Payne—Aldrich tariff, declaring it the best tariff the nation had ever had. 3) He refused to greet the public.

America Overseas

Taft tried to help American business in other countries. He tried to convince Americans and Europeans to lend money to the Chinese to buy back railroads owned by Russia and Japan. When the Russians and Japanese objected, Taft tried to help Americans build railroads in China. He hoped to strengthen China against Japan.

Taft tried to push through the Senate treaties with two Central American nations, Honduras and Nicaragua. The treaties would protect loans made by United States bankers to businesses in those countries. Taft's administration was accused of pushing other countries around with the promise of money. Taft was accused of *dollar diplomacy*. The United States Senate refused to ratify the Central American treaties.

8. Why was Taft accused of dollar diplomacy?

1) In attempting to strengthen China against Japan, he tried to convince Americans and Europeans to lend money to the Chinese to buy back railroads owned by Russia and Japan. When that failed, he tried to help Americans build railroads in China. 2) He tried to push through treaties with Honduras and Nicaragua to protect the loans made by United States bankers.

How does government backing for loans help Americans do business in new nations that do not have strong business or government organizations?

The Republicans Divide

9. What issue divided the Republicans?

1) The issue of how much the government should do divided the Republicans. 2) The liberal group wanted more laws to protect the people. 3) The conservative group was afraid to change the system of business and power.

President Taft did not seem to be able to sell his ideas to Congress or to the people. Some Republicans thought of him as a loser. They began to look for another candidate for the presidency in 1912. The political party that had supported Progressive policies as long as Theodore Roosevelt was the leader now split into two groups. There were those who wanted more laws to protect people—the *liberals*—and those who were afraid to change the system of business and power too much—the *conservatives*.

What Taft had done was to cause members of his own party to move in one direction or the other. The Roosevelt appeal that had held the Republican party together was gone. Taft's presidency following Theodore Roosevelt highlighted the growing importance in a big, complicated nation of a President who could think and speak to and for the people.

The Return of Roosevelt

10. Why did Roosevelt organize the Progressive Party?

Roosevelt knew he could not get the Republican nomination.

Some of the people who wanted more changes through government action tried to nominate Senator Robert La Follette from Wisconsin in 1912. La Follette's illness early in 1912 and the reappearance of Theodore Roosevelt changed these plans. Roosevelt had returned from a hunting trip in Africa and made it known that he would run against Taft for the Republican nomination. The reformers in the Republican party offered him their support.

The convention delegates had to be recognized, or certified, by a committee. The committee was made up of Taft supporters. It soon became clear that the party organization, or machinery, was in the hands of those who wanted no more change in America. They intended to nominate President Taft.

Roosevelt decided to take the most dramatic action of all. He left, or bolted, his political party and organized a new one. When asked how he felt, he replied, "I feel stronger than a bull moose." The new party was officially named the Progressive party. But it was known from that moment on as the Bull Moose party.

The unpopularity of Taft and the return of Theodore Roosevelt made people think about the importance of a President's personality. Perhaps it was important to vote for the personality that could help the people like new laws.

The Progressive Party Platform

11. In what areas did the Progressive Party want change?

Theodore Roosevelt's ideas about improving America had changed. In 1912, he spoke about a square deal for everyone. He talked

574

about the need to use government more often to make the American way of life as good as possible for each person.

He now talked of changing by law some of the customs of owners, workers, voters, and farmers. Roosevelt no longer wanted just to stop bad behavior. He no longer wanted to leave business as free from control as possible. He wanted to force America to make life better for its poorer people.

The Progressive party platform of 1912 listed the changes Roosevelt and his followers thought should be made. They included direct voting by the people for senators (the Seventeenth Amendment) and the initiative, referendum, and the recall of government officials, including judges, for poor behavior. It also included the following: equal voting rights for women; a limitation on money donated by people to campaigns and the publication of lists of all who gave before and after elections; laws to prevent industrial accidents, diseases caused by jobs, and unemployment; laws to set health and safety standards for various jobs; laws against night work by women, and for an eight-hour working day for women and young people; a six-day work week for all workers; payment to workers and their families for accidents and death related to jobs; payment of money to retired people from saving funds paid by the employer and the worker and collected by the government (social security); industrial and agricultural schools for job training; promotion of trade unions; and public ownership (through the government) of natural resources to be open to all people to encourage development and some profit on a fair basis.

The Election of 1912

When the voters went to the polls in November 1912, they could choose from among four candidates. Three of the four were considered reformers—Theodore Roosevelt, the socialist Eugene V. Debs, and the Democrat Woodrow Wilson. Only Taft seemed to represent the voter who wanted no change.

Woodrow Wilson had won the nomination of the Democratic party over William Jennings Bryan. Wilson had been a college professor, president of Princeton University, and governor of New Jersey. His nomination was described by the newspaper reporter William Allen White:

> "I had met Wilson at Madison, Wisconsin, two years before. I had watched his career as governor of New Jersey, when he had, by sheer intellectual strength, given his state the primary and the direct election of United States senators. Wilson was for workmen's

1) The Progressives wanted changes in election procedures and voting rights. 2) They wanted changes in workers' rights. 3) They wanted industrial and agricultural schools for job training. 4) They wanted public ownership of natural resources.

12. Why did Wilson win the presidential election of 1912?

1) The Democratic party was not split. 2) Wilson was able to appeal to people who wanted change but were afraid of Roosevelt's drastic new ideas.

compensation, child-labor laws, and the whole Progressive program. He stood as a progressive Democrat just as La Follette, Roosevelt, and others in the Republican party had become. . . .

"I had no great personal liking for Wilson. When I met him, he seemed to be a cold fish. I remember I came home from the meeting at Madison, Wisconsin, and told Mrs. White that the hand he gave me to shake felt like a 10-cent pickled mackerel in brown paper—irresponsive and lifeless. He had a highty-tighty way that repulsed me. When he tried to be pleasant he creaked. But he had done a fine liberal job in New Jersey. I liked the way he gathered the Irish politicians about him and let them teach him the game in his political fights. In every contest he rang true. So, as the convention dragged on my respect and admiration for Wilson grew. . . ."

The election results showed that 11 million of the 15 million voters wanted some kind of reform. Debs, the socialist, got almost one million votes. Wilson won the election because his party was not split. He was able to appeal to people who wanted change but were afraid of Theodore Roosevelt's drastic new ideas. Wilson got the votes of all of the Democrats and a good many of the Republicans, too. It was clear that more government action to correct the nation's problems was what most voters wanted.

Checking the facts

1. What qualities did Taft lack as President?
2. What was accomplished during Taft's administration?
3. Why were the Republicans divided at their convention?

3. WILSON TAKES OVER

None of the reformers spoke out for Blacks or for Native Americans. Blacks were beginning to get together from time to time, but they were not a solid group of voters. In fact, many did not vote at all.

A Progress Report on Blacks

13. How far had Blacks come in the 50 years since Emancipation?

In 1913, during President Wilson's first year in office, Black conventions were called in several states to celebrate the 50th anniversary of the freeing of the slaves. Three states—New York, New Jersey, and Pennsylvania—voted tax money for public celebrations.

Although progress had been made by many individual Blacks, as a group Blacks were still treated badly in both the North and the South. Records show that by 1913 Blacks owned 550,000 homes and ran 937,000 farms and 40,000 businesses. More than 70 percent could read, a sharp change from the 5 percent who could read at the time of emancipation.

Blacks believed that their situation had improved. One poem written for the celebration was *Fifty Years* by James Weldon Johnson. It looked both backward at what had been accomplished and forward to how far Blacks still had to go.

> Just fifty years—a winter's day—
> As runs the history of a race;
> Yet, as we now look o'er the way,
> How distant seems our starting place!
>
> Courage! Look out, beyond, and see
> The far horizon's beckoning span!
> Faith in your God-known destiny!
> We are a part of some great plan.

In the early 1900's, many Black families owned their own houses and farms in the United States. Over one million Blacks attended public schools and 35,000 taught in these schools.

1) Many owned their own homes, farms, and businesses and had savings. 2) More than 70 percent could read, compared with 5 percent in 1863. 3) Over one million Blacks were enrolled in public schools.

Is the poem a realistic picture? What do you think of its message?

577

14. What did the NAACP accomplish?

1) Its members held protest rallies and collected petitions calling on the government to end its Jim Crow policies. 2) Those in favor of segregation gradually lost support in the administration.

The new administration began to segregate government facilities. In the Post Office and the Treasury Department, in which many Blacks worked, barriers were set up between offices. Separate lunch rooms and rest rooms also were set up for Blacks. The leaders of the NAACP met with Wilson and asked him to form a National Race Commission. But Wilson refused, saying, "It will take a very big man to solve this thing." The NAACP held protest rallies and collected petitions calling on the government to end its Jim Crow policies. Those in favor of segregation finally lost support in the administration. Their policies gradually were ended.

Wilson's Ideas

15. What did Wilson believe that government should do for America?

1) The government should provide strong presidential leadership as the unifying force of a complex system. 2) Industrial success should still be protected, but the government should also pass laws that would provide safe, healthy working conditions for people.

Woodrow Wilson had definite ideas about what government could or should do for Americans. He had written three major works—*Congressional Government, The State,* and *Constitutional Government in the United States.* Wilson believed that Congress needed strong leadership from the President. "We have grown more and more to look to the President as the unifying force of our complex system, the leader of both his party and the nation."

Wilson believed that Americans should be proud of their industrial success. But he believed that Americans should work hard to do away with the evils that had become a part of American life. Wilson was not as exciting a speaker or as dramatic a personality as Theodore Roosevelt. He sounded more like a preacher, but many Americans liked what he had to say.

Wilson gave America credit for caring about people in trouble and for trying hard to do something about them. He said: "America is great in its moral force." But Wilson also pointed out why some people were hurt:

> ". . . There has been something crude and heartless
> and unfeeling in our haste to succeed and be great.
> Our thought has been 'Let every man look out for
> himself, let every generation look out for itself.' While
> thinking this, we reared giant machinery which made
> it impossible for any but those who stood at the levers
> of control to have a chance to look out for themselves."

Wilson called for a New Freedom. (See chart, page 580.) It differed from Roosevelt's program by focusing on people who had less power and fewer chances to succeed. Wilson thought that government should pass laws that would provide safe, healthy working conditions for people. The system itself was not to be thrown away. Private property was still to be protected.

Which traditional American values was Wilson talking about in his speech? Notice that Americans have always had both pride in success and guilt about the people who are hurt.

Wilson believed that America was a special nation with a special duty to provide both freedom and justice at the same time. He sounded a good deal like Thomas Jefferson. But unlike Jefferson, he had to deal with a modern, industrial way of life.

Woodrow Wilson not only had high ideals, he was also practical. He knew that to achieve ideals a President needs votes in Congress. Votes in Congress come from a political party that stands behind its leader. Wilson had that support from the Democratic party to build on during his first four years in office.

In the beginning of his presidency, he spoke in person to a joint meeting of Congress. Wilson was the first President since Jefferson to speak to both houses of Congress. He used this approach because he knew he was better at making formal speeches than he was in person-to-person meetings with senators and representatives.

The Tariff and the Income Tax

Wilson used his power to face the tariff question that had always caused so much trouble. He believed that some businesses used the high tax on overseas goods as a way of keeping others from competing with them. If tariffs were lowered, then big, American businesses would have to compete with foreign businesses. New or smaller American businesses would have a chance to catch up. Wilson believed that competition was the key to keeping the economic system strong and making it fairer at the same time.

Wilson spoke out publicly against any special power group that would try to change the tariff in a selfish way. He kept Congress in session through a long, hot summer. He worked with it on every part of the tariff bill. When the Underwood Tariff of 1913 was passed, it was the first move in half a century toward freer trade with foreign countries.

Because the government would collect fewer taxes on imported goods under the Underwood Tariff, Wilson proposed and Congress attached to the bill a *graduated tax* on incomes over $3,000 a year. As incomes increased beyond $3,000, they were taxed at higher percentages. This graduated income tax was a major step in Wilson's plans for a society with new opportunity for people with less income. Since government services were needed, the people who needed them least and could afford them most should pay more for them.

The Banking System

Every 20 years or so there had been a major problem with banks in America. Banks had loaned too much money. Businesses and

16. Why did Wilson address both Houses of Congress?

1) He knew that to achieve ideals a President needs votes in Congress. 2) He knew that he was better at making formal speeches than he was in person-to-person meetings.

17. Why did Wilson favor lower tariffs?

1) American businesses would have to compete with foreign ones, making the economic system stronger and fairer. 2) Newer or smaller American businesses would have a chance to catch up because prices would be lower.

18. What was the graduated income tax?

1) A tax on income that increases at higher percentages as income increases.

19. How would Federal Reserve banks prevent bank panics?

Why should a President have inside experience and understanding of how American politics works?

579

Wilson's New Freedom, 1913-1917

LEGISLATION	SOME PROVISIONS
Underwood Tariff Act 1913	Reduced tariffs more than any other tariffs passed in 50 years.
Federal Reserve Act 1913	Established 12 Federal Reserve Banks which serviced only member banks, not private or business concerns. Helped insure a strong and stable banking system.
Clayton Antitrust Act 1914	Strengthened the older Sherman Antitrust Act by trying to insure fair business practices and fair competition.
Federal Trade Commission 1914	Advised and regulated industries involved in interstate and foreign trade.
Smith-Lever Act 1914	Provided federal money for rural education.
Federal Farm Loan Act 1916	Enabled farmers to borrow money more easily.
Smith-Hughes Act 1917	Provided federal money for vocational education in rural and urban areas.

1) Local banks could borrow from them when they needed more money. 2) They would keep banks from charging high interest rates for reserve loans.

farms had used the money to grow. Then many of those businesses and farmers found they had produced more than they could sell.

Prices dropped and profits dropped. There was not enough money to pay the interest on the loans. Banks needed the interest on those loans to pay their depositors and to lend money to other borrowers. Word got out that banks were short of money. Depositors panicked and tried to withdraw their money. Banks called in their loans sooner than borrowers had expected. Many people could not repay the bank.

Therefore, in 1913, Wilson proposed setting up special banks so that local banks could borrow from them when they needed more money. These special, or Federal Reserve banks, would keep banks from loaning too much by charging them high interest rates for reserve loans.

20. What were the provisions of the Federal Reserve Act?

The Federal Reserve Act created 12 Federal Reserve regions. Each had a Federal Reserve bank and a board to supervise the banks. Regions seemed best because each part of the United States was

What is the importance of having the correct amount of money in circulation for buyers and sellers?

almost like a separate country in its land, resources, population, and types of business. The President was given the power to appoint the members of the board. When the board believed that new businesses, new farm lands, and more products and jobs were needed, the Federal Reserve banks would lend money at a lower rate of interest.

The Federal Reserve system was also going to be responsible for getting paper money into circulation. In that way, when buying and selling had to be encouraged, more money could be released. When there was too much gambling on risky business and farming, then less money could be made available.

Farmers also benefited. A banking system for them was set up in 1916 by the Federal Farm Loan Act. Farmers could get loans over a long period of time to help them recover from losses and to prevent financial disaster from one season's bad weather and crop failure. Farmers who formed cooperatives could get even larger federal loans. By encouraging farmers to share their risks, Wilson helped make it possible for them to sell their crops in the huge national and international markets.

The Trusts

The Sherman Antitrust Act of 1890 had been used by Roosevelt and Taft to break up some big business organizations. Wilson believed that the best way to keep big businesses under control was to make them compete with one another.

Wilson proposed, and Congress passed, the Clayton Antitrust Act of 1914. For the first time, a law allowed the government to investigate two or more businesses that charged the same prices. Similar prices might be caused by price-fixing in order to charge more to the customers. The Clayton Antitrust Act also made it illegal for a corporation to tell its customers not to buy from its competitor. The law also made it impossible for corporations in the same kind of business to have the same people on their boards of directors. A Federal Trade Commission was set up to investigate the behavior of corporations and to keep them competing with each other. By regulating big businesses, Wilson believed that smaller businesses would be able to compete for customers.

Workers

Congress accepted Wilson's proposal and kept labor unions from being regulated as large corporations under the Clayton Antitrust Act. In addition, Wilson used the interstate commerce clause of the Constitution to have a law passed forbidding the sale of goods

1) Twelve regional Federal Reserve banks were created. 2) The President appointed the members of the Federal Reserve Board that supervised the banks. 3) The board could lend money at a lower rate of interest if it believed that it was needed to stimulate business. 4) The board was responsible for controlling the circulation of paper money.

21. How did farmers benefit from the Federal Farm Loan Act?

1) They could get loans over a long period of time to help them recover from crop disasters. 2) Cooperatives that shared risks could get even bigger loans.

22. How did the Clayton Antitrust Act help smaller businesses?

The Federal Trade Commission was set up to investigate price fixing, unfair advertising, and interlocking directorates.

23. What laws did Wilson propose to aid workers?

From what you know about how businesses got big, to what extent do you think the Clayton Antitrust Act could or should protect smaller businesses?

581

1) He persuaded Congress not to regulate labor unions as large corporations under the Clayton Antitrust Act. 2) He used the interstate commerce clause of the Constitution as a basis for a law forbidding the sale of goods made by child labor. 3) The Adamson Act gave interstate railway workers eight-hour days. 4) Federal money was spent for career or vocational education programs for industrial and farm workers. 5) Federal money was used to build highways.

made by child labor. Another law proposed by Wilson gave interstate railway workers the eight-hour day (the Adamson Act of 1916).

Federal money was spent for career or vocational education programs for industrial and farm workers. Federal aid to highway-building marked the beginning of the nation's official enchantment with the automobile.

Woodrow Wilson believed that these laws helped to keep American organizations from getting so powerful that people would not have a chance to get into the system. He gave New Freedom to more people. Wilson hoped that he had made the government more open to newcomers—like the earliest days of the expanding nation in the 1800's.

Checking the facts

1. How did Wilson regard the government and the economic system?
2. How did Wilson put his beliefs into practice?
3. What was the status of Blacks in America in 1913?
4. How did the Federal Reserve system work?

4. NEW LEADERSHIP OVERSEAS

24. Why did Wilson treat the nations of Central America differently from other small nations?

1) He wanted to prevent local warfare that would damage the Panama Canal. 2) American and European businesses did not want riots or revolutions to erupt after they had invested money.

As President, Wilson took an active part in foreign affairs. He agreed with Theodore Roosevelt that the United States should continue to be a force for good in the world. This meant helping democracy, expanding free trade, and keeping the peace. Doing all three turned out to be very difficult.

Wilson believed that the United States must not push around smaller nations. Smaller nations, like smaller businesses, needed to be given a chance to grow.

Wilson announced that the United States would not put pressure on Latin American countries. Dollar diplomacy would be replaced by treating less wealthy and less industrialized nations as equals. For example, Wilson insisted that American ships pay tolls to use the Panama Canal just as the ships of other nations did.

But Wilson did not keep to his word in Central America. Americans watched Central American countries quite closely for two reasons. They wanted peace in the area so that local warfare would not damage the Panama Canal. And American and European businesses had invested money in the countries of Central America. They did not want revolutions or riots to disrupt profitable plantations and mines.

Wilson Takes Action Against Mexico

A revolution that overthrew Porfirio Diaz, the dictator of Mexico, occurred in 1911. When Wilson became President, Francisco Madero, Diaz's successor, had just been overthrown. General Victoriano Huerta (WAIR-tah) had declared himself president of Mexico. Wilson refused to recognize Huerta as Mexico's leader because he had murdered Madero.

Wilson found himself in a disagreement with business leaders in America and Europe. They wanted the United States government to leave Huerta and Mexico alone for as long as Huerta ran Mexico smoothly. Wilson, however, believed that the United States should not support a dictator who had murdered his way into office.

There were Mexicans who disliked Huerta, but they also resented the American President's interference in their affairs. Wilson interfered by sending American troops into Mexico in 1914, after a few American sailors had been arrested. Wilson told Congress that the army was going to Mexico "to help the people secure their liberty."

When a new revolution broke out in Mexico, Wilson sided with one of the revolutionary leaders, Francisco "Pancho" Villa (VEE-yah). This leader had taken control of Mexico City. Villa had declared himself ready to work with the United States.

But two other revolutionary leaders proclaimed themselves president. In 1915 the United States, Argentina, Brazil, Chile, Guatemala, and Uruguay recognized Venustiano Carranza (ve-noos-ti-A-no kar-RAN-za) as president of Mexico. Villa began to attack Americans in northern Mexico to embarrass the Mexican government. He crossed into New Mexico, burned a town, and killed a number of Americans. By this time, public opinion demanded that United States troops cross into Mexico to capture Pancho Villa.

Wilson put General John J. Pershing in command of the cavalry that rode into Mexico in 1916. However, Villa was never caught.

Wilson had made an important point about moral government. He had also learned that it was impossible to control another nation's politics from the outside. Americans wanted to deal with countries that were both peaceful and democratic. When countries were one or the other, but not both, it was always a problem for Americans to decide what to do.

25. Why did Wilson find himself in disagreement with American and European business leaders over Mexico?

1) They wanted the United States government to leave Huerta and Mexico alone as long as he ran the country smoothly. 2) Wilson thought that the United States should not support a dictator.

26. Why did Wilson send United States troops to Mexico?

1) He sent troops after a few American sailors had been

Pancho Villa, seated on the left, is shown with another Mexican revolutionary leader, Emiliano Zapata, on the right.

Where is the United States taking actions today to try to help a nation that wants peace and democracy?

583

arrested and again to capture Pancho Villa.

27. Why did an assassination involve so many nations in a war?

1) The feelings of nation against nation had built up over hundreds of years of competition for land, ports, and trade. 2) The central powers of Germany, Austria–Hungary, and Turkey fought the Allied Powers of Great Britain, France, and Russia to keep the other side from becoming too powerful.

How World War I Began

Before 1914 the American government had not taken an active role in Europe. During the time when the United States was involved in Mexico, most of the nations of Europe were at war. It was the biggest, bloodiest, and most costly war in the history of the world. How did so many nations become involved?

The Great War, as people at that time called it, came about because nations were linked to other nations in many ways. The new machinery and new industries meant that people in these modern nations bought and sold goods and services to each other. Even the United States, across the ocean, was concerned about being able to sell to England and to Europe. European nations had fought each other for land, ports, and trade for hundreds of years. By 1914 that old competition and lack of trust were now linked with the new competition for markets in which to sell the goods produced by modern industry. Nations also were competing for the natural resources that came from acquiring colonies, particularly in Africa.

The feelings of nation against nation had built up in Europe for a long time. The actual fighting broke out in 1914 when a Serbian patriot who hated Austria assassinated the Archduke Franz Ferdinand, heir to the Austro-Hungarian throne. All of a sudden, Franz Ferdinand, and the city of Sarajevo (sara-YEA-voe), in which the murder occurred, became familiar names to Americans. (See map, page 589.)

Within weeks the nations of Europe began to line up into two groups, or *alliances*. The Central Powers of Germany, Austria-Hungary, and Turkey, and the Allied Powers of Great Britain, France, and Russia, fought each other for control of Europe, Africa, and trade. One of the reasons for fighting was to keep the other side from becoming too powerful. There was another reason, too. All of Europe seemed ready for a war.

What Should the United States Do?

28. Why did the United States have difficulty in remaining neutral?

1) Americans often sided with the countries from which their families had emigrated. 2) Most of America's trade was with England and France, because the British navy blockaded German ports.

Americans wanted to continue buying and selling everywhere in the world. They also wanted to keep out of what they believed was Europe's war. Wilson wanted to keep Americans from taking sides—that is, to keep them neutral. Wilson and many others believed the United States could stay at peace and could also continue to sell to the nations at war. When the war was over, the United States would be the richest and the most powerful force for good in the world.

The United States stayed neutral for almost three years of the Great War. Neutrality was difficult for many Americans because they

Have you ever been neutral in an argument between two sides? Why is it hard to be truly neutral and still care?

World War I, 1914-1918

EVENT	DATE	WHERE	OUTCOME
Archduke Franz Ferdinand is assassinated	June, 1914	Bosnia	Archduke Franz Ferdinand is killed in the city of Sarajevo. This is the spark that sets off World War I.
War is declared in Europe	Aug., 1914	Europe	Germany declares war on Russia and France, Britain declares war on Germany and Austria.
Battle of the Marne	Sept., 1914	France	German advance on Paris is halted at the Marne River by the Allies.
Sinking of the *Lusitania*	May, 1915	Off the coast of Ireland	This British liner is sunk by a German submarine without warning; 1,195 people die, 128 are Americans.
Zimmermann telegram	Feb., 1917		In this message, Germany instructs Mexico that if war between Germany and the United States breaks out, Mexico should attack the United States and take back the lost territories of New Mexico, Texas, and Arizona. When the United States finds out about this message, American sympathies move more toward war against Germany.
Congress declares war on Germany	April, 1917		After war is declared, the United States begins its war effort and mobilization of its armed forces and industries.
American troops arrive in Europe	June, 1917	France	American soldiers fight under the command of General John J. Pershing.
American forces take Cantigny	May, 1918	Cantigny, France	American troops stop the German advance in France at Cantigny.
Allied forces hold Germans at Chateau-Thierry	May, 1918	Chateau-Thierry, France	American soldiers help the French hold the Germans back at Chateau-Thierry.
American troops hold back Germans at Belleau Wood	June–July, 1918	Belleau Wood, France	American soldiers and marines hold back Germans during six days of fighting.
Germans fall back at Reims	July, 1918	Reims, France	This battle, also known as the second Battle of the Marne, is the decisive battle of the war. The Germans retreat.
Germans are defeated at St. Mihiel	Sept., 1918	St. Mihiel, France	After three days of ground and air attacks, the French, American, and British forces defeat the Germans in this battle.
Allied forces defeat Germans at Meuse-Argonne	Sept.–Nov., 1918	Meuse-Argonne, France	Over one million combatants are engaged in this battle; 120,000 Americans are wounded. The Germans are pushed back 30 miles.
Germans sign armistice	Nov., 1918	Compiegne, France	In this armistice, the Germans agree to evacuate France, Belgium, Luxembourg, and Alsace-Lorraine. They agree to surrender artillery and land to the Allies.

These were face-to-face battles with modern weapons. How do you think TV reporting changes how people feel about war?

often sided with the countries from which their families had emigrated. More than one third of the 92 million Americans were either foreign born or the children of immigrants.

As the months went by, Americans began to take the side of the Allies. Most of America's trade was with England and France because the British navy kept all ships out of, or *blockaded,* German ports. Business with the Allies grew by 400 percent. When the Allies could not pay their bills on time, American bankers loaned them money.

The Shock of German Submarines

29. Why did the German U-boats attack an Allied passenger ship?

The Germans thought that the passenger ship was also carrying munitions.

Then the Germans used their new weapon. It was a boat that could move under water and fire bombs, or torpedoes, and that could not be seen from the surface. These *Untersee,* or U-boats, were used for sneak attacks. No warning was given to allow crews to get to their lifeboats before their ships were sunk. The U-boats had a terrifying effect on everyone. The Germans published notices in newspapers warning passengers not to travel on the *Lusitania,* a British ship they claimed was carrying munitions. When a U-boat sank the ship in May 1915, American newspapers and the American public were shocked. Of 1,200 passengers, 128 Americans were killed. Suddenly Europe's war seemed closer.

Wilson protested to the German government but decided not to take other action. Almost a year later, a French ship, the *Sussex,* was torpedoed. The United States protested again. That was in 1916, the year in which Wilson ran for his second term. He attracted many votes from reformers who had supported Theodore Roosevelt and the Republicans. The Democratic party campaign slogan was "He kept us out of war." Wilson's record of reform and his hope for peace were enough to give him another four years in the White House.

America at War for Lasting Peace

30. What events prompted the United States to enter the war against the Central Powers?

1) Germany declared that their submarines would attack all shipping. 2) The German minister of foreign affairs sent a note to the President of Mexico promising land to Mexico if it would enter the war against the United States.

The Germans declared in 1917 that their submarines would attack all shipping boats. They knew the United States would probably enter the war on the Allies' side, but they believed their U-boats could bring rapid victory.

The United States did declare war on Germany—only a few weeks after Wilson was informed that Zimmermann, the German minister of foreign affairs, had sent a message to President Carranza of Mexico. The British got hold of the message, decoded it, and sent it to the United States. The Zimmermann note promised to give New

586

Mexico, Arizona, and Texas to Mexico if Mexico would enter the war against the United States. The note was printed in American newspapers, causing much excitement in the United States. In April 1917, after Europe had fought three long and horrifying years of battle, the United States prepared to join the fight.

Wilson was truly sincere when he said that America entered the war to save Western civilization. The only reason for fighting and dying, he said, was to create a new and a better life for all people: "The world must be made safe for democracy. . . . We have no selfish ends to serve. We desire no conquest, no dominion."

Two months later General John J. Pershing was made commander of the American troops—the American Expeditionary Force. He went to France to make plans for the arrival of the American army. A reporter for a Chicago newspaper described a ceremony that took place at a cemetery that honored France's heroes:

> "General Pershing advanced to the tomb and placed upon the marble slab an enormous wreath of pink and white roses. Then he stepped back. He removed his cap and held it in both hands in front of him. The bright sunlight shone down on his silvery grey hair. Looking down at the grave, he spoke in a quiet, impressive tone four simple, all-meaning words: 'Lafayette, we are here.' "

The American army arrived in France to the tunes of popular war songs—"Over There," "It's a Long, Long Trail," and "Keep the Home Fires Burning." The Great War was the most emotional experience of almost everyone of that generation. They really believed that they were going to end war forever.

They were united in that effort. With the help of the American government and its Committee on Public Information, they came to believe that the Germans alone had caused the fighting. It took a great deal of one-sided persuasion, or *propaganda*, to convince Americans about the enemy.

The battles themselves cost many lives. World War I was fought by foot soldiers in trenches. When big cannons were added to modern weapons and fired at close range, the result was shocking. Six thousand out of 8,000 American marines died in one major battle at Belleau Wood in France, and there were many more battles. (See chart, page 585.) The American Expeditionary Force fought with the Allies in the last offensives of the war—the second battle of the Marne, at Soissons (swa-SON), Saint-Mihiel (SAN-mee-YEL), and at Meuse Argonne (MUZ ar-GON).

"Uncle Sam" posters called Americans to enlist in the army during World War I.

31. What type of war was it?

It was a trench war fought by foot soldiers.

While men were fighting in World War I, women were working in heavy industry.

In your opinion, what are the differences between fighting to take territory and fighting to preserve free governments?

587

In 1918, under the French commander Marshal Foch, the Allied armies finally attacked along the entire line dividing the two forces. The Germans were defeated at every point. Their king, or kaiser, resigned his throne. An agreement to stop fighting was signed. This agreement, or *armistice,* came on November 11, 1918.

Wilson Plans for Peace

Woodrow Wilson had a detailed plan for peace. Through his Fourteen Points, Wilson hoped to do away with the most repeated causes of war. He called for an end to secret treaties between nations which make other nations afraid and jealous. He stated that the conquest of another nation's territory must be ended. He said that certain groups of people had the right to have their own government. He called for freedom of the seas and for reducing military supplies.

Wilson's fourteenth point stated his most famous idea. It called for an organization of nations. This League of Nations would settle disagreements before they led to war.

The Treaty of Versailles

The conference to work out a general peace settlement was held at Versailles (vair-SIGH), near Paris. The major decisions were made by the Big Four—the leaders of the United States, Great Britain, France, and Italy. But Wilson could not get the European leaders to agree to most of his ideas for a peace settlement. The Treaty of Versailles was a harsh document. The first article did call for a League of Nations. But Germany and Austria lost some of their own land and colonies. They had to agree to pay huge sums for war damages and their armies and navies were restricted. Also, Germany had to accept responsibility for starting the war.

Wilson put all his hopes in the League. But the nation that would not agree to join the League or sign the Treaty of Versailles was the United States. Americans were exhausted by the war. They did not feel, as Wilson did, that they had won the chance to take responsibility to make the world better. Most Americans felt they had won the right to go back to their side of the Atlantic Ocean and forget the horror of war. Wilson could not convince enough Republicans to vote for the treaty or for the League. Senator Henry Cabot Lodge, the chairman of the Senate Foreign Relations Committee, could not convince the President to include the amendments many Republicans believed necessary. Wilson had not bothered to take the Republicans to the peace conference or to ask for their advice. They fought him and his ideas for peace.

These Black soldiers are being awarded the Distinguished Service Cross for bravery in the war. One of the most famous Black fighting units was the 369th Regiment.

32. Why did the United States refuse to join the League or sign the treaty?

1) Americans were exhausted by the war and believed that they had earned the right to go back home and forget about Europe. 2) Wilson had not taken any Republicans to the peace conference, nor had he consulted them. This angered the Republicans, who then refused to vote for the League or for the treaty. 3) Wilson refused to include amendments that the Republicans thought were necessary.

What failed—Wilson's idea, his practical plan, or both?

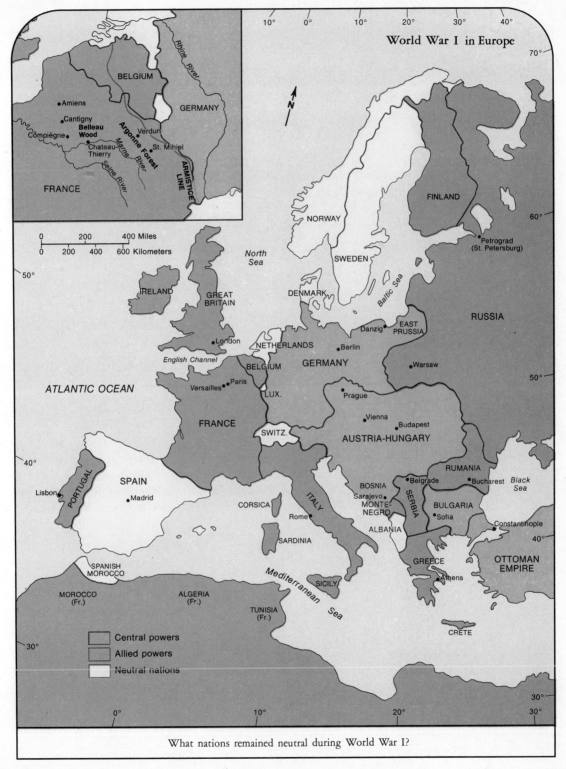

World War I in Europe

Inset map (France):
BELGIUM
Rhine River
GERMANY
• Amiens
• Cantigny
Belleau Wood
• Compiègne
• Verdun
Argonne Forest
• St. Mihiel
• Chateau-Thierry
Marne River
ARMISTICE LINE
FRANCE
Seine River

Main map labels:
NORWAY
FINLAND
SWEDEN
Petrograd (St. Petersburg)
North Sea
IRELAND
GREAT BRITAIN
DENMARK
Baltic Sea
RUSSIA
Danzig
EAST PRUSSIA
• London
NETHERLANDS
• Berlin
GERMANY
• Warsaw
ATLANTIC OCEAN
English Channel
BELGIUM
LUX.
• Versailles • Paris
• Prague
FRANCE
SWITZ.
• Vienna
• Budapest
AUSTRIA-HUNGARY
RUMANIA
• Bucharest
Black Sea
PORTUGAL
• Lisbon
SPAIN
• Madrid
CORSICA
ITALY
• Rome
BOSNIA
• Sarajevo
• Belgrade
SERBIA
MONTE-NEGRO
BULGARIA
• Sofia
• Constantinople
SARDINIA
ALBANIA
GREECE
• Athens
OTTOMAN EMPIRE
SPANISH MOROCCO
Mediterranean Sea
SICILY
MOROCCO (Fr.)
ALGERIA (Fr.)
TUNISIA (Fr.)
CRETE

Scale:
0   200   400 Miles
0   200   400   600 Kilometers

Legend:
Central powers
Allied powers
Neutral nations

What nations remained neutral during World War I?

589

The nations that remained neutral during World War I were Norway, Sweden, Denmark, the Netherlands, Luxembourg, Switzerland, Albania, Spain, and Spanish Morocco.

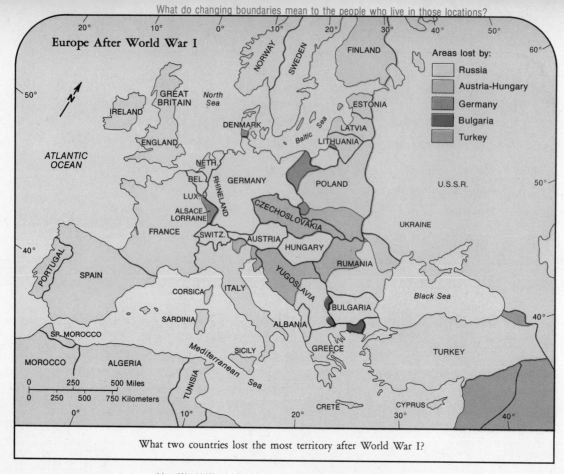

Europe After World War I

Areas lost by:
- Russia
- Austria-Hungary
- Germany
- Bulgaria
- Turkey

What two countries lost the most territory after World War I?

After World War I, Russia and Turkey lost the most territory.

33. How did Wilson's term end?

1) The United States signed its own peace treaty with Germany. 2) Wilson suffered a stroke on a nationwide trip trying to get Americans to tell their senators to vote for the treaty.

Wilson traveled across the nation by train to try to get Americans to tell their senators to vote for the treaty. The Senate rejected the treaty and the United States did not join the League. Wilson became seriously ill during the trip. He had a stroke, which left him partially paralyzed.

Woodrow Wilson recovered enough to finish his term in office. He had achieved more through laws at home than through power abroad. Wilson was remembered for his practical plans and his ideal that the American government lead America and the rest of the world in making people freer to try to help themselves.

Checking the facts

1. How did Wilson's foreign policy with small nations break down with Mexico?
2. Why did the Great War come about?
3. Why did the United States get involved in World War I?

Wilson believed in using government to take away the obstacles to freedom. What gets in the way of people's, groups, and nations' ability to choose how to improve their lives?

PUTTING IT ALL TOGETHER

UNDERSTANDING THE MAIN IDEAS

1. What had the Progressives accomplished under Roosevelt's leadership?
2. How did Taft differ from Roosevelt in his view of the presidency? What were the results of his presidency?
3. How did Woodrow Wilson's beliefs influence the actions he took as President?
4. What were Wilson's contributions to the nation?

ACTIVITIES

1. What would Theodore Roosevelt say about the kind of government action taken today? Answer this question in a brief essay. Make an outline of your ideas before you begin to write.
2. Read about one of the famous battles of World War I. Why do you think that war created such a great impression in the memory of the Western world? Incorporate your response to this question in a book report.
3. Compare pictures and cartoons of Theodore Roosevelt and William Howard Taft with those of the President today. How are the cartoons and pictures the same? How are they different? Do they get their message across in the same way? What do you think makes an effective political cartoon?

BOOKS TO READ

Graham, Shirley, *Booker T. Washington* (New York: Julian Messner, Inc., 1955).

Gurney, Gene, *Flying Aces of World War I* (New York: Random House, Inc., 1965).

Hoyt, Edwin P., *The Phantom Raider* (New York: Thomas Y. Crowell, 1969).

Leckie, Robert, *The Story of World War I* (New York: Random House, Inc., 1964).

Rouveral, Jean, *Pancho Villa: A Biography* (Garden City: Doubleday and Co., Inc., 1972).

chapter 23
America Tires of Improving
1918–1930

1. A LITTLE CHANGE, A LOT OF FEAR
2. THE PEOPLE'S REPRESENTATIVES AND THE PEOPLE
3. GOOD TIMES, BAD TIMES

INTRODUCTION

No nation of free people moves in only one direction at a time. Even when people share many values, differences are bound to arise. For example, some people may be pleased with changes that have taken place. But others may think that there has been the wrong kind of change, too much change, or not enough change.

In the period during and just after World War I, there seemed to be less direction than there had been before the war. Few people knew what the goals of the nation were. This was a sharp contrast to the days of Theodore Roosevelt and Woodrow Wilson. Both of these Presidents had very clear ideas about what kinds of action Americans should take at home and abroad. They were able to convince Americans of the need to take action. After the war, America's leaders were of another type. They were not too con-

	1919	1920	1921	1923	
Who?	President Woodrow Wilson	Americans	Warren G. Harding	Calvin Coolidge	
What?	provides for a League of Nations	listen to the first regular commercial radio broadcast	becomes the twenty-ninth President	becomes the thirtieth President	
Where?	at the Treaty of Versailles in France	in Detroit, Michigan	of the United States	of the United States	

Would you describe the feelings of people you know today as for or against change? What kinds of improving are they interested in?

cerned with taking action to bring about change. As you read about this time in America's history, think about the following questions:

1. What seemed to be the main goals of the American people during the years after World War I?
2. How did they go about achieving these goals?
3. What changes took place in American life after World War I?
4. How did these changes influence the way that Americans live today?
5. What role did the government play after World War I?

1. A LITTLE CHANGE, A LOT OF FEAR

The nation had struggled during World War I. It tried to grow enough food and make enough guns and ammunition. Everyone had helped in the war effort. Women had gone to work on farms and in factories. Some had become trolley conductors and police officers. People loaned money to the government by buying bonds that would be paid back with interest after the war was over.

By 1918 Americans had grown tired of trying to make themselves and the rest of the world better. What Americans wanted was a chance to relax and enjoy their prosperity. Despite this feeling of being tired, the spirit of reform did not die out completely. There were two major reform movements that won victories in the years after the war. Both became amendments to the Constitution.

No Liquor

There were many people in the nation who believed that the cause of war and evil was liquor. With their support the Eighteenth

1. What was the mood of America after the war?

1) Americans were tired of trying to make themselves and the rest of the world better. 2) Americans wanted to relax and enjoy their prosperity. 3) Some of the reform spirit did not die out completely.

2. What was the prohibition period?

1924	1925	1927	1929	1929
Native Americans	John Scopes	Charles Lindbergh	Herbert Hoover	Americans
are made full citizens	is tried and convicted for teaching evolution	makes the first solo airplane flight	becomes the thirty-first President	lose millions of dollars
of the United States	in a school in Tennessee	across the Atlantic Ocean	of the United States	in the stock market crash

How can the people of a free nation keep up their energy and spirit for improving over a long period of time?

People look on with mixed emotions as a prohibition agent destroys kegs of whiskey. Do you think prohibition was constitutional? Why or why not?

Prohibition was the time when the Eighteenth Amendment made the selling of alcoholic beverages illegal.

Amendment was approved in 1919. It made the selling of alcoholic drinks illegal. The period of forbidden drinking was called *prohibition*. But people soon realized that the law against drinking was hard to enforce. Many people made their own liquor. Professional criminals smuggled liquor into the country. They made huge sums of money from people who were not going to obey the law.

Women and the Vote

3. How did the nation become convinced that women should have the right to vote?

The work done by women during the war convinced people that they had earned the right to equal citizenship.

The other reform movement that won a victory after the war was woman's suffrage. The movement to give women the vote had been moving slowly until Alice Paul, a young Quaker with a doctorate from the University of Pennsylvania, entered the struggle. Paul had been in England where she had worked with the British feminists. She organized the Women's party which began to work for a national constitutional amendment giving the vote to women. The party quickly had over 50,000 members. This development

Prohibition raised the question of whether it should be against the law for people to do damage to themselves.

encouraged the National Woman Suffrage Association, organized by Susan B. Anthony and Elizabeth Cady Stanton in 1869, to take action. In 1915 the new president of the association, Carrie Chapman Catt, announced a six-year timetable in which to gain the vote for women. During this time, World War I resolved the issue. The work done by women during the war convinced people that they had earned the right to equal citizenship. The Nineteenth Amendment giving women the right to vote became law in 1920.

Some people had mixed feelings about the Nineteenth Amendment. A senator assured people that they need not worry about letting women vote. He reasoned that the vote "has not made women like men. They still love their homes and children just the same as ever." Some women argued against the vote. They said that women influenced their husbands' voting and therefore husbands' votes represented wives' votes, too. One woman argued that "the ballot will (not) help the wage-earning woman. Women must resort to organization . . . and trade unions." She argued that the vote had not prevented lower pay for women in the four states—Wyoming, Colorado, Utah, and Idaho—that already had women voters. In spite of the opposition, many women used their new right by voting for the first time in the election of 1920.

Jeannette Rankin of Montana was the first women elected to Congress. She served at the time women got the vote.

Blacks in the South

In the years from 1910 through the 1920's, millions of southern Blacks moved from rural areas to cities. They moved first to southern cities where there was cheap housing. The Black poor lived along the railroad tracks near the factories or along the rivers. These areas were run down. They had poor water supplies and sewer systems. There were no high-rise tenements as in New York. Blacks lived in shacks like the ones sharecroppers lived in on farms. In southern cities there was not one Black ghetto but, rather, servants' quarters in the same neighborhood as their employers'.

In southern cities Blacks provided skilled services for Whites, such as barbering and dressmaking. But as the years went on, Whites got those jobs, and many Blacks had to take jobs doing unskilled work. In the 1920's, 70 percent of the steelworkers in the city of Birmingham, Alabama, were Black. Leadership among southern Blacks went to those who had money and could buy property. Land was still a major symbol of power in the South. To own real estate in the city was everyone's goal. Middle-class Blacks—lawyers, doctors, and skilled tradespeople—were leaders in their communities.

In city neighborhoods middle-class Black women formed organizations to help other Blacks. One group was the Atlanta Neighborhood Union. It provided playgrounds for children and a health center near the two Black colleges—Morehouse and Spelman.

4. What was life like for southern Blacks after the war?

1) Many had moved to the cities where they lived in cheap housing near industry or their employers.
2) By the 1920's, 70 percent of the steelworkers in Birmingham were Black.
3) Some Blacks were in the professions and were community leaders.
4) Middle-class Black women formed organizations, such as the Atlanta Neighborhood Union, to help other Blacks.

Why is the location of Black housing important to our understanding of Blacks and Whites in the North and South?

The Blacks in the North

5. *Why were the Blacks in the North unhappy after the war?*

They had moved into northern cities to work in war jobs. After the war was over, those jobs were given to returning White veterans.

Many Blacks had moved North during World War I. The states of Alabama, Louisiana, Mississippi, and Tennessee actually had a loss of Black citizens during the war. In northern cities, such as Chicago and New York, Blacks moved into the old neighborhoods, or ghettos, immigrants had left.

Among Blacks there was disappointment that many of the wartime jobs that they had had in the North did not last. Employers would often fire Blacks and give their jobs to White veterans. Once the war was over, there was little attempt to get more rights and power for Blacks. Black reformers tried 25 boycotts of public transportation. But their efforts to end segregation on buses and trolleys failed.

Two new Black leaders appeared during this postwar period. They spread their messages to the new city dwellers in the developing Black ghettos of the big northern and western cities—New York, Chicago, Detroit, Cleveland, and Los Angeles. One was Asa Philip Randolph who became a union organizer—especially of the men who worked as porters on the Pullman sleeping cars. Randolph made harsh fun out of America's willingness to win a war in Europe and its unwillingness to work at solving its racial problems at home.

Marcus Garvey organized the Universal Negro Improvement Association to help Blacks in America and in Africa.

The other well-known Black leader in this postwar time was Marcus Garvey. He was born in Jamaica, an island in the Caribbean. He spoke for Black strength and power. Marcus Garvey's message was that there was no hope that Blacks would get fairness in America. Therefore, they should go back to Africa. "Get up you mighty race—you can accomplish what you will. . . . Africa for the Africans at home and abroad" was his message. Garvey was respected by many Black Americans. He was the head of the Universal Negro Improvement Association. He used signs and symbols to make Blacks feel pride in being black. He designed uniforms, gave sermons, and held parades. In 1921 Garvey declared a Republic of Africa with himself as President.

In addition to helping Blacks feel better about themselves, Garvey was successful in collecting a great deal of money from people who worked to help Blacks. Business cooperatives were formed so that Black people could share the cost of running businesses. Garvey started Black factories. He also formed a steamship company, called the Black Star Line.

Blacks in the Arts

The 1920's was a period in which Black writers, singers, and musicians become popular. Their work was praised by both Blacks

Why did post–World War I Black leaders look upon Blacks as a group to be organized rather than as individuals to be helped?

King Oliver's Creole Band performed in the 1920's. Louis Armstrong, second from right, later became a popular solo jazz trumpet player.

and Whites. These artists wanted to help other Blacks. Famous Black writers who lived in Harlem in New York City were Langston Hughes, Countee Cullen, Claude McKay, Jean Tooner, and James Weldon Johnson.

Jazz, a mixture of African and West Indian rhythms and religious music, was born in New Orleans, Louisiana. Black musicians such as Louis Armstrong spread the sound of jazz throughout the nation. People flocked to listen to Black jazz bands. Because of the influence of jazz on the time, the 1920's is often called the "Jazz Age."

The Red Scare

Americans were relieved that the war was over. Now they could take up their lives where they had left off. They turned against everything foreign. Foreigners in the United States were thought of as suspicious. Many Americans were worried that the recent revolution in Russia would spread to the United States. The Russian Revolution, which started in 1917, had overthrown the ruler, or tzar (SAR). At the end of 1917, the Bolsheviks, or Communists, took over the government. They did not allow private ownership of property.

During the 1920's Americans became suspicious of anyone who criticized the American government or the American system of property-owning and business. They were afraid that people might try to set up a government-owned, or *Communist*, system in the United States.

Members of the Communist party were called "Reds." The period

6. How did the "Red Scare" prompt Americans to act outside the law?

1) People suspected of being Communist spies were arrested, their homes were searched without court orders or warrants. 2) At their trial, Sacco and Vanzetti were not given proper treatment under American law.

How does an idea catch on that all critics of the government or of the economy are tied to the enemy?

597

in America's history when so many people were arrested as Communist spies was known as the "Red Scare." About 6,000 people were arrested during the peak of the scare in 1920. Their homes were searched without court orders, or warrants.

Fear and hatred were aimed particularly at new immigrants who had not yet become citizens. Some of them belonged to labor groups that wanted to change the American system of government. Some wanted no government at all. People who believe this are called *anarchists.*

When strikes occurred many people panicked. They thought that foreign revolutionaries, or *radicals*, were going to ruin the country. The fear became a kind of madness. In 1920 two men robbed a shoe factory in Massachusetts and killed a guard. Two Italian immigrants, Nicola Sacco and Bartolomeo Vanzetti, believed to be anarchists, were arrested and jailed for the crime. The trial was run unfairly. The judge joined in accusing the two men. They were kept in jail for seven years, and were finally executed in the electric chair.

Whether or not Sacco and Vanzetti were guilty, their treatment was not proper under American law. But fear of Communists and fear of foreigners combined to cause some Americans to act outside the law.

Limits on Immigration

7. Why did the number of immigrants drop?

Many Europeans tried to come to America during the years after

Ben Shahn painted this picture in protest of the Sacco-Vanzetti case. Sacco and Vanzetti are shown in the center, handcuffed.

World War I. Jobs were scarce and the land was still suffering from having been used for battlefields. In 1919, 110,000 immigrants arrived, followed by 430,000 in the next year and 805,000 in 1921.

Many Americans, even those who had been immigrants themselves, were afraid of these newcomers. They pressured their representatives in Congress to keep out immigrants from countries that might have "Red" or leftist or just different ways of thinking or behaving.

A new immigration law set up limits for each country that might send immigrants to the United States. These limits, or *quotas,* were supposed to keep the *ethnic*, or nationality, balance as it was in 1920. That is, of the 150,000 immigrants a year that were to be allowed into the country, more could come from Great Britain and northern Europe (France, Germany, Scandinavia, Switzerland) than would be allowed to come from other places. What actually happened was that all immigration dropped. Few people wanted to come from the countries that had the higher quotas. Italians and Greeks waited for years before they were allowed to come to the United States.

Mexican Immigration

The number of Mexicans who came to live in the United States more than doubled in the 1920's. Almost 500,000 Mexicans came during this time. This was almost 3 percent of the total Mexican population. American law discriminated against eastern Europeans. But Mexicans were able to enter for a period of about five years without any trouble.

Some Mexicans came to escape the continual fighting during the revolutions in their country. But most came for jobs. Sometimes they were hired by or signed contracts with American companies before they left Mexico. This contract labor paid lower wages than Americans got but much more than could be made in Mexico. Most of the Mexicans came to work in the mines, on the railroads, and on the large farms of the West. In 1920 the largest numbers came to live in Texas. Others went to California, Arizona, Colorado, New Mexico, Oklahoma, and Kansas. Although many Mexicans were able to get jobs in the United States, they were not accepted into most communities. Many preferred to stay by themselves so that they could follow their customs and be close to their friends. A Mexican song and prayer popular at the time tells how many Mexicans felt:

> "Goodbye, my beloved country. Now I am going
> away;

1) A new immigration law set up a quota for each country based on the 1920 ethnic or nationality balance. 2) Few people wanted to come from the countries that had the higher quotas.

8. What were the arrangements under which many Mexican Americans came to the United States?

1) Mexicans signed contracts with American companies before they left to work in the mines, on the railroads, and on the large farms of the West. 2) Contract wages were lower than what Americans got but were higher than in Mexico.

From your knowledge of American history, when people come to a new nation just for jobs, what difficulties are likely to arise?

"I go to the United States, where I intend to work. . . .

"I go sad and heavy-hearted to suffer and endure; My Mother Guadalupe, grant my safe return. . . .

"I go to the United States to seek to earn a living. Goodbye, my beloved land; I bear you in my heart.

"For I am not to blame that I leave my country thus; the fault is that of poverty, which keeps us all in want."

A New Kind of Intolerance

9. How did the actions of the Ku Klux Klan relate to its goals?

Even when the Red Scare was over, a number of organizations kept attacking foreigners and anyone else they felt was not American enough.

The Ku Klux Klan took advantage of this situation to launch new attacks against immigrants and anyone who was not White, Anglo-Saxon, or Protestant. The Klan had almost disappeared after the Blacks in the South had been kept from voting. But now they had a new cause. They set up a national organization with a national magazine. They sold robes and masks. Almost 2 million Americans became Klan members in the early 1920's. The organization had strength in the North and the South. Atlanta, Georgia, was the Klan headquarters. But Chicago and Indianapolis had larger Klans than those of other cities.

In 1926 members of the Ku Klux Klan marched in Washington, D.C. How did the Klan threaten American unity?

The Klan argued that modern ways of living were ruining the simpler way of life that had existed on farms and in small towns in America. The Klan wanted the nation to return to a style of living in which everyone knew everyone else and all had similar backgrounds. The Klan appealed to some real desires and real worries of many Americans.

The Klan used secrecy and violence to enforce its ideas. Jews, Catholics, foreigners, and Blacks were its targets. Most Americans did not buy its message of hatred. They spoke out against the Klan. Newspapers printed accounts of the tarring and feathering, the whipping, and hanging that Klansmen carried out under the protection of their masks.

Problems After the War

One of the problems in this postwar period was that organizations that really wished to help strengthen America by correcting some of its mistakes were also attacked by those who were afraid. Some people thought every reformer was a Communist.

600

Some people were worried about the crowded conditions in the cities where newcomers from the South, both Black and White, were competing for jobs. Cities in America after World War I were changing. They were developing more variety. They also were facing more problems. Some people connected the variety to the problems. Instead of trying to learn how to build better houses and transportation, they tried to move away from the strangers or to keep them out.

Many Americans blamed "the other people" for the existence of the very rich and the very poor in the crowded cities. There was a good deal of sadness that the war had neither cured the problems of society, nor made American democracy perfect.

1) The Klan wanted the nation to return to a style of living in which everyone knew everyone else and had similar backgrounds.
2) The KKK tarred and feathered and whipped Jews, Catholics, and foreigners. In addition to these injustices, Blacks were also hanged.

Checking the facts

1. How did the formation of laws and organizations reflect the mood of the people after World War I?
2. What were the cities like in this postwar period?

2. THE PEOPLE'S REPRESENTATIVES AND THE PEOPLE

10. How did people's attitudes regarding government change during the postwar period?

They voted in two Presidents who thought that there was enough popular representation to preserve individual liberty.

America was the home of a variety of people. But in the 1920's some of those people turned on each other. They even got their

This view of New York City was painted by Georgia O'Keefe in the 1920's. What was her impression of the city?

Why do some people always have to blame some person or group for every problem? Why is it difficult to accept complicated causes for good times and for times of trouble?

representatives in Congress to pass laws limiting the variety of people who could come to America. In the cities they lived in neighborhoods with people like themselves. If they had enough money, they moved out of the cities to the suburbs to live with people like themselves. Variety did not mean togetherness.

What had happened to another ideal, that of representing every person in government in order to preserve individual liberty? Roosevelt and Wilson and their political parties had worked hard to make the government the protector of liberty. They had also tried to control the big corporations that now ran much of the country's manufacturing, buying, selling, investing, and hiring.

In the postwar period the people voted for two Presidents who thought that there was enough popular representation. Those two Presidents also believed that the government should not regulate or control business. Businesses should be left alone. They believed that the ones that were run well would survive. The ones that were run poorly would go out of business. The ones that got bigger deserved more business. And the smaller ones would have to try harder or go out of business.

Harding Becomes President

11. Why was Harding the President for the times?

He was lazy and seemed unable to make a decision. But a great many people seemed to be tired of improving anyway.

Warren Harding was elected President in 1920. He had been the owner and editor of a newspaper in Ohio. He also had been a United States senator for one term. Harding was a handsome man. He looked like a President is supposed to look. This image was his greatest advantage. His greatest disadvantage, as described by his best friend, was that he "just did not like to work." By 1920 many people had had enough of reform. They chose a man from the Republican party who would not push anyone to do anything.

Harding was not only lazy. He seemed unable to make a decision. He let his cabinet officers run the country. Some of them were fine managers. But few of his advisers had any new ideas about how to improve society. Many people were tired of improving anyhow.

What Did the Harding Administration Do?

12. How was the Harding administration able to pay back most of the war debts?

It spent little money.

Harding's secretary of the treasury wanted to reduce taxes paid by rich people and corporations. This plan was supposed to make more money available to expand businesses and hire more workers. He had no plan, however, to help the people who had little money. Nor did he have a plan to help the farmers. Now that the war was over, farmers were in trouble. Europeans could grow their own food again. This left American farmers with too much to sell, or a *surplus*. There was a new tariff, the Fordney-McCumber Tariff of 1922, which was aimed at helping some new businesses by raising

What is meant by "Harding created a vacuum. Others filled it and used the power."

duties on imports. The new taxes were on rayon, china, toys, and chemicals.

The Harding administration did not spend much money. It managed to pay back most of the money that had been borrowed during the war years. For this it was praised by those who had jobs, and those who ran large businesses, and those who had bought war bonds.

Harding's biggest problem came from some of his old Ohio friends. He got jobs for these friends in Washington. Some of his friends were dishonest, and their deals became known to the public. The scandals that took place ruined Harding's reputation. The worst scandal took place in 1922. Secretary of the Interior Albert B. Fall sold government oil reserves (from The Teapot Dome Reserve in Wyoming) to private business and took huge payments for doing so. Fall's crime was uncovered, and he went to prison. But Harding was blamed.

13. Why was the Harding administration criticized?

1) Fall, his secretary of the interior, sold government oil preserves to private business and took huge payments for doing so. 2) Fall went to prison, but Harding was blamed.

Harding felt that his friends had betrayed him. While returning to Washington from a trip in the summer of 1923, he died of a heart attack. Calvin Coolidge, the Vice-President, became President. Coolidge was able to convince many Americans that the Republican party was now in the hands of honest people in spite of the Harding scandals. The Republicans and Calvin Coolidge won the election of 1924.

Coolidge Takes Over

What was the reason behind Coolidge's success at the polls? More people had jobs in 1924. The United States controlled more land and resources than all of Europe put together. Many people agreed with Coolidge that "the business of America is business." Coolidge believed that the government should represent the wealth and health of the nation. The best thing that government could do was to leave the system alone. For people who were enjoying reasonable success, this was a worthwhile belief.

The Roaring Twenties

Not all Americans were content with letting the system alone. They were disappointed that World War I had not made the world fairer or more democratic. They used their art as writers, poets, and painters to tell the world how they felt. The happy-go-lucky mood of many Americans made many artists leave home for other places, such as Paris, France. The postwar period was a loud, fast-moving time. People were most concerned with themselves. They liked to go dancing and to the movies just for the fun of it. They liked lively music and going places in fast cars. They made heroes

Calvin Coolidge, as Vice-President, was untouched by the Harding scandals. He won the presidential election of 1924.

Can you look at America's success and problems at the same time? Why do some people only look at one or the other?

603

Babe Ruth played baseball for the New York Yankees. His 714 home runs got him elected to the National Baseball Hall of Fame.

out of the airplane pilots and sports personalities of the day. They liked all kinds of achievement, such as the building of skyscrapers. This time came to be known as "the Roaring Twenties."

The Movies

By the middle of the 1920's the movies had become the fourth largest industry in the nation. By 1927 there were 20,500 motion picture theaters. Eighteen million people could go to the movies at one time.

It was not only large cities that had movie theaters. About half of them were in towns that had fewer than 5,000 people. Almost everyone went to the movies.

The theaters in large cities were very fancy buildings. They were often large enough to hold full symphony orchestras and pipe organs. Between showings of movies there were stage shows with dancers, singers, and comedians.

The early movies were silent. They were films of stage plays without the words. An organ or a piano player accompanied the film as it was shown. This was done to create a mood. The first film to have a dramatic story line and use the camera for special effects was *The Birth of a Nation*. It was produced in 1915. This was a feature film, not a short subject. People who came to see it were charged $2.00, the same price paid for a stage play. The story showed the Ku Klux Klan in a favorable light and produced an angry response from Black Americans. From a technical point of view, however, the movie did show how historical stories were well-suited to movies.

14. Why did movie studios move to California?

Talking pictures were such a success that filmmakers wanted to make them all year. The California weather was good for year-round movie making.

By 1927 filmmakers were able to put film, voice, music, and sound effects together. The first sound motion picture was *The Jazz Singer,* starring Al Jolson. It was an immediate success. Filmmakers wanted to make more "talking pictures." To do this they needed to film all year. And so film studios moved from New York and New Jersey to California because of its good weather. The town of Hollywood, California, became the moviemaking center. Movies gave people the sensation that they were going around the world, for example, to the North African desert in *Beau Geste* and *The Sheik*. They took them back in time, as in *Robin Hood* and *The Three Musketeers*. Movies became an everyday part of American life.

The Automobile

15. How did Ford's plan make it possible for the average American to afford a car?

For many Americans the greatest adventure was the automobile. It created exciting new possibilities in their lives. They could go whenever and wherever they pleased. With a car they could live far from their jobs.

Henry Ford took the car, invented by the French, and thought of a way to produce it in great numbers. Ford's plan called for a moving assembly line where each worker would do one small job that added to the building of the whole car. This plan cut the costs of producing cars. They could then be sold at a price that many people could pay. By 1914 Ford's workers put a car together in 93 minutes. By 1925 the Ford factory made 9,000 cars a day, each selling for less than $300.

Frederick Taylor showed factory managers how careful planning could cut down the number of steps that each worker had to make in manufacturing an item. Minutes were saved by using Taylor's method. Minutes multiplied by many workers meant saving hours. Saving hours meant making more profits. There were some serious drawbacks to these advances, however. Working fast at only one job caused trouble among factory workers. They got bored and took days off or slowed down. Ford raised the pay for his factory workers from $2.00 a day to $5.00 a day—and solved the problem.

The output of automobiles more than tripled between World War I and 1923. By 1929 there were almost as many private cars on the road as there were families in America—23 million.

Automobiles helped other businesses to grow. Tires, spark plugs, paint, glass, rubber, nickel, and oil had to be produced for cars. Roads had to be built. The number of miles of roads almost doubled between 1921 and 1929. New jobs in gas stations, roadside restaurants, and hotels were created to serve tourists. Housing construction in the suburbs speeded up to meet the demands of people moving to obtain more space. With the growth of suburbs came real-estate developers, insurance brokers, and branch banks.

Mass production of the automobile gave a boost to the advertising business. Do you know why?

1) He developed the moving assembly line where each worker would do one small job that added to the building of the whole car. 2) The line saved time and money in production, thus bringing down the cost of each car.

The Radio

The first radio station, KDKA, went on the air in Pittsburgh in 1920. By 1927 there were 732 stations across the nation. Radio made it possible for people all across the country to hear the same music, the same sermons, and the same speeches by the President of the United States. Public opinion could now be influenced quickly, for better or for worse. Listening to the radio became a regular family activity.

The Airplane

Airplanes had been used successfully for combat in World War I. After the war manufacturers continued to work at making better planes. What spurred on the age of the airplane, however, was the first nonstop flight across the Atlantic Ocean by aviator Charles A.

16. What effect did the radio have on Americans?

1) Radio made it possible for everyone to hear the same music, the same sermons, and the same speeches. 2) Public opinion could now be influenced quickly, for better or for worse.

17. Why did Lindbergh's flight excite Americans?

What changes in the way Americans live were caused by the airplane?

605

Charles Lindbergh became a national hero when he made his famous flight. How would this feat affect transportation?

Compare this flapper's style of dress with the women pictured in Chapter 19. How had women's lives changed since the late 1800's?

Lindbergh. He was 25 years old when he made that famous flight. On May 20, 1927, he took off in his gasoline heavy plane *The Spirit of St. Louis*. Lindbergh landed in Paris 33 hours and 39 minutes later.

Lindbergh's flight excited Americans more than did any other event in the 1920's. Perhaps the most important aspects of his adventure were that he said he would do it and that he did it alone. Lindbergh expressed values that Americans admired. He was an individual, not a giant profit-making business. He was handsome, brave, and quiet. He made Americans feel proud again.

Changing Attitudes Toward Women

One of the biggest changes during the 1920's was in the behavior of women. Women had played an important part in the war. They never went back to their old ways of dressing, looking, and acting. Both men and women changed their attitudes about what women could and should do.

Working women no longer came solely from families in which women had to work so that the family could eat. In the 1920's many married women whose husbands had jobs were also working. Not every aspect of women's new activities was serious. Shorter skirts, smoking, wearing makeup, and going to nightclubs were the most noticeable aspects of women's changing behavior in the 1920's.

Obviously happiness of the individual was thought to be the most important goal of the 1920's. How far America had drifted from Theodore Roosevelt's national goals and Woodrow Wilson's ideal of national goodness!

Checking the facts

1. How did the Harding and Coolidge administrations reflect the nation's feelings about government and business?
2. What changes did new inventions make in the American way of life?
3. How had the role of women changed during the years following World War I?
4. How did this change affect the work force?

What do you today think about the flappers? How have attitudes about women changed since the 1920's?

THE AGE OF THE AUTOMOBILE

Think of your life without cars, trucks, or buses. How would you get to school, to the store, or to a friend's house? How would food and other items get to the stores? It is hard to imagine life without these forms of transportation. But the automobile is a recent arrival on the American landscape. In 1893 a single-cylinder motor carriage, put together by bicycle builders made its appearance. In 1900 there were only 8,000 cars in the United States. The roads were made for horse drawn carriages. There were no drive-in restaurants or gas stations. There were no quick trips to the next town or city.

In 1908 Henry Ford started work on a new car that would change the way Americans lived. He began to increase the number of cars available to the public by focusing on the production of one model. This car was called the Model T. The rapid growth in the production of this car gave rise to new industries and jobs. Besides the building of cars, other new products were needed. Services for cars and trucks were set up. These included gas stations, repair shops, and retail outlets to sell the cars. The towns and states had to build roads.

With the building of new roads, towns that were isolated before were now connected. The car and the roads connected Americans to one another in a new way. By 1929, the United States was producing 4.6 million cars and 771,000 trucks. This was 85 percent of all the cars and trucks produced in the world. In one generation the automobile had changed the way Americans worked, where they lived, and how they played.

3. GOOD TIMES, BAD TIMES

The war years were years of movement from farm to city and from city to city. They were years when cities grew in area by adding on, or annexing, the suburbs and small towns nearby. The cities grew in population. The smaller cities in the South showed the influence of the nation's new industrial life. They were connected with the rest of the nation through networks of transportation systems and big businesses.

1) Lindbergh's was the first individual nonstop flight across the Atlantic. 2) He said that he would do it, and he did it alone. 3) Lindbergh expressed values that Americans admired.

The Cities Grow in the South

The cities that grew in the South during the war years were tied to the new national railroad system. Atlanta, Georgia, was a railroad center as well as the home office of the Federal Reserve bank. It saw a great increase in population. Some older cities that were shipping centers declined in population. Among these were Charleston, South Carolina; Savannah, Georgia; and Mobile, Alabama. Market towns that were not railroad centers, such as Augusta, Georgia, and Montgomery, Alabama, also lost population. Only the port cities had any sizable foreign-born population. Even there it was never more than 10 percent of the whole.

The cities that were tied to industry because they could supply oil grew the fastest. People moved to those cities for jobs. The cities of Fort Worth and Houston in Texas had oil refineries. Houston was also a major port for shipping cotton and oil.

Houston soon became the largest city in the Southwest. Dallas, Texas, was a center for food processing and clothing. Dallas also prospered because it was chosen as the site for the Federal Reserve bank in that large southwestern district.

Despite the growth of southern cities, in 1920 three quarters of the population of the South still lived in small communities. However, urban life was becoming the way of life and the standard of living that many people wanted. And many southerners were on the move. A school survey in Memphis, Tennessee, showed that only about 2 percent of the White parents had been born in that city. Even the most powerful people in southern cities had probably migrated from somewhere else in the South.

America Continues to Expand

During the 1920's many Americans were attracted to activities that were big, powerful, and splashy. In that period people worried less about those who were not represented in America's important decisions. They also put aside thoughts about those who did not have a fair share of America's opportunities.

There was a boom in inventions and a boom in investing. People who had money bought stocks in businesses. The businesses used the money to expand. They expected that there would always be customers for whatever goods and services they could produce.

Everyone got "hot tips" on what stock to buy. More than a million Americans borrowed money to buy stock. They hoped to sell their stock at high prices and thereby make enough money to repay their loans and make profits, too.

The People Choose

The presidential election of 1928 came during a period of prosperity. Calvin Coolidge chose not to run for another term. The Republicans ran a man who was well-known for his ability as a manager. Herbert Hoover was an engineer. He had been in charge of the successful program to bring relief, medicine, food, and clothing to Europe during and after World War I. He had served in the cabinets of Harding and Coolidge as secretary of commerce.

The Democrats chose Governor Al Smith of New York as their candidate. Smith was a Catholic, and he favored getting rid of prohibition. He was a lively personality who contrasted sharply with the bland but efficient Herbert Hoover. Smith promised to provide services that city people wanted: schools, parks, and water, and good administrators to deliver services and to listen to people.

The nation had no reason to change leaders. Business looked good. Most people were content with their lives. And many people thought that Smith was very different from the leaders that they were used to. Hoover and the Republicans won a smashing victory. It almost seemed as if the Democrats could not recover from the loss. However, a close look at the results showed that two groups of voters had supported Smith: people who lived in the cities— many of them immigrants and Catholic—and farmers who could no longer sell their crops for good prices.

Herbert Hoover became President during an unfortunate time. How did he deal with the nation's problems?

The Great Crash

During the 1920's some events were taking place at home and abroad that Americans failed to pay attention to. American farmers were unable to sell their crops. Farms and businesses in Europe were also having trouble finding buyers. None of these changes stopped the excitement of the 1920's. A great many Americans had faith that somehow there would always be buyers for American products. And so they continued to borrow in order to invest in American businesses.

Many Americans were satisfied with the lives that they led. The dream of owning property, of owning one's own home, had become real for many Americans. Many of these people were the children and grandchildren of immigrants. They had believed in the system of opportunity and hard work. Now they had what they wanted.

The sense of satisfaction that people felt made the shock of bad news that much greater. On October 24, 1929, so many people began to sell their stocks in businesses that there were almost no buyers for them. This was the sharpest drop the stock market had ever suffered. It was a stock market crash.

20. What caused the stock market to crash?

1) Farmers and businesses were producing more than they could sell. 2) When people became aware of the surplus, they began to sell their stocks in business. 3) There were not enough buyers for the stock.

In order to understand enough to vote intelligently people should know more than whether they "feel happy." Where should a voter go for information? When should a voter get that information?

609

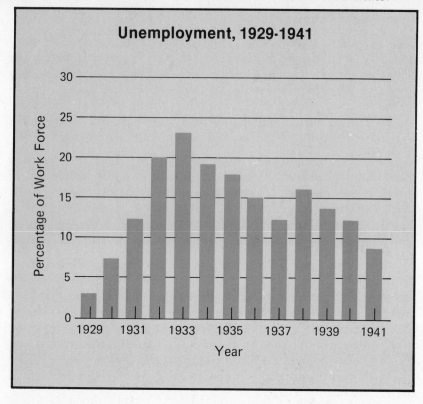

Unemployment, 1929-1941

Percentage of Work Force

Year

Several people tried to tell one another that if everyone acted as if the future *were* going to be all right, then it *would* be all right. After all, they argued, faith in the future causes people to build businesses, buy stocks, houses, and cars. The mayor of New York City even asked the movie houses to show cheerful movies. But nothing worked to build up confidence. Within less than a week the dollar value of the stock of America's most important businesses had dropped 77 percent.

Business Slowdown

When the future seems dark, owners of factories produce less. Factories that produce less need fewer workers. When workers are laid off from their jobs, they do not buy automobiles, radios, and washing machines. This in turn causes less production and more layoffs. There are fewer consumers with money to buy products. These conditions signal a business depression. And a business depression is what happened in Europe and America after the stock market crash of 1929.

The depression lasted over seven years. There were signs of it everywhere—empty shops, smokeless factory chimneys, people begging for money on the streets. The writer Frederick Lewis Allen

21. What were the effects of the stock market crash?

1) Factories produced less, workers were laid off, people could not buy; this situation caused less production and more layoffs.
2) The depression lasted over seven years.

Faith and trust in each other are important to the nation's future. In how many ways?

said that in a ten-block walk in a rich section of New York City, a person would be asked for money four or five times. Railroads, the first sign of growing prosperity after the Civil War, had shorter trains. There were fewer goods, or freight, to ship, and fewer people had money to go anywhere.

Who Was Hurt?

To be without a job for the first time in one's life and have no hope of getting one were frightening. To have a house and a car and no cash was strange. How long could people go on believing that some day they could pay their bills and that some day they, too, would be paid for their services?

It was not a personal feeling that someone was out to get you. But it was a hopeless feeling. Every day in cities there were long lines of people waiting for bread given by charity groups. There were people selling apples on street corners. Some people wandered the city streets or huddled together to keep warm. They had the feeling that the situation was beyond their control.

People who had been thrown out of their homes because they could not pay the rent grouped together in shacks made of packing boxes. These shantytowns could be seen outside the city limits. They were nicknamed "Hoovervilles." Americans had just recently voted for candidates who did not believe in government action. However, they blamed Hoover and the Republicans for not trying to help them. Homeless people drifted from park bench to park bench or from town to town. They tried to find food and a place to sleep.

To make matters worse, a severe *drought*, or a long period without rain, hit the area from Texas to the Dakotas beginning in 1930. Dust storms blew away the rich topsoil of the farming regions in this area. Once the land was useless, farmers and their families began to leave.

People who had been rich now found themselves without cash. They had to let their servants go, and then the servants starved. Many lived on handouts from relatives who had cash.

Among workers in the worst situation were the coal miners. When the mines shut down, there was no one to turn to. There were no stores and no skilled workers with whom one could trade. Some lived on dandelions and the roots of weeds. Blacks suffered because they had little. Blacks in northern cities had been hired last and were fired first. They lost much that they had recently gained.

Hoover's Plan for Recovery

Herbert Hoover knew that the first step was to build confidence. Americans would have to begin to trust the future in order to start

22. How did the depression affect American life?

1) Some lived by waiting in bread lines supplied by charity groups. 2) Those who had lost their homes lived in shantytowns made of packing boxes.

This picture was taken during the depths of the economic depression. What emotions does this woman's face express?

What kind of action was needed to help the nation's unemployed?

again. People had to get back to work. Businesses had to start up production again.

Hoover knew that people in every kind of job in every region of the country would have to do something. He asked business people to work together to pay decent wages and to set fair prices. He promised them that if they got together, the government would not use the antitrust laws against them. Hoover asked that farmers form cooperatives to sell their crops. Then they would compete less with each other and could keep their prices high enough. He let the government buy surplus wheat and cotton and store it, giving farmers good prices for those crops.

Hoover also wanted the Federal Reserve bank to get more money into circulation. He said that banks would have to lend more so that business could expand and hire more workers. He asked people who could to give more to charity.

Hoover's recovery plan left a great deal of the work to the cities and states. But they did not have enough tax money coming in to help. However, Hoover believed that the federal government should not do more. Although he knew what action was needed, he thought that it would be wrong for the federal government to do more than help people to get started. For example, Hoover agreed that farmers could borrow money from the government to buy seed and buy food for their cattle. But he was opposed to having the federal government give food and money directly to farmers. Hoover even agreed to a higher tariff, the Hawley–Smoot Tariff of 1930. Its aim was to promote American production by making it hard for foreign businesses to compete with American businesses. But by 1930 Europe was also suffering a depression. Hoover failed to realize that American and European countries needed to trade to pull themselves out of the depression.

For people on breadlines and those who were frightened, Hoover was not doing enough. The Americans who supported Harding and Coolidge in the 1920's switched their votes in the 1930's.

Old Progressives, city voters, farmers, and Blacks all looked for new leadership. Did anyone have a plan?

Checking the facts

1. What factors helped the cities of the South grow?
2. What caused the business depression?
3. Why did people become discontented with Hoover?

The depression occurred in Europe too. Why do Americans need other nations to be successful?

PUTTING IT ALL TOGETHER

UNDERSTANDING THE MAIN IDEAS

1. What seemed to be the main goals of the American people after World War I?
2. How did they go about achieving those goals?
3. What changes took place in American life after World War I?
4. How did these changes influence the way that Americans live today?
5. What role did the government play after World War I?

ACTIVITIES

1. What action are women taking in your community to achieve more recognition for themselves? What opposition is there? What arguments are used by each side? Prepare a brief oral report on this topic. Then present it to your class.
2. How much effort should newcomers to America make to speak standard English and learn Anglo-American customs? What should parents teach their children about the customs and beliefs of their ancestors? Should parents require children to practice ethnic customs? Write a brief essay in which you answer these questions.
3. Read a book about one of the famous people of the 1920's. Why was that person so popular? Incorporate your findings in a brief book report.
4. Write a short essay on the topic: What causes changes in fashions or fads? Compare the fashions and fads of the 1920's to those of today. How are they different? How are they similar?

BOOKS TO READ

Katz, William Loren, *From the Progressive Era to the Great Depression* (New York: Watts Publishing Co., 1974).

Meltzer, Milton, *Langston Hughes: A Biography* (New York: Thomas Y. Crowell, 1968).

Peare, Catherine Owens, *The Herbert Hoover Story* (New York: Thomas Y. Crowell, 1965).

chapter 24
The Government Leads

1932–1937

1. A NEW DEAL
2. PLANNING ON A LARGE
   SCALE

INTRODUCTION

The terrible depression made it certain that the voters would change political parties in the election of 1932. What was unexpected was the excitement the Democratic candidate caused among the American people. This chapter is the story of Franklin Delano Roosevelt's plan, or New Deal, for America. As you read, try to answer some of the following questions:

1. How did Americans try to solve their problems during the depression?
2. How did government spending of tax dollars help private citizens?
3. Whom should government help today?

	1931	1932	1933	1933-1938	
Who?	Japanese troops	Franklin Roosevelt	Adolf Hitler	President Roosevelt	
What?	invade China and conquer	is nominated presidential candidate	becomes chancellor	introduces New Deal programs	
Where?	Manchuria	at the Democratic Convention	of Germany	in the United States	

1. A NEW DEAL

Franklin Delano Roosevelt had been brought up to be a public leader. His family had education, money, and a history of political action. By the time of the 1932 election, Roosevelt had had a great deal of political experience. He was his party's choice for Vice-President in 1920. He had held national office as Woodrow Wilson's assistant secretary of the navy. He had survived an attack of infantile paralysis, which left him crippled in both legs at the age of 40. Instead of leaving public life, he worked hard in the Democratic party organization. He was in his second term as governor of New York, and 50 years old, when he ran for President. As a political candidate, Roosevelt was the right person, in the right place, at the right time.

1. What experience did Roosevelt have in government?

1) He had served as Wilson's assistant secretary of the navy. 2) He was in his second term as governor of New York when he ran for President.

Faith in Roosevelt

Franklin Roosevelt captured the imagination of the American people. He was handsome. He had overcome a personal handicap. He was a superb public speaker. And he sounded confident. He knew that Americans had to have faith in the future. Businesses had to take a chance on new investments, and consumers had to be willing to buy. He knew that Americans who differed from each other would have to believe that the whole of America was worth working for and paying for. His most difficult job was to convince Americans that they could solve their problems.

2. Why did Roosevelt have the faith of the American people?

He believed that if Americans worked together, they could make a better future.

Where does such faith come from? In a free country, it must come freely from individuals. But it has to have something to attach itself to. Franklin Roosevelt did not have answers to the problems of America, but he cared about the people who had problems. He sounded as if people working together could make the future better. The American people attached their faith to Roosevelt. He won the election of 1932 by a popular vote of almost 6 million. He won the electoral vote of all but six of the states. The Democratic party was now the party in power.

1934	1935	1936	1937	1938
Native Americans	Congress	American workers	Franklin Roosevelt	German troops
are allowed to own tribal lands	passes the Social Security Act to help people	complete the Hoover Dam	becomes President for a second term	occupy the Sudetenland
in the United States	in the United States	on the Colorado River	in the United States	in Czechoslovakia

FDR reminded people that they could trust each other. He also had the kind of personality that made people want to trust him. What kind of leader can you trust?

In his Inaugural Address, Roosevelt gave the people hope.

"This great Nation will endure as it has endured, will revive and will prosper. So, first of all, let me assert my firm belief that the only thing we have to fear is fear itself—nameless, unreasoning, unjustified terror which paralyzes needed efforts to convert retreat into advance."

Roosevelt's First 100 Days

"This nation asks for action." But what kind? The new President gathered around him a group of people who had ideas about what might be done. No one had one big plan to include all the parts of the economy. But Roosevelt knew that Hoover's plan had failed. Asking people to cooperate and to give small government loans was not enough. Roosevelt decided there had to be action on every part of the economy. There had to be help for every group that demanded it. Action had to come right away. A great many people who wanted to help came to Washington to think up new ideas. They felt free to try new ways.

Roosevelt organized a separate executive office of the President. It was made up of people who worked directly for the President and helped him form new ideas for new laws. Usually this was the job of Congress. Now Roosevelt often sent a draft of a bill to Congress along with his request for a law.

Within his first 100 days in office, Roosevelt took advantage of the excitement from the campaign and his election. He got Congress to pass a long list of laws to give a boost to a number of different parts of the nation's economy. (See chart, page 617.) Roosevelt believed the government owed every American at least enough help for survival and "getting along." This list of actions reached a great many people very quickly.

Relief Programs

Roosevelt realized that solving the causes of problems was going to take too long. First, the people who were suffering needed relief. A social worker, Harry Hopkins, was made head of relief projects. The government set aside $500 million for getting direct aid to individuals. The relief agency spent money giving food, clothing, housing, fuel, and medicine to people who were in need.

People were grateful for relief, but they wanted a chance to work for what they got. Hopkins planned a program in which the government would make work available to them. The plan called for hiring people to do jobs that private business ordinarily did not

Roosevelt had been crippled by polio. He used special devices to help him stand while speaking to an audience.

3. How did Roosevelt get relief to those who were suffering?

1) A relief agency was created. It spent $500 million for food, clothing, housing, fuel, and medicine for people who were in need.
2) People were hired to do jobs that private business ordinarily did not do.
3) The W.P.A. funded artists, musicians, and actors.

616

The New Deal, 1933-1938

ACT OR AGENCY	SOME PROVISIONS
Civilian Conservation Corps (CCC) 1933	Established work camps for conservation.
Agricultural Adjustment Act (AAA) 1933	Decreased farm surplus by limiting production. Established banks to lend money to farmers at low interest rates.
Federal Deposit Insurance Corp. (FDIC) 1933	Insured bank deposits.
Tennessee Valley Authority (TVA) 1933	Established a government corporation to develop the resources of the area.
National Recovery Administration (NRA) 1933	Helped industry set up fair codes of cooperation. Gave labor more power in labor disputes.
Public Works Administration (PWA) 1933	Set up public projects to provide employment and increase business activity.
Civil Works Administration (CWA) 1933	Made work for the unemployed.
Works Progress Administration (WPA) 1935	Set up large-scale national work programs.
National Youth Administration (NYA) 1935	Provided work for needy students.
Social Security Act 1935	Gave financial help to the unemployed and the aged.
Food, Drug, and Cosmetic Act 1938	Required makers of foods, drugs and cosmetics to list products' ingredients.
Fair Labor Standards Act 1938	Established minimum wages and hours for workers in interstate trade. Prohibited children under 16 to work.

do. These were jobs such as raking leaves and building public playgrounds and swimming pools.

Unemployment was a real worry to the administration. The American people placed a high value on hard work and opportunity. Hopkins showed the President stories of people in professions who were out of work. These people included musicians, dancers, artists, actors, and lawyers. Many of them found that when other people had no cash, they quickly stopped paying for music lessons and lawyers' fees. Older people and the handicapped were also among the first to be laid off when jobs were in short supply.

Roosevelt's response was to use tax dollars to pay these people to work. Groups of artists, musicians, and actors found that their work was paid for by the government. Working artists were often placed in small towns. Some exciting work was done with tax dollars under the Works Progress Administration (WPA).

FDR's plan was to tax people who have money and then use this money to pay others to do work. What are the advantages and disadvantages of this method? Is this method better for a short-term or a long-term solution?

617

Frances Perkins was the first woman appointed to the presidential cabinet. Previously, she had worked to improve conditions in industry.

Secretary of Labor Frances Perkins was the first woman to hold a cabinet position. She told the story of an elderly lawyer who was unable to find clients. He got a WPA job as assistant caretaker at a small seaside park. He did double the work anyone could have expected of him. He supervised children's play and made himself useful and agreeable to the whole community:

"I had occasion to see him from time to time," Mrs. Perkins said, "and he would always ask me to take a message to the President. He thanked the President for a job, which paid him $15 a week and kept him from starving to death. It was an honorable job that made him feel useful and not like a bum, he would say with tears in his eyes. . . ."

Public Building Projects

Other kinds of jobs were the big construction projects or public works, such as dams, roads, and post offices. These projects took tax money, which had been raised across the country, and hired people in those areas that most needed jobs. The Public Works Administration was the agency that supervised the projects.

Young men who could not get jobs or job-training were helped by the Civilian Conservation Corps (CCC). The age limit was 18 to 25, and the jobs were in planting forests and developing national parks. These jobs made new resources for the nation where no private business could afford to do them.

One of the main promises of the New Deal was that money would quickly get into the hands of individuals. With money in hand, they would have buying power. Their buying would help business which would then be able to rehire the people they had laid off.

Government in Banking, Business, and Farming

4. How did Roosevelt's approach differ from Hoover's?

Roosevelt never failed to try an idea because of a belief that the government should not do too much.

Quick ways of hiring people were only a short-term kind of action. What could be done to prevent the bank panics and bank closings that seemed to come in 20-year cycles? What could be done to help business plan so that there would not be so much cutthroat competition? What could be done to keep American farmers from producing more than they could sell? These were some of the questions with which Roosevelt had to deal.

As Roosevelt's programs appeared, it became clear that he wanted government to take action in banking, business, and farming. He knew that under the Constitution the federal government had the

618

power to make rules and use its tax dollars. Government could create businesses, set working conditions, and change farming, if the lawmakers agreed.

Roosevelt took any action he thought might work. He never failed to try an idea because of a belief that the government should not do too much. This was a different approach from the one taken by Hoover. If only some of the actions worked, that was fine with Roosevelt. If some worked for only a short while, then that was fine too. If some failed, then Roosevelt was ready and willing to try something else.

Banking

When Roosevelt first took office, he closed all the banks. Soon after, he sent in government examiners to find out which banks had enough reserves and good management. Banks that met these standards were allowed to reopen. Others never did, and people who had put their money in them lost every penny.

To keep that kind of loss from happening again, Congress passed a law that insured bank accounts in properly run banks. These banks would become members of a government-sponsored insurance business, the Federal Deposit Insurance Corporation, or FDIC. If something went wrong and a bank could not cover its deposits, then the government insurance agency would pay the depositor up to a certain amount in any one account. A person could have many such accounts in more than one bank.

5. What laws did Congress pass to protect investments?

1) Congress established the Federal Deposit Insurance Corporation. If a member bank could not cover its deposits, the FDIC would insure the deposit up to a certain amount. 2) It set up the Home Owners Loan Corporation to prevent people's homes from being taken away if they had trouble paying their mortgages.

After the stock market crash of 1929, people panicked and withdrew their savings from banks. How did the government remedy this situation?

Do you think the FDIC is a good use of government power? Why?

The government set up a similar organization to make sure that people's homes would not be taken away if they had trouble paying the mortgage. This was the Home Owners Loan Corporation (HOLC). Home owners' loans were provided to cover such an emergency.

Business and Labor

6. What did the NRA codes accomplish?

1) These voluntary codes encouraged businesses to keep wages up and to produce as much as possible. 2) NRA agreements helped to end child labor and allowed workers to organize for better pay and better working conditions. 3) The National Labor Relations Board watched over and kept fair relations between workers and owners.

Amelia Earhart was the first to fly alone from Honolulu to California. In 1937 she attempted to fly around the world but her plane was lost in the South Pacific and was never recovered.

The Roosevelt administration was worried about what businesses did to each other when there were not enough customers for everyone. Franklin D. Roosevelt felt that businesses in the same industry ought to be allowed to set up codes of correct behavior to which each separate business would agree. These codes were supposed to keep businesses healthy without hurting the workers. If all businesses agreed to allow trade unions to organize their workers and to bargain with their employers, then the workers could be paid more. Businesses would not be able to use cheap labor as a way of cutting costs.

The codes were to be voluntary, but they were supervised by the federal government. This plan took form in the National Recovery Administration, or NRA. Any business that agreed to the codes would get a Blue Eagle to display on their business paper and in their advertising. The NRA pledge was called "We Do Our Part." It was supposed to persuade businesses to compete less with each other, to keep wages up, and produce as much as possible. Many businesses, however, found it easier to make profits by raising prices and producing less. With more machinery and fewer workers, they could do better business. By doing this, businesses were not helping productivity or employment.

The most favorable results of the NRA codes were in the field of labor. The NRA agreements helped do away with child labor. They allowed workers to organize for better pay and better working conditions. A government committee, the National Labor Relations Board, was set up to watch over and keep fair the relations between workers and owners.

The right to organize stated in Clause 7a of the NRA codes was used by labor leaders to persuade workers to join unions. It was clear that only those people who got together and spoke up as a group were heard. Union leaders argued about the best way to get the most union members the most power in a corporation.

The craft-workers union, the American Federation of Labor, left out the growing number of fairly unskilled machine operators. The A.F. of L. was also spread out among many different corporations. Because of these factors, it seemed that the A.F. of L. might not grow in numbers. The president of the mine-workers union, John

L. Lewis, had the idea that all people who worked for one employer should belong to one union. If these workers went out on strike they could force a whole corporation to stop doing business.

The Lewis group called themselves the Committee for Industrial Organization. They formed their own labor organization in 1935—called the Congress of Industrial Organizations, or CIO. In 1935 the law made it all right for unions to organize, bargain for what the workers wanted, as a group, and strike. No employer could fire a worker for such activities (Wagner Act). This was the beginning of the great strength of labor unions in America.

Farming

When Roosevelt came to deal with the problems of farmers, he made a daring move. He recognized the farmers as a group that must be helped. But most importantly, he knew that American farmers grew too many crops to get a good price. American farmers were not making enough money to pay for their machines and still have a profit.

7. Why was the Agricultural Adjustment Act necessary?

1) The Agricultural Adjustment Act was necessary to deal with the problems of farmers. 2) Farmers were growing more goods than they could sell. 3) They couldn't make enough money on what they did sell to pay for their machines.

What does a nation do about growing too much food? In America there was too much food for the people who could buy it. A very rich family cannot eat more food than one that is just well-off. Farmers could not give away extra food to the poor at home or abroad. The farmer has to sell it at harvesttime to someone who can afford to store it until there is a shortage. The middleperson can send it to places that need it and can pay for it.

Franklin D. Roosevelt's plan to help farmers, called the Agricultural Adjustment Act, had three main parts. First, there was to be a cut in production and a rise in prices. Second, a plan was started to pay farmers to plant less in the future. Third, a plan was started to keep the soil from wearing out by not planting every farm field every year.

People reacted strongly to Roosevelt's plan. Some people said it was wrong not to grow all the food one could. Many thought it was wrong to destroy crops and animals in order to lower the supply and raise the prices.

Many objected to the Agricultural Adjustment Act because they felt the government took too much action. No matter how well it might work, they argued, the plan interfered with the freedom of individuals and the power of the states.

Native Americans and the New Deal

The people who were poor before the depression struck suffered the most in the 1930's. Native Americans were among this group.

8. Why was the Indian Reorganization Act of 1934 controversial?

Why is it so hard to make plans for farming? Why are there so few families left on small farms?

This picture shows Taos children doing a "Hoop Dance" to the beat of a drum on a reservation in New Mexico.

1) Collier's plan called for the creation of tribal organizations in which Native Americans could appoint leaders who would discuss plans and make formal contracts with the federal government. 2) Some tribes were broken into rival groups and were less likely to join with each other than they were to deal with the government in Washington. 3) The idea of tribal councils and shared tribal land did not accord with the ideas of all tribes.

Hunger, disease, and the lack of organization in Native American communities were serious problems. Roosevelt and his advisers needed to take action to find a solution.

When John Collier became Commissioner of Indian Affairs, government action toward Native Americans was changed. Collier believed that tribal organization was important. Tribes could appoint leaders who could discuss problems and plans with the federal government. They could make formal contracts.

This idea was something similar to the original treaties between Native Americans and the early government of the United States. It also gave the different tribes the organization they needed to be heard. Organized groups received help. People who acted alone very rarely made great changes during the depression.

Collier knew that many Native American tribes were broken up into rival groups. They were less likely to join with each other than they were to deal with the government in Washington.

Many Native Americans tried to stop Collier, and some tribes voted against his plans. Tribes that owned land rich in minerals, such as oil, were not interested in putting that land into a common pool.

Actually, a majority of tribes turned down Collier's ideas as stated in the Indian Reorganization Act of 1934. One of the most outspoken Native Americans against the idea of tribal organization was J. C. Morgan. He was a Navajo who had been sent away to boarding school. He had graduated from Hampton Institute in Virginia. Morgan had returned to the Navajo reservation to help his people learn modern ways in education and sanitation. When Collier spoke out against boarding schools, Morgan replied, "If it was not for boarding schools, we would not be here today." Morgan attacked Collier for trying to keep the Native Americans backward.

In what ways is it better for each Native American tribe to keep its own identity? In what ways is that almost impossible?
What advantages are there to Native Americans of working together as "Indians"? What problems does that cause for the tribes?

HOW TO CONDUCT AN INTERVIEW

Observing how people act is one way of getting information. Reading books and newspaper or magazine articles is another way. Hearing people talk is a third way. There is still another way of getting information—asking people questions. We call this interviewing.

Interviewing requires getting people to tell their opinions or share their experiences with you. To conduct a good interview, the interviewer should follow certain rules:

1. Decide on a topic.
2. Write out your questions in advance. Leave space to write down the answers. Do not trust your memory.
3. Ask simple and clear questions. For example, a good question might be: What kind of job do you have? This can be followed by another question: Tell me, what do you do on your job? Do *not* ask more than one question at a time.
4. Be polite. Tell the person the purpose of your interview. Ask the person for permission to be interviewed. If the person refuses, thank him or her. Everyone has the right not to be interviewed.
5. Do not press the interviewee. If a person you are interviewing says that he or she does not wish to answer the question, say "all right, let us go on to the next question."
6. Ask the person if you can identify him or her in the future. If the person says no, accept this.
7. When the interview is over, thank the person. Read over the interview immediately to be sure you have recorded everything. Now you have a record of how your questions were answered. If you interview a number of people with the same questions, then you can count the number of questions people agree on and disagree on. Then you will have conducted an opinion survey.
8. Practice interviewing. Try to interview your grandparents, parents, classmates, or teachers. For example, in Chapters 23 and 24 you have gathered some information on the depression. You might find it interesting to interview people who experienced the depression first-hand. What kinds of questions would you like answered?

Morgan was elected tribal chairman of the Navajos in 1938. In 1942 he lost the tribal election to Chee Dodge. Dodge believed in restoring tribal traditions. This followed the ideas of John Collier. Native Americans of many tribes tried different ways of following both ideas. They wanted full citizenship. They wanted a part in modern American life. They also wanted to keep their traditions and group beliefs.

What were the advantages and disadvantages of going to school on the reservation to the child, to the tribe, and to the American nation as a whole?

623

Checking the facts

1. How was Roosevelt different from Hoover in his approach to helping people?
2. What actions did Roosevelt take to provide relief for those who were suffering?
3. What actions did Roosevelt take to insure a better future for the people?

2. PLANNING ON A LARGE SCALE

9. Why was there argument over the ownership of the hydroelectric plant at Muscle Shoals?

1) Some said that government should not own a business. 2) The owners of private electric power companies were afraid that the government would sell electricity at such a cheap price that they would not be able to make a fair profit.

Up to Roosevelt's time, one plan for developing a whole area of the country, the Tennessee River Valley, had never received presidential support. Roosevelt saw the plan as a wise use of the power of the federal government.

The Tennessee River ran through seven states. During World War I, the government had built a plant to make explosives near the waterfall at Muscle Shoals, Alabama. The location was important. The force of the waterfall turned the *turbines.* The turbines generated electricity to run the machines.

When the war was over, there was much argument over the ownership of the *hydroelectric* plant. Some said the government should not own a business. Presidents Coolidge and Hoover refused to let a government-owned business compete with private businesses. The owners of private electric power companies were afraid the government would sell electricity at such a cheap price that they would not be able to make a fair profit.

The TVA

10. What would the Tennessee Valley Authority do?

1) It would carry out plans to build other dams, nitrate fertilizer factories, give advice to people in the area on how to take care of the soil, develop new industries, and then train workers. 2) It could use its power to work across state lines and its money to start new ventures.

Roosevelt favored government control of the hydroelectric plant. He agreed with a plan to build other dams and nitrate fertilizer factories. He also agreed to give advice to people in the area on how to take care of the soil, and to plan for the development of new industries and the training of workers. Roosevelt thought one government agency, the Tennessee Valley Authority, should carry out all of these plans. It could use its power to work across state lines, and it could use its money to start new ventures.

He saw the TVA as planning the total environment: people, land, and resources. It would be a new use of government. Many people opposed the TVA. They were afraid of government going into businesses that had been owned privately. Others supported the TVA because they thought something new had to be done.

Government planning caused private business to complain. But private businesses are not supposed to get together because they could then raise prices or hurt other businesses. Can you think of a fair way to do regional planning?

During the New Deal, the TVA built many dams. The Norris Dam, located on the Clinch River in Tennessee, was the first dam built by the TVA in 1936. It still is used today to control flooding and to generate electricity.

Planning for a Safe Future

The most important action taken by government at this time was for an insurance plan. It would help people have money to live on when they could not work. The plan was explained in the Social Security Act of 1935.

11. What was the purpose of the Social Security Act of 1935?

It pooled money from the workers and their employers to help the workers to live when they were no longer able to work.

The United States was one of the last of the world's industrial nations to have a plan of social security. It was paid for by each worker's wages and an equal amount from his or her employer. Both payments were required. Both payments were collected by the government.

When a worker was temporarily out of work, the government would send a check each month from the pool of savings of all the other workers in the plan. The idea of pooling money from workers to help each other out when needed was, in this country, a new use of law. The government handled all the bookkeeping and check-writing, as well as the collecting of the money. As more services came to people out of Washington, more people went to Washington to work for the bureaus that made sure the services were performed. These managers, or administrators, were referred to as government by committees, or bureaus—government bureaucracy.

In what way is social security a reminder of why it is helpful to be a member of an organized society?

FDR's fireside chats brought him into the homes of many Americans. How do you think these "chats" affected his popularity?

12. What did the First Lady do for others?

She traveled across the country and wrote reports reminding the nation of the problems of Blacks and the poor.

How to Get Support?

Franklin Roosevelt knew that his ideas on government action were expensive and different. If they were to succeed, the voters would have to tell their representatives in Congress to pass the necessary laws. Congress would never make such changes without being sure that their voters liked what the President was doing.

To reach the people, Roosevelt used the newspapers, the telegraphed news services, and, most of all, the radio. These were the mass media. He held press conferences twice a week every year. He let all the newspeople crowd up to his desk and fire questions at him. He called reporters by their first names. He exchanged jokes with them, and he answered their questions.

Franklin D. Roosevelt used his time with reporters to explain the way he saw the problems of the nation and the way he wanted to solve them. His explanations were like lessons, and he was a masterful teacher.

On the radio, Roosevelt spoke to Americans in "fireside chats." He could talk to millions as though they were his family in his living room.

Justice William Douglas of the Supreme Court said:

"He was in a very special sense the people's President, because he made them feel that with him in the White House they shared the presidency. The sense of sharing the presidency gave even the most humble citizen a lively sense of belonging."

Eleanor Roosevelt, the First Lady, became a well-known public personality in her own right. She traveled across the country and wrote reports on what she saw. She was especially aware of the problems of Blacks and the poor.

She visited the camps of migrants from the Oklahoma Dust Bowl, and she called the attention of the nation to them. Eleanor Roosevelt did the same kind of work in behalf of Black sharecroppers evicted by landlords who wanted to avoid sharing AAA benefit payments with them. She listened to the problems of youth and helped to create the National Youth Administration.

Eleanor Roosevelt's concern for Blacks, and the President's desire to get Blacks to vote and be part of the government, were well known. On one occasion, the famous Black singer, Marian Anderson, was not allowed to sing in a concert hall in Washington. One of Franklin Roosevelt's cabinet officers arranged for her to sing from the steps of the Lincoln Memorial.

Some People Were Against FDR's Methods

Many people became used to the idea that if something went wrong, the government should pass a law to prevent it. One of the President's advisers said: "We are trying to reform the structure of things rather than trying to reform the people." This was different from other Presidents. Many people thought the methods Roosevelt used to get problems solved was wrong. Some thought there was too much government action. Others thought the Constitution really didn't give Congress and the President the power to make so many changes.

Those who had money during the depression never forgave Roosevelt because he got the money for his programs by raising their income taxes. Roosevelt was outspoken in his belief that government should redistribute the income in the nation after the people had earned their salaries, or wages. He believed that those who had more should be taxed more. The government would then run programs to spend the money in ways that would get it to those who needed more.

The people who did not like Roosevelt's ways appealed to the Supreme Court. They said the federal government had used unconstitutional powers. In a series of court cases, many of the programs of the New Deal were stopped.

Eleanor Roosevelt shakes hands with a blind worker who is operating a loom.

FDR and The Supreme Court

In spite of his victory in the 1936 election, Roosevelt did run into difficulty with the Supreme Court. The majority of the Supreme Court had ruled that the New Deal laws about business were interfering even with businesses that operated within one state (the Schechter Poultry Case). By 1937 Roosevelt was worried that most of the New Deal acts would lose in the Supreme Court. He felt that many of the justices were so old they did not understand that the American people's thinking had changed.

Roosevelt thought he had a good idea. His plan was to get a law passed that would add one justice to the Supreme Court for every justice over the age of 70 who had been on the Court for ten years or more. The law did not pass. Roosevelt received very poor notices in the press. But, as it turned out, Roosevelt was able to appoint a new justice. And others on the Court began to vote in favor of the New Deal programs that were brought before it.

13. Why did Roosevelt try to change the Supreme Court?

He believed that many of the justices were so old that they did not understand that the American people's thinking had changed.

The Depression Goes On

By Roosevelt's second term in office, people were still out of work. There were not enough government jobs. The private businesses

14. What helped the economy to become more healthy?

Why do economists measure the number of *permanent* jobs to see if the nation is going to be able to employ all of its citizens who can and want to work?

During the 1930's many farmers suffered from the depression. Scores of families left their farms and went to California to work as migrant workers.

The government began to buy from private business in order to sell, lend, or give away goods to some of the European countries that were fighting a horrible war.

were not expanding fast enough to employ more of the people. The depression continued both in cities and on farms.

On the Farms

Farmers who sought to renew their bank loans found that payment, or else security on all their personal property, was demanded without regard to the needs of wife and family. One report read:

> "Prices of farm products had fallen to almost nothing, oats were ten cents a bushel, corn twelve cents a bushel, while hogs, the chief cash crop in the Corn Belt, were selling at less than two and one half cents a pound. In the fall of 1932 a wagon load of oats would not pay for a pair of shoes."

People were discouraged. It wasn't until the government began to buy more from business that the economy began to recover. The government began to buy more in order to sell, loan, or give goods to European allies who were fighting a horrible war.

Checking the facts

1. What were Roosevelt's plans for developing the Tennessee Valley? Why did some people oppose those plans?
2. What methods did Roosevelt use to make his plans known to the public? Why were his methods successful?
3. What issues brought Roosevelt into conflict with the Supreme Court?

Giving away work or food is not a long-term solution. Businesses have to make money to pay taxes for the government to be able to help. In what way is every person's job tied to every other person's job?

PUTTING IT ALL TOGETHER

UNDERSTANDING THE MAIN IDEAS

1. How did Americans try to solve their problems during the depression?
2. How did government spending of tax dollars help private citizens?
3. Whom should government help today?

ACTIVITIES

1. Franklin D. Roosevelt saw the federal government as the place to which groups of people took their problems and ideas for improvement. The government would then decide among all the needs of all the groups what action to take and how much tax money to spend on each. People who were not organized into groups were not heard. This activity asks that you make a list of all the organized groups that are mentioned in one issue of your local newspaper or in a national magazine. Who belongs to these groups? What do they hope to achieve? Prepare a report of your research and present it to your class.
2. You and another classmate might invite to speak to your class an officer of a group that tries to represent individuals that might not otherwise be heard. Some of these groups are the League of Women Voters, Common Cause, a local historical society, etc. Some questions you might ask of the group officer are: What brought individuals together into the group? Who were the original leaders? Does the organization still work on the same issues as it did at the beginning?
3. Prepare to interview two people who remember Franklin D. Roosevelt and the New Deal. Make sure to prepare your questions well in advance. Once the interviews are concluded, pool your responses. Were most of the responses about FDR himself? Which of his New Deal policies did people remember? Present your findings in a brief oral presentation to the class.

BOOKS TO READ

Graves, Charles P., *Eleanor Roosevelt* (New York: Dell Publishing Co., Inc., 1968).

Hickok, Lorena A., *The Story of Franklin D. Roosevelt* (New York: Grosset and Dunlap, Inc., Publishers, 1968).

Meyers, Elisabeth P., *Madam Secretary: Frances Perkins* (New York: Julian Messner, Inc., 1972).

chapter 25
A World War for Survival

1939–1945

1. THE UNITED STATES RESPONDS
2. WHAT THE WAR DID TO AMERICA
3. WARTIME AND MINORITIES AT HOME

INTRODUCTION

Americans had spent more than a generation trying to improve the way of life in the United States. They wanted work and a secure future for everyone. In 1933, the same year FDR took office, a man became dictator of Germany who intended to help his country in another way. He planned to conquer all the nations in Europe. The freedom of the United States was threatened as well.

Adolf Hitler and the National Socialist party in Germany were, from the beginning, the object of disapproval for most Americans. The Nazis' program to kill every Jew in Germany was a horror to the world.

The years of Roosevelt's second term were years of war in the rest of the world. Italy and Japan were also on the march. Italy attacked the African nation of Ethiopia in 1935. In 1936 Germany and Italy formed an alliance and withdrew from the League of Nations. Japan invaded China in 1937. Germany took over the nation of Austria

	1939	1940	1941	1941	
Who?	The British and French	German troops	Americans	American soldiers	
What?	declare war	conquer and occupy	enjoy full comercial television	join the allies in the fight against facism	
Where?	on Germany	France	in the United States	around the world	

Why is it important to know that FDR and Hitler came to power during the depression? What does the contrast between the two nations tell you about the American way?

in 1938 and most of Czechoslovakia in 1939. In that year Germany and Russia signed an agreement not to attack each other. No one in Europe seemed able to stop Germany's aggression.

Finally, on September 1, 1939, Germany invaded Poland. Great Britain and France declared war on Germany. The Second World War had begun. As you read about America in World War II, keep the following questions in mind:

1. How did Americans respond to the threat of dictatorships abroad?
2. How did Roosevelt unite the American people behind the war effort?
3. In the war years what happened to minorities in America?

1. THE UNITED STATES RESPONDS

The United States' attitude toward World War II was very different from that of World War I. In 1939 there was no question about which side was right or wrong. Hitler and the dictator in Italy, Benito Mussolini, were out to destroy the free nations of the world.

The Role of the United States

The question for the United States was how to help the French and British and still keep American troops out of the fighting. In 1937 Congress said that the United States would not loan money to nations at war, and it would not sell guns to them. In this way, it was hoped that the United States would not be drawn into the war because of business connections.

But Americans could not ignore the illegal and immoral acts of Germany and Italy, the *Axis Powers*. (The axis meant an imaginary

1. How did the United States agree to help its allies?

The United States agreed to help France and Britain by selling them arms if they sent their own ships to pick up the supplies and paid cash for them.

1942	1943	1944	1945	1945
American forces under General Douglas MacArthur	The Axis powers	The Allies	Harry S Truman	American planes
are driven out by the Japanese	are defeated	launch an invasion of Europe	becomes the thirty-third President	drop atomic bombs
from the Philippines	in North Africa	from Normandy, France	of the United States	on Hiroshima and Nagasaki in Japan

What had the United States learned from its World War I experience? Why was this war different?

631

line drawn between the capital cities of Berlin and Rome.) When France and Great Britain, the Allies, declared war on Germany, the United States declared itself willing to sell arms to nations at war. This was on the condition that the Allies sent their own ships to pick up the supplies and paid cash for them.

Americans debated their role in the war. Was it better to stay out of the war? Or was it better to help the Allies to make sure that they won? Even after Germany invaded Poland, President Franklin D. Roosevelt still planned to keep America out of the fighting overseas.

The Election of 1940

2. Why was Roosevelt elected to a third term of office?

1) Some believed that it would be a poor idea to change leaders during the war. 2) Willkie was like FDR in many ways.

Roosevelt ran for a third term as President in 1940. No one in the history of the United States had ever done that. The Democratic party reasoned that it would be a poor idea to change leaders while the world was at war. But many Democrats worried about breaking the tradition of two terms.

The Republicans ran a man who had been a Democrat, but thought Roosevelt's programs, especially TVA, were too much for government to do. Wendell Willkie was, however, very concerned about the problems of jobs and security and had the same point of view about the war as FDR. Willkie made a campaign issue out of the third term. "Just think," he said, "here is a candidate who assumes that out of 131 million people, he is the only absolutely necessary person." Roosevelt did not even reply. He ignored the issue and let others talk about it.

These are Russian children in a Nazi concentration camp. The sign in Russian reads, "Entering this camp or talking across the wire is forbidden under the threat of being shot."

Willkie won almost 45 percent of the popular vote—more votes than any Republican had ever won. However, he only won an electoral majority in ten states. These were mostly farm states of the Midwest. Roosevelt had won a third term as President.

The War Is Felt at Home

By the time Roosevelt won the election, Hitler and the Nazis had conquered Denmark, Norway, Holland, Belgium, and France. Americans were frightened. Congress voted to spend money on military goods, and Roosevelt spoke to the nation. He stressed the need for Americans to work hard to produce the guns, clothing, food, and other supplies needed to help Great Britain. Clearly, Germany had planned all along to attack the United States. Only Great Britain stood between Hitler and America. German rockets were bombing England almost daily. Americans wondered how long the British would be able to hold out against the attacks. Under Roosevelt's plan, America would lend, or lease, supplies to Great Britain and the other Allies. The leaders of Britain could pay

What were the differences between FDR and Willkie? How do you feel about a third term for a government official?

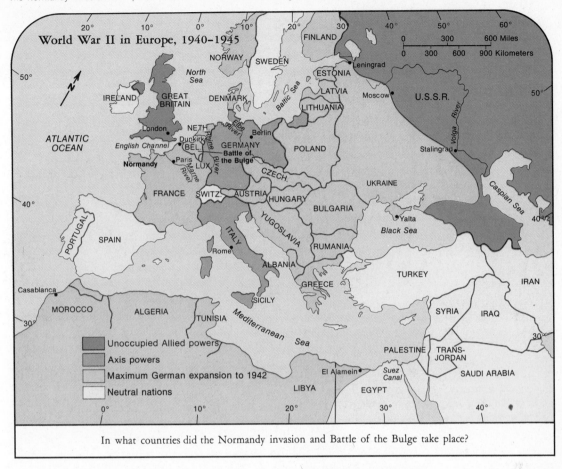

World War II in Europe, 1940–1945

In what countries did the Normandy invasion and Battle of the Bulge take place?

for them later. In response to Roosevelt's plan, Congress passed the Lend-Lease Act in 1941. Within a year, the United States sent $30 billion worth of supplies overseas. Roosevelt explained the plan to the American people:

> "We must be the great arsenal of democracy. For us this is an emergency as serious as war itself. We must apply ourselves to our task with the same resolution, the same sense of urgency, the same spirit of patriotism and sacrifice, as we would show were we at war. . . ."

In the summer of 1941, President Roosevelt met with the British Prime Minister, Winston Churchill, on a ship in the Atlantic Ocean. There the two leaders signed the Atlantic Charter. The United States and Great Britain agreed to a peaceful world in which the nations who won the war would not keep any territory gained in fighting. The charter also promised that all nations would be free to decide on their own form of government after the war.

What was so unusual about the Atlantic Charter?

Franklin D. Roosevelt and Prime Minister Winston Churchill of Great Britain, both seated, are shown during the signing of the Atlantic Charter.

3. Why did it take an attack on Hawaii to bring the United States into the war?

1) Some Americans were against war. 2) Some Americans were against Jews and in favor of the Nazis. 3) Some Americans thought Germany was going to win. 4) Some Americans were only interested in their own country.

Not all Americans were in favor of their country playing a part in the war. There were over 700 organizations in the United States that opposed the nation's helping any side. Their reasons for opposing aid to Great Britain differed. Some were against war. Some were against Jews and in favor of the Nazis. Others thought Germany was going to win. Some were only interested in their own country. In the meantime, Jews and opponents of Hitler in Germany were being killed in concentration camps. Some Jews got out of the country before Hitler closed the borders. Most were not that fortunate. Six million Jews would not leave or could not leave Europe. They eventually died in what has become known as the *holocaust*.

What finally brought the United States to declare war? The Japanese attacked the American naval base at Pearl Harbor, Hawaii, on December 7, 1941.

America Enters the War

4. Why did Roosevelt consider the attack on Pearl Harbor to be an "unprovoked and dastardly attack"?

In that one sneak attack, 2,335 American soldiers and sailors were killed and 1,178 were wounded. Over 200 planes were destroyed or damaged, along with eight battle ships, three cruisers, and three destroyers. At the moment of the attack, two Japanese ambassadors were sitting in the office of the American secretary of state to talk about peaceful agreements.

On the morning of December 8, President Roosevelt dictated a message to be delivered to Congress:

> "Yesterday, December 7, 1941—a day which will live in infamy—the United States of America was suddenly and deliberately attacked by naval and air forces of the Empire of Japan.
>
> I ask that the Congress declare that since the unprovoked and dastardly attack by Japan on Sunday, December 7, a state of war has existed between the United States and the Japanese Empire."

Japan had signed an agreement with Germany and Italy that each nation would help any of the others in the event of war. When the United States declared war on Japan on December 8, 1941, Germany and Italy declared war on the United States.

At the moment of the attack, two Japanese ambassadors were sitting in the office of the American secretary of state to talk about peaceful agreements.

Checking the facts

1. How did the United States support the Allies in the early years of World War II?
2. How did Americans react to the war in Europe?
3. What event brought Americans into the fighting?

2. WHAT THE WAR DID TO AMERICA

Americans no longer had any question about going to war. They knew it was a war for survival. They did not know how difficult it was going to be to win.

The age for being drafted into the armed forces was set between 20 and 44. More than 31 million men were registered, and almost 10 million men were drafted. Another 5 million volunteered, or enlisted. Over a quarter of a million women enlisted for duty in all the branches of the armed forces. They did not go into combat, but the WAC's (Women's Army Corps) and the WAVES (Women Appointed for Voluntary Emergency Service) did important work throughout the war.

On the Home Front

As Americans had learned in World War I, it takes organization to fight a war. Everyone in the nation felt the impact of the war. Food was needed for the armed forces and for America's allies.

What is the purpose of this World War II poster?

Don't miss your great opportunity..

THE NAVY NEEDS YOU IN THE WAVES

What do the figures on the number of volunteers in the armed forces tell you about World War II?

635

The war effort at home created many jobs for women and minorities in industry. This woman is working in a munitions factory.

5. Why were the Americans having difficulty fighting in the Pacific?

1) They had lost Pearl Harbor as a supply base. 2) The war was fought between ships trying to find each other in the Pacific Ocean and soldiers fighting hand to hand in the island jungles.

Thirty percent of all the meat was bought by the government. People were told how much sugar, coffee, meat, and butter they could buy. Each person had a part, or *ration*. Tires and gasoline were also rationed.

Factory production soared. By 1943 airplane factories produced 5,500 planes every month. Before the war that number was 200. Labor unions called off strikes. Fifty million men and 20 million women went to work in government jobs. There were now jobs for everyone because of the war. Businesses that made war goods expanded. They built new factories because they knew they could sell everything they produced. Workers got an average of $45 a week for a 45-hour work week. The depression was cured by enormous government spending of tax money for products that were needed.

The cost of the war from 1940 to 1943 was a little more than the total cost of government from the day George Washington became President to 1940. The government borrowed money to pay for all the supplies it needed. People bought war bonds. School children bought defense stamps from their savings each week. Even this was not enough. Income taxes on people and corporations became higher and higher.

The Fighting

Within five months of the attack on Pearl Harbor, the Japanese had captured the Philippine Islands. The American Generals Douglas MacArthur and Jonathan Wainwright, with what was left of their American and Filipino soldiers, had to be ordered to Australia. With Pearl Harbor gone as a supply base, there was no way to fight the Japanese. The troops on the Bataan Peninsula and the island of Corregidor on the west side of Manila Bay were the last to get out.

Information about the pain of the terrible injuries, the fear of death, and the feeling of losing the war were widespread. People read about the battles in the newspapers and magazines. They saw pictures of the dead and wounded.

The war in the Pacific was fought between ships trying to find each other in the ocean. On land, marines and soldiers fought in hand-to-hand combat in the jungles, and they fought from island to island. The Japanese were stopped from taking Australia, an American ally, and both sides suffered terrible losses.

The War in Europe

It took the United States until 1942 before it had enough troops, arms, supplies, and ships to move into the European war. The

6. How was Italy taken?

World War II in the Pacific

EVENT	DATE	WHERE	OUTCOME
Japan attacks China	July, 1937	China	Nationalist and Communist Chinese fight back against Japanese.
Japan attacks Pearl Harbor	Dec. 1941	Pearl Harbor, Hawaii	Many Americans are killed and ships destroyed. The United States declares war.
Japan attacks Pacific Islands	1941–1942	Islands between Australia and India	The Japanese seize most islands between Australia and India to use as military bases.
Battle of Midway	June, 1942	Midway Island	It is a major American victory over the Japanese. The threat to the United States' west coast and Hawaii is eliminated.
Guadalcanal	Aug., 1942	Solomon Islands, New Guinea	Many naval and land battles occur. Finally American forces push Japanese forces out of Guadalcanal.
Battle of the Philippine Sea	June, 1944	Mariana Islands	The greatest naval-air battle of World War II is fought. Japan suffers heavy losses.
Battle of Leyte Gulf	Oct., 1944	Leyte and Luzon	Naval battles are won by the Americans. This is the largest sea battle in history. The Japanese navy is destroyed.
Iwo Jima and Okinawa	Feb., 1945	The islands of Iwo Jima and Okinawa	The bloodiest battles of the war are fought here. The Japanese air force is destroyed.
Bombing of Japan	Aug., 1945	Hiroshima and Nagasaki	Many Japanese die from the atomic bomb dropped by the Americans. Japan surrenders.

military plan was to land troops in North Africa, clear the Mediterranean Sea of the enemy, and attack Italy. Italy was the southernmost point of the Axis Powers, and it was the weakest chain in the Axis defense system.

It took six months of hard fighting in North Africa before the Allies could begin the invasion of Italy. Italy was first bombed by planes. Then troops parachuted in and landed in boats. The army that invaded Italy in July 1943 was made up of British, American, French, Canadian, and Polish troops.

1) Troops were landed in North Africa to clear the way to Italy. 2) After 6 months of hard fighting in North Africa, the Allies were able to bomb Italy from their bases in North Africa, and land troops.

7. *What was the importance of D-Day?*

There continued to be debate among the Allies about the invasion of Europe from the south. Why was it part of the plan?

637

In the Normandy invasion, troops and supplies came by ship and were taken inland by truck. Barrage balloons overhead protected against enemy aircraft.

1) It was invaded by the largest force in history. 2) It marked the beginning of the recapturing of French territory.

When the Italians surrendered, the Germans were left to defend the country. Over 350,000 Allied soldiers were killed, wounded, or reported missing in the battle for Italy. It was June 1944 when Rome, Italy's capital, fell to the Allies.

In 1943 Roosevelt, Churchill, of Great Britain, Chiang Kai-shek (CHANG–kai–shek), of China, and Joseph Stalin, the dictator of Russia, met and planned a new attack on Hitler's armies. The attack was to be launched from Britain across the English Channel onto the beaches of Normandy, France.

The invasion force of American, British, and Canadian soldiers was under the command of an American, General Dwight D. Eisenhower. After a number of delays due to the weather, the Allied troops finally landed in France on D-Day, June 6, 1944.

Four thousand transports, landing boats, and warships carried more than 130,000 troops across the English Channel. It was the largest invasion force in the history of war.

World War II was also an air war. American bombers flew from bases in England over Europe. These huge planes, called flying fortresses, were used for daytime bombing of German-occupied Europe. The British Royal Air Force did the nighttime bombing raids. They were designed to make an area safer before sending in ground troops.

Checking the facts

1. How did Americans organize themselves in the effort to win the war?
2. Which side won the first battles of World War II in the Pacific?
3. What was the Allied plan for the invasion of Europe?

3. WARTIME AND MINORITIES AT HOME

8. What conditions led to race riots in the cities?

The war for survival of America was seen by everyone as the war for survival of freedom. Eventually, the talk about freedom in the world also caused talk about freedom in the United States.

During the war, Black and White Americans came from farming areas of the South to northern cities. They hoped to find jobs that

Up close, a war is full of bloodshed and terror. Step back and look at charts and maps. What picture do you get?

World War II in Europe, Africa, and the Americas

EVENT	DATE	WHERE	OUTCOME
Germany and Italy form Axis Alliance	Oct. 1935		Mussolini hopes to acquire an African empire; he joins with Hitler in an alliance.
United States passes the Neutrality Acts	1935 and 1937		These acts give the President power to decide whether or not arms should be sold to nations at war.
Britain and France declare war on Axis powers	Sept. 1939		Britain and France declare war when Germany invades Poland. Britain and France had signed a treaty guaranteeing the freedom of Poland.
Declaration of Panama	Oct. 1939	Panama City	The United States and other countries of the Americas established a safety zone around the Americas. Nations at war could be barred from this zone in an attempt to defend the Western Hemisphere.
Blitzkrieg attacks by Germans over Europe	1940	Denmark, Norway, France, Belgium, Luxemburg, Netherlands	Using bombers, tanks, and infantry, Germany managed to sweep across Europe as far as Greece.
British evacuate Dunkirk	May-June 1940	Port of Dunkirk in Northern France	The British army is trapped by the Germans and carry out a desperate evacuation by motor and fishing boats.
Battle of Britain	Aug.-Oct. 1940	Britain	The Germans bomb Britain heavily and constantly until the Royal Air Force is able to repel them and save Britain from conquest.
Lend-Lease Act	March 1941	United States	This act allows the President to lend military equipment to Britain and the other allies.
Siege of Stalingrad	Aug. 1942	Russia	Russian forces save the city of Stalingrad from the German assault. The Russians also regain territory lost to the Germans.
Allies win in North Africa	Oct. 1942– May 1943	Egypt, Morocco, Algeria, Tunisia	Generals Eisenhower and Montgomery defeat Rommel and his forces. 250,000 German troops surrender and the fighting in North Africa ends.
Italy surrenders	Sept. 1943		When the Allies land in Italy, it surrenders. The Germans quickly advance but are eventually defeated by the Allies.
Normandy invasion	June 1944	Northern coast of France	General Eisenhower launches this invasion into German-held Europe. From Normandy, Allied ground and air forces battle their way through France and Belgium.
Battle of the Bulge	Dec. 1944	Belgium	The Germans slip between Allied lines creating a "bulge." However, General Patton drives the Germans back. This battle delays the Allied entry into Germany.
Germany surrenders	May 1945	Germany	The Allied forces close in on Germany and force its surrender.

MILEAGE RATION

Food and other items were rationed during the war. Ration stamps were issued to all Americans. Why was rationing necessary?

1) Blacks and Whites had come from the farming areas of the South to northern cities hoping to find jobs that paid well. 2) There were factory jobs, but the cities were not prepared for the influx of people. 3) In those terribly crowded areas Black and White Americans took their anger out on each other.

would pay well. They expected to be able to have better housing, better food, and better education for their children.

The northern cities did have factory jobs, but the cities were not prepared for the crowds of people. There was not enough housing or schools. Food was rationed. There were not enough parks for children to play in and activities for the adults. In these terribly crowded areas, Black and White Americans—many of them new-comers—took their anger out on each other. There were race riots in many cities. Both Blacks and Whites started fighting. Black leaders felt the time had come for Blacks to speak up. Many Black organizations such as the NAACP and the National Urban League began to show unusual unity among themselves for the first time.

The Blacks

9. Why did Roosevelt appoint a Fair Employment Practices Committee?

1) Asa Philip Randolph had planned a march on Washington, D.C., to demonstrate for equal rights for Blacks in jobs, the armed forces, and in

Black churches, clubs, and newspapers asked Americans to give Blacks equal chances in jobs, the armed forces, and in government programs to train the unemployed. If this didn't happen, they would ask that Americans stop talking about freedom and fairness in the world.

Even before America entered World War II, Asa Philip Randolph planned a march on Washington, D.C. Randolph had long been a promoter of peaceful, organized, public protests. He was head of

For Blacks, World War II was an important time for change. Why?

the Brotherhood of Pullman Car Porters and knew how successful physical, peaceful action by large groups could be.

President Roosevelt and other government leaders who wanted to help Blacks were afraid of a march during wartime. They wanted the people of the nation to pull together, not apart. The President sent for Randolph and two of his best known and most powerful supporters, Walter White of the NAACP and T. Arnold Hill of the National Urban League. In the meeting, FDR insisted he was doing his best and planned to do more for Blacks. But he felt the march had to be called off.

Walter White knew the President well. It is reported that the President asked him, "How many people will really march?" The answer was "No less than 100,000." FDR then asked what they wanted. The Black leaders wanted an executive order that would make it illegal to discriminate against anyone in either war industries or apprentice programs. Roosevelt agreed to their demands. On the day the order was issued, June 25, 1941, Randolph called off the march. Later, Roosevelt appointed a Fair Employment Practices Committee to make sure the order was carried out.

All during the war, Black organizations continued public protests. In 1943 the Congress of Racial Equality (CORE) organized a sit-in at a restaurant in Chicago. It was followed by sit-ins in Baltimore and St. Louis. Black people sat at tables in those restaurants and quietly insisted on being served.

The Black newspapers spoke out against prejudice in factories and in the army. They called for a double "V"—victory at home and overseas. These papers sent reporters as war correspondents to both Europe and the Pacific. They wrote about the troubles between Black and White soldiers and civilians.

Blacks fought in segregated units during the war. For the first time, they were also in combat units in the Navy, the Marines, and the Air Corps. Over one million Blacks were drafted during World War II.

During the war, new magazines published by Blacks for Blacks appeared. John H. Johnson started *Negro Digest* in 1942. He also published *Ebony,* a monthly picture magazine, and *Jet*, a weekly news magazine. These magazines wrote about the achievements of Blacks in America. Blacks were shown in advertisements. Manufacturers wanted to sell products to the growing number of Blacks who had money to spend on luxury goods.

Blacks began to be promoted into important jobs in big corporations, especially in the banking and insurance businesses. Once in jobs of authority, these leaders helped set up training programs for others. More Blacks joined the modern American business world.

government programs to train the unemployed.
2) Roosevelt agreed to issue an executive order making it illegal to discriminate against anyone in war industries or in apprentice programs. 3) Randolph called off the march.

1) CORE organized sit-ins at restaurants in Chicago, Baltimore, and St. Louis. 2) Black newspapers called for a double "V"—victory at home and overseas. 3) For the first time, Blacks served in combat units, but they were segregated. 4) Several Black magazines were formed to write about the achievements of Blacks. Blacks were shown in advertisements. 5) More and more Blacks became part of the modern business world.

10. What other gains did Blacks make during the war?

Asa Philip Randolph organized the Pullman car workers into a union. He also fought for desegregation of the armed forces.

Newcomers to California

During the years of the depression, 350,000 refugees from the Dust Bowl of the Southwest came to California. They came to escape the drought which made farming impossible in their area. The Californians called them Okies and Arkies and complained that they were lazy and unreliable. By 1939 these same people went to work in shipyards and defense plants. They made money and began to live the way other Californians did. Then they treated the Mexican migrant workers as badly as they had been treated. The Mexicans were paid 20 cents an hour and lived in labor camps.

Japanese-Americans

There were thousands of Japanese-Americans. Some were born in Japan but had become American citizens. They were called Issei (ee-ZYE). Their children were, of course, American citizens, born in America. They were known as Nisei (nee-ZYE). In 1942, just two months after Pearl Harbor, the Army commander on the west coast sent a message to Washington, D.C. In it he stated that the large Japanese population in the West, particularly in California, was a real military danger. In response, a number of newspapers and members of Congress in both parties demanded that all American citizens of Japanese descent be removed from the west coast area. They feared the Japanese-Americans would help Japanese troops if there was an invasion of the mainland of the United States.

President Roosevelt went along with the idea. In 1942 relocation centers were set up in Utah, Wyoming, Arizona, and Colorado. The Japanese-Americans were kept there until after the war. They were not physically punished but they lost their homes and jobs. They remained loyal to the United States.

By February 1943 the Nisei asked to be allowed to serve in the army. One Japanese-American, Mike Masaoka, spoke at a congressional hearing:

> "In this emergency, as in the past, we are not asking for special privileges or concessions. We ask only for the opportunity and the right of sharing the common lot of all Americans, whether it be in peace or in war. This is the American way for which our boys are fighting."

Roosevelt: A Fourth Term!

In 1944 Franklin Roosevelt wanted another term as President and got it. His vice-presidential running mate was Harry S Truman,

Mexican citizens were recruited for jobs during the war. They are giving the "V" sign for victory.

11. How were Japanese-Americans treated during the war?

1) They were moved from the West Coast to relocation centers in Utah, Wyoming, Arizona, and Colorado. That forced move brought about the loss of their homes and their jobs. 2) The *Nisei* were allowed to form their own combat unit that fought in Italy.

What caused other Americans to allow the unfair treatment of Japanese-Americans during the war? How can this kind of action be prevented?

a senator from Missouri. The Republicans ran the governor of New York, Thomas E. Dewey. The only campaign issue was the length of time Roosevelt had been in office. However, many of the American people did not seem to mind. They were pleased with Roosevelt's running of the war. In the election, Roosevelt got 2,357,000 more votes than Dewey and took the electoral college vote in 36 of the 48 states.

The war was not over yet. Germany was still fighting hard. In December 1944, the Germans attacked an area between Belgium and Luxembourg. (See chart, page 639.) They created a huge bulge in the Allied troop lines. In the Battle of the Bulge that followed, many soldiers died, but the Allied line finally held. (See map, page 633.) By March 1945, the Allies had crossed the Rhine River into Germany, and they were making their way to Germany's capital, Berlin. The Russians, also an American ally, marched in from the east toward Berlin.

The war in Europe was nearing an end. But Franklin D. Roosevelt did not live to see it. He died on April 12, 1945. Less than one month later, Adolf Hitler committed suicide, and the Germans surrendered. May 8, 1945, was declared V-E Day for victory in Europe.

Finishing the War Against Japan

The United States expected to have to invade Japan and occupy all the major islands before the Japanese government would surrender. The battles for the islands of Iwo Jima and Okinawa near Japan cost many American lives. (See map, page 644.) The Japanese used suicide planes and seemed to be ready to fight on and on.

When the Japanese refused to surrender, President Truman made an important decision. He gave the command to drop the new atomic bomb on two Japanese cities. Although it would kill and injure many people, Truman believed that the invasion by American ground troops would cost many more lives. It was an impossible decision, but Truman felt he had to make it. The bombs that were dropped on Hiroshima and Nagasaki killed thousands of Japanese. Some 80,000 died at Hiroshima. The price was terrible but the Japanese surrendered. V-J Day was August 14, 1945.

The World After the War

The end of World War II left the United States with great ability to produce machines, food, and new scientific discoveries. The American people had given all their energy to the war effort. However, Americans were not at ease with one of their allies. A new dictatorship in the Soviet Union was now in control of Eastern

The 442nd Regimental Combat Team was made up of Japanese-Americans. They fought in Italy and southern France.

12. Why did Truman authorize the use of the atomic bomb?

He thought that it would save American lives, as many as were lost taking the islands of Iwo Jima and Okinawa.

13. What made the Allies uneasy with the Soviet Union?

It was a dictatorship, and it controlled Eastern Europe at the end of the war.

The atomic bomb was developed in America because Germany was known to be working on it. The decision to drop the bomb on Japan was not in the original plan. Does that make a difference in judging the decision?

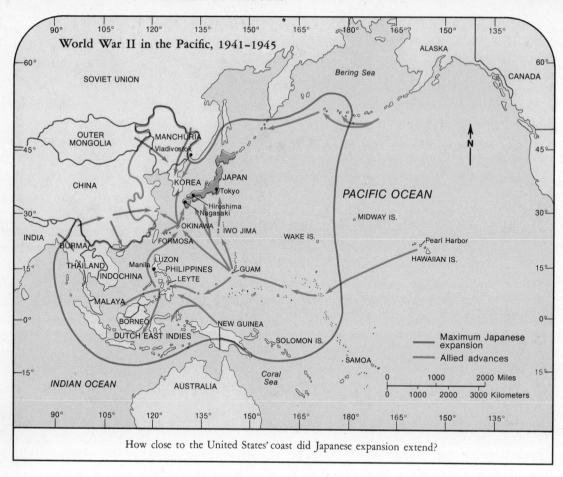

World War II in the Pacific, 1941–1945

How close to the United States' coast did Japanese expansion extend?

Europe. General Eisenhower and President Truman did not want to anger the Russians. After all, they had fought well against the Nazis. Churchill of Great Britain felt differently. He warned that the Russian presence in Eastern Europe was a new problem.

The rise of communism threatened the entire free world. American leaders would have to deal with this new threat.

In the postwar years, the American people had to face a challenge to their entire system. How would they react?

Checking the facts

1. While the United States was fighting for freedom in Europe and Asia, what was happening to freedom at home?
2. What were the major factors in the Allied victory?

How big is the Pacific Ocean? What did its size have to do with the way the war was fought and the way in which it ended?

PUTTING IT ALL TOGETHER

UNDERSTANDING THE MAIN IDEAS

1. How did Americans respond to the threat of dictatorships abroad?
2. How did Roosevelt unite the American people behind the war effort?
3. In the war years, what happened to minorities in America?

ACTIVITIES

1. Franklin Roosevelt had charm, a good voice, and the ability to inspire people. Are there political leaders today to whom you listen? If you can, listen to an elected official on a TV news show. What does that person do to reach his or her audience? What does that person do to make the audience trust the speaker? Incorporate your impressions in a brief essay.
2. World War II has been the subject of many movies and books. Choose one of these and write an analysis of it. What does the movie or book try to spotlight? Is it concerned with heroes, strategy, or the battle of good against evil? Include your findings in a brief written report.
3. Interview someone who fought in or lived through World War II. What does he or she remember the most? Where was he or she when the news was broadcast about the attack on Pearl Harbor? The death of FDR? How did the war affect his or her life?

BOOKS TO READ

Bliven, Bruce, Jr., *From Pearl Harbor to Okinawa* (New York: Random House, Inc., 1970).

Houston, Jeanne Wakatsuki, and Houston, James D., *Farewell to Manzanar* (New York: Bantam Books, 1974).

Levinger, Elma E., *Albert Einstein* (New York: Julian Messner, Inc., 1962).

Martin, Ralph G., *President from Missouri: Harry S Truman* (New York: Julian Messner, Inc., 1973).

Meltzer, Milton, *Never to Forget: The Jews of the Holocaust* (New York: Harper and Row, 1976).

Snyder, Louis L., *First Book of World War II* (New York: Watts Publishing Co., 1968).

chapter 26
Preserving: A New Challenge

1945–1960

1. TAKING ON THE CHALLENGE
2. HOW MUCH CHALLENGE?
3. HOW MUCH PROBLEM
   SOLVING?
4. HOW AMERICANS LIVED IN
   THE 1950's

INTRODUCTION

When World War II ended in August 1945, Americans were excited and relieved. As soon as Italy, Germany, and Japan were conquered, people wanted to get back to their civilian lives. Rationing ended. Many who could afford them hoped to get new refrigerators or new cars. They could also travel abroad for the first time in six years. The thrill of travel by airplane became possible for more people. The aviation industry had grown quickly during the war. More planes and pilots available meant travel overseas would cost less than it had before the war.

In the midst of victory celebrations and hope for a bright future, it was hard to take the news that the world was now challenged by a new double enemy—communism and the Soviet Union. Americans were tired of foreign places and fighting. It was hard for many Americans to realize that a strange belief in a far-off country could actually harm America.

	1945	1945	1949	1950-53	
Who?	Delegates from 50 nations	Communist troops	Communists led by Mao Tse-tung	American soldiers	
What?	set up the United Nations at a meeting	remain in many nations	gain control of the government	fight North Korean and Chinese Communist troops	
Where?	in San Francisco, California	of Eastern Europe	in China	in the Korean War	

Why was the end of World War II different from the end of World War I?

Averill Harriman, ambassador to the Soviet Union, and George Kennan, a Russian expert in the State Department, had warned President Roosevelt not to trust the Soviet leader. Their predictions about what the Soviet Union would do after the war proved accurate. The Soviet leader, Stalin, had promised Roosevelt and Churchill that the Soviet Union would form democratic governments in the countries of Eastern Europe that its army occupied. Instead, Stalin killed or imprisoned democratic leaders in countries such as Poland, Hungary, and finally, Czechoslovakia. The Soviet Union turned Eastern Europe into a Communist empire.

Harriman, Kennan, and other experts had recommended that the United States keep its army in Europe and Asia. General George Patton wanted to attack the Soviet Union right after the war. Most Americans, however, wanted to "get the boys home by Christmas." And home they came.

The death of Franklin Roosevelt caused many Americans to worry. What would the new President Harry Truman do? Truman was well-known in the Senate but not to the American public. Besides, no leader looked very important to many Americans compared with their memory of FDR.

What Americans wanted was to feel secure. But Truman and the nation saw that there was no way to separate the security of America and its democratic allies from the new challenge of Soviet communism, which preached against the democratic way of life. As you read this chapter, think about the following questions:

1. How did Truman meet the challenge of communism?
2. What was the reaction of Americans to the Korean War?
3. How did Senator Joseph McCarthy first attract public attention in the United States?
4. What improvements were made in American life during the 1950's? For whom?

1953	1956	1956	1957	1958
Dwight Eisenhower, a former World War II general	Russian troops	Egypt and Israel	Black Americans	Fidel Castro
becomes the thirty-fourth President	crush a revolt against communist control	wage war	benefit from a new civil rights law	leads a rebellion against the government
of the United States	in Hungary	in the Middle East	in the United States	in Cuba

If FDR had wanted to deal with Russia at the same time as he dealt with the war, what might he have done? With what results?

647

1. TAKING ON THE CHALLENGE

In September 1945, one month after the Japanese surrender, President Truman turned to the job of making America more democratic and thus more secure. He announced a long list of reforms, which he called the Fair Deal.

The Challenge of Making America Secure

1. What did Truman do to promote equal opportunity?

1) He wanted new rules against racial discrimination in all federal government jobs and in businesses working for the federal government. 2) He ended segregation in the armed forces by executive order.

Truman wanted to increase the benefits of the New Deal. He asked for higher minimum wages. He also asked that more people be protected by the social security insurance plan. He wanted more federal tax money to build public housing that could be rented at lower rates than private housing; more money to tear down crumbling buildings in the slums of the big cities; more aid for education and health; and more money to bring electricity and jobs to rural regions of the nation, as TVA had done in the Tennessee Valley. Truman also wanted new rules against racial discrimination in all federal government jobs and in businesses working for the federal government. Before the war was over, Truman ended segregation in the armed forces by executive order.

2. What caused inflation after the war?

1) Labor unions wanted better pay for their workers. 2) People competed with one another to buy goods that were not made during the war. 3) Competition for scarce goods caused inflation.

Labor union workers also had plans for their security. They wanted to keep the better pay that they had earned during the war. After the war prices went up because people had money to spend. But there were few nonmilitary goods and services to buy. People competed with one another to buy goods that were not made during the war. Many factories could not make enough of these goods right away. They needed time to change their equipment from making tanks and airplane engines to making cars and refrigerators. Competition for scarce goods caused inflation, or rising prices. Workers wanted their wages to go up when prices rose. In the first year after the war, there was a series of major strikes.

The Voters Say No

3. Why did Americans vote for a Republican Congress in 1946?

1) Many voters probably blamed the party in power for allowing so many strikes and for rising prices. 2) When the voters thought of the Democratic party, they thought of higher taxes and government policies to solve social problems.

In 1946 there was an election for Congress. Truman found that his plans were threatened. The voters elected more Republicans than Democrats to both the House and the Senate. Why? Probably many voters blamed the party in power for allowing so many strikes and for rising prices. Spending more money to help the poor did not appeal to many American voters.

Truman also worried about strikes. He ordered the army to run the coal mines. In this way, the strike would not keep the nation's industries from having enough fuel to produce goods. Truman also threatened to order the army to run the railroad. His threat prevented a railroad strike. Truman's actions might have showed the voters that there was not one political party for labor and one

What had happened to the United States that had made strikes so costly? Notice how long inflation has been a problem.

against it. But most people remembered the labor policies of the New Deal. When the voters thought of the Democratic Party, they thought of higher taxes and government policies to solve social problems. And they thought that they had had enough of both.

Despite the President's objection, or *veto*, in 1947 the new Congress passed a new law. It took away some of the power of the unions. It gave the President the right to ask the courts to issue an order to delay a strike. There was to be an 80-day "cooling off" period. During that time information could be gathered and the two sides could meet to settle their disagreements without a strike. This law was called the Taft–Hartley Act. It also allowed people to work without joining unions. Nonunion workers would get the same pay and work rules as those negotiated for union workers by their leaders.

4. What were the provisions of the Taft-Hartley Act?

1) The President could ask the courts for an 80-day "cooling off" period to allow time for the two sides to try to settle their dispute. 2) It allowed nonunion members to get the same pay and work under the same rules negotiated by the union.

Foreign Policy

Truman got more support from Congress for his foreign policy. In his first year in office he led the United States into a new world organization for peace. The United Nations got *bipartisan* support, or support from both parties, in Congress. Unlike the days of Woodrow Wilson and the League of Nations, Americans had begun to realize that they were permanently international.

5. Why did the United Nations get bipartisan support in Congress?

Truman recognized that nations that had many poor people might become Communist. Communists preached against private ownership of capital and the machinery of production. Nations in which the rich did little to help the poor were easy targets for Communist propaganda. Communist nations believed that communism would help the poor. But they did not trust the people with freedom of choice. Truman spotlighted the lack of trust under communism. He offered American aid to nations that were democratic, or kept freedom of choice for their people. The United States would help free nations to create new jobs, to protect themselves with American arms from attack by the Soviet Union, and to preserve the freedom to vote and to hold property.

By 1953 both the United States and the Soviet Union had built hydrogen bombs. How could the accumulation of these bombs threaten world peace?

The Truman Doctrine

The Truman Doctrine was stated by the President in a message to Congress in March 1947. Greece and Turkey needed help. They stood between the Soviet Union and the Mediterranean Sea. Through invasions by the Eastern European countries of Albania, Bulgaria, and Yugoslavia, which the Soviet Union controlled, Stalin was trying to force Greece to become Communist. His threat to invade Turkey threatened freedom in that country, too. If the Soviet Union forced Greece and Turkey to become members of its

Truman made his foreign policy clear. Do you agree with the idea of aid to democracies? In what ways could that help America?

649

President Truman signs a bill providing aid to European countries. How did the Marshall Plan discourage communism in Europe?

Americans had begun to realize that their country had become permanently international.

Communist empire, the Soviet Union would control the Mediterranean. Then it would be a direct threat to France, Italy, and other nations in Western Europe.

President Truman told Congress that total dictatorships, or "*totalitarian* governments spread and grow in the evil soil of poverty. . . . They reach their full growth when the hope of a people for a better life has died. We must keep that hope alive!"

He accepted George Kennan's idea that the United States should keep communism from spreading to Western Europe. The policy was called *containment*. The first act of containment was to give aid to prevent aggression and poverty.

The Marshall Plan

The United States would give aid to keep other nations peaceful and free. In that same year, 1947, Secretary of State George C. Marshall announced a plan to give money to Great Britain and to all other European nations. This money would help to rebuild factories, houses, and transportation that had been destroyed in the war. This money for capital improvements would help former allies and Germany and Italy, former enemies, to become strong, to provide jobs, and to prevent communism. The Western Europeans accepted the Marshall Plan. The same offer was made to the Soviet Union and the nations of Eastern Europe. But the Communists turned it down.

America was spending its money in peacetime to help other nations create jobs for their people. This was a new approach to foreign policy. It was a way of keeping alive the values of liberty and opportunity in the world.

The Communist Challenge

6. What did Tito prove?

By refusing to accept Soviet control, he proved that a nation could be communist and oppose the Soviet Union.

How far did the Soviet Union's influence spread? In 1948 the Czech Communist party, with the help of the Soviet Union, took over the democratic nation of Czechoslovakia. In Italy the Communist party almost won an election in 1948. But American foreign aid and public appeals made by Italian Americans to their relatives and friends and by the Catholic Church to its members finally convinced many Italians to vote against the Communists. In Yugoslavia there was slightly better news. The Communist government of Marshal Josef Broz Tito broke away from the Soviet Union. Tito remained a Communist. But he refused to accept Soviet control. With aid from the United States, Yugoslavia showed the world that the Soviet Union could be opposed.

In what ways does the Marshall Plan teach that "doing good" and watching out for our national interest do not have to be opposite policies?

Why is the postwar map so important for understanding why the United States spends so much money on weapons?

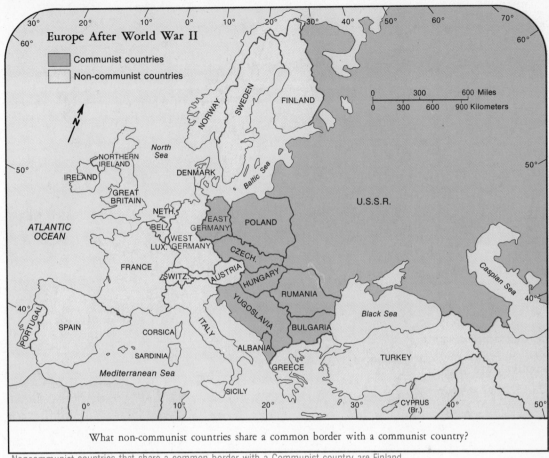

Europe After World War II

Communist countries
Non-communist countries

NORWAY
SWEDEN
FINLAND
North Sea
NORTHERN IRELAND
IRELAND
DENMARK
Baltic Sea
GREAT BRITAIN
NETH.
BEL.
EAST GERMANY
POLAND
U.S.S.R.
LUX.
WEST GERMANY
CZECH.
ATLANTIC OCEAN
FRANCE
SWITZ.
AUSTRIA
HUNGARY
RUMANIA
Caspian Sea
YUGOSLAVIA
BULGARIA
Black Sea
PORTUGAL
SPAIN
CORSICA
ITALY
ALBANIA
GREECE
TURKEY
SARDINIA
Mediterranean Sea
SICILY
CYPRUS (Br.)

300   600 Miles
300 600 900 Kilometers

What non-communist countries share a common border with a communist country?

Noncommunist countries that share a common border with a Communist country are Finland, West Germany, Austria, Italy, Greece, and Turkey.

The Challenge in Germany

The place where the free world and the Communist world met was Germany. Germany had been occupied and was controlled by the four major allies of World War II. The United States, England, and France worked together in their occupation zones in western Germany. In 1948 the English and the Americans decided to merge their zones. They also decided to use one currency. In this way they could rebuild their parts of Germany under the Marshall Plan. The French continued to administer their zone independently. But they used Marshall Plan money to rebuild it. The Soviets objected to the joint action on the part of the English and the Americans. They did not want Germany to be rebuilt. They wanted the German people to pay for rebuilding the Soviet Union. The Soviet Union had lost so many people and suffered so much damage during the war that Hitler started.

The Soviets did not rebuild their occupation zone in eastern Germany. Instead, they took the food produced by German farmers in

7. Why didn't the Soviet Union work with the United States, England, and France in rebuilding Germany?

1) The Soviets wanted the German people to pay for the rebuilding of the Soviet Union. 2) The Soviets took entire factories and plants in their zone and shipped them to the Soviet Union.

The Soviets really helped defeat Germany and suffered greatly. How is that past shown in the map of Germany and the zones?

651

During the Berlin blockade, 1948–1949, the United States and Great Britain airlifted supplies into West Berlin.

8. How did the Truman administration break the Berlin blockade?

1) It ordered the air force to fly supplies to the citizens of the English, American, and French zones of Berlin.
2) Eleven months later the Soviets lifted the blockade.

the East and sold it to the Russian people. They took whole factories and plants in the eastern zone and shipped them to the Soviet Union.

As an expression of its opposition, the Soviet Union closed the borders of its zone of occupation. This meant shutting off the city of Berlin, which had been the capital of Germany. Berlin was 150 miles (240 kilometers) inside the Soviet zone in eastern Germany. (See map, page 651.) At the end of the war, Berlin was occupied by the four allied powers. Like the rest of Germany, it was divided into four zones. The Soviet action prevented the English, American, and French zones in Berlin from receiving supplies from western Germany.

This was a serious challenge, but it was not a military action. What should the United States, England, and France do? The commander of the American occupation forces, General Lucius Clay, believed that the Soviet action should be considered a challenge, if not an act of war. "If we mean to hold Europe against communism, we must not budge," he said.

Why was the Berlin blockade such an important move to the United States and to the Soviets? What was new about "challenges" that are not "acts of war"? In what ways are challenges hard to live with?

The American response to the Berlin blockade was to fly supplies to the citizens of the English, American, and French zones of Berlin. The risk was that the Soviet Union might shoot down the planes. But supplying food and medical supplies was the Truman administration's way of taking action "short of war." The airlift worked. Eleven months later the Soviets lifted the blockade. But the Soviet zone of Berlin remained a hostile border.

Support at Home

Truman's actions were popular among Americans. America had helped to strengthen both democracy and capitalism. The United States had also stood up to Soviet action. The Republicans in Congress voted to support the President.

Congress did give President Truman the necessary support to set up a system of group defense, or *collective security*, to defend the West against the Soviet Union. This meant entering into a military alliance with the noncommunist governments of Western Europe. The Western nations took the Soviet threat seriously. They met together to draft the North Atlantic Treaty.

9. Why was the North Atlantic Treaty drafted?

The Western nations took the Soviet threat seriously, and they set up a system of collective defense to defend Western Europe against the Soviet Union.

Politics at Home

Truman came up for election to the presidency in November of that same year, 1948. Many politicians and newspaper columnists thought he would lose to the Republican candidate, Governor Thomas Dewey of New York. But they had not counted on the voters' reaction to the Fair Deal.

Truman was elected in 1948 for a term of his own. How great would the challenges at home and abroad become in four years?

Checking the facts

1. How did the Taft-Hartley Act come to be enacted?
2. How did Truman meet the Communist challenge abroad?

2. HOW MUCH CHALLENGE?

The new combination of the Soviet empire and Communist belief continued to threaten the Western nations. In 1949 delegates from ten Western European nations (Belgium, Britain, Denmark, France, Iceland, Italy, Luxembourg, Norway, the Netherlands, and

10. What were the provisions of NATO?

This poster honors the victory of Mao Tse-tung in the Chinese revolution.

1) All member nations pledged that an attack on one of them would be considered an attack on all of them.
2) Each nation promised support against aggression, including support from armed forces.

11. How was the Security Council of the United Nations able to vote on "police action" to restore peace in Korea?

The Soviet representatives were not there to veto collective action. They were boycotting the Security Council to protest the exclusion of the communist regime as the representative of China.

Portugal), Canada, and the United States met in Washington D.C. They all signed the treaty of alliance that Congress had supported the year before. The treaty established the North Atlantic Treaty Organization (NATO). All member nations pledged that an attack on one of them would be considered an attack on all of them. Each nation promised support against aggression, including support by armed forces.

Joining an organization designed only to prevent war by military readiness was a new move into a permanently international world. It was also a new recognition by the United States and others that Russia had to be warned. The Western allies had taken up the Soviet challenge. And challenge it was. The Soviet Union tested its first atomic bomb in that year.

Communism in Asia

Just when the American people hoped that containing the Soviet Union in Europe would contain communism, Communist beliefs gained victory. It was in Asia. There had been a long civil war in China between the Nationalists and the Communists. The Nationalists were the government leaders who had been the allies of the United States in World War II. Their leader was Chiang Kai-shek. The United States did not want to become involved in that civil war. But the Truman administration finally sent money and arms to the Nationalists to oppose the Soviet Union's support of the Communists.

In 1949 the Chinese Communists under their leader Mao Tse-Tung won the war. Chiang and the Nationalists were forced to leave the Chinese mainland. They set up their government on the island of Formosa. Americans were shocked. How and where would communism be contained in Asia?

The Line Is Drawn in Korea

The place was the peninsula of Korea. It bordered both China and Russia.

Korea was split into two occupied zones at the end of World War II. The Russian zone of North Korea had a Communist government. The American zone of South Korea had a noncommunist government. After Soviet and American troops withdrew, each Korean government claimed that it had the right to govern the whole of Korea.

In June 1950 the North Koreans with Soviet support crossed the occupation border and attacked South Korea. The United States decided not to act alone. It asked the Security Council of the United

To be a leader or even an educated voter, why do you have to know about civil wars in other countries?

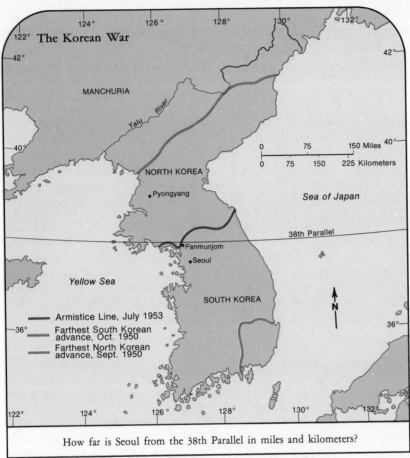

The Korean War

124° 126° 128° 130° 132°

122° The Korean War

42° 42°

MANCHURIA

Yalu River

40° 40°

NORTH KOREA

• Pyongyang

Sea of Japan

38th Parallel

• Panmunjom
• Seoul

Yellow Sea

SOUTH KOREA

N

— Armistice Line, July 1953
— Farthest South Korean advance, Oct. 1950
— Farthest North Korean advance, Sept. 1950

36° 36°

122° 124° 126° 128° 130° 132°

How far is Seoul from the 38th Parallel in miles and kilometers?

Seoul is approximately 45 miles, or 75 kilometers, from the 38th parallel.

Nations to take action against North Korea. At that time the Soviet Union was not attending Security Council meetings. Its representatives claimed that they would not come back until the Chinese Communists were allowed to represent China in the United Nations. Each of the five permanent members of the Security Council (the United States, Britain, France, China, and the Soviet Union) had the right to veto, or to prevent, United Nations' actions against an aggression. China was still represented by the Nationalists who supported the United States. And the Soviet representatives were not there to veto collective action. Therefore, the council voted to take "police action" to restore peace in Korea.

The armed forces of ten nations, including mostly South Koreans and Americans, formed the United Nations force under General Douglas MacArthur. The UN force was able to push the North Koreans back beyond the 30th parallel line dividing the two halves of Korea. MacArthur believed that the United Nations had to enlarge its police action. He believed that the UN force could unite Korea by driving the Korean Communists from the North. In

12. Why did Truman remove MacArthur from his command in Korea?

Notice how, step by step, the Korean War became a tangle. Why was it so hard for Americans to understand that war?

655

1) The UN approved MacArthur's plan to conquer North Korea. But six weeks after his arrival there, the Chinese crossed the border and attacked the UN forces. 2) MacArthur wanted to bomb China, but Truman did not want a war with the vast country. 3) MacArthur told American newspapers about his disagreement with the President.

October 1950 the United Nations approved his plan to conquer North Korea. Later that month, MacArthur and his troops reached the northern border of the Korean peninsula, the border shared with China. Within six weeks, the Chinese crossed the border and attacked the UN force. How was communism to be contained?

President Truman and General MacArthur disagreed. MacArthur wanted to fight the Chinese by bombing their territory and stopping their invasion. Truman wanted to keep the Chinese from taking over Korea. But he had no intention of going to war with the world's most heavily populated nation. MacArthur told American newspapers of his disagreement with the President. Truman ordered him to return to America and took away his command.

13. What actions did the United States take in trying to contain communism?

1) The army drafted many men, and the budget for military expenses was increased 400 percent. 2) NATO formed an army under the World War II American General Dwight Eisenhower. 3) The United States signed security treaties with the Philippines, Australia, and New Zealand. 4) Japan became an ally.

The Korean War scared most Americans. Protecting Koreans did not have the same appeal as protecting old allies like Britain and France. But the war in Korea seemed to be necessary to prevent a Communist victory in Asia. And the United States government decided that it would have to take that responsibility. The army drafted many men. Some men had fought in World War II. The budget for military expenses was increased 400 percent.

More Armies; More Treaties

The Korean War convinced the Truman administration that the United States would have to contain communism in Western Europe, in Asia, and throughout the world. NATO formed a joint army under the World War II American General Dwight Eisenhower. The United States signed security treaties with the Philippines, Australia, and New Zealand. Even the Japanese, the recent enemy, became an ally of the United States against the new enemy, communism.

The Challenge at Home

14. How did Americans disagree on what to do about communism?

1) Some did not want war no matter who the enemy was. 2) Some believed that anyone who supported Truman against MacArthur or who did not want to go to war against communism must be a communist.

The year 1951, Truman's last year as President, was a year of angry debate within the United States about American foreign policy. Some people blamed Truman for not giving enough support to the Nationalist Chinese. Admirers of MacArthur thought that the United States should fight China for a total victory.

On the other side of the debate were several different opinions. Some did not want more war, no matter who or what the enemy was. Others thought it was impossible to conquer the land between the Black Sea and the Pacific Ocean. And there were a few who thought that communism was a good idea because it seemed to promote social justice—even if the price that was paid was a loss of liberty.

The Korean war frightened Americans. Why?

People on each side of the debate tended to think that everyone on the other side was exactly alike. Some believed that anyone who supported Truman against MacArthur or who did not want to go to war against communism must be a Communist. Many Americans began to be suspicious of each other.

Americans were afraid of an enemy who had opposing beliefs. How could a nation fight against an idea? Some Americans were afraid to criticize their government for fear of being thought disloyal. Other Americans were afraid to support the government because at least one senator was saying very loudly that "Truman was soft on communism."

Senator Joseph McCarthy

One man took advantage of the fear and suspicion. He was Senator Joseph McCarthy of Wisconsin. As early as 1950, he began making public speeches that the State Department contained many Communists. McCarthy made broad statements claiming that he was right because Communists were "consistently found at the time and place where disaster strikes America and success comes to international communism." McCarthy claimed that the United States "lost China" because American officials who served there were Communists. They had written reports that praised the economic policies of the Chinese Communists. Therefore, said McCarthy, they had to be Communists.

His critics said that he was branding people with "guilt by association." They reminded Americans that in this country people are innocent until proved guilty. But the Senate was not a court of law, and McCarthy did not have to prove his charges. However, his accusations from the floor of the Senate got into the newspapers. Then suspicion swept the United States. People who refused to sign government loyalty oaths lost their jobs in such unrelated fields as college professors, violinists in symphony orchestras, actors, and writers.

When McCarthy was most popular, Senator Margaret Chase Smith, a Republican from Maine, had the courage to speak against his methods. She accused McCarthy of hiding behind senatorial privilege. Members of Congress could speak on the floors of both houses without being sued for trying to ruin someone's reputation (libel). Senator Smith said:

> "Those of us who shout the loudest about Americanism by making accusations are all too frequently those who, by our own words and acts, ignore some of the basic principles of Americanism—The right to criticize. The right to hold unpopular beliefs. The right to protest. The right of independent thought."

15. How did McCarthy promote his views?

1) He made his accusations about communists in American government from the Senate floor, where those charges did not have to be proved 2) His charges got into the newspapers.

Why do Americans sometimes refuse to let others speak? What can result from this lack of tolerance? Is it a threat to the American way?

657

Margaret Chase Smith, Republican senator from Maine, risked her political career by speaking up against McCarthy.

16. Why were Americans ready for change in 1952?

1) Many were upset about the Korean War. Twenty-five thousand Americans had died in a war that had no victors.
2) Ike promised to go there, suggesting that the war would soon be over.
3) Congressional investigations had revealed that some people in Truman's administration had taken bribes.

A strange thing had happened in the minds of many Americans. They had made a connection between people who pointed out America's problems because they wanted to solve them and Communists who pointed out America's problems because they wanted to destroy the American way of life. People who had been reformers were linked together by some Americans with people who thought that the American system would never improve and ought to be given up.

This hysterical fear reminded many Americans of the anti-German propaganda during World War I and the "red scare" after it. Many made that connection when they learned that citizen groups were going through school libraries, taking books off the shelves that criticized America in any way. For a time Americans lost their faith in freedom of speech and their faith in each other.

The Election of 1952

By the end of Truman's time in office, many Americans were upset. In addition to "McCarthyism," they were upset about the Korean War. Some 25,000 American soldiers had died in Korea in a war that had no victors. It looked as if American troops would have to stay in that far-off land, neither winning nor losing the war. Many people were not sure what the war was for.

By the time the campaign for President had begun in 1952, congressional investigations revealed that some people in Truman's administration had taken bribes. His appointments secretary and two officials in the Justice and Treasury departments were convicted and sentenced to prison. This was too much. The nation decided it wanted a change.

The Republican party did not run McCarthy or one of his supporters for the presidency. They offered the nomination to General Eisenhower who had never been an active member of the party. Eisenhower, however, was a popular hero. He reminded people of victory over the old enemy, Hitler. That was an enemy that Americans could understand. For Vice-President the Republicans chose a senator who had become known for his attacks against Communists in the government. He was Richard M. Nixon.

The Democrats ran the governor of Illinois, Adlai E. Stevenson. Stevenson was a witty, soft-spoken man who tried to show the American public how complicated the Communist challenge really was. Some people did not like Stevenson's wit. Life did not seem funny. Some Americans thought that he made the world sound too complicated.

When Eisenhower announced that "If elected, I will go to Korea,"

Adlai Stevenson was a popular leader. Why did he lose in 1952?

Americans felt relieved. They could turn their problems over to this smiling, fatherly, famous man. He would take care of things.

The slogan "I like Ike" suggested that some Americans hoped for a simple, quick solution to their problems abroad. Helping people at home had taken a back seat to "doing something about Korea." Many people liked Eisenhower and hoped that he would somehow make things better.

A record number of Americans—approximately 61 million—voted in 1952. Stevenson won more popular votes than had any candidate before that election. But Eisenhower won more than that. He was elected President.

Checking the facts

1. What circumstances led to American involvement in Korea in the 1950's?
2. What is meant by "the McCarthy era?"

During the presidential campaign, Eisenhower's supporters wore buttons such as this one. Do you think campaign advertising is effective?

3. HOW MUCH PROBLEM SOLVING?

Eisenhower did go to Korea in December 1952, one month after he was elected. By the end of his first six months in office, in July 1953, the United Nations and the North Koreans signed a cease-fire agreement. However, this cease-fire, or *armistice*, was not the same thing as peace.

The two sides agreed to a dividing line between the two armies. An area was set aside. Both sides agreed not to enter it. This *demilitarized zone* was an admission that the two sides would probably never trust each other and never give up their desire to win. The Americans were relieved that the shooting war was over, even if there was no victory. American troops stayed in South Korea to protect it from being attacked. American aid to South Korea stayed in the budget of the federal government.

17. What was the importance of the demilitarized zone?

Setting aside an area in which both sides agreed not to enter was an admission that neither side would probably ever trust the other nor would ever give up its desire to win.

McCarthyism Under Eisenhower

Did Senator McCarthy relax his attack on government once the Republican party came to power? No. He attacked even harder. For two years he continued to hold congressional hearings, some of which were televised. Because these hearings were not court trials, he could accuse government workers and members of the army of being Communists or Communist sympathizers. Often he did not even give any evidence for his accusations.

18. How did McCarthy lose his power?

We have had to face the same kinds of problems for a long time. Is it hard for people to care about solving the same kinds of problems year after year?

659

This picture shows Joseph Welch, lawyer for the army and Senator Joseph McCarthy. McCarthy is pointing out areas of supposed Communists in the United States. How did McCarthy's "red scare" affect Americans?

1) Americans finally began to question him when his attacks suggested that no one in the government was hard enough on communism. 2) In December 1954, the Senate of the United States voted "that this conduct of the Senator from Wisconsin, Mr. McCarthy, is contrary to senatorial traditions and is hereby condemned."

Americans finally began to question McCarthy when his attacks suggested that *no one* in the government was hard enough on communism. His attacks began to look as if they were aimed at President Eisenhower. But Eisenhower was popular with the American people. And his reputation as a fighter for freedom in World War II was more powerful than McCarthy and McCarthyism.

The Senate held televised hearings during which McCarthy attacked some army officers. In December 1954, the Senate voted "that this conduct of the senator from Wisconsin, Mr. McCarthy, is contrary to senatorial traditions and is hereby condemned." From that moment on, Joseph McCarthy lost his power. Americans were beginning to remember the importance of defending free speech and the free press.

Eisenhower's Foreign Policy

19. *Why did Eisenhower make an "open skies" proposal to the Soviet Union?*

1) He believed that the communist nations and the free nations could coexist in the world without destroying each other with nuclear weapons. 2) He suggested a plan that would allow each nation to take aerial photographs of the other to ensure that the other side was not preparing for war.

Eisenhower kept Truman's policy of containment. But he added the idea that the American system of democracy, capitalism, and free trade could exist with the Soviet and the Chinese systems of dictatorship and public ownership of property. Eisenhower believed that the Communist nations and the free nations could live in the world without destroying each other with nuclear weapons. This was called *peaceful coexistence*. The big question was whether the Soviet and Chinese leaders could be trusted to compete with the United States without beginning a hot war.

At a meeting in Geneva, Switzerland, in 1955, Eisenhower suggested a plan allowing each nation to take aerial photographs of the other. In this way each nation could be sure that the other side was not preparing for war. This "open skies" prosposal became part of

Was peaceful coexistence a change from the Truman Doctrine?

what the press called "the spirit of Geneva." But it did not last long. In October 1956 the Hungarians revolted. They had been controlled by the Soviet Union since World War II. The Soviets sent in their army to crush the revolution. The United States did not risk going to war to stop the Soviet Union in Hungary. Its unwillingness to help the Hungarian freedom fighters was debated in the United States. The possibility of an all-out war with the Soviet Union seemed too great a risk. The competition with the Russians was going to be a long one. But a cold one.

The Cold War Spreads

The 1950s were confusing years for Americans. Eisenhower's action in Korea seemed less important as the United States faced the cold war in place after place. Following World War II, a period of competition and hard feelings between the Soviet Union and non-communist countries like the United States existed. It was called the *cold war*. The United States built up its army in case the Soviet Union or its allies attacked the United States. But when the Soviets took action, it was not directly against the United States. Americans did not want to be the police force in every part of the world. America wanted and needed friends around the world. It was hard to compete with the Soviets, who were lining up friends on their side. The Soviet Union and the United States sent aid. They made investments in other countries. Foreign aid was good for business. Although many Americans believed that foreign aid could not ensure friendship and support, they realized that it had become part of the cold war.

Every action that one side took was considered competition by the other. In October 1957 the Soviet Union sent the first satellite into orbit in outer space. It was called "Sputnik." All over America people knew its name. People wondered how the Soviet Union had managed to get so far ahead of America in science. By the next year the United States had launched its first space vehicle, Explorer I.

With the space program and the military buildup, the government had become involved directly in many parts of the American economic system. Whole factories depended on government contracts. University faculties depended on government grants. Jobs were created in private businesses that had won government contracts. And money was being spent on military goods and space equipment to make the Soviet Union too afraid to start a war.

The Challenge for Fair Treatment at Home

President Eisenhower was one of many Americans who believed that the New Deal and the Fair Deal had spent too much government money. Congress sent Eisenhower 150 bills for financial aid

20. How did the cold war influence the American economic system?

The space and military buildup to compete with the Soviet Union involved the government in many aspects of the economic system.

Millions of American tax dollars went toward the building of rockets for the space program.

The threat of the atom bomb and the cold war changed the lives of many Americans. How have similar threats influenced your life?

661

In 1957 President Eisenhower sent in the national guard to ensure that Black students would be admitted to Little Rock Central High School.

to education, housing, and rebuilding cities. He vetoed all of them. However, Eisenhower cared a great deal about giving everyone equal rights to a good education and equal treatment in the courts. These were basic rights of citizens, or civil rights. They were the American guarantees of liberty and opportunity.

21. What gains did Blacks make in civil rights during the Eisenhower administration?

1) In *Brown* v. *Board of Education of Topeka* in 1954, the Supreme Court ruled that separate schools for Blacks were unconstitutional. 2) When nine Black students were refused admission to the all-White Central High School in Little Rock, Arkansas, in 1957, he sent the national guard to make sure that the students would be admitted and would not be hurt. 3) Black organizations held successful sit-in demonstrations at segregated restaurants and boycotted segregated buses.

Eisenhower appointed Governor Earl Warren of California to the post of chief justice of the Supreme Court. Under Warren's leadership, the Court made a number of important decisions in the area of civil rights. The first of these major decisions was *Brown* v. *Board of Education of Topeka (Kansas)* in 1954. The court ruled that separate schools for Black Americans was unconstitutional. The Court ruled that "separate but equal" schools did not provide equal opportunity for Black students. No separate school could be truly equal for Blacks. The 1896 decision of *Plessy* v. *Ferguson* had ruled that "separate but equal" was constitutional. It was reversed almost 60 years later.

Many of the civil rights decisions of the Warren Court were based on the Fourteenth Amendment to the Constitution. It guaranteed *equal protection* under the law to every citizen. Equal protection was interpreted by the Supreme Court to mean that the government and agencies receiving government money must give fair and equal treatment to all citizens. Schools were agencies of state government. Therefore, the Court declared, they had to provide equal education.

Nine Black students were refused admission to the all-White Central High School in Little Rock, Arkansas, in 1957. Governor Orval Faubus refused to protect those students from the mobs outside the school. Eisenhower sent the national guard to make sure that the students would be admitted and would not be hurt.

The 14th amendment protects the American way because it now applies to every citizen. How does it protect you?

Black lawyers, civil rights leaders, and church leaders began using new tactics during the last few years of Eisenhower's presidency. They wanted to call attention to laws and practices that took away their civil rights. Blacks were excluded from housing in White neighborhoods. Many businesses, professions, and private clubs in the nation were closed to Blacks. Action was taken by civil rights groups, such as the Southern Christian Leadership Conference, the Congress of Racial Equality, the Urban League, and the Student Nonviolent Coordinating Committee. The first peaceful sit-in demonstration took place at a segregated lunch counter in Greensboro, North Carolina. A boycott of buses was organized by Martin Luther King, Jr. in Montgomery, Alabama. Blacks argued that restaurants that got their licenses to do business along with police and fire protection from city governments had no right to keep out Black citizens who helped to pay for those governments. Governments that created public transportation paid for by taxes had no right to force Blacks to sit in the back of buses or trolleys. As civil rights demonstrations spread throughout the country, lawyers for the National Association for the Advancement of Colored People defended peaceful protesters who had been arrested for exercising their civil rights.

More Communist Action and American Reaction

During the latter part of the 1950's the long-range plan of Communist nations became clear. They were giving aid to poor countries, especially to those that had been part of the empires of the Western European world. Asian, African, and Latin American countries were the targets. Communism was tied to the struggle against colonialism. The Soviet Union and China sent their citizens to work among the poor. They wanted the people of Latin America, Africa, and Asia to regard them as friends. They spoke out against private property, especially property owned by foreigners in the West. Year by year the spread of Communist aid to *third-world* countries grew. By 1958 Soviet and Chinese Communists were urging these nations to establish Communist dictatorships—by revolution if necessary.

In that year China bombed the islands off its coast occupied by the Nationalists. The Chinese Communists wanted to remind the Nationalists and the Americans that those islands and Formosa were Chinese territory. China restated its claim. Then it left the world to wonder when and how it would pressure those islands to join the Communist People's Republic of China. In 1959 China took control of Tibet. That nation stood between China and India. China claimed that its actions in Tibet simply restored old borders that had kept China secure.

22. What were the third-world countries?

There were poor nations in Asia, Africa, and Latin American that had been part of the empires of the Western world.

23. What actions did China take to assert itself?

1) China bombed the Nationalist-controlled islands off its coast to remind the Nationalists and the Americans that those islands were Chinese territory.
2) China took control of Tibet, claiming that it was simply restoring old borders.

A Vietnamese rice farmer plows his field as French troops make their way to the front line in 1954.

The Domino Theory

Western nations were afraid that the Chinese would move south into the Indochinese peninsula. That land had been part of the French empire. But the French lost a long war against jungle, or guerrilla, fighters and had pulled out in 1955. The United States had given aid to the French. Eisenhower and his advisers believed that if one territory fell to communism, then the one next to it would be weakened and fall, and then the next, and the next—like a row of dominoes that leaned on one another.

The *domino theory* became part of American foreign policy. When the French pulled out, leaving Indochina divided, the United States began to send aid and advisers to the government of South Vietnam. The United States was afraid that if an election were held in Vietnam in 1956, the Communists who controlled North Vietnam would win. Vietnamese in the south agreed with the Americans. They refused to participate in the election.

The Middle East and Cuba

In 1956 another area of the world became involved in the cold war—the Middle East, where much oil was. The "Eisenhower Doctrine" for the Middle East was to guarantee support to noncommunist nations in the area. But many noncommunist nations in the Middle East had sworn to destroy the democratic nation of Israel. The Arab states believed that Israel had no right to form a state in land that they claimed belonged to the Arab Palestinians. The United States supported Israel. Through the United Nations it had helped to form the state of Israel in 1948. All of the Arab states refused to recognize Israel. But only some of them claimed

24. Why did the United States send aid and advisers to the government of South Vietnam?

1) The French pulled out of Indochina after losing a long war against guerrilla fighters. 2) Eisenhower believed in the domino theory, that if one territory fell to communism, then the territory next to it would be weakened and fall, and so on.

25. What were the cold-war alliances in the Middle East?

1) The United States supported Israel and the nonrevolutionary states of Jordan, Saudi Arabia, Lebanon, and Iran. 2) The Soviet Union opposed Israel and gave military equipment to the revolutionary Arab states.

Why does it help to know that Vietnam was part of our cold war foreign policy?

to be revolutionary—Egypt, Iraq, and Syria. The Eisenhower administration continued to support Israel. It also gave some military assistance to the nonrevolutionary states of Jordan, Saudi Arabia, Lebanon, and Iran. The Soviet Union opposed Israel and gave military equipment to the revolutionary Arab states.

And in 1959 still another trouble spot appeared. A revolution brought Fidel Castro to power in Cuba. This island was only 90 miles (144 kilometers) off the coast of Florida.

26. Why did the United States hesitate about supporting Castro?

1) American businesses had invested in Cuba.
2) Americans bought a great deal of Cuban sugar and tobacco.

The United States hesitated to support Castro. American businesses had invested in Cuba. Americans bought a great deal of Cuban tobacco and sugar. The government that Castro overthrew, however, had become unpopular with the people. Castro became known as a Communist. What should the United States do? Is it wrong to interfere with the government of another country? Is it wrong not to give support to revolutions which overthrow dictators? What if the new revolutionary leader, like Castro, wants to help the poor but intends to be a dictator as well? The United States decided not to support Castro. The Soviet Union did. Foreign policy toward poor nations of the third world had grown increasingly complicated as the cold war progressed.

Living in a world with what seemed to be a permanent enemy was frightening and costly. Americans were torn between wanting to help people at home and wanting to help people abroad. In some ways, however, they just wanted to hold on to what they already had.

Checking the facts

1. What ended the McCarthy era?
2. How did Eisenhower conduct his foreign policy regarding communism?
3. What actions did Eisenhower take in support of equal rights?

4. HOW AMERICANS LIVED IN THE 1950's

The automobile and the highway made it possible in the 1950's for many factories to move away from the cities, where the poor lived. Factories were moved to the suburbs, where the middle-class managers lived. And white- and blue-collar workers in the offices and in the factories moved there, too. Discrimination prevented Blacks from buying houses in many suburbs. And so they either

27. How did the move to the suburbs affect Blacks?

1) Discrimination prevented Blacks from buying houses in many suburbs. 2) There was little public transportation, which meant that they could not get jobs unless they had cars to drive there.

One of the problems facing foreign policy decision makers is how to deal with governments that have different values. How would you answer the questions in the third paragraph?

Suburbs began to pop up in many cities during the 1950's. Many consisted of tract homes such as these. All the homes were built from the same architectural plans.

lost their jobs or had to travel long distances to get to work. If they did not own cars, it was often impossible for them to get to work. Very little money had been spent to provide public transportation to the suburbs.

For the first time in American history, the poor and the newcomers could not find the low skilled jobs that had always provided support for those groups. In the New York City area alone, 80 percent of the jobs created between 1952 and 1957 were in the suburbs.

More Education

28. How did educational opportunity improve?

1) By 1960, 50 percent of adults were finishing high school. 2) There was a 50 percent rise in the number of young people going to college. 3) There were 9 million adults enrolled in continuing education courses.

Americans who could afford it seemed to want a higher quality way of life. They wanted better homes and better cars. They also wanted better education. The number of high school graduates had never been so high. At the end of the war, about one in every three adults had finished high school. By 1960 the number had increased to almost one in two. There was a 50 percent rise in the number of young people going to college. And there were 9 million adults enrolled in continuing education courses.

Puerto Ricans Come to America

29. Why did Puerto Rican immigration drop off after 1953?

The newest group of newcomers to the United States were the Puerto Ricans. There had been some Puerto Ricans in the United

After the wartime migration of Blacks to northern cities, many factories moved to the suburbs. How does the employment situation faced by Blacks compare with the situation faced by southern Europeans in the 1890's?
Why has the goal of education fitted in so well with American values?

States since the early 1800's. More had come after the United States won Puerto Rico in the Spanish-American War. The greatest number came after World War II. In the first year after the war, about 40,000 more Puerto Ricans came to the mainland United States than left it to return to the island. In 1953, the peak year, the number reached 70,000. After that it dropped year by year, as businesses in the United States found themselves unable to sell all they could produce. When they began to lay off workers, it was often the last hired, including Puerto Ricans, who lost their jobs. Many went home.

Puerto Ricans were different from other newcomers. Puerto Ricans were American citizens when they arrived. And the government had made plans to help them settle before they left home. The government of Puerto Rico set up a Migration Division in the Department of Labor. It worked with governments and businesses in 115 mainland towns and cities. The aim was to make sure that Puerto Ricans had jobs and housing when they arrived.

By careful planning, workers from Puerto Rico would go where there were shortages of labor. And American businesses could not hire Puerto Rican workers at wages lower than the legal rate. Sixty-nine percent of Puerto Ricans on the mainland lived in New York City in 1960. However, there were also Puerto Ricans in cities and on farms throughout the nation.

Before Puerto Ricans came to the mainland, they were given a booklet. Entitled *Guide to the Traveler*, it explained how important it was to learn English, what kinds of clothing were needed in each climate zone, what family papers were needed for entrance into school, how to get a driver's license, and the problems of buying on the installment plan. This is the kind of aid that earlier immigrants had to find out for themselves. What was so different was that the Puerto Ricans were Americans. They got the information at home and from their government.

By the time that the Puerto Ricans arrived, the policy was to integrate everyone in public housing projects. Puerto Ricans were spread all over the city rather than living near each other. Public housing was supposed to be better and fairer than ghetto housing. But scattered housing also made it hard for Puerto Ricans to offer each other neighborhood support. Puerto Ricans were the only Roman Catholics who did not have their own churches in their own language with the differences in the service that they were used to.

Puerto Ricans had a major problem because many of them arrived in the city after so many industries had moved to the suburbs. Like Blacks who had migrated to cities before them, Puerto Ricans had

In 1959 Hawaii was admitted as the fiftieth state. Students at the Kuhio School in Hawaii are shown reacting to the news.

1) The United States was not able to sell all it produced, causing the layoff of workers. 2) Many Puerto Ricans lost their jobs, for they had been the last hired, and they returned home.

30. What problems did Puerto Ricans encounter?

1) They were spread all over the city in public housing, which made it hard for them to offer each other neighborhood support. 2) They were in competition with Blacks for scarce work in the city. 3) Puerto Ricans with dark skins found that they were treated as badly by White Americans as Blacks were.

When the nation was expanding, newcomers who had skills began to benefit. Why have the Puerto Ricans faced so many problems since they immigrated to the mainland?

Mobile learning centers such as this one were created to help Puerto Ricans learn English. What are the advantages of these centers?

no cars and no money. They could not get jobs in the suburbs. The rivalry between Blacks and Puerto Ricans for scarce work in the city was serious. Tight competition for jobs existed in the needle trades, hotels, hospitals, and other places in which some low-skilled workers could begin to learn skills.

Puerto Ricans also had problems with the civil rights movement. Many Americans had begun to encourage integration of the races. This seemed only natural to the Puerto Ricans who came from a society in which skin color was not a problem. But Puerto Ricans who had dark skins found that they were treated as badly by White Americans as Blacks were. It began to be important to look and sound different from Blacks. Instead of joining the civil rights movement and learning English, many Puerto Ricans stayed away from Blacks. Many decided that it would be better to continue to speak Spanish.

Puerto Ricans began to organize when they saw that the Black power movement had shifted from integration to independence as a goal. Puerto Ricans who intended to remain in the United States realized that they would have to organize to get power, too.

The Mexican Americans

31. What problems were Mexican Americans having?

They all received low wages. The "braceros" contracted to work for low wages; the "wetbacks" had to work for low wages because they were illegal immigrants.

In the years of World War II and immediately after, Mexican Americans were also having trouble. Their difficulty came from some special conditions in the market for cheap labor in the Southwest. And they also suffered from being seriously divided among themselves.

One of their leaders who described the situation was Ernesto Galarza. Galarza had come to the United States in 1911. He was highly educated. He got a job with the American Federation of Labor. Galarza directed research and education for the National

What were some of the differences between the Black experience and the Puerto Rican experience in the eastern cities in the fifties?

Many poor Mexican immigrants went to work on farms and ranches. In what ways was their experience different from the experience of poor workers who immigrated to the cities?

Mexicans line up to apply for permission to enter the United States to work legally.

Farm Union. He believed that the main thing that Mexican Americans had in common was the low wages that they received. He believed that until the labor unions organized the farm workers, the Mexican Americans were still going to suffer.

In addition to the Mexican Americans who had lived in the United States for some time, there were two other groups of workers from Mexico. There were those who came as groups of contract laborers. Their contracts had been made between United States employers and the Mexican government. There were even treaties that encouraged this kind of labor contract. These workers were called "braceros." Although their work was legal, they were paid low wages that helped to keep all wages low.

The other low-wage group consisted of illegal immigrants who crossed the wide border and took whatever work they could find and whatever wages they could get. They were called "wetbacks" in the 1950's because they swam across the Rio Grande into the United States. They and their employers were hated both by the other Mexican Americans and by other workers who realized that 60,000 unskilled jobs in southwest Texas alone and another 20,000 on the giant farms and corporate ranches in the San Joaquin Valley of California would go to the cheapest labor available.

Another split among Mexicans was the one between city people and farmers. Those who moved into the big cities, such as Los Angeles, San Antonio, and Chicago, learned to live like city people. They began to feel closer to other city people than they did to other Mexican Americans.

The experience of urban Mexicans was closer to the experience of other immigrants than it was to that of farm workers. Why did place of residence and kind of job prove more important to some groups than did their national origins?

In the 1950's Elvis Presley became an instant idol to millions of American teen-agers. One of his popular hits was "You Ain't Nothin' but a Hound Dog."

The End of the 1950's

32. Why did Kennedy's slim victory pose a problem?

It was not clear what the American people wanted the government to do.

Life in America had changed. And the attention of America's leaders seemed to be on many subjects at one time. The 1950's were a time when many Americans realized how many problems there were. Many wanted to hold onto what they had, both at home and overseas. The poor, Blacks, women, Mexican Americans, and Native Americans were beginning to organize. At least they were beginning to realize that they would have to organize in order to improve their lives.

The election of a new President in 1960 was a very close one. John F. Kennedy, a senator from Massachusetts, won over Eisenhower's vice-president, Richard M. Nixon. But how would the new President interpret his slim victory? Did the American people want the government to try to solve more problems? Would the 1960's be a new time to "try to improve"?

Checking the facts

1. How were the Puerto Ricans different from other immigrants in the United States?
2. Why were the Mexican American workers having trouble getting help?

Why does pop culture cut across ethnic lines?
Why are the fifties hard to summarize? What kinds of variety did America contain at that time?

PUTTING IT ALL TOGETHER

UNDERSTANDING THE MAIN IDEAS

1. How did Truman meet the challenge of communism?
2. What was the reaction of Americans to the Korean War?
3. How did Senator Joseph McCarthy first attract public attention?
4. What improvements were made in American life during the 1950's? For whom?

ACTIVITIES

1. Examine a map of the world. How were the dividing lines between Communist sections and free sections drawn in Germany, Korea, and Vietnam?
2. Read an article in your local newspaper about communism today. In what ways does the challenge to America look the same? Are there ways in which the challenge seems different? Place your findings in a brief written report.
3. Look at political cartoons about the Soviet Union. What is the message of the cartoonist to the reader?
4. Interview two adults over the age of 45. What do they remember about Senator Joseph McCarthy and President Eisenhower? Prepare a series of questions to ask your interviewees. Then place your findings in a report, to be delivered orally to your class.

BOOKS TO READ

Goettel, Elinor, *America's Wars—Why* (New York: Julian Messner, Inc., 1972).

Goldman, Eric F., *The Crucial Decade and After: America, 1945–1960* (New York: Random House, Inc., 1956).

Holland, Ruth, *The Forgotten Minority* (New York: Thomas Y. Crowell, 1969).

Sterling, Philip, and Brau, Maria, *The Quiet Rebels* (Garden City: Doubleday and Co., Inc., 1976).

chapter 27
Improving By Finding New Ways

1960–1966

1. KENNEDY'S 1,000 DAYS
2. THE GREAT SOCIETY

INTRODUCTION

By 1960, Americans knew what the challenges were—both at home and abroad. But they were not sure what they could do to meet those challenges. Could the United States make another push to do more for the poor and the elderly? Could the United States keep up its military strength, which would be needed if the Russians decided to cause more trouble? Helping the poor meant spending money on aid that could have helped the economy to grow. Creating jobs was a slow kind of help. But it was a real solution. New jobs would come by letting business pay lower taxes. But business would have to be trusted to build new factories and hire the poor.

Did anyone believe that the United States could continue to improve? In 1960 the new President, John F. Kennedy, believed that it could. And his belief was contagious. He was handsome and young and spoke well. Kennedy became President in 1961. He was 43 years old, the youngest President elected in the history of

	1961	1961	1962	1963	
Who?	John F. Kennedy, a senator from Massachusetts	The government of communist East Berlin	Khrushchev and Kennedy	President Kennedy	
What?	becomes the thirty-fifth President	builds a wall	disagree over Soviet missile bases	is assassinated while riding in a motorcade	
Where?	of the United States	separating East Berlin from West Berlin	in Cuba	in Dallas, Texas	

After two generations of trying to improve their country and the world, many Americans knew a great deal about the modern world. Why is it important to know about the events of your own time?

the United States. He clearly believed that it was the American way to solve problems. Kennedy called for new action on a "New Frontier." In his inaugural address he said about communism: "Let us never negotiate out of fear. But let us never fear to negotiate. Let both sides explore what problems unite us instead of belaboring those problems which divide us. . . ." And he called on Americans to work together on a new beginning with leaders from a new generation. "And so, my fellow Americans, ask not what America will do for you, but what together we can do for the freedom of man."

Kennedy believed that problems don't go away by themselves. Thinking and caring people must try to solve them. He had faith in Americans. Many Americans were excited about Kennedy. But many Americans wondered whether anything could be done. As you read about the 1960's, think about the following questions:

1. Were there any new ideas about dealing with communism abroad and opportunity at home?
2. How could the American people pay for new government programs to help the disadvantaged?
3. How could the American people create new jobs?

1. KENNEDY'S 1,000 DAYS

The President and Congress

President Kennedy hoped to be able to carry the excitement of his New Frontier to Congress. However, many conservatives in Congress thought that too much spending would not help America's economy or its problems. Congress did vote for a higher minimum wage law, a drug control law, and federal aid to back mortgages

1. Which of Kennedy's bills did Congress pass to help the economy?
Federal aid to guarantee mortages on housing to create construction jobs and a higher minimum wage law.

1963	1964	1965	1965	1966
Lyndon Johnson	Three civil rights workers	Dr. Martin Luther King, Jr.	American troops	Women
becomes the thirty-sixth President	are killed	organizes a drive to get Blacks registered to vote	are sent to support the government	form the National Organization of Women (NOW)
of the United States	in Mississippi	in Selma, Alabama	of South Vietnam	in the United States

To many Kennedy was the most exciting President since FDR, even though the problems that he faced were different from those faced by Roosevelt. In what ways were their problems different?

President Kennedy, on the left, and his Vice-President, Lyndon Johnson, are shown here. Why did Kennedy choose Johnson as his running mate?

James Meredith gained national attention when he tried to gain admission to the University of Mississippi.

on housing. Housing was a key to a healthy economy because it created construction jobs.

Kennedy was unable to get Congress to pass laws for medical care to the aged, federal aid to education, and strong civil rights for Blacks. The education bill could not get past representatives from the richer states. Those states were not allowed as much money per pupil as were poor states. There were also problems over giving aid to private and church schools. The American Medical Association, the doctor's lobby, came out strongly against government aid to older people, or medicare.

Kennedy had talked of "getting the economy moving again." This meant new jobs through increased business investment and more trade. He wanted to cut taxes to give people more money to spend. Congress did not agree. Congress did support his plan to work with European countries to lower tariffs. This made it possible for goods to be traded more freely across the Atlantic.

Civil Rights

The civil rights movement changed in method and focus in the early 1960's. Before that, particularly in the 1950's, the National Association for the Advancement of Colored People had sponsored case-by-case court action. Individual law suits were the group's method of bringing about racial integration.

In the 1960's people marched and protested for voter registration in the South. College students from all over the country were the core of what became known as "freedom workers." In 1961 a Black man from Mississippi, James Meredith, sued in the federal courts for admission to the state university. When the governor refused to obey the court order and allow Meredith admission, President Kennedy sent in federal marshals and troops to enforce it.

In the next few years several hundred White and Black freedom workers took "freedom walks" through Mississippi. This was their way of showing that they believed in integration. They also worked to get southern Blacks registered to vote. Fighting broke out, and three freedom workers were killed. The nation was made aware of how hard it was to change old ways. Many southerners who supported civil rights were upset over strangers coming into their states. They pointed out that the northerners came from cities where there were segregated housing and job discrimination.

Action Against Cuba

One of the places that Eisenhower and Kennedy talked about when they met prior to Kennedy's inauguration in 1961 was Cuba. Since

March 1960 Eisenhower had directed the American intelligence service, the Central Intelligence Agency, to bring together the large number of Cuban exiles in the United States. They were to be trained to return to Cuba to help the Cuban people fight against the Castro government. Kennedy continued this policy.

Then the CIA decided to push for a plan of invasion. There was great disagreement among the President's advisers. Some believed that the United States should not back such an invasion. That would be doing what the United States criticized the Russians for doing. Others said that it was too late to stop the invasion. The Cuban exiles had been trained and armed.

Kennedy had been in office only 77 days when he made the decision to go ahead with the plan. His military advisers said that in a few weeks the Castro government would have Soviet airplanes. Then any action would be too late. He ordered the landing at a place called the Bay of Pigs on April 17, 1961. The 1,400 Cuban invaders ran into severe opposition that they had not anticipated. They expected air support from the United States. But the Kennedy administration had counted on an uprising against Castro in Cuba as soon as the invasion began. No such uprising took place. Castro had quickly rounded up a quarter of a million people to make sure that there was no aid to the invaders. The invasion failed.

The Bay of Pigs invasion caused the Kennedy administration great embarrassment. The President went on television and took complete responsibility for the disaster. He said that the United States had learned that trying to win over communism was a "new and deeper strugle. . . ."

Action in Indochina

Eisenhower had discussed with Kennedy the fighting between Communists and noncommunists in Laos, a country in Southeast Asia. If the Communists won, he thought that noncommunist governments in the area would also fall. The Southeast Asia Treaty Organization (SEATO) could not be counted on to help. Eisenhower believed that the area should be protected—with an American army if necessary.

President Kennedy responded to the situation in Southeast Asia. He committed more aid to the government of South Vietnam. A special force, known as the "Green Berets," was sent to advise the South Vietnamese army.

Some people were afraid that Americans could do no better in a guerrilla war than the French had done. (The Communists had defeated the French in 1954.) Others believed that only the United States could save Southeast Asia from communism.

2. How did the Bay of Pigs invasion cause the Kennedy administration great embarrassment?

1) The CIA had trained Cuban exiles in the United States for an invasion of Cuba. 2) The 1,400 Cuban invaders ran into severe opposition that they had not expected. The United States did not provide air support because it had counted on an uprising against Castro. 3) The invasion failed.

The Green Berets are a special branch of the United States armed forces, trained in guerrilla warfare.

The President has to deal with many parts of the world at one time. Why is it important to know the steps through which the United States government became involved in Vietnam?

675

New Ideas

3. What new ideas did Kennedy put into action?

1) He established the Peace Corps, an organization that sent Americans to less developed countries to help build hospitals and schools and to teach modern methods of health care, farming, and the use of tools. 2) He announced that within ten years the United States would put an American on the moon. Congress voted money for rocket development and for the training of astronauts. In 1962, John Glenn became the first American astronaut to orbit the earth.

4. How did Kennedy get the Soviet Union to remove its missiles from Cuba?

1) The United States called for meetings of the OAS and of the UN Security Council and blockaded shipments of supplies to Cuba. The Soviets became convinced that Kennedy would invade Cuba if necessary. 2) The United States told the Soviets that they had 24 hours to decide to pull out or the United States would take action in three days.

5. What did the United States and the Soviet Union do to keep the competition from becoming a hot war?

Not every situation that President Kennedy acted on was an old problem. He caught the imagination of the world with several new ideas. One was to send Americans to less developed countries to help build schools and hospitals. An organization called the Peace Corps was set up in 1961. The members of the Peace Corps, mainly young people, lived in foreign villages and taught in schools. They also taught modern methods of health care, farming, and the use of tools.

To take up the Soviet challenge in outer space, Kennedy announced that within ten years the United States would put a man on the moon. He asked Congress to vote money for rocket development and for training astronauts. In 1962 John Glenn became the first American astronaut to orbit the earth.

Cuba Again

In July of 1962 the Soviet Union began to supply Cuba with nuclear missiles capable of destroying the United States. The CIA reported that there were 5,000 Soviet specialists in Cuba and missile bases were visible from the air. It was not clear what the Soviet leader Nikita Khrushchev (krews-TSHEF) had in mind.

The United States government had to decide whether to blockade Cuba with ships or to send aircraft to destroy the missile sites. When the decision was made, Kennedy went on television and called the Soviet action a deliberate challenge to the United States. He called for a meeting of the Organization of American States (OAS)—the nations of the Western Hemisphere—and asked the secretary-general to call a meeting of the Security Council of the United Nations. All shipments of supplies to Cuba were to be stopped by the United States navy. Then the world waited.

Word came that the Russians were willing to take the missiles out of Cuba if the United States would promise not to invade the island. The President's brother, Attorney General Robert Kennedy, was his chief adviser. He gave a message to the Soviet ambassador in Washington. The message said that the Soviet Union had 24 hours to decide to pull out. If not, the United States would take action within three days.

The Soviet Union finally gave in. The United States had stood up to the challenge and avoided war.

At Peace with an Enemy

In order to avoid any misunderstandings with the Soviet Union, Kennedy spoke out for more discussions between the two govern-

How would you compare the Berlin airlift and the Cuban missile crisis?

The United States and the Soviet Union develop new weapons and at the same time sign treaties that limit their use. Why?

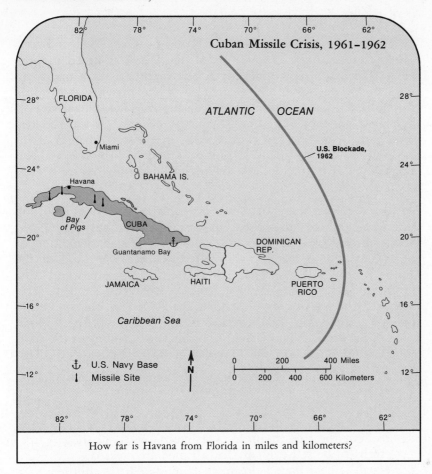

Cuban Missile Crisis, 1961–1962

ATLANTIC OCEAN

U.S. Blockade, 1962

FLORIDA

Miami

BAHAMA IS.

Havana

Bay of Pigs

CUBA

Guantanamo Bay

DOMINICAN REP.

PUERTO RICO

JAMAICA

HAITI

Caribbean Sea

⚓ U.S. Navy Base
Missile Site

N

| 0 | 200 | 400 Miles |
| 0 | 200 | 400 | 600 Kilometers |

How far is Havana from Florida in miles and kilometers?

1) They signed the Nuclear Test Ban Treaty. 2) They set up a direct telephone line between the White House and the Kremlin. 3) The United States agreed to sell its surplus wheat to the Soviet Union.

Havana is approximately 200 miles, or 320 kilometers, from Florida.

ments. He believed that each aspect of the United States' relationship with the Russians should be acted on separately. In September 1963 a treaty was signed banning the testing of nuclear weapons. It was called the Nuclear Test Ban Treaty. In August 1963 a direct telephone line was set up between the White House and the Kremlin in Moscow. This "hot line" would make it possible for both governments to communicate immediately. It would prevent wars that might be begun by mistake.

The President also agreed that the United States would sell surplus wheat to the Soviet Union. This agreement helped the Soviet Union to feed its people. It also helped American farmers to get higher prices for their wheat. It signaled a new relationship between the two nations. The United States and the Soviet Union began to cooperate in matters of trade, culture, and scientific research. It was important to both sides to keep their competition as far from a hot war as possible. It was hard for many Americans to understand the need for both sides to talk and do peaceful business.

How did the Kennedy administration continue Eisenhower's policy of peaceful coexistence?

A March for Jobs and Freedom

Race was a major issue during the Kennedy years. Medgar Evers, a Black leader of the NAACP in Mississippi, was killed in June 1963. The nation was shocked. A few months later a march on Washington was held. The main idea of the march was to focus national attention on the demands of Blacks. The official title of the march was the "March for Jobs and Freedom." It was the idea of the same man who had threatened such a march when Franklin D. Roosevelt was President. A Philip Randolph of the Brotherhood of Sleeping Car Porters told Kennedy that "The Negroes are already in the streets."

Nothing like that march had ever happened before. Over 200,000 Americans gathered in the nation's capital on August 28, 1963. Most were Blacks, but thousands of Whites joined them. One of the leaders of the march was Walter Reuther, the head of the United Automobile Workers. The entire march was peaceful. The 5,000 police had only to direct traffic. President Kennedy later met with the leaders of the march: the Reverend Martin Luther King, Jr., Randolph, Reuther, Roy Wilkins of the NAACP, John Lewis of the Student Nonviolent Coordinating Committee (SNCC), and Floyd McKissick of the Congress of Racial Equality (CORE).

The Reverend Martin Luther King, Jr., spoke from the Lincoln Memorial about his dream of equality:

> "I have a dream that one day this nation will rise up, live out the true meaning of its creed 'We hold these truths to be self-evident that all men are created equal.' . . . I have a dream that my four little children will one day live in a nation where they will not be judged by the color of their skin but by the content of their character."

There were Blacks who also spoke out against King and Kennedy. Peaceful integration was not their goal. Under their new leaders, members of a group called the Black Muslims spoke out for "Black power." Malcolm X was their most outspoken leader. He spoke of pride in being Black. "Black is beautiful," he said. There was now a split in the leadership among Blacks. Some worked for integration. Some worked for bringing Blacks together to demand the right to make their own decisions.

Spanish-Speaking Americans

The 1960's were years of action for Spanish-speaking Americans as well. But there were differences not only in their history but also in their attitudes and their ideas of what to do. There were some

Dr. Martin Luther King, Jr., used the methods of nonviolent resistance to fight for civil rights for Blacks.

1) César Chávez led a six-year strike against the owners of the California vineyards. 2) The Spanish Americans of New Mexico were trying to get the land back that was granted them in the treaty ending the Mexican War. 3) Puerto Ricans in New York formed an organization to promote education.

6. What did the various Spanish-speaking American groups work for?

Martin Luther King, Jr., and Malcolm X disagreed about American society. How did each help Blacks in America?

WHO IS LA RAZA?

When the federal government formed the Office of Spanish-Speaking American Affairs in the Department of Health, Education and Welfare, it obviously faced the problem of differences in attitudes and goals of the Mexican Americans, Spanish Americans, and Cuban Americans they were trying to help. The Director of that government office asked in a speech, "Who is *la raza?*" The words mean "the people." Armando Rodriguez tried to speak for all the groups. "I found that the Spanish-speaking population groups are referred to as Spanish Americans, Latinos, Hispanos, Spanish-speaking Americans, Spanish-surnamed Americans, Americans of Spanish or Mexican descent. . . . But whatever we are called, we are *la raza*, a name that unites us linguistically and culturally. I have also found out that there are approximately 10 million of us, that more than 80 percent of us live in urban communities like Chicago and Miami, and that more than 70 percent of us are in the three states of New York, Texas, and California. I also found that the states of Michigan, Illinois, Indiana, New Jersey, Ohio, Wisconsin, and Iowa are the fastest growing areas for settlement of Spanish speakers in the country."

who worked for unity among all Spanish-speaking Americans. They believed that they would have more power if they could unite and vote for the same candidates. For the most part each Spanish-speaking group in each area of the country took action for its own benefit.

The migrant farm workers in California were finally organized into the National Farm Workers Association. The association became part of the AFL-CIO labor union. The best known leader of the farm workers was César Chávez. He knew the importance of both unity and publicity. In 1965 he led a strike by the grape workers in the California vineyards. The strike lasted six years and was helped by a nationwide boycott of California grapes by consumers across the country.

The Spanish Americans of New Mexico had a very different feeling about their situation. Their ancestors had actually held land that was part of the United States. They had had official land grants from the Spanish and Mexican governments. An organization was formed by the descendants of those families to get back or get paid for the land that had been taken away from them. Although all the historical records had been destroyed, the Alianza Federal de Mercedes (Federal Alliance of Land Grants) worked to search out and lay legal claims to that land. Reies López Tijerina (RAY-ez LO-pez tee-heh-REEN-a), the leader of the Alianza, said they were not interested in integration. They wished "to be left alone."

Through years of hard struggle, César Chávez was able to organize California grape pickers into an important union called the United Farm Workers.

These Puerto Rican youths belong to an ASPIRA club. What was one of the goals of this organization?

7. What were the signs of better living for a great many Americans?

Less unemployment, higher wages, and educational opportunity were positive signs.

8. Why did some believe there was a conspiracy involved in Kennedy's assassination?

1) Some wondered whether the accused killer Lee Harvey Oswald was hired by people who thought Kennedy had done too little. 2) Some believed that Kennedy had been killed by those who thought that he had done too much. 3) Others blamed Kennedy's assassination on a plot by the Cubans.

In New York Puerto Ricans formed a very different kind of organization, called ASPIRA. It was begun by second-generation New Yorkers who held professional jobs. ASPIRA's goals were centered around education. The organization formed clubs in the high schools of New York and held workshops to help students plan for the future. One of the goals of ASPIRA was to motivate students to go on to professional or vocational training and skilled jobs. A second goal was to study the Puerto Rican heritage, traditions, and leaders so that students could develop pride in their cultures. The third goal was to train community leaders to work in neighborhoods and in local organizations. ASPIRA worked with parents as well as with individual students and groups.

America in 1963

The year 1963 was also a time of better living for a great many Americans. Only 5 percent were unemployed. The weekly pay average was four times what it had been for their parents during the depression. Prices were higher, but the way most people lived, their *standard of living*, was higher than ever before.

One of the measures of the improvement of life is educational opportunity. More than ten times as much was spent on education than a generation before. Fifty percent of all Americans of college age were in a college or university. In 1900 it had been 4 percent. At the beginning of Kennedy's presidency, it had been 40 percent.

Kennedy Is Killed

The Kennedy years were years of excitement and debate. Some people admired the young President. Some thought he talked too much about taking action. In the midst of the debate, a shocking event took place. On November 22, 1963, John F. Kennedy was assassinated as he rode in a motorcade in Dallas, Texas. The investigation that followed declared that the assassin had acted alone. But the nation debated about a conspiracy. People wondered whether the accused killer, Lee Harvey Oswald, was hired by people who thought that Kennedy had done too little. Some believed that Kennedy had been killed by those who thought that he had done too much. Others blamed the assassination on a plot by Cubans. Americans were frightened.

Even those who opposed Kennedy realized that he had brought hope to people. At least he believed problems could be solved. The shock and disappointment over his death were felt most deeply in the United States. But people all over the world also mourned.

Checking the facts

1. How did Kennedy meet the challenge of communism?
2. How did Kennedy use Eisenhower's idea of peaceful co-existence with Communist nations?
3. What progress were minority groups making during Kennedy's administration?

2. THE GREAT SOCIETY

The man who succeeded John F. Kennedy in 1963 was Lyndon Baines Johnson, a Texan. It was questionable whether Johnson could have been elected to the presidency on his own. No southerner had been elected since before the Civil War. Besides, Johnson was neither an effective speaker nor a television personality. Johnson was the most powerful legislator of his time. As the majority leader of the Senate, he had been able to get both Democrats and Republicans to support Eisenhower's foreign policy.

Johnson had the good will of most Americans when he took office on November 22, 1963. When he ran for the presidency in 1964, the combination of the nation's sadness at Kennedy's death and Johnson's work with Congress gave him a landslide victory.

Johnson's aim as President was to finish the job begun by the New Deal. Johnson described the "Great Society" in his State of the Union message on January 2, 1965. He gave a long list of what

9. What did "the Great Society" propose as the first test for a nation?

The test proposed was the equality of the people.

President Johnson is shown here signing one of his Great Society bills into law. What did Johnson hope to achieve?

681

Elderly Americans were one of a number of groups of people to benefit from the Great Society programs.

action he expected the United States government to take at home and abroad. "The Great Society asks not only how much but how good; not only how to create wealth, but how to use it; not only how fast we are going, but where we are headed. It proposes as the first test for a nation: the equality of its people."

Laws Passed

There were four major laws that Kennedy had wanted but could not get Congress to pass. Johnson got them all passed.

Medical care (or medicare) for the elderly was first. The American Medical Association hired 23 full-time lobbyists to stop passage of that bill. But the President, said one historian, "countered with personal telephone calls and invitations to the White House. He twisted arms and he twisted hearts." He got the bill through Congress and then flew to Independence, Missouri, to sign medicare into law. Independence was the home of 89-year-old ex-President Harry Truman. Truman had asked for such a law in 1945. Johnson wanted Truman to be part of the signing ceremony. Medicare gave hospital insurance to people over 65. The program was helpful and expensive. It increased the number of people in hospitals by 3 percent, or 100,000 patients each week.

Money for Education

10. What did Johnson achieve for education?

There were 40 bills for education passed into law while he was President.

Only a few days after the success of Medicare, Johnson asked Congress for $1 billion for public and parochial schools. The President got that bill in 87 days. While Johnson was President there were 40 bills for education alone—more than in American history.

The Right to Vote

11. Why was the Voting Rights Act of 1965 necessary?

The Fifteenth Amendment guarantees all citizens the right to vote; but in practice southern Blacks were not allowed to register, and many were frightened away from voting.

Next was the voting rights bill. Although 20 percent of the voting-age population in the South was Black, only 7.5 percent of those Blacks were registered to vote. The Fifteenth Amendment guaranteed all citizens the right to vote. In practice southern Blacks were not allowed to register, and many were afraid to vote.

The Voting Rights Act of August 1965 sent federal registrars to the South in order to make it possible for Blacks to register. Any action that kept anyone from registering to vote became a federal offense.

War on Poverty

Lyndon Johnson had been poor, and he never forgot it. He set up an Office of Economic Opportunity and declared "war on poverty."

There was money to give special training to people who did not have the skills to get jobs. Over one million children from poor families were given special lessons in the Head Start preschool program. The Neighborhood Youth Corps paid for 500,000 part-time jobs for teenagers. A Peace Corps for Americans was established. It was called Volunteers In Service To America, or VISTA. Over $9 billion was used to help Appalachia, a poverty-stricken rural area in the Southeast.

Johnson had huge success with Congress. At the end of the first session of Congress, 89 of the 91 major bills that he sent to Congress had been passed and signed into law. Lyndon Johnson told the nation what its unfinished business was—making sure that disadvantaged people got special help.

Many Americans believed that if enough money were spent on education, housing, and health services, the problems of society would go away. The Great Society was the period of the greatest government action. A long road had been traveled since Theodore Roosevelt had used government to make the American system work better.

The British rock group, the Beatles, helped shape the tastes of young people in the 1960's.

Women in the 1960's

The Great Society meant hope for women as well. Women had been able to vote since 1920. But many women wanted the right to make the same choices that men could make. These choices were about jobs—with equal pay and an equal chance at promotion—about education, about owning property, about getting bank loans. Women also wanted guarantees of fair treatment in stores, in churches and synagogues, in unions, clubs, and at home.

12. What were the goals of NOW?

To push for the right of women to do whatever they were qualified to do and to educate women to believe that they could do more.

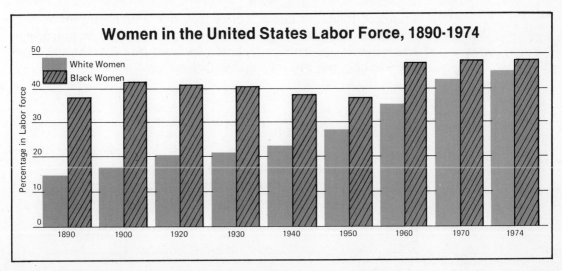

Women in the United States Labor Force, 1890-1974

Most Americans had hope for the Great Society. They hoped that it would fulfill the great American ideal of liberty and justice for all. How far did the Great Society get? What did we learn from this experiment?

683

Betty Friedan was an early leader of the women's movement.

In 1966 the National Organization for Women (NOW) was formed. It had two purposes. One was to push for the right of women to do whatever they were qualified to do. The other purpose was to educate women to believe that they could do more. Women by working together could help all women, rich and poor, Black and White.

This movement among women was different from the drive for voting rights and jobs that happened 50 years before. Betty Friedan, NOW's first president, pointed out that the new women's movement was for all women, not just for those who had to or wanted to work outside the home.

The women's movement, she said, was not against men. If women and men were not locked into set jobs and set ways of acting, then both men and women would be free to make choices as individuals.

There was growing support for the women's movement. But many women did not want to change their lives in any way. They were afraid that they would lose the protection that they believed society gave to married women. They were afraid that changes in what women did would change the way that men felt about them.

"We do not speak for every woman in America, but
we speak for the right of every woman in America to
become all she is capable of becoming—on her own
and/or in partnership with a man."

It was clear that the belief in fair treatment and guaranteed rights in America was held by many people. It was also clear that each civil rights group had a different job to do because not every minority was in the same position.

President Johnson's Great Society took new action paid for by federal taxes. That new action, however, was based on the old American value of opportunity. Johnson believed that government must provide help not given by individuals or groups.

Checking the facts

1. What goals of Kennedy's did Johnson meet?
2. What were the accomplishments of the "war on poverty"?
3. How had the thinking changed in the women's movement in the mid-1960's?

PUTTING IT ALL TOGETHER

UNDERSTANDING THE MAIN IDEAS

1. What did Kennedy accomplish in dealing with communism?
2. What did minorities accomplish in their fight for equal opportunity?
3. What government programs were developed to help the disadvantaged in the United States?

ACTIVITIES

1. Research the work of a civil rights movement currently in the news. Find out the nature of the group's work and its goals. Does the group want equality of opportunity from now on, or a special chance to catch up? Or does the group want both?
2. Write an essay on the following topic: How much of a civil rights program involves changing public opinion? How much involves passing laws?
3. Write a persuasive statement to convince people in your neighborhood to donate some time and skill each month to neighborhood projects. You might want to work with another classmate in preparing your statement.
4. Draw an outline map of Asia for this activity. Locate the following on your map: India, Southeast Asia, Indonesia, Japan, the Philippines, and Korea. Make sure to include Vietnam, Laos, and Cambodia on your map. Use this map to show the places where the United States was involved in military action. Was the purpose of the action to fight an enemy or protect an ally? Create a key with appropriate symbols for your map.
5. It is generally agreed that the United States has more improvements it would like to make than it has money to pay for them. Discuss this issue in class. What do you think Americans should spend their tax money on? For what do you think Americans might volunteer time and skill without pay?

BOOKS TO READ

Drotning, Philip T., *Up From the Ghetto* (New York: Thomas Y. Crowell, 1972).

King, Martin Luther, Jr., *Why We Can't Wait* (New York: Harper and Row, 1964).

Meltzer, Milton, ed., *In Their Own Words: A History of the American Negro, 1916–1966* (New York: Thomas Y. Crowell, 1967).

Roberts, Bruce, and Roberts, Nancy, *Where Time Stood Still: A Portrait of Appalachia* (New York: Macmillan Publishing Co., 1970)

chapter 28
More Challenges for Americans

1964–1978

1. JOHNSON AND VIETNAM
2. GOVERNMENT ACTION AT
   HOME AND ABROAD
3. PRESERVING IN ORDER TO
   IMPROVE

INTRODUCTION

No other President and Congress had spent so much money on so much action to improve life in America. Lyndon Johnson was proud of the projects that were going to bring about the Great Society. He enjoyed using the power of the presidency to sell ideas to the people and to talk Congress into action. However, the methods he used in taking action at home did not work in dealing with foreign affairs. The late 1960's were a time of American involvement in Vietnam. The effort first to win and then just to end the war caused people of both political parties to worry about the quality of leadership. At the same time, Americans were worried about the rise in prices and the cost of solving the nation's problems. Illegal action by government officials added to the troubled picture. Americans looked again at government leaders and programs. Americans began to turn toward themselves for possible answers. As you read this chapter, think about the following questions:

	1967	1968	1969	1970	
Who?	Israelis and Arabs	Dr. Martin Luther King, Jr.	American astronauts	Four students	
What?	fight the Six-Day War	is assassinated	are the first humans to land	are killed by the National Guard	
Where?	in the Middle East	in Memphis, Tennessee	on the moon	at Kent State University	

History shows us that events and people form a web of interconnections. No person or event can be understood in isolation from other people and events.

1. What questions faced Americans as they became more deeply involved in the war in Vietnam?
2. How did programs aimed at helping the poor suffer because of spending on the war?
3. What kinds of illegal action did the Nixon administration take part in?
4. How did Presidents Ford and Carter plan to deal with the nation's problems?
5. What kinds of citizen action have appeared since 1960?

1. JOHNSON AND VIETNAM

It was President Johnson and his advisers who increased the number of American armed forces in Vietnam. They were even more convinced than Eisenhower and Kennedy that communism had to be stopped in Southeast Asia. In August 1964, North Vietnamese boats attacked an American destroyer in the Gulf of Tonkin. A few days later, American jets bombed the boat bases in North Vietnam. Congress approved this action brought about by the President's order. This approval—called the Tonkin Gulf Resolution—gave Johnson broad powers to continue the war. The President, therefore, was able to take action without consulting Congress on every move. He only had to ask Congress for money, not for troops.

1. What did the Tonkin Gulf Resolution allow Johnson to do?

The resolution gave him broad powers to continue the war without consulting Congress on every action.

Fighting in Vietnam

The North Vietnamese troops were hard to spot. To the Americans they looked and acted like the allies in South Vietnam. In addition, there were two groups of enemies. There were the North Vietnamese under the leadership of Ho Chi Minh (hoe-chee-MIN). He had

2. Why did the Americans have difficulty fighting in Vietnam?

1972	1973	1974	1975-1976	1978
Richard Nixon	Native Americans	Richard Nixon	Palestinians and Lebanese Christians and Moslems	President Carter
is the first U.S. President to visit	seize the reservation	resigns as President	fight a civil war	signs treaty giving Panama eventual control of the canal
China	at Wounded Knee, South Dakota	of the United States.	in Lebanon	in Panama

Who was responsible for escalating the Vietnamese War?

1) The North Vietnamese troops were hard to spot because they looked and acted like the allies in South Vietnam. 2) The Vietcong, the South Vietnamese who were on the side of the north, didn't look or act any differently. 3) It was difficult to support an anti-communist government led by dictators who were using government money to make themselves rich. 4) Guerrilla fighting was new to Americans, who insisted on trying to use bombing against it.

been the leader of all the Vietnamese in the war against the French in the 1950's. He was a Vietnamese hero. There were South Vietnamese who were on the side of the North. They were the Vietcong. In the streets they did not look or act any differently from the rest of the people the Americans saw every day.

The United States had another serious problem in supporting the South Vietnamese government. Its leaders were anti-communist, but they were not in favor of democracy. In fact, the leaders were dictators who were using their power to imprison their own citizens who criticized them. Many Ameicans wondered whether or not the government of South Vietnam was worth helping.

The kind of war being fought in Vietnam was new to Americans. It was guerrilla fighting. The Vietcong soldiers lived in underground tunnels. They wore no recognizable uniforms. They mounted sneak attacks against American troops, night and day, from every direction. Many advisers told President Johnson that bombing does not work against guerrilla troops. But the advice against bombing was ignored. On February 7, 1965, the Vietcong raided a camp of American military advisers, killing and wounding many. This event gave Johnson the excuse he needed to send in jets to bomb the North Vietnamese. These air strikes continued for the rest of the year. When the Vietcong started to bomb American air bases in South Vietnam, Johnson sent in soldiers to protect them. By April 1965 there were 33,500 American soldiers in Vietnam under the command of General William Westmoreland. More soldiers were sent in during the next year.

Americans React

3. How did Church and Johnson differ on America's role in Vietnam?

1) Church thought that if the people of South Vietnam would not support the government in power, there was little that the United States could do to save that country from communism. 2) Johnson chose to overlook complaints against the South Vietnamese, because the Soviets were supplying war materials to the North Vietnamese.

Critics of the American part in the war were outspoken. Their criticism took the form of demonstrations. Students on college campuses spoke out the loudest and longest against the war. They did not want to have to fight for a cause in which they did not believe. Some felt it was not right for the United States to be involved in this war. Senator Frank Church of Idaho, one of the first senators to speak out against the war said, "There are limits to what we can do in helping any government overcome a Communist uprising. If the people of South Vietnam will not support the government in power, we cannot save it." But President Johnson asked Congress for money to finance a greater war effort. The House of Representatives approved Johnson's request within 48 hours, with only 10 representatives voting against it.

Johnson was convinced that communism had to be stopped by war. He saw the leaders of South Vietnam as people who were fighting against communism. Johnson chose to overlook the complaints against the South Vietnamese leaders. The fact that the Russians were supplying war materials to the North Vietnamese was proof to the President that the war in Vietnam was really a war against Soviet power.

The American action in Vietnam grew and grew. Close to 5,000 American soldiers were killed in 1966. More men died in 1967 than in all the years of the war up to that time. Thousands of Vietnamese civilians were killed as well. On television the President told the American public his reasons for sending more and more troops to Vietnam: "We did not choose to be the guardians at the gate, but there is no one else."

American action in Vietnam lasted longer than in World War II or in Korea. And the protests continued. College students burned their draft cards. Some 10,000 left the country to live in Canada rather than go to Vietnam.

Riots at Home

The questions facing Americans about Vietnam were too real and too frightening. Americans fought each other. In the summer of 1967, a series of riots hit major Black ghettoes in New York and Minneapolis. But the worst riots were in Boston, Newark, and Detroit.

During the 1960's many college students demonstrated against American involvement in Vietnam.

Blacks were disappointed at the reality of the civil rights movement. In Newark, for example, the unemployment rate was twice as high as the figure for the whole nation. In addition, there were twice as many Blacks out of work as Whites in Newark. The Great Society got money to the people enrolled in programs. But it was not able to get skills to enough of the unskilled. It was not able to get permanent jobs in private business for the poor.

It was not just a matter of race. In Detroit, the White mayor had been elected with the support of Black voters. There was a large Black middle class that had prospered by working in the automobile industry. But in Detroit poor Whites and Blacks joined together in rioting. There were 1,600 fire alarms in 11 days in 1967. Forty-three people died and 7,000 were arrested. One street three miles (4.8 kilometers) long was burned to the ground. The poor had burned their own neighborhoods.

Over 100 cities in 32 states suffered riots during the summer of 1967. What had caused them? There were many reasons given. They included the frustration over the war, the rise in prices caused by the cost of the war, and the lack of believable explanations from the President. Was the war really worth fighting when troubles still existed at home? Why didn't the Great Society work faster?

Why do people believe that they can improve their lives? Whom do they have to trust?

The late Hubert Humphrey had a long and varied career in the government. In 1968 he ran as the Democratic candidate for President.

4. *Why were Kennedy and King considered to be symbols of hope?*

1) Robert Kennedy showed concern for Blacks, the poor, and young people. 2) King believed in a better future for all and supported peaceful action.

5. *How was Nixon elected in 1968?*

1968—Election Year

By 1968, it was time for a presidential election, and the news was bad. During the Vietnamese New Year's celebration, called Tet, 60,000 of the Vietcong carried out a sneak attack on Saigon, the capital city of South Vietnam. The Americans had to fight hard to drive the Vietcong back. Many lives were lost. By April 1968, there were 549,000 American troops in Vietnam. Almost 23,000 had died there. By June 23, 1968, the war had become the longest in American history. After many years of fighting, the Vietcong were not showing any signs of giving in. But Americans were getting tired of what they saw as a hopeless situation.

The Democratic party spoke out against the war and President Johnson. Two Democrats challenged Lyndon Johnson's right to seek reelection. Senator Eugene McCarthy of Minnesota filed for the first primary, in New Hampshire. Instead of getting the expected 20 percent of the Democratic vote, McCarthy got 42 percent to Johnson's 48 percent. This showed that many Americans had turned against Johnson and the war.

Then Robert F. Kennedy, the late President Kennedy's brother, announced his candidacy. In spite of the programs of the Great Society, the Vietnam War had become the major issue in the campaign. Lyndon Johnson went on television and delivered two announcements. First, he had ordered less bombing in Vietnam. Second, he announced his decision not to run for reelection. Vice-President Hubert Humphrey, a long time supporter of civil rights and help for the needy, then entered the Democratic race for the nomination.

1968—Two Assassinations

There were two people in the nation who still seemed to be symbols of hope. For many of the Blacks, the poor, and the young people, Robert Kennedy became a political hero. For many Blacks and Whites in America, the Reverend Martin Luther King, Jr., was the great hope for the future. He believed in a better future for all and supported peaceful means of taking action. Within a few months of each other, King and Kennedy were killed by assassins. King was killed on April 5, 1968, by a man, James Earl Ray, whose motive was unclear. Kennedy was killed on June 5 by a young Arab, Sirhan Sirhan, who said he did it "for my country."

The peaceful leadership of those who were offering hope to the American people seemed to be gone. Among the national leaders still anxious to try to improve America were Hubert Humphrey and Eugene McCarthy. They wanted to end the war and aid the poor. When Humphrey won the Democratic presidential nomi-

Why is it important to understand why Nixon was elected in 1968?

nation, McCarthy and his antiwar supporters refused to help the Democrats in the campaign. It was not until five days before the actual election that the Democrats began to pull together.

The Republicans nominated Richard M. Nixon. With the Democrats divided, Nixon was almost assured of victory. Nixon won the election of 1968, but not by a landslide. He was the first President in 120 years to start his term of office with the other party in control of both houses of Congress.

Nixon offered the American people a kind of relief. He promised to bring the nation together and get the troops out of Vietnam. He caught the mood of the nation. Many people were exhausted from the war and the conflict it had brought, both abroad and at home. They wanted time off from action.

1) The Democrats did not work together. When Humphrey won the Democratic nomination, McCarthy and his antiwar supporters refused to help him. 2) Nixon promised to bring the nation together and to get the troops out of Vietnam.

Nixon and Vietnam

One of Nixon's campaign promises was to end the war in Vietnam. To reach that end he began to withdraw American troops from Vietnam. By 1970 the number of American soldiers there was down from 543,000 to 340,000. People thought they had reason to hope for an early peace. Peace talks were being held in Paris, France, between the Americans and the North Vietnamese. But neither side would give in. The United States wanted promises from the North Vietnamese that the South Vietnamese would be treated fairly after the Americans went home. One aspect of fair treatment was free elections, the United States argued. The North Vietnamese wanted the United States troops to leave the country and leave the peace to them. The representatives of North Vietnam insisted on a new government in South Vietnam. The talks dragged on with neither side willing to give in.

6. What issues separated the United States and the North Vietnamese at the Paris peace talks?

1) The United States wanted promises from the North Vietnamese that the South Vietnamese would be treated fairly after the Americans went home; the United States also wanted free elections. 2) The North Vietnamese wanted United States troops to leave the country and leave the peace to them; they wanted a new government in South Vietnam.

Americans were disappointed that getting out of Vietnam was taking so long. The number of war dead had reached 44,000. And the news was getting worse day by day. Then the President announced that 200,000 American soldiers would have to be kept in Vietnam for years. Americans were shocked that the South Vietnamese could not take over the war by themselves. The leaders of the South Vietnamese government had put 80,000 of their own people in jail for speaking out against the government. That same government demanded more arms and more money from the United States.

It seemed as if the war would never end. Nixon sent American troops into the neighboring country of Cambodia. It was, he said, an effort to stop the supply of food and guns that were getting into Vietnam via North Vietnamese hiding in Cambodia.

7. What were the reactions to the Cambodian invasion?

Why were the United States demands on North Vietnam unrealistic? (free elections; fair treatment of the south by the north)

691

1) The news sparked huge demonstrations, both on and off the college campuses, against Nixon's actions. 2) The House of Representatives voted to remove American troops from Cambodia.

What can you tell about the war from this map? What cannot be shown here?

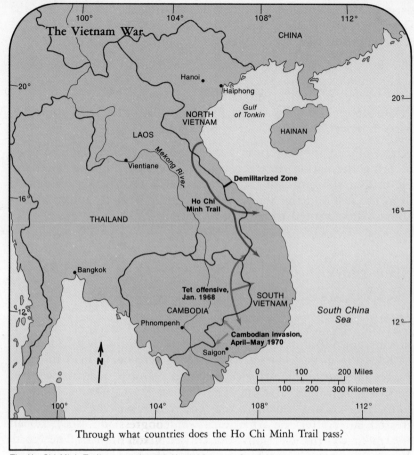

The Vietnam War

CHINA

Hanoi

Haiphong

Gulf of Tonkin

NORTH VIETNAM

HAINAN

LAOS

Mekong River

Vientiane

Demilitarized Zone

Ho Chi Minh Trail

THAILAND

Bangkok

Tet offensive, Jan. 1968

CAMBODIA

SOUTH VIETNAM

South China Sea

Phnompenh

Cambodian invasion, April–May 1970

Saigon

N

0   100   200 Miles
0   100   200   300 Kilometers

Through what countries does the Ho Chi Minh Trail pass?

The Ho Chi Minh Trail passes through North Vietnam, South Vietnam, and Laos.

The news of the Cambodian invasion sparked huge demonstrations against Nixon's actions. Students on college campuses across the nation held rallies against the war. Many protest meetings became violent. At Kent State College in Ohio, an antiwar protest got out of control. The National Guard was called in and four students were killed.

Protests against the war were taking place in other places besides college campuses. The Senate finally took action to try to stop the war that had never been declared. The House of Representatives voted that American troops must leave Cambodia. After all, they said, it was Congress that had the right to declare war, and Congress had never declared this one.

Nixon Loses Support

8. How did Nixon lose the support of many Americans?

Not all of the news about the fighting in Vietnam had reached the American public. Word about the army's actions in Vietnam began

How many years after Americans first went to Indochina did Congress take action to limit the war?

to "leak" into the American press. President Nixon, who demanded absolute loyalty from everyone, began to suspect people in government of giving out classified information. He seemed to believe that Americans who were against the war were plotting against him with the help of some newspapers. In June 1971, newspapers across the United States began to print secret military papers. These papers were a history of the American involvement in Vietnam. They were "leaked" to the newspapers by Daniel Ellsberg. He once worked for the army. Although the papers did not involve the Nixon administration, the President tried to stop their being printed. The Supreme Court denied Nixon's request to suppress the Pentagon papers, as the documents were called.

1) He tried to stop the Pentagon papers from being published. 2) He set up a special investigative unit that bypassed both the FBI and the CIA. 3) He angered Blacks by opposing the busing of children to integrate public schools. 4) Prices, including the price of oil, were rising rapidly. 5) Unemployment was on the rise.

Nixon began to discuss using burglary and other illegal methods to stop people who were telling the public too much. A special investigation unit was set up by the President. It reported directly to him, bypassing both the Federal Bureau of Investigation (FBI) and the Central Intelligence Agency (CIA). Because it was supposed to stop leaks at all costs, the group was nicknamed the "Plumbers."

Nixon was losing the support of many Americans. Blacks were angry because he opposed busing children to schools outside their area in order to help racial integration of the schools. Everyone was concerned because prices were high. The oil-producing countries of the world were organized. These countries were able to set high prices for their valuable resource. Americans had to pay the high prices if they wanted to heat their homes. Unemployment was also on the rise. A poll at the time of the congressional elections of 1970 reported "the presidency of Richard Nixon hit bottom." Only 30 percent of the American people thought he was doing a good job.

Checking the facts

1. How did Americans react to the United States' lengthy involvement in Vietnam?
2. Why was the involvement in Vietnam the longest in United States history?

2. GOVERNMENT ACTION AT HOME AND ABROAD

Over 12,000 student antiwar protesters marched on Washington in the spring of 1971. Nixon's attorney general, John Mitchell, ordered the local police, the National Guard, and the army to break up any large groups of people. They used billy clubs and tear gas.

9. How did Nixon react to opposition?

1) When antiwar protesters marched on Washington in 1971, the local police, the national guard, and the army broke up the demonstration and arrested 12,614 people.
2) The President's White House staff made a list of his political enemies and had the FBI investigate them to see whether they could be pressured in any way.

In four days, 12,614 people were arrested, including spectators standing on sidewalks. There was not enough room in the jails, so the government put up a stockade in the football stadium. Many of these arrests were made without formal charges. The federal courts stepped in at this point. The courts ruled that the civil rights of the protesters had been taken away illegally, and ordered their release.

By the spring and summer of 1971, Nixon was very worried about the opposition. He was convinced that anyone who criticized the war was disloyal to the nation, as well as disloyal to him. He wanted to get back at anyone who was critical of him. The President's White House staff made a list of Nixon's political enemies. The FBI was supposed to check on these people to see if they could be pressured in some way. For example, the tax collectors of the Internal Revenue Service were asked to do extra checkups on people whom the President thought were enemies.

Nixon in China and Russia

10. What were the results of Kissinger's visit to Peking?

1) The United States recommended that the People's Republic of China be admitted to the United Nations. 2) Trade between China and the United States resumed for the first time since 1949. 3) Nixon announced that he had accepted an invitation to visit Peking.

In other ways 1972 appeared to be Nixon's best year. It was the year he opened up peaceful ways to talk with both the Chinese and the Russians. In July 1971 Nixon sent his secretary of state, Henry Kissinger, to Peking, the capital of China. His job was to begin talks with the government of the People's Republic of China. Then the United States recommended that the People's Republic be admitted to the United Nations. Trade was allowed between the United States and mainland China for the first time since 1949. That was the year the Communists had taken over control of China.

Nixon announced that he had accepted an invitation to visit Peking. People hoped that this move toward friendly relations with mainland China would not hurt the Nationalist Chinese government on Formosa (Taiwan). But that was not possible. When the United Nations voted the People's Republic into membership, the United Nations also voted the Nationalist Republic of China out.

11. What did Nixon's trip to Russia accomplish?

1) The United States and the Soviet Union agreed to work together in space, share programs in public health, cancer and heart research, and pollution control.

Nixon went to China in February 1972. He also planned a spring trip to the Soviet Union. This was to keep the Russians from being nervous about an agreement between the United States and China.

In between the Chinese and Russian meetings, the North Vietnamese set off a huge invasion force in South Vietnam. The United States started bombing the northern cities again. The terrible fighting made both sides ready to talk about peace. In addition, the Russians did not want their meeting with Nixon ruined by more fighting in Vietnam.

Nixon's meeting with the Russians produced a variety of agreements. The United States and the Soviet Union would work to-

694

gether in space, share programs in public health, cancer and heart research, and pollution control. They agreed to limit the number of guided missiles for five years. However, the agreements did not mean that the competition between the nations was going to end.

Election Year—1972

The year Nixon had to run for reelection was the year of his China and Russia trips, a year of poor trade abroad for American goods, and the year of his increased fear of criticism and illegal action about the civil rights of protesters. Despite the good public reaction to his trips abroad, Nixon was worried that he might not get reelected in 1972. His supporters set up a special group that would work for his reelection. It was called the Committee to Reelect the President, later to be nicknamed CRP or CREEP. A group of burglars headed by the CRP's chief of security was sent to break into the Democratic party headquarters at the Watergate Hotel in Washington. They were looking for evidence to embarrass the Democrats. The five burglars were caught. But few people thought it was big enough news to hurt Nixon's reelection campaign. The President's friend and former attorney general, John Mitchell, then head of CRP, said, "We want to emphasize that the people involved were not operating either on our behalf or with our consent."

Nixon had been elected on a promise to end the war in Vietnam. But 17,000 Americans had been killed there since his election in 1968. There were still 139,000 troops in Vietnam by 1972, although the fighting had almost stopped. Two weeks before the November election, Secretary of State Henry Kissinger announced that "peace was at hand."

Nixon won reelection over a badly split Democratic Party. Their leader on the home issues was Hubert Humphrey. But the party's nomination went to Senator George McGovern of South Dakota. McGovern had been outspoken against the war, but he was not a good campaigner. In the election, Nixon won every state's electoral vote except those of Massachusetts and the District of Columbia. The Democrats held onto Congress, however.

What did the 1972 election results mean? The voter turnout was the lowest in 24 years. Only 55 percent of the registered voters went to the polls. The country no longer had its mind on the Great Society. People were depressed by the war in Vietnam and unimpressed with the Democratic party leadership. There was news of war between the Israelis and the Arabs in the Middle East. American support of Israel caused trouble with the Arabs. The United States had to rely on them for oil. And the Russians were supplying the Arabs with arms to fight Israel.

During a visit to the People's Republic of China in 1972, President and Mrs. Nixon stood at the Great Wall.

12. Why was Nixon re-elected in 1972?

1) The fighting had almost stopped in Vietnam, and Kissinger announced that "peace is at hand." 2) The Democratic party was badly split. 3) People were depressed by the war and unimpressed with the Democratic leadership.

McGovern's tax plan disturbed employed Americans who were worried about high prices and taxes. Were the issues clear in the election campaign of 1972? Were the personalities strong?

695

The Vietnamese War was reported on TV daily. Did television influence American perceptions of the war?

Many American soldiers who fought in Vietnam were wounded or killed. The rugged Vietnamese countryside made the removal of the wounded very difficult.

The War Ends

Instead of the war in Vietnam being over, the peace talks in Paris broke down. President Nixon then started a massive bombing raid against military targets right in the middle of North Vietnam's cities. Many civilians were killed. Ninety-eight American crewmen from downed bombers were captured. Nixon's promise of peace seemed to be false. Americans who had voted for Nixon were now against him. Everyone agreed that the people who fought in Vietnam had fought bravely. No one criticized those who obeyed the draft. But even some of those who fought bravely began to realize that the war was impossible to win. Finally, late in January 1973, the two sides agreed to end the war.

Americans did not feel victorious. The Communist government would certainly take over the whole of Vietnam as soon as the Americans left. Some 46,000 Americans had died in the war and 300,000 were wounded. Over $100 billion that might have gone to build a better society had been spent. What was left was a giant debt and high prices—the conditions of inflation.

Worst of all, said one writer for the *New York Times*, people in America had stopped trusting the judgment of their leaders. They stopped believing that their leaders were telling the truth. One writer called it "a decline in respect."

Watergate Breaks Wide Open

In the summer of 1973, the details of Watergate were brought out into the open. Under the leadership of Sam J. Ervin, Jr., the Senate

13. What were the results of the war?

1) Americans did not feel victorious, for the North Vietnamese would certainly take over the whole of Vietnam as soon as the Americans left. 2) Forty-six thousand Americans had died in the war and three hundred thousand were wounded. 3) Over $100 million that might have gone to build a better society had been spent. 4) A giant debt and high prices remained, fueling the forces of inflation.

14. Why did Nixon resign from the presidency?

The Senate hearings on TV helped to inform many Americans that their leaders had acted illegally and had lost trust in the American way. How did TV coverage of the Watergate hearings compare with the televised coverage of the McCarthy hearings?

Investigating Committee disclosed how the President and his advisers had tried to cover up the facts of the break-in at Democratic headquarters at the Watergate. The people in the office of the President had deliberately lied to the American people. Nixon's attorney general had hired Archibald Cox, a Harvard law professor, to investigate the whole Watergate affair. Cox demanded that the President turn over all the tape recordings he had made of his private conversations. Nixon was afraid to give up the tapes because they might contain the truth about Watergate. So he fired Special Prosecutor Cox. But the United States Supreme Court ruled that the President must turn over the tapes anyway.

The House of Representatives Judiciary Committee took up the question of who was guilty in the Watergate affair. The committee declared the President to be an unindicted, officially unaccused, co-conspirator in the Watergate cover-up. His two chief aides, John Erlichman and H. R. Haldeman, went to jail. The House Judiciary Committee then voted three articles of impeachment to recommend to the Congress. The first article stated that Nixon "made it his policy" to cover up the Watergate burglary. This was obstruction of justice. The second accused agents of the President, including the White House "Plumbers," of planned burglaries and unlawful eavesdropping—part of a "pattern of massive and persistent abuse of power for political purposes." The third charge was contempt of Congress for defying requests for information made by the Judiciary Committee. The President of the United States had been formally accused of obstruction of justice, abuse of power, and contempt of Congress.

1) The Senate Investigating Committee disclosed how the President and his advisers had tried to cover up the facts of the break-in at Democratic headquarters. 2) The attorney general hired special prosecutor Cox to investigate the whole Watergate affair. 3) Cox demanded that the President turn over the tape recordings of his private conversations, and Nixon fired him. 4) The Supreme Court ruled that Nixon had to turn over the tapes. 5) The House of Representatives Judiciary Committee voted three articles of impeachment to recommend to the House, accusing the President of obstructing justice, abusing power, and contempt of Congress.

Senators Sam Ervin, center, and Howard Baker, second from the left, led a Senate committee investigation into the Watergate affair. How did their efforts help bring about President Nixon's resignation?

Before Congress could vote on the recommendation of the Committee, Richard Nixon resigned on August 8, 1974. This was the first time in the nation's history that a President had resigned.

15. What did Ervin mean when he said, "Never elect anyone to office who does not believe in the system"?

1) The American system was founded on trust in others. 2) Nixon used power illegally because he thought he was right and better for the country than was anyone else.

Even people who had supported the war and Nixon's lack of action on home problems were horrified. Americans argued with each other. Was it just Nixon, or was it a long history of too much power in the hands of one person? In trying to improve America, President Johnson had used great power. In trying to help, the Warren Court had used its power to further the rights of the less powerful. But the power was also used by people who did not trust other Americans. Nixon used power illegally because he thought he was right and better for the country than anyone else.

How could the nation be sure that such unconstitutional behavior would never happen again? Senator Ervin was asked, "What is the lesson to be learned from the Nixon years?" Ervin said, "Never elect anyone to office who does not believe in the system."

Checking the facts

1. What resulted from Nixon's trip to Russia and China?
2. What circumstances led up to Nixon's resignation from the presidency?

3. PRESERVING IN ORDER TO IMPROVE

16. How did Americans react to Nixon's pardon?

1) Some agreed with Ford that it would help put Watergate behind the country and that Nixon's resignation was enough punishment. 2) Some thought that it was wrong for the former President to go unpunished while others went to jail.

When Nixon resigned in August 1974, the Vice-President, Gerald Ford of Michigan, became President. Ford was welcomed as an honest man who had served for 25 years in the House of Representatives. Ford faced the nation's shock over Richard Nixon as well as the cost of the Vietnam War. One of Ford's first acts was to pardon Nixon for any criminal offenses he might have committed. President Ford said that he believed the pardon would help America "put Watergate behind them." Some people agreed. They felt that Nixon's resignation was enough. To others, however, it seemed wrong that the former President could go unpunished while others went to jail. Many resented the presidential allowance that Nixon received. It was the same as what he would have received if he had retired with honor.

Ford as President

Ford believed that the United States did not have enough money to try to solve the nation's remaining problems. He explained that money for government help and government jobs comes from taxes.

Taxes in turn come mostly from profits of private business and the wages of people who work. New expenses would therefore cause higher taxes. If there are not higher profits to provide those taxes, then businesses must charge higher prices. Higher prices in turn take more of the people's wages. Ford said Americans already had too many debts to pay. There were the debts of the Great Society and the Vietnam War. Ford believed that a choice had to be made between paying debts and creating new government programs to help the needy. Because of his attitude toward government spending, Ford became another of the veto Presidents. He refused to sign bills for most new programs. He refused to sign bills to continue funding for many Great Society programs. They went out of business.

Other government leaders disagreed with Ford. Although the debts were high, something still had to be done to hire the unemployed and to help the poor with health care, education, and housing. In 1975 Senator Hubert Humphrey of Minnesota co-sponsored the Humphrey-Hawkins Bill. This proposal set a goal for much greater employment. If private industry could not provide jobs for the unemployed, then the government would have to do so. Black leaders gave their support to Humphrey's point of view. This bill was a reminder of the promises of Franklin D. Roosevelt, John F. Kennedy, and Lyndon B. Johnson.

No one disagreed with Ford's insistence that debts should be paid. People knew that private businesses had to make a profit so the government could have the tax money to provide needed services. There was disagreement, however, on how much profit businesses were making. There was disagreement on whether the poor could wait for the debts to be paid. Therre was also disagreement about how to get American workers to produce more to help keep prices down. The needy were disappointed that Gerald Ford did not offer much hope. Hope for opportunities in the future has always been an important American value.

One of the groups most in need of a sense of hope in the future was the Native Americans. Groups such as the American Indian Movement (AIM), founded in 1970, focused the attention of the public on Indian problems. An outbreak of violence on the Pine Ridge Indian reservation in South Dakota took place in 1975. The dispute stemmed from a disagreement between supporters of AIM and the tribal chief of the Oglala Sioux, Richard Wilson. Other Native Americans demanded that former tribal lands be returned to them. Claims by Native American groups had been made in Wisconsin, Massachusetts, and New York.

By the spring of the American Bicentennial celebration, Americans were discouraged with their national leaders. Johnson, in spite of the Great Society, had led the nation into the worst of the Vietnam

Gerald Ford was sworn in as President after Nixon resigned. What difficulties did Ford face as President following the Watergate affair?

He believed that a choice had to be made between paying the debts of the Great Society and the Vietnam War and creating new government programs to help the needy.

1) Johnson had led the nation into the Vietnam War. 2) Nixon had committed the worst abuse of presidential power in the history of the nation. 3) Ford seemed to have no sense of a future worthy of hope. 4) Congress had supported the war effort in Vietnam, had taken a long time to find out the truth about Nixon, and had not overridden the Nixon–Ford vetoes of programs designed to help the needy.

18. Why were Americans discouraged with their national leaders?

How many arguments of a similar nature can you find in this week's newspapers? What are people trying to do to improve? to preserve?

War. Nixon, in spite of bettering relations with China and the Soviet Union, had abused the power of the President in the worst fashion in the history of the nation. Gerald Ford, for all his good intentions, seemed to have no sense of a future worthy of hope. Americans were not just unhappy with Presidents, they were also disappointed with Congress. Congress had supported the war effort in Vietnam. It had taken a long time to find out the truth about Nixon. Congress had not overridden the Nixon-Ford vetoes of programs to help those who needed to be helped. When the 1976 election came near, Americans were frustrated with the people in government. They were in the mood for a change. The Democratic candidate, Governor Jimmy Carter of Georgia, ran against President Ford.

Jimmy Carter

In his campaign Carter talked about the nation's ability to pay its debts. Carter himself was a successful business person and farmer. He knew the importance of selling to foreign nations. He knew about the false pleasure in higher profits if they are based on higher costs. He worried about higher wages without more production. He spoke about higher oil prices and the increasing need for petroleum for American industry, farms, transportation, and homes. In fact, for many Democrats who were used to the Roosevelt and Johnson list of people who were going to be helped by the government, Jimmy Carter sounded like a conservative Republican. He said that money should be saved in the government, so that taxes could be lowered. Then private businesses could afford to invest money and create new jobs.

In his campaign Carter also talked about improving life in America. Carter said improvement could mostly be brought about by getting jobs for the unemployed in private businesses. Carter's biggest appeal as a candidate was that he was an outsider. To Americans discouraged with past leaders, he spoke about not having connections in Washington. He sounded like the Populists of the late 1800's. He appealed as a southerner and as a farmer.

Carter wrote a book called *Why Not the Best?* in which he told the American people first to believe in themselves. Good people could manage good government. The second step was to elect someone new. Carter was the newest candidate of all. When the election results came in, Carter was the winner.

Improving, Preserving, and Debating

Americans still have a list of problems they want solved. Now the debate is on—who should solve those problems? How shall the American people pay for the solutions?

1) Money should be saved in the government so that taxes could be lowered. 2) Improvement of life in America could be brought about mostly by getting jobs for the unemployed in private business.

19. What points did Carter make during his campaign for the presidency?

In January 1976 President and Mrs. Carter walked in their inaugural parade. What qualities do you think helped Carter become President?

Choose any one of the following problems and try to answer two questions: who, and how.

Pollution and the control of pollution continues to be one of the most outstanding problems facing Americans. Warnings about the dangers of aerosol spray cans to the environment were issued in 1976. Scientists maintained that the gases used in spray cans could eventually destroy a shield of protective elements surrounding the earth. The Environmental Protection Agency (EPA) continues to bring pressure on industries, such as the auto producers, to make their products less polluting. The results of their efforts have been mixed. However, Americans as a whole, seem to be showing greater support for individual efforts to improve the quality of the nation's environment.

The federal government has more money, but many big programs managed from Washington turned out to be wasteful. The programs took too many people to run them. A program that worked in one town with one group was not right for another group somewhere else. Today people are trying to take the responsibility for their own neighborhoods. A National Alliance of Neighborhoods is lobbying for government funds for the people themselves to use. They wish to improve their housing and help each other.

Poor neighborhoods, however, can often be too poor to help themselves. In times when jobs are scarce and new jobs are in the suburbs, housing and mass transportation are tied to skill-training. People who can learn new skills and can help themselves must be identified. Those who cannot, must be helped in other ways. Minorities need to be helped to go into business themselves. Jesse Jackson of People United for Self Help (PUSH) and Leon Sullivan of the Opportunities Industrialization Centers (OIC) are working toward this goal. They want to raise money and get bank credit for Blacks to go into business, as well as for job training.

There is much debate by and about those who have jobs. Unions strike for higher wages and other people complain of high prices that the higher costs of union labor are passing on to the consumer. Unions are pushing for shorter work weeks for the same amount of pay. Others say that if workers would produce more per hour, more goods and services could be sold more cheaply at a profit. This would make it possible to hire more workers because lower prices would create more customers.

Farmers still want higher prices guaranteed in advance for the gamble they take in growing food. Farmers talk of going on strike to keep food off the market and force prices up. But, at the same time, consumers cannot afford higher prices for food.

Women now realize how long it takes people, including other women, to accept them as equal. Many states have refused to ratify an Equal Rights Amendment to the Constitution. Yet there is growing agreement that women are taking and will continue to

Ralph Nader, a lawyer, has worked for improved safety and quality of consumer goods.

Reverend Jesse Jackson's programs and lectures have helped many young Blacks.

Which of the six themes about the American way can you identify in each of the debates discussed here?

701

In January 1978 many farmers rallied in the nation's capital to bring their demands to the President's attention.

20. Why was Carter having difficulty getting Congress to pass his energy program?

1) Congress was not consulted before the President introduced the plan. 2) Carter had not become enough of an insider to know how Congress worked.

21. What were the terms of the Panama Canal Treaty of 1978?

1) The Panama Canal and the Panama Canal Zone will be turned over to Panama by the year 2000. 2) The security of the area remains a concern of the United States and the nations of the Western Hemisphere.

take an equal part in responsibility for support of themselves and their families. The number of women in jobs has increased by 37 percent over the past ten years. More and more women are finding jobs that once were reserved for men only.

President Carter and Legislation

Upon taking office President Carter showed an understanding of the nation's problems. He seemed to know how complicated they were. One of Carter's first programs was to deal with the nation's energy problem. In April 1977, President Carter presented his energy program. This program would include solutions for all parts of each problem. For example, everyone knows that oil prices and oil exploration, natural gas prices and exploration, nuclear power plants, automobile standards, pollution control, coal prices, train and pipeline transportation, shipping costs, and relations with Israel and the oil-producing Arab nations are all tied into the "energy problem."

One part of Carter's program was to give a tax "break" to anyone willing to insulate his or her home in order to preserve heat and therefore use less fuel. Carter also wanted to spend government funds on finding ways of using the sun to give much-needed energy.

But Carter ran into a Congress that wanted to be consulted in advance. This was the Congress that had used its power in causing the removal of Richard Nixon from office. It was in no mood to give up that power.

In addition, now that Jimmy Carter was President, he could not claim to be an outsider. And yet he did not seem to be enough of an insider to know just how to get Congress to vote for his solutions. No one in Congress owes a newcomer anything. On the other hand, everyone in Congress owes representation to the special interests of the voters back home. It is difficult, Carter found, to get a whole program on energy when the people expect their congressional representatives to protect their special energy needs.

The Panama Canal—A New View

In the Carter administration, the Panama Canal was also looked on as part of a bigger, more complicated picture. The Panama Canal once represented American power in Central America during Teddy Roosevelt's administration. American companies had built it. The American government has supervised its operations from its opening in 1914 until 1978. Yet the Panama Canal is located in Central America. And the people of those nations had new power and plans for their own independent futures. Wasn't it time for the United States to give up its claim in this area? President Carter thought

702

so. He worked hard to make it happen. Many Americans disagreed with him over this issue. They believed that the shift to cooperation would be seen by America's enemies as a loss of strength. But the Senate finally passed the Panama Canal Treaty in 1978. In June 1978, Carter flew to Panama and jointly signed the treaty with Panama's chief of government. As a result of this treaty, the Panama Canal and the Canal Zone will be turned over to Panama by the year 2000. The security of the area remains a joint concern of the United States and all nations of the Western Hemisphere.

The American Way

Americans seem to be committed to taking a hard look at the facts. They demand honest answers from their representatives. Americans seem united in wanting to preserve the economic strength of the country—with the liberty and opportunity that made America grow. But programs must be paid for.

Americans, however, also know that those who have less skill, poorer housing, and less opportunity must have continuing chances to better their lives. They need to help plan for themselves. Scientific management by experts in government, business, and unions is no longer enough. Government regulations against wrongdoers must not make new ideas too costly or too time-consuming to develop. Americans look again to liberty in combination with trust and justice to decide how to get the most results for the money.

The last quarter of the twentieth century sees a new dedication to America's values—the American way. Americans who know their history have respect for the years of trial, error, success, failure and hope.

Americans are still a variety of people, united by their love of liberty, their desire to manage their own lives, and their search for new opportunities and fairer treatment of everyone. Some kinds of expansion and bigness worked well. Some kinds hurt people along the way. But through majority rule and representation with sharp attention to minority rights, Americans are wiser about government action and citizen action. Both are the American way.

22. What is the American way?

Checking the facts

1. What issues did Ford have to face when he took office?
2. Why was Carter elected?
3. Why was Carter having difficulty mobilizing the country around his programs?

What problems would you handle through government action? Which level of government? Why? What problems would you handle through community action—by citizens helping each other? Why? Are the six themes about the American way part of your life this week? How?

703

PUTTING IT ALL TOGETHER

UNDERSTANDING THE MAIN IDEAS

1. What questions faced Americans as they became more deeply involved in the war in Vietnam?
2. How did programs aimed at helping the poor suffer because of government spending on the war?
3. What kinds of illegal actions did the Nixon administration take part in?
4. How did Presidents Ford and Carter plan to deal with the nation's problems?
5. What kinds of citizen action have appeared since the 1960's?

ACTIVITIES

1. List three aspects of life in America that you wish were fairer. Then write an essay in which you answer the following questions: How do you think reform could happen? Should government do anything? If so, what? How would your ideas protect people's freedom to try something new? To better themselves? If you wish, ask two adults you know these same questions.
2. The 1960's are still recent history. Often recent history is the hardest to understand. It is so close that personal feelings can interfere with judgment. What do the people you know remember about Presidents Kennedy and Johnson? Dr. Martin Luther King, Jr.? Vietnam? Prepare an interview in which you present a series of questions to interviewees. Can you make any generalizations based on the responses?
3. Using sources in your school or local library, look up the recent history of one nation in Africa, Asia, or Latin America. Was it ever part of an empire? Which country controlled it? To whom does it sell its products? Who is represented in the government? Place your findings in a brief written report.

BOOKS TO READ

Gersh, Harry, *Women Who Made America Great* (New York: J. B. Lippincott Co., 1972).

Schusky, Ernest, *The Right to be Indian* (San Francisco: Indian Historian Press, 1970).

REVIEWING THE UNIT

BUILDING VOCABULARY

The following is a list of some of the vocabulary words in Unit Six:

referendum	propaganda	ration
lobbyist	armistice	inflation
rebate	ghetto	bipartisan
dollar diplomacy	quota	containment
graduated tax	turbine	cold war
alliance	holocaust	domino theory

Define five of the vocabulary words listed above and use each one in a complete sentence.

BUILDING SOCIAL STUDIES SKILLS

Turn to the maps on the pages given here. Then complete the following activities:

1. Page 651—By the end of World War II, the Soviet Union occupied various countries in Eastern Europe. Stalin had promised Roosevelt and Churchill that these countries would be allowed to have democratic governments. Some Americans, such as Averell Harriman and George Kennan, had warned Roosevelt not to trust Stalin. Look at the map and locate the Eastern European countries occupied by the Soviet Union. Are the countries democratic or Communist? Did Stalin tell the truth?
2. Page 677—Using the scale on the map, explain why the presence of Soviet-supplied missiles in Cuba posed such a threat to the United States.

BUILDING WRITING SKILLS

Choose one of the following topics and write a paragraph comparing and contrasting the ways in which the United States government handled the issue.

a. The Panama Canal: President Roosevelt in 1903, President Carter in 1978
b. Woodrow Wilson and the League of Nations, Harry S Truman and the United Nations
c. The reasons for United States involvement in World War II, the reasons for United States involvement in Vietnam

Presidents of the United States

President and Party	Number of Terms	Years of Term	Home State
George Washington (Fed.)	2	1789–1797	Virginia
John Adams (Fed.)	1	1797–1801	Massachusetts
Thomas Jefferson (Dem.-Rep.)	2	1801–1809	Virginia
James Madison (Dem.-Rep.)	2	1809–1817	Virginia
James Monroe (Rep.)	2	1817–1825	Virginia
John Quincy Adams (Rep.)	1	1825–1829	Massachusetts
Andrew Jackson (Dem.)	2	1829–1837	Tennessee
Martin Van Buren (Dem.)	1	1837–1841	New York
William H. Harrison (Whig)	1(d.1841)	1841–1845	Ohio
John Tyler (Whig)			Virginia
James K. Polk (Dem.)	1	1845–1849	Tennessee
Zachary Taylor (Whig)	1(d.1850)	1849–1853	Louisiana
Millard Fillmore (Whig)			New York
Franklin Pierce (Dem.)	1	1853–1857	New Hampshire
James Buchanan (Dem.)	1	1857–1861	Pennsylvania
Abraham Lincoln (Rep.)	2(d.1865)	1861–1869	Illinois
Andrew Johnson (Dem.)			Tennessee
Ulysses S. Grant (Rep.)	2	1869–1877	Illinois
Rutherford B. Hayes (Rep.)	1	1877–1881	Ohio
James A. Garfield (Rep.)	1(d.1881)	1881–1885	Ohio
Chester A. Arthur (Rep.)			New York
Grover Cleveland (Dem.)	1	1885–1889	New York
Benjamin Harrison (Rep.)	1	1889–1893	Indiana
Grover Cleveland (Dem.)	1	1893–1897	New York
William McKinley (Rep.)	2(d.1901)	1897–1905	Ohio
Theodore Roosevelt (Rep.)			New York
Theodore Roosevelt (Rep.)	1	1905–1909	New York
William H. Taft (Rep.)	1	1909–1913	Ohio
Woodrow Wilson (Dem.)	2	1913–1921	New Jersey
Warren G. Harding (Rep.)	1(d.1923)	1921–1925	Ohio
Calvin Coolidge (Rep.)			Massachusetts
Calvin Coolidge (Rep.)	1	1925–1929	Massachusetts
Herbert C. Hoover (Rep.)	1	1929–1933	California
Franklin D. Roosevelt (Dem.)	4(d.1945)	1933–1949	New York
Harry S Truman (Dem.)			Missouri
Harry S Truman (Dem.)	1	1949–1953	Missouri
Dwight D. Eisenhower (Rep.)	2	1953–1961	New York
John F. Kennedy (Dem.)	1(d.1963)	1961–1965	Massachusetts
Lyndon B. Johnson (Dem.)			Texas
Lyndon B. Johnson (Dem.)	1	1965–1969	Texas
Richard M. Nixon (Rep.) resigned 1974	2	1969–1977	California
Gerald R. Ford (Rep.)			Michigan
Jimmy Carter (Dem.)	1	1977	Georgia

Women in America

Unit 1 to 1783	Margaret Brent	*Landowner and Business Agent* — Arrived in Maryland four years after its founding, and as a landowner requested to vote
	Anne Bradstreet	*Poet* — Arrived in the Massachusetts Bay Colony with John Winthrop; wrote poetry published in London
	Deborah Sampson	*Soldier* — Enlisted in the Revolutionary War disguised as a man
	Mercy Warren	*Author* — Wrote plays poking fun at the British during the Revolutionary War
	Phillis Wheatley	*Poet* — First published, Black, female, poet
Unit 2 1783–1836	Elizabeth Ann Seton	*Religious Leader* — First American born saint, she was the founder of the Sisters of Charity of St. Joseph
	Prudence Crandell	*Educator* — Made an unsuccessful attempt to establish the first school for Black girls in Connecticut
	Sacajawea	*Guide* — Led Lewis and Clark across the Louisiana Purchase
	Sarah Remond	*Physician and Abolitionist* — Became a speaker for the Female Anti-Slavery Society and studied medicine in Europe
	Sarah Hale	*Editor* — Publicized women in the magazines she edited, including *The Ladies Magazine* later, *Godey's Ladies Magazine*
Unit 3 1836–1850	Dorothea Dix	*Reformer* — The first person to bring the problems of the insane to the public's attention
	Margaret Fuller	*Writer* — Wrote for the *New York Tribune* and authored books
	Sarah Bagley	*Labor Leader* — Led a group of women protesting conditions in the mills, later organized working women
	Jessie Benton Frémont	*Explorer* — Traveled with John Fremont in the Southwest
	Eliza Spaulding	*Pioneer* — One of the first European women to cross the Rockies; she worked with the Nez Percé Native Americans in Oregon
Unit 4 1850–1877	Susan B. Anthony	*Women's Rights Advocate* — Called the first Women's Rights Meeting and devoted her life to working for full rights for women
	Jane Addams	*Reformer* — Set up Hull House in Chicago
	Mary Baker Eddy	*Founder of the Christian Science Church* — Wrote books on the philosophy of science and religion
	Sojourner Truth	*Abolitionist and Feminist* — Ex-slave who spoke to groups on the need to abolish slavery and give equality to women
	Harriet Tubman	*Abolitionist* — Conductor on the Underground Railroad
Unit 5 1877–1900	Elizabeth Blackwell	*Physician* — The first women to graduate from medical school in the United States
	Mary Cassatt	*Painter* — American Impressionist painter who studied in France
	Maria Mitchell	*Astronomer* — She discovered a new comet
	Clara Barton	*Nurse* — Founder of the American Red Cross
	Lydia Pinkham	*Businesswomen* — Successfully sold Lydia E. Pinkham's Vegetable Compound by mail order
Unit 6 1900–	Hellen Keller	*Writer* — Blind, deaf, and dumb from birth, she overcame these handicaps to write and speak on behalf of the handicapped
	Mary McLeod Bethune	*Educator* — Established a school for Black girls in New Orleans, later the Bethune-Cookman College; advisor to F.D. Roosevelt
	Frances Perkins	*Secretary of Labor* — First woman to serve in a presidential cabinet
	Amelia Earhart	*Pilot* — First woman to fly across the Atlantic Ocean
	Margaret Meade	*Anthropologist* — Studied people of the Pacific islands
	Martha Graham	*Dancer* — Established a new style of modern dance

GLOSSARY

abolition—the antislavery movement (340)

accounting—keeping track of costs (503)

acquit—to dismiss a defendant as innocent (444)

agriculture—the planned growing of food (12)

aliens—foreign immigrants who have not yet become citizens (258)

alliance—a union, or joining together by agreement, of two or more nations (584)

ally—a nation joined in an alliance (513)

amendments—additions to the Constitution (206)

amnesty—a pardon (441)

amphibious—the ability to move on both land and sea (374)

anarchists—people who want no government at all (598)

annex—to join to a larger group, such as a nation (363)

anthropologist—a scientist who studies how and why behavior develops among groups of people (12)

appropriation—money set aside for a specific use (257)

arbitration committee—a group of owners and workers who come together to settle disputes (549)

archaeologist—a scientist who studies the life and culture of ancient people (29)

armistice—a cease-fire; a signal to stop fighting (659)

armory—a place where arms are stored (422)

assimilate—to take in and make part of oneself (464)

astronomy—the study of stars, planets, and heavenly bodies (12)

Axis Powers—the alliance of Germany, Italy, and Japan in World War II (631)

bicameral—a two-house legislature (169)

bilingual—having a knowledge of two languages (495)

bipartisan—from both political parties (649)

blacklist—a list of people who are not allowed to work in a certain industry (334)

blockade—an action taken to keep someone or something out (586)

bond—a government loan paid for by borrowing money from the people (170)

bosses—political leaders who control political candidates in big cities (522)

botanist—a scientist who studies plants (11)

boycott—a refusal to buy an item (145)

bribe—money paid illegally to get what one wants (257)

buffer—something that lessens the chance of conflict between two things, such as neutral zone between nations (357)

calumet—a pipe bowl used by Native Americans (25)

capital—money for investment (247)

carpetbagger—a northerner who went South after the Civil War to help run the state governments (444)

cartographer—a person who makes maps (92)

caucus—a closed or secret meeting (308)

checks and balances—a system worked out to keep any one of the three branches of government from becoming too powerful (198)

circuit courts—regional courts (246)

civil law—laws made by the government (93)

civil servant—a person who works for the government (314)

civil service—government jobs (525)

clan—a family group (20)

closed shop—a company that hires only union personnel (517)

708

coalition—a combination of individuals and groups with different interests (260)

cold war—a period of competition and hard feelings between the Soviet Union and non-Communist countries (661)

collective security—group defense (653)

communism—a system of government in which everything is owned by the government (597)

compact—an agreement (88)

compact theory—the theory that the nation was formed by an agreement among states or the citizens of the states (259)

compensation—pay to workers injured on the job (546)

compromise—a method of give and take to arrive at an agreement (199)

concession—something given up or yielded (253)

confederacy—a loose grouping of clans, tribes, or other groups (23)

congregation—a group of people all belonging to the same church (85)

conquistadores—the people who came from Spain to conquer the New World and find gold there to support the Spanish Empire (52)

conservative—a person who does not want major changes to occur in government or society (574)

constitution—a written plan of government (101)

containment—a policy to limit the spread of communism (650)

Continental Divide—a ridge at the top of the Rocky Mountains from which water flows east to the Mississippi River and west to the Pacific Ocean (269)

contraband—stolen goods; also, a runaway slave who joined the Union army (432)

corporation—a group of persons permitted by law to act as one person to carry on business (463)

covenant—an agreement (88)

credit—the allowing of a debt to be paid in installments over a long period of time (473)

dark horse candidate—a candidate for office who is unknown or a last-minute choice (369)

demilitarized zone—an area into which army or military people are forbidden to go by agreement between sides (659)

democracy—rule by the people (258)

depression—a time when prices go down and jobs are scarce (303)

dialect—a way of speaking that is different from standard speech (495)

dollar diplomacy—a policy of the government to influence other countries with the promise of money (573)

domino theory—the idea that if one country went Communist, its neighbors would also become Communist (664)

duty—a tax on goods coming into a country (561)

economy—the whole system of producing, distributing, and using goods and services in a country (183)

embargo—the forbidding of all trade, or trade of a specific item, with a country (273)

encomienda system—a system of land ownership in which the owner of the land ruled over the people living on it (52)

epidemic—the uncontrolled spread of disease (348)

equal protection—the constitutional guarantee that every person would be treated the same (662)

equator—an imaginary line running around the midpoint of the earth between the North and South poles (11)

ethnic—sharing a common heritage (490)

executive—the President or the department in the government headed by the President (18)

excise tax—a tax on the sale of goods (247)

factions—special-interest groups (250)

factor—in business, an agent or middle person (123)

federalism—a system of local, state, and national governments (198)

fugitive—a person who is wanted by the law (386)

gauge—the width between railroad tracks (331)

geologist—a scientist who studies land formations (8)

glacier—a large sheet of moving ice (8)

graduated income tax—tax system in which the more one earns, the higher the taxes one pays (579)

greenbacks—printed money without gold or silver backing its value (525)

guerrilla warfare—fighting carried on by small groups that attack by surprise (141)

hard money—money worth as much in buying or purchasing power when it is repaid as when it was borrowed (526)

hierarchy—a ladder of power (206)

hogan—a dome-shaped house built of logs and mud (27)

holocaust—the killing of Jews in Europe before and during World War II (634)

homespun—a coarse fabric spun at home and worn by colonists (95)

humanism—a set of beliefs that hold that human reasoning can be used to understand life and that human accomplishments are important (42)

hydroelectricity—electricity produced by water power (624)

impeach—to bring to trial (444)

impressment—the forcing of sailors into naval service (252)

indentured servant—a person who was contracted to work for a certain amount of time in exchange for passage to America (80)

indigo—a plant from which blue dye is produced (123)

inferior courts—lower courts (205)

inflation—a period of rising prices because more money is needed to buy the same amount of goods (169)

initiative—a process by which voters can present laws directly to the state legislature or the electorate for approval

injunction—a legal order from a court, that directs someone to do or not do something (511)

interstate—between states (283)

isthmus—a narrow neck of land connecting two other, larger, land bodies (11)

judicial review—the power of the Supreme Court to decide if an action by a government is constitutional (261)

judiciary—the court officials who interpret the law and settle disputes about them (181)

kickback—an illegal payment to someone for securing a contract (522)

levee—a raised embankment usually built to prevent flooding (347)

liberal—a person who wants more laws to protect people (574)

livery—a uniform (245)

lobbyist—a person who tries to convince legislators to support a particular position (419)

longitude—a measure of distance east or west on the earth (39)

machine—the group of bosses who control a political organization (522)

majority—more than half of a group (401)

market system—a system of buying and selling (284)

marketing cooperatives—farmers who organize together to sell produce at higher prices (506)

medieval system—a system in which lords were to get titles to the land that could be handed to their sons (106)

mercantile system—a system by which the colonies would produce goods and trade them only with England (107)

mercenary—a soldier who is hired to fight (157)

merger—joining companies into one organization (475)

mesa—a hill with steep sides and a flat top (26)

militia—a volunteer army (153)

milpa system—a system of cutting down trees on hilly

land and burning the stumps in order to make the land more fertile (16)

minority—less than half of a group (401)

monopoly—exclusive control of an item by a company, which results in the fixing of prices and the elimination of competition (150)

muckracker—a person who exposes corruption and the problems of the poor in order to encourage the government to take action (490)

mythology—a set of stories a culture develops to explain early history and beliefs (14)

nationalism—the idea that when the language, religion, and customs of a nation are imporant and unique enough, that nation has a right to independence (70)

nomad—a person who has no permanent home but, as a way of life, wanders across large areas of land in search of food and pasture (25)

nonimportation agreement—the colonists' agreement not to buy goods that came from England (146)

null and void—declared unconstitutional (259)

nullify—to cancel (259)

parochial schools—schools set up or run by a church (346)

patent—a guarantee given by the federal government that protects the rights of an inventor by preventing anyone else from selling the invention for a certain length of time (278)

patronage—a system of rewarding people who help an official get elected (314)

patroon system—a Dutch system of settlement that gave huge land grants to people who would bring 50 settlers to the New World (99)

peaceful coexistence—Communist and free nations living together without trying to dominate one another through warfare (660)

philanthropy—giving money to help other people (487)

piedmont—back-country area or land at the base of mountains (126)

platform—a statement of political positions (416)

pooling—the act of companies putting all their profits together and dividing them evenly at the end of the year (475)

popular sovereignty—the right of people in a particular area to make decisions about all issues (378)

prairie—a large area of open grassland (25)

prehistoric—the time before people developed a system for writing down their history (8)

presidio—the Spanish word for "fort" (52)

profit—the extra money left after bills have been paid (76)

Prohibition—in the United States the period between 1919 and 1933, when it was illegal to sell alcoholic drinks (594)

propaganda—communication for the purpose of influencing the thinking, emotions, or actions of people (587)

pueblo—the Spanish word for "village" (26)

pyramid—a large triangular-shaped structure, sometimes used in religious ceremonies (14)

quarantine—to isolate those who are or may be infected to keep disease from spreading (502)

quota—a set limit (490)

radicals—individuals who advocate extreme political, social, and economic changes (598)

ratify—to agree to; to approve (184)

ration—an assigned portion of food or provisions distributed, as during wartime (636)

rebates—money returned (553)

recall—to remove elected officials before their terms are over (543)

referendum—the process by which the voters approve or disapprove of a bill by voting on it directly (543)

representative assembly—a group of people who meet to make decisions on behalf of other people (81)

reservation—an area of land set aside for Native Americans (320)

revelation—a special message believed to be from God (392)

rider—a provision, not likely to pass on its own, attached to a bill so that it may be passed by the legislature and will become a law (376)

scalawags—people from the South who aided carpetbaggers after the Civil War (444)

settlement house—a community center, often in the poorer section of a town, that provides instruction, recreation, and advice to people in the area (501)

secede—to leave the Union (317)

segregate—to separate people, usually by race (352)

shaman—a person who is thought to have supernatural powers (20)

slum—the poorer section of a city (338)

Socialist—a person who believes that the people should own the means of producing and distributing food and goods, which should be operated by the government (567)

sod—the upper layer of earth containing grass and plant roots (461)

soft money—money that is worth less when it is paid back than when it was borrowed (525)

sovereignty—the right of a people to govern themselves (198)

specie—gold or silver used as money (303)

speculator—a person who buys land to make a profit (412)

spoils system—the giving of jobs by newly elected officials to people who helped the officials get elected (314)

squatter—someone who settles on land before he or she has a legal right to the land (378)

standard of living—the level of necessities and comforts found in the way the majority of people live (680)

strike—a refusal by workers to work in order to get more money or better working conditions (335)

subsidy—government financial support (282)

suffrage—the right to vote (339)

tariff—a tax on imports (184)

temperance—a movement to eliminate the sale and use of liquor (343)

tenant farmers—farmers who rent the land (462)

tenement—a type of building occupied by many people in the early 1900's (492)

tenure—protection from being fired (504)

terrain—the physical shape of land (404)

theological school—a school to train people in religion (346)

third world—underdeveloped or emerging countries in Latin America, Africa, and Asia (663)

tidewater—a low-lying coastal area (120)

totalitarian—relating to control of government by a dictator (650)

transcontinental—across the country, from coast to coast (448)

trust—separate businesses under the control of one board of trustees (475)

turbine—a kind of engine operated by the pressure of water or steam (624)

turnout—a strike (334)

turnpike—a toll road (281)

vertical operation—an organization that includes every step of the manufacturing and delivery process (471)

veto—the right to reject something (649)

wampum—shell beads used by Native Americans for money, decoration, and pledges of friendship (22)

ward—a neighborhood political group (521)

Western Hemisphere—North and South America (298)

wholesaler—a person who buys a large amount of goods to resell (279)

writ of assistance—a document allowing police to search someone's home or property (146)

712

INDEX

Italicized page numbers refer to a picture.

Plymouth Company, 74, 86, 89
Pocahontas, 77-78
Poe, Edgar Allen, 343
political conventions. *See* conventions, political
political leaders in the cities, 451, 521-522
political parties, 523-524
Polk, James K.
as President, 370-375, 383
poll taxes, 239
pollution, 701
Polo, Marco, *36*, 37
Ponce de León, 33, 38-39
Pontiac's war, 141
popular sovereignty, 378, 412, 414, 415, 418, 419
Populists, 526-527
Portsmouth Peace Conference, 562
Portuguese expeditions, 38-40
possessions, American, *530*, 531
Post Office Department, 572
Powhatan, Chief, 76, 77
Powhatan confederacy
and Jamestown settlers, 76-77
massacre by (1622), 81
President of the United States, 220-224
disability and succession, 222, 233, 237, 239-240
election of, 221, 232, 260, 308
impeachment of, 224
powers of, 223
relationship of people to, 245-246, 256-257
selection of candidates, 308-309
two-term limit, 238
See also conventions, political
Presidents of the United States
Adams, John, 256-260
Adams, John Quincy, 310-312
Arthur, Chester A., 525
Buchanan, James, 416, 418
Carter, Jimmy, 702-703
Cleveland, Grover, 511, 524, *525*, 526, 529
Coolidge, Calvin, 603, 609
Eisenhower, Dwight D., 659-662
Fillmore, Millard, 387, 411
Ford, Gerald, 698-700
Garfield, James A., 525
Grant, Ulysses S., 444, *445*, 446
Harding, Warren, 602-603
Harrison, William H., 364
Hayes, Rutherford B., 446, 511
Hoover, Herbert, 609, 611-612

Jackson, Andrew, 314-320, 363, 364
Jefferson, Thomas, 260-262, 264-274
Johnson, Andrew, 440-441
Johnson, Lyndon B., 681-684, 686-690
Kennedy, John F., 670, 672-680
Lincoln, Abraham, 423-424, 426, 428, 430, 431-432, 434, 436-438
McKinley, William, 527, 530-532
Madison, James, 289-290, 293
Monroe, James, 297-298
Nixon, Richard M., 691-698
Pierce, Franklin, 412, 414
Polk, James K., 370-375, 383
Roosevelt, Franklin D., 615-628, 632-635, 642-643
Taft, William Howard, 571-574
Taylor, Zachary, 383-384, 387
Truman, Harry S, 643-658
Tyler, John, 365-367, 368, 370
Van Buren, Martin, 363, 364
Washington, George, 242-255
Wilson, Woodrow, 576, 578-584, 586-588, 590
See also elections, presidential
press, the: freedom of, 118
primary elections, 542-543
privateers, 158
Proclamation of 1763, 142
Progressive party, 574, 575
Progressives, the, 541-546, 568.
prohibition amendment, 235-236, 593-594
repeal of, 237-238
Public Health, 502-503
Public Works Administration, 618
Pueblos, the, 7, 26, *27*
revolt of, 54
Puerto Ricans on the mainland, 666-668, 680
and Blacks, 667
formation of ASPIRA, 680
housing for, 667
problems for, 666-667
See also Spanish-speaking Americans
Puerto Rico: U.S. control of, 531
Pure Food and Drug Act, 554
Puritans, 85, 104, 108
Connecticut colony of, 101
and hard work, 91

and Harvard College, 91
importance of schooling to, 91, 105
leaving England, 90-91
opposing James I's religious views, 85-86
pressured by Charles I, 89-90
See also Massachusetts Bay; Pilgrims

Quakers, the, 108, *130*
and abolition movement, 340
in New Jersey, 108, 109
opposed to slavery, 110, 130
in Pennsylvania, 109-110
Quartering Act, 145
Quebec
Americans' failure to take, 157
colony founded in, 66, 67
defeat of French in, 137

Radical Reconstructionists, 441-444
radicals, 598
radio, the, 605
railroads, the, 331, 403-410, 447-449
Blacks segregated from Whites on, 527
builders of, 404-406
in Chicago, 405-406
and the cities, 408-409, 460-461
commission of specialists to set rules for, 544-545
effects of, on agriculture, 407-408
and the farmers, 522
fights for control of, 450
financing of, 407
and the Hepburn Act, 553
improved equipment, 404
in the Midwest, 344
miles of track, 390-403
and nationwide business, 468
in New England and mid-Atlantic states, *331*
politics and, 412
refrigerated cars, 469
state regulation of, 544
transcontinental, 448
Raleigh, Walter, 60
and the Roanoke Island colony, 60, 62
Randolph, Asa Philip, 596, 640-641, 678
Randolph, Edmund, 195, 201, 204, 209, *245*
rationing, 636
recall process, 543
reconstruction, 440-446
Lincoln's plan for, 440-441
and Radical Constructionists in Congress, 441-444

White reactions to, 445-446
Reconstruction Acts, 442, 444
Red Scare, 597-598
referendum, 543
reform movements, 340-343
American Temperance Union, 343
antislavery, 340-341
Brook Farm community, 341
election of senators by the people, 543
improving quality of public education, 341
management of cities, 543
prohibition, 235-236, 593-594
Roosevelt, Theodore, 548-555. *See also* Roosevelt, Theodore
schools of deaf and blind, 341, 343, 353
secret ballots, 542-543
settlement houses, 501
specialists in government agencies, 544-545
in state governments, 543-544
women's suffrage, 236, 543, 594-595
workers' compensation, 546
for working children and women, 546
religion
Anne Hutchinson's persecution for her beliefs, 103
Maryland Toleration Act, 100-101
separation of White and Black churches in the South, 353-354
See also church, the; Puritans; Separatists
religion, freedom of, 4
in the colonies, 101, 102, 110
representation, 187, 192-193, 251, 538
and compromise, 301-306
in Franklin's Albany Plan of Union, 132
in General Court of Puritan Massachusetts, 93
in House of Burgesses, 81, 82
how it works, 193
and liberty, 199
slavery and, 202-203, 305
taxation without, 143, 145, 151
and veto power of Pennsylvania settlers, 110
Republicans, the, 250, 256, 258, 414-415, 423, 444, 524, 525, 527, 552, 558, 571, 574, 588, 603, 609, 632, 648
split in party, 574

reservations for Native
Americans, 449, 465-466
breaking up of, 464-465
Reuther, Walter, 678
Revere, Paul, *154*
Revolution, French, 251-252
Revolutionary War. *See*
American Revolution
Richman, Julia, 496
Riis, Jacob A., 490-491, 537
riots (1967), 689
roads, 281, 282, 283, *287*
Roanoke Island colony, 60,
62
"Roaring Twenties," 603-
606, 608, 609
airplane, the, 605-606
automobile, 604-605, 607
changing attitudes toward
women, 606
Rockefeller, John D., 477,
486
Rockefeller, Nelson A., 239
Rocky Mountains, 369, 378
Rolfe, John, 77-78
Roman Catholic Church
in France, 64
split between England
and, 58-59
Roman Catholics, and Que-
bec Act, 151
Roosevelt, Eleanor, 626
Roosevelt, Franklin D., 238,
615, *616*
Atlantic Charter signed by
Churchill and, 633
banks closed by, 619
death of, 643, 647
elected to fourth term,
642-643
and Fair Employment
Practices Committee,
641
fireside chats of, *626*
Inaugural Address, 616
and Lend-Lease Act, 632-
633
as President, 615-628,
632-635, 638, 642-643
press conferences of, 626
and proposed Black march
on Washington, 641
and Social Security Act,
625
and Supreme Court, 627
and the TVA, 624
See also New Deal
Roosevelt, Theodore, 531,
537, 547-571
action of, on strike by coal
miners, 549
action of, on trusts, 549,
550, 552-553
background of, 547-548
beliefs about foreign na-
tions, 556
and creation of Depart-
ment of Commerce and
Labor, 550
on forests and national
parks, 554-555

and "Gentleman's Agree-
ment" with Japan, 564
and Hepburn Act, 553
involved in Latin Ameri-
can affairs, 560-561
and the Panama Canal,
557-560. *See also* Pan-
ama Canal
as President, 547-571
and Progressive Party,
574-575
reforms by, 548-555
with Rough Riders in
Cuba, 531
Roosevelt Corollary to Monroe Doctrine, 561
Russia, 562
agreement with Germany,
631
Alaska purchased from,
448
Nixon in, 694
rise of communism in,
644
treaty with, on fishing
rights, 297
See also Soviet Union
Russian Revolution, 597
Russo-Japanese War, 562

Sacajawea, *269*
Sacco-Vanzetti case, 598
San Jacinto, battle of, 363
Santa Anna, Gen. A. L. de,
361-362, 363, 374
Santa Fe Trail, 359, 360, 361
scalawags, 444
schools. *See* education
Scotch-Irish settlers, 114
Scott, Gen. Winfield, 320,
373, 374-375, 412
secession, voting for, 422,
423-424.
Second Continental Con-
gress. *See* Continental
Congress, Second
Sedition Act, 258, 259
segregation, 352-354, 447-
448, 527, 569, 578
and boycotts of public
transportation, 596,
663
end of, in armed forces,
648
in government facilities,
578
of World War II fighting
units, 641
See also discrimination
Senate, the, 202, 212-213
electing senators, 235,
543, 572
Separatists, 85, 87
settlement houses, 501
settlements in North America, 73-115
in Carolina, 106-107
Catholic colony of Mary-
land, 99-101
of the Dutch, 99

formation of London
Company and Ply-
mouth Company, 74
Germans in, 113-114
Jamestown, Va., 73-84
Jews in, 114
Massachusetts Bay, 90-95
Oglethorpe in Georgia,
111
Plymouth Colony, 86-89
and Proclamation of 1763,
142
Puritans in Connecticut,
101
Quakers in New Jersey,
108, 109
Quakers in Pennsylvania,
109-110
Scotch-Irish, 114
Swedes and Huguenots in,
113
Williams in Rhode Island,
102
See also colonies, North
American
Seven Years War. *See* French
and Indian War
Seward, William, 448
Shays' Rebellion, *186*, 187,
202
Sherman, Roger, 202
Sherman, Gen. William
Tecumseh, 437, 438
march through Georgia,
437
Sherman Antitrust Act, 523,
550, 572, 581
shipbuilding, 105
ships, American, 257, 289,
332, 333-334, 366
seized by the British, 252,
272-273, 289
silver
discovery in the West,
450, 459
search for, by European
explorers, 45, 47, 48
Sinclair, Upton, 553
Sioux, the, 25
battle of Little Big Horn,
449
battle at Wounded Knee,
466
sit-ins, 641, 663
Slater, Samuel, 278
slave trade, 351
auction, 377
banned in District of Columbia, 385
British and American re-
lations over, 366
in New England triangle
of trade, 105, 127
slavery, 40, 120-121, 123,
186, 412
abolition of, 233, 278, 441
abolition movements, 278,
340-341
and annexation of Texas,
364, 367, 370
Black, in Virginia, 82-83

and Compromise of 1850,
385-386, 412
cotton and, 278, 350-351,
352, 359, 364, 391
Dred Scott decision, 418,
420
and Emancipation Proc-
lamation, 432
first Black slaves in New
World, 46
and free Blacks, 352-353
and Fugitive Slave Act,
386, 417
import tax on slaves, 219
Jefferson on, 186
and Lecompton Constitu-
tion, 418
in Mexico, 359, 360
and the Missouri Compro-
mise, 303-306
as national moral issue,
387
Native American slaves in
Spanish colonies, 53
and the Northwest Ordi-
nance, 304
opinions about, 130
and Philadelphia Anti-
Slavery Society, 340
as political issue between
the North and South,
364, 367, 369, 375-378,
383-384, 385-386, 387,
413-414
and popular sovereignty.
See popular sovereignty
Quaker belief about, 110,
130
question of, in territory
acquired from Mexico,
375-378
and representation, 202-
203, 305
revolts led by Denmark
Vesey and Nat Turner,
317
runaway slaves in Union
army, 432
slave ships, *120*
and tobacco growing, 83,
121
and the Underground
Railroad, *416*, 417
in Virginia, 82-83
and Wilmot Proviso, 376
women in antislavery
movement, 341
Slidell, John, 372
Smith, Alfred E., 609
Smith, John, 76
Smith, Joseph, 392-393
Smith, Margaret Chase, 657
smuggling, 146, 148, 149
Social Security Act, 625
Socialist party, 567
Sons of Liberty, 146, 147
and Boston Tea Party,
149-*150*
South, the
Black Codes of, 352, 442
Blacks in (1920's), 595

PHOTO CREDITS

Sources have been abbreviated as follows:
BA—Bettmann Archives
BB—Brown Brothers
CP—Culver Pictures
LC—Library of Congress
NYPL—New York Public Library
UPI—United Press International
WW—Wide World Photos

X T—State Capitol Building, Phoenix. X BL—Henry B. Belville, Courtesy Hampton Institute. X BR—Ford Archives/Henry Ford Museum. 1T—Independence National Historic Park Collection. 1BL—Pugsley Union, South Dakota State College. 1BR—NASA.

UNIT 1: 3—HRW Photo by Russell Dian. 4—©Nicholas Foster 1976, Image Bank. 5—Peter Vadnai, Editorial Photocolor Archives. 10—American Museum of Natural History. 11—Franklin McMahon, Jr. 14—Art Institute of Chicago. 15—©David Ryan, Uniphoto. 19—From the Collection of the University Museum, Philadelphia. 21T—LC. 21B—Museum of the American Indian, Heye Foundation. 22—Smithsonian Institution. 24—Mohawk-Caughnawaga Museum. 27—Bruce Davidson, Magnum Photos. 28—Museum of Natural History. 30—Tony Linck. 34—*The Memorial History of Boston*, by Justin Winsor, 1881. 36—Bodlein Library. 39—CP. 40—Vivian Fenster. 42—The Master and Fellows of Magdelene College, Cambridge. 43—NYPL, Rare Book Division. 45—Uffizi Gallery. 47—American Museum of Natural History. 48—Hispanic Society of America. 50—Bradley Smith. 58—Walker Art Gallery, England. 59—Woburn Abbey Collection. 60—National Maritime Museum, England. 63—Tiroler Landesmuseum Ferdinandeum, Innsbruck. 65—Cornell University Library. 66—NYPL, Rare Book Division. 68—National Gallery of Art. 69—American Heritage Publishing Company. 75—Colonial Williamsburg. 77T—LC. 77B—National Portrait Gallery. 79—LC. 80—CP. 84—Metropolitan Museum of Art, Gift of Edgar William and Bernice Chrysler Garbisch. 86—Woolaroc Museum. 87—Pilgrim Hall. 90—American Antiquarian Society. 94—Shelburne Museum. 95—Worcester Art Museum. 99—Courtesy Scribners and Sons. 100—NYPL, Picture Collection. 104—Historical Pictures Service. 106—BA. 109—Thomas Gilcrease Institute of American History and Art. 111—National Gallery of Art. 112—LC. 116—HRW Photo by Michael Provost. 120—National Maritime Museum, England. 123—Folger Shakespeare Library. 126—LC. 129—NYPL, Prints Division. 130T—New-York Historical Society. 130B—NYPL, Prints Division. 131—Insurance Company of North America. 134—NYPL, Picture Collection. 137—Collection of Peter Winkworth. 141—CP. 143—John Carter Brown Library. 144—Mansell Collection. 147B—Metropolitan Museum of Art. 147TR—CP. 152—CP. 153—Shelburne Museum. 154—Boston Museum of Fine Arts. 155—White House Historical Society. 157—Yale University Art Gallery. 158—CP. 159—White House Historical Society. 163—Historical Society of Pennsylvania. 164—Collection of Gilbert Darlington. 168—Anne S.K. Brown Military Collection. 172T—CP. 172B—National Gallery of Canada, Ottawa. 174T—Valley Forge Historical Society. 174B—NYPL, Picture Collection. 175T—CP. 175B—Mount Vernon Ladies Association. 176—U.S. Naval Academy Museum. 178T—National Archives. 178B—Old Print Shop. 179—Virginia State Library. 182—Henry Francis duPont Winterthur Museum. 184—CP. 186—CP.

UNIT 2: 192—Image Bank. 193—Beryl Goldberg. 196—Independence National Historical Park Collection. 197—Historical Society of Pennsylvania. 199—Bowdoin College. 201—NYPL, Picture Collection. 202—National Collection of Fine Arts. 204—NYPL, Picture Collection. 207—Independence National Historical Park Collection. 208—New-York Historical Society. 210—New-York Historical Society. 244—Metropolitan Museum of Art. 245—Continental Insurance Company. 246—Chase Manhattan Bank Money Museum. 247—National Gallery of Art. 249—National Gallery of Art. 250—Maryland Historical Society. 252—BA. 253—NYPL, Picture Collection. 254—Chicago Historical Society. 255—Metropolitan Museum of Art, Gift of Edgar William and Bernice Chrysler Garbisch. 257—Boston Athenaeum. 260—Sandak. 261—NYPL, Picture Collection. 267—Architect of the Capitol, Washington. 269—CP. 270—Montana Historical Society. 272—Yale University Art Gallery. 276—BA. 280—Yale University Art Gallery. 282—Maryland Historical Society. 283—Museum of the City of New York. 285—New-York Historical Society. 289—LC. 293—Anne S. K. Brown Military Collection. 294—Peale Museum. 296—*Pictorial History of the Negro in America* by Langston Hughes

and Milton Meltzer, 1968. Used by permission of Crown Publishers, Inc. 302—Collection of James Campbell, Courtesy American Heritage Publishing Company. 305—Corcoran Gallery of Art. 306—LC. 307—National Academy of Design. 311—Boston Museum of Fine Arts. 313—The Hermitage. 316—CP. 312—Woolaroc Museum.

UNIT 3: 326—WW. 327—BA. 330—Boston Museum of Fine Arts. 331—BA. 333—Marine Historical Association, Inc., Mystic. 335—*Frank Leslie's Illustrated Newspaper.* 336—Museum of the City of New York. 339—Granger Collection. 340T—Granger Collection. 340B—Granger Collection. 341T—Granger Collection. 341B—Sophie Smith Collection. 345—NYPL, Map Division. 349—Cincinnati Historical Society. 350—LC. 358—de Young Memorial Museum. 359—Texas State Archives. 363—Daughters of the Republic of Texas Museum. 362—Courtesy Mrs. Bill Arthur and Mrs. Al Warner. 365—LC. 368—Whitman Mission National Historic Site. 372—CP. 375—John Mix Stanley Collection, H. J. Lutcher Stark, Courtesy *Life.* 377—BA. 379—California Historical Society. 384—State Street Trust Co. Boston. 392T—California State Library. 392B—LC.

UNIT 4: 400—Joshua Tree, Editorial Photocolor Archives. 401—UPI. 405—New-York Historical Society. 408—Chicago Historical Society. 411—Mariner's Museum, Virginia. 414—Yale University Art Gallery. 416—Cincinnati Art Museum. 417—CP. 419—Lincoln University Library. 421—Chicago Historical Society. 429—Seventh Regiment Fund, Inc. 433—LC. 435—Collection of Mr. & Mrs. Charles J. Sinnott, Courtesy *Life.* 441—LC. 442—CP. 445—Granger Collection. 448—Photography Collection Suzzallo Library, University of Washington. 450—Taft Museum, Cincinnati. 451—CP.

UNIT 5: 456—A T. and T. 457—Sears Roebuck. 461—Nebraska State Historical Society. 463—McKay Collection, Montana Historical Society. 466—Oklahoma Historical Society. 472—Singer Company. 473—CP. 475—Chicago Historical Society. 482—Museum of the City of New York. 486—Photo ©Arnold Newman. 488—BA. 490—Bancroft Library University of California. 491—Addison Gallery of American Art, Phillips Academy. 492—BA. 494—LC. 497—CP. 498—BA. 504—Sears Roebuck. 510—BA. 515—BB. 517—BB. 520—LC. 525—BA. 526—Granger Collection. 529—CP.

UNIT 6: 538—Office of Economic Opportunity. 539—George Gardner. 542—CP. 545—Granger Collection. 548—LC. 549—New-York Historical Society. 553—Warsaw Collection of Business Americana. 558—Culver Pictures. 568—CP. 569—NYPL, Picture Collection. 571—Smithsonian Institution. 577—BB. 583—CP. 587B—Granger Collection. 588—National Archives. 594—CP. 595—WW. 596—UPI. 597—CP. 598—Kennedy Gallery. 600—CP. 601—LC. 603—BA. 604—Photoworld/FPG. 605—Smithsonian Institution. 606T—BA. 606B—CP. 609—LC. 611—LC. 612—WW. 616—WW. 618—WW. 619—UPI. 620—BA. 625—Tennessee Valley Authority. 626—*Philadelphia Inquirer.* 627—WW. 628—BA. 632—G. D. Hackett. 634—UPI. 635—National Archives. 636—UPI. 638—U.S. Coast Guard. 640—NYPL, Picture Collection. 641—UPI. 642—Denver Public Library, Western History Department. 643—U.S. Army Photo. 649—U.S. Airforce Photo. 650—Harry S Truman Library. 652—UPI. 658—UPI. 659—NYPL, Picture Collection. 660—Black Star. 661—NASA. 662—UPI. 664—Robert Capa, Magnum. 666—Alpha Photo/FPG. 667—UPI. 668—UPI. 669—UPI. 670—WW. 674T—NYPL, Picture Collection. 674B—UPI. 675—WW. 678—UPI. 679—Hap Stewart. 680—Aspira. 681—WW. 682—Editorial Photocolor Archives. 683—Capitol Records. 684—UPI. 689—John Henry Sullivan, Jr., Photo Researchers. 690—WW. 695—Editorial Photocolor Archives. 696—WW. 697—WW. 699—UPI. 700—Rick Bloom, Uniphoto. 701T—Fred Ward, Black Star. 701B—Laurence Fried, Magnum. 702—UPI. 703—Joseph Muench.